Kimberly Willey

A HISTORY OF Israel

A HISTORY OF Israel

From the Bronze Age Through The Jewish Wars

WALTER C. KAISER, JR.

Nashville, Tennessee

0-8054-6284-8 (hc)

Published by Broadman & Holman Publishers, Nashville, Tennessee
Page Design and Composition: TF Designs, Mt. Juliet, Tennessee

Dewey Decimal Classification: 933
Subject Heading: ISRAEL \ JEWS--ISRAEL
Library of Congress Card Catalog Number: 97-9718

Library of Congress Cataloging-in-Publication Data

Kaiser, Walter C., Jr.
A history of Israel : the Old Testament and its times / Walter C. Kaiser Jr.
p. cm.
Includes bibliographical references.
ISBN 0-8054-6284-8 (hc)
1. Bible. O.T.--History of biblical events. 2. Jews--History--To 70 A.D.
I. Title.
BS1197.K251998
221.9'5—dc21

97-9718
CIP
r97

2 3 4 5 02 01 00 99 98

Dedicated to
Cyrus H. Gordon
With deep appreciation

to
a mentor,
longtime friend,
teacher of teachers,
and
a second Cyrus to scores of fellow students

CONTENTS

List of Maps

Preface

It is a daunting task, if not a presumptuous one, to assume that one person could cover the expanse of data, times, issues, and complexities involved in the scope of a history of Israel such as you now hold in you hands. Nevertheless, it is important that each generation give an accounting of itself in a stewardship of its own understanding of what was committed to their day. By the grace of God, we have endeavored to give as accurate an accounting of ourselves in these matters as possible.

This is the best and the worst of all times to attempt such a project as this. Rarely, in the history of reconstructing Israel's past, has there been as great skepticism about the usefulness, much less the possibility, of such a task. The reviews of this volume, I am well aware, could be scurrilous from some quarters, for the debate has often taken on acrimonious tones that are barbed with personal attacks on various writers in the field. But this must not be a reason for silence; another generation has arisen that wants to make up its own mind on these matters without having the issue prejudged for them. Furthermore, all scholarly works are subject to a more intensive review than those that will appear in the scholarly journals—it will be the review of the Lord of history in the final day.

It is with an eye to that review that we have dared to do the unthinkable—as judged by the "biblical minimalists" (a term some think is a sneering epithet, but it is used here only to indicate the role the Bible has played for this school of thought). The unthinkable is this: We have dared to use the Bible as a source in the construction of Israel's history! That is not judged to be a proper move for serious scholarship today by at least one influential school of thought. But it is judged still to be proper in many circles.

Our approach will be to take the Bible on its own terms, just as we have taken all the epigraphic materials from the ancient Near East as reliable—until they were proven to be otherwise. It is the principle found in the system of American jurisprudence that will be employed in this text: The text is innocent until proven guilty. All too many begin with the thesis that because the biblical text has been used by religious bodies, the Bible must be judged guilty and untrustworthy until proven innocent.

Accordingly, it is not that conservative scholars are not critical in their approach to the materials they use; rather, the difference between the conservatives and their scholarly counterparts is precisely where the use of the critical tools enters into their argument. If we start with the assumption that the results of the various critical methods are assured, unless counterarguments can be brought against the methods, the resulting claims made about the text will be vastly different from the competing methodology of conservatives. Contrariwise, a conservative will begin with a different warrant: that the Bible is to be generally accepted because of the claims the text makes for itself and the way these claims have been received these many centuries. But these claims are subject to the critical methodologies at the level of a rebuttal; which, if shown to be true, must negate the claim made in the text.[1] Note, however, where this rebuttal appears: It is not part of the data with which we begin, nor is it part of the warrants with which we proceed, but it comes as a rebuttal just before the claim is announced.

Therefore, it is unfair and improper to conclude that researchers who use the Bible in constructing a history of Israel are less informed, more naive, and less capable of using the critical tools than those who refuse to consider anything in the Bible to be worth reporting in a history until the Persian period. Both use the same methodologies and read the same literature; the difference is only in where they appear in the procedure.

It is hoped that the current emphasis on plurality and care about being correct socially, racially, and politically also will be extended to

1. For a further explanation of this important distinction based on Stephen Toulmin's *Uses of Argument* (Cambridge: Cambridge University Press, 1958), see Walter C. Kaiser Jr., *Toward Rediscovering the Old Testament* (Grand Rapids: Zondervan, 1987), 68–79.

the evangelical partners in the conversation that all too frequently have been deliberately left out of the dialogue. Here is the real test of liberal thinking!

It only remains to thank my colleague, Dr. Gary Pratico, chair of the division of biblical studies at Gordon-Conwell Theological Seminary, South Hamilton, Massachusetts, for his generous counsel and suggestions for this manuscript. I am likewise deeply indebted to the board of Gordon-Conwell Theological Seminary and to the family of the late Colman M. Mockler for the generous provisions of the chair I hold named "The Colman M. Mockler Distinguished Professor of Old Testament." The gracious terms set for this chair have allowed me to do the research and compose this volume over the past years. It is also a pleasure to acknowledge John Landers for his patient editorial work and Broadman & Holman Publishers for suggesting this project in the first place. A special word of appreciation is also due to Charles Lee, my Byington scholar, who assisted me in composing the Scripture and author indicies. It has been a pleasure working with all these persons. The responsibility for the errors that remain are mine and not those of my colleagues.

My hope is that this work may stimulate the interest of many others to press on in our research of the historical understanding of the people of this land and book. To that end, we commend these pages to the glory of God.

ABBREVIATIONS

AASOR	Annual of the American School of Oriental Research
AJSL	American Journal of Semitic Languages
ANET	Ancient Near Eastern Texts Relating to the Old Testament, ed. James Pritchard
ANEP	Ancient Near Eastern Pictures Relating to the Old Testament, ed James Pritchard
ARAB	Ancient Records of Assyria and Babylon, D. D. Luckenbill
ASTI	Annual of the Swedish Theological Institute
AUSS	Andrews University Seminary Studies
BA	Biblical Archaeologist
BAR	Biblical Archaeology Review
BASOR	Bulletin of the American Schools of Oriental Research
Bib Sac	Bibliotheca Sacra
BCE	Before the Common Era
BETS	Bulletin of the Evangelical Theological Society
BR	Bible Review
CAH	Cambridge Ancient History
CBQ	Catholic Biblical Quarterly
CE	Common Era
CRAI	Comptes-rendus Acad. Inscr. et Belles-Lettres
CT	Christianity Today
CTM	Concordia Theological Monthly
DOTT	Documents of Old Testament Times, D. Winton Thomas
EB	Early Bronze Age

EQ	Evangelical Quarterly
GTJ	Grace Theological Journal
HAT	Handbuch zum Alten Testament
HTR	Harvard Theological Review
HUCA	Hebrew Union College Annual
IEJ	Israel Exploration Journal
JANES	Journal of the Ancient Near Eastern Society of Columbia University
JAOS	Journal of the American Oriental Society
JARCE	Journal of the American Research Center in Egypt
JBL	Journal of Biblical Literature
JCS	Journal of Cuneiform Studies
JEA	Journal of Egyptian Archaeology
JETS	Journal of the Evangelical Theological Society
JNES	Journal of Near Eastern Studies
JNSL	Journal of Northwest Semitic Languages
JPOS	Journal of Palestinian Oriental Society
JSOT	Journal for the Study of the Old Testament
JSOTSup	Journal for the Study of the Old Testament Supplement Series
JPS	Jewish Publication Society
JSS	Journal of Semitic Studies
LR	Lexington Review
MDAIK	Mitteilungen des deutschen archaologischen Instituts
MB	Middle Bronze Age
NIV	New International Version
NEASB	Near East Archaeological Society Bulletin
PEQ	Palestinian Exploration Quarterly
RB	Revue Biblique
RHPR	Revue d'histoire et de philosophie religieuses
TynB	Tyndale Bulletin
UF	Ugarit-Forschungen
VT	Vetus Testamentum
VTSuppl	Vetus Testamentum Supplement Series
WTJ	Westminster Theological Journal
YNES	Yale Near Eastern Studies
ZAW	Zeitschrift für die alttestamentliche Wissenschaft
ZDPV	Zeitschritft des deutschen Palastina-Vereins
ZPEB	Zondervan Pictorial Encyclopedia of the Bible

Introduction

"An increasingly modish—virulent?—strain of biblical scholarship concludes that the Bible is useless for reconstructing the history of ancient Israel. If this history can be reconstructed at all, it must be based solely on archaeological evidence as interpreted by anthropological models."[1] Fortunately, not all researchers hold this view. But the times have surely changed and the chains that mark off the legitimate playing field for using the Bible in reconstructing the history of Israel have been successively moved back towards the postexilic times of the Persians or even later.

At one time, only Genesis 1–11 was held to contain nothing of historical worth by many scholars. Then at the beginning of this century, William Foxwell Albright moved the lines back to the patriarchal era. He declared that the patriarchal materials in Genesis 12–50 contained a historical core of information that could be trusted. But this thesis began to give way by the middle of the 1970s in the view of many. Two scholars[2] raised so many questions about Albright's alleged evidences for the historicity of this period that a general disaffection among some scholars began to take place.

1. Hershel Shanks, "The Biblical Minimalists: Expunging Ancient Israel's Past," *BR* 13.3 (June 1997): 32.

2. Thomas L. Thompson, *The Historicity of the Patriarchal Narratives* (Berlin: de Gruyter, 1974) and John van Seters, *Abraham in History and Tradition* (New Haven: Yale University Press, 1975). Thompson now teaches at the University of Copenhagen and van Seters teaches at the University of North Carolina.

The lines were moved once again up to the time of the Exodus and the conquest of Canaan. The study of this era has resulted in a real donnybrook. John Garstang thought the issue was settled in the 1930s when he excavated Jericho, announcing that the destruction of that key city in the conquest had occurred about the spring of 1400. But he was judged to be wrong by later colleagues. Subsequent excavations by Kathleen Kenyon reversed Garstang's opinions, and the debate was on.

In the 1950s, Yohanan Aharoni argued that instead of an Israelite conquest of the land, there was a "peaceful infiltration" into Canaan. Simultaneously, Albrecht Alt and Martin Noth were coming to the same conclusion. Eventually the question became not whether Israel took the land of Canaan by force or by peaceful penetration, but whether there was any evidence for a nation of Israel at all! Fortunately, Pharaoh Merneptah's Stela, dating from the thirteenth century, included a reference to the word *Israel* with a determinative sign (indicating what kind of word it was) after it for a people. As Hershel Shanks commented, "But for this accidental find [by Sir Flinders Petrie], the biblical minimalists might have won the day among mainstream scholars, who often feel defensive about maintaining the historicity of obviously tendentious biblical narratives."[3]

But the minimalists did not concede the case, even on these strong grounds. One argued that it was only a geographical term, and not an ethnic designation, while another argued that this "Israel" had no relationship with the group we know then, or now, as Israel.[4] On these grounds, not only was the Bible an unreliable historical source, but so was the hieroglyphic stela of Pharaoh Merneptah! There seemed to be no end of hubris.

The lines were moved again: this time to the era of the united monarchy of Kings David and Solomon. But that era also was not impervious to skeptical thinking. Philip R. Davies found that the "House of David was built on sand" and David himself was "as real as King Arthur!"[5] What makes such a disclaimer all the more surprising is that it came in the face of the Tell Dan eighth-century stela found in 1993, which told of the victories of "[Jeho]ram son of Ahab, King of Israel"

3. Hershel Shanks, op. cit., p. 38.

4. The first view belongs to Gosta Ahlstrom, *Who Were the Israelites?* (Winona Lake, Ind., Eisenbrauns, 1988) and the second belongs to Robert B. Coote, *Early Israel: A New Horizon* (Minneapolis: Fortress, 1990).

5. Philip R. Davies, "'House of David' Built on Sand," *BAR* 20 (1994): 55 as cited by Hershel Shanks, op. cit., p. 39.

and "[Ahaz]iah son of Jehoram, [ki]ng of the House of David."[6] This confirmed the existence of a dynasty of King David. However, the rebuttal was that there was not a word divider dot between Beth and David; thus, Beth David was to be read as a toponym much as Bethlehem was a place name. And if this could be said of David, not much more could be said for the divided kingdom which followed from the end of the tenth to the sixth centuries.

So the discussion has gone in this fast-moving debate. Recently it has taken on a political aspect. Keith Whitelam recently published *The Invention of Ancient Israel: The Silencing of Palestinian History*.[7] His argument is that the whole idea of an ancient Israel was an "invention" created to exclude a Palestinian history. Thus, Israel itself was a fiction, and any search for it was both illegitimate and useless.

Is it any wonder that many are hesitant to attempt to write a history of Israel at this time? Indeed, our main source for many of the events of this history is the Bible itself. But if it is to be totally discounted, must we not also, for the same reasons, discount and disregard the ancient histories of Herodotus and Josephus? Then, why should we treat any of the claims of the ancient hieroglyphic and cuneiform monuments with any more respect? Eventually this type of deconstruction will land us in a solipsism in which only we ourselves exist and no more!

The history of Israel you are about to read has taken a different approach which we explain in the first chapter. We have treated the biblical text along with the other written materials from the ancient Near East as innocent until proven guilty by the evidence. Moreover, the archaeological evidence will enlarge our understanding of many of the key events and the times in which the episodes of the eras occurred. Ancient Israel was not an "invention" or an attempt to suppress a Palestinian history; it was and continues to be the basis and roots for much that is found in the three major religions of the world: Judaism, Christianity, and Islam.

Rather than moving the lines farther and farther back in time in an effort to find the lowest common denominator on which all scholars can agree, it is high time that we dig into the evidence in a more vigorous manner and test whether the things believed are indeed sustained by the facts, times, culture, and epigraphical materials themselves. We

6. See Avraham Biran, "'David' Found at Dan," *BAR* 20 (March/April 1994): 26–39; and David Noel Freedman and Jeffrey C. Geoghegan, "'House of David' Is There!" *BAR* 21 (1995): 78–79.

7. Keith W. Whitelam, *The Invention of Ancient Israel: The Silencing of Palestinian History* (New York: Routledge, 1996).

would be the major losers if we rejected the information we have in favor of a safer consensus that would earn us the plaudits of colleagues. Neither academic, religious, nor political approval should be our motivating force as we turn each piece of evidence for its contribution to this history. Only the truth should be our final resting place, for in no other haven are we credible as scholars and as mortals.

1

The Current State of Old Testament Historiography

According to the modern consensus in the field, the volume you are holding in your hands is a book that should, according to modern standards, never have seen the light of day. For example, J. Maxwell Miller, writing in 1994, summarized his view about the possibility of writing or conducting a study of the history of Israel : "In view of the wide range of approaches and views, . . . it is impossible to present a reconstruction of the history of Israel that represents scholarly consensus. There simply is no consensus at the present moment."[1]

No Consensus

Interestingly enough, however, the disagreement among scholars is not so much over the "facts" in the field; rather, it is over how one should interpret those facts, and with what sorts of presuppositions one

1. J. Maxwell Miller, "Introduction to the History of Ancient Israel," *The New Interpreter's Bible*, ed. Leander Keck (Nashville: Abingdon, 1994), 257. Among the key contributors to this discussion are: Thomas L. Thompson, *Early History of the Israelite People* (Leiden: Brill, 1992); Philip R. Davies, *In Search of Ancient Israel* (Sheffield, 1992); John Van Seters, *Prologue to History* (Yale, 1992); Norman Gottwald, *The Tribes of Yahweh: A Sociology of the Religion of Liberated Israel* (Maryknoll, N.Y.: Orbis, 1979); A. Mazar, *Archaeology of the Land of the Bible* (New York: Doubleday, 1990); and Israel Finkelstein, *The Archaeology of the Israelite Settlement* (Jerusalem: Israel Exploration Society, 1988). For a convenient summary and critique of the minimalist view of history, see Baruch Halpern, "Erasing History: The Minimalist Assault on Ancient History," *Bible Review* 11.6 (1995): 26 – 35, 47.

may legitimately approach the study of Old Testament history. Because of these two major areas of disagreement, a variety of methods for the study of the Old Testament (hereafter abbreviated as OT) has emerged, with little or no consensus exhibited among any of the articles or complete monographs on the subject.

No Agreed-upon Definition of History

The problem is, however, much more serious than that; it has gone so far as to be uncertain just what is the definition or nature of history itself. Is history-as-account (rather than the other sense of history-as-event, which is not treated here for the moment) the selective rearrangement into a meaningful narrative of what people have said, done, and thought in the past? If so, one would presume that history would rest primarily on textual accounts from that past, supplemented by contemporary inscriptions and artifacts from archaeology. But times have changed. The view that seems to have temporarily gained ascendancy is to give credence to particular perceptions of reality (usually those of educated, upper-class, male scribes) that may not be in line with contemporary concerns of those from the underclasses, ethnic minorities, or feminist groups. Dependency on any written documents, much less the use of biblical materials for constructing the history of Israel, is just out of the question.

Added to this is a further complication: In the eyes of some writers on this topic, the Bible is suspect as being a religious document more concerned about getting across a "privileged point of view" than it is in representing fairly the real state of affairs. Is this a legitimate conclusion based on any fair appraisal of all the materials that are available to us? Should the Bible be excluded as a source from which to write a history of Israel?

No Priority Given to the Bible as a Source

Keith Whitelam is sure that the Bible should not be given a primary role as a source in the formulation of a history of Israel. He asserts: "The standard treatments of the history of Israel, constrained as they are by the biblical texts, are set in the mold of political histories concerned with the unique event and unique individual. . . . However, the continued conviction that the biblical text remains the primary source for all periods of history means that many historians perpetuate this unnecessary restriction in their consideration of other forms of potential evidence."[2]

Of course, it is agreed that in the real technical sense of the term, the Bible is no more a history book than it is a science textbook, law book, ethics manual, or even a systematic theology. It is not organized according to the formats of these disciplines, nor is any one of these approaches the major reason why the Bible was written. But that is different from the argument that asserts that the Bible purports to include a chronicle of real events from the ancient Near East, against which backdrop the revelation of God was communicated. The work of Yahweh in the OT is depicted as being a part of history itself.

Why are moderns so skeptical about the whole prospect of writing a history of anything, much less a history of Israel? And why is it that the tensions rise almost to a breaking point when it involves the Christian Scriptures and the presence of God in that narrative? The answers to these and related questions must be found in an analysis of some modern fallacies that have arisen since the days of the Enlightenment in the eighteenth and nineteenth centuries. These arguments are accelerating so rapidly and affecting a discipline like the history of Israel so dramatically that it is breathtaking.

Some Modern Fallacies

Fallacy No. 1: History cannot include the unique, the miraculous, and the intervention of the divine. One of the most prized principles of modernity is the principle of analogy that assumes that all historical phenomena must be subjected to an analogous explanation, i.e., one that explains events in terms of other known happenings. But should the event that is being examined claim to be unique, involve the intervention of God, or be a miraculous occurrence, it is immediately disqualified by this Enlightenment definition. Instead, it contends that there are no other analogous happenings by which such unique, divine, or miraculous events could be measured, inspected, and evaluated.

Because of this feature, W. G. Dever asserted that "the Bible contains no real historiography in the modern sense. . . . The modern notion of a disinterested secular history would have been inconceivable to Biblical writers."[3] J. Maxwell Miller repeated the same sentiment when he described the three basic differences between the "critical"

2. Keith W. Whitelam, "Recreating the History of Israel," *JSOT* 35 (1986): 55.

3. W. G. Dever, "Recent Archaeological Discoveries and Biblical Research," *BAR* 16 (1990): 53.

historian and his or her "precritical" counterpart: The contemporary historian's approach tends to differ from that of his earliest counterparts in three ways: he generally takes a critical stance toward his sources; (2) he is inclined to disregard the supernatural or miraculous in his treatment of past events; (3) he is very much aware of his own historicity and, accordingly, of the subjectivity and tentative character of his own historical conclusions."[4]

But two objections can be made to this preemptory disregard for potential materials for historical construction that have any reference to a deity, the unique, or the miraculous. First, it follows the somewhat arbitrary definition of history that was established in the Enlightenment. In that case, as C. Westermann observed, "The Old Testament has no concept of history, in the sense that history is only *history* that can be documented and that follows a verifiable course governed by causal laws."[5] But beside such a cavalier redefinition of what does and does not constitute history, it has a second flaw. The principle of analogy is not applied evenly to all other ancient documents. The presence and activities of the gods in inscriptions, such as the Mesha Inscription and the Behistun Stone, or in "histories" such as Herodotus's, did not automatically eliminate them from being considered as accurate sources for the histories to which they contribute, despite the references to the god Chemosh in the Mesha Inscription, the Delphic Oracle in Herodotus, and the plethora of instances in which Ahura Mazda appears on the Behistun Stone.[6] It would be possible to multiply these examples many times over, for it found frequent usage in the ancient Near East.

It is understandable, of course, that scholars reexplain the events ascribed, for example, to Chemosh, but would it necessarily follow that biblical sources should receive the same treatment? queried V. Philips Long.[7] At this point, the matter seems to settle on a personal decision whether one sides with the biblical claims or with the critical assumptions. But the issue is not to be left at the doorsteps of starting presup-

4. J. M. Miller, *The Old Testament and the Historian* (Philadelphia: Fortress, 1976), 12 – 13.

5. C. Westermann, "The Old Testament's Understanding of History in Relation to That of the Enlightenment," in *Understanding the Word: Essays in Honor of Bernard W. Anderson, JSOTSup* 37; ed. J. T. Butler, E. W. Conrad, and B. C. Ollenburger (Sheffield: JSOT Press, 1985), 207.

6. See the engaging article by Edwin Yamauchi, "The Current State of Old Testament Historiography," in *Faith, Tradition and History*, ed. A. R. Millard, J. K. Hoffmeier, and D. W. Baker (Winona Lake, Ind.: Eisenbrauns, 1994), 1 – 36, especially pp. 27 – 28, where Yamauchi notes Herodotus's appeal to the Delphic Oracle and the presence of 69 references to Ahura Mazda on the Behistun Inscription.

7. V. Philips Long, *The Art of Biblical History* (Grand Rapids: Zondervan, 1994), 125 – 127.

positions, for this only masks the fact that presuppositions are of various types and operate at several levels.[8]

William Abraham has pointed to another way out of this impasse in his *Divine Revelation and the Limits of Historical Criticism*.[9] The problem, as Abraham analyzed it, is that the principle of analogy is too narrowly based if it is defined as being restricted to my own personal experience. There are just too many real events that lie outside the realm of my own experience; therefore, this principle must operate within a wider context. Analogical thinking can only operate as far as the network of my background beliefs allow it to do so. To put the matter more sharply, events must be caused by choices or actions of personal agents or natural forces, or a combination of the two. But where personal agency is involved, Abraham insightfully reminds us, the historian may adopt a *formal conception* of the correlation (which would allow both human and divine agency) or a *material conception* of the correlation (which would limit it to terrestrial causes, while disallowing divine causation).

The actions of God in the story of Israel's history are not bolts out of the blue but, instead, belong to a complex of interrelated acts, a veritable network of happenings. Thus, to believe in God's intervention into the complex of events on this earth is not to affirm randomness, or the esoteric, but it is to enjoy the principle of correlation on a much wider base than a limited material conception would allow.

Fallacy No. 2: History cannot include anything that does not have external documentation. Another fallacy is the rejection of everything in Scripture for which there is no external documentation or external corroboration. So serious are scholars about this principle that they refuse to begin their history of Israel in those periods that they judge to be without such external evidences. Accordingly, Miller and Hayes[10] see no history prior to the time of the judges, while Soggin and Whitelam[11] start their reconstruction of Israel's history with David and Solomon.

8. A point made by V. A. Harvey, *The Historian and the Believer: A Confrontation Between the Modern Historian's Principles of Judgment and the Christian's Will to Believe* (New York: Macmillan, 1966), 84.

9. W. Abraham, *Divine Revelation and the Limits of Historical Criticism* (Oxford: Oxford University Press, 1982) as cited by V. Philips Long, *The Art of Biblical History*.

10. J. Maxwell Miller and John H. Hayes, *A History of Ancient Israel and Judah* (Philadelphia: Westminster, 1986). The same could be said for Martin Noth, *The History of Israel*, tr. from the 2nd ed. by Stanley Goodman (New York: Harper & Brothers, 1958), which has been one of the standard textbooks in this field for many seminaries and universities over the years.

11. J. A. Soggin, *A History of Israel: From the Beginnings to the Bar Kochba Revolt*, tr. John Bowden (London: SCM Press, 1984). K. W. Whitelam, *The Just King: Monarchial Judicial Authority in Ancient Israel* (Sheffield: JSOT Press, 1979).

The most radical of all is Garbini,[12] who rejects the entire OT except some elements from the Persian and Hellenistic eras.

But such a reduction of usable historical data to those materials that are verifiable from existing artifacts or epigraphical remains could lead to premature foreclosing of the case. For example, Yamauchi reminds us that it was not until 1932 that we had any external verification for the exile of Jehoiachin in Babylon from the tablets of E. Weidner. Nor did we get attestation for Pontius Pilate until 1961 or for the procurator Felix until 1966, or the "house of David" until the Aramaic stele fragment was found at Tel Dan and published in 1993.[13]

Often the absence of evidence, such as the uncertainty of archeological periods on some tells, may not be a lack of evidence at all. It may only indicate the randomness of our knowledge of the past, or a telltale sign that our methodologies for recovering the past are still in need of development. For example, the conquest of Canaan by the Israelites is more frequently denied today because sites such as Jericho, Ai, and Gibeon do not provide any evidence of any Late Bronze materials. But, to take Gibeon for the moment, Late Bronze materials were found in its cemetery. And it is conceded that the modern village of El-Jib sits unexcavated on the mound of Gibeon, so how can this site be used as evidence that it was not in existence during the days of Joshua? All the evidence may not be in yet, so "no evidence" may only be a witness that there is no evidence as yet. Meanwhile, the debate continues over the interpretation of the data from Jericho and over the proper location of Ai.

Fallacy No. 3: History cannot include narratives about individuals, but must focus on nations instead.[14] Here is another arbitrary restriction that is introduced by formal definition. Why would the histories of individuals, families, and tribes be excluded from consideration, unless this, too, is another remnant of the Enlightenment, as Westermann noted, that, "at the basis of this critique is the assumption that familial affairs have no place in *historical-political* events, which have to do instead with the nation, not with the family."[15] No doubt, this is the reason for the reluctance for many modern histories of Israel to commence prior to the times of the monarchy when a nation first appears on the scene.

12. G. Garbini, *History and Ideology in Ancient Israel* (London: SCM, 1988).

13. E. Yamauchi, "The Current State," pp. 26–27.

14. While point one in this argument does not have the apparent force and importance that the previous points one and two have had, it is nevertheless an important point since some have raised this as another roadblock in the process of constructing a history of Israel.

15. C. Westermann, "The Old Testament Understanding," p. 211 as cited by Yamauchi, "The Current State," p. 28.

But such a tactic is hardly fair to the large bulk of materials found in the OT that represent matters prior to the emergence of a geopolitical unit in the nation.

Fallacy No. 4: History must not focus on individuals as shapers of the times, but on sociological factors that attempt to discover general laws and large-scale societal forces that influence historical change. Some sociological approaches to history attempt to maintain a balance between the individual, the particular, the unique, and the complementary search for general laws that shape history. But most, like Karl Marx's assessment, charge that individuals play a minor role in history.

This diminishing of the role of the individual in exchange for material/economic or related forces as the real driving forces in history is what leads many of these sociological approaches to history to end up as antiliterary and antitextual.[16] The preference is for impersonal processes, rather than human agents, to have control over the destinies of mortals. Once again, there is an attempt to supersede the "limiting constraints" of the text by alleging that the text is merely a witness to itself and not to any historical reality! But in place of the text's view of reality, another must be substituted—which usually ends up being the sociohistorian's own view of reality.

Added to this mistake, another is now possible: the anachronism of projecting one's present history back on to the past. For example, some liberation motifs have been retrojected over the ancient history of the Exodus of Israel from Egypt in such a way that the past is practically swallowed up by the present concerns, no matter how right they may be in and of themselves. But is such a procedure a fair reading of what happened back then? In a contrary but astonishing move, as Andrew Hill and Gary Herion noted, the role of personal faith is excluded from the discussion of sociopolitical processes as an unworthy participant in the discussion.[17]

Fallacy No. 5: History writing must not give logical and necessary priority to written evidence over material culture. Recently, a greater emphasis has been placed on nontextual evidence and the development of models based on this evidence, leading to the statement of anthropological and

16. See the balanced discussion of V. Philips Long, *The Art of Biblical History*, pp. 135–142. Long attributes the first introduction of the distinction between *idiographic* (describing the separate, the distinct, the individual) and the *nomothetic* (lawgiving) to Wilhelm Windelband, rector of the University of Strassburg, in his inaugural address in 1894 entitled, "History and Natural Science." Long, pp. 135–136.

17. Andrew Hill and Gary Herion, "Functional Yahwism and Social Control in the Early Israelite Monarchy," *JETS* 29 (1986): 277 as cited by V. Philips Long, *The Art of Biblical History*, p. 141.

sociological models that show little or no consideration of the textual evidence.[18] Typically, assumptions based on archaeological assumptions are made about ethnicity, to the disadvantage of what is claimed in biblical or ancient texts. Thus, it is claimed that a Transjordanian site, such as Dibon, could not have been involved in Transjordanian conquests in the Bronze Age, for it was not occupied in this century. However, as K. A. Kitchen has shown,[19] the name does appear as *tbn* in a list of conquests across the Jordan by Rameses II. Since the site of Dibon was known to Rameses' scribes, it is a fallacy to assign priority to the archaeological evidence that counters the evidence found in the textual materials. This same phenomenon can be illustrated from many other similar instances in the recent past endeavors of writing the history of Israel.

APPROACHES TO THE STUDY OF THE HISTORY OF ISRAEL

Currently, there are about five major schools or approaches to how one may evaluate the historical worth of the written and material evidences for a history of Israel and how one goes about reconstructing that history. The five schools are: the Traditional Approach, the William F. Albright and John Bright Baltimore School, the Albrecht Alt and Martin Noth School, the Norman Gottwald School, and the Non-Pan-Israelite Tribal Confederation School. Each of these merits at least a brief discussion, since interaction with each view will follow in this history.

APPROACH NO. 1: THE TRADITIONAL SCHOOL

It was possible for John Bright to assert in 1956 that "Protestant fundamentalism has been singularly unproductive of late where history writing is concerned."[20] But that estimate would need to be drastically revised today with the contributions of F. F. Bruce, R. K. Harrison, Kenneth A. Kitchen, E. H. Merrill, Charles F. Pfeiffer, E. R. Thiele, and L. J. Wood.[21]

---

18. Richard S. Hess, "Fallacies in the Study of Early Israel: On Onomastic Perspective," *TynB* 45.2 (1994): 339–354.

19. K. A. Kitchen, "The Egyptian Evidence on Ancient Jordan," in *Early Edom and Moab: The Beginnings of the Iron Age in Southern Jordan*, ed. P. Bienkowski (Sheffield Archaeological Monographs, 7; Sheffield: J. R. Collis, 1992), pp. 21–34, especially 27–29.

20. John Bright, *Early Israel in Recent History Writing* (London: SCM, 1956), 27.

21. F. F. Bruce, *Israel and the Nations: From the Exodus to the Fall of the Second Temple* (Grand Rapids: Eerdmans, 1963); R. K. Harrison, *A History of Old Testament Times* (Grand Rapids: Zondervan, 1957); K. A. Kitchen, *Ancient Orient and the Old Testament* (Chicago: InterVarsity, 1966); E. H. Merrill, *Kingdom of Priests: A History of Old Testament Israel* (Grand Rapids: Baker, 1987); C. F. Pfeiffer, *Old Testament History* (Grand Rapids: Baker, 1973); E. R. Thiele, *The Mysterious Numbers of the Hebrew Kings* (Chicago: University of Chicago, 1953); L. J. Wood, *A Survey of Israel's History* (Grand Rapids: Zondervan, 1970).

The traditional approach has tended to argue that the text of Genesis to Kings embodies the only ancient, continuous written source that deals directly with Israel's origins. Similarly, the Ezra-to-Chronicles account essentially repeats the same material; however, it commences in earnest with King David. The materials depicted in all these books are taken at face value on the principle that the text is innocent until it is proven guilty by external facts. Therefore, the history of Israel is the story of the patriarch Jacob and his family, which was later renamed Israel, and which multiplied into a nation of 600,000 fighting men, plus women and children, who wandered in the wilderness for forty years after escaping Egypt, and finally conquered Canaan under Joshua.

But the traditional approach has been subjected to a number of difficult problems. One of the main difficulties, critics charge, is that the chronological framework of the Bible does not "square" with the evidence coming from a number of other sources. For instance, the Bible would seem[22] to require a fifteenth-century (Late Bronze Age) date for the conquest of Canaan, but archaeologists are saying of late that they have found little or no evidence of any Late Bronze Age occupation or destruction of the ruins of such key cities as Arad, Heshbon, Jericho, or Ai.

John Bimson has sought to counter this objection by advancing the proposal that the destruction levels, attributed to the Hyksos at the end of the Middle Bronze Age in the mid-sixteenth century, be redated to the late fifteenth century and reassigned from the Hyksos to the Israelites.[23] But few archaeologists have been attracted to this resolution of the problem; they claim that Arad, Heshbon, and Ai show no archaeological evidence of Middle Bronze occupation or destruction. The traditional position remains marginalized, as much as it ever was, despite its desire to become a full partner in the current discussions.

Approach No. 2: The Albright/Wright/Bright Baltimore School

This school has argued for the general trustworthiness of the account in Genesis to Kings, but it never meant by this that all the details of Scripture were accurate and true.[24] Whenever the Bible did not corre-

22. The operative phrase here is "would seem." For more detail, see below chapters 9 – 11.
23. John Bimson, *Redating the Exodus and Conquest* (Sheffield: *JSOT*, 1978).
24. John Bright, *A History of Israel* (Philadelphia: Westminster, 1981); William Foxwell Albright, *From Stone Age to Christianity* (New York: Doubleday, 1957); idem., "The Biblical Period," in *The Jews: Their History, Culture and Religion* I, ed. L. Finkelstein (New York: Harper and Row, 1949), 3 – 69; and George Ernest Wright, *Biblical Archaeology* (Philadelphia: Westminster, 1962).

late with archaeological interpretations, this school felt free to depart from the Bible in favor of the external evidence without searching for any harmonization of the two sets of data. Accordingly, John Bright's *A History of Israel* (first edition 1959, second edition 1972, third edition 1981, with a fourth edition to be published in 1996 or 1997 posthumously) treated the patriarchs as figures connected with movements of the Amorites around 2000 B.C.—with a negotiable margin of eight hundred years.

This approach is the result of a compromise between the Bible's version of what happened and a reconstruction of the extrabiblical evidence. It understands the Bible primarily through the eyes of a modified historical-critical approach to the Bible. Since none of the details of the Bible are taken in a literal fashion, any problems that appear from the alleged contradictions with the Bible are not causes for concern. Thus, the Exodus is placed in the thirteenth century during the days of Rameses II (ca. 1279–1213 B.C.), shortly before the stele inscription mentioned the people of Israel in Canaan at the time of Merneptah's fifth year as pharoah.

Since Bright died in March 1995, a fourth revision of his *History*, which became an established textbook in its generation, is underway by an editorial group. Bright's *History* has been translated into German, Spanish, and Japanese.

APPROACH NO. 3: THE ALT/NOTH SCHOOL

Alt and Noth expressed extreme doubt that the overall outline of events found in Genesis to Kings contributes very much to its historicity.[25] In fact, according to them, this biblical outline is probably a "revisionist" form of history. Instead, using historical-critical analysis of the text, only a few older literary units and traditions survived the revisionists' hands, according to this school. Even archaeological evidence can contribute very little when tested against models of ancient historical parallels, ethnographic, and sociological studies.

Noth, therefore, chose instead to base his work on studies about the ancient Greek and Italian tribal leagues known as amphictyonies, on the sociological theories of Max Weber, and on extensive traditio-critical analysis of the Bible. In the judgment of Albright, Alt and Noth stressed

25. Albrecht Alt, *Kleine Schriften zur Geschichte des Volkes Israel I-III* (Munich I, 1968; II, 1964; III, 1968). A selection of these articles is available in English translation in idem., *Essays in Old Testament History and Religion* (New York, 1966); and Martin Noth, *Geschichte Israels* (Gottingen: Vandernhoeck & Ruprecht, 1950, 2nd ed, 1954 = *The History of Israel* [New York: Harper and Row, 1958, 2nd ed. 1960].)

three guiding principles in forming their histories: (1) they rigidly applied the methods of form criticism, (2) they constantly emphasized the factor of etiology in explaining the origin of tradition, and (3) they held tenaciously to the view that certain names and tales adhered to certain geographical locations (*Ortsgebunden*, "tied to places").[26]

But all three guiding principles could be faulted, argued Albright and Bright. Literary forms in and of themselves could not be the final arbiters of what was or was not historical. The classification of the literary form did not automatically render a verdict on a text's historicity. Moreover, the etiological factor is often a secondary formation with little or no evidence that it ever was primary. Finally, traditions can and do shift locations, for they are more "tied to people" (*Volksgebunden*) than they are "tied to places" (*Ortsgebunden*).

Alt and Noth tended to build one theory on top of another as they skipped over the patriarchs and the Exodus as being without any historical reality and spoke instead of the ancestors of Israel as probably being seminomads who ranged between the fingers of the desert and Canaan searching for pastures until they finally settled down and took up agriculture. These tribes then formed an amphictyonic league around a central shrine. Thus, there never was a conquest of Canaan until Saul and David's time.

Besides the problems already noticed, the whole amphictyonic model, once a reigning concept among scholars, is now completely rejected. Weber's theories about seminomads are also suspect as is the heavy dependence on form criticism to supply historical data.

Approach No. 4: The Norman Gottwald School

Gottwald did not choose to go the route of using historical-critical analysis of the Scripture or to side with the Max Weber-Alt-Noth assumption that the nomadism of ancient Palestine was essentially different from the social structures of the peasant farmers or city dwellers of Canaan.[27] Instead, he based his conclusion on what he regarded as the results of ethnographic studies. These studies allegedly showed that

26. W. F. Albright, "The Israelite Conquest of Canaan in the Light of Archaeology," *BASOR* 74 (1939): 11–23 as cited by J. Bright, *Early Israel in Recent History Writing*, pp. 89–104.

27. This school is not exclusively that of Gottwald, but George Mendenhall, who gave its largest impetus, would not care to be grouped in this category any longer. However, the sociological model has developed far beyond Gottwald's original horizon. For example, one would link the name of Israel Finkelstein, *The Archaeology of the Israelite Settlement* (Jerusalem: Israel Exploration Society, 1988) with many features in this school as well.

seminomadic herding was not an intrusive element from the desert fringe; it was derived from sedentary agriculture in ancient Palestine.

Accordingly, Gottwald, followed in part an article in *Biblical Archaeologist* written by George E. Mendenhall in 1962, which claimed that Israel did not enter Canaan as conquerors, but as nomads. Israel arose from the indigenous Canaanite population. Overshadowed by Egypt, oppressed by the rulers of the city-states in the lowlands, the peasants finally had enough and staged a revolt at the end of the Late Bronze Age as they retreated to the hill country to form an egalitarian tribal society under the aegis of a new Yahweh.[28]

Gottwald's work rested almost entirely on social theory, again building one theory on top of another. But as for a peasant revolt, instead of a conquest of Canaan, there is not one word in the Bible or in any other epigraphic material which suggests such ever took place. While Gottwald succeeded in attracting only a large number of liberation theologians, two of the concepts he stressed have remained: (1) Israel, most contemporary scholars agree, probably emerged from an indigenous Canaanite population, and (2) from here on out, explanations about Israel's so-called conquest and occupation of Canaan must have ethnographic and sociological research behind them if they wish to be considered by the reigning scholarly community. A few voices could still be heard, however, for grounding discussions of Israel's origins in epigraphy and archaeology, but they are quickly being marginalized in the academy.

Approach No. 5: Non-Pan Israelite Tribal Confederation Schools

Each of the four previous schools argue for some kind of tribal confederation from which a united Israelite monarchy would emerge during the days of Israel's united monarchy of Saul, David, and Solomon. But a growing number of scholars regarded the whole supposition as contrived, openly expressing their doubts that such a state of affairs ever existed. Among those who doubted this construction were J. A. Soggin, J. M. Miller, J. H. Hayes, J. Van Seters, and T. L. Thompson.[29]

28. N. Gottwald, *The Tribes of Yahweh: A Sociology of the Religion of Liberated Israel* (Maryknoll, N.Y.: Orbis, 1979).

29. J. A. Soggin, *A History of Israel: From the Beginnings to the Bar Kochba Revolt* (London: SCM, 1985); J. M. Miller and J. H. Hayes, *A History of Ancient Israel and Judah* (Philadelphia: Westminster, 1986); John Van Seters, *Abraham in History and Tradition* (New Haven: Yale, 1975); idem., *The Hyksos: A New Investigation* (New Haven: Yale, 1966); idem., *In Search of History: Historiography in the Ancient World and The Origins of Biblical History* (New Haven: Yale, 1983); and T. L. Thompson, *Early History of the Israelite People* (Leiden: Brill, 1992).

Miller and Hayes felt the whole previous approach was incorrect. Israel and Judah, they argued, were separate peoples only temporarily joined under David and Solomon and perhaps some later kings. In fact, even David and Solomon were legendary figures, brought about by the "re-imag[ing]" of the Genesis-to-Kings account, which was done in order to idealize Israel's past, by the editors of Chronicles-Nehemiah, for theological reasons.

Thompson was no less severe: the whole story about the rise and fall of the Israelite monarchy was constructed out of whole cloth during the Persian period as an attempt to ingratiate themselves with the Persian rulers. Since the Persians, so Thompson reasoned, had benevolent policies that honored national gods and traditions, the Jews living in Persia decided they had better get both quickly. So the editors of Genesis-to-Kings created a tradition, using the name *Israel*, a term having nothing to do with Judah, as they retrojected back into time a Jerusalem cult and temple along with a legendary David and Solomon. All of this was constructed from a few older traditions, but all of it was so obviously reworked that it was almost unrecognizable by all until recent scholarship uncovered the ruse.

Thompson will allow that the dynasty founded by Omri has the most authentic items in its accounts, but certainly nothing before the ninth century is trustworthy or reliable for historical construction.

Thompson is so skeptical that it seems as if skepticism has gone about as far as it can go; it even attracted the criticism of Miller. In fact, Miller doesn't mind Thompson's calling into question David and Solomon's historicity, but when he questions the general setting of those times, Miller declares he has gone too far. When one casts off the total construct of the Bible with its general chronology, it succeeds only in calling everything into question.

The Present Approach to the History of Israel

"One might almost gain the impression," conceded Bright in a moment of unusual candor, "that each scholar selects from the traditions that which his best judgments and his predilections allow him to regard as historical—often little enough—and discards the rest. It is without doubt the most pressing problem confronting the historiography of Israel that the question of method as it applies to this problem be given an answer."[30] Surely he is correct. Even more so, now that

30. John Bright, *Early Israel in Recent History Writing*, p. 15.

postmodernity (the recent view of life that, among other things, eliminates absolute truth in favor of truth being that which is in the eye of each beholder) has agreed that all persons follow their own preferences. However, is it not necessary for those who are truly postmodern to have those predilections governed by so-called facts, standards, or rules of evidence? Can one construction be just as good as another, so long as it can find a popular note on which to hang its theory and command a significant number of those scholars who belong to the current power block?

But this does not mean an evangelical history of Israel may contend that what is good for the goose is good for the gander and go and do likewise! Some in this camp may complain: Why should we be judged differently and on a stricter set of standards by reviewers and peers? But such action will advantage all parties very little.

On the contrary, the present history of Israel will adopt the methodology of using the present chronology and statement of the history of this nation as set forth in the biblical texts as our starting point and working assumption. If and when the external evidence clearly refutes that construct, in part or in whole, only then will we abandon it and adopt that for which there is stronger attestation.

The type of argument used here will be that set forth by Stephen Toulmin.[31] Toulmin observed that arguments have a number of components: data, warrants, and backing. Because arguments are so complex, Toulmin advises us to chart the argument so that the function of each component becomes clear.[32] In historical studies, arguments typically involve the following components:

31. Stephen Toulmin, *Uses of Argument* (Cambridge: Cambridge University Press, 1958).

32. Many have built on Toulmin's approach, including Nigel M. de S. Cameron, *Biblical Higher Criticism and the Defense of Infallibilism in 19th Century Britain* (Lewiston: Edwin Mellen, 1987), 276–289; David H. Kelsey, *The Uses of Scripture in Recent Theology* (London: SCM, 1975), pp. 122–138; William Abraham, *Divine Revelation and the Limits of Historical Criticism* (Oxford: Oxford University Press, 1982), chap. 6; V. A. Harvey, *The Historian and the Believer: A Confrontation between the Modern Historian's Principles of Judgment and the Christian's Will to Believe* (New York: Macmillan, 1966), 43–64; and Walter C. Kaiser Jr., *Toward Rediscovering the Old Testament* (Grand Rapids: Zondervan, 1987), 68–72.

Given:	so, **Q** (Qualifier— necessarily, presumably, possibly)	Therefore, **C** (conclusion)
		unless **R**
D(Datum/data)	since **W** (Warrant) on account of **B** (Backing)	(Rebuttal)

It is important to notice that the difference between the historical-critical models and an evangelical model for constructing historical narrative is not the given of the data under investigation. And certainly it is not even the use of the tools and techniques of criticism. Rather, it is *the place where they appear in the argument*. Is historical criticism a *warrant* for reading the text, or is it to be reserved as a *qualifier*, that is, a *condition* of rebuttal? Accordingly, an evangelical model would go like this: Given the **Data**: the biblical narrative and text; so the **Qualifier** presumably, since the **Warrant** that what the Bible says is true, on account of the **Backing** that Jesus held this view, the text makes such a claim for itself, and the church has received it as such for these centuries; therefore, the **Conclusion** is that the narrative and chronology of the text is to be trusted; unless a **Rebuttal** is made in the form of counter-arguments questioning either the warrants or the backing, in which case a new argument must be introduced to justify the move from that data to conclusion.

The historical-critical argument, instead, goes like this: Given the **Data** of the phenomena culled from Scripture, so the **Qualifier** presumably, since the **backing** that historical-criticism is generally valid, and the Bible is a book like any other to which historical criticism applies; therefore, the **Conclusion** is that the narrative is composite, unless a **Rebuttal** can come in the form of counterarguments, such as ones that show that the evangelical interpretation is inherently more likely. Again, notice where the critical investigation of the text was introduced into the process of argumentation.

In order to carry out this program of reading the Bible historically, we will need to divide our task into two parts: first, we must understand the claims that the text is making for itself; and secondly, we must test the historical truth claims that the text makes for itself. These tests will examine both for *internal* consistency and *external* consistency with all of the known evidence available at this time.

2

Ancient Israel in Its Geographical Context

"To write the history of ancient Palestine," advised Gösta W. Ahlström, "can be nothing other than an attempt to present a probable picture based on such different kinds of source material as archaeological remains . . . and written material, as well as to indicate how the climate and physical structure of the country and its natural resources played a certain role in influencing different types of life style."[1] Accordingly, the second half of Ahlstrom's statement of agenda will be addressed in this chapter, which will seek to deal with the matters of the physical structure and climate of the country in order to locate the scene where most of the action of the history of Israel will transpire.

The Name of the Land

The most common name in the Old Testament for the land where the history of Israel takes place is Canaan. The earliest known reference to Canaan comes from a letter from Mari (on the Euphrates) in the eighteenth century B.C.[2] Egyptian inscriptions from the time of

1. Gösta W. Ahlström, *The History of Ancient Palestine* (Minneapolis: Fortress, 1993), p. 61.

2. G. Dossin, "Une Mention de canaanéens dans une lettre de Mari," *Syria* 50 (1973): 282. Among the more recent geographies, one should mention, Yohanan Aharoni, *The Land of the Bible: A Historical Geography*, tr. by Anson F. Rainey, rev. ed. (Philadelphia: Westminster, 1979); Denis Baly, *Basic Biblical Geography* (Philadelphia: Fortress, 1987). Added to these are the following atlases: Yohanan Aharoni and Michael Avi-Yonah, *The Macmillan Bible Atlas*, rev. (New York: Macmillan, 1977); L. H. Grollenberg, *Atlas of the Bible* (Nashville: Nelson, 1957); Thomas V. Briscoe, *Broadman & Holman Bible Atlas* (Nashville: Broadman & Holman, 1998); Carl G. Rasmussen, *The Zondervan NIV Atlas of the Bible* (Grand Rapids: Zondervan, 1989); J. Rogerson, *Atlas of the Bible* (New York: Facts on File, 1985); Barry Beitzel, *The Moody Atlas of Bible Lands* (Chicago: Moody, 1985); and J. B. Pritchard, ed., *The Harper Atlas of the Bible* (New York: Harper and Row, 1987).

Amenhotep II (1400s B.C.) mention a *ki-n-ᶜ-nu*, while a statue of Idrimi of Alalakh also refers to "the land of Canaan" *(ma-at ki-in-a-nim)*.[3]

The etymology of the name Canaan is unknown, but a later development may have connected it with the crimson dye industry that originated in that area and was known in Hurrian as *kinaḫḫu*.[4] This crimson and dark purple color was also called *kinaḫḫu* by the Sidonians, but they do not seem to have called the country by this same name. Thus the term for the crimson and textile industry came to designate the people of Canaan. By the time of the Iron Age, the designation *Canaanite* had changed to mean a "merchant," or "tradesperson"(cf. Prov. 31:24; Isa. 23:8; Zech. 14: 21), but it does not seem that it was meant as an ethnic term.

In the biblical narrative, Canaan is the son of Ham (Gen. 10:6), who became the ancestor of the Canaanites. Canaan is described as being the father of Sidon, the Hittites, Jebusites, Amorites, Girgashites, Hivites, Arkites, Sinites, Arvadites, Zemarites, and Hamathites (Gen. 10:15–18). While some recent scholars fear that such a list that represents the Canaanites as extending from Anatolia (Asia Minor, or present-day Turkey) to Nubia in Africa to be "unrealistic," there is no reason to doubt this list at the present time.

Genesis 10:19 also describes the borders of Canaan as "reach[ing] from Sidon toward Gerar as far as Gaza, and then toward Sodom, Gomorrah, Adamah, and Zeboiim, as far as Lasha." Thus, the description once again moves down the coastal area and then moves inland south of the central hill country to the five cities around the southeastern end of the Dead Sea. When this set of boundaries for Canaan is compared with those given in Numbers 34:2–12, a greatly enlarged area is announced in the passage in Numbers. There the boundaries extend from the "Wadi Egypt" (known today as the Wadi el-ᶜArish, the present-day southern border established after the Six-Day War of 1967), just below the Gaza strip in the south, to a spot above Byblos in the north. The eastern boundary would embrace the Transjordanian territory of Golan, Bashan, and Damascus, but then follow the Jordan River below the Sea of Galilee. It is interesting to note that the name *Canaan*, or the land of promise, is not used in the Bible for Transjorda-

---

3. Jack Sasson, "On Idrimi and Sarruwa," in *Studies on the Civilization and Culture of Nuzi and the Hurrians in Honor of Ernst R. Lachman*, eds. M. A. Morrison and D. I. Owen (Winona Lake, Ind.: Eisenbrauns, 1981), p. 323 dates the inscription to the thirteenth century B.C.E.

4. See Ephraim A. Speiser, *Oriental and Biblical Studies: Collected Writings of E. A. Speiser*, eds. J. J. Finkelstein and M. Greenberg (Philadelphia: University of Pennsylvania, 1967), pp. 324–325.

nia south of the Yarmuk River (what is most of the present-day state of Jordan).

The other name for this same territory is much more debated because of the possible connotations it carries in present political negotiations between the Israelis and the Palestinian Arabs: it is Palestine. It would appear that the term is derived from the Akkadian *palaštu*, *pilištu*, or Egyptian *p-r-st*, referring to the "Philistines."[5] But this term was at first limited to what is today known as the Gaza strip, where the Philistines once abode. By the time of the Greek historian Herodotus, it applied to the people or territory of the coastal plain from Gaza to Mt. Carmel. In the Roman period, the name was expanded to include the interior of the country (along with the coastal areas), as it became the official name for the province after A.D. 135, for the name Judea was being dropped from current usage.

The Geography of the Land

The land on which the history of Israel and Judah was played out occupies about 9,500 square miles, an area the size of the state of Vermont or the country of Belgium. It reaches from the Mediterranean Sea on the west, the Arabian desert on the east, to the Lebanon and Anti-Lebanon mountains on the north and the Sinai Desert on the south. In all, the land extends about one hundred and fifty miles from north to south and less than seventy-five miles in width. Due to its lack of any individual geographical identity, it was doomed to be the land-bridge, meeting place, and contested battlefield of the successive empires of Egypt, Assyria, Babylonia, Medo-Persia, the Hellenistic world, and Rome.

Our general orientation towards the land should always be facing toward the east, just as it was for an ancient Near Easterner, whereas modern western map orientation usually faces north, with the cartography reflecting this by placing north at the top of the map. Therefore, as one approached the land of the Bible from the often-stormy Mediterranean Sea, the land would appear to spread out before the traveler in four successive strips: (1) the coastal plain, (2) Galilee and the central hill country, flowing in a southerly direction from the Lebanon range, (3) the Jordan Rift Valley, continuous with the Bekaa Valley, continuing south of the Dead Sea in the Arabah, and (4) the Transjor-

5. Donald J. Wiseman, "Two Historical Inscriptions from Nimrud," *Iraq* 13 (1951): 21–26 points to the fact that *pilistu* may refer to Palestine in general. Certainly the name *palaštu* is known from an inscription by Adad-nirari III from the end of the 19th century B.C.

danian highlands as the southern continuation of the Anti-Lebanon mountains in Phoenicia/Lebanon on into the Moab-Edom plateau. The only major interruption of this general north-south orientation of the geographical features of the land is the protrusion from the Mediterranean Sea and into the interior by way of Mt. Carmel, which then drops off into the Esdraelon and Jezreel Valleys, which flow in a northwest-to-southeast direction toward the southern end of the Sea of Galilee.

The Coastal Plain

The first strip or ribbon of land would be the coastal plains of Philistia (today called the *Gaza strip*) and Sharon. At the southern end of these coastal plains is the Wadi el-ᶜArish, which empties into the Mediterranean Sea about thirty miles south of Raphia. This wadi is the present natural border between Israel and Egypt as set at the end of the 1967 war. It is also known from Assyrian inscriptions, where the wadi is called Nahal Musur, as Joshua 15:4 called it, "the Brook of Egypt."

The width of this plain varies from a few hundred feet wide at the foot of Mt. Carmel to about thirty miles wide near Gaza. The Bay of Accho, just north of Mt. Carmel, is the only good natural harbor on the coast, although there were other poorer (in the natural sense) ports such as Gaza, Ashkelon, Joppa, and Dor along this narrow ribbon of land bordering the sea. Later, Herod the Great would turn the old site of Strabo's Tower, just south of Dor, into the successful artificial harbor of Caesarea.

This coastal plain was subdivided into four plains: Acre in the north, Dor and Sharon in the middle, and Philistia in the south.

The *Plain of Acre* extended some twenty-five miles north of Mt. Carmel and was only five to eight miles wide. It did not play a major part in Israel's history and seemed at times to be more closely linked to the Phoenician kingdom of Tyre than to Israel.

The plains from Mt. Carmel to Joppa were known as the *Plain of Dor* and the *Plain of Sharon*. These marshy sites were fertile but poorly drained in ancient times. Both plains together were some fifty miles long and about ten miles wide. The hills to the east drained onto these plains, leaving mostly extensive marshes. At the southern end of Sharon was an almost impenetrable oak forest. This may be the reason why Israel never settled the only portion of the coastline that she ever had effective control over.

From Joppa to Gaza, it became the *Philistine Plain*, which was better suited for agriculture, since it became increasingly arid as one moved south, finally merging into the desert. The land gradually rose to three-hundred-feet-high gentle ranges. This area is thick with fruit orchards, olive trees, and grain fields.

One of the most famous international highways passed through these coastal plains; it was called the *Via Maris*,[6] "the Way of the Sea." It came up the coast from Egypt and then turned up and inward at the Carmel ridge, slipping through the Megiddo pass on down into the Esdraelon Valley towards Jezreel, forming the main arc of the Fertile Crescent (see below for a definition of this designation) that moved troops and commerce between Egypt to Mesopotamia through Israel and Syria.

Galilee and the Central Hill Country

A long range of limestone hills, moderately high but ruggedly contoured, form the backbone of the land. There are two main divisions to this natural north-south extension of the Lebanon mountains from the north: (1) Galilee, north of the Esdraelon and Jezreel Valleys, and (2) the central hill country, which extends from the valleys just mentioned almost to Jerusalem, forming Samaria, and the Judean hill country.

The Judean hill country extended from the northern environs of Jerusalem south to the Negev desert. *Ephraim*, named for the dominant tribe of Israel in the central hill country of Samaria, inhabited the mountains north of Jerusalem.

Farther north, Galilee was divided into two parts: northern or *Upper Galilee*, and *Lower Galilee*. Upper Galilee was more rugged and rose to almost four thousand feet, interspersed with fertile valleys, while Lower Galilee also had the same fertile valleys, though it was less rugged.

A radical break intersected the two Galilees from continuing this mountainous spine into Samaria and the Judean hill country: the Esdraelon and Jezreel Valleys. Here a flat, fertile plain spread almost eighteen miles across the face of Mt. Carmel. The Esdraelon Valley was linked by Mt. Carmel's four passes. In fact, there are four fortresses which guard the routes across Mt. Carmel, each spaced about five miles apart: Jokneam in the north, and then descending in a southerly direction: Megiddo, Taanach, and Ibleam. Of these four routes, the one past

6. This nomenclature, of course, is somewhat anachronistic, since it comes from much later times. However, it has become so entrenched in the literature that it is simpler to refer to these areas by the more popular designations for ease of communication.

Megiddo was clearly the most important, as the Egyptian report from the first campaign of Thutmose III concluded: "The capturing of Megiddo is the capturing of a thousand towns."[7]

The Esdraelon Valley was like the coastal plain with its interior valley floor, but it tilted gently toward the southeast, south of the Sea of Galilee, to a point where it reaches a depth of several hundred feet below sea level. In the east central side of this valley was the small city of Jezreel, later a summer palace site for the Ephraimite kings of northern Israel. At the far eastern end was the city of Beth-shean, and at the far western end were the four passes across Mt. Carmel. To the northwest of this valley stood Mt. Tabor while the eastern end of the valley was outlined by Mt. Moreh to the north and Mt. Gilboa to the south.

South of Esdraelon, or Jezreel Valley, the central hill country continued as Ephraim or Samaria. The most significant cities of this area are Shechem, Dothan, Tirzah, and Samaria. Shechem was located on a pass between the twin peaks of Mt. Ebal (3,083 feet) and Mt. Gerizim (2,889 feet). This central hill region was composed mostly of red, porous limestone (*terra rossa*) and dolomite with chalk in the foothills. South of Shechem was a broad, domed region with its highest point of 3,332 feet being at Jebel Asur (biblical Baal Hazor) near Bethel. The towns in this region were Shiloh, Mizpah, Gibeon, and Bethel. It was the southern part of this region that the tribe of Benjamin occupied. Two major east-west fault lines conveniently cut through this part of the country, giving good routes into the interior of the country: the first came up from the western foothills in the Valley of Aijalon along the route called "the ascent of Beth-horon" and led to a point just northwest of Jerusalem, while the second followed a double fault line from the other direction (i.e., from the region of Jericho), one leading to Gibeah and Michmash, the other leading more directly into Jerusalem.

The Judean section formed the southern and final extension of these hills that began in the Lebanon mountains, stretching from around Jerusalem to Beersheba in the Negev. In earlier biblical times, a good portion of this area was covered with forests, for its western slopes were especially well watered and ideal for growing grapes, olives, grain, and other similar products. Important cities and towns in this area included Jerusalem, Hebron, Bethlehem, Tekoa, Beth-zur, Tekoa, and Debir.

Parallel to the Judean portion of the central hill country was the *Shephelah* (meaning "lowland," "piedmont"), a section on the western

7. James B. Pritchard, ed., *Ancient Near Eastern Texts Relating to the Old Testament* (Princeton: Princeton University Press, 1950), p. 237.

slopes that separated the Philistine Plain from the Judean highlands. Because of its significance as a military buffer between the Gaza strip (where the Philistines dwelt for most of the earliest biblical period) and Judah, and also because of its rich agricultural productivity, it was a hotly contested piece of real estate throughout most of Israel's history. The five cities of the Philistines made up the famous Pentapolis of Ashdod, Gath, Ekron, Ashkelon, and Gaza.

The eastern edge of the Judean hill country, framed by the highlands and the Dead Sea, was the *Wilderness of Judah*. This area was usually a very inhospitable area, except for just after the rainy season when the grass would provide pasturage for the flocks and herds. Otherwise, the area was arid, barren, riddled with caves and steep precipices.

On the southern edge of the Judean highlands, the land quickly merged with the *Negev* (meaning "the dry land"), stretching from the east-west depression of Beersheba to an oasis at the extreme southern limit of the country near Kadesh-barnea. This high plateau had little rainfall; therefore, it sustained only a few scrubs and some grasslands.

The Jordan Rift Valley

One of the most interesting geological formations on earth is this major fault line, or rift, that extends from the mountains in Syria, through the Sea of Galilee, the Jordan River, the Dead Sea, the Arabah, and the Red Sea, all the way to Lake Malawi in Africa. This deep cut in the earth's surface marks the geographical—and often cultural—rift between the hill country on the west and the Transjordanian highlands on the east. The biblical name for the Jordan Rift Valley is the *Arabah*, or in modern Arabic, *el-Ghor*.

The Jordan River has its sources in three headwaters on the more-than-9,000-foot-high Mt. Hermon in the north. The river takes its rise from the foot of Mt. Hermon, around the city of Dan and continues above sea level until it enters a lagoon that used to be called Lake Huleh before it was drained and used for farming. (Now there is a decision to return it to a lake.) On the western side of the river from Lake Huleh to the Sea of Galilee stood the city of Hazor, precisely where the roads to Hamath and Damascus crossed the Jordan. From Hazor south, the river dropped off precipitously, so much so that in ten miles, when it reaches the Sea of Galilee, it is almost 700 feet below sea level.

The *Sea of Galilee* is a freshwater lake, seven miles wide and about thirteen miles long. It has variously been known as the *Sea of Gennes-*

aret, *Sea of Tiberias*, and *Sea of Chinnereth*. It has always supported a strong fishing industry.

The Jordan River continues for another sixty-five miles south as the crow flies, although it meanders about two hundred miles in actual length. The valley the river passes through on its journey averages about ten miles wide and has a tropical climate. As the river approaches the *Dead Sea*, it takes on the character of a virtual desert, except for a few natural springs, such as the ones near Jericho. The valley now drops so suddenly, often one hundred fifty feet at a time, that it forms jagged, eroded, gray marly flats known in the Bible as the *Zor*— that section of thick growth along the riverbanks where wild animals, including lions, prowled in earlier times in the area called in Scripture "the pride of the Jordan."

The Dead Sea (also known as the *Salt Sea, Sea of Arabah*) is the lowest spot on the face of the earth. It is about eight miles wide and some fifty miles long with an average depth of almost 1,300 feet below sea level at the northern end. At the southern end, below the projection from the eastern shore known as *el-Lisan*, "the tongue," the average depth is from ten feet to only three to four feet in more recent times.

Draining into the Dead Sea are the eastern tributaries, modern *Wady Mujib*, the biblical River Arnon, and the *Wady Hesa*, usually identified with the biblical River Zered. The only input of water on the western shore comes from *En-gedi*, "spring of the goats," a freshwater spring that has created an oasis.

From the Dead Sea, the Arabah, or Great Rift, continues toward the *Gulf of Aqabah*. The land rises rapidly, attaining a height of 650 feet above sea level some forty miles north of the gulf. On the gulf itself was located the port city of *Elath*, from which ships sailed for the east African coast, India, and South Arabia.

The Transjordanian Highlands

Running like a wall alongside the Jordan Valley are the highlands east of the Jordan River. This elevated stretch of land runs from Mt. Hermon in the north all the way to the shores of the Gulf of Aqabah in the south. This highland country can be divided into five main regions by four streams: (1) The *Bashan Plateau* north of the *Yarmuk River*, that empties into the Jordan just south of the southern outlet for the Sea of Galilee (a territory also known as the Golan Heights), (2) *Gilead*, which is situated between the *Wadi Zerqah* (biblical *Jabbok River*) and the Yarmuk, (3) the *Plateau of Ammon*, (4) the *Tableland of*

Moab, bisected by the Wadi Mujib (biblical *River Arnon*), and (5) the *mountains of Edom*, south of the Wady Hesa (biblical *Zered River*).

The wadis or canyons of the Hasa (Zered), Mujib (Arnon), Zerqah (Jabbok), and the Yarmuk all emptied either into the Dead Sea or the Jordan. So steep and so perpendicular were their canyons (e.g., the Arnon has 1,600-foot-high canyon walls in spots) that they formed natural barriers for human contact. Hence, they became natural boundaries for the various regions in Transjordania.

Bashan was famous for its fat cattle and fabled bulls; well watered with a rich basalt soil, as well as basalt rocks, signs of volcanic activity in the past. Bashan, unlike the rest of Transjordania, gently rises to the east in the mountains of Hauran; thus the rainfall is abundant on this ascending slope. Gilead, on the other hand, turned its lesser, but still significant, rainfall into thick forests along with an olive and grape culture. Gilead was more directly connected with Israel than most other areas east of the Jordan.

On the southeastern edge of the Jabbok River stood the chief city of the Ammonites, Rabbath-ammon, itself on the edge of the desert. This region traded hands between the Ammonites and the Moabites. The Moabites inhabited the area east of the Dead Sea, farming a plateau of land about twenty miles wide between that locked-in body of salt water known as the Dead Sea and the desert.

The land of the Edomites becomes more and more arid as one progresses south from the River Zered, with Bosrah as its chief city. Edom (from *ʾdm*, "red") no doubt derived its name from the Nubian red sandstone of the region. This region is divided into three parts: (1) *Paran*, west and southwest of the Arabah, (2) *Seir*, the mountainous region east of the Arabah, and (3) *Teman*, which is east of Seir.

The Bible Lands

What is generally considered as the Bible lands is an ellipse of over five million square miles (reaching from the Phoenician colonies on the Atlantic Ocean to India).[8] While little is known, or even necessary for our interests, of the far-flung colonies going out to the Atlantic Ocean, it is important to grasp something of the enormous scope against which the events of Israel's history were played out. Thus, to understand the Hebrew Bible and its history, one must know some-

8. This estimate was given by William Foxwell Albright, "The Impact of Archaeology on Biblical Research," in *New Directions in Biblical Archaeology*, eds. David Noel Freedman and Jonas C. Greenfield (Garden City, N.Y.: Doubleday, 1969), p. 3.

thing of the geography and composition of the Near East. Moreover, the very location of Israel profoundly affected what was to happen to her over the centuries, for she sat uncomfortably in the middle of what the Egyptologist James H. Breasted dubbed the "Fertile Crescent" (including Egypt, Palestine, Mesopotamia, Anatolia, and Armenia; or to use modern names: Egypt, Lebanon, Syria, Turkey, Jordan, Iraq, and Iran). In this area of river valleys, mountain heights, deserts, and oases, at times ascending to almost 17,000 feet in the mountains of Armenia and plunging to 1,300 feet below sea level in the depths of the Dead Sea, came the very matrix of humankind, a veritable cradle for civilization itself.

In this role, the area of Palestine-Syria served as a land bridge between the continents of Asia and Africa. As such, the land that Israel occupied was the point of contact between the various succeeding empires in Egypt and those of Asia. It is little wonder, then, that Israel's history is so inextricably tied up in international relationships between these great rivals and centers of power in antiquity. Each of these major powers is worthy of a short sketch to set the background for our discussion of the history of Israel.

EGYPT

Ever since the sixth century B.C., Egypt has been called "the gift of the Nile." This is because it survives on the narrow ribbon of land that follows this river that originates from the Blue Nile and the White Nile, both beginning near the equator until they converging to flow for the next 1,900 miles northward to the Mediterranean Sea. In the last 750 miles to the sea, after having traversed six major cataracts of treacherous and unnavigable rapids in the preceding section, the Nile River flows through the territory known as "Upper Egypt," which ends at ancient Memphis (or modern Cairo). Here the river breaks into a fertile triangular delta, known as "Lower Egypt." [9]

Until the Aswan Dam was built in A.D. 1970, Egypt had depended on the Nile River for its life-giving moisture and fresh layer of fertile mud each year, for only in Lower Egypt did it ever rain, and then only eight inches in Alexandria on the Mediterranean Sea to one inch a year at Cairo, where Upper and Lower Egypt meet. Therefore the major event each year was the annual inundation that would begin early in

9. J. Baines and J. Malek, *Atlas of Ancient Egypt* (New York: Facts on File, 1982). Also see A. S. Van der Woude, ed., *The World of the Bible: Bible Handbook*, vol 1tr. by S. Woudstra from the Dutch (Grand Rapids: Eerdmans, 1986). A. Gardiner. *Egypt of the Pharaohs: An Introduction* (New York: Oxford University Press, 1961).

July and reach its peak in October. But this flood affected only the narrow ribbon of land that bordered the Nile, leaving approximately only one-thirtieth of the total land area of that nation where people could live and plant crops.

While Upper and Lower Egypt were separate in their earliest history, from about 3100 B.C., a ruling family from Upper Egypt united the two parts and started a series of dynasties that lasted for some three thousand years. Tradition assigns this role of unification to Menes, who is pictured wearing a crown with the symbols of both Upper and Lower Egypt.

An Egyptian historian named Manetho (ca. 275 B.C.) established the dynastic division of Egypt's history, designating the families first, second, third, etc. dynasties along with their approximate dates. While much remains in flux on the dates, the usual division of the key dynasties has taken this form: [10]

Old Kingdom	Dynasties III-VI	ca. 2650–2100 B.C.
First Intermediate Period	Dynasties VII-XI	ca. 2200–2000 B.C.
Middle Kingdom	Dynasties XI-XII	ca. 2000–1800 B.C.
Second Intermediate Period	Dynasties XIII-XVII	ca. 1800–1541 B.C.
New Kingdom	Dynasties XVIII-XX	ca. 1541–1085 B.C.
Late Period	Dynasties XXI-XXXI	ca. 1085–332 B.C.

Egypt has one of the longest and most venerable national existences in the ancient Near East. In part, that may account for the fact that her history is more entangled with that of Israel than any other country in that part of the world, for more than six hundred references to Egypt appear in the Old Testament.

10. Absolute precision cannot be hoped for in these dates; thus there will be variation, depending on the system appealed to. The dates used here are those in *Cambridge Ancient History*, 3rd ed., ed. by I. E. S. Edwards et. al. (Cambridge: Cambridge University Press, 1973), vol. 2, part 1, p. 308. These *CAH* dates are accepted by George Steindorff and Keith C. Seele, *When Egypt Ruled the East* (Chicago: University of Chicago Press, 1957), pp. 274–75 as cited by Eugene H. Merrill, *Kingdom of Priests: A History of Old Testament Israel* (Grand Rapids: Baker, 1987), pp. 58–60, n. 5. For alternative dates for the Eighteenth Dynasty (1533–1303 B.C.), see William W. Hallo and William K. Simpson, *The Ancient Near East* (New York: Harcourt Brace Jovanovich, 1971), pp. 300–301.

Mesopotamia

At the opposite end of the Fertile Crescent from Egypt lays Mesopotamia, the land "between the rivers": the Tigris River on the east and the Euphrates River on the west. To the north and northwest, the terrain was mountainous and hilly, serving as the originating source for the two great rivers that generally marked the boundaries of this land. Canals were dug from the rivers so the water could be drawn to irrigate the agricultural fields. The great difference, however, was that the Tigris and Euphrates were a lot more capricious than the Nile, for their floods were not so seasonal and predictable as were those of the Nile.[11]

The ancient alluvial plain in the south was formed by centuries of soil being deposited along the way and at the mouth of these rivers in the Persian Gulf. While Egypt was insulated from outside influences and invasions, Mesopotamia was a sitting duck for marauding tribes that descended from the mountains to the north and east.

The homeland of the patriarchal ancestors of Abraham, Isaac, and Jacob were located in northwestern Mesopotamia, along a northern tributary of the Euphrates called the Balih, with its main city called Haran. It was from here that Abraham began his journey to the land of promise, having earlier left Ur of the Chaldees.

Mesopotamia was the home of several of the great empires of Bible times. Beginning around 3000 B.C., a literate and advanced people called the Sumerians entered parts of Mesopotamia and built their cities near established residences of earlier village settlers beginning around 2850 B.C. and lasting until about 2360 B.C. Gradually these early sites expanded into city-states, the more important of which were Ur, Erech, Lagash, Eridu, and Larsa. These city-states were sort of theocracies, ruled by a god. The actual administrator of each city-state was known as a *lugal*, "great man," while the "priest" was known as the *ensi*. How these two offices related to each other is not always clear, but in time, the role of the *lugal* took the ascendancy as one city-state subjected the others to its rule. Accordingly, the *ensi* of the conquering city-state would predominate the others and their gods, assuming in some cases the role of the *lugal* as well.

The city was the home of the gods, for a temple perched atop a mound resembling a mountain would tower over everything else in the city. These staged towers were known as ziggurats, of which some sev-

11. A. L. Oppenheim, *Ancient Mesopotamia: Portrait of a Dead Civilization* (Chicago: University of Chicago Press, 1964); H. W. F. Saggs, *The Greatness That Was Babylon: A Sketch of the Ancient Civilization of the Tigris-Euphrates Valley* (New York: Hawthorne Books, 1962).

enty still remain to some minimal height. Mounted at the very pinnacle of each was the temple to the deity that was favored in that city, with a central pair of stairs and two other sets of stairs coming from each side connecting the worshipers from the city with the sky-bound location of the god's temple.

The Sumerians have given to us samples of some of the earliest writing known to humankind, usually dated about 3100 B.C. The Sumerians produced an epic and mythic literature that promoted their religion. They also had remarkable achievements in advanced methods of irrigation, the use of the wheel for ox- and ass-drawn carts, an extended network of trading partners for cultural exchange, development of the cuneiform (wedge-shaped) writing, and the origination of a mathematical sexagesimal (i.e., based on units of sixty) system for weights, measurements, and time. Their architectural skills as observed in their temples and public buildings were monumental achievements as well.

Soon after the Sumerians arrived in Mesopotamia, the Akkadians entered from the northwest. Both groups began arriving around 2360 B.C. and dominated the region until about 2180 B.C. The Akkadians entered as peacefully as did the Sumerians, adopting much of the Sumerian culture. The Semitic language of the Akkadians differed from the language of the Sumerians, which some think may have had Indo-European antecedents; nevertheless, the Semitic Akkadians adopted the Sumerian syllabic cuneiform script to write their own language. In this way, and others that were to follow, the two groups merged to such an extent that it is sometimes difficult to distinguish the identity and distinctive contribution of each.

The most noteworthy event came in the twenty-fourth century B.C. when an Akkadian named Sargon seized power over all of Sumer and established a line of Semitic rulers. Sargon hailed from the city-state of Kish, but he made Akkad his capital after bringing all of Sumer down to the Persian Gulf under his control. His was the first empire in history.

Mention should also be made of Hammurabi, the famous sixth king of Babylon's first dynasty and founder of the first Amorite Empire in Mesopotamia. Hammurabi is best remembered for his law code, which was inscribed on an eight-foot-high stone monument in Akkadian cuneiform. Some of the laws in Hammurabi's Code resemble those in the Hebraic law codes.

This area, which is known in modern times as Iraq, became home to the feared and brutal conquerors known as the Assyrians, followed later by the Neo-Babylonian Empire. The history of Mesopotamia can be outlined briefly as follows:

The Early Dynastic Period	ca. 2800–2500 B.C.
The Akkadian Period	ca. 2360–2180 B.C.
III Dynasty of Ur	ca. 2200–2000 B.C.
The Amorite Period	ca. 1894–1595 B.C.
The Kassite Period	ca. 1595–1175 B.C.
The Period of Assyrian Domination	745–626 b.c.
The Neo-Babylonian Period	626–539 B.C.
The Period of the Achaemenids	539–332 B.C.

If Egypt was a strong power anchoring the Fertile Crescent's post on the south and west, then Mesopotamia provided the balancing power in the east.

Anatolia, Asia Minor-Armenia

Some of the hardiest settlers in the ancient world came to the north and northwest of the Fertile Crescent, an area almost entirely tucked away in mountainous land areas with inadequate rainfall. Especially prominent in the second millennium were the once-obscure peoples known as the Hittites. They were centrally located in an area later to be called Turkey. So powerful were they at that time that they forced Egypt to come to terms with them as equals.[12]

In the early part of the first millennium, Urartu set up a strong Armenian kingdom that made Assyria sweat militarily in the eighth century. This kingdom was north of the Lake Van and Lake Urmia region, near the Zagros Mountains.

12. Donald J. Wiseman, ed., *Peoples of Old Testament Times* (Oxford: Claredon, 1973).

Syria-Phoenicia

North of the land of Israel was Syria-Phoenicia, a land that could be divided just like Palestine into four regions, all extending generally in a north-south orientation. There was a narrow plain that ran along the coast, providing a number of excellent harbors for the Phoenicians who were to become some of the greatest seafarers in antiquity. This region quickly gave way to rugged western mountains called the Lebanon range, followed farther east by a valley formed along the Leontes River. From this valley rose a second mountain range in the east known as the Anti-Lebanon range, capped by the 9,100-foot-high, snow-covered Mt. Hermon, the highest peak in all of Syria-Palestine. This range dropped off on the east again into a high desert-like plateau, where the oasis at the city of Damascus made that site famous as it later became the capital of the kingdom of Syria, another rival to Israel in the days after the monarchy under kings David and Solomon.

These were some of the main players and the stage on which the drama of the history of Israel would be enacted. Every component had some part to play, whether it was the geography, the climate, the culture, politics, or aspirations of each of the players.

3

Ancient Israel in Its Archaeological Context

The earliest dwellings[1] that exhibit any type of permanence in the Levant (i.e., the eastern end of the Mediterranean Sea) belong to the Neolithic ("New Stone" or Late Stone) Age and date back to somewhere between the seventh and fifth millennia B.C. It is with these cultures that the story of the history of these lands, and especially of Israel, can begin. But some strands of the story are even prior to the Neolithic period.

The Paleolithic Period

Prior to the Neolithic Age, our knowledge, understanding, and dating procedures are sketchy. The Paleolithic (i.e., the "Old Stone") Age is usually divided into the Lower, Middle, and Upper Paleolithic. The earliest remains of any human culture are usually discovered along the Syro-African Rift: the Olduai Gorge in east Africa and the Ubeidiya in the Jordan Valley, south of the Sea of Galilee. The Lower Paleolithic is marked by the chipped stone tool industry, for the great geological Rift Valley system was carved out at this time. This system runs from

1. "Village" life is generally associated with the chalcolithic period. "Village" in its technical sense (as opposed to "city" or "urban" settings of the Late Chalcolithic to Early Bronze periods with their clearly defined architectural traditions, city planning, regional and international commerce as evidence in the material culture) is really a term reserved for latter periods; thus we speak here of dwellings only.

the Orontes Valley in Syria, the *Beqaᶜ* of Lebanon, the Jordan Valley, down through the Arabah, the Red Sea, and extending into eastern Africa at the equator. The Lower Paleolithic is given the name of the *Acheulian* as a cultural designation.

The earliest identifiable site in the Lower Paleolithic is near *ᶜUbeidiya*, close to the southern end of Lake Tiberias/Sea of Galilee on the western shore.[2] The animal bones from this site showed a strong affinity with the African animals: elephant, hippo, crocodile, giraffe, bear, boar, bison, and many species of birds. The stone tools were mainly chopping ones, crudely fashioned, along with flake tools that exhibited the same primitive appearance.

Another site probably belonging to this same period is known at Abu Khas in Jordan, located on a high acropolis above Pella, a few miles southeast of *ᶜUbeidiya*. No bones were found at this site, but the tools were similar in construction and appearance.

Very little is known of the *Middle Acheulian*, but the *Late Acheulian* is represented by a number of sites. These include a number of new stone tools, but most of the occupations are quite small, measuring one hundred meters or less, while a few attained quite large proportions.[3]

The Middle Paleolithic is favored with some six hundred sites in part of the Wadi el-Ḥasa drainage system in Jordan. Nearly two-thirds of the sites located in the Kerak region belonged to the Middle Paleolithic.[4] Other abundant sites have been found in northern Jordan, Syria, Lebanon, and Israel.

The Upper Paleolithic or Epipaleolithic (the latter term emphasizes the continuity of techniques in the manufacture of stone tools) is dominated by the *Natufian culture*, so called from the caves of Wadi en-Natuf, where it was first discovered. Based on radiocarbon testing, a date of about 10,500–8,500 B.C. is assigned to the Epipaleolithic Period.

The amazing advance that this culture evidenced was the presence of flint sickles used to harvest wild grains and probably cereal crops that were now being grown by that time. There is strong evidence of the use of grinding stones (especially mortars and pestles) for processing food.

2. M. Stekelis, *Excavations at ᶜUbeidiya*; M. Stekelis, O. Bar-Yosef and T. Schick, *Archaeological Excavations at ᶜUbeidiya, 1964–1966* (Jerusalem: 1969).

3. M. Stekelis and D. Gilead, "Ma`ayan Barukh: A Lower Paleolithic Site in Upper Galilee," *Mitekufat Haeven* 8 (1966) and G. Rollefson, "The Late Acheulian Site at Fjaje, Wadi el-Bustan, Southern Jordan," *Paleorient* 7/1 (1981): 5–21.

4. G. Rollefson, "Chipped Stone Artifacts from the Limes Arabicus Surveys," *The Roman Frontier in Central Jordan*, ed. S. Parker (Oxford, 1987), 759–92.

The Natufian culture tended to locate near permanent stands of wild cereals, which resources allowed them to establish permanent settlements for the first time. Thus, numerous Natufian hamlets are found in the Levant. Rather than finding the small camps of the previous periods, Natufian settlements consisted of well-made circular semisubterranean dwellings spread out over several thousand meters, providing housing for up to one hundred people or more.

During the closing phases of the Natufian culture, regional clusters and cultures developed in Palestine, such as the *Harifian* in the Negev and the *Khimian* in northern Palestine. The latter had already moved into the Neolithic period.

The Neolithic Period

While it was customary in the past to distinguish this period from preceding ones by the appearance of "polished stone tools" (hence, the "New Stone Age"), the most important development is the so-called economic revolution that occurred as humankind switched from relying on hunting and gathering to now introducing animal and agricultural husbandry.[5] The use of wild cereals was now supplemented with sowing, growing, and harvesting cereal grains near one's own domicile. Another principle change was the acquisition of animal protein, mainly in the form of meat supply from domesticated goats by the middle of the seventh millennium, though gazelle, wild pig, and other animals continued to be hunted. But by the sixth millennium, pigs, sheep, and dogs had been added to the list of domesticated animals. The third change that occurred in this Natufian culture came toward the end of the sixth millennium: the separation of the pastoral economy of goats and sheep to the arid steppes and desert regions, leaving the agricultural and animal husbandry of cattle and pigs to live on and work the moister and more fertile areas of the Levant.

The only other distinguishing mark dividing this period of the Neolithic (usually dated ca. 8500–4300 B.C.) is the distinction between the Aceramic (or Prepottery) Neolithic and the Ceramic (or Pottery) Neolithic. The date for dividing these two phases is, as with many of the dates in this murky and fairly obscure past, quite controversial. The division of this long period usually follows four subdivisions (the dates are based on uncalibrated carbon 14 readings):

---

5. Some would ascribe this transition from hunting and gathering to the introduction of animal and agricultural husbandry to the Mesolithic period rather than the Neolithic.

Prepottery Neolithic A (henceforth PPNA)	ca. 8500–7500 B.C.
Prepottery Neolithic B (henceforth PPNB)	ca. 7500–6000 B.C.
Pottery Neolithic A (henceforth PNA)	ca. 6000–5000 B.C.
Pottery Neolithic B (henceforth PNB)	ca. 5000–4300 B.C.[a]

a. The dates used here are those of Amihai Mazar, *Archaeology of the Land of the Bible: 10000–586* B.C.E. (New York: Doubleday, 1992), 30.

One of the most remarkable permanent settlements is to be found in the lowest levels of the site of Tel es-Sultan, ancient Jericho. It must have had a long existence, for the Neolithic culture at Jericho is represented by some forty-five feet of remains, spread over six and one-half acres of the mound west of the local spring. The accumulation of debris for PPNA is nine to ten meters and three to four meters for PPNB. Some samples from the later levels at ancient Jericho—if radiocarbon dating can be trusted—have yielded dates of about 6800, 6250, and 5850 B.C.[6]

The Neolithic town from the PPNA and PPNB periods of Jericho was protected on the western edge of the mound by a massive, strong wall made of huge stones. It stood to a height of almost six meters with a broad trench or fosse hewn out of the rock on the outer side of the wall. A massive tower within the wall measured eight and one-half meters in diameter and was preserved to a height of seven and seven-tenths meters, with a solid stone core and a steep stairway leading to its top. Kathleen Kenyon suggested it was part of a fortification system, but O. Bar-Yosef thought it was intended to protect the settlement from the massive runoff of water and silt from the wadi to the west. However, Bar-Yosef's explanation did not explain the function of the round tower.[7]

The houses were made of pounded earth and mud bricks or stone, with clay floors, plastered with lime and burnished. Some houses evidenced traces of reed mats covering the floors. Clay figurines of animals and the mother goddess were found.[8] There were also statues of

6. Kathleen M. Kenyon, *Digging up Jericho* (Frederick A. Praeger, Inc., 1957), 74.

7. This chronology is a matter of some controversy. Some wish to date these fortifications to the Early Bronze Period. While this is not necessarily where the mainstream of archaeologists are, it is important to note that this controversy does exist and should therefore be held with some degree of tentativeness.

clay on reed frames, always in groups of three, seeming to point to some type of ancient triad in the divine family of father, mother, son.

Of special interest in the PPNB were the groups of plastered human skulls usually buried under house floors with the facial features modeled in clay and shells used for the eyes. Such plastered skulls were discovered at Jericho, Ain Ghazal, Beisamoun (in the northern Jordan Valley) and at Tell Ramad near Damascus. The most extensive find of seven skulls was found at Jericho, many with natural outlines of cheeks, brows, and lips. Depictions of the whole human body were also occasionally found, that is, at Jericho and at Ain Ghazal ("Spring of the Gazelle").

Did these point to some type of ancestor worship? Or were they used for some cultic purpose? No one knows. Interestingly enough, Amihai Mazar suggested that these plastered forms "may suggest a belief that man was created by being molded in clay—an idea that finds expression in the creation story in the Book of Genesis, and that is to be found in the ancient myths of the Sumerians and Egyptians."[9]

Although Jericho of the prepottery period is practically unrivaled for its extensive revelations about that culture, village life is known from all over the Fertile Crescent as early as the seventh millennium B.C. For example, in the highlands of eastern Iraq is the mound of Jarmo. It also exhibits a prepottery culture with tools and vessels of stone. Traces of grains seem to support the case for the development of agriculture here, while bones of sheep, goats, pigs, and oxen argue for the domestication of animals. From this point on into the later half of the fifth millennium, villages are confirmed as existing all over western Asia. They exist, for example, in the Yarmuk Valley, then at Byblos, Ras Shamra, Tell Judeideh in Phoenicia and Syria and at Hassuna, a site near Mosul in Mesopotamia and at a number of places in the Upper Tigris region. The earliest villages in Egypt were those at Fayum in the north and at Tasjan in the south.

The most significant innovation that divides the Neolithic period into two main parts is, of course, the invention of pottery. Once it was learned how to add tempering materials such as straw or pieces of stone to the clay, it was possible to produce portable containers. Thus pottery became one of the major tools of the archaeologist for distinguishing the various chronological eras and cultures.

---

8. J. Garstang, "Jericho: City and Necropolis, Fifth Report," *Annals of Archaeology and Anthropology* 23 (1935): 143–84.

9. Amihai Mazar, *Archaeology of the Land of the Bible* (New York: Doubleday, 1992), 47–48; cf. Ruth Amiran, *Bulletin of the American Schools of Oriental Research* 167 (1962): 23–25.

Just how pottery was invented is unknown. It may have resulted from earlier uses of clay for plastering floors and sunken basins. But once humans learned to add tempering materials such as straw or pieces of stone to the clay, it was possible to make portable containers. The earliest attempts at making pottery probably occurred late in the seventh millennium B.C., as the finds at Ain Ghazal tend to confirm. Pottery, then, now becomes one of the major tools that the archaeologist will use for defining geographic areas and chronological ranges that are to be correlated with similar ancient cultures.

The Neolithic pottery was fired at low temperatures, made on mats, whose impressions can still be seen on the bottoms of many of the vessels, and exhibiting fairly crude and simple handmade forms. There were bowls, deep kraters, storage jars, and small closed jars. The decorations or designs consisted of triangular motifs, zigzag lines, and herringbone patterns, all of which were applied either by paint or by incisions.

The Chalcolithic Period

What followed the Neolithic period was labeled the Chalcolithic (from the Greek *chalcos*, "copper," and *lithos*, "stone") Age. It was not only the fact that copper was used, but the technological process of smelting the ore to produce the metal that was the great achievement of this era.

The Chalcolithic sites tended to cluster along the wadi banks in the peripheral areas of Israel. For example, in the northern Negev, over seventy sites belonging to this period were found within a 110–kilometer stretch along the banks of the Beersheba Brook and its continuation, the Besor Brook. Another concentration was found on the banks of the Gerar Brook, which leads off into the Shephelah from the Besor Brook. Another chain of Chalcolithic settlements was found along the Jordan Valley, Teleilat Ghassul being the main administrative and economic center for that area, if size and the span of an estimated thousand-year occupation are indicative of such.

A hoard of 436 fantastic copper objects in the "Cave of Treasure"[10] wrapped in a mat (thus giving them exceptional preservation) provide some of the best work known in this era. Included were crowns, scepters, mace heads, vessels and tools, found in a cave in Nahal Mishmar,

10. P. Bar-Adon, *The Cave of Treasure: The Finds from the Caves in Nahal Mishmar* (Jerusalem: 1980).

a remote cave on a cliff face in the Judean desert (north of Masada). The copper objects in this cache were well made, illustrating the first appearance of the "lost wax" (*cire perdue*) process. In this process, metal was poured into the casting that had been formed by the wax, as wax was melted out of the casting to make room for the liquid metal. The copper in this group had a small amount of arsenic and other trace elements. This could not have come from the mines in the Arabah or in Cyprus; the closest source was probably in the mountains of Armenia, near the former Russian-Turkish border.

A second cache of copper artifacts was collected from Kfar Monash, near Tel Aviv. It included some eight hundred small copper plates, which still has archaeologists guessing as to their use.

Among the many sites known in this period, Teleilat Ghassul (dating to ca. 3500 B.C.) stands out as the key site and the main culture of the Chalcolithic period. It is a fifty-acre site overlooking the northeastern end of the Dead Sea with ten occupational phases. Its buildings betray some degree of planning, for they were "broad houses," rectangular in form, measuring three and one-half by twelve meters, with "the entrance in the middle of the long walls." These rectangular houses were attached to one another at their narrow sides, like English "row houses," creating several paralleled chains of houses. Large adjacent courtyards included silos, possibly serving as pens for animals such as sheep.[11]

The center of life must have been the temple, for its ritual seems to have been highly organized. The wall paintings on the white plastered walls (often with numerous coats of plaster; twenty in one case) of the temple and other shrines were elaborate and highly symbolic. Designs such as an eight-pointed star, a bird, and various geometric figures painted in red, black, and white, along with strange elephant-like masks, must have served some purpose now lost to us.[12]

One isolated Chalcolithic temple was found above the oasis at En Gedi, on the western shore of the Dead Sea. In a large courtyard surrounded by a stone fence stood a ceremonial water basin. The temple itself was a five-by-twenty rectangular "broad room," with an entrance in the long wall facing the courtyard. Opposite the entrance was a horseshoe-shaped affair of stone, where animal bones and ash were

11. It should be noted that "broad-room dwellings" or public structures are most often associated with the urban settings of the Late Chalcolithic or even more frequently with the Early Bronze.

12. For an artist's beautiful reconstruction of some of these designs and descriptions given here, see *National Geographic* (December 1957): 834 ff.

found in circular pits in what surely was a place where sacrifices were made.

The hallmark of Chalcolithic pottery was the lug handle, a ropelike decoration made of clay bands with finger impressions on jars. The large pithoi were among the largest ever made in Palestine. Other forms included large kraters, bowls with flat bases, the cornet, a V-shaped cup with a long pointed base, and the pottery churn used for churning butter.

The real flowering of earliest culture seems to have begun in Upper Mesopotamia. There the Hassuna culture marked the transition from the Neolithic to the Chalcolithic period with a distinctive type of painted pottery, called *Samarra Ware*—a pottery decorated with monochrome geometric animal and human figures of excellent rendition.

To put all of this into the context of the wider perspective of Mesopotamia and Egypt, it should be noted that civilization in the fourth millennium got its start in Lower Mesopotamia. There was a sequence of predynastic cultures that moved from the early fourth into the third millennium. In descending order they were known as the *Obeid* (ca. 3500 B.C.), the *Warka* (ca. 3500–3000 B.C.), and the *Jemdet Nasr* (ca. 3000–2800 B.C.). During the *Obeid*, a system of dikes and drainage ditches was installed to take over the bottom land of Lower Mesopotamia. The *Warka* period saw the development of platforms on which the mud-brick temples could be placed above the level of the flood waters. All sorts of new techniques were now evident, including ovens for firing pottery, the wheel, exquisite cylinder seals, and the epoch-making invention of writing—coming some time before 3000 B.C.

Meanwhile, the Egyptian cultures of this period did not evidence the same level of cultural achievement in the fourth millennium. Prior to the rise of the first dynasty in the twenty-ninth century, some cultures were named after sites in Egypt: the *Badarian*, the *Amratian*, and the *Gerzean*. All three exhibit a rather meager and poor culture compared to the Chalcolithic in Mesopotamia. In part, Egypt's isolation, a positive feature in her security, worked against her in cultural achievements. What pottery she had was artistically and technologically inferior to that found in Mesopotamia. No monumental buildings have been found, and houses were made of reed mats and mud.

The Chalcolithic period was a time of enormous achievement, but it was uneven and tended to favor Mesopotamian sites, with the main exception being Teleilat Ghassul.

The Early Bronze Period

Somewhere around 3300 B.C., the Ghassulian culture came to an abrupt and enigmatic end.[13] Most of the Chalcolithic centers, such as those near Beersheba, in the Judean desert, Teleilat Ghassul, and the temple at En Gedi, were abandoned and remained unoccupied. In fact, the entrance to the En Gedi temple was blocked. This, along with the hiding of the Nahal Mishmar treasure, imply some traumatic event, but no evidence for any violence is found at any of these sites, so the mystery remains.

Early Bronze I

The Early Bronze period (ca. 3300–3050 B.C.; henceforth EB I) is not as sharply defined or commonly agreed on by all scholars. For example, some of the pottery (particularly, the "gray burnished ware"), labeled "Late Chalcolithic" by others, was contemporary with what other groups designated as "Early Bronze I." This led to subdividing the period into EB IA, EB IB, and EB IC by G. Ernest Wright in 1958. Kathleen Kenyon, however, suggested the term *Proto-Urban* to denote Wright's EB IA and EB IB, but that was not universally accepted either. Furthermore, what Wright called EB IC lacked any true contents; thus, the best solution seemed to be to use the term EB I to include all pre-urban settlements of the Early Bronze Age.

Some studies have shown that almost one-third of the EB I settlements were established on Chalcolithic sites. But there was also a corresponding shift from the preferences of location in the Chalcolithic period such as the Judean Desert in the Beersheba wadi system, the Jordan Valley, and the Golan heights, to different parts of the country, such as the coastal plain, the central hill country, the Shephelah, and the northern plains. Most of those former Chalcolithic sites were abandoned, as already mentioned.

Very few EB I sites have been excavated to a sufficient extent to allow any sort of thorough study of their plan or architecture. What we do know is that in the northern part of the country there is a tendency to build curvilinear, elliptical, apsidal, or round structures. This architecture, which was practically unknown in the Chalcolithic period along with the gray burnished pottery, some think may evidence a foreign immigration in this period.

---

13. The Early Bronze chronology is a veritable "powder keg." The dates adopted here (ca. 3300–2300 B.C.) are those of Amihai Mazar, *Archaeology*, p. 91. See his chart of "Comparative Stratigraphy of Early Bronze Sites" on p. 109.

International relations also had begun to assert themselves, for while the Sumerian culture influenced Egyptian culture during its Late Gerzean and Pre-Dynastic periods, relations between Canaan and Egypt are in evidence in the late Pre-Dynastic period. Egyptian pottery and flint blades from the Gerzean culture have also turned up in EB I contexts. It is these "international" connections of material culture that will be one of the defining features of urban/city dwelling in the Early Bronze, especially the EB II and III.

One of the best illustrations of this mutual interaction between the two countries comes from Tel Erani, on the southwestern coastal plain, west of Lachish. Egyptian pottery and stone vessels from the late Pre-Dynastic and First Dynasty are most abundant in these strata at that coastal site. Especially significant is a jar fragment incised with the name of Narmer, the first Egyptian pharaoh.

Meanwhile, EB I pottery originating in Palestine has turned up at several sites in the eastern delta of Egypt. Even more important is the stone palette of King Narmer, probably the most important artifact from the First Dynasty in Egypt, which shows the pharaoh smiting Asiatic enemies and depictions of him (shown as a bull) conquering a fortified city surrounded by a city wall and towers.

The combination of this evidence would suggest that there was a strong Egyptian presence in southern Palestine during this period, but it came to an end in EB II. This makes a chronological correlation possible between EB I and Egyptian history. The only other problem is that the date for the accession of the First Dynasty ranges from 3200 to 2900 B.C. Most today, however, accept 3100 B.C. as the best date for the accession of Narmer to the throne of Egypt.

Early Bronze II and III

Early Bronze II and III (henceforth EB II, EB III) is dated about 3050–2300 B.C., and takes up the major part of the Bronze Age, extending some seven to eight hundred years in all. It was this period that saw the emergence of cities with their now-familiar intensive fortifications. The inception of this era with its corresponding mark of urbanization is usually correlated with the third king of the First Dynasty of Egypt, Djer, about 3050 B.C. The transition to EB III from EB II is dated to the end of the Second Dynasty, about 2700 B.C., continuing until the end of the Sixth Dynasty, the same dynasty whose third pharaoh in that Sixth Dynasty, Pepi I, was noted for having conducted military raids against numerous cities in Palestine. EB II and EB

III are also contemporaneous with, or even slightly later than, the Sumerian Dynastic period as well as the rule of the Akkadians in Mesopotamia.

Sometime during the First and Second Dynasties, Egypt's interest shifted to her naval connections with Byblos in Phoenicia. The port of Byblos became an important gateway through which Egyptian influence could enter the Upper Levant. Thus, the recently discovered (1960s) Tell Mardikh (=Ebla), south of Aleppo, with its two thousand complete tablets and some seventeen thousand fragments, pointed to a highly literate and thriving society during this period. Ebla may well have been the bridge between Mesopotamia, the Levant, and Egypt in this era.

What is impressive in this era of EB II and EB III is the large number of fortified cities such as Dan, Hazor, Qedesh in Galilee, Beth Yerah, Beth-Shean, and Megiddo in the north, and Jericho, Lachish, and Tell el-Hesi in the south. Other major cities lay along the main trade and travel routes. But in addition to these excavated towns, there were another 260 sites in western Palestine, with the most densely packed areas being the coastal plain, the hills of Samaria, the Shephelah, and the Jordan Valley. Twenty of these sites exceeded 20 acres comprising a total of 750 acres, or about half of all the built-up land of the period. Mazar lists the most prominent in this group as Beth-Yerah (55 acres), Yarmuth (40 acres), Tell el-Hesi (25 acres), Ai and Arad (each about 25 acres). Another 36 towns average over 12 acres each, and about 160 smaller settlements no more than 1.5 acres each. Therefore, Mazar estimates that the urban area of the EB included about 1,500 acres, giving a population of 150,000, using an assumed coefficient of 100 persons per built-up acre.[14] This concentration of the population in the hill country of Galilee, Samaria, and Judah was a distinctive early part of the Bronze Age, and usually said to be without parallels in the later stages of the Bronze Age. Meanwhile, Transjordania had numerous Bronze sites. For example, Bab edh-Dhra' was one of the largest of five sites located in dry riverbeds leading down to the Dead Sea on its eastern bank.

Remarkably, extensive EB II settlements have been found in the Negev and southern Sinai. For example, in the vicinity of St. Catherine's Monastery in southern Sinai, I. Beit-Arieh found some fifty EB II sites and excavated six of them. Here, clustered around a main route running along a wadi where water and pastures could be found, were EB

14. Amihai Mazar, ibid., pp. 111–112.

II settlements. Another chain of sites was found further north of this site in the Negev. Their houses were similar to the "broad room" type of structures found at earlier sites.

What is notable about the Early Bronze sites is their fortification system. Walls surrounding the sites, some three to four meters thick, with horseshoe-shaped towers, were seen at Arad,[15] Taanach, Ai, Jericho, Yarmuth, and Megiddo (Stratum XVIII). In the latter part of EB II and EB III, the walls tended to thicken and to be strengthened, some reaching seven or eight meters in width. Now elongated, rectangular towers also begin to appear at points where the fortifications were the weakest along with earthwork glacis (an artificial solid steep slope) composed of layers of dirt and crushed lime, to strengthen the foundations of the city wall and to prevent easy access to the wall by the enemy's siege equipment.

City gates also began to appear at Tell el-Farʿah (in the north), Beth-Yerah, Ai, and Arad. The gate area was flanked by two large square towers built of mud bricks. In some cases, a "bent axis" was added to impose an added difficulty on any attacker who tried to take the city at the point of the city gate.

But why were these monumental fortifications necessary? Was Egypt the feared enemy? There is no evidence of Egyptian military activity in Palestine from the beginning of the First Dynasty to the time of Pepi I in the Sixth Dynasty. The only other possible source of fear would be other Early Bronze city rulers.

The temples of this era were similar to the "broad room,"[16] known from Chalcolithic and EB I temples and from domestic architecture. There were three EB III temples at Megiddo, each measuring seventeen by eighteen meters with walls one and eight-tenths meters thick. The temples had an open porch with two pillars, leading into a broad hall, some fourteen meters wide by nine meters long. A raised dais at the back of the hall no doubt was for a pedestal for the statue of the god; each temple had its own deity.

A unique building is found in the granary at Beth-Yerah. It was a 30-by-40-meter building with outer walls about 10 meters wide. Foundations for nine circular silos measuring 10 meters wide were sunk into

15. The Early Bronze city of Arad, as published by Ruth Amiran, *Early Arad* (Jerusalem, 1978), is a wonderful site from which to illustrate the architectural and cultural traits of a "city" in the technical sense of the word. EB I was an unfortified 25–acre city, but EB II had a wall around the city, 2.4 meters wide and 1,200 meters long, erected on ridges surrounding the crater-like area in the center that contained a well or a central water reservoir.

16. The "broad room" design had a wide number of uses, of course. It had been used already for private dwellings, public buildings, and temples along with a number of other uses.

the outer walls, giving about eight meters in diameter for each silo. If we assume that each silo was seven meters high, each could hold 200 to 250 cubic meters of grain, with a total capacity for all nine silos of 1,800 to 2,250 cubic meters—some 1,400 to 1,700 tons of wheat or some other grain. That figure is astounding, for it would take something like 5,600 to 6,800 acres of land to fill this granary, assuming again an average grain production of 0.25 tons per acre. Again, if Beth-Yerah's fifty-acre city had a population of 4,000 to 5,000 people, and assuming further that each person ate about 0.14 tons of grain per year, they would consume only about 70 percent of the grain, leaving the rest to be traded or stored long-term.[17]

The best-known pottery of the EB III period is called "Khirbet Kerak ware," after the site of Khirbet Kerak (Beth-Yerah) where it was first described. This ware was handmade with a thick body and then fired at rather low temperatures. A heavy slip was applied and then highly burnished, the color of the slip being controlled by the fire. This pottery was red on the inside, but the outside was either all black or black with red around the rim. It is best represented in the northern part of the country (Megiddo, Beth-Shean, Hazor, and Beth-Yerah), with few representatives found in the south. Similar pottery, however, is known at Ebla, east of the Orontes River and in parts of Anatolia.

Once again, the collapse of the era of EB II and EB III was rather sudden. The collapse may have been caused by Egyptian raids, as attested in a hymn found in the tomb of the Egyptian general Uni (ca. 2300 B.C.), who talks about destroying thousands in the "land of the sand dwellers." But it may have been caused by invasions from the west Semitic "Amorite" tribes from Syria. Perhaps various factors contributed to the demise of this culture.

Early Bronze IV/Middle Bronze I

The period of decline that set in following the collapse of EB II and EB III parallels the same kind of interlude that Egypt faced in the First Intermediate period (dynasties VII-XI). This decline occupied some three hundred years—years when Palestine saw rather sparse population and when agriculture tended to give way to the pastoral life of herding. This period of decline will be called Early Bronze IV (hence-

17. Amihai Mazar, ibid., pp. 127–129 for all of these assumptions and amazing calculations.

forth EB IV) and Middle Bronze I (henceforth MB I), with this jointly named period dated about 2300/2250–2000 B.C.[18]

The composite name for this period is somewhat of a compromise for the terminological chaos that exists. W. F. Albright and G. E. Wright distinguish between EB IV and MB I. Others have combined the two periods and come up with their own designations, such as "the caliciform culture" (Olga Tufnell, named after one of the most common pottery vessels of this period) or "the Intermediate Early Bronze-Middle Bronze Period" (K. M. Kenyon).

Urban life began to revitalize only in about 2000 B.C., at the beginning of the Middle Bronze Age II. This coincided with the emergence of the Middle Kingdom in Egypt.

Meanwhile, the period we examine in the interim has very few major sites to its credit; even where these few sites do exist, there is a sparse occupational level for some seven hundred years!

The most distinctive form of pottery was the "caliciform," named after its shape. Cemeteries have been the main source for the story of the pottery found in this period. These are usually broken down into three main groups: the Transjordanian, the Northern, and the Southern. Some pottery shapes are found in all three settings, that is, a number of types of goblets, anphoriskoi (small jars with handles), "teapots," and lamps with four spouts. The Transjordanian group is mainly attested at Bad-edh Dhra'; the Northern group at the Qedesh cave in Upper Galilee and in cemeteries in the Jezreel Valley, such as those near Megiddo, Hazor, and Beth-Shean. The Southern group is represented by small finds in the hill country of Judah, the Shephelah, Negev, and the Sinai.

Since cemeteries supply the bulk of the material for the EB IV/MB I period, it is important also to note that there are three types of burial in this period. These are the shaft tombs, witnessed to in western Palestine; megalithic dolmens covered by tumuli, seen in the Golan heights and in Upper Galilee; and the built-up tumuli, typical of the central Negev.

Most of the cemeteries have shaft tombs. These are vertical shafts cut into the rock that lead to an underground burial chamber. Some of the shafts are circular, such as those at Jericho, and they descend to depths of six meters.

---

18. Even more controversial than the previous archaeological periods is the EB IV and MB I. Here both the nomenclature and the chronologies are vigorously debated. Once again, for the sake of consistency and uniformity in this presentation, we have adopted the dates suggested by Amihai Mazar, *Archaeology*, p. 151–173.

The megalithic dolmens are structures that have the appearance of being tables made out of two or more vertical basalt blocks roofed over by large rock slabs. A heap of stones usually cover over these dolmens, creating a tumulus (i.e., stone structures in which the dead are laid). It would appear from the tomb evidence, and the absence of the rich EB II-III urban cultural traditions, that the new character of this "nomadic interlude" needs to be factored in as a decisive moment in the description of these times.

The Negev tumuli tended to be built-up circular cairns with an inner central cell where the body was placed along with gifts, presumably for the persons' afterlife. These tumuli were not placed apart from the settlement, but they were found inside the settlement, between the houses. On inspection, many of these were found empty, as if they were only used temporarily or as a temporary place of burial until the bones could be removed and put into a secondary internment.

EB IV/MB I are not so well attested as some of the other periods we have investigated here. This may evidence a population decline and an interlude in the progress of culture and civilization in Palestine. Into this kind of world the biblical narrative sets the times of the patriarchs in Genesis 12–50. This may account for the fact that Abraham, Isaac, and Jacob could move so freely in this land with little or no political hindrances.

The puzzle remains, however. Who were the people of Palestine during the EB IV/MB I? Was there a radical break from the preceding period? The dominant view is that the country was invaded by West Semitic seminomadic tribes from Syria and Mesopotamia known as the "Amurru" (Sumerian "MAR.TU"). Others have contended that an Indo-European group was responsible for the break in culture and the new peoples in the land. Another view, currently gaining support among scholars, considers the massive invasion as improbable but stresses the indigenous nature of the culture and the people. This later view emphasizes an autochthonous pastoral group of nomads who had been living in the country, but who now stepped into the vacuum created by the collapse of the cities. Regardless of which answer finally triumphs, the end of the Bronze Age was one of the great crises in the history of that part of the Levant.

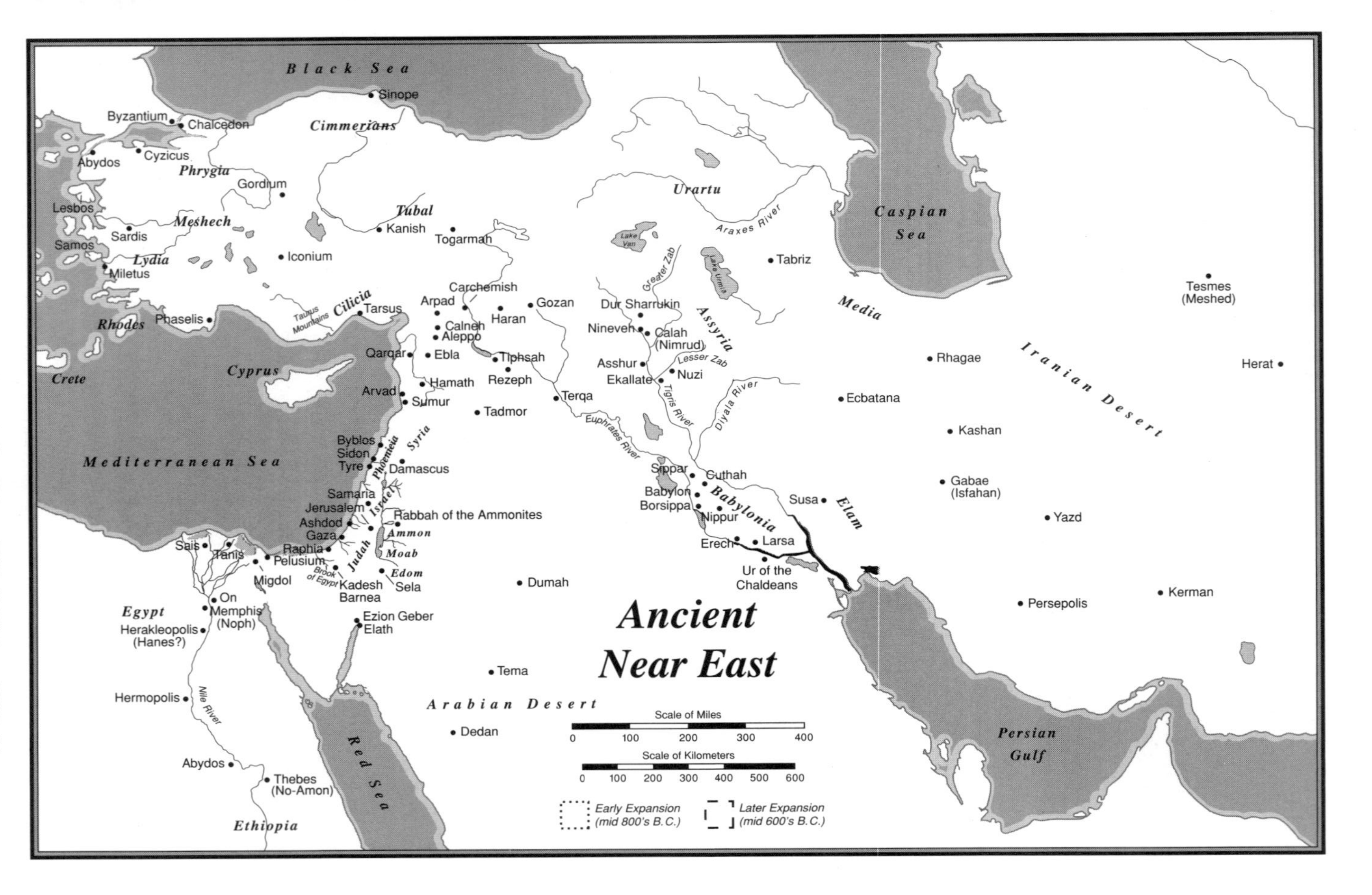

From *Holman Bible Handbook* (Nashville: Holman Bible Publishers, 1992), 54.

Part I

The Patriarchs and the Residence in Egypt

THE MIDDLE BRONZE AGE AND THE PATRIARCHS

Before the twentieth century, the history of Israel usually commenced with the call of Abraham, but those days were numbered when, over one century ago, Julius Wellhausen (1844–1918), the widely acclaimed reconstructor of early Israelite history, declared that "no historical knowledge" of the patriarchs could be obtained from Genesis. Abraham, Isaac, and Jacob were a mere "glorified mirage" projected back from later Hebrew history.[1]

Not until the 1940s to the 1960s was a successful challenge made to Wellhausen's estimates of the historical worth of the patriarchs. Two scholars were especially responsible for reversing the current of thought by setting the stories of the patriarchal age against the ancient Near Eastern backgrounds found in the Middle Bronze II Age (henceforth MB II): William Foxwell Albright (1891–1971) and Cyrus Herzl Gordon (1908–).[2]

But that state of affairs has changed again since the mid-1970s. A small group of contemporaries, but with most adamant voices,

1. Julius Wellhausen, *Prolegomena zur Geschichte Israels* 6th edition (Berlin: de Grutyer, 1927), 316; reprinted as *Prolegomena to the History of Ancient Israel* (New York: Meridan Books, 1957).

2. See Cyrus H. Gordon, "Biblical Customs and the Nuzi Tablets," *BA* 3 (1940): 1–12; idem, "Hebrew Origins in the Light of Recent Discoveries," *Biblical and Other Studies*, ed. A. Altmann (Cambridge, Mass., 1963), 3–14; William F. Albright, *Archaeology, Historical Analogy and Early Biblical History*, chapt. II: "The Story of Abraham in Light of New Archaeological Data" (Baton Rouge, Louisiana, 1966), 22–41.

composed of scholars such as Thomas L. Thompson, John Van Seters, and Donald B. Redford, have reexamined the evidence that Albright and Gordon used, they rightly found that some of the material which Gordon and Albright relied on did not demonstrate what these earlier scholars thought it did in every case. [3] But Thompson, Van Seters, and Redford failed to examine all the evidence, and as Kenneth A. Kitchen concluded, they probably "set the clock back 100 years. . . [for] like Wellhausen, they concluded that the stories of the patriarchs are fictional creations—dating to the Babylonian Exile (6th century B.C.) or later—and are historically worthless."[4]

So where do we go from here? Was this a real period in the history of Israel, or was it a fabrication, as has been argued by some on both ends of the twentieth century? First, let us look at the Middle Bronze II period and then examine the specific claims of the biblical text of the patriarchs.

MIDDLE BRONZE IIA

Once again there are about as many theories about the age designation, many of the same type, as those for the change of some of the previous archaeological periods. The best advice seems to be to call this period MB IIA (2000–1800/1750 B.C.).

The case for the theory of a mass invasion of Amorites or "sand people" into Palestine during this time frame can be abandoned for lack of hard evidence. The settled population seems to be about the same groups as they were in the EB IIIII periods. Even the amount of Egyptian influence in this period is hard to assess. True, Pharaoh Mentuhotep II (ca. 2061–2010 B.C.) of the Eleventh Dynasty was able to unite most of Egypt behind him to fight the Nubians and Libyans. This same dynasty reopened the turquoise mines in Sinai. It was left to the founder of the Twelfth Dynasty, Amenemhat I (ca. 1991–1962 B.C.) to enter fully into the international scene after the stagnant years of the First Intermediate period. But this pharaoh was not so strong as it might appear at first, for he built the "wall of the ruler" in the Wadi Tumilat of the Egyptian delta to prevent the infiltration of the "Asiatics," called

3. See Thomas L. Thompson, *The Historicity of the Patriarchal Narratives* (Berlin: de Grutyer, 1974); John Van Seters, *Abraham in History and Tradition* (New Haven: Yale, 1975); and Donald B. Redford, *A Study of the Biblical Story of Joseph* (Leiden: Brill, 1970).

4. Kenneth A. Kitchen, "The Patriarchal Age: Myth or History?" *BAR* 21 (Mar/Apr 1995): 48–57, 88–95; the quote is from p. 48.

the "sand-dwellers."[5] Meanwhile in Mesopotamia, the Amorite kingdoms were taking the lead beginning in Ur III (2060–1950 B.C.).

Our only knowledge of an explicit Egyptian military expedition through Palestine (called in the Egyptian texts "*Retenu*") was found on an inscription by Khu-Sebek about Pharaoh Senwosret III (ca. 1878–1842 B.C.). This pharaoh directed a campaign to Palestine and reached *s-k-m-m*, usually identified with Shechem. Egypt's interest remained in Phoenicia and not in the southern part of the Levant, where the patriarchs would graze their flocks.

Two interesting pieces that come from Egypt during the time of Amenemhat I and Senwosret I are the "Tale of Sinuhe"[6] and the "Instruction of Amenemhet." The "Instruction" may have been written as propaganda to justify the fearful repression that followed Amenemmes I's death, while the "Sinuhe Tale" ends by praising Senwosret I as a merciful king. Some have argued that Sinuhe may have left town because he was involved in a conspiracy against the crown.

Whatever is the true reason for his leaving, Sinuhe secretly left Egypt, crossing the wall in the northeast, and continuing on up to Gubla (= Byblos). From there he went further east to Qedem and was persuaded by a prince, Ammi-enshi, in Upper Retenu (Syria) to stay and marry his daughter. This he did and was subsequently made Ammi-enshi's military commander, living in the country of Yaa (an unknown location). After many years he longed to return to Egypt so he could be buried in his homeland. Sensosret invited him to return and he became a courtier in his government. In the meantime, Sinuhe had described the "good land" in Retenu with all of its products and with the cultivation of figs, vines, olives, and cattle raising in the settled land of Upper Retenu.

The other piece of source material for this period are the so-called "Execration Texts" from around the end of the Twelfth Dynasty. Written on clay figurines or jars are curses against cities and their rulers in Syro-Palestine. There are three groups of Execration Texts:

1. The earlier group, called the Berlin Group, was found at Thebes and consists of 289 inscribed sherds mentioning nineteen

5. The Egyptian term ʿ*3mw*, usually translated "Asiatics," is not an ethnic term, for it is used of various peoples. Philologically the term ʿ*3mw* is not related to the Hebrew ʾ*mry*, "Amorite," or the Akkadian term *amurru*. Instead, it may be connected to the Egyptian ʿ*3m*, "boomerang, throwing stick," which is used in some texts to describe enemies. So Gösta W. Ahlström, *The History of Ancient Palestine* (Minneapolis: Fortress, 1993), 165, n. 3.

6. See M. Green, "The Syrian and Lebanese Topographical Data in the Story of Sinuhe," *Chronique d'Egypt* 58 (1983): 38–59. For "The Instruction of King Amenemhet" see Pritchard, *Ancient Near Eastern Texts*, pp. 418–19.

different cities and their rulers (sometimes mentioning more than one ruler or prince for each place!). Those names that have been identified include, among others, Ashkelon, Jerusalem, Beth-Shean, Rehob, and Byblos.

2. The Brussels Group is a younger set of curses found at Sakkara and lists some sixty-four Palestinian places or peoples. This list is more wide ranging and more extensive than the Berlin list.
3. The third group is made up of 175 pieces of curses on bowls and three figurines found at Mirgissa in Nubia. Usually, this group is dated about the same time as the Berlin group because the phraseology is so similar.

The Execration Texts do not mention some cities: Ugarit, Megiddo, Jericho, and Qatna; these cities may have been on friendly terms with the Egyptians. We do know that Tuthotep was an Egyptian official who was stationed at Megiddo during Senwosret III's term of office. He may well have been in charge of collecting grain, wine, and cattle for shipping to Egypt. A statute of Tuthotep was found at Megiddo, as were some Egyptian seals from the office of the vizier found at Jericho. This latter piece of evidence suggests that Egypt's sphere of influence reached far into the interior of the Jordan Valley.

But the point from these texts is clear. The towns or cities that the patriarchs are supposed to be in contact with during the alleged period of MB IIA do, in fact, often turn out to be the very cities that are mentioned in these texts. This is a presumption in favor of the text's authenticity rather than its being a late fabrication from some distant time such as the Exile.

MB IIA is marked by an almost total revolution in every aspect of its material culture: settlement patterns changed, urbanism increased, pottery took on new distinctive forms, metallurgy changed, and different burial customs emerged.

The innovation of the fast potter's wheel and likely improved firing techniques brought a large variety of new and elegant shapes such as large dipper juglets, carinated thin bowls, and flat large bowls. The times seemed to take a leap forward in the Middle Bronze Age.

The Bible's Chronological References for the Patriarchal Age

The Bible places the times of the patriarchs between the twenty-first and nineteenth centuries B.C.[7] First Kings 6:1 noted that Solomon

7. Some indeed may question whether it is necessary to include the full range of biblical texts that comment on the patriarchal chronology, but we think it is necessary if we are to represent the text's own method of presenting this data while staying alert to all the external evidences that are available as well.

began the construction of the temple in the fourth year of his reign (usually dated about 967 B.C.), some 480 years after the Exodus from Egypt (which would put the Exodus at 1447 B.C.). Exodus 12:40 summed up the total years in Egypt as 430 (making the entrance of Jacob's family into Egypt as 1877 B.C.). The total number of years that the patriarchs spent in Canaan comes to 215 years; thus, Abraham's journey from Haran into Canaan came sometime in 2092 B.C., when he was seventy-five years old.

Two variations to this chronology exist in the biblical text. One is a minor difference of thirty years or less, for Genesis 15:13 predicts that Abraham and his seed will spend four hundred years in Egypt instead of the four hundred and thirty of Exodus 12:40. But this may simply be a case of rounding out the numbers, which in any event does not significantly change the picture. The other variation is major. The Greek Septuagint text for Exodus 12:40 added the words "and Canaan" to the fact that Israel spent four hundred and thirty years in Egypt. This would reduce total years by two hundred and fifteen, making Abraham's journey from Haran into Canaan in 1877 B.C. and not in 2092 B.C. Evangelical scholars, as is true of other scholars, are divided on which text tradition should be adopted: some, like Kenneth Kitchen, tended to place the patriarchal tradition in the nineteenth to seventeenth centuries B.C. (Cyrus Gordon was even a bit later than that); others, like this writer, rejected the Septuagintal textual reading, considering it secondary and incorrect, preferring instead to stay with the Hebrew Masoretic tradition. Usually what is even more determinative of the dates for this period than the biblical data is the date for the Exodus, with most of modern scholarship preferring a thirteenth-century date over the fifteenth century B.C. in that, in the view of the majority, this fits better with what we know about Egypt. This latter point will be discussed later.

The Origin of the Patriarchs

What value is to be attached to the Bible's claim that Abraham went from Ur of the Chaldeans in Lower Mesopotamia to Haran in Upper Mesopotamia and from there to Canaan?

Abram's "native land," or "birthplace," on the basis of Genesis 11:28, 31 and 12:1, seems to be "Ur of the Chaldeans," for his brother Haran died while their father Terah was still alive prior to the time when Terah, Abram, Sarai, and Lot left Ur to go to Haran. The only other time this "Ur of the Chaldeans" is used is in the covenant given in Genesis 15:7, where Yahweh says to Abram: "I am Yahweh who brought you out of Ur of the Chaldeans *(ʾûr kaśdîm)* to make you heir of this land" (author's translation). Never again is this place mentioned until Nehemiah 9:7, and later repeated in Stephen's speech in Acts 7:2.

The Septuagint version rendered what in Hebrew is phonetically the earlier form of "Ur of the Kasedim" as Ur of the *chaldaioi*, "Chaldeans." The change from the *-sd* to *-ld* is normal for neo-Assyrian and Neo-Babylonian; thus, Hebrew would appear to preserve the earlier form. This does not relieve the problem, however, for if Chaldeans were related to the "Kaldu" of the cuneiform inscriptions, as many surmise, they were Arameans from Upper, not Lower, Mesopotamia, who do not appear in the Assyrian texts until the ninth century B.C. If that is true, it appears that the term *Chaldean* is not to be linked to the Kaldu.[8] What it is to be identified with, however, is unknown at this time.

The southern city of Ur, of course, is now well known to us from the excavations of Sir Leonard Woolley.[9] He found Ur to be a thriving city in the third millennium B.C., particularly during the Third Dynasty of Ur. But as this dynasty ended, the town was destroyed by the Elamites just before 2000 B.C. It did spring back from this devastation and was a trading and religious center until the end of Hammurapi's reign (ca. 1792–1750 B.C.) and then passed into almost total eclipse for almost a thousand years, reappearing only in the Neo-Babylonian period. On the biblical chronology, Abram would have left prior to the Elamite destruction of the city.

But can this southern Ur be the "birthplace" of Abram? Does not the biblical text identify Haran rather than Ur l (Gen. 12:1; 24:4, 7) as Abram's "native land" (*ʾereṣ môledet*), which would point to Upper, not Lower, Mesopotamia? True, *môledet* can mean "birthplace" or the like, but it must in some cases be translated "family" or "descendants." Thus, the word in itself is not determinative.

Prior to our twentieth century's promotion of the fame of the southern Ur that was excavated by Woolley, Ur was commonly identified with Urfa, Syriac Orrhai, now called Edessa, about twenty miles northwest of Haran. C. H. Gordon thought this indeed might be possible, but he pointed also to another Ur, the town called Ura in the Hittite terri-

8. Xenophon in his *Anabasis* IV.iii.4 and *Cyrop*, III.1.34 mentions "Chaldeans" in the north who were together with the Kardouchoi (or Kurds) as neighbors of the Armenians, as cited by Roland de Vaux, *Early History of Israel* (Philadelphia: Westminster, 1978), 189, n. 13.

9. Sir Leonard Woolley, *Abraham, Recent Discoveries and Hebrew Origins* (London: 1936). Most scholars would hotly contest most, if not all, that Woolley attributed to the biblical traditions in this work.

tory, from which the Ras Shamra Texts said merchants came to trade in Ugarit.[10]

Regardless of whether the southern or northern town eventually proves to be the correct identification, Abram must not be depicted as a nomadic shepherd tending a few straggly sheep and goats, but as a merchant prince who "trades" with monarchs and needs a security force of some 318 men to oversee his capital investments, his herds.

The Names of the Patriarchs

Another way to attack the problem of the dating of the patriarchs, and even to locate their origins, is to note the form of the names themselves. Isaac, Jacob, Joseph, and even Abraham's son by Hagar—Ishmael—all begin with an i/y- prefix that scholars of northwest Semitic languages call "Amorite imperfective" names. Such names with an i/y- prefix were common to the Mari archives of the early second millennium B.C.

Even more interesting is the fact that there is a tendency for names that are common in the patriarchal era (e.g., Serug and Nahor) to appear at the end of the third and beginning of the second millennium B.C. in Lower Mesopotamia before they appear later in Upper Mesopotamia.[11] De Vaux commented on this phenomenon by saying:

> Abraham's great grandfather is called Serug and a *sa-ru-gi* is mentioned in a document from Tello which dates back to the Third Dynasty of Ur. Abraham's grandfather and one of his brothers were called Nahor and the personal name *Na-ha-rum* occurs in four documents of the same period, probably coming from Nippur. The name Jacob, which is an abbreviation of *Yaᶜqôbh -ʾEl*, appears in several different forms . . . in four Kish documents, about a century before Hammurabi, . . . and in the two Tell Harmel documents of the same period. It also appears as *Ya-ku-ub-El* and even in the abbreviated form of *Ya-ku-bi* in the texts of the First Dynasty of Babylon.[12]

This data has not gone unquestioned. P. Kyle McCarter announced:

10. Cyrus H. Gordon, "Abraham of Ur," in *Hebrew and Semitic Studies Presented to* G. R. *Driver* (Oxford: 1963), 77–84; idem., "Abraham and the Merchants of Ura," *JNES* 17 (1958): 28–31. This thesis was critiqued by A. Saggs, "Ur of the Chaldees: A Problem of Identification," *Iraq* 22 (1960): 200–209. Gordon's reply came in the first article named in this footnote. Another city called Ura is found in Armenia, mentioned in the fourteenth-century archives from the Hittites. It is about 190 miles north of Haran, but that does not appear to be within traveling distance of Ugarit, according to some.

11. Roland de Vaux, ibid., p. 191, and nn. 24, 25, 26.

12. Ibid., p. 191.

> [T]here is no reason to believe that its use [Amorite imperfective names] diminished after the Middle Bronze Age; in the Late BronzeAge, it is well attested in Ugaritic and Amarna Canaanite names [Late Bronze Age]. Thus, while it is true that the name 'Jacob' is very common in the Middle Bronze Age, it is also found in Late Bronze sources, and related names occur in both Elephantine (fifth century B.C.) and Palmyrene (first century B.C. through third century A.D.) Aramaic. [13]

But Kenneth Kitchen vehemently denied McCarter's evidence, saying that i/y- prefix names were known already in the third millennium, as Ebla attests. But in the second millennium B.C., out of a repertoire of some 6,000 names from the first half of the second millennium B.C., 16 percent of the 1,360 names beginning in i/y are of the Amorite imperfective type. When the Late Bronze Age (late second millennium B.C.) archives of Amarna and Ugarit are examined, only 2 or 3 percent of all the names beginning in i/y- prefix are Amorite perfectives. In the Iron Age it drops even more dramatically to 0.5 percent. Moreover, McCarter's Palmyrene example is of a Jew called Jacob! Kitchen concluded, "This type of name, that of all the patriarchs except Abraham, does belong mainly to the Patriarchal Age. . . the early second millennium B.C. or Middle Bronze Age."[14] Of course, none of these names can be associated with any one of the patriarchs directly, but the fact that they share the very types of names that are unique to the time that they claim to be living in is a point in favor of their general reliability. If the stories had been invented in much later times, such as those of the Babylonian Exile, the use of such names would have been most unlikely since they had little or no currency in that era.

Abraham and the Four Great Eastern Kings

Genesis 14 is one of the most hotly contested chapters in this whole period. It contains the account of the campaign led by four kings—Kedorlaomer of Elam, Tidal king of the Goiim, Amraphel of Shinar, and Arioch of Ellasar—against the five kings of the cities bordering the southeastern end of the Dead Sea: Bera of Sodom, Birsha of Gomorrah, Shinab of Admah, Shemeber of Zeboiim, and the king of Bela, also known as Zoar. For twelve years, these five kings had been subjects of Kedorlaomer, but they all revolted in the thirteenth year (Gen. 14:1–4).

---

13. P. Kyle McCarter, "The Patriarchal Age," in *Ancient Israel*, ed. Hershel Shanks (Washington, D.C.: Biblical Archaeological Society, 1988), 11.
14. Kenneth Kitchen, "The Patriarchal Age: Myth or History?" pp. 90, 92.

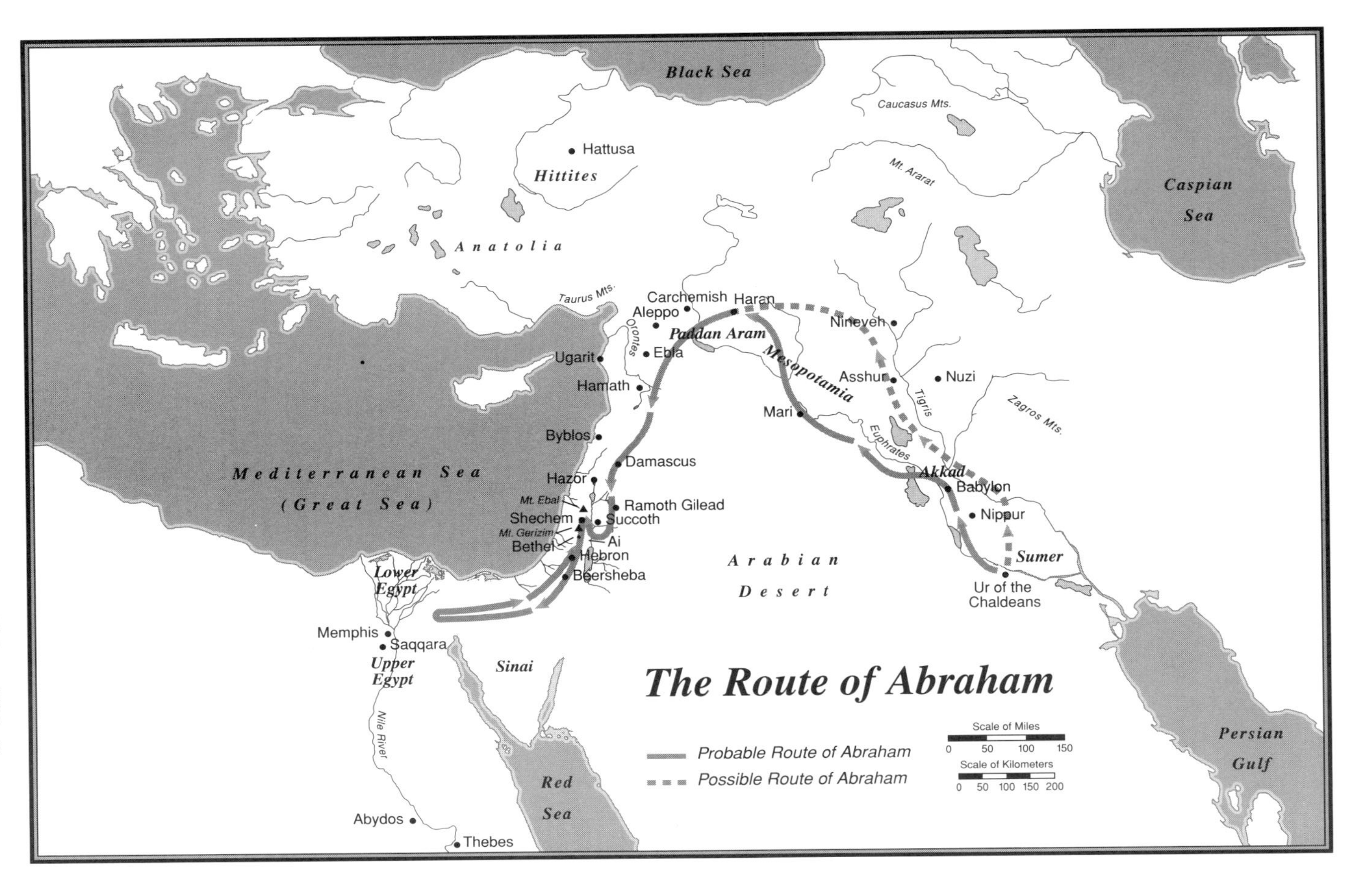

From *Holman Bible Handbook* (Nashville: Holman Bible Publishers, 1992), 61.

In the fourteenth year, Kedorlaomer came with his three allies and defeated the five kings of the plain, taking Abraham's nephew Lot as one of their hostages with them. Abraham pursued the four kings and sprang a surprise night attack against the four kings at Dan. He chased them as far as Hobah, north of Damascus (Gen. 14:15), recovering his relative Lot, along with the other people, and all the goods that had been taken from the five cities that bordered the Dead Sea.

A significant number of scholars of good reputation have defended the description of this military campaign in Genesis 14 as being historically authentic, or in some cases in most of its detail.[15] But it has had its fair share of detractors as well, especially literary critics who view the chapter as a late composition with possible early genuine elements.

Most will agree that even if positive identification of the four Mesopotamian kings has not as yet been possible, the chapter certainly does provide a rather detailed geographical description of the invasion, using words that occur nowhere else in the Bible and place names that only occur here, often with an appositional explanation of a better known, but later, place name, placed alongside the rare geographical term. For example, the word used in Genesis 14:14 is *ḥănîkîm*, occurring only here in the Old Testament. This word, however, has been found in the Egyptian Execration Texts from the nineteenth century B.C. and in one of the fifteenth century Taanach Letters, where it means "armed supporters, or retainers." The Genesis text explains this unusual phrase by the expression "born in his household," or "members of his household from birth." This may signal the fact that these armed retainers were tied to their master by military obligations. It is difficult to see how someone could fabricate this text, say in the postexilic period, and deliberately use a word that was not in ordinary use.

The response, of course, is to say it was a "deliberate archaism" to make it appear old, just like the phrase "Abram the Hebrew" (Gen. 14:13) was alleged to be as well. It is likewise alleged that the word *rĕkûš*, "possessions" (Gen. 14:11, 12, 16, 21) is another late word since it also appears in the postexilic books. But that may be circular reasoning, for it begs the question as to which came first, the use in Genesis 14 or the uses in the postexilic age.

---

15. For instance: William F. Albright, "A Third Revision of the Early Chronology of Western Asia," *BASOR* 88 (Dec. 1942): 33–36; idem., "Abraham and the Caravan Trade," *BASOR* 163 (1961): 49–54; Kenneth Kitchen, *Ancient Orient and the Old Testament* (Chicago: InterVarsity, 1966), 43–47; F. Cornelius, "Genesis XIV," *ZAW* 72 (1960): 1–7; and E. Speiser, *Genesis: Anchor Bible Commentary* (Garden City, N.Y.: Doubleday, 1964), 105–109.

But there is more. The place names listed in this chapter are startlingly unique, often with explanatory glosses alongside these ancient names to help guide the later reader. Thus "Bela" is explained as being the same as "Zoar" (v. 2), "En Mishpat" is the same as "Kadesh" (v. 7), and "the Valley of Shaveh" is the same as the then-current "King's Valley" (v. 17). If this is, as some have claimed, "deliberate archaizing" of the text, it appears that the writer doth protest too much. But if it were an event that took place approximately in the twentieth century B.C. and then was recorded only later in Mosaic times in the fifteenth century B.C., it is reasonable that names of places had to be updated to that time in order to make sense to the reader.

The names of the four kings from Mesopotamia, though surprisingly still unidentified with a known historical personage from that part of the world, have a ring of authenticity about them that few will deny.[16] Kedorlaomer of Elam is clearly an Elamite name, for it has the Kudur type name that is common there (Kudur/Kutur + X): in fact, both elements of Kedorlaomer are authentic Elamite elements. Arioch of Ellasar exhibits the similar name *Arriyuk(ki)* or *Arriwuk(ki)*, which is attested at both Mari and Nuzi as a Hurrian name. But the name of his kingdom, Ellasar, still has not been linked with any known principality in that time. Tidal of the Goiim, or "nations," is equivalent to the name of four Hittite kings named Tudhaliyas. The kingdom of Goiim is much more vague and may relate to a similar term that was applied in the first millennium to the Cimmerians and then to the Medes. The name "Amraphel" is less clear, though there have been unsuccessful attempts to link it to Hammurapi. Surely his kingdom of "Shinar" is used to denote Babylon, or Mesopotamia in general in the Bible (similar to "Sangar" in Egyptian and "Sanhar" in cuneiform). Thus, Genesis 14 could only fit in the period it intends to portray: this is a most unlikely period if it were arbitrarily retrojected back into history almost a millennium and a half later. Indeed, the recent discovery of the Hurrian capital may be the first break in this case.

Nevertheless, doubts about the text's overall historicity persist. Roland de Vaux is extremely pessimistic about the ultimate credibility of the text. He complained: "There are certainly gaps in our knowledge of the history of the Ancient Near East, but we know quite enough to

16. For the discussion in this section, see Roland de Vaux, *Early History of Ancient Israel*, pp. 218–19; Kenneth Kitchen, "The Patriarchal Age," pp. 56–57, along with the footnotes in both these articles for further evidence.

be able to say that it is historically impossible for these five cities south of the Dead Sea to have at any one time during the second millennium been the vassals of Elam, and that Elam never has been at the head of a coalition uniting the four great near eastern powers of that period."[17] But Kenneth Kitchen countered with an opposing estimate: "There is one—and *only* one—period that fits the conditions of Genesis 14—the early second millennium B.C. Only in that period did the situation in Mesopotamia allow for shifting alliances; and only then did Elam participate actively in the affairs of the Levant, sending envoys not only to Mari but as far west as Qatna on the Orontes in Syria."[18]

Kitchen explained how the situation changed drastically after the eighteenth century B.C. in Mesopotamia. With the triumphs of Hammurapi of Babylon and Shamsi-Adad I of Assyria, the land was dominated just by these two powers: Assyria and Babylon. Only in the two centuries from 1550–1350 B.C. did they share power with Mitanni, but there were none of the rival city-states, for they had vanished forever. Likewise in Anatolia in the north there were drastic changes as well, for competing chiefs and cities were absorbed into the Hittite kingdom that dominated the scene until somewhere around 1200 B.C. In the first millennium, the Levant was run by Aramean and neo-Hittite states at first, then by Israel, the Philistines, and Phoenicians later on, ultimately all falling to the Medo-Persian Empire in the end. Thus, Genesis 14 could only fit in the period it portends to portray; this is a most unlikely period if it were arbitrarily retrojected back into history almost a millennium and a half later!

Life during the Times of the Patriarchs and Matriarchs

Around the middle of the twentieth century A.D., we were much more confident in our descriptions of life during the times of the patriarchs and matriarchs. But much of that confidence has eroded because too much emphasis was put on sociological and cultural structures that seemed to be uniquely similar to those mentioned in the Nuzi, Mari, and Alalakh Tablets. Therefore, the alleged parallels between matters such as teraphim, sale of birthrights, deathbed blessings, "sistership"

17. Roland de Vaux, *Early History of Ancient Israel*, p. 219.
18. Kenneth Kitchen, "Patriarchal Age," p. 57.

documents, Hittite land-sale contracts, and the like have, by and large, been removed from the table for discussion.[19]

This does not mean, however, that all has been lost or that nothing remains from this period. Kenneth Kitchen has again led the way by pointing to several new factors that are unique to the Middle Bronze Age and the times of the patriarchs.

For example, Kitchen detailed the escalating price of slaves from ancient Near Eastern sources to demonstrate that the price paid for Joseph (twenty shekels of silver according to Gen. 37:28) is properly slotted for the Middle Bronze age. During the Akkad Dynasty (2371–2191 B.C.), a slave brought between ten and fifteen shekels of silver, but the price dropped to ten during the Third Dynasty of Ur (2113–2006 B.C.). But in the second millennium, the price of slaves rose to twenty shekels, as witnessed by the Hammurapi Code, the Mari Tablets, and elsewhere. This increase continued in the fourteenth and thirteenth centuries as it crept up to thirty shekels at Nuzi and Ugarit, a price that matched the identical period in biblical history of the Mosaic law, where Exodus 21:32 asks thirty shekels for a slave. Five hundred years later, the Assyrian market was fetching fifty to sixty shekels a head (the identical price that the Assyrian king Pul put on the head of every Israelite for their ransom, "fifty shekels of silver"; see 2 Kings 15:20). The ultimate inflation came in the Persian period with prices soaring from ninety to one hundred and twenty shekels. The point is clear: "If all these figures were invented during the Exile (sixth century B.C.) or in the Persian period by some fiction writer, why isn't the price for Joseph 90 to 100 shekels, the cost of a slave at the time when the story was supposedly written? And why isn't the price in Exodus also 90 to 100 shekels? It is more reasonable to assume that the biblical data reflect reality in these cases."[20]

Another line of evidence for the correct positioning of the patriarchs in the early second millennium, Kitchen suggests, is to be found

19. See the original suggestion of E. A. Speiser, "The Wife-Sister Motif in the Patriarchal Narratives," in *Biblical and Other Studies*, ed. A. Altmann (Cambridge: Harvard University Press, 1963), 15–28. Especially important for the Nuzi material is M. J. Selman, "The Social Environment of the Patriarchs," *TynB* 27 (1976): 119–21. Other scholars who remain unconvinced by Speiser's handling of the Hurrian material, especially on the sistership documents, are C. J. M. Weir, "The Alleged Hurrian Wife-Sister Motif in Genesis," *Transactions of the Glasgow University Oriental Society* 22 (1967–70): 14–25; John Van Seters, *Abraham in History and Tradition* (New Haven: Yale University Press, 1975), 71–78; D. Freedman, "A New Approach to the Nuzi Sistership Contract," *JANES* 2 (1970): 77–85; and S. Greengus, "Sisterhood Adoption at Nuzi and the 'Wife-Sister' in Genesis," *HUCA* 46 (1975): 5–31.

20. I am indebted to Kenneth Kitchen, "The Patriarchal Age," p. 52, for this whole argument as well as the final quotation.

in the form and structure of the covenants exhibited in Genesis as compared to those stretching from the third to the first millennium in the ancient Near East. Had the covenant form been drafted in any other time than the early second millennium, it would have taken a drastically different sort of arrangement of the possible component parts, such as the title, witnesses, stipulations, curses, blessings, deposit provisions, and prologue.[21] In short, a typology of treaties and covenant forms provides another sort of factual basis for locating the patriarchal materials in precisely the times they claim to have occurred.

Patriarchal Livelihoods

Abraham, Isaac, and Jacob are often described as sheperds of rather large herds of sheep and goats (Gen. 12:8; 13:3, 18; 18:1–10; 24:67; 31:25, 33, 34). But were they, on this account, true bedouin (a name meaning "men of the desert"), raising camels and wandering over huge areas of terrain? The name *bedouin* may be overly specific and too technical for its application to the patriarchs.[22] But usually the case about their being bedouin is made to rest on this question: Are the many references to camels in the patriarchal stories anachronistic? For example, camels are mentioned fifteen times in the story of Rebekah's marriage (Gen. 24). Are these references to camels misplaced in time and space?

There seems to be more than passing evidence that the camel already was domesticated by patriarchal times in the first half of the second millennium B.C.[23] Support for this concept is gathered from archaeological evidence of skeletal remains along with illustrations of camels at excavation levels belonging to the third and second millennia B.C. The response is to doubt if such evidence proves domestication of the camel at this period—and if it does, then it must be a reference either to the one-humped camel or dromedary rather than the two-

21. See the color-coded bar graphs that Kitchen produced in "The Patriarchal Age," pp. 54–55 that accompanies his argument for the substantial difference in the different time periods.

22. For some, the lifestyle of the pastoral nomads of Mari is most useful for providing insights into the patriarchal lifestyle. Especially significant in this regard are the works of two scholars: V. H. Matthews, *Pastoral Nomadism in the Mari Kingdom, ca. 1850–1760* B.C. (Cambridge: Cambridge University Press, 1978); and M. B. Rowton, "The Physical Environment and the Problem of the Nomads," in *La Civilisation de Mari. Xve Recontre Assyriologique Internationale*, ed. J. R. Kupper (Paris: Société d'Édition "Les Belles Lettres," 1967), 109–121; idem., "Urban Autonomy in a Nomadic Environment," JNES 32 (1973): 201–215; idem., "Enclosed Nomadism," *Journal of the Economy and Social History of the Orient* 17 (1974): 1–30.

23. For a defense of the early use of the camel, see J. P. Free, "Abraham's Camels," *JNES* 3 (1944): 187–193; J Morgenstern, "The Ark, the Ephod and the Tent," *HUCA* 17 (1942–1943): 255–259, n. 174; and Kenneth Kitchen, *Ancient Orient and the Old Testament* (Chicago: InterVarsity, 1966), 79–80.

humped camel. But some of the arguments are needlessly tedious and soon become boring.

Now were the patriarchs merely donkey drivers who led caravans? The patriarchs did break their journey almost always on caravan trails, but that hardly proves anything one way or another. Others have tried to suggest that the name *Hebrew*, as in "Abram the Hebrew" (Gen. 14:13), like the name *Habiru/Apiru*, really meant "dusty," for that is how donkey drivers who followed their animals appeared. But all of this is more speculative than factual. The donkeys in the biblical text are either part of the patriarch's herds, or they are used as mounts to be ridden.

A better argument can be made for the patriarchs as those who used their herds as means of "trade."[24] Three texts use the Hebrew verb *saḥar*, meaning "to trade" (Gen. 34:10, 21; 42:34). And trade they did, with the likes of monarchs such as the pharaoh of Egypt or Abimeleck of the Philistines. Such high circles hardly suggest the typical picture of the patriarchs as seen in most church materials or plays—a person in a bathrobe-type of dress with a kiaffka on his head.

On the contrary, some stock can be put in the fact that they were in the royal courts of that day to do business, acting as an early form of "merchants," using as their trading capital the sheep and goats they carried with them as they moved to the various pasturelands.

The Religious Beliefs and Practices of the Patriarchs and Matriarchs

Even though Genesis never used the term, ever since Albrecht Alt, scholars have been referring to the cult of the "god of the father/s" among the patriarchs.[25] Allegedly, the deities of the patriarchs were variously named: "Fear of Isaac," or "Kinsman of Isaac" (Gen. 31:42, 53); "Shield of Abraham" (Gen. 15:1); and the "Mighty One of Jacob," or the "Bull of Jacob" (Gen. 49:24–25). Therefore, it is argued, with the exception of El Shaddai, the names worshiped by each of the patriarchs signified the cult of that clan.

But Alt's thesis has not gone uncontested. Whereas the Genesis documents are usually not trusted for the construction of the history of the period, these metaphorical references to Israel's one true God are sud-

24. See Cyrus H. Gordon, "Abraham and the Merchants of Ura," *JNES* 17 (1978): 28–31; L. R. Fisher, "Abraham and his Priest-King," JBL 81 (1962): 264–270.

25. A. Alt, *Essays on Old Testament History and Religion* (Oxford: 1966), 1–77.

denly adopted lock, stock, and barrel and made into competing entities of their own against any monotheistic worship of God.

On the contrary, while both Yahweh and Elohim were known as alternative names for the same deity worshiped by all three patriarchs, as Exodus 6:3 makes clear, the patriarchs witnessed in their day the nature and character of El Shaddai more directly and intimately than they did the character of Yahweh.[26]

The patriarchs erected altars (Gen. 12:7, 8; 13:18; 26:25; 33:20; 35:7) and offered sacrifices to God. While they held special spots as sacred and holy to God, there is little or no evidence that they regarded certain stones or trees as sacred in and of themselves. And as a sign of the covenant, they circumcised their sons (Gen. 17:9–14). While the Egyptians (Gen. 34), the Edomites, Ammonites, Moabites, and certain Arabs practised circumcision (Jer. 9:24–26), the timing and the meaning of the rite differed widely among these peoples—usually performed as a puberty rite at age twelve for many of these other nations.

---

26. M. Haran, "The Religion of the Patriarchs: An Attempt at a Synthesis," *ASTI* 4 (1965): 51–53, n. 34.; Thomas McComiskey, " The Religion of the Patriarchs: An Analysis of *The God of the Fathers* by Albrecht Alt," in *The Law and the Prophets*, ed. John H. Skilton (Philadelphia: Presbyterian and Reformed, 1974), 195–206.

5

The Story of Joseph: Settlement in Egypt

There is no reason to doubt that a person called Joseph really existed or that his story found in Genesis 37–50 accurately reflects the period of Egyptian history that falls somewhere after 1870 B.C. Like the names *Isaac*, *Jacob*, and *Ishmael*, the name *Joseph* belongs to the early Amorite Prefective onomastic type, even though there are no extrabiblical texts from the second millennium B.C. with this name, much less evidence of Joseph's personal existence from documents of that period. Nevertheless, a number of details emerge from his story and its times that have the ring of authenticity about them.

Joseph's Story

Joseph's story falls into three parts: Joseph and his brothers in Canaan, Joseph alone in Egypt, and Joseph in Egypt with his brothers. Each part involves a conflict narrative with the overall point being the final reconciliation that emerged from the tangled threads of the story.

In the first part, Joseph was the younger, but favored, brother who wore a sort of patrician's coat and dreamed what appeared to be bizarre dreams of grandiose glory. Understandably, the brothers resented this and plotted to get rid of their brother, who flaunted his dreams of supremacy over them. Instead of killing him outright, they put him in a pit (through his brother Reuben's intervention); then they sold him to a caravan of Midianite (also called Ishmaelite) traders (through Judah's intervention), who in turn sold him to a private owner in Egypt named Potiphar.

The second part of the story details how Joseph rose to a favored position in Potiphar's household. However, despite Joseph's expert handling of matters, Potiphar's wife turned on him because he refused to have sex with her. Once again, Joseph suffered at the hands of others and, this time, he landed in prison.

Joseph's predicament is so similar to the famous Egytological story named "The Tale of the Two Brothers" (or, "The Story of Anubis and Bata") recovered in A.D. 1860 that many have thought this part of the Joseph story was borrowed from it. But the differences are just as apparent: the two stories share the Egyptological setting but not total literary equivalence. "The Tale of Two Brothers" was written on papyrus in the cursive style of Egyptian writing called "hieratic." Anubis, the older brother, was married and owned his own farm. Bata was the ward of his older brother Anubis. Bata tended Anubis's cattle, plowed his fields, and harvested his crops. Bata was a righteous man and blameless in every way. However, one day as he came in from the fields, Anubis's wife, who had been pestering him to have sex with her, suddenly jumped up and threw her arms around Bata saying, "Come on now, sleep with me just this once, and I will sew some new clothes for you." But Bata wrenched free of her grasp and ran back to his work in the fields. Unfortunately, all the house servants were out of the house that day; thus, no one could verify or deny either person's story.

Anubis's wife decided that a preemptive strike would be the best way to salvage the situation. She took to her bed and aroused her husband's sympathy when he returned in the evening to find her still in bed complaining that she had been attacked by his brother Bata. Anubis hid behind the door of the barn, waiting to kill Bata as he brought the cattle back into their quarters. But the cattle, so the story avers, tipped Bata off that his brother was waiting behind the door. Thus, Bata narrowly escaped being killed.[1] Potipher's wife played the same ancient part with Joseph and had him imprisoned on nothing more than her word (Gen. 39:7, 12, 17–19).

---

1. "The Tale of the Two Brothers" is from Papyrus 10183 in the British Museum, usually known by its former owner as the D'Orbiney Papyrus. It was written by the scribe Ennana, who was a pupil of the scribe of the treasury of Pharaoh Kagboi. A hieroglyphic text is conveniently available in Alan H. Gardiner, *Late-Egyptian Stories* (Bruxelles: Edition de la Fondation Egytoplogique, 1932), 9–30. For a popularized synopsis of this story, see Victor H. Matthews and Don C. Benjamin, *Old Testament Parallels: Laws and Stories from the Ancient Near East* (New York: Paulist Press, 1991), 41–45.

Even in prison, Joseph prospered and was given a responsible position. When an opportunity arose to interpret the dreams of two state prisoners, Pharaoh's butler and baker, he correctly interpreted the dreams of both men, urging the one whose dream turned out to be favorable for his release that he should mention Joseph's plight to the pharaoh. Much later, however, the chief baker suddenly recalled his forgotten promise to Joseph when the pharaoh himself had a dream that needed interpretation. As a result of his being able to interpret the dream, Joseph was released from prison and this time given a prestigious place in Egypt's government.

The third part of the Joseph narrative describes his reconciliation with his brothers as they come down to Egypt to buy grain during the time of unprecedented famine—a famine that lasted seven years throughout much of the ancient Near East.

THE ENTRANCE INTO EGYPT

More than once, famine seems to have driven persons from Syro-Palestine into Egypt for relief from the severe drought. For example, an earlier text claims that Abraham went down into Egypt because of a famine in Canaan in his day (Gen. 12:10). There is also the well-known tomb painting of Khnum-hotep at Beni Hassan, from the reign of Sesostris II (at the beginning of the nineteenth century B.C.), showing the arrival of thirty-seven Asiatics, men, women, and children, being led by their chief Ibsha (also read as Abi-shar).[2] The many-colored striped dress of these thirty-seven Asiatics was all the more interesting in light of the part that Joseph's coat played in his story.

But even more interesting is the report that comes from the eighth year of the reign of Pharaoh Merneptah. In this letter, the Pharaoh allowed the bedouin tribes from Edom (the Shasu) to gain access into the land of Egypt "to keep them alive and to keep their cattle alive."[3]

Accordingly, in the Joseph story, the move of his father and his brothers to Egypt was not an unprecedented act, given the dire emergency that precipitated its move, but such moves must have been something that occurred again and again in Egypt. Such incidents must have increased, not decreased in times when there was a weak government

2. P. E. Newberry, *Beni Hassan I* (London, 1893), Plate XXVIII, XXXXXXI. This tomb painting is reproduced in *Ancient Near East in Pictures*, no. 3; the text in *Ancient Near Eastern Texts*, p. 229a. Now also see Alice V. Baines, "The Function of Iconography as Autobiographical Narration in the Tomb of Knemhotep at Beni Hasan (Tomb 3)," *JNSL* 21/2 (1995): 1–24, especially the diagram of the registers on pp. 23–24.

3. James Pritchard, ed. *ANET*, p. 259a.

and lax border controls in Egypt. Usually these groups did not penetrate beyond the delta region, but there were occasions when some Asiatics went beyond the Nile delta and settled in Egypt for an extended period. During the Second Intermediate period, for example, settlements of this kind must have played a part in the Hyksos's seizure of power in the land.

Joseph's Dreams

People throughout the ancient Near East attributed great significance to the presence and interpretation of dreams.[4] Egyptians seem to have exceeded even the standard set by their neighbors. Egyptian literature from the Middle Kingdom up to the Roman period records an extraordinary number of dreams, often along with guides or manuals for their interpretation.[5] The significance of dreams in the Joseph story, again, suits the general expectation of that era.

Most will acknowledge that the dreams of Pharaoh and his officials have a very strong Egyptian flavor (Gen. 40–41). The officials' dreams are closely tied in with what takes place in the court, while Pharaoh dreams of cows feeding on the banks of the Nile. The "reeds" among which the cows grazed is an Egyptian word, *ʾāḥû* (Gen. 41:2, 18). However, even though it is an Egyptian word, there is evidence that it may have entered into western Semitic speech at a very early stage, as the Ugaritic *ʾaḥ* attests.[6]

As for the "seven heads of grain, full and good," as opposed to the "seven other heads [that] sprouted—withered and thin and scorched by the east wind" (Gen. 41:22–23), it must be remembered that the Egyptians associated variations in the water level of the Nile River at its flood stage directly with the productivity of the land. So sensitive was Egypt's dependency on the flood reaching a height of twenty-five to twenty-six feet above zero datum at the first cataract at Elephantine that the crops for the year could be calculated in accordance with the number of feet that the flood reached. For instance, if the flood was only twenty or twenty-one feet above normal, instead of the anticipated twenty-five or twenty-six feet, then crop production would be off

4. A. L. Oppenheim, *The Interpretation of Dreams in the Ancient Near East, with a Translation of an Assyrian Dream-Book* (Philadelphia: Transactions of the American Philosophical Society, n.s., 1956) 46, 3.

5. S. Sauneron, *Les songes et leur interpretation dans l'Egypt ancienne* (Paris: Symposium of Sources Orientales, 1859) as cited by Roland de Vaux, *The Early History of Ancient Israel*, p. 303, nn. 36, 37.

6. Roland de Vaux, ibid., p. 304.

by 20 percent! A greater decline in the level of floodwaters would bring even a greater drop in productivity. On the other hand, if the floods went to thirty feet (20 percent above what was needed), it would sweep away dikes and canal banks, resulting in loss of life as these embankments of the villages would be wiped out as well.[7]

The fall-off in the level of the flood seems to be connected with the changes in the wind, for a prophecy of Nefer-rohu declares: "The rivers of Egypt are empty. . . . The south wind will oppose the north wind." [8] Apparently it was the south wind that dried up everything in Egypt, but the biblical writer mentioned the "east wind" (Gen. 41:6, 23, 27) instead of the "south wind." Amazingly, however, the Greek Septuagint, a translation made in Egypt itself, does not mention the "east wind" in its text of verses 6, 23, or 27. It simply says that the heads of grain were "destroyed by the wind."[9] It would appear that "south wind" is what should be read in all of these instances, or that a superior form of the Hebrew text, which omitted the direction of the wind, was witnessed to by the third century B.C. Septuagint Greek translation.

The "wise men" (Hebrew *ḥarṭummîm*, Gen. 41:8, 24) that Pharaoh consulted to interpret his dreams accurately reflects the Egyptian *harʿtôm*, meaning "chief reader" in Egypt.[10] These individuals were trained to interpret texts and to study spells of magicians. In some texts they do figure as magicians, just as Exodus 7:11, 22; 8:3; and 9:11 depict them.

Egyptian Names and Terms

Joseph was given the Egyptian name of *Zaphenath-Paneah* (Gen. 41:45). Once again, this name has not been directly attested, but it has often been acknowledged to be a real Egyptian type of name meaning "(the god) has said: he will live." The equivalents of this name, however, do exist with Isis, Amon, or Osirus, being "the god [who] is say[ing]: he will live." So far, these names have not been found prior to

7. John A. Wilson, *The Culture of Ancient Egypt* (Chicago: University of Chicago Press, 1951), 10–11.

8. *ANET*, p. 445a.

9. This observation is made by Roland de Vaux, *op. cit.* p. 304, n. 44. He also noticed that in the plague of locusts (Exod. 10:13) and the crossing of the sea (Exod. 14:21), the Septuagint again has *notos*, the "south" wind, instead of the "east wind." It appears as if the word "east wind" was substituted for "south wind" early on by a copyist who may have used his knowledge of Palestine to replace the real situation in Egypt.

10. As in this whole section, the works of J. Vergote, *Joseph en Egypt, Genese, chap 37–50 à la lumière des études égyptologiques récentes* (Louvaine: Publicationa Universitaires, 1959), 80–84; Also see J. M. A. Janssen, "Egyptological Remarks on the Story of Joseph in Genesis," *JEOL* 14 (1955–1956): 63–72.

the Twenty-first (or in one case, the Twentieth) Dynasty. There is no reason to conclude, as some have done, that the Joseph story, therefore, must have been written in the time of Solomon since Solomon is a contemporary of the Twenty-first Dynasty. Must we presume that we are now in possession of all the available data and that there is nothing more to be learned from any future evidence?

Joseph's Egyptian wife was named Asenath (Gen. 41:45, 50; 46:20). She was a daughter of Potiphera, a priest of On, or Heliopolis. The meaning and form of her name are still unattested, but they may well be connected with the divine name *Neith*. Her father's name, Potiphera, is fairly well attested, again from the Twenty-First Dynasty onward, as *Pẓ-dǰ-pẓ-rʿ*, meaning something like "It is the [god] Re who has given birth to him." His name seems to be the same name as Joseph's master, Potiphar, though a few think that Joseph's master's name was a transcription of the Egyptian title, unless Potiphar reflects the Egyptian *Pẓ-dî-pẓrʿ*: "It is the [god] Horus who has given."[11]

In Genesis 41:43, a cry comes forth from the people as Joseph is on his way to his investiture in Pharaoh's court. They cry *ʾabrēk*, meaning something like "Make way!" or "Bow down!" This has been explained by referring to the Egyptian *ib-r.k*, literally, "the heart to you," perhaps signifying "Attention!" That Egyptian form does occur in the Ramesside period of Egypt three times, but most Egyptologists doubt that is what is intended here in the Joseph narrative. Therefore, we are not certain what this expression really means, though the sense of it and its proper location in Egyptological settings seems to be secure.[12]

Likewise, the oath Joseph used as he accused his brothers of being spies, "As surely as Pharaoh lives" (Gen. 42:15, 16), indeed has another Egyptological ring to it once again, but it has not been attested, so far, earlier than the Twenty-first Dynasty. This formula is, at any rate, nicely paralleled by the well-known Hebrew oath, "As surely as the Lord/or my lord the king/ lives."

The Egyptological Culture of Joseph

Joseph lived to an ideal Egyptian age, 110 years (Gen. 50:22, 26). There are twelve examples of such longevity in the Nineteenth Dynasty and seventeen in the Ramesside period.[13] After these periods,

11. J. Vergote, *Joseph en Égypte: Gènese Chap. 37–50 à la lumière des études égyptologiques récentes* (Louvaine: Publications Universitaires, 1959), 147–50.
12. Ibid., pp. 135–141.
13. G. Lefebvre, "L'âge de 110 ans et le vieillesse chez les Egyptiens," *CRAI* , pp. 106–119.

that number appears less frequently. However, this same ideal age of 110 did appear in the Old Kingdom and Middle Kingdom and in the Eighteenth Dynasties, once for each period. Therefore, it was not unknown in the earlier periods, as some have tried to infer on the basis of our present statistics.[14]

At the death of Jacob, Joseph's father, he was embalmed, as was the custom of the Egyptians (Gen. 50:2–3). Some dispute, however, has arisen over the length of time required for embalming. Typically, it required seventy days in Egyptian literature, but verse 3 seems to say that it only took forty days in Jacob's case. Instead, verse 3 also mentions that the mourning period for Jacob was seventy days. Either the text combined the mourning and the completion of the embalming process, or the process was deliberately cut short by request of the Hebrew family. Joseph was also placed in "a coffin" (Gen. 50:26) after he had been embalmed, another custom that was alien to Israel's early history, but again was at home in Egypt.

Titles in the Joseph Story

Potiphar, one of Pharaoh's officials, was known as "the captain/commander of the guard" (Gen. 37:36; 39:1; 40:3; 41:12; Hebrew *śar haṭṭabbāḥîm*), who must have worked in "the house of the captain of the guard" (Gen. 41:10). J. Vergote is sure the Hebrew root *ṭ-b-ḥ*, here translated as "guard," is more accurately rendered in Hebrew (cf. 1 Sam. 9:23–24) and Egyptian (*wdpw*) as "cook," or better still as "butler." This title is attested as early as Middle Kingdom texts.[15]

Likewise, Joseph is said to have functioned as "chancellor" or "lord of the household" (Gen. 41:40; 45:8). This title is similar to two such titles found in the Onomasticon of Pharaoh Amenope. Thus the Hebrew might reflect something like *mr-r3 pr wr*, "the chief attendant/administrator."

Some have argued that it is better to seek a Semitic usage for explaining such titles rather than an Egyptological one. For example, it is contended that seven times in 2 Kings 25:8–20, and seventeen times in Jeremiah 39, 40, 41, and 42, *rab haṭṭabbāḥîm* occurs as a title.[16] The final solution here must await further discoveries.

14. J. Vergote, *Joseph en Égypt*, 200–201 and the reference there also to J. M. A. Janssen, "On the Ideal Lifetime of the Egyptians," in *Oudheidkundige Medelingen uit het Rijksmuseum van Oudheden te Leiden*, nouv. Ser. 31 (1950), 33–44.

15. J. Vergote, *Joseph en Égypte*, pp. 31–35.

16. Roland de Vaux, op. cit., pp. 301–302 argued this way against the contentions of J. Vergote, *Joseph en Egypte*, pp. 203–213, who placed the story of Joseph in the Eighteenth Dynasty, probably written by Moses. In fact, concluded de Vaux, Joseph just says that he was appointed "lord" (Hebrew *ʾadôn*) of all of Pharaoh's household and "administrator" (*môšēl*) of the whole land. de Vaux thinks the terms were not meant to be precise, but only that Joseph had great power in Egypt.

Place Names in the Joseph Story

It is said that Jacob came to Egypt with all his family and settled in the land of "Goshen" (Gen. 45:10; 46:28–29; 47:1). But so far, the name *Goshen* has not turned up in any Egyptian reference and may not be an Egyptian name for the area, but rather a Semitic name. But given the references to other places in the land of Goshen, such as Pithom,[17] the land of Goshen can be securely identified with the area where these sites exist.

Genesis 47:11 also refers to Goshen as the "land of Rameses," which many immediately label as an anachronism, since the name *Rameses* belongs to the Nineteenth Dynasty, i.e., the thirteenth century B.C. But the same data could be read just the opposite way, as we prefer to do, meaning that the names of the two store cites built by the Israelites, named Pithom and Rameses (Exod. 1:11), and the reference to the "land of Rameses" (Gen. 47:11), contain older names that were later also used as names of the pharaohs of the Nineteenth Dynasty.

Another geographical matter is raised by the proximity of the place where Joseph's brothers settled in the land of Goshen or Rameses to the residence of the pharaoh himself (e.g., Gen. 45:10; 46:28–29 compared with 47:1). Nothing, however, in these texts need mean anything more than the fact that the family of Joseph was closer to him in Goshen than it had been in Canaan!

Therefore, the discussions as to what period of time the capital of any of the pharaohs was located in the delta region may be an exercise in futility, for that may not have been what was intended by the expressions of nearness to Joseph.

It is true, of course, that the Hyksos had their capital in the delta at Avaris (=Tanis). But during the Eighteenth Dynasty, the capital was situated at Thebes in Upper Egypt, at least until the Amarna era of Pharaoh Akhenaton (=Amenhotep IV). Thebes was a good distance from the delta. One pharaoh did have a second capital at Memphis during the Eighteenth Dynasty. However, in the Nineteenth Dynasty, a capital was built in the delta, Pi-Ramses, probably to be identified with Qantir ["Bridge"], south of Tanus. Here the pharaohs of the Nineteenth and Twentieth dynasties resided until the Twenty-first Dynasty (of the days of the monarchy in Israel) moved the capital to Tanis and then in the next dynasty to Bubastis.

---

17. Pithom means the "house/temple of [the god] Atum," Egyptian *Pr-Itm*, located either at Tell er-Retabeh ["Broomhill"], or eight and one-half miles east at Tell el-Maskhutah ["Mound of Idols"], both in the Wadi Tumilat.

The Egyptological background for the Joseph narrative is well enough established to merit its inclusion in the historical narrative, as the Hebrew text of the Bible claimed. It fits at the end of the Middle Bronze IIA period of the patriarchs.

Moreover, Joseph's story is our only explanation for why Jacob's family and the nation of Israel found themselves in Egypt for the next 430 years. Just as the cultural background, terms, and geographical references shifted from Babylon to Canaan as the text of Genesis moved from Genesis 1–11 to Genesis 12–36, so now the cultural background, terms, and geographical references shifts to Egypt in Genesis 37 to the exit from Egypt in Exodus 15.

The Joseph stories exhibit an overwhelmingly Egyptological context that fits this period of the eighteenth century B.C. setting for the story. Joseph provided the eponymous ancestry for the tribal units of Ephraim and Manasseh, thereby supplementing the genealogical data of the earlier Genesis record by adding two names to the twelve-tribe list in place of his own name (the tribe of Levi was not usually counted among the twelve). As one of Jacob's sons, he was also able to preserve the family during the critical years of the famine that hit much of the Near East during the final years of their father Jacob, who by this time had been renamed Israel—the eponymous ancestor of the nation whose history is the subject for much of the work that follows.

Part II

The Sojourn In Egypt, the Exodus and Sinai

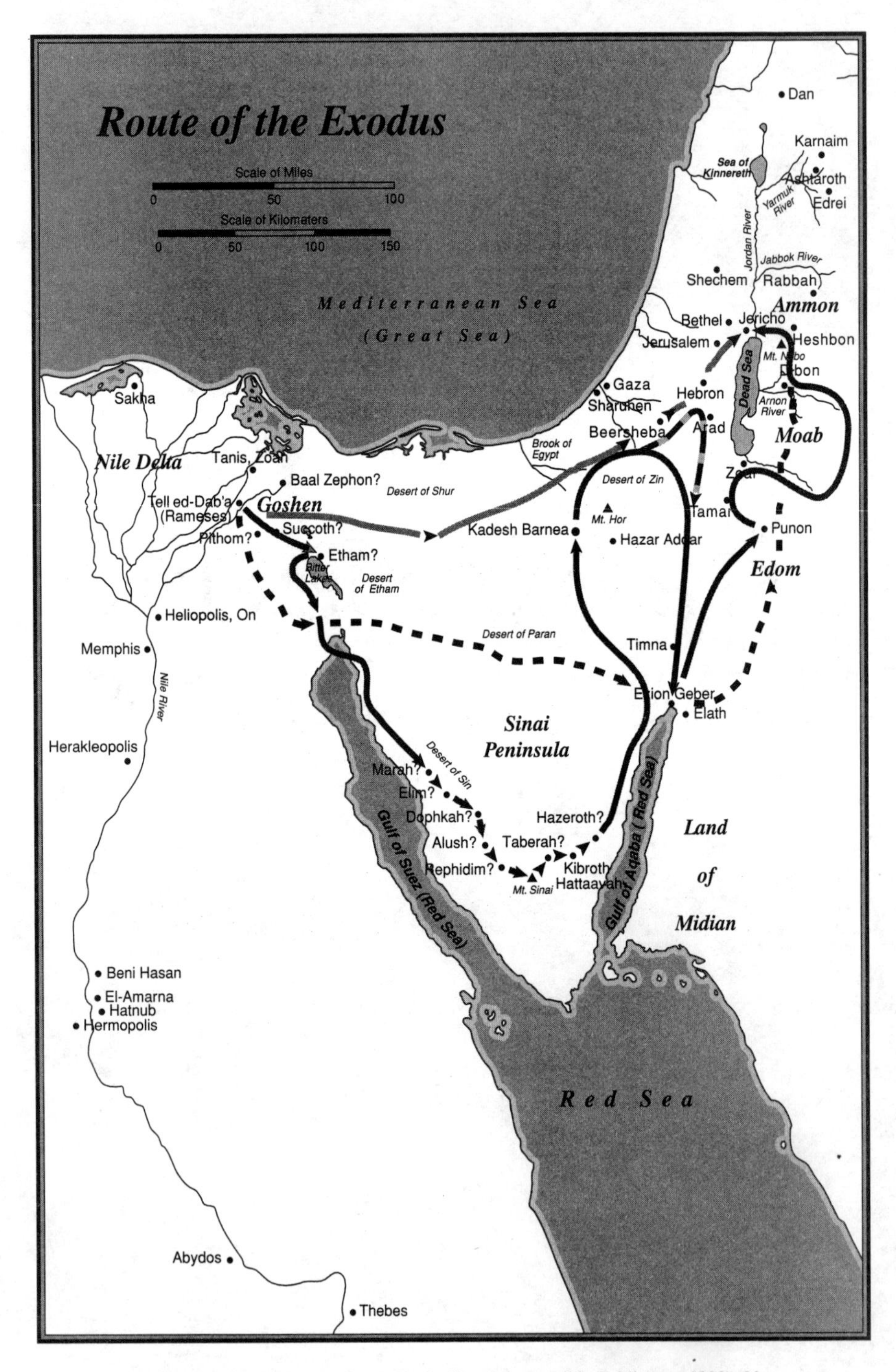

From *Holman Bible Handbook* (Nashville: Holman Bible Publishers, 1992), 82.

6

The Man Moses and His Mission

Several hundred years of relative silence separate the end of the story of Joseph in Genesis 37–50 from the beginning of the Book of Exodus where the story is picked up once again. After Jacob had migrated to Egypt with his family to remain through the rest of the seven-year famine, the text of Scripture supplies no details other than to tell us that a new king "who did not know about Joseph" began to oppress the Israelites (Exod. 1:8). The new king took this action because of the great increase in the Israelite population.

The Hyksos and the King Who Did Not Know Joseph

The Joseph narrative seems to indicate that Jacob and his sons descended into Egypt to live there in the middle of the illustrious Twelfth Dynasty, (ca. 1875 to 1850 B.C.). Some argue that the "new king who did not know about Joseph" (Exod. 1:8) was Amosis (1570–1546 B.C.), the founder of the Eighteenth Dynasty, and that three hundred years had passed before the Israelites began to be oppressed by the Eighteenth or Nineteenth Dynasties.[1] Joseph's death is usually put at about 1775 B.C. But if Israel's enslavement only began under the new pharaoh of the Eighteenth Dynasty, then the prediction of Genesis 15:13 that Israel would be enslaved and *mistreated* for *"four*

1. This is the argument of John Rae, "The time of the Oppression and the Exodus," *BETS* 3 (1960): 58–69. It appears to be well thought out and most reasonable.

hundred years" would be wide of the mark by hundreds of years.[2] Thus, if the Eighteenth Dynasty (or even the Nineteenth Dynasty as is more often preferred today) initiated the oppression, they would have been afflicted only for about one hundred years, or less. The pharaoh of the oppression has not been correctly identified as being either of these two possibilities.

Who, then, was the pharaoh of the oppression if it was not the founder of the Eighteenth or Nineteenth Dynasty? One clue can be found in the Hebrew text of Exodus 1:8, *wayyāqām . . . ʿal Miṣrāyîm*, which is usually incorrectly rendered as new king "came to power in Egypt," or "arose over Egypt." However, in Hebrew text, the verb *qum* plus the preposition *ʿal* often is rendered "to rise against" (Deut. 19:11; 28:7; Judg. 9:19; 20:5, 2 Sam. 18:31; 2 Kings 16:7), but it never is given the meaning of assuming the throne of a nation in a peaceful and friendly manner.[3]

If it was not Amosis of the Eighteenth Dynasty, then who could have been this pharaoh of the oppression of Israel? Answer: An Asiatic people whom the Egyptians knew as the Hyksos,[4] "rulers of foreign lands."[5] The Hyksos swept into Egypt at a time of Egyptian political instability. Since these invaders had the distinctive advantage of such advanced weapons as the war chariot and the laminated or composite bow, they overthrew the native Egyptian dynasties some time around

2. Genesis 15:13 reads: "Then the LORD said to [Abram], 'Know for certain that your descendants will be strangers in a country not their own, and they will be enslaved and mistreated four hundred years.'"

3. This is John Rae's observation, "The Time of the Oppression," pp. 60–61.

4. The Egyptian term *Hyksos* has been used as an ethnic term for this period in Egyptian history, and then it was applied too loosely to fortifications, pottery, and weapons. In recent times, however, the earthen works or *glacis* can no longer be identified exclusively with the "Hyksos," for they are found in nearly every excavated site in Syria-Palestine. The terms *Amorite* or *Canaanite* are judged to be more serviceable. See B. Mazar, "The Middle Bronze Age in Palestine," *IEJ* 18 (1968), 65, 97; and John Van Seters, *The Hyksos: A New Investigation* (New Haven: Yale University Press, 1969). There is no doubt that elements of the Western Semitic peoples did infiltrate Egypt in the Fifteenth Dynasty and dominated it until they were expelled at the end of the Seventeenth Dynasty. The recent Austrian excavations at *Daba`a* in the delta, not far from the Hyksos capital of Avaris, have brought to light much typical Palestinian Middle Bronze II A/B material (ca. 1800 B.C.), confirming the Asiatic presence in Egypt. Nevertheless, no evidence exists to support the notion that the Hyksos occupation fully coincided with the period that the Israelites spent in Egypt. The Egyptian records and archaeological investigations have turned up no certain link so far. See Roland de Vaux, *The Early History of Israel*, tr. David Smith (Philadelphia: Westminster Press, 1978), 75–81. Also on the Hyksos, see D. B. Redford, "The Hyksos Invasion in History and Tradition," *Orientalia* 39 (1970): 1–51; and T. Save-Soderbergh, "The Hyksos Rule in Egypt," *JEA* 37 (1951): 53–71.

5. It does not appear that Manetho's etymological explanation of the Greek word *Hyksos* is correct, for he derived it from the title for the invading forces, *hq3w hsw.t*, "rulers of foreign countries." These same words were used for several centuries as the designation for bedouin leaders in Syria and Palestine.

1730–1710 B.C. And from that time until the revolt of Amosis, founder of the Eighteenth Dynasty in 1570 B.C., the Hyksos exercised absolute control in northern Egypt, establishing their capital in the Nile delta at Avaris, and later over much of Egypt.

We are beholden to an Egyptian priest named Manetho, who wrote fifteen centuries after the event. According to Manetho, the last independent sovereign of the Thirteenth Dynasty was Dudi-mose (also called Tutimaios). It was during his reign that:

> an unknown people came unexpectedly from the east and invaded our country and seized it by force without any difficulty, capturing the leaders, burning towns, razing the temples, and treating the inhabitants with terrible cruelty, cutting men's throats and leading the women and children into captivity. They even made one of their people, Salitis, king. This prince set up his court at Memphis.[6]

Five other kings are listed by Manetho, each of whom was "more and more determined to extirpate the Egyptian people. The whole of this nation is known as the Hyksos, that is, the shepherd kings." So Manetho was the first to call this nation the Hyksos. From Manetho's list of the Hyksos kings and from the fragmentary Turin Papyrus, the names and reigns of this hostile nation divide up into four dynasties, from the Fourteenth to the Seventeenth Dynasties, but the information is incomplete and so confused that we are unable to determine if there is any overlap with contemporary Egyptian dynasties as well.

Some of the proper names among the Hyksos were undoubtedly Semitic (e.g., *Yaqub-el, Yaqub-har, Anat-el*). Other names, however, cannot be easily explained by any known ethnic group. This group of peoples was known variously as "Asiatics" (the Amu), "inhabitants of the sands," or "people of Retenu." They appear to have adopted the Egyptian god Seth as their main deity. The Seth cult came originally from Upper Egypt, but then spread to the delta region. Seth was a storm god, who was given the dress and characteristics of a Syrian god. Thus, he was identified with Baal and given Anat or Astarte as a spouse. On this slim basis, many regarded the Hyksos as Semitic.

To argue that Israel, a Semitic people, to be sure, was in some way part of the Hyksos movement in Egypt is to leave unanswered why the Israelites did not leave Egypt *with* the Hyksos when they were expelled around 1570 B.C. Or to put the same question differently, why did the

---

6. The sources that Manetho used are now lost to us, as is Manetho's work, but the text can be found in Josephus, *Contra Apionem*, I XIV, 75–82.

Egyptians not also expel the Hebrews when they drove out the Hyksos if the two were associated with each other? Would not the Egyptians have vented their hatred of the Hyksos on the Israelites? But there was a difference: the fact that the Hyksos had persecuted the Israelites meant that they were separate from them and were not the object of the Egyptian expulsion.

Accordingly, the "new king who did not know about Joseph" must have been a Hyksos ruler who arose some time between 1730 and 1710 B.C. This meant that the oppression of Israel lasted for some three hundred years, a figure much closer to the four hundred predicted in Genesis 15:13. If a brief period of relaxation of the oppression came after the expulsion of the Hyksos, then the Egyptians of the Eighteenth Dynasty soon discovered that it was to their advantage to continue the oppression of the Jews begun under the Hyksos. Such an identification of the Hyksos as the "new king" that knew not Joseph also would explain the fact that in Exodus 1:9–10, the "new king" said about the Israelites, "Look how numerous and powerful the Israelite people are than we. Come, let us deal shrewdly with them lest they continue to increase, and it happens that when a war breaks out, they will join our enemies and fight against us and then leave our country" (my own translation; contrast the unwarranted NIV). In no way could the number of Israelites exceed that of all the native Egyptians of either the Eighteenth or Nineteenth Dynasties, but they could easily equal and probably eventually exceed the number of the Hyksos, depending on how soon after their ascendancy to the throne the Hyksos enforced their oppressive measures.

The date for the Hyksos can be fixed with a fair degree of exactness by the "Stele of the Year 400," found at Tanis.[7] This stele celebrates the fourth centenary (about the year of 1330 or 1320 B.C.) of the inauguration of the cult of Seth. The stele must have been brought to Tanis from Avaris (if the two cities are not the same site), the former capital of the Hyksos. The conclusion is that the inauguration of the worship of Seth on a national level must have begun four hundred years earlier in 1730–1720 B.C., thereby also marking the arrival of the Hyksos at approximately that same time.

It does not appear that the Hyksos rule consisted of a succession of sovereign rulers reigning over a completely unified Upper and Lower Egypt. Instead, there is evidence that the leaders of the Hyksos at

---

7. This stele is illustrated in P. Montet, "La stele de l'an 400 retrouvée," *Kêmi* 4 (1931), Plate XI, and pp. 191–215. The text of the stele can be found in *ANET*, pp. 252–253.

Avaris-Memphis were leaders of a federation of rulers over various parts of Egypt. For instance, the royal scarabs from dynasties fourteen to seventeen cannot always be classified under any one or two of the contemporaneous dynasties existing at that time.

The revolt that overthrew the Hyksos hegemony was organized in Upper Egypt at Thebes, five hundred miles south of the Hyksos capital of Avaris, in the delta area where Israel dwelt during their Egyptian sojourn. It is documented in the Papyrus Sallier I,[8] which records what is perhaps a legend based on some kernel of truth about the next to the last king of the Seventeenth Dynasty, Seqnen-Re.[9] Seqnen-Re received an insulting communiqué from the Hyksos king Apophis in Avaris that the animals in the hippopotamus pool at Thebes, some five hundred miles away, were preventing him from sleeping. The papyrus is incomplete, but the mummy of Seqnen-Re did evidence a severe head wound from which the ruler died, inflicted, if one were to guess, by the Hyksos. Seqnen-Re's son, Kamose, continued the struggle against the Hyksos, as witnessed by two stelae found at Karnak.[10] But it was Kamose's brother, Amosis, the founder of the Eighteenth Dynasty, who actually finished the job of driving out the Hyksos from Egypt. The only extant document recording the expulsion from Egypt, the preservation of which James B. Pritchard called "an irony of history," is a document from a certain obscure captain of a Nile vessel. This captain, named Ah-mose, served under Amosis and fought several times against Avaris until the city eventually fell.[11] The document ends with this anticlimactic note: "Then Avaris was despoiled. Then I carried off spoil from there: one man, three women, a total of four persons. Then his majesty gave them to me as spoils."

THE OPPRESSION

Three separate pogroms (organized destructions or massacres) were carried out against the Israelites: (1) the slave labor of building the two store cities (Exod. 1:11–12), (2) the order for the midwives to kill all newly born male babies (Exod. 1:15–22), and (3) the order that Israel was to gather its own straw to make bricks while maintaining the same quota as before (Exod. 5:6–23).

8. *ANET*, p. 231.

9. This spelling is that of Roland de Vaux, *The Early History of Israel*, p. 81; Sir Alan Gardiner, *Egypt of the Pharaoh* (Oxford: At the Claredon Press, 1961), 442, spelled it "Sekenenre."

10. See P. Montet, "La stèle du roi Kamosé," *CRAI*, 1956, 112–120; also in *ANET*, pp. 232–33; 554–555.

11. *ANET*, pp. 233–34.

The Egyptological coloration of the biblical narrative is evident in several details preserved in the text. We have seen already how the migratory patterns of seminomads, especially during times of famine, is graphically illustrated by the report of an Egyptian border official in the thirteenth century B.C. He reported that Edomite peoples had been granted permission to move into the Nile delta region in order "to keep them alive and to keep their cattle alive."[12]

The process of making bricks described in Exodus 1:13–14 and 5:12–21 is graphically documented in Egyptian art and texts. A wall painting in the tomb of the vizier Rekhmire during the Eighteenth Dynasty (ca. 1460 B.C.) showed foreigners making and carrying bricks. The inscription read, "The captives whom his majesty has brought to build the temple of Amon at Thebes . . . making bricks to reconstruct the stores [of Amon]."[13] The overseer of the brick-making slaves was known as a *śar*, "slave master," the same term used in Hebrew and the name that appears on this famous wall painting at Thebes during the reign of Thutmose III. The rank of this "slave master" is indicated in the painting by the heavy whip he carries and by the Egyptian hieroglyphic determinative of the head and neck of the giraffe.

A leather scroll from the fifth year of Rameses II's reign in the Nineteenth Dynasty mentioned the quota of two thousand bricks for each of the forty workers. This is an exceptional number, but an extraordinary number of construction projects demanded an unimaginably large number of bricks.

The names of the two midwives, Shiphrah and Puah, are also of more than passing Egyptological interest. Both names appear to be Semitic rather than Egyptian. Shiphrah is found as *Sp-ra*, "fair one," or "beauty," in an eighteenth century B.C. list of Egyptian slaves.[14] Puah, on the other hand, probably reflects the Ugaritic *pǵt*, meaning "girl," or "splendid one."[15]

The delivery stools the women used were literally "two stones" (cf. Egyptian *ḏb.ty*), which are pictorially represented in the hieroglyphic

12. *ANET*, p. 259.

13. Kenneth A. Kitchen, "From the Brickfields of Egypt," *Tyndale Bulletin* 27 (1976): 137–47; N. De G. Davis, *The Tomb of Rekh-mi-re' at Thebes* (New York, 1943), especially I, p. 55; II, pl. lviii-lix. On brickmaking, see C. F. Nims, "Bricks without Straw," *BA* 13 (1950): 22–28.

14. W. F. Albright, "Northwest-Semitic Names in a List of Egyptian Slaves from the Eighteenth Century," *JAOS* 74 (1954): 222–33, especially p. 229.

15. C. H. Gordon, *Ugaritic Textbook* (Rome: Pontifical Biblical Institute, 1965), Glossary No. 2081.

writings and in the art of that day showing a woman giving birth by sitting on two stones and a midwife both in front of her (to catch the baby) and behind her.

The two store cities which Israel built for the Egyptians were for the storage of provisions and perhaps for armaments as well. The location of one of the cities, Pithom (*Pr-Itm*), "House of [the god] Atum," has variously been located and equated with Tanis, Avaris[16] or with Tell er-Retabeh, "Broomhill," another name, according to some, for Heliopolis. Others have equated Pithom with Tell el-Maskhuta, "Mound of the Idols," a site that is also in the Wadi Tumilat, as is Tell er-Retabeh. The other site, Per-Rameses, "House of Rameses," has more recently been located at or near Qantir, "Bridge" (also known as Khatana or Tell el Daba), about twelve miles south of Tanis.[17]

The point that is usually made about the name of the store city Rameses, of course, is that this city must have been constructed during the reign of one of the pharaohs of the Nineteenth Dynasty named Rameses, presumably Rameses II. But this is not necessarily so, as is usually thought by most scholars, for the name *Rameses* is in fact much older than the 1300s B.C., as the late date theory [18] of the Exodus holds. William F. Albright argued that: The Ramesside house actually traced its ancestry back to a Hyksos king whose era was fixed 400 years before the date commemorated in the '400 year stele' of Tanis. The great-grandfather of Rameses II evidently came from an old Tanite family, very possibly of Hyksos origins, since his name was Sethos (Suta) . . . Ramesses II established his capital and residence at Tanis, which he

16. P. Montet, "Tanis, Avaris et Pi-Rameses," *RB* 38 (1930): 5–28. And A. Gardiner, "Tanis and Pi-Ra`messe: A Retraction," *JES* 19 (1933):122–28.

17. M. Bietak, *Tell el-Daba* (Vienna, 1975), 2. 179–220; also in English, M. Bietak, *Avaris and Piramesse* (Oxford, 1979).

18. For most of this century, two major positions on the date of the Exodus have vied with each other for the allegiance of the scholarly community: the early date of the fifteenth century (ca. 1450 B.C.) and the late date of the thirteenth century (ca. 1250 B.C.). The late date points to this evidence: the names of the store-cities that Israel constructed, Pithom and Rameses (Exod. 1:11), that reflects Pharaoh Rameses II of the thirteenth century B.C.; many of the sites ostensibly conquered by Israel (Heshbon, Arad, Ai, Hebron) or mentioned in the conquest stories (Gibeon, Jarmuth) were not occupied in the Late Bronze Age; and the Merneptah Stele only mentions "Israel" in Canaan by 1220 B.C. The early date responds by noting that Rameses is an old name preserved in the patriarchal period of Genesis as well; Israel did not burn or destroy any cities except Jericho, Ai, and Hazor, all three of which are hotly contested over what remains there, site identification, or dating vacillations; and the Merneptah Stele cannot tell when Israel entered the land, only that they were there by the 1220 B.C. date. It is unlikely, without further dramatic archaeological and epigraphic finds that this debate will be easily resolved.

named 'House of Ramesses' and where he built a great temple of the old Tanite, later Hyksos god Seth."[19]

This supposition that the city of Rameses is simply a modernization of an obsolete place name, as happened, for example, in the case of the place Dan in Genesis 14:14 (which we learn from Josh. 19:47 and Judg. 18:29 had an earlier designation of Laish) is hardly applicable here, for in none of the places where Rameses is mentioned (Gen. 47:11; Exod. 1:11; 12:37; Num. 33:3) is a more ancient name for the site given.

Moses and the New Kingdom in Egypt

The Eighteenth and Nineteenth Dynasties rebounded from over a century and a half of foreign rule under the Hyksos. From a political and archaeological point of view, the expulsion of the Hyksos marked the end of the Middle Bronze Age and introduced the Late Bronze Age (ca. 1550–1200 B.C.). This break between the Middle and Late Bronze can be seen not only in the change in the material remains of the culture, but also in such breaks with the previous Egyptian tradition of building pyramids as tombs for the pharaohs; from the Eighteenth Dynasty on royal tombs were "hidden" in the mountains in place of the mammoth pyramids that had dotted the landscape since the days of the Old Kingdom.

The fourteen kings of the Eighteenth Dynasty and the four kings of the Nineteenth Dynasty with their approximate dates[20] are as follows:

Eighteenth Dynasty	
Amosis	1570–1546
Amenhotep I	1546–1526
Thutmose I	1526–1512

19. William F. Albright, *From Stone Age to Christianity*, 2nd ed. (Garden City: Doubleday Anchor Books, 1957), 233. Charles F. Aling, "The Biblical City of Ramses," *JETS* 25 (1982): 129–137 denied this case made by Albright, but accepted by John Rea, "Time," p. 62, as well as by Leon Wood, *A Survey of Israel's History* (Grand Rapids: Baker, 1970): 93 ff. and by Gleason L. Archer, *A Survey of Old Testament Introduction* (Chicago: Moody, 1964), 207–208.

20. The dates given here for the New Kingdom are those of the authoritative *CAH*: T. G. H. James, "Egypt: From the Expulsion of the Hyksos to Amenophis I," *Cambridge Ancient History*, 3rd ed., I. E. S. Edwards et. al. (Cambridge: Cambridge University Press, 1973), vol. 2, part I, p. 308. Also see William C. Hayes, "Egypt: Internal Affairs from Tutmosis I to the Death of Amenophis III," *CAH* 2, 1, pp. 315–21. For alternative dates, see William W. Hallo and William K. Simpson, *The Ancient Near East* (New York: Harcourt Brace Jovanovich, 1971), 300–301. Also Sir Alan Gardiner, *Egypt of the Pharaohs*, pp. 177–280.

Eighteenth Dynasty	
Thutmose II	1512–1504
Hatshepsut	1503–1483
Thutmose III	1504–1450
Amenhotep II	1450–1425
Thutmose IV	1425–1417
Amenhotep III	1417–1379
Amenhotep IV	1379–1362
Smenkhare	1364–1361
Tutankhamon	1364–1352
Ay	1352–1348
Horemheb	1348–1320

Nineteenth Dynasty	
Rameses I	1320–1318
Seti I	1318–1304
Rameses II	1304–1236
Merneptah	1236–1223

The Late Bronze Age witnessed the destructive military confrontations between Egypt, Mitanni, and the Hittite kingdoms.[21] The presence of Egyptian cultural objects found in Palestine and Syria are just as frequent as the Syro-Palestinian cultural objects found in Egypt, bearing further testimony to the fact that this was a period of great international exchange. Thus, the ebb and flow of the fortunes of war and politics have left certain graphic marks on all of these countries.

It is during the early days of this period that Moses appeared on the scene. The command that all male babies were to be killed must have

21. See Harry A. Hoffner, "The Hittites and Hurrians," in *Peoples of Old Testament Times*, ed. Donald J. Wiseman (Oxford: At the Claredon Press, 1973), 197–228; and Keith N. Schoville, "Canaanites and Amorites," in *Peoples of the Old Testament World*, eds. Alfred J. Hoerth, Gerald L. Mattingly, and Edwin M. Yamauchi (Grand Rapids: Baker, 1994), 157–182.

come during the days of the second monarch of the Eighteenth Dynasty, Amenhotep I, if Moses was born about 1526 B.C. Such an order would have been most effective in reducing the perceived threat that had frightened the leaders of Egypt had it not been for the courageous actions of the two midwives, Shiphrah and Puah. It is doubtful that they were the only women available for midwifing for what was fast approaching two million or more persons.[22] Accordingly, it may be surmised that these two midwives were the representatives for something like a midwives' federation.

The scheme devised by Moses' parents (Exod. 2:1–10), who are said to be the Levitical couple Amran and his wife Jochebed, for saving him from this edict of death has been told often. After hiding Moses for three months in their Israelite home in the delta area where the Israelites were living, his mother built a basket of papyrus coated with bitumen and pitch in the shape of an Egyptian barque ark and put Moses in it at the very place where Pharaoh's daughter was known to come to bathe, all under the watchful eye of Moses' older sister Miriam. Moses was rescued by the princess and taken to the palace to be raised, after Miriam offered to find a wet nurse for the Hebrew boy, who was, though not told to the princess, the boy's mother.

Whether the princess was the renowned Hatshepsut is a matter of speculation. There is no doubt, however, that the chronology suggested here would fit nicely with her, and that she was a most unusual person for her times, possessing a strong personality and unusual gift of leadership, which she eventually used to claim the throne for herself. But since she was not a male, her claim on the throne could only be legitimized by her marriage to a son of the pharoah ruling at that time—a son born to Thutmose I from a lesser wife. Thutmose I took the legal title of Thutmose II, but he was weak in body and personality, leaving Hatshepsut free, for all intents and purposes, to rule as she saw fit for most of his reign.

Moses' experience is often compared with that of a Mesopotamian legend about Sargon of Agade.[23] In this account, Sargon's mother put her baby in a basket and placed him in the river. Ultimately, Sargon was found by Akki, a drawer of water, who then raised Sargon as his

22. The number of six hundred thousand males of fighting age (Exod. 12:37) indicates a total population of some two and a half million. Many regard this number as an impossible exaggeration, but using Malthus's formula that population doubles every twenty-five years, the figure is more than justifiable for the 430 years they were in Egypt. The two midwives obviously could not meet the childbearing needs for the entire community. Could they not just as well have been the representatives for the whole profession?

23. *ANET*, p. 119.

own son. Later, Sargon became his gardener. Then Sargon became the great king of early Sumer.

In yet another parallel Sumero-Akkadian text, a child is found and given to a nurse, who keeps him for three years, for which she is given a salary. Then he is adopted and given an education as a scribe.[24] The similarities with the Moses story are striking indeed.

The name Moses is, as might be expected, Egyptian. It is comparable to those theophoric types found frequently in Egypt such as Ah-mose, Ptah-mose, Thut-mose and the like, meaning "the [god] ______ is born." The short form of Moses' name (*mśy* or *mśw*) is found frequently in the New Kingdom documents.

Moses was not the only Egyptian name found during the New Kingdom times. Merari (Exod. 6:16) reflects the Egyptian *Mrry*, "beloved;" Phinehas (Exod. 6:25) renders Egyptian *P3-nḥsy*, "the negro," or "copper colored [one]."[25]

Moses was raised and educated in the palace of Egypt, thereby gaining one of the finest educations possible in that day. Not only would he be introduced to a spectrum of languages needed for life in the court, but he would also be taught a variety of other subjects, as may now be surmised from the schoolboy materials which we have discovered.

One unusual Egyptian text, Papyrus Anastasi I, is a rather rare source of our knowledge of the geography of Palestine, its roads, and its peoples. Its text is a letter from the Egyptian scribe Hori to another Amenemopet, dated in the latter part of the thirteenth century B.C. Hori begans by chastising Amenemopet for failing to calculate what the army needed in Phoenicia (?). But then he went on to describe the geography of Palestine and Phoenicia. If Moses was introduced to documents or training such as this, it is no wonder that he had such advance understanding of the terrain, peoples, and situations he would encounter as he moved through the Sinai Desert into Transjordania and into Palestine.

Granting for the present a 1446 B.C. date for the Exodus (see the case for this in the next chapter), the birth of Moses in 1526 must have fallen in the very year of Amenhotep I's death. Amenhotep was succeeded by Thutmose I, the man who must have been responsible for the infanticide decree; for while Moses was in danger, Aaron, his older

24. B. S. Childs, "The Birth of Moses, " *JBL* 84 (1965): 109–122. The text is in B. Landsberger, *Die Serie ana ittisu* (Materialien zum sumerischen Lexikon, I) (Rome, 1937), 43–47.

25. A. Gardiner, "The Egyptian Origin of Some English Personal Names," *JAOS* 56 (1936): 189–197; J. G. Griffiths, "The Egyptian Derivation of the Name Moses," *JNES* 12 (1953): 225–231; and P. Montet, *L'Egypt et la Bible* (Paris, 1959), 34–36.

brother by three years (Exod. 7:7), did not appear to have been exposed to the same peril.

Thutmose I (1526–512) was a commoner who married the king's sister. As already mentioned, Thutmose II (1512–1504) was married to Hatshepsut. He, however, died young under circumstances that are not altogether clear. In the meantime, he had named his son Thutmose III (1504–1450) as coregent and heir. He, in turn, became known as one of the most illustrious and energetic rulers of this dynasty. Thutmose III was a son of a concubine, and he too married his half sister, the daughter of Hatshepsut and Thutmose II. The first twenty years of his reign began when he was a minor and thus were dominated by his overbearing mother-in-law, Hatshepsut. While she was not supposed to rule, there is no doubt where the power actually resided. However, when she died, Thutmose III conducted some sixteen campaigns in Palestine alone. He reacted so strongly to his mother-in-law Hatshepsut that he had every reference to her expunged from all the monuments in Egypt.

If the chronology suggested here is correct, then Moses was reared as a foster son of Hatshepsut. Moses' self-imposed exile began in 1486 B.C., when he was forty years old (Acts 7:23). Thutmose III had been in power for eighteen years and the now-aged Hatshepsut would have died only three years later after Moses fled the land of Egypt. For forty years Moses lived with the Midianites in the region of Arabia and Sinai. When Thutmose III died in 1450 B.C., and was succeeded by his son Amenhotep II (1450–1425 B.C.), Moses was able to return to Egypt now that "the king of Egypt [had] died" "who wanted to kill [him]" (Exod. 2:23; 4:19). Thus, Amenhotep II was the pharaoh of the Exodus.

This chronology identifies Thutmose III as the pharaoh who sought Moses' life for what he had done in Egypt because he was the only ruler *to live long enough* to fit the pattern of the one who sought Moses' life for the whole *forty years* that he lived in Arabia with Jethro of Midian. In fact, of all the rulers in the Eighteenth and Nineteenth Dynasties, only two reigned long enough to fit this pattern: Thutmose III (1504–1450) and Rameses II (1304–1236). But Rameses II is typically identified as the pharaoh of the Exodus by those who hold the other main view of the date of the Exodus, placing the Exodus too late on everyone's views of the date of the Exodus to satisfy any theory if placed after Rameses II's death in 1236 B.C. Thus, Thutmose III fits best as the pharaoh who wanted to take Moses' life and Amenhotep II is the pharaoh of the Exodus.

Amenhotep is a good fit for a number of reasons. First, while most of the kings of the Eighteenth Dynasty had their principal residence at Thebes, far from the Delta,[26] Amenhotep resided at Memphis much of the time. This gave Moses easy access and proximity to the throne without going too far from Goshen, as the text seems to demand. Second, Amenhotep's power did not pass on to his oldest son, but instead, it came to a younger son named Thutmose IV.

This line of succession had been implied in the famous dream stele found between the forepaws of the great Sphinx at Giza.[27] While the young prince rested there after hunting in the Giza area, so the inscription claims, the god Harmakhis Kheper-Re-Atum appeared to him in a dream and promised him the throne if he would clear away the sand that had partially covered the Sphinx. The obvious implication is that Thutmose IV had not expected to inherit the throne. The inscription is generally judged to be an authentic restoration of a substantially identical text commissioned by Thutmose IV.

If Thutmose IV came to the throne in 1425 B.C., and if he was not over twenty-five at the time (according to the highest estimates by scholars), then he was born at the earliest in 1450 B.C., just three to five years before the Exodus. The mummy of Thutmose IV has been found in his tomb, number 35 in the Valley of the Kings at Thebes. He is estimated to be between twenty-five to thirty-three years of age at his death. If we take an average of twenty-nine as the age of his death in 1417 B.C., then he was about twenty at his accession to the throne and was born at about the time of the Exodus, though a more recent estimate places the age the mummy at thirty-five to forty years old.[28] Thus, he could hardly have been hunting at the age of one to eleven.

But Thutmose IV did have several brothers who may have been older than he, one of whom appears to have been a victim of the tenth plague, of the death of the firstborn. Webensenu must have been the eldest son of Amenhotep II since he was granted burial in the royal tomb, but his brothers were not so honored. It is reasonable to conclude that Webensenu was the firstborn prince who was killed before the

26. William C. Hayes, "Egypt: Internal Affairs from Tuthmosis I to the Death of Amenophis III," *CAH* 2.1, 315–21. In addition to this data, it was often the custom that the pharaohs of the Eighteenth Dynasty would assign the governance of Memphis to the crown prince. See Donald B. Redford, "A Gate Inscription from Karnak and Egyptian Involvement in Western Asia during the 18th Dynasty," *JAOS* 99 (1979): 277.

27. *ANET*, p. 449 for the text of this dream stele.

28. Charles F. Aling, "The Sphinx of Thutmose IV and the Date of the Exodus," *JETS* 22 (1979): 97–101, especially p. 98, n. 9. See now also G. Brunton and R. Engelbach, *Gurob* (London, 1927), pl. LI for the list of the princes of Dynasties XVIII and XIX.

Exodus in the tenth plague. The second son of Amenhotep II was Khaemwaset, who is recorded as having married, and therefore must have outlived his older brother. But Khaemwast's death in the last years of Amenhotep II's reign opened the way for Thutmose IV unexpectedly to come to the throne. Thus, while the Sphinx Stele cannot be taken as direct proof of the death of the firstborn, enough evidence has been brought to light by Egyptologists to support the early date of the Exodus and the fact that indeed Thutmose IV did not expect to succeed his father to the throne. Even though we do not know for sure which was the eldest of the two brothers of Thutmose IV, or even exactly when it was that each died, we do know that Thutmose IV would not have been the next pharaoh under any natural expectations of succession.

Moses and the Midianites

According to Exodus 2:21, Moses married Zipporah, the daughter of the Midianite Jethro. Later, in Numbers 12:1, it seems that Moses also married a Cushite woman (i.e., an Ethiopian), an act that brought criticism from many, including his own brother Aaron and his sister Miriam. Some have attempted to combine the two narratives by noting that Moses' wife came from Cushan, which is placed in parallel with Midian in Habakkuk 3:7, either because the two peoples were one by virtue of blood relationship, or by a common abode. Also, in Judges 1:16 and 4:11 Moses' in-laws are not called Midianites, but Kenites. Rather than easily assuming, as critical scholarship has often done, that there are two parallel traditions here, the solution may well rest, as some have suggested, along the lines that "Kenite" is the name of a status, not a tribe, and means "smith." Thus Hobab, the son of Jethro (also called Reuel in Num. 10:29), was a member of a group of traveling metalworkers belonging to the Midianites.[29]

This is not the only place where the Midianities appear in the biblical record. They appear as the camel caravaneers or merchants that came upon Joseph's brothers in Genesis 37:28, 36. Jacob's sons sold their brother Joseph to these Midianites, who in turn sold him in Egypt to Potiphar, one of Pharaoh's officials. The Midianites also appear in the Balaam narrative in the stories about Baal Peor (Num.

29. William F. Albright, "Jethro, Hobab and Reuel," *CBQ* 25 (1963): 1–11. Both names Hobab and Jethro occur in Ugaritic: Cyrus H. Gordon, *Ugaritic Textbook* (Rome: 1965), Glossary No. 918 (*Hbb*) and No. 1170 (*Ytr*).

25:6–9),[30] in the war against Midian (Num. 31), and in the Gideon story (Judg. 6–8). The animosity that existed against the Midianites in the episode narrated in the Book of Numbers can scarely serve as the motivating cause for inventing the existence of such a people. It would favor, instead, their being expunged from the record. Thus, we conclude that the Midianites/Kenites were a well-defined group in the ancient world of that day.

Geographers place Midian in Arabia, just southeast of the Gulf of Aqabah. Here it was that Moses stayed with Jethro during his forty years of self-imposed exile. However, the Midianites were great vagabonds who pastured their sheep all over the Sinai peninsula as well as Arabia (cf. Exod. 3:1; 18:27).

Moses' father-in-law, Jethro, made a declaration of his faith in Yahweh in Exodus 18:1–10. Jethro declared the greatness and power of Yahweh as he heard what God had done for Moses and his people in the plagues and Exodus from Egypt. While some argue on the basis of Exodus 18:11–12 that Jethro officiated at the offering of a sacrifice to Yahweh, the Hebrew text simply notes that he "brought" (*wayyiqqaḥ*) a burnt offering and a fellowship offering. The word used here is the customary word for proffering or providing an animal for sacrifice; it is never used in the Old Testament in the sense of "to offer." Thus, there is no basis for concluding, as some have, that the Midianite priest Jethro officiated here in Exodus 18:12, but he did worship and fellowship with Moses and Aaron "in the presence of God" as a joint expression of their common faith in the same God.

---

30. For a recent archaeological find of Balaam of Pethor and a discussion of its relevance to the historical question, see Walter C. Kaiser Jr., "Balaam Son of Beor in Light of Deir `Allah and Scripture: Saint or Soothsayer?" in *Go to the Land I Will Show You: Studies in Honor of Dwight W. Young*, ed. by Joseph Coleson and Victor Matthews (Winona Lake, Ind.: Eisenbrauns, 1996), 95–106.

7

THE EXODUS FROM EGYPT

The Exodus from Egypt was to Israel what the *Odysee* was to the Greeks or the stories about the Pilgrim fathers and the Revolutionary War is to Americans. Nor was it to be forgotten that Yahweh was the one who had "brought [Israel] up out of Egypt and the house of bondage," for that formula, or a variation thereof, occurs 125 times alone. Thus Israel's national identity was intimately tied up with their deliverance from the land of Egypt in the great Exodus. But such an undertaking did not come off without a hitch, for the opposition that accompanied it was one of the main reasons why the people should never forget what Yahweh had done.

MOSES VERSUS PHARAOH

Even though Moses' nemesis, the Eighteenth Dynasty pharaoh Thutmose III, was gone, his dealings with Amenhotep II would not be easy, or merely routine. Within months of having received his call to return to Egypt, thereby ending his self-imposed exile in Midian of forty years, Moses encountered a very strong and determined king in Amenhotep II.

Amenhotep II had ascended the throne when he was eighteen years of age, in 1450 B.C. He was already, by his own accounts, an expert handler of ships, a skilled user of the bow, and one who prided himself on his horsemanship. Moses first requested that Pharaoh permit Israel to take a three-day journey into the desert to offer sacrifices to the Lord

(Exod. 5:1–3) was turned down abruptly (Exod. 5:4–11). This more moderate request had the effect of preparing Pharaoh for a more difficult entreaty for permission for a permanent departure from forced labor, but instead Pharaoh Amenhotep II was not even amenable to this milder form of permission to leave for merely three days, much less a request with enormous economic and political implications.

Thus, the use of force was going to be necessary if this potentate was to yield to any request whatsoever. Ten severe plagues were brought upon the country with increasing levels of hardship. These manifestations of power are now known to us as the "plagues" of Egypt, but that word is used only six times[1] to describe these ten judgments on the land and the people of Egypt. Instead, the text prefers to use the words *wonders*, *signs*, or *miraculous works* of God to describe what took place.

The Order of the Plagues

The arrangement of the first nine plagues has long been the focus of discussion. Jewish exegetes such as Rashbam (Rabbi Samuel ben Meir), who lived in northern France in the twelfth century, recognized that only certain of the plagues were introduced and preceded by warnings to Pharaoh, while others were not. In the thirteenth century Bahya ben Asher and in the fiftteenth century Don Isaac Abrabanel described a repetitive pattern in the one who brought on the plagues. They noted that the first nine plagues can be neatly divided into three groups of three plagues each. Within each group, the plague opens with the same formula: thus in the first, fourth, and seventh plagues, Moses is instructed that he will find Pharaoh on the river bank the next morning where he is to deliver a message. In the second, fifth, and eighth plagues (the second in the group of each of these sets), Moses is told that he will find Pharaoh at his residence (presumably in Memphis) and there he is to once again proclaim to him the next plague. Finally, in plagues three, six, and nine, Pharaoh is given no announcement or warning, but the plague is merely sent without any further ado. Another way to put it is this: In the first three plagues (in their order of events described in the text), Moses' brother Aaron holds out his staff as the effective instrument for initiating the plague. In plagues four, five, and six, the first two are brought on by God and the third by

1. Surprisingly few Hebrew terms are used for the plagues in this narrative. Only in Exodus 9:14 is the word (*maggēpôt*, "plagues") used. In Exodus 8:2 *nōgēp*, "plague," is found, while in Exodus 12:13 it is *negep*, "a hit," "pestilence." Exodus 11:1 has *negaʿ*, "stroke," and Exodus 9:3, 15 have *deber*, "pestilence." The NIV uniformly renders all these as "plague."

Moses. In plagues seven, eight, and nine, all three are brought on by Moses holding out his arm with his staff. These various patterns indicate that the plague narratives were tightly woven in their composition and were articulated with a consciousness of the total group of plagues, rather than being randomly associated.

Natural Explanations of the Plagues

All sorts of attempts have been made to offer natural explanations for the plagues. These explanations may be categorized as cosmic, geological, and seasonal. The cosmic explanation posits a comet that twice made contact with the planet earth during the second millennium B.C., thus explaining the parting of the Red Sea and the theophany of Mt. Sinai. Accordingly, the plague of hail was a shower of small meteorites, and the death of the firstborn and the opening of the waters for the people to cross over were caused by earthquakes.[2]

The second attempt to explain these events is geological. It is thought that a violent eruption of the volcano of Santorini around 1447 B.C. caused a tidal wave that wiped out the Egyptian army in the lagoon of Sirbonis. The plagues, it is speculated, were the results of the aftereffects of these eruptions and the ensuing tides.[3]

The most detailed attempt to place the plagues into a seasonal sequence from a natural point of view is that of Greta Hort.[4] Her argument is that the first nine plagues resulted from an unusually high inundation of the Nile which began in July and August. The red color of the Nile was caused by silt from the equatorial rains that filled the White Nile (coming from east-central Africa, present-day Uganda), the Blue Nile, and the Atbara River, both of which flow with tons of red soil from the basins of both of these rivers. In addition to this discoloration, a type of algae, known as flagellates—small organisms called Euglana sanguinea and their bacteria—absorbed a great deal of oxygen from the water, thereby causing the fish to die.

The frogs, which normally inhabit the banks of the Nile, sought other refuge, now that the waters were so putrefied from the second plague that came in August. The unusual inundation of the Nile led to a heavy increase in the mosquito population in October and November as a third plague.

---

2. I. Velikovsky, *Worlds in Collision* (New York: Macmillan, 1951), 63–106.
3. A. G. Galanopulos, "Die äegytischen Plagen und der Auszug Israels aus geologischer Sicht," *Das Altertum* 10 (1964): 131–37.
4. Greta Hort, "The Plagues of Egypt," ZAW 69 (1957): 84–103; 70 (1958): 48–59.

When the floods started to subside, a large outbreak of *Stomoxys calcitrans* occurred, a tropical and subtropical species of flies that bite both men and beasts. This fly multiplied by each laying six to eight hundred eggs in dung or rotting vegetable decay, and then attacked humans and their animals by biting at their lower extremities. In December and January, the flies disappeared almost as quickly as they came, but the rotting heaps of dead frogs left in the grass and the soil were full of the microbe *Bacillus anthracis*, which now affected the cattle that were put out to graze in January, thereby sending the fifth plague of cattle murrain.

The sixth plague of boils was symptomatic of the anthrax, which was carried by the fly *Stomoxys calcitrans*. It infested both the houses and the animal sheds of the Egyptians. This was followed in February by violent hailstorms just as the flax and barley were coming into head. And given the exceptionally damp year, as the locusts left northern Arabia, the flies were driven by a wind into Egypt, the eighth plague. About this same time, the thick deposit of powdery red soil began to be blown about by the sirocco winds, causing the plague of darkness, the ninth plague. Meanwhile, the Israelites, who were living in the Wadi Tumilat of the delta region, were unaffected by this affliction, as this depression in the Nile Valley gave them protection from the force of the sirocco blowing elsewhere in Egypt.

In all of these explanations, the element that is missing is the aspect of the "wonderful" or supratemporal. Thus, while the seasonal approach that affects the Egyptian ecosystem offers some insights into the order and perhaps even some or all of the mechanisms that were used, it cannot explain everything—especially the death of the first-born in the tenth plague.

It is noteworthy, however, that the plagues as a whole differ radically from the curses found in Leviticus 26 and Deuteronomy 28. In those curse lists, Israel would suffer terror, consumption, fever, crop failure, defeat at the hands of their enemies, unnecessary fear, wild beasts consuming their children and cattle, death by the sword, and such hunger that they would eat the flesh of their own children according to Leviticus 26:14–26, along with confusion, inflammation, madness, blindness, social chaos, military defeat, etc. in items added to the list found in Deuteronomy 28:15–60. The plagues visited on Egypt, however, are quite different. Except for pestilence, boils, and locusts, the disasters to be visited on Egypt are more in keeping with the ecological system of that country than of Syria-Palestine. Herein is the strength of Greta Hort's suggestions.[5]

The Plagues and the Egyptian Pantheon

Another pertinent suggestion needs to be added here. According to Numbers 33:4, "The LORD executed judgments" against their gods (KJV). Accordingly, the plagues can be seen as a series of attacks on the Egyptian pantheon. The plague of blood, the first plague, was directed against the god Khnum, creator of water and life; or against Hapi, the god of the Nile; or even against Osiris, whose bloodstream was the Nile. The second plague, the plague of the frogs, was directed against Heket, goddess of childbirth, represented as a frog. The fifth plague, against the cattle, might have had in mind Hathor, the mother and sky goddess, who took the form of a cow; or against Apis, symbol of fertility, who took the form of a bull. The seventh and eighth plagues (hail and locusts) were opposed to Seth, who manifested himself in wind and storms, or against Isis, goddess of life, or even against Min, who was worshiped as a god of fertility. Min is an especially good candidate for these two plagues, for he was widely revered in a "coming-out-of-Min" celebration at the beginning of harvest. Darkness, the ninth plague, on the other hand, was directed against such deities as those associated with the sun—Amon-Re, Aten, Atum, or Horus. Finally the death of the firstborn[6] could well be associated with Osiris, the judge of the dead and patron deity of the Pharaoh.

One weakness of interpreting the plagues *solely* as a biblical polemic against the Egyptian deities is that it leaves the third, fourth, and sixth plagues (mosquitoes, flies, and boils) unaccounted for. Nevertheless, there is enough of a connection that some Egyptians might have noticed that the very realms over which some of their most esteemed deities reigned had been so vacated that their worshipers were left without protection.

---

5. Ziony Zevit, "Three Ways to Look at the Plagues," *BR* 6 (1990): 16–23, 45. See also J. V. McCasland, "Signs and Wonders," *JBL* 76 (1957): 149–52; J. L. McKenzie, "God and Nature in the Old Testament," *CBQ* 14 (1952): 18–39; 124–45; D. J. McCarthy, "Moses' Dealings with Pharaoh: Ex. 7, 8–10, 27," *CBQ* 27 (1965): 336–47.

6. Mordechai Gilula, "The Smiting of the Firstborn: An Egyptian Myth?" *Tel Aviv* 4 (1977): 94–95 notes three or four cases where the "slaying of the firstborn" (Egyptian *smsw*, "firstborn") occurs in pre-Mosaic texts about the death of the firstborn of the gods. They occur in the Pyramid Texts and Coffin Texts.

The Tenth Plague and the Passover

As already noticed, the tenth plague is treated differently than the previous nine plagues. On the very night that God would deliver the Israelites from Egypt, he struck the firstborn of Egypt with the scourge of death (Exod. 12:31, 41–42) while the Israelites celebrated their first Passover.

Thus, our sole source for any study of this feast of the Passover comes from Scripture alone. Yet this feast is dependent on the event of the tenth plague for its historical justification. The instructions for this feast, communicated through the elders, were these:

1. Preparations were to begin on the tenth day of the month of Abib (Exod. 12:3);
2. The head of each household was to select a lamb or a kid according to the number of people who would be present (v. 4);
3. The animal was to be a year-old male that was without any defects (v. 5);
4. Each animal was to be slaughtered at twilight on the fourteenth day of the month (v. 6);
5. The blood of each animal was to be applied to the doorframe of each dwelling (v. 7);
6. That night each family was to eat the roasted lamb or kid (v. 5) along with bitter herbs and unleavened bread (v. 8);
7. The meat was to be roasted whole with the legs and head intact and the washed entrails left inside: it was not to be eaten raw or boiled in water (v. 9);
8. All leftovers were to be burned so that nothing was left to be profaned by putrefaction or superstitious abuse (v. 10); and
9. The meal was to be eaten with an air of haste and expectancy; thus, the people's long robes were to be tucked in their belts, their sandals left on, and their staffs kept ready at hand (v. 11).

The etymology of *pesaḥ*, "Passover," is disputed because it is uncertain. Some derive it from a Hebrew root meaning "to leap, limp, hobble" (as Jonathan's lame son in 2 Samuel 4:4; or in the ambivalent fencesitting on Mt. Carmel done by the Israelites in 1 Kings 18:21), but the explanation given in Exodus 12:13, 23, 27 is that Yahweh "passed over," "left out," or "protected" the dwellings of the Israelites. Yahweh struck Egypt, but He spared those Israelites who were under the protection of the blood of a substitute lamb. The Feast of Unleavened Bread was closely connected with Passover, yet it was treated as a separate feast. For seven days, following the Passover celebration, the people were to eat unleavened bread (i.e., bread without yeast) to commemorate the *haste* with which they had to leave Egypt.[7]

THE EXODUS FROM EGYPT

The staging area of assembly and the point of departure from Egypt on the fifteenth of Nisan was the city of Rameses (Exod. 12:37), a site that is best identified with Qantir instead of the remoter but more popular identification, Tanis, which is sixteen to seventeen miles northeast of Qantir. Tanis would have been on the extreme northern side of Goshen, which also argues for Qantir being the better identification for Rameses.

The fleeing Israelites did not take the most direct route from Egypt to Canaan. In fact, Israel was warned not to take the shortest route going through Qantara and the "land of the Philistines" in the Gaza strip in Exodus 13:17.[8] A middle route that headed across the Negev to Beersheba (whose advocates incorrectly assume that Mount Sinai is Gebel Helal near Kadesh-Barnea) was also available, but it does not appear that Israel chose this alternative either. The route they selected was a southeasterly route that led from the wilderness east of modern Ismailia to the southern extremities of the Sinai Peninsula.

From Rameses, then, Israel journeyed to Succoth, a site generally identified with the Egyptian *Ṯeku*, the present Tell el-Maskhutah at the mouth of the Wadi Tumilat, near the modern town of Ismailia. This was one of the gateways to the desert.[9] It is of more than passing interest that this gateway into the desert was the route used by escaping slaves. One letter, written at the end of the thirteenth century B.C., was used as a model letter to instruct schoolboys. It is believed to have been the work of a frontier official at Teku. In this letter, the official relates how he pursued two runaway slaves. At Teku, the slaves headed south. He followed them, but when he arrived at the "fortress" (*ḫtm*), he received news that the runaways had crossed the fortifications to the

7. See J. B. Segal, *The Hebrew Passover from the Earliest Times to A.D. 70* (London: Oxford University Press, 1970); Roland de Vaux, *Ancient Israel: Social Institutions*, vol. 1 (New York: McGraw-Hill, 1965).

8. See Trude Dothan and Moshe Dothan, *People of the Sea: The Search for the Philistines* (New York: Macmillan, 1992), 205–208, who demonstrate that at Deir el-Balah (a few miles south of Gaza) there was an Egyptian fortification, recalling the plans of residencies constructed in the fourteenth century B.C. of the el-Amarna period along with the distinctive "Amarna blue" vessels that are extremely rare in Canaan. All of this testified to the reason why Moses did not take this route in the Exodus.

9. Edward Naville, *The Store-City of Pithom and the Route of the Exodus* (London, 1885), p. 23, suggested that Succoth was a district and not a city; the district of the *Teku* is near Tell el Maskhutah. Both identifications, however, are pointing to the very same area.

north of Migdol of Seti. Thus, he had to give up the chase.[10] What is significant here is that three of the names on the route of the Exodus appear in this account and in the same order, if the equations are correct: *Ṯeku* = Succoth; *ḫtm* = Etham; and Migdol of Seti = Migdol. (Other difficulties, however, do exist. These will be treated in what now follows.)

The number of people traveling with Moses at this time is said to be "about six hundred thousand men on foot, besides women and children" (Exod. 12:37). This would mean a total entourage of over two million people. All attempts to whittle down this number, such as explaining that the word for "thousand" (Hebrew *ʾeleph*) as meaning here "clan," "family unit," or "tribe" (as it does mean in Judg. 6:15), fail to meet the standard of consistency with other contexts.[11] For example, Exodus 38:25–27 required a half-shekel for every one of the 603,550 fighting men, which amounted to "100 talents and 1,775 shekels." Since there are 3,000 shekels to a talent, then 3,000 times 100 equals 300,000 plus 1,775 totals 301,775 shekels. With half a shekel demanded for each man, 301,775 times 2 equals 603,550 fighting men, a number that matches a later count in Numbers 1:46 and approximates the one in Numbers 26:51. Along with this vast number of people who fled Egypt was the "mixed crowd" (Exod. 12:38), that no doubt included some Egyptians, who must have been persuaded by the spectacle of the plagues that fell upon their nation (Exod. 9:20; they "feared the word of the LORD"). Some of this group may have been among the "rabble" (same Hebrew word) mentioned in Numbers 11:4.

After Israel left Succoth, the route of the Exodus, according to Exodus 13:20, took them to Etham, at the edge of the desert. The exact location of Etham is unknown. Many have associated it with the Egyptian city of Khetem (spelled *ḫtm* in Egyptian, meaning "fort" or "fortress"). But this equation is philologically unsatisfactory since the Hebrew *aleph* is not used to render the Egyptian *ḫ*. Moreover, the best known "fortress" in the area was the fortress of Sile, near modern Kantarah, but that road would have taken the Israelites in the opposite direction they were to go, since Sile is located at the beginning of the road leading to the land of the Philistines (cf. Exod. 13:17). Naville, more convincingly, suggested that Etham is the region of Atuma, a

10. Papyrus Anastasi V, XIX, 2–XX as translated in *ANET*, p. 259b.

11. See George E. Mendenhall, "The Census Lists of Numbers 1 and 26," *JBL* 77 (1958): 52–66; and the "Introduction," of Ronald Allen, "Numbers," in *The Expositor's Bible Commentary*, 12 vols., ed. Frank E. Gaebelein (Grand Rapids: Zondervan, 1990) 2: 686–91.

desert that begins at Lake Timsah and extends west and south of it, where Asiatic bedouins from the land of Atuma grazed their flocks.[12]

The command to "turn back" (Exod. 14:2) apparently meant a change in direction or even a temporary setback for Israel, but which way did they go? Finegan has Israel turning back west and going south to get around the bulging upper part of the large Bitter Lake. He would then see them as going southeastward between the mountain range Jebel Jenefel and the large and small Bitter Lakes, all connected by water with the Gulf of Suez as the pharaonic canal that ran through the Wadi Tumilat.[13] Kitchen rejected this reasoning and had Israel go north-northwest, then north toward Qantara, but this northern retreat would have taken them right into the jaws of Egyptian power and toward the divinely forbidden coastal route.[14]

The place Israel "turned back" to was "near Pi Hahiroth, between Migdol and the sea" (Exod. 14:2). Pi Hahiroth has not been identified as yet. In Hebrew it means "the mouth of the canals," but it may be an Egyptian name *P3 (rt) hatḥrt*, "House or temple of Hat-Hor," *p(i) Ḥrt*, "Temple of Ḥrt," or even *P3* Hir, "the Hir-waters [of a canal or lake]."[15]

The Migdol mentioned here may be the ruins of a square tower on a height known as Jebel Abu Hasan overlooking the southern part of the small Bitter Lake. [16] It was at this point that Pharaoh, assuming that Israel was hopelessly entangled on their own dead-end trail, decided to give chase to the fleeing slaves.

Israel was now camped at the sea, opposite Baal Zephon. This Baal was the Baal from Ras Shamrah, Ugarit, no doubt introduced into Egypt by Canaanite sailors. But this site also is without positive identification, even though some wish to place it on a northern projection at Daphnai, Tell Defenneh.[17]

At this point the people had arrived at the "Red Sea" (Exod. 13:18), which in Hebrew was *Yam Sûph*. Now most scholars will complain about equating *Yam Sûph*, "Sea of Reeds" (Egyptian *ṭwf*, "reeds"), with the Red Sea, feeling that the place chosen for the crossing of this "sea"

---

12. Edward Naville, *Pithom*, p. 24.
13. Jack Finegan, *Let My People Go: A Journey Through Exodus* (New York: Harper and Row, 1963), 85
14. Kenneth Kitchen, "Exodus, The," *ZPEB*, ed., Merrill C. Tenney (Grand Rapids: Zondervan, 1975) 2: 428–32.
15. C. DeWitt, *The Date and Route of the Exodus* (London, Tyndale, 1959), 17.
16. Jack Finegan, *Let My People Go*, p. 86, records the discovery of this place made by Jean Cledat. It contained carvings and texts, some with the names of Seti I and Rameses II.
17. Kenneth Kitchen, *ZPEB* 2: 430.

was a "papyrus lake" that was a shallow body of water, in which the Egyptian chariots got bogged down.

Although some claim that the Red Sea did not have any "reeds," the term *Yam Sûph* is used elsewhere to designate the Red Sea and the Gulf of Aqabah (Exod. 10:19; Num. 33:10–11; Num. 14:25; Deut. 1:40; 1 Kings 9:26). Having said that, it is still necessary to note that the Red Sea proper (Gulf of Suez, the western arm that surrounds the Sinai Peninsula) appears to be too far south to have served as the spot where Israel crossed over. And when they crossed over *Yam Sûph,* Israel was in the "Desert of Shur" (Exod. 15:22), which is the northern part of the Sinaitic Peninsula but not as far south as the Red Sea. Therefore, some argue that a better location for this *Yam Sûph* would be the waters of the Bitter Lakes, themselves deep enough for the miraculous claims of the text.

The Date of the Exodus

In dating these events, it has become almost axiomatic among archeologists and biblical scholars to assert that the Israelites left Egypt around 1270–1250 B.C. and entered Canaan around 1230–1220 B.C., toward the end of the Late Bronze Age (1550–1200 B.C.); this is the generally accepted date (GAD). Yet this conclusion has a number of problems connected with it.

The four major arguments in earlier scholarship in favor of the Late Date (thirteenth century B.C.) for the Exodus are these:

1. The absence of sedentary populations between 1900 and 1300 B.C. in Transjordania, according to Nelson Glueck;
2. The construction of the two store cities named Pithom and Rameses during the reigns of either Seti I (1308–1290 B.C.) or Rameses II (1290–1224 B.C.);
3. The archaeological evidence for massive and widespread devastation of Canaanite towns and cities in thirteenth-century Canaan; and
4. An inscription from the fifth year of Pharaoh Merneptah (1224–1216 B.C.) celebrating an Egyptian campaign into Canaan in which he mentions "Israel" as a people he encountered there.

Each piece must be investigated carefully to determine the accuracy of its claims.

The surface surveys by Nelson Glueck of Transjordania in the 1930s led him and most scholars to deny the traditions preserved in Numbers

20–25 of the presence of strong kingdoms in Edom and Moab during the time Israel was moving into Canaan.[18] However, this objection may now be safely scrapped, for Glueck's conclusions have been seriously modified, even though Glueck's conclusions are still being cited by many scholars. Further surveys and excavations in Transjordania have brought to light, for example in 1963–1966, eighteen sites from the Middle Bronze II and almost as many from the Late Bronze. Again in 1975 another fourteen Transjordanian Middle Bronze II sites were located along with six Late Bronze settlements.[19] Ahlström concluded, "What this shows is that the opinion of Nelson Glueck about Transjordania being depopulated in the LB period is not in agreement with the facts."[20] Thus, this problem must be removed from the current list of objections to a fifteenth-century B.C. Exodus and conquest of the land. Transjordania was, contrary to previous strong denials, occupied at the time that the Israelites claimed they encountered peoples and opposition from these lands.

The second issue concerned the name of one of the store cities built by the Israelites. The name of the store city built by the Israelites, called Rameses in Exodus 1:11, also raises the specter of the name *Rameses* occurring in the even-earlier Joseph narratives in Genesis 47:11. The usual assumption is that this city was named after Rameses II of the Nineteenth Dynasty. There is no question that Rameses II built or rebuilt a city with the use of the *ʿapiru* slave labor, for Leiden Text 348[21] allows such without expressly making the assertion. But to claim that the city of Exodus 1:11 is the same city, which was built at the same time, or that the *ʿapiru* were the Israelites is another matter.

Years ago Albright showed that the Ramessides did not originate with the Nineteenth Dynasty but that they could, in fact, be traced back to the Hyksos ancestry.[22] A wall painting from the time of Amen-

---

18. Nelson Glueck, "Explorations in Eastern Palestine and the Negeb," *BASOR* 55 (1934): 3–21; *BASOR* 86 (1942): 14–24.

19. Moʿawiyah Ibrahim, James Sauer, and Khair Yassine, "The East Jordan Valley Survey, 1975" *BASOR* 222 (1976): 54; Terence M. Kerestes et. al., "An Archaeological Survey of Three Reservoir Areas in Northern Jordan, 1978," *Annual of the Department of Antiquities, Jordan* 22 (1977–78): 108–135, tables 1, 2, and 3; and Gerald L. Mattingly, "The Exodus-Conquest and the Archaeology of Transjordania: New Light on an Old Problem," *GTJ* 4/2 (1983): 245–62. Also J. M. Miller, "Archaeology and the Israelite Conquest of Palestine: Some Methodological Observations," *PEQ* 109 (1977): 87–93

20. Gösta W. Ahlström, *The History of Ancient Palestine* (Minneapolis: Fortress Press, 1993), 220–21.

21. Moshe Greenberg, *The Hab/piru* (New Haven: American Oriental Society, 1955), 56, n. 162.

22. William Foxwell Albright, *From the Stone Age to Christianity* (Garden City, N.Y.: Doubleday, 1957), 223–24.

hotep III (1417–1379 B.C.) has the name of the vizier Ramose appearing, again showing that the name Rameses antedates the Nineteenth Dynasty.[23]

The other problem with naming this city after this monarch of the Nineteenth Dynasty is that there does not appear to be enough time, even in the long reign of this monarch, to allow for the Egyptians to mistreat the Israelites, and for them to continue to multiply and to fill the land despite that mistreatment. Rameses II would need to rule more than the sixty-eight years he attained in order to allow for the years of construction, the decree to kill all the male babies, and the first eighty years of Moses' life. Thus, the city could hardly have been named for Rameses II.

Some conservative scholars have suggested that Exodus 1:11 is a modernization of the name of the city in Exodus 1:11 since the original name of the city, used when the Israelites built the city, was no longer used.[24] While this is a distinct possibility, the suggestion is unnecessary since the name appears earlier. Also, the same argument would need to be extended to other earlier passages such as the one in Genesis 47:11. Accordingly, the name of the city Rameses cannot be used to date the Exodus due to its earlier use both in external and internal sources.

The third issue is that the massive destruction of several Canaanite cities dates to the thirteenth century and not to the fifteenth century B.C. Now there is incontrovertible evidence for thirteenth-century destructions. But is it true that the only known historical event to fit these destructions, that is, anywhere near this thirteenth century, is the Israelite conquest?

We have no inscriptional evidence from any of these Canaanite sites that might indicate the identity of the invaders. The only extant texts describing any political or military activity in this period are the Tell el-Amarna Tablets. Only sixteen of the almost four hundred letters mentions the enigmatical *ʿapiru*. But scholars have resisted equating the *ʿapiru* with the Hebrews. Ahlström warned, "We cannot derive a reliable picture of the social conditions of Palestine during the Amarna period from these texts, but it is clear that social unrest and disturbances did occur. It is impossible, however, to find a peasant revolt being referred to in these letters, as has been maintained by

---

23. Gleason Archer, "An Eighteenth-Dynasty Rameses," *JETS* 17 (1974): 49–50. This wall painting and name of Ramose is also cited in Hayes, "Internal Affairs," in *CAH* 2.1, pp. 342, 405.

24. Charles F. Aling, "The Biblical City of Rameses," *JETS* 25 (1982): 136–37.

[G. E. Mendenhall, Norman K. Gottwald, J. M. Halligan, or R. G. Boling]."[25]

But there is an even more important argument against assigning these thirteenth-century destructions of Canaanite cities and towns to the Israelites. The Israelites were told not to destroy any of the cities they conquered: the only exceptions were Jericho, Ai, and Hazor. As for Hazor, Yigael Yadin, who excavated the site, at first argued that Hazor suffered an extensive conflagration around 1400 B.C., but then Yadin lowered that date to the thirteenth century.[26] Some still think Yadin's original date is the more acceptable date.[27] The case for a 1400 B.C. destruction of Jericho is likewise just as strong as the 1400 B.C. date for the destruction of Hazor, despite the subsequent ravages of weather and the debate over chronological issues at Jericho. This will be treated in more detail in the chapter on the conquest. Ai, the third city that the Bible claims was among the only three sites that were burned and destroyed by Israel, continues to be a mystery because of the uncertainty of its location. Recently, Ai has been tentatively identified with Khirbet Nisya, a site one mile southeast of Bireh, rather than with et-Tell. [28]

Since no way exists at present to distinguish between LB Canaanite and LB Israelite culture,[29] and since Israel distinctly refrained from destroying the towns she would later want to occupy with the sole exceptions of Jericho, Ai, and Hazor, the thirteenth-century destructions must be attributed to the numerous attacks that came to Israel during the period of the Judges, among which the Sea Peoples rank as some of the most devastating around 1200 B.C.

The final piece of evidence to be considered in the question of the date of the Exodus is the inscription set up by Pharaoh Merneptah

25. G. W. Ahlström, *The History of Ancient Palestine*, p. 241. The works he referred to in footnote 2 on that page are: G.E. Mendenhall, "The Hebrew Conquest of Palestine," *BA* 25 (1962): 66–87; N. K. Gottwald, *The Tribes of Yahweh: A Sociology of the Religion of Liberated Israel, 1250–1050 BCE* (New York, 1979); J. M. Halligan, "The Role of the Peasant in the Amarna Period," in *Palestine in Transition: The Emergence of Ancient Israel*, eds. D. N. Freedman and D. F. Graf (Sheffield, 1983), 15–24; and R. G. Boling, *Judges:* Anchor Bible (Garden City, 1970), 12.

26. Y. Yadin, "Further Light on Biblical Hazor," *BA* 20 (1957): 44. The change is complete in Yigael Yadin, "Excavations at Hazor, 1955–1958," *The Biblical Archaeologist Reader 2*, eds., David Noel Freedman and Edward F. Campbell Jr. (Garden City, N.Y.: Doubleday, 1964), 224. However, A. Bentor, the new excavator of Hazor, will have no part in this former dating by Yadin!

27. John J. Bimson, *Redating the Exodus and Conquest* (Sheffield, JSOT Supplement Series 5, 1978), 192–94.

28. David Livingston, "Location of Biblical Bethel," *WTJ* 33 (1970): 20–44 and idem, "Traditional Site of Bethel Questioned," *WTJ* 34 (1971): 39–50, which was a response to Anson Rainey's, "Bethel Is Still Beitin," *WTJ* 33 (1971): 175–88.

29. In modest measure, of course, the material cultures can be distinguished, but not at the sites mentioned in the conquest narratives.

(1236–1223, but also given as 1224–1216) to celebrate his campaign into Canaan. In it he mentioned "Israel" as a group he confronted, a group already settled there by 1220 B.C.[30] But how could the Israelites be a serious foe for Merneptah if they had just arrived in the land? Even more astounding is the claim that the reference to "Israel" could not have meant the whole of Israel—that is, the twelve tribes—because Israel was not so constituted at this time.[31] But how this fact became known is a mystery, for no sources are cited to demonstrate this foundational concept on which many a theoretical house on the history of Israel will be built in the last third of the twentieth century.

The general line of reasoning for the late date of the Exodus prefers to make Rameses II the pharaoh of the Exodus since he reigned the longest in the Nineteenth Dynasty—1304–1236 B.C. But it is impossible for Rameses II to fulfill that role since he should have followed a pharaoh who had at least a forty-year reign in order to cover the forty years that Moses was a fugitive in the land of Midian. But Rameses II was preceded by Seti I, who only reigned from 1318–1304, just as Seti I's predecessor, Rameses I, only reigned from 1320 to 1318 B.C. Thus Merneptah, not Rameses II, must be the pharaoh of the Exodus for this theory. Even if the Exodus came in Merneptah's first year (1236 B.C.), the conquest would not begin, on that calculation, until 1196 B.C., which creates another series of problems, namely, that the period of the elders, the times of the judges, Eli, and Samuel must all be completed before about 1050 B.C. This calls for some astounding abbreviation and condensation of materials mentioned in the conclusion to the Book of Joshua, the whole Book of Judges, and the beginning of the Book of Samuel.

A more promising path, supported by the available archaeological and historiographical methods, is to adopt the fifteenth-century B.C. date for the Exodus and to locate it in the Eighteenth Dynasty. The statement of I Kings 6:1 affirmed that the Exodus was 480 years before Solomon began to build his temple in 967 B.C.[32] That would place the Exodus at 1447 B.C. and the conquest at 1407 B.C. Such a proposal is almost universally rejected today, with the date most frequently mentioned being 1260 B.C., or somewhere before 1220 B.C.[33]

---

30. The text is found in Pritchard, *ANET*, pp. 376–78.
31. Roland de Vaux, *The Early History of Israel*, p. 390.
32. The chronology adopted here is the one to which most biblical scholars are quietly coming, namely, the one proposed by Edwin R. Thiele, *The Mysterious Numbers of the Hebrew Kings* (Grand Rapids: Eerdmans, 1965), 28.
33. John Bright, *A History of Israel*, 3rd ed. (Philadelphia: Westminster, 1981), 123–24.

In order to accommodate the 480–year figure of Scripture, it is generally argued that this was not a literal figure, but one that projects an ideal of 40 years for a generation, with some twelve generations being thereby indicated. In reality, however, as the argument continues, a generation was more like 25 years. Thus 12 times 25 gives the total of 300, not 480 that the biblical writer came to. Therefore, 967 B.C. plus 300 real years equals 1267 B.C. for the Exodus and not 1447 B.C. No evidence, however, is given for this approach to chronological computation in the ancient Near East or in the Bible. Furthermore, such facile theories about the length of time a generation lives, or how aggregate numbers of years are excerpted from fuller records when a lesser number is in mind,[34] all fail to account for the other facts such as the judge Jephtah; he chided the Ammonites for not contesting the territorial rights to land that was won in Moses' defeat of Sihon and the Ammonites 300 years prior to the time of Jephthah's judgeship (Judg. 11:15–27). If Jephthah's defeat of the Ammonites is placed about 1100 B.C., his reference to 300 years would again place the Exodus around 1400 B.C. Here is corroborating evidence for the 480–year claim made in 1 Kings 6:1. Thus, the case for the early date is not so weak as it has often been made out to be. It has some very strong claims to be considered as fully legitimate as any of its contenders have enjoyed in the past.

The Amarna Age and the Amarna Tablets

In 1887 some 350 tablets were discovered at Tell el Amarna, about 180 miles south of Cairo. Later finds increased this total to just under 400 tablets. The tell is the modern site of the capital of the ninth king of the Eighteenth Dynasty, Amenhotep IV (Akhenaton), named Akhetaten ("the horizon of Aten/Aton"). Amenhotep IV was the proponent of the cult of the sun god Aten or Aton, whom he declared to be the sole god and in whose honor he changed his own name to Akhenaton or Akhenaten. This was not a strict monotheism, for the pharaoh was still regarded as a god.

The most important aspect of this discovery is the tablets that form part of the royal archive. About three hundred of these letters were written by Syro-Palestinian scribes in the Akkadian language with a mixture of Canaanisms and a few Hurrian words added. About forty of

34. This is the argument of the otherwise conservative Kenneth Kitchen, *Ancient Orient and the Old Testament* (London, Tyndale, 1966), 74–75.

the letters show Egypt's diplomatic contacts with Babylon, Mitanni, Cyprus, and the Hittite King Suppiluliuma. The letters cover the time of Amenhotep III and his son Amenhotep IV.

Of special note are the people called the *Habiru/ʿapiru*, written in Akkadian as the SA.GAZ. In the past, some have tried to equate the *ʿapiru* with the word for "Hebrew" (*ʿbrî*); the disturbances these princes from Syro-Palestine write about take place about the time of the conquest of Canaan (ca. 1400–1370 B.C.)[35] But the attractiveness of that theory gave way as soon as it was discovered that the *ʿapiru*/SA.GAZ were found in other texts, as far afield as Babylon, Mari, Nuzi, Boghazkoi, and back as far as the Third Dynasty of Ur; it appears that the word is a social and descriptive term rather than an ethnic one. In that sense, there still may be some connection between the *ʿapiru* mentioned in the Amarna correspondence and the Hebrews, especially those involved in southern and central Canaan. In that case, the name would have been used as a derogatory epithet.

Support for this view can be found in the fact that letters which came from the southern area of Canaan were written from cities that were late in being captured by Israel, including Megiddo, Gezer, Ashkelon, and Acco. There are no letters from the cities Joshua captured early on, such as Jericho, Bethel, Gibeon, and Hebron.

It is objected, however, that even this limited equation cannot be made, for the *Habiru/ʿapiru* are represented as being residents already in the land of Canaan, whereas the Hebrews were invaders. The answer to this complaint is that by the time of the Amarna Letters, the Hebrews were indeed residents themselves, with Joshua's conquest over, and the various tribes occupying a good deal of their allotted areas. It is also objected that Abdi-Hepa indicated that Jerusalem was in imminent danger of falling to these Habiru, whereas that city was never one of Joshua's objectives. But again, if Joshua's campaign was past, Abdi-Hepa's concerns may have been simply stirred by what seemed to be happening all around him—almost as if his city had been one of the few survivors. Others note that the names of the officials in the letters do not match those of the Book of Joshua. For example, the king of Jerusalem in Joshua 10:3 is Adoni-zedek, but in the Amarna correspondence it is Abdi-Hepa. But again, Joshua's nomenclature is

35. H. H. Rowley, *From Joseph to Joshua* (New Haven: American Oriental Society, 1950), 46–56.

earlier than that of the letters. Furthermore, leaders can come and go rather quickly in troubled times.[36]

These letters, then, show that the ʿ*apiru* fought mainly against those areas on the perimeter of the Israelite conquest. However, there is a remarkable harmony between the cities mentioned in the conquest and the cities and towns from which the letters originate. Only four towns that existed in the hill country of Canaan are mentioned in these letters, a fact that can be attributed to the dominance of Shechem and Jerusalem over the area. But as Eugene H. Merrill concludes, "Is it not more reasonable to assume that the reason for the silence is that all interior Canaan was in Israelite hands by this time except Shechem and Jerusalem, the picture given by the Bible itself?"[37] That would seem to be a reasonable conclusion.

---

36. An alternative view refuses to see any equation between the ʿ*apiru* and the Hebrews but places Joshua's conquest just prior to the time of the *Habiru*. Meredith Kline, "The Ha-Bi-Ru—Kin or Foe of Israel?" *WTJ* 20 (1957): 54–61. Kline argues correctly that the word *Hebrew* is not a social connotation but an ethnical one, going back to Eber, ancestor of Abraham; besides, there is a philological difficulty in deriving "Hebrew" from ʿ*apiru* or *Habiru*. Joshua's main conquest had been completed by the time the *Habiru* raiders entered Canaan.

37. Eugene H. Merrill, *Kingdom of Priests: A History of Old Testament Israel* (Grand Rapids: Baker, 1987), 108.

8

The Sinai Sojourn

After the Exodus from Egypt, the most important event that happened in the live of the newly constituted nation was the stay at Sinai. This lasted almost a year. After their arrival at Sinai around 1447 (Exod. 19:1), the Israelites were given some fifty-eight chapters of legislation and instruction; this includes the second half of the Book of Exodus (chap. 20–40), all of Leviticus (chap. 1–27) and a good deal of the Book of Numbers (chap. 1–10). Finally, their departure from Sinai is given in Numbers 10:28.

There can be little doubt that this was a most decisive time in the life and experience of the nation. Here Yahweh gave his people the Sinaitic Covenant. As part of his gift to the people, he gave the decalogue or "ten words" (Exod. 20); the civil code called the "Book of the Covenant" (Exod. 24:7) or "Covenant Code" (Exod. 20:22–23:23); the ceremonial code with its legislation on the tabernacle and its ministers (Exod. 25–31 and 35–40) and the institution of the sacrifices, feast days, and related matters on worship (Lev. 1–27). To all of these mainly legal texts must be added Deuteronomy, which is connected to the same period of time.

The Location of Mt. Sinai

The general route that Israel took, according to the majority view up to recent times, ran south generally along *Yam Sûph*, the Red Sea, for approximately one hundred miles and then diagonally inland about fifty miles toward modern Jebel Musa (Mt. Sinai). There Israel remained for nearly one year. From that point, their journey led north to Kadesh-barnea (*Tell el-Qudeirat*) at the southern extremity of Canaan, a trip that should have taken no more than eleven days (Deut. 1:2) but stretched out into thirty-nine years!

The most important issue in determining the route of the Exodus is the location and identity of Mt. Sinai. Several mountains have been associated with Sinai besides the traditional one of Gebel Musa: Jebel Halal, Ras es-safsah, Gebel Serbal, and a mountain near Al-Hrob.

Some have tried to locate Sinai in the north of the Sinai Peninsula at Jebel Halal.[1] Jebel Halal is about twenty-five miles to the west of Kadesh, but this would have required the Israelites to take a middle route across the Sinai. Also, Kadesh was never associated with Sinai but with the Wilderness of Paran (Num. 13:26). Moreover, Kadesh was three stages in the journey away from Sinai (Num. 11–13), a fact that also disqualifies it from being the Mt. Sinai meant in the text.

An extinct volcano called Hala el-Bedr, the "crater of the full moon," is near Al-Hrob; this volcanic mountain east of the Gulf of Aqabah has also been advocated as the site for Sinai. But this suggestion as the location for Mt. Sinai would not make sense out of the route of the Exodus. Even though there are a number of references to thick smoke and a blazing fire in connection with the theophany on top of Mt. Sinai (Exod. 19:18; Deut. 4:11b-12a; 5:23–24; 9:15), the critical element missing in all these descriptions that are alleged to be elements of a volcanic eruption is the flow of lava.[2]

An even less-attested suggestion for the location of Sinai is Gebel Serbal, near the oasis of Feiran, about thirty miles northwest of Jebel Musa. However, it does not have a wilderness at its base. This site is about six miles from Pharan, which some have connected to the ancient name of Rephidim, a location based on a gloss of Exodus 17:6, which says that the water at Rephidim was situated "at Horeb," the other name for Sinai.

Thus the choice seems to be between three peaks located in the southern end of the Sinai Peninsula: Gebel Musa (7,362 foot elevation at the southern end of plain er-Raha), Ras es-safseh (6,738 feet at the northern edge of the plain) and a third peak, Jebel Katherina, which is the highest of all—8,550 feet. But Jebel Musa seems to be the preferred

1. C. S. Jarvis, "The Forty Years' Wanderings of the Israelites," *PEQ* (1938): 25–40; J. Gray, "The Desert Sojourn of the Hebrews and the Sinai-Horeb Tradition," *VT* 4 (1954): 148–54.

2. J. Koenig, "La localisation du Sinaï et les traditions des scribes," *RHPR* 43 (1963): 2–30; 44 (1964): 200–235.

site because of the imposing granite formations of this massif and the presence of the extensive plain at its base. Furthermore, when Justinian had the monastery and basilica of St. Catherine erected at the foot of Jebel Musa, the "mountains of Moses," in the middle of the sixth century, this seemed to formalize a tradition that can be traced back to at least the fourth century.

The Journey to Sinai

As Israel departed from the eastern shore of *Yam Sûph*, after watching the overthrow of the Egyptian chariotry, they paused to give praise to God (Exod. 15:1–21). For the next three days they traveled without finding water. This must indicate that Israel moved inland for some distance, for normally they would have found water in several places near the Red Sea before coming to Hawarah.

The "Desert of Shur" mentioned in Exodus 15:22 is the whole district ranging from Egypt's northeastern frontier eastward into the northwestern quarter of the Sinai Desert and extending southward to the mountains of Sinai. Shur means "wall," a place mentioned several times in Genesis (16:7; 20:1; 25:18). In Numbers 33:8, however, this area is called the "Desert of Etham," perhaps reflecting the Egyptian word for "fort" (*ḫetem*). It is not unusual for a Near Eastern place to have two different names, especially since the meaning of "wall" may have referred to the defensive line of "forts" along the Egyptian border.

Local Arabs traditionally place Israel's first stop at Ain Musa, "the Springs of Moses," a site not mentioned in any biblical text. It is a source of sweet water and about sixteen to eighteen hours' journey (about forty miles) north of the site of Marah, "Bitter," the first stop mentioned in the text. The journey from Ain Musa to Marah was some forty miles. At first, the fleeing people would have been confronted with a stony desert nestled between the waters of the Gulf of Suez far to their right and the mountain chain of El Ruhat on their left. After nine more miles, they arrived at the desert plain called el Ati, a white, glaring stretch of sand that eventually turned into hilly country with sand dunes rolling down to the coast, all devoid of water.

Thus Israel came upon Marah, a site generally identified with Ain Hawarah. This site is notorious for its salty, brackish water. Edward Robinson described its well as being a "basin six or eight feet in diameter, and the water about two feet deep. Its taste is unpleasant, saltish, and somewhat bitter. . . . The Arabs . . . consider it the worst water in all these regions."[3] At God's direction, Moses cast a piece of wood into

3. Edward Robinson, *Biblical Researches in Palestine*, (Boston: Crocker and Brewster, 1857–60), 2:96.

the pool, and it became sweet and drinkable. Ferdinand de Lessups, builder of the Suez Canal, was told by Arab chiefs that they put a thorn-bush into some types of water to make it palatable. Maybe so, but it may also be that the actual healing of the waters had as little to do with the wood as did the salt that Elisha used to heal the Jericho spring in 2 Kings 2:19–22; both may have been tests of obedience and an opportunity to demonstrate the power of God.

Israel journeyed on to Elim (Exod. 15:27), located in the large and beautiful valley of Ghurundel, about seven miles south of Ain Hawarah. This tract of land lies between the Wilderness of Shur and the Wilderness of Sin and contains the Wadi Ghurundell and two other wadis: Wadi Useit and Wadi Tayibeh. In the rainy season, there is a constant torrent of water running down to the Red Sea, but this slows dramatically in the dry season. The grass is thick and high with many tamarisk, acacias, and palm trees in Wadi Ghurundel. This site had at least twelve wells to supply the people and their herds.

The next site, the Desert of Sin, is problematical as to its exact location. The next stop after the Desert of Sin, according to Numbers 33:12 is Dophkah, meaning "smeltery," a name to be connected with the Eighteenth and Nineteenth dynasties. Egyptian turquoise and copper-mining are centered at Serabit el-Khadim. This would place the Desert of Sin to the south and east of Elim, either (1) along the coastal plain of el Markha (a site favorable to easy travel and avoidance of the Egyptian mining settlements) or (2) the inland Debbet er Ramleh, which forms a crescent between Serabit el-Khadim and the et-Tih plateau (a site favored because it is in a direct line between Elim and Sinai; it is a better-watered area and its name of the Desert of et-Tih is similar in sound to the Hebrew "Desert of Sin"). Most prefer the second option, though there are advocates of the first, arguing that the inland route was too rugged. It was at this point where the food supply gave out, for the people had brought enough food for only one month. That is exactly how long they had been on the road, for Exodus 16:1 noted that it was now the "fifteenth day of the second month," exactly one month since they had left the two Egyptian store cities. Here the divine provision of manna began and continued for the next forty years.

The people rested at Dophkah and Alush (Num. 33:12–14) before they came to Rephidim. This site is best identified with the large Wadi Refayid, in southwest Sinai, instead of with Wadi Feiran. At Rephidim, the people found their water depleted. Even though the region contained a few springs, apparently they were depleted and were insufficient for all their needs. This led to the famous water-from-the-rock scene in Exodus 17:1–7. Also at Rephidim, the Israelites were attacked by a roving band known as the Amalekites. While the Amakelites' normal range of habitation was in the northern part of the Negev, around Kadesh (Gen. 14:7; Num. 13:29; 14:25, 43), here they must have ventured further south than usual to take advantage of looting the rear guard of the sick, elderly, and young (Deut. 25:17–19). Amalek was the son of Eliphaz (Esau's eldest son) by a concubine named Timna (Gen. 36:12), who became a "chief" or "clan" in the tribe of Esau (Gen. 36:15).[4] Thus, the Amalekites were distant cousins to the Israelites. They surely had to go a long way out of their way and their own territory to engage Israel in battle. Moses commissioned a young man named Joshua from the tribe of Ephraim to direct the battle against the Amalekites.

It was at Rephidim that Moses was visited by his father-in-law, Jethro. After Jethro arrived in camp, he gave some suggestions to Moses on organizing the officials over thousands, hundreds, fifties, and tens in order to relieve Moses of the strain of the work (Exod. 18:1–27).

The next stop was at Mt. Sinai (Exod. 19:1–2). Here Israel arrived in the third month of their journey (Exod. 19:1), "on the very day," meaning probably the same day of this month as that of the first month they had started—the fifteenth day of the month. The people would remain here for eleven months and five days, for they departed on the twentieth day of the second month, a year later (Num. 10:11). During this time the Sinai Covenant was given to them with the Law and orders of service for the worship of Yahweh.

The Sinaitic Covenant

Before this moment in her history, Israel had had no experience in self-government; in fact, she had no laws of her own and no identity as an organized people. During her long encampment at Sinai, the people were welded together as they were given a sense of identity and mission as a nation in the undisturbed confines of the desert.

It has become a commonplace with scholars, since the middle of the nineteenth century, to interpret the various covenants and the idea of covenant itself in the light of numerous ancient Near Eastern treaties of vassalage from the second and first millennia B.C. Especially paradig-

4. One confusing aspect of this identification is that the eastern kings from Mesopotamia are credited with devastating "the whole territory of the Amalekites" (Gen. 14:7). Unless this is a mere modernization of an ancient name, the Amalekites must have existed even before Esau, with some of Esau's descendants joining them later on.

matic were the treaties between the great Hittite king and his vassals during the fifteenth to the thirteenth centuries (1450 B.C. to 1200 B.C.). This comparison was first made by George E. Mendenhall,[5] who was followed by Klaus Baltzer,[6] Meredith G. Kline, and Kenneth A. Kitchen.[7] The same comparison that the Hittite treaties exhibited was soon refined and extended to include other treaties being discovered in Syria and Mesopotamia, but now covering a period from the seventeenth to the thirteenth centuries B.C. The argument was that these forms would have been known to the Israelites and therefore used by them to express the relationships between God and his people.

The vassalage treaties present the closest parallels with the Sinai Covenant. They include two fifteenth-century treaties from Alalah in Syria and the group of Hittite treaties from 1450 to 1200 B.C. While there are slight differences, they all have the same basic structure. They consist of the following six elements:

1. *Preamble*. The great king gives his name and the titles of his office.
2. *Historical Prologue*. The suzerain rehearses the historical basis for the treaty, with emphasis on his acts of benevolence on behalf of the vassal, thereby incurring motives and obligations of gratitude from the vassal.
3. *Stipulations*. Here were the conditions imposed by the great king with the requirement of a loyalty oath in which the vassal promised to come to the aid of the great king in time of war.
4. *Preservation and Public Proclamation of the Covenant*. Copies of the treaty were to be preserved in the temples of both countries, and to be read publicly in the vassal state once a year.
5. *Witnesses to the Treaty*. Gods of both countries were invoked as witnesses to the treaty.

---

5. G. E. Mendenhall, "Covenant Forms in Israelite Tradition," in *The Biblical Archaeologist Reader*, eds. Edward F. Campbell Jr. and David Noel Freedman (Garden City, N.Y.: Doubleday, 1970), vol. 3, pp. 38–42, a reprint of the article that first appeared in *BA* 17 (1954): 50–76; idem.,*The Law and Covenant in Israel and the Ancient Near East* (Pittsburgh: Biblical Colloquium, 1955).

6. Klaus Baltzer, *Das Bundesformular* (Neukirchen und Vluyn, 1960); idem., *The Covenant Formulary in Old Testament, Jewish, and Early Christian Writings* (Philadelphia: Fortress, 1970).

7. Meredith G. Kline, *The Treaty of the Great King: Deuteronomy* (Grand Rapids: Eerdmans, 1963). Interestingly enough, though Kline was one of the first to apply Mendenhall's insights to the form of the whole Book of Deuteronomy as necessarily being written in the second millennium, and not the first millennium as critical form and literary source criticism demanded, scant attention was paid to this discovery. Credit is usually given to Kenneth Kitchen, who also came to the same conclusion in his book, *Ancient Orient and the Old Testament* (Chicago: InterVarsity, 1966), three years later.

6. *Sanctions*. Blessings will result from obedience to the treaty, but curses will fall on the vassal who is unfaithful.

Though the parallel is in no sense perfect, the Sinaitic Covenant does exhibit the first three elements of the vassalage treaty form. The Sinai Covenant begins with a *preamble*, "I am Yahweh your God" (Exod. 20:2a), without listing any titles as in the Hittite treaties. It is enough to say that God is Yahweh. Verse 2b-c is equally brief in its *historical prologue*: "who brought you out of the land of Egypt, out of the house of slavery." The *stipulations* follow in verves 3–17 with the Ten Commandments.

Other elements of the suzerainty treaties are absent from the Sinai Covenant, while it does contain additional elements such as the dramatic enclosure of Yahweh in a cloud, smoke, thunder, and trumpet blasts along with the sealing of the covenant in blood. Therefore, a direct dependence on the Hittite treaties cannot be assumed, but it does belong to the same general pattern for this type of covenant.

W. Beyerlin believes, however, that the three final missing elements of such vassalage treaties in the Sinaitic Covenant can be found in Exodus 24:3– 8. Thus, *provision for preservation* was made in Exodus 24:4a: "Moses then wrote down everything the LORD had said." The witnesses, Beyerlin believes, are the "twelve stone pillars representing the twelve tribes of Israel" (v. 4c), which were erected to take the place of witnesses. The sanctions, presumably, are those announced in verses 6–8, where the people pledge to "do everything the LORD has said" as they are sprinkled with blood.[8] The positive point that all can agree on is that there is a connection between the Decalogue and Exodus 24:3–8.

Not only does Exodus 20–24 follow the structure and contain the essential elements of the classic suzerain-vassal treaties attested in the royal archives of the Hittites from Boghaz-koi (ancient Hattusas), but the entire Book of Deuteronomy exhibits all six elements of this classic structure. Moreover, to the consternation of modern criticism, the Book of Deuteronomy matches the second millennium structure of the treaties from Alalah and the Hittites rather than those that derive from the first millennium (the neo-Assyrian treaties of the seventh century). This is disturbing news for those who had placed most of the Book of Deuteronomy in a D document that was "piously" "forged" by some scribe(s) in King Josiah's day and placed among the rubble of the temple, hoping it would be "discovered" in the temple cleansing that took place in 621 B.C.

8. W. Beyerlin, *Herkunft und Geschichte der ältesten Sinaitraditionen* (Tübingen, 1961), 59–78.

Unfortunately for this long-held theory about its dating and origins, Deuteronomy has all six elements of the classic treaty form, whereas the historical prologue and the blessings and sanctions disappear from the first millennium forms exhibited in the Neo-Assyrian treaties.[9] Thus on grounds of Formgeschichte analysis, Deuteronomy must be dated in the days of Moses (i.e., the second millennium B.C.) and not in 621 B.C.

Moses used as a model for the revelations communicated to him the patterns that emerged from the seventeenth to fourteenth centuries, since they were models with which he and his people were familiar. Thus, he used a vehicle the people knew so that he could be instructive and clothe the theological truths of the covenant relationship that Yahweh had with Israel in the familiar garb of international suzerainty vassal treaties.

But should the Sinai legislation be spoken of as a "covenant"? The Hebrew word *berit* is almost always translated as "covenant," but this can be most misleading in a number of contexts. *Covenant* is usually understood as a mutual contract between two partners. But if one of the partners is God, then it cannot be a contract between two equal partners.

Little will be gained by trying to analyze *bĕrît* etymologically, for its origins are obscure, and comparisons with Akkadian and other languages have yielded very few tangible results. The expression in Hebrew for making a covenant or concluding one is *kārat bĕrît*, "to cut a covenant." Often the word to "swear" is used in parallelism with *bĕrît*; thus covenant making was in the form of an oath. It was accompanied by a rite in which the one(s) making the oath passed down an aisle formed by animals that had been cut in half (Gen. 15 and Jer. 34:18–21), presumably invoking the same fate on the covenant maker as that which befell the animals now forming the aisle through which the oath maker walked. On some occasions, both parties passed between the pieces, as it were, making it a bilateral oath and a joint responsibility, as in the case of Solomon and Hiram (1 Kings 5:12) or David and Jonathan (1 Sam. 23:18). But this mutual commitment by means of a *bĕrît* clearly will not fit the cases of Abraham or David. There, only Yahweh passed between the pieces—not the patriarch Abraham or the monarch David! And surprisingly, in Exodus 34:10, 27, only Yahweh "cuts a *bĕrît*" with Moses and the people; the people never join in to "cut a *bĕrît*"! The only difference was that with the

9. See the unanswered argument of Meredith G. Kline, *Treaty of the Great King. The Covenant Structure of Deuteronomy: Studies and Commentary* (Grand Rapids: Eerdmans, 1963).

Sinai Covenant there were obligations to obey; no such conditions were attached to the Abrahamic or Davidic Covenants.

The Book of the Covenant

The title for this section of Exodus 20:22–23:33 derives from 24:7. In many ways, this amounted to Israel's earliest civil legislation, which took the principles of the moral law and illustrated them in real situations that could arise in the nation's communal existence. Each of the commandments in the moral law of the Ten Commandments provided a superstructure for specific legislation that made the principle practical. Accordingly, the commandment "You shall not murder" is given explicit application in Exodus 21:12–14:

> "Anyone who strikes a man and kills him shall surely be put to death. However, if he does not do it intentionally, but God lets it happen, he is to flee to a place I will designate. But if a man schemes and kills another man deliberately, take him away from my altar and put him to death."

The laws in the Book of the Covenant are very similar at times to those found in other ancient Near Eastern law codes[10] such as the codes of Ur-Nammu (ca. 2060 B.C.), Eshnunna (ca. 1700 B.C.), Lipit Ishtar (nineteenth century B.C.), Hammurapi (ca. 1700 B.C.), and the Hittite law codes from approximately the fourteenth to twelfth centuries B.C. While there are no examples of direct borrowing, the topics covered and many of the sanctions tend to parallel each other rather closely at times.[11]

A major distinction between the different laws found in the Old Testament is the form given to two different types of laws. Albrecht Alt[12] observed that the two general types of laws were absolute or apodictic laws, such as those in the Ten Commandments having a "you shall" form, and the conditional, casuistic, or case law type that begin with "if a person." In the apodictic or absolute form, there were no "ifs" involved; it was absolute, categorical language based on the character

10. These law codes can conveniently be found in James Pritchard, *ANET*, pp. 159–98.

11. The most comprehensive commentary on the Covenant Code and its dating to the time *prior* to the settlement of the tribes in Canaan, along with a refusal to argue that the laws were merely adopted from pagan sources, is S. M. Paul, "Studies in the Book of Covenant in Light of Cuneiform and Biblical Law," *VT Suppl.* 18 (1970): 101–102 especially. On the modern relevance of these laws, see, with some qualifications, James B. Jordan, *The Law of the Covenant: An Exposition of Exodus 21–23* (Tyler, Tex.: Institute for Christian Economics, 1984).

12. Albrecht Alt, *Essays on Old Testament History and Religion* (Oxford: University Press, 1966), 81–132.

of God, which was, of course, unchanging. The Decalogue is the best example of the apodictic form. Also the Holiness Law of Leviticus 19–22, with its "Be holy because I, the LORD your God, am holy," is another illustration of this absolute form.

Case law was different. It took up various situations and built precedents for specific cases that demanded practical wisdom in applying the absolute principles from the moral or absolute law.

Israel had a unique understanding of law: they conceived of all law as a result of special revelation, thereby taking the form of an expression of the will of God. Even though all of Israel's laws were addressed to the community as a whole, the Law itself singled out the individual and addressed each person as an individual with a direct divine imperative, as in the Decalogue: "You (sg) shall . . ." Accordingly, Israel's religion and ethics took on a personal aspect, a meaning, and a dignity usually unattested elsewhere in the ancient Near East.

THE CEREMONIAL LAW

Israel's ritual laws were codified in Exodus 25–31, 35–40, Leviticus 1–27, and Numbers 1–10. In this section of the Bible, the following topics were treated: the ark and the tabernacle (Exod. 25–27), the priestly vestments (Exod. 28), the ordination of priests and related matters (Exod. 29–31), sacrificial laws (Lev. 1–7), the consecration of the priesthood (Lev. 8–10), teaching on clean and unclean (Lev. 11–15), the Day of Atonement and the principle of the life being in the blood (Lev. 16–17), laws on holiness (Lev. 18–26), and religious vows (Lev. 27).

The worship of Yahweh required a distinction between the sacred and the secular, the holy and the common. It meant especially a recognition of the presence of Yahweh and the preparation for entering into that presence.

The ark of the covenant was the most central symbol in the ceremonial law, for that is why it is mentioned first even though it was kept in the innermost recesses of the tabernacle: in the Holy of Holies. For a holy deity who had no form or physical image to represent him, the nearest that the Old Testament would come would be in the ark of the covenant that symbolized the immanence of Yahweh. Thus he was not remote or distant, but he dwelt in the midst of his people, for whenever the ark was taken up, the people chorused: "Rise up, O LORD! May your enemies be scattered; may your foes flee before you." Whenever it came to rest, they said, "Return, O LORD, to the countless thousands of

Israel." Yahweh's abiding presence went with the people wherever they went. In the destruction of the temple, however, the ark was lost and never mentioned again in Israel's history.

The tabernacle[13] was a movable dwelling where Yahweh met his people in worship. It was constructed during the wilderness period and continued to function almost up to the time when Solomon dedicated the temple in his fourth year (967 B.C.). It was a model of simplicity, having only a few pieces of furniture that functioned to point to a few basic theological concepts. By the first month of the second year after the Exodus (ca. 1445 B.C.), the tabernacle had been erected.

The tabernacle was variously named, including the "tent of meeting" (*ʾōhel môēd*) and the "tabernacle" (*miškān*), from the associated verb *šākan*, "to dwell." Accordingly, the tabernacle was a movable "dwelling" where Yahweh and his people met each other. This tent, or tabernacle, occupied the center of the camp during the wilderness wanderings. As such, its architecture focused on the presence of Yahweh who inhabited the inner sanctum of the sanctuary, the Holy of Holies. Surrounded by an open court, the taberncle itself was composed of two rooms: the *ʾûlām* (i.e., the main room), or "Holy Place," and the *dĕbîr*, or "Holy of Holies." In this innermost part of the tabernacle dwelt Yahweh's glory, symbolized by the cloud by day and the pillar of fire over it by night. The first-century A.D. Jewish historian Josephus[14] considered the entire sacred area to portray the earth, i.e., in its court; heaven, in its Holy Place; and the innermost heaven, the Holy of Holies. Such may well have been the ancient Israelite understanding of the tabernacle as providing an extension of the heavenly realm into the earthly, even as 1 Kings 8:27 seemed to affirm: "But will God really dwell on earth? The heavens, even the highest heaven, cannot contain you. How much less this temple I [Solomon] have built!" The presence of God, as seen in the structure of the tabernacle, was of great significance to Israel.

Along with the high demands of the Law of Yahweh were the provisions for reconciliation in case of failure. One of the most detailed provisions was made in the sacrificial system. A formal theology of sacrifice, or its origins, are nowhere presented in Israel's history or documents. But there were three basic purposes in the sacrifices: (1) to

13. See Frank M. Cross Jr., "The Priestly Tabernacle," *The Biblical Archaeologist Reader*, eds. G. Ernest Wright and David Noel Freedman (Garden City, N.Y.: Doubleday, 1961): 201–228.
14. Josephus, *Antiquities*, III, vi. 4.

offer a gift to Yahweh; (2) to enjoy communion and fellowship with Yahweh; and (3) to atone for sin.

The whole burnt offering symbolized a total consecration to Yahweh in love and praise (Lev.1:7; 6:8–13). The cereal offering was a gift or tribute to God (Lev. 2:1–16; 6:14–23). The peace or fellowship offering expressed the desire for communion with God (Lev. 3:1–17; 7:11–21). The sin or guilt offering was made for all the sins for which the offerer was genuinely sorry and repentant (Lev. 4:1–5,13; 6:24–30).[15] All of these sacrifices were tied into the tabernacle and formed the heart of Israel's worship patterns as a nation.

The Journey from Sinai to Kadesh-barnea

One month after the tabernacle was erected, preparations were made for the tribes to move out of Sinai on to their destination in Canaan (Num. 1:1). The actual journey commenced twenty days later on the twentieth day of the second month of the second year (Num. 10:11–12). Thus, the stay of almost one year at Sinai came to an end.

Most of the places mentioned in the itineraries of Numbers and Deuteronomy are unknown to us today. This does not mean they are the result of scribal embellishments, as some would have us believe, for why would the alleged embellishments have dealt in fictitious place names that anyone in that part of the world could have immediately recognized? Some of these place names are now beginning to turn up in lists found on the walls of Egyptian pharaohs and officials, as we will mention in the Transjordan record.

The first encampment was at Taberah (*Kibrôt Hatta*ʾ*avâh*; Num. 11:3, 34), which was only three days journey from Sinai. But this site is unknown as yet, as is Hazeroth (Num. 11:35). But the site of Kadesh-barnea is now identified with Tell el-Qudeirat, located in the Desert of Zin, almost fifty miles south-southwest of Beersheba (Num. 20:1). From this site, Moses sent out the twelve spies into Canaan. The spies traveled all the way north to Rehob, no doubt the same as Beth Rehob, just west of Dan, or twenty-five miles north of the Sea of Galilee. Indeed, if "the entrance to Hamath" (Num. 13:21) is to be equated with Lebo Hamath (modern Lebweh), then the spies made it all the way to the headwaters of the Orontes River, one hundred miles north of the Sea of Galilee.[16]

---

15. For a fuller discussion on these matters, see Walter C. Kaiser Jr., "The Book of Leviticus: Introduction, Commentary, and Reflections," in *The New Interpreter's Bible* (Nashville: Abingdon Press, 1994), I: 983–1191.

16. Yohanan Aharoni, *The Land of the Bible* (Philadelphia: Westminster, 1979), 72–73.

On their way back, apparently, the spies encountered the Anakim, a giant race, which was enough to dampen the spirits of all but two of the twelve spies. They also picked a huge cluster of grapes at Eschol ("cluster") from Hebron (possibly the same site as the patriarchal site of Mamre or Kiriath Arba; Gen. 13:18; 23:2; Josh. 14:15) to demonstrate the fruitfulness of the land, even though they advised against engaging in battle or entering the land.

Though two of the spies, Caleb and Joshua, counseled that Canaan could be taken, the other spies argued that the place was populated by giants and the populace lived in cities with walls up to heaven. Thus, the conquest that could have been was now delayed from about 1445 until about 1407 B.C. When the people learned that they were doomed to wander around until that unbelieving generation had died off, they determined on their own to launch an attack on the southern hill country. This ill-advised venture occasioned a humiliating defeat as Israel was repulsed and chased to Hormah (modern Tell el-Mishash), about eight miles east of Beersheba. When Yahweh did not go with the troops, they were as vulnerable as the others, if not more so.

From Kadesh-barnea to the Plains of Moab

Not until the fortieth year of Israel's wanderings were plans made to march into Canaan; only, this time they would penetrate the land from the east rather than repeat their ill-fated and ill-advised attempt made on the south some thirty-eight years previously. In order to reach this entry point, however, Israel would need to traverse Edomite and Moabite territory.

Moses, therefore, sent messengers to the king of Edom requesting permission to travel up the King's Highway through Edom, promising not to do anything other than to use it as an in-transit route. All appeals to their familial relationships and the like fell on deaf ears. (Edomites were descendants of Jacob's twin brother Esau, who occupied the land following his separation from his brother Jacob, according to Genesis 32:3.) The people would need to circumvent the lands of Edom and Moab. Thus Moses left Kadesh and made camp in Hor, where Aaron died (Num. 20:28–29). If this mountain is northeast of Kadesh, as some think, it explains why the king of the Canaanite site of Arad became nervous and launched his own preemptive strike against Israel. (Presumably, Arad is Tell el-Milh, sixty miles northeast of Kadesh, instead of Tell 'Arad, which apparently did not exist until Solomon's day.) Israel secured a victory over Arad at Hormah, the same place where they had been defeated some thirty-eight years previously.

Moses then turned south, perhaps changing his mind about attacking from the south along the way of the Atharim (or "the way of the spies"), bypassing Edom to the east on a trek of more than one hundred miles to Elath on the Gulf of Aqabah, and then two hundred miles back north to the plains of Moab.

Most place names in this list remain an enigma to us today, but there is some progress to report. The route must be pieced together from the narratives in Numbers 21 and Numbers 33. In general, Israel went east from Hor to Zalmonah, near Edom's borders (Num. 33:41), then about eighteen miles southeast to Punon (Feinan), where the copper mines were, then on to an unknown Oboth (Num. 21:10; 33:43). It seems they would have gone down to the Gulf of Aqabah and then up on the east side of Edom, sticking to the "desert road of Moab" rather than the Arabah road or the King's Highway.

The list in Numbers 33 appears on the surface to be a routine listing of sites along the route of the Exodus. Yet the list of Transjordanian cities noted from their move from the Arabah near Elath to the plains of Moab is amazing in light of recent finds. Such sites as (1) Iyyim, (2) Dibon, (3) Almon-diblathaim, (4) Nebo, (5) Abel-shittim, and on to (6) the Jordan River (Num. 33:45b-50) are all patiently listed.

It is not unusual to find a large group of detractors who would regard such depictions as unsophisticated, naive, or useless for historical construction. For example, Gösta Ahlström declared, "It is quite clear that the biblical writers knew nothing about events in Palestine before the tenth century B.C.E."[17]

However, Charles R. Krahmalkov[18] has shown that matters are otherwise than these scholars have hastily concluded. Krahmalkov points to three Egyptian maps of the road from the Arabah to the plains of Moab. The earliest of these is from the reign of Thutmosis III (ca. 1504–1450 B.C.), inscribed on the temple wall at Karnak as part of what is called the "Palestine List." According to this list, the route from the south to the north is precisely the way the Israelites listed their

17. Gösta Ahlström, *The History of Ancient Palestine* (Sheffield: Sheffield Press, 1993), 45. He is not alone, for Thomas L. Thompson opined, "Israel's own origin tradition is radically irrelevant to writing . . . a history [of Israel's origins]" (Sheffield: Sheffield Press, 1987), 47. Likewise, Robert B. Coote concluded, "The Scriptures do not contain an historical account of Israel's origin and early history," in *Early Israel: A New Horizon* (Minneapolis: Augsburg/Fortress Press, 1990), 141.

18. Charles R. Krahmalkov, "Exodus Itinerary Confirmed by Egyptian Evidence," *BAR* 20 (1994): 54–62.

route in Numbers 33, involving at least four of the same stations along the way: Iyyim, Dibon, Abel, and Jordan.

The other two maps date to the reigns of Amenophis III (ca. 1387–1350 B.C.) and Rameses II (ca. 1279–1212 B.C.) and come from the mortuary temple at Soleb and the west side of the entrance to the great hall of the temple of Amon at Karnak, respectively. The Rameses list is the more significant, for it names four stations for this area in its forty-nine-name topographical list: Hernes, Qarho (an alternate name for Dibon, as attested by the Mesha Stone), Iktanu, and Abel. Therefore, in an otherwise unknown place called Dibon, we have two inscriptions giving us irrefutable historical evidence for the existence of such a city at the very time that the biblical text claims it was there. Krahmalkov's amazing summary is this:

> In short, the Biblical story of the invasion of Transjordan that set the stage for the conquest of all Palestine is told against a background that is historically accurate. The Israelites' invasion route described in Numbers 33:45b-50 was in fact an official, heavily trafficked Egyptian road through Transjordan in the Late Bronze Age. And the city of Dibon was in fact a station on that road in the Late Bronze Age.[19]

As the march continued up the east side of Edom, Moses requested permission of Sihon, the Amorite king, to pass, but Sihon attacked Israel instead. To the north of Sihon's kingdom lay Og of Bashan, and he, too, was soundly defeated by Moses and his warriors. So quickly did Israel move that they came to Og's capital city of Edrei, some thirty miles east-southeast of the Sea of Galilee, before he was able to intercept them. There the giant king was slain (Num. 21:35), and all sixty of his cities taken (Deut. 3:4). Thus, Israel now controlled all of Transjordania from the Arnon Valley in the south to Mount Hermon in the north, some 150 miles apart.

Balaam and the Affair of Baal of Peor

It was apparent by now to Balak, king of Moab, that Israel was a force to be reckoned with, for he would be the next to fall. Balak then took the unusual step of hiring Balaam, a widely known diviner, so it would

19. Ibid., p. 58.

appear, from Pethor. Pethor is probably the same city as Pitru known from Akkadian texts, a site near the Upper Euphrates River.[20]

The task of Balaam was to put a curse on Israel so they could be more easily defeated by Moab. However, despite a number of attempts on King Balak's part to get Balaam under as fine a set of circumstances as possible in order that he might be able to curse Israel, Balaam was unable to curse Israel. Frustrated at his inability to claim so handsome an honorarium as was offered to him, Balaam seems to have retired in the area long enough to give military advice to the Moabites, who seemed to have been collaborating in those days with the Midianites (Num. 25; 31:8, 16). Thus, when the attack was launched against Moab, Balaam was found among the dead.

The long years of wandering and waiting were now over. Moses could now give his attention to the conquest of Canaan.

20. For a recent archaeological find of Balaam of Pethor, see Walter C. Kaiser Jr., "Balaam Son of Beor in Light of Deir ʿAllah and Scripture: Saint or Soothsayer?" in *Go to the Land I Will Show You: Studies in Honor of Dwight W. Young*, ed. by Joseph Coleson and Victor Matthews (Winona Lake, Ind.: Eisenbrauns, 1996), 95–106.

Part III

The Israelite Occupation of the Land

From *Holman Bible Handbook* (Nashville: Holman Bible Publishers, 1992), 134.

ENTRANCE INTO THE LAND OF CANAAN

One of the most dramatic stories ever told about the origins of a nation's existence now began to unfold as the Hebrews moved toward the goal of occupying the land.[1] A journey that could have taken no more than eleven days, from Sinai to the southern border of Canaan (Deut. 1:2), had now stretched out for thirty-eight more years. However, the story of Israel's entrance and occupation of the land is "the most difficult problem in the whole history of Israel"[2] in the scholarly world of the twentieth century. The controversy about that story is played out on two separate screens: the screen of the biblical text and the screen of the archaeological remains. Each of these is significant, but precedence must always be given to textual study, for the text is the historian's primary source of information. Archaeological artifactual materials, while important and significant, are subject to a wide range of interpretations when supporting epigraphic materials are not found in context with these pieces of external evidence.

THE SO-CALLED DEUTERONOMIC HISTORY

Israel's movement into Canaan and its premonarchical experience is told in what many scholars prefer to call the deuteronomic account of Israel, in which the coming to full national stature in the monarchy

1. The discussion of the Conquest will be separated from the question of the entrance into the land.
2. Roland de Vaux, *The Early History of Israel*, p. 475.

under Saul, David, and Solomon is recounted. The deuteronomic collection is said to consist of five books of the Hebrew Bible:

1. Deuteronomy, which serves as the introduction and sets the theological norm for the rest of the story;
2. Joshua, which describes the conquest of Canaan and the division of its territory among the tribes;
3. Judges, which deals with life during the early days of the confederacy;
4. Samuel, which continues the story while depicting its struggles with the Philistines and the establishment of the monarchy under Saul and David; and
5. Kings, which completes the story of the monarchy to its tragic and lamentable end in the Babylonian exile in 587 B.C.

In addition to giving the details as to how the monarchy emerged and grew, this material also tries to make theological and rational sense out of the trauma of the Exile that came at the end of this process.

The narrative from Joshua to Kings is a unified and continuous telling of Israel's story. But it was not a narrative that was content to rehearse the dry facts of the situation; instead, each of the "books" used its story to make theological points based on the narration of the events. Each "book" was convinced that it was the nation's sin that had, in each case, brought the people and its succession of leaders into harm's way.

This does not mean, as some have concluded, that Deuteronomy existed at one time as a separate and independent "book" apart from the Torah, for that would be claiming more than what we have in evidence to support such an assertion. But it is to argue that Deuteronomy is just as necessary to the five books of the Torah as it is to the four books of Joshua-Kings. In effect, then, Deuteronomy links the two sections of the canon together, Torah and the Earlier or Former Prophets (as the four books of Joshua, Judges, Samuel, and Kings were known in the Hebrew canon).

One major deviation from most contemporary scholarship must be noted if we are to be fair to our own principles of historiography: that the text must first be taken on its own terms until it is proven guilty. That is, Deuteronomy lays claim in its own presentation of things by asserting that it had been written *before* the awful litany of events that ensued, rather than as a theological apologetic for what happened as a retrospective analysis. It came as a warning that Yahweh would judge Israel and her history if she did not measure up to the high standards and calling that God had set for her. But it also came as God's word of promise that Yahweh's salvation would even transcend Israel's failure, for the covenant that Yahweh had made with the patriarchs rested solely on Yahweh's promise to fulfill his word. To be sure, the nation must believe and obey if any one generation was to participate in the benefits promised beyond the trauma of the Exile, but in no way did any of its provisions depend on the nation's performance pro or con.

The Structure of Joshua 1–11 and the Annals of Thutmose III

It is "rapidly becoming a consensus,"[3] that instead of a conquest of the land of Canaan, one should picture the Israelites as abandoning a former nomadic lifestyle and the assuming of a more sedentary life in the hill country by the Israelites sometime around 1200 B.C.[4] Accordingly, the "conquest narratives" of Joshua 1–11 are accorded very little historical credibility, but are usually regarded as etiological stories (the study of causes or reasons why stories were told) which were shaped more by theological and ideological principles than by the realities of events that took place. Robert Coote will declare flatly that "these periods [of the Exodus and the Conquest as described in the Old Testament] never existed."[5] Likewise, John Van Seters will aver that "the invasion of the land of Canaan by Israel under Joshua was an invention of DtrH [a deuteronomistic historian]."[6] It would seem that the matter should rest at that point, especially if there is a new emerging consensus on the question that has been so hotly debated for almost the entirety of this century.

Nevertheless, leaving the archaeological question to one side for the moment, what can be said about the literary structure of Joshua 1–11? Are there any textual clues that might substantiate or challenge that is approaching a consensus?

There are! Van Seters, in the article already mentioned, headed off in the right direction to solve this problem when he investigated the

3. William G. Dever, "'Hyksos,' Egyptian Destructions, and the End of the Palestinian Middle Bronze Age," *Levant* 22 (1990): 79, n. 3.

4. The material for this section follows the pattern set in a chapter by the same title by James K. Hoffmeier, "The Structure of Joshua 1–11 and the Annals of Thutmose III," in *Faith, Tradition and History: Old Testament Historiography in Its Near Eastern Context* (Winona Lake, Ind.: Eisenbrauns, 1994) 165–79.

5. Robert Coote, *Early History: A New Horizon* (Minneapolis, Minn.: Fortress, 1990), 3.

6. John Van Seters, "Joshua's Campaign and Near Eastern Historiography," *JSOT* 2 (1990): 12.

three Assyrian texts from Sargon II, Esarhaddon, and Ashurbanipal in his article "Joshua's Campaign of Canaan and Near Eastern Historiography." But as Hoffmeier correctly pointed out, he restricted his search, contrary to the title of his article, to the end of the eighth and the beginning of the seventh centuries, thus allowing these sources neatly to support his dating of Joshua's campaigns to the deuternomistic history period of the first millennium.[7] Another work by K. Lawson Younger made a much more extensive investigation of the records from Egypt, Mesopotamia, and Anatolia from the second and first millennia B.C.,[8] which fills out the picture much better. Notice should also be given to the fact that my colleague Jeffrey Niehaus has similarly answered Moshe Weinfeld's selective use of first millennium Assyrian texts to support his dating of the deuternomistic history (D) to a seventh-century date. Niehaus showed that there were literary prototypes to those Weinfeld used from the first millennium.[9]

The entry point into this new analysis of the structure of Joshua 1–11 is to be found in two pieces of text: Joshua 10:28–42 and Joshua 11:10–14. Both of these texts exhibit a significant difference from the material in Joshua 6:1–10:27. Younger and Hoffmeier both point to the recent studies in Egyptian historiography by Anthony Spalinger and Donald Redford.[10] Spalinger argued that military scribes accompanied the king on campaigns and reported on the events in a "daybook," or what Grapow had called a "daybook style" (Tagebuchstil), which can still be found as early as Papyrus Bulaq 18 from the Thirteenth Dynasty, with vestiges still evident in Papyrus Anastsi III from the late Nineteenth Dynasty.[11] Daybooks are somewhat like logbooks that record day-to-day activities. Redford collected some sixteen examples of such daybooks.

---

7. James K. Hoffmeier, ibid., p. 166.

8. K. Lawson Younger Jr., *Ancient Conquest Accounts: A Study in Ancient Near Eastern and Biblical History Writing (JSOT Sup* 98; Sheffield, JSOT Press, 1990): 226–28. Younger was the first to compare Joshua 1–11 with ancient Near Eastern military writings.

9. Jeffrey Niehaus, "Joshua and Ancient Near Eastern Warfare," *JETS* 31 (1988): 37–50. Moshe Weinfeld, *Deuteronomy and the Deuteronomic School* (Oxford: Clarendon, 1972; repr. Winona Lake, Ind.: Eisenbrauns, 1992).

10. Anthony Spalinger's dissertation and articles were the first to make use of the Annals of Thutmose III since Martin Noth's article in 1943 ("Die Annalen Thutmose III als Geschichsquelle," *ZDPV* 66 (1943): 156–74). Spalinger's dissertation was published as *Aspects of the Military Documents of the Ancient Egyptians* (*YNES* 9; New Haven, Conn.: Yale University Press, 1982). Idem., "Some Notes on the Battle of Megiddo and Reflections on Egyptian Military Writing," *MDAIK* 30 (1974): 221–29; idem., "A Critical Analysis of the 'Annals' of Thutmose III (*Stucke* VVI)," *JARCE* 14 (1977): 41–54.

11. H. Grapow, *Studien zu den Annalen Thutmosis des Dritten und zu ihnen verwandten historischen Berichten des Neuen Reiches* (Berlin: 1947), 50–53.

Here is the point of the comparison: while the Book of Joshua does not number his campaigns or date them by the regnal year of his leadership, it does use many of the same stereotypical formulas or expressions. In Joshua, the following syntagmatic analysis was worked out by Younger and Hoffmeier. It involved the following themes or expressions:

1. departure of Joshua from a conquered city;
2. all Israel was with him;
3. arrival at the next city;
4. brief description of the military encounter with the city (siege, assault, taken, etc);
5. Yahweh gives the town and its king into the hand of Israel;
6. an attempt is made to date the campaign or its duration
7. the city, its king, and its people are smitten with the sword;
8. description of the extent of the destruction of the population;
9. comparing the present destruction (and the execution of its king) with a previous victory, usually the immediately preceeding one;
10. an additional note about the campaign; and
11. taking of booty.

These eleven statements may now be noted as to how they fit the seven cities or episodes that were listed in Joshua 10:28–39:[12]

	Makedah 28	Libnah 29–30	Lachish 31–33	Eglon 34–35	Hebron 36–37	Debir 38–39	Hazor 11:10–14
1		x	x	x	x	x	?
2		x	x	x	x	x	x
3		x	x	x	x	x	x
4	x	x	x	x	x	x	x
5		x	x				x
6	x		x	x			
7	x	x	x	x	x	x	x
8	x	x	x	x	x	x	x
9	x	x	x	x	x	x	

12. This chart is after the one in Hoffmeier, "The Structure of Joshua 1–11," p. 168.

	Makedah 28	Libnah 29–30	Lachish 31–33	Eglon 34–35	Hebron 36–37	Debir 38–39	Hazor 11:10–14
10			x			x	x
11							x

The similarites between the "daybook" and these two texts from Joshua are striking. But a further comparison between Thutmose III's campaign and Joshua's first campaign is likewise instructive.[13]

Annuals of Thutmose III	Joshua 1–6
1. Divine commission to conquer and march on Palestine 647.1–649.1	1. Divine commission to conquer and the assurance of victory (Josh. 1:1–18)
2. Thutmose calls for a war counsel to receive an intelligence report 649.3–652.11	2. Joshua dispatches spies to bring an intelligence report on Jericho (Josh. 2)
3. The march through the Aruna Pass to Megiddo 652.13–655.9	3. The march through the Jordan River (Josh. 3:1–17)
4. Setting up camp south of Megiddo and preparation for war 655.12–656.16	4. Setting up camp at Gilgal and preparation for Yahweh war (Josh. 4:19–:5)
5. The battle and siege of Megiddo 657.2–661.13	5. The siege of Jericho (Josh. 6:6–14)
6. The surrender of Megiddo and presentation of tribute to Thutmose 662.8–663.2	6. The fall of Jercho and booty dedicated to Yahweh (Josh. 6:15–25)

Therefore, based on the evidence from the New Kingdom era in the second millennium B.C., the very time when Israel left Egypt, the structure for Joshua 1–11 is very similar to that of the Egyptian daybook tradition. It must have been adopted by the Israelite scribes who used it to record the events of Joshua 1–11. In addition to the daybook structure, it is important to note that both Joshua 1–11 and Thutmose III's Annals also use long narratives to describe the most significant campaigns along with the short, terse, and abbreviated reports in stereotypical formulas. This new evidence should give pause to what would

13. The chart again is from Hoffmeier, "The Structure," p. 174. All references to the Annals of Thutmose III are to *Uruk IV* (K. Sethe, *Urkunden der 18. Dynastie*, pp. 1–1226 and W. Helck, *Urkunden der 18. Dynastie*, pp. 1227–1954).

otherwise rapidly become a consensus against the validity of the text's reports of a conquest.

JOSHUA, THE NEW LEADER OF ISRAEL

Joshua occupies comparatively little space in the Hebrew sources. He is introduced as Moses' successor and the conqueror of the land of Canaan (Deut. 1:38; 3:21, 28; Josh. 1). Besides the places where he figures in the book bearing his name, he is only mentioned in Exodus 17:8–16; 1 Kings 16:34, which refers to Joshua 6:26; once more in 1 Chronicles 7:27 in the genealogy of Ephraim; and once in Nehemiah 8:17. He also appears among the ancestors of Israel in Ecclesiasticus 46:1–6. This is a surprisingly low number of occurrences, considering how significant a role he played in the nation's life and history. Yet from a biblical standpoint, it is not all that surprising, for the credit for what happened never rested with any mortal but with Yahweh who was effecting the deliverances.

Joshua belonged to the tribe of Ephraim. It was among this hill country tribe that he was given an estate (Josh. 24:29–31; cf. 19:49–50; Judg. 2:8–9). He first appeared in Exodus 17:8–16 as the leader of the forces repulsing the Amalekites who attacked Israel at Rephidim. While Moses supported his young lieutenant with hands raised in prayer as he watched the progress of the battle from the hill, the young warrior led his troops in their first shakedown battle that was to prepare him for what was to come in the conquest of Canaan.

All his days he led Israel, after Moses' death. At the end of his days, he was buried in Ephraim at Timnath-serah.

THE SPIES AND RAHAB OF JERICHO

Prior to crossing the Jordan River, Joshua sent two spies to reconnoiter the land they were about to enter. They came to Jericho and entered the inn of one named Rahab, who may also have been a prostitute (Josh. 2:1; Heb. 11:31).[14] It was customary in those days that innkeepers were to be a sort of unofficial CIA or KGB for the king and to report whatever they overheard, especially when the customers "got in their cups" and their tongues were loosened with intoxicating drinks.

14. W. L. Moran, "The Repose of Rahab's Israelite Guests," *Studi sull'Oriente e la Bibbia* Genoa, 1967, pp 273–284, which contains a full bibliography on Rahab. Also see D. J. Wiseman, "Rahab of Jericho," *TynB*.14 (1964): 8–11, who argues on the basis of Akkadian that Rahab was an "innkeeper" and not a "prostitute"; but see the Greek of Hebrews 11:31.

The king of Jericho, after being warned that the spies had infiltrated the city, sent messengers to seize the spies; but Rahab hid the spies in the newly gathered stalks of flax that were drying on the roof of the inn. Rahab got rid of the messengers by lying to them, saying that the spies had just left the city. Later Rahab allowed the spies to escape that night by letting them down through a window of her house, which must have been built between the double walls of the city. The spies promised Rahab that she and her family would be spared for her courageous act if she would tie a red rope to her window as a sign of the location of her place when the Conquest began. As a reward for what she had done, Rahab and her family were indeed spared when Jericho was destroyed (Josh. 6:22–25).

The spies hid in the hills for three days while the messengers of the king of Jericho continued to search for them. Then they crossed the Jordan and reported to Joshua that Yahweh had delivered the whole country into their hands (Josh. 2:24). The form of the verb that the spies use here in their report is the Hebrew perfect tense of the verb that stresses the fact that "Yahweh has [already] delivered [the inhabitants of the land of Canaan into their hands]." To argue, however, that this is a formula of "holy war,"[15] as some do, is to make two mistakes: (1) Nowhere does the Bible talk about "holy wars," but refers (in texts like Deut. 20) to the wars of Yahweh; and (2) this formula, with its past tense, ("Yahweh has delivered") does not occur in Torah texts like Deuteronomy 20.

De Vaux and others wanted to argue that this story of Rahab and the spies was not in accordance with the fall of Jericho in Joshua 6. In the latter account, de Vaux claimed, the city was taken by the power of God, not as Joshua 2 represented it—because Rahab betrayed her city. Moreover, he continued, there would be no reason for displaying a red cord from the window of Rahab's house if her home was built on the city wall that collapsed; for her house would have collapsed as well. Therefore, he hypothesized, Rahab's story belonged, instead, to the literary genre of spy stories. Thus, just as Moses had sent scouts from Kadesh to reconnoiter the land (Num. 13–14) and to scout out the land of Jazer (Num. 21:32), so Joshua sent spies to Jericho (Josh. 2) and men to Ai (7:2–3). Later the Danites would send men to look over Laish (Judg. 18:2–10) as well. In most of these cases, especially where the stories are preserved in a good state, de Vaux cautioned, the scout's report was followed by an attack against the territory. Therefore,

15. Roland de Vaux, *The Early History of Israel*, pp. 597–98.

de Vaux thought that the conclusion of the spy story was suppressed in order to feature the miracle of the collapse of the walls of Jericho (Josh. 6).[16]

Surely this is a gratuitous conclusion, for the story contains none of the conflicts in the account that de Vaux has imagined. Nowhere does the text claim that all the walls collapsed. And even if it had, was it not possible that Rahab and her family could still have survived and the sign still be visible in the manner in which the walls fell? Even his citing of the literary genre of spy stories does not fit, for not all the stories de Vaux cites follow the pattern he imagines; consequently, he must say that some of the spy stories are not in a good state of preservation. How does he know these things? Where does one get that kind of information?

More desperate are the conclusions of M. Noth and W. Rudolph[17] that the whole story about Rahab is without any basis whatsoever in history, but it is simply an etiology explaining why a Canaanite group named the "house of Rahab" survived in Israel. (An etiology is the "study of causes," that is, an attempt to explain the origin or reasons for a situation, name, or happening. Nowadays it is used more frequently in medical science where etiologies refer to the causes of diseases.)

What, then, would make us think that the story of Rahab and the spies is an etiologic story? It must be that Joshua 2 and 6 do not record all the same facts. But why must we think that they are required to repeat the identical information if the documents belong together? And there is where the rub comes: they are not thought of as one document, but as stories representing different traditions. But that must be more of an assumption and a hypothesis than the evidence that what we have in the text before us seems to be a continuing and unified story that presumes all of the parts of the story to make up the whole. It is gratuitous to assign the tradition of Rahab to an earlier tradition and the tradition about the collapse of the walls of Jericho to a later time without some kind of controlling evidence; otherwise, the story of Rahab does come first merely on the grounds of the sequence of events represented in the text.

---

16. Roland de Vaux, ibid.
17. M. Noth, *Josua* (HAT) 2, pp. 22–23, 29–31; W. Rudolph, *Der 'Elohist' von Exodus bis Josua* (BZAW, 68) 1938, p. 169.

The Wars against Sihon and Og in Transjordania

Israel had been forced to circumvent the lands of Edom and Moab after being denied permission to pass through them. Moab's northern border varied, but, usually, it was set at the Arnon River running due east from the upper end of the Dead Sea. The Moabites had dispossessed the earlier inhabitants called the Emim, a subgroup of the Anakim, of the race of the Rephaim. Apparently, they belonged to a race of giants, whose exact origins are unknown.[18]

When Israel arrived at Dibon Gad, she was confronted by the hostile Amorites who controlled, at that time, the Transjordan between the Arnon and the Jabbok Rivers. Whether these Amorites were descendants of an earlier migration of Canaanite Amurru is difficult to determine, but it seems likely. Moses requested permission to follow a route through the Amorite lands to Beer, Mattanah, Nahaliel, Bamoth (all unknown sites today), and finally to Pisgah, a high plateau overlooking the Dead Sea and much of Canaan (Num. 21:21–31). Since this route passsed near the Amorite capital of Heshbon, Sihon, king of this area, was adamant that Moses and Israel should not go this way. Instead, Sihon launched an attack on Israel at Jahaz, some twenty miles from Heshbon. Jahaz is in the direction of the desert, for at the time of Eusebius,[19] it was believed to be between Medeba and Dibon. Surface explorations of Heshbon (*Ḥešbôn*) have yielded potsherds dating from before the Iron Age. Late Bronze pottery has been found at Jalud, a site some six miles southeast of Medeba and a Middle Bronze tomb was found at Nebo.[20]

Israel quickly seized Heshbon, slew Sihon, and occupied all the Amorite lands from the Arnon to Jazer, northeast of Jericho. But that did not settle things for another Amorite ruler to the north of the kingdom of Sihon, Og of Bashan, stood as a potential enemy. De Vaux incorrectly argued that this story was added to Numbers 21, being clearly borrowed from Deuteronomy 3:1–7 in his judgment.[21] While it does duplicate the story of Sihon, there is no prima facie reason why it should not stand in its own rights as a separate happening, unless more persuasive evidence is found that it replicates something already having occurred.

---

18. Conrad L'Heureux, "The Ugaritic and Biblical Rephaim," *HTR* 67 (1974): 265–74.
19. Eusebius, *Onomasticon*, 104, 11. Also see the Moabite Stone, lines 19–20 where Mesha took back Jahaz and attached it to Dibon.
20. Roland de Vaux, *The Early History of Israel*, pp. 564–65, cites W.F. Albright, *BASOR* 49 (Feb 1933), p. 28 and S. Saller and B. Bagatti, *The Town of Nebo* (Jerusalem, 1949): 24–29, plates 4–6.
21. Roland de Vaux, ibid.

Technically, Bashan lay north of the Yarmuk River, but at the time of Israel's conquest it must have included territory to the south of the Yarmuk as well. Bashan and Gilead were well-watered plateaus with good stands of trees, pastures, and farmlands. Israel struck Og and Bashan so quickly that they were not intercepted until Israel was at their capital city of Edrei, some thirty miles east-southeast of the Sea of Galilee (=*Der`a* on the frontier between Syria and Jordan). Once again, Israel won; Og, the giant king[22] was slain and his sixty cities were taken (Num. 21:35; Deut. 3:4). Thus, prior to Israel's entrance into the land of Canaan they had conquered and now controlled all the Tranjordanian Amorite lands from the Arnon Valley in the south to Mount Hermon in the north, a stretch of almost 150 miles. So desirable was this land that Reuben, Gad, and the half tribe of Manasseh decided to settle here rather than cross over the Jordan to Canaan. However, they promised to aid the rest of the tribes in the conquest of the land before returning to their families in the Transjordan area.

The Crossing of the Jordan and the Camp at Gilgal

Israel camped on the east side of the Jordan River at Shittim. About the time of the spring floods, when the river had flooded over its banks, word came to the people that they were to prepare to cross over the river (Josh. 3:1–17). The signal for the crossing was to be the moving out of the Levites carrying the ark of the covenant before them, but the people were to keep their distance of almost a thousand yards behind the ark in order to recognize and respect the sacred things. The people were also to consecrate themselves, for they would witness amazing things on the morrow when they crossed the river.

What happened was a miracle of timing, though the event in itself was natural enough—an event that would be observable several times more in later history. Upstream, the waters undercut the high dunes on the bank of the river, thus causing them to collapse and thereby dam up the river. Thus, the Israelites walked dry-shod over what had been an overflowing, flooded river.

The Arab chronicler Nowairi noted that on the night of December 7–8, 1267, the dunes upstream from the bridge at Damieh collapsed, causing the river to stop flowing from midnight until ten o'clock the

22. According to Deut. 3:11, Og's bed could be seen at Rabbah of the Ammonites = Amman, sixty or more miles to the south. His bed was fourteen and one-half feet long. Og was one of the last of the dolomens, a race of giants that lived in Palestine.

next morning.[23] Nowairi's account is similar to that of Joshua 3:16: "The water from upstream stopped flowing. It piled up in a heap a great distance away, at a town called Adam in the vicinity of Zarethan, while the water flowing down to the Sea of the Arabah (the Salt Sea) was completely cut off. So the people crossed over opposite Jericho."

Twelve men were chosen from each of the twelve tribes to carry twelve stones from the middle of the Jordan River (Josh. 4:1). These were to be set up at the spot where the first encampment took place on the west bank of the Jordan. The purpose of the stones was to provoke a question from the children: "What do these stones mean?" (Josh. 4:6). The answer was to be an occasion for reminding the nation of the time when they crossed over the Jordan dryshod, while the waters of the Jordan were cut off at the command of God (Josh. 4:7, 22–24). According to Joshua 5:1, news about the drying up of the Jordan to enable the Israelites to cross over the river spread among all the Amorite kings of the west and the Canaanite kings along the seacoast, so that they became dispirited and frightened over the prospect of facing the Israelites.

But Joshua had more important matters on his mind, for all that generation that had crossed over had been born during the forty years they had been in the wilderness since they had left Egypt. But they had not been circumcised. Thus the command went out from Yahweh to Joshua to make flint knives and to circumcise that whole generation of men. As a sort of pun on the whole event, the locale was called Gibeath Haaraloth, "hill of foreskins" (Josh. 5:3), for there Yahweh "rolled away the reproach of Egypt from [them]." The campsite was called Gilgal, a Hebrew word that sounds like the Hebrew word *gālal*, "to roll away." Thus, they were consecrated prior to entering the land of promise.

The First Passover in the Land

On the fourteenth day of the month, Israel paused that evening to celebrate the Passover, followed by the feast of unleavened bread. On that day the daily provision of manna ceased (Josh. 5:10–12). The roasted ears of grain probably were an oblation of firstfruits (Lev. 2:14; 23:14). For the first time, the people ate the produce of the land of Canaan and ceased eating the manna. Indeed, a new era had begun.

---

23. Nowairi, *Vie de Bibars*, fol. 31. F-M. Abel, *Géographie de la Palestine*, I, p. 481, incorporated a translation of this text from Nowairi in his geography, as did other works. John Garstang, *Joshua, Judges: Foundations of Bible History* (London: 1931), 137, reported a similar event that took place in July 1927, in which an earthquake stopped up the river at the dunes of Damieh for twenty-one and one-half hours. Garstang claimed to have quoted eyewitnesses who said they too had walked over "dry-shod," but no independent confirmation of an earthquake exists for this period of time.

10

The Conquest of Canaan

The conquest of Canaan raises some of the most complex issues in biblical historiography. These issues are historical, methodological, and theological.

The *historical* problem appears first. Our only direct literary source, for all intents and purposes, is the biblical narrative found throughout Joshua and the first chapter of Judges. But modern historiography attempts to write a "secular history" of Palestine. How is it possible to write a "secular history" when our main sources are what secular historians dismiss as "theocratic literature"? We ought to respond to this problem as follows: Why should we force the biblical evidence to purge itself of its so-called "theocratic point of view" in order to qualify as "history"? Or why should it even have the "secular" history attached to it? This tends to force the Bible out of the picture by definition.

This, then, leads to the *methodological* problem. Since the past generation, this problem has been stated as a twofold question: To what degree should the archaeological evidence be used to counter the biblical evidence, and vice versa? How are these two sets of data related to each other?

Finally, there is the *theological* problem. The central event in Israel's recitation of the great acts of God in her past is Yahweh's redemption of Israel's people from Egyptian bondage and Yahweh's subsequent granting them victory over the Canaanites as they speedily conquered the land. These two affirmations of the Exodus and the Conquest were at the heart of the nation's existence and of her credo (see, for example, Deut. 26:5–9). But if these events have no basis in the facts or happenings in history, is not Israel's faith, as well as our faith, without foundation or substance? As G. Ernest Wright concluded: "In Biblical faith, everything depends upon whether the central events [i.e., the exodus-conquest-settlement] actually occurred."[1] Therein lies the conundrum of the issues involved in the history of the conquest.

The Regnant Theories on the Entry and Settlement of the Land

There are four main theories of how the people entered and settled the land. The "Unified Military Conquest" Model. The "Peaceful Infiltration" Model (were already formulated in the 1920s and 1930s). The "Peasants' Revolt" or "Sociological" Model, which was shaped in the 1960s. Now in the late 1970s and 1980s has come a fourth theory from Israel Finkelstein that is a variation on the "Peaceful Infiltration" Model: i.e., the origins of the Israelite settlers go back to the end of the Middle Bronze Age when the network of villages in the hill country broke apart and people dropped out of the sedentary rural framework in favor of a lengthy pastoral period when people took to the margins of society known as the agricultural settlement or the Pastoralist Groups Model.[2]

The Conquest Model was espoused by William Foxwell Albright and his American students, along with a number of Israeli scholars such as Yehezkel Kaufmann and Yigael Yadin. The Peaceful Infiltration Model was first proposed by Albrecht Alt in the 1920s and is influential in the German school, with scholars such as Martin Noth and now partially with Israel Finkelstein. The Peasants' Revolt Model was first proposed by George Mendenhall in the 1960s, but then it was elaborated and carried beyond what Mendenhall had proposed by Norman Gottwald. Each model must now be examined in some detail.

The Conquest Model

Yehezkel Kaufmann[3] insisted that the descriptions of the Conquest in Joshua and in Judges 1 were in accord with historical reality, even

---

1. G. Ernest Wright, *The God Who Acts: Biblical Theology as Recital* (Naperville: Blessings, 1952), 126.

2. Israel Finkelstein, *The Archaeology of the Israelite Settlement* (Jerusalem: Israel Exploration Society, 1988), 336–56.

3. Y. Kaufmann, *The Biblical Account of the Conquest of Palestine* (Jerusalem: Magnes, 1953); idem., "Traditions Concerning Early Israelite History in Canaan," *Scripta Hierosolymitana* (Jerusalem) 8 (1961): 303–334.

though they were at times shrouded in legend. While he accepted the need for literary criticism, Kaufmann rejected all suggestions that Joshua and Judges were part of a six- or seven-volume Torah or that these books were part of a deuteronomistic history. On the contrary, a real conquest under the joint operation of all the tribes of Israel was carried out in Canaan. In Kaufmann's view, Joshua was an excellent strategist and tactician who kept the twelve tribes unified during the Conquest, always took the offensive, and made surprise attacks, giving the enemy no opportunity to recover and recoup. Nor was the picture gained from Judges 1 any different from that provided in Joshua, for it is an early description of what took place in the beginning of the period of the judges after Joshua's death. It was a historical continuation of the story of Joshua.

Four kinds of war ensued in the takeover of the land: (1) wars of conquest (Num. 21 to Judg. 1), ending with the capture of Bethel in Judges 1:22–26; (2) wars in which the Canaanites were not expelled or captured, but subjected to forced labor (Judg. 1:27–35); (3) wars of liberation at the beginning of the monarchy (Judg. 3–1; Sam 31); and (4) the imperial wars of David and Solomon.

Kaufmann is faulted by the scholarly establishment, however, for failing to accept the results of literary criticism and the findings of the history of traditions as well as paying no attention to all extrabiblical and archaeological evidence.[4]

W. F. Albright[5] also contended for an actual conquest, which he dated to around 1220 B.C. Cities like Debir (which he identified with Tell Beit Mirsim), Bethel, and Lachish have left evidence of being destroyed at approximately that time, only to be followed, with or without interruption in habitation, by a less prosperous form of occupation—presumably by the same Israelites who were responsible for the destruction of those same cities. Albright rejected the theory of a peaceful and gradual entry of nomadic groups of Israelites into Canaan, for he was convinced that there was a real conquest of the land.

Albright was followed in America by his disciples. G. Ernest Wright,[6] for example, argued that the way to reconcile the account

4. For example, R. de Vaux, *The Early History of Israel*, pp. 477–78; J. Bright, *Early Israel in Recent History Writing* (London, 1956), 56–78.

5. W. F. Albright, "The Israelite Conquest of Canaan in the Light of Archaeology," *BASOR* 74 (1939): 11–23; idem., *The Biblical Period from Abraham to Ezra* (New York, 1963), 24–34.

6. G. E. Wright, *The Westminster Historical Atlas of the Bible* (Philadelphia: Westminster, 1956), 39–40; idem., *Biblical Archeology* (Philadelphia: Westminster, 1962), 69–84; idem., "The Literary and Historical Problem of Joshua 10 and Judges 1," *JNES* 5 (1946): 105–114; idem., "Archaeology, History and Theology," *Harvard Divinity School Bulletin* 28 (1964): 85–96.

given in Joshua 1–11 with Judges 1 was to note that Joshua attacked a limited number of cities in southern Canaan, while leaving the Conquest to be completed by local groups later on. Another Albright disciple was John Bright,[7] who thought that the archaeological evidence, while not definitive in its own right, did swing the argument in favor of the historical authenticity of the biblical accounts. The Albright heritage continued to "play out," to a certain extent, in William G. Dever. Dever received his doctorate from Harvard University in 1966 under G. E. Wright's supervision with a dissertation on the Early Bronze IV/Middle Bronze period in Palestine. He worked closely with the Gezer expedition as director from 1966–1971, 1984, 1990, followed by other expeditions.

So where did Dever stand on the conquest issue? In a recent interview,[8] Dever allowed that "all archaeologists today" have rejected the Israelite Conquest of Canaan as described in the Bible. Nevertheless, he saw the presence of some conflict even if one held to a peasant revolt or a social revolution. Furthermore, he affirmed, the "only destruction that I would want to connect with incoming Israelites might be the one at Bethel. The one at Hazor is now dated too early by Yadin's own student and disciple."[9] But when push came to shove, Dever would not say that the Bible's account of the Conquest was completely wrong. For him the Bible pointed to two accounts of the origins of Israel—the one in Joshua and the one in Judges. The account in Judges, Dever averred, minimized a simple military campaign and, instead, referred to a two-century-long cultural struggle between Israel and Canaan. Joshua, however, glorified the military career of a single individual and, therefore, could not be easily reconciled with the archaeological evidence as it presents itself today, contended Dever.[10] Thus, Dever fits within the Conquest Model, but with many nuances that had already begun to emerge in his mentor, G. E. Wright, before Dever's death.

In a similar manner, Amihai Mazar used components of this view to explain his own theory of the Conquest. He contended that in the cases of southern Transjordania, Arad, Ai, Yarmuth, and Hebron, there was an "outright conflict between the archaeological findings and the con-

7. John Bright, *Early History*, 87–89; idem., *History of Israel*, 117–120.

8. Hershel Shanks, "Is This Man a *Biblical* Archaeologist?" *BAR* 22.4 (1996): 37. See William G. Dever, *Archaeology and Biblical Studies: Retrospects and Prospects* (Evanston, 1974) and idem., *Recent Archaeological Discoveries and Biblical Research* (University of Washington Press, 1990).

9. Ibid., p. 37.

10. Ibid., p. 38.

quest narratives," while in the case of Lachish, Hazor, and Bethel, "archaeology does not contradict these stories."[11] Thus, Mazar concluded that the Book of Joshua digested a number of successive local clashes to yield a tradition of a single conquest. But for him the process was much more complex than that: it was some three hundred years of Egyptian domination in clashes between mostly weak and poor Canaanite city-states that eventually were replaced by a new national entity named Israel.

The conclusion that there must have been a violent irruption into the land by Israel, regardless of how schematized the Joshua narratives were, was shared by J. A. Soggin[12] and Paul Lapp.[13] Almost all of Albright's followers, however, thought the master may have exaggerated the significance and importance of the archaeological evidence. They, nevertheless, felt inclined to agree with his Conquest Model and the general story line of Joshua, more than with the other models that were being set forth.

The Peaceful Infiltration Model

The German school of Albrecht Alt and Martin Noth[14] put forth a different theory based on the history of traditions and on patterns of territorial distributions in the land. For them the Israelites entered the land peacefully for the most part. While there may have been some sporadic exceptions, generally speaking, the pattern was a peaceful one in which these people came in search of new pastures in those territories that had not been incorporated into the system of city-states or that were not heavily populated. This pattern of peaceful penetration is confirmed by the biblical story of the Gibeonites and the absence of any battles in the central part of Canaan in the Joshua stories. If this school is asked, "But where, then, did the conquest stories of Joshua 2–11 originate?" the answer will be that they were etiological stories; that is, stories to explain why something is the way it is "until this day"! Thus, stories were invented to explain why Jericho was in ruins in that day, as was Ai, or why a cave in Makkedah had its entrance sealed with

11. Amihai Mazar, *Archaeology of the Land of the Bible: 10,000–586* B.C.E. (New York: Doubleday, 1992), 334.

12. J. A. Soggin, "Ancient Biblical Traditions and Modern Archaeological Discoveries," *BA* 23 (1960): 95–100.

13. P. Lapp, "The Conquest of Palestine in the Light of Archaeology," *CTM* 38 (1967): 283–300; idem., *Biblical Archaeology and History* (New York, 1969), 107–111.

14. A. Alt, *Die Landnahme der Israeliten in Palästina* (Leipzig, 1925); M. Noth, *Das Buch Josua* (HAT), 1953; idem., *History of Israel*, tr. from 2nd ed., Stanley Godman (New York: Harper and Brothers, 1958), 68–84.

great stones. But they claim that Joshua played little, if any, role in all of this.

As the people of Israel moved from a seminomadic to an agrarian way of life, their occupation of Canaan (*Landnahme*) led to intermittent fighting over a long period as the quest for new territory extended into the period of the settlement proper (*Landesausbau*). According to Noth, this process took almost two hundred years, from the second half of the fourteenth century B.C., coming at the end of the Amarna Age, until about 100 B.C. Noth, like Alt, was not too impressed by the archaeological data, for the destruction levels that the Albright school had appealed to were just as easily attributable to the internecine conflicts between the city-states themselves, if not also to the invasion of the Sea Peoples around 1200 B.C.

Manfred Weippert took up the same Peaceful Infiltration Model and modified it slightly by arguing that the Israelite tribes had to be divided into two groups: (1) the tribes from the Leah group, along with the groups of Bilhah and Zilpah, entered first in a peaceful manner; (2) but the Rachel group, representing the house of Joseph mainly, came later and introduced the cult of Yahweh and the idea of holy war, the armed conquest led by Joshua.[15]

This theory of a peaceful infiltration has been rather severely criticized for its "nihilistic" views of the biblical text and of the archaeological external evidence and for its too frequent recourse to etiology as the explanation for what it does recognize in the biblical text.[16] Others, such as Brevard Childs, demonstrated how the formula "until this day" rarely had an etiological function for justifying an existing fact, but in most cases it simply served as a personal confirmation by the writer of what the narrator was reporting.[17] But none of this settled the debate: the debate ground on despite the assertion of theories and the counterassertions that were offered.

The Peasants' Revolt Model

G. E. Mendenhall[18] stood the problem of the Conquest on its head. He asserted, first of all, that the ancestors of the Israelites were not

15. M. Weippert, *Die Landnahme der israelitischen Stämme in der neuren wissenschaftlichen Diskussion*, (Göttingen, 1967), 14-51; idem., *The Settlement of the Israelite Tribes in Palestine* (Naperville: Allenson, Inc., 1971, especially p. 146.

16. W. F. Albright, "The Israelite Conquest," *BASOR* 74 (1939): 11–23; Y. Kaufmann, *The Biblical Account*, pp. 70–74; J. Bright, *Early Israel*, pp. 79–110.

17. B. S. Childs, "A Study of the Formula, 'until this day,'" *JBL* 82 (1963): 279–292.

18. G. E. Mendenhall, "The Hebrew Conquest of Palestine," *BA* 25 (1962): 66–87.

nomads or even seminomads, for the contrast between nomadic and agrarian peoples did not exist in the ancient Near East. Instead, the "tribe" was a result of a social unit, not genealogical descent. The real conflict was not between seminomadic herdsmen and settled farmers, but between villagers and city dwellers. That was the conflict in Canaan. The Hebrews are treated in the Bible the same way that the Habiru are treated in the contemporary history; thus, they must share some of the same origins as the Habiru. Accordingly, instead of arguing for any large-scale immigration of peoples, Mendenhall conjectured the farmers, herdsmen, and peasants united to revolt against the Canaanites who lived in the city-states. This on-going conflict was suddenly brought to a head when a group of escaping prisoners from Egypt arrived at Canaan's west bank with a belief in a new God, Yahweh. Israel, then, was not an ethnic group but a religious community, with some ethnic unity acquired by marriage, now bound together by resistance from the city-states that refused them entry. As a result, the lid was blown off everything as kings and cities alike were demolished and liquidated in the revolt of these peasants in a contest of control with the city-states.

Norman Gottwald exploited and extended this theory while building his theory on sociological grounds.[19] Gottwald also hypothesized that there was a class struggle between the peasants of Israel and the nobility of Canaan. This movement began with the Amarna Age Apiru/Habiru providing a model for the peasants to emulate. The peasants were bound together by cultic, sociopolitical, and military interests, a group Gottwald called Elohistic Israel. Out of this coalition or Apiru emerged Elohists who formed a group that called itself Israel and now worshiped a new God called Yahweh.

But as J. Maxwell Miller complained, this whole theory was a "modern construct superimposed upon the biblical traditions."[20] Likewise, Mendenhall's theory of the tribe, which really was responsible for kicking off this line of thinking, was also foreign to the representation given in the Bible, where blood ties are the basis for affinity and not sociological factors.[21]

19. Norman Gottwald, *The Tribes of Yahweh* (Maryknoll, N.Y.: Orbis, 1979), 210–219.

20. J. Maxwell Miller, "The Israelite Occupation of Canaan," in *Israelite and Judean History*, ed. John H. Hayes and J. Maxwell Miller (Philadelphia: Westminster, 1977), 279.

21. See some of the other vigorous criticisms of Gottwald's theories in Walter R. Winfall, "The Tribes of Yahweh: A Synchronic Study with a Diachronic Title," *ZAW* 95 (1983): 197–209; Frederic R. Brandfon, "Norman Gottwald on the Tribes of Yahweh," *JSOT* 21 (1981): 101–10; Eugene H. Merrill, *Bib Sac* 138 (1981): 81–82; Marvin L. Chaney, *JBL* 103 (1984): 89–93. A good overview of recent sociological approaches to Israelite history and literature appears in Walter Brueggemann, "Trajectories in OT Literature and Sociology of Ancient History," *JBL* 98 (1979): 161–85.

The Agricultural Resettlement of the Pastoralist Groups Model

Israel Finkelstein has recently given a modification of the Peaceful Infiltration Model of the Conquest. He accepts the fact that there may be a kernel of historical veracity in the biblical tradition about the Exodus and Conquest, for certain elements of the settlers may have come from outside the country, and perhaps from the south. But simultaneously with these movements, there is the distinct possibility that certain groups who settled in the hill country in the Iron I period originated directly from the Canaanite society of the lowlands; at least, that is what the archaeological evidence seems to suggest to some.[22]

Things came to a head as the number of settlers increased and the lands for agriculture no longer sufficed. This brought settlers into conflict with the Canaanite centers in the hill country to determine who was to control the best lands. This resulted in the destruction of several cities, which were isolated from the network of the lowland Canaanite urban centers. Bethel was destroyed in just such a conflict. Other sites, such as Shechem and those in the territory of Manasseh, continued to coexist with the new settlers well into the Iron I period.[23] The process of Israelite settlement probably lasted, on this model, up to the end of the eleventh century B.C. Finkelstein sees no archaeological evidence to support dating the beginning of Israelite settlement earlier than the twelfth century B.C. But as the Israelites became stronger and more consolidated into tribal units, argued Finkelstein, they established their own interregional institutions, the most important being at Shiloh.

Each of these four theories has exerted enormous influence over large segments of the interpreting community. The Conquest Model strikes us as giving a more even hand to both types of evidences from internal textual sources and external archaeological sources. Of course, to argue that the biblical description of the Conquest is impossible because it requires or presupposes the presence of the supernatural is to stand opposed to that which is central to biblical faith: God must bare his holy arm and do what seemed impossible. But should the external evidence contradict the claims made in the text, then, and only then, should alternative models and explanations be sought. So, what is the state of the evidence on this question of the Conquest from these two sets of data?

22. Israel Finkelstein, *The Archaeology of Israelite Settlement*, p. 348.
23. Ibid., p. 349.

The Jericho Campaign

The conquest of Jericho was chosen as the best primary objective for a successful strategy for conquering the whole land. The hill country in southern Canaan was controlled by the fearsome giants who had intimidated the original group of spies Moses had sent out thirty-eight years earlier. The plan now was to penetrate the land just north of the Dead Sea and take on Jericho, a heavily fortified city. This would open access to the center of the land, thereby adopting the principle of "divide and conquer."

The stories of Jericho are among the best-known and most-loved in the Old Testament. They are also central to the whole argument of a Conquest Model and to any accompanying affirmations of biblical faith about the reliability and accuracy of the Exodus and Conquest accounts. However, with very few exceptions, most scholars today doubt if anything like what the Bible describes took place at this site.

This is remarkable, for the first archaeologist to excavate Jericho reported that his findings confirmed the biblical narrative. John Garstang excavated Jericho from 1930 to 1936. He argued that City IV came to a violent end around 1400 B.C., based on pottery types found in the destruction debris, the dates of the Egyptian scarabs with Eighteenth Dynasty pharaohs on them from nearby tombs, and the absence of Mycenaean potteryware (an imported pottery found at some sites by this time). Garstang concluded:

> In a word, in all material details and in date the fall of Jericho took place as described in the Biblical narrative. Our demonstration is limited, however, to material observations: the walls fell, shaken apparently by an earthquake, and the city was destroyed by fire, about 1400 B.C. These are the basic facts resulting from our investigations. The link with Joshua and the Israelites is only circumstantial but it seems to be solid and without a flaw.[24]

Garstang's conclusions evoked such controversy that he requested another rising English archaeologist, Kathleen Kenyon, to review and update his findings in the 1950s. Kenyon failed to support Garstang and reverted to an earlier conclusion arrived at by the Austro-German expedition of Ernst Sellin and Carl Watzinger completed in 1907–1909 and 1911; Jericho, they concluded, had been destroyed by the end of the Middle Bronze Age, about 1550 B.C.; the city had been unoccupied from that mid-sixteenth-century B.C. date throughout the

24. John Garstang, "Jericho and the Biblical Story," in *Wonders of the Past*, ed. J. A. Hammerton (New York: Wise, 1937), 1222.

whole Late Bronze period (1550–1200 B.C.), except for a small area occupied in the fourteenth century B.C. Kenyon also added that the double wall which Garstang had associated with the Israelite invasion around 1400 B.C. was, in fact, to be dated one thousand years earlier to the Early Bronze period.[25] Based on Kenyon's report, it seemed that the biblical account must now be written off as so much religious rhetoric and folklore.

Not much happened to resolve this dilemma over the next twenty-five years. Kenyon died in 1978, but her final report on Jericho was not published until 1981 and 1983.

More recently, Kenyon's results have been scrutinized by Bryant Wood, then of the University of Toronto. Wood concluded that Kenyon was right about one thing: the double wall on top of the tell was an Early Bronze wall and did not belong to City IV, as Garstang had concluded. But on the 1400 B.C. dating for the fall of City IV, and the circumstances under which it fell, Garstang was more than vindicated by the published results of Kenyon after her death.[26] City IV, however, all agreed was violently destroyed by a conflagration that suggested the presence of a prior earthquake and a resulting fire. Kenyon noted :

> The destruction was complete. Walls and floors were blackened or reddened by fire, and every room was filled with fallen bricks, timbers, and household utensils; in most rooms the fallen debris was heavily burnt, but the collapse of the walls of the eastern rooms seems to have taken place before they were affected by the fire.[27]

Just as amazing was Kenyon's recovery of six bushels of grain in one season alone, just as Garstang had gathered large amounts as well. Thus, City IV did not fall after a long period of starvation, as was the case with so many ancient cities, but with plenty of supplies still remaining. Nor did the attackers plunder this most valuable commodity in antiquity (one that often was used as a medium of exchange), for

---

25. Kathleen Kenyon, "Some Notes on the History of Jericho in the Second Millennium B.C.," *PEQ* (1951): 101–138; idem., *Digging up Jericho* (London: Ernst Benn, 1957), 262; *idem.*, "Jericho," in *Encyclopedia of Archaeological Excavations in the Holy Land*, vol. 2 , ed. Michael Avi-Yonah (Englewood Cliffs, N.J.: Prentice Hall, 1976), 551–564.

26. Bryant G. Wood, "Did the Israelites Conquer Jericho?" *BAR* 16/2 (1990): 45–59. Wood was refuted by Piotr Bienkowski, national curator of Egyptian and Near Eastern Antiquities at the National Museums and Galleries, Liverpool, England, in his article entitled "Jericho Was Destroyed in the Middle Bronze Age, Not the Late Bronze Age," *BAR* 16/5 (1990): 45–6, 69. Bienkowski was answered in that same issue by Wood, "Dating Jericho's Destruction: Bienkowski Is Wrong on All Counts," pp. 47–49, 68.

27. Kathleen Kenyon, *Excavations at Jericho*, Vol. 3: *The Architecture and Stratigraphy of the Tell*, ed. Thomas A. Holland (London: British School of Archaeology in Jerusalem, 1981), 370.

if these were the results of the Israelite invasion, the explanation is easily at hand: the city had been put under the ban, for everything in it was devoted to the Lord (Josh. 6:17–18); nothing was to be taken.

Moreover, the timing of the attack was wrong from a military point of view, for it normally would have come just before the harvests, when grain supplies were at their lowest levels, or the grain was just about ready to be harvested from the field, only now it would feed the attackers as they laid siege to the city. However, Rahab was drying freshly harvested flax on the roof of her house (Josh. 2:6), thereby agreeing with the fact that the Israelites crossed the Jordan River just at the spring flood stage (Josh. 3:15) and at the time of the celebration of the Passover, prior to attacking the city (Josh. 5:10).

But what about the walls that came tumbling down, now that Garstang's identification of the walls proved to be incorrect? Kenyon was able to show that City IV had an impressive fortification system with its own walls. A stone revetment wall rose fifteen feet from the base of the mound. On top of this revetment were remnants of a mud brick wall, preserved to another eight feet. Holding the revetment wall was a gigantic, earthen-packed embankment or rampart with plastered face that reached all the way to the top of the mound. On top of this rampart was another city wall.

But where the lower revetment wall originally stood, there is evidence that the walls did indeed "fall down flat" (Josh. 6:20). Kenyon found that *outside* the revetment wall, in her excavation on the west side of the city, the bricks of the city wall had fallen outward. The amount of red mud bricks found outside the wall in Kenyon's eighty-foot balk would have been sufficient to build a wall six and one-half feet wide and twelve feet high. The fact that the bricks fell outside the stone revetment wall explains how it was possible for each man "to charge straight in [to the city]" (Josh. 6:20), for the debris had formed a sort of natural bridge to scale what was left of the walls.

What date is to be assigned to City IV? Kenyon, Sellin, and Watzinger declared it fell in 1550 B.C., but Garstang and Wood put it at 1400 B.C. Which was correct?

Wood pointed to one carbon-14 sample taken from a piece of charcoal found in the debris that yielded a date of 1410 B.C., plus or minus forty years! Several scarabs (small Egyptian amulets shaped like a beetle with an inscription, often of the pharaoh's name) gave a continuous series extending from the Thirteenth (eighteenth century B.C.) to the Eighteenth (early fourteenth century B.C.) Dynasties. In the Eighteenth Dynasty, three royal names occur: Hatshepsut (ca. 1503–1483 B.C.), Thutmosis III (ca. 1504–1450 B.C.), Amenhotep III (ca. 1417–1379 B.C.), and a seal from Thutmosis III.

The most common rejoinder is that the scarabs of the Eighteenth Dynasty were very common and tended to be kept as heirlooms, remaining in circulation for a long time. But Wood noted that this critique, while true enough for Thutmosis III and Amenhotep III, would not explain the presence of Hatshepsut's scarab. She was maligned after her death, as her name was defaced and removed from all public documents. Accordingly, her scarabs are neither numerous nor retained as good luck charms. Hence its presence here at Jericho is a good indicator of the 1400 B.C. date for City IV, the one that Joshua destroyed as the Conquest began.

Even the ceramic evidence points to the distinctive styles of Late Bronze I. While the pottery of Middle Bronze II is similar to Late Bronze I, yet there were subtle but real differences in the pottery styles.[28] Thus, based on arguments from radiocarbon dating, scarab dating, stratigraphy, and ceramic typology, archaeologists and biblical historians could exhibit more openness to the possibility that Jericho was destroyed about 1400 B.C. In much the same way as the Bible declared, Jericho's City IV was found by the archaeologists: with the booty of the city being left intact and the walls having collapsed toward the exterior of the city and not to the interior, as would be the case if they had been battered down by an invader under normal circumstances of most military invasions.

THE CENTRAL CAMPAIGN

After Jericho fell, Joshua sent spies on to the next Canaanite fortification, which was at Ai, "near Beth Aven" (7:2). This is one of the most detailed of all the conquest stories, and according to some scholars, the most probable, since, as they put it, "It contains no miraculous elements. Unfortunately, however," de Vaux lamented, "the story is not supported by archaeological evidence."[29]

Ai has long been identified with Khirbet et-Tell, about a mile to the southeast of Bethel (while Josh. 7:2 has it to the "east of Bethel"). The name of "Ai," *ʿay*, is clearly related to *ʿiy* (plural *iyyim*), meaning a

28. Bienkowski took strong exception to Wood's statements in this regard, "Jericho Was Destroyed," p. 49, but Wood came back and adequately answered every one of Bienkowski's objections, ibid., p. 47.

29. Roland de Vaux, *The Early History of Israel*, p. 614.

"ruin," or a heap of ruins. Thus, its identity rests on its being a ruin and its proximity to Bethel, which itself has been equated with Beitin since 1838 by the American topographer Edward Robinson.

Robinson equated Beitin and Bethel because of the similarity of the names (assuming the well-attested shift from the Hebrew *l*, *lamed*, in Bethel to the Arabic *n*, *nun*) in Beitin. He also based it on the *Onomasticon* of Eusebius's (A.D. 269–339) where Eusebius (later revised and amplified by Jerome) stated that Bethel lay "at the twelfth Roman milestone from Aelia" (Jerusalem) on the east side of the road to Neapolis (Shechem-Nablus).[30]

Beitin, however, does not lie at the twelfth Roman mile marker as Eusebius and Jerome indicated, but at the *fourteenth!* Moreover, there is not a mountain east of Beitin, between Ai and Bethel, as Genesis 12:8 ("hills east of Bethel . . . with Bethel on the west and Ai on the east") required.

However, all is not lost. There is a site that fits all these topographical requirements for the site of Bethel rather than the one that is traditionally used. It is Bireh, just 550 yards south of the twelfth Roman mile marker. It has a prominent mountain, Jebel et Tawil, "the tall one," to the east of town. It lies on the east-west geographical border between Benjamin and Ephraim. That site, according to Livingston, would be a better candidate for Bethel.

But with what site, then, would Ai be identified? "A small site east of Bireh, Khirbet Nisya," answered David Livingston. It has a valley to the north of it, which descends into the Wadi Suwinit, going down to Jericho, with a hill on the far side, just as Joshua 7:2 and8:10–13 had it. On the west is a ridge that could hide a force waiting in ambush, without being seen either from Bireh (=Bethel) or Khirbet Nisya (=Ai) (Josh. 8:9, 12–13).

Khirbet Nisya has yielded a wide range of sherds from the Chalcolithic (fourth millennium) and Early Bronze (third millennium) to the Middle Bronze II as well. Since on most chronologies the Middle Bronze extends from 1900 to 1550 B.C., Bimson and Livingston suggest that the end of the Middle Bronze be moved from 1550 to around 1420

30. David Livingston, "The Location of Biblical Bethel and Ai Reconsidered," *WTJ* 33 (1970): 20–44; idem., "Traditional Site of Bethel Questioned," *WTJ* 34(1971): 39–50. See the response to this by Anson F. Rainey, "Bethel Is Still Beitin," *WTJ* 33 (1971): 175–188. See also Edward Robinson, *Biblical Researches in Palestine I* (Boston: Crocker and Brewster, 1856), 449–450; also John J. Bimson and David Livingston, "Redating the Exodus," BAR 12 (1987): 66, n. 36 where they cite J. Alberto Soggin in his *Joshua* (London: SCM, 1972), 102–103 that this transformation of the Hebrew *lamed* does not always represent an original Arabic *nun* where there are terminations of *-el* and its derivatives.

B.C., since the date for the cutoff point was somewhat arbitrarily fixed, being tied to the expulsion of the Hyksos from Egypt. But the fall of any of the Canaanite cities cannot be tied to the activity of the Eighteenth Dynasty pharaohs pursuing the Hyksos into Canaan, for as Donald Redford has pointed out, the beginning of the Eighteenth Dynasty was simply unable to carry out campaigns against fortified cities in Canaan.[31]

But if the Egyptians did not conquer these cities in Canaan in 1550 B.C., when were they conquered, then who did conquer them if not the Egyptians? Bimson and Livingston answer that the Middle Bronze should end about 1400–1420 B.C. Thus, they would lower the cutoff point for the Middle Bronze Age by 150 years, a move not terribly unreasonable given the fact that artifacts cannot be dated by radiocarbon half life methods or pottery typology any closer than within one hundred years or so. This proposal has not been greeted with any enthusiasm. However, as the theory stands, it is likely that the Middle Bronze II date for the destruction of Khirbet Nisya should be lowered to around 1400 B.C. and attributed to the Israelite invasion under Joshua, not to the Egyptians.

Nothing is said about Israel's encounter with Bethel at this time, but it may be assumed that, as with many other Canaanite cities, the people were destroyed, but their city was spared, ready to be occupied by Israel after the Conquest was completed. Later, in the Book of Judges, it does indicate that the Ephraimites did in fact take Bethel, but this seems to take place after Joshua's death (Judg. 1:22–26). But even then, a Bethelite allowed the Israelites to enter his city, with the result that the population was destroyed, except for the collaborator, while the city itself was spared.[32]

THE TREATY WITH THE GIBEONITES

The country of Canaan was now cut almost in half. Joshua turned north, without any noticeable opposition, to Shechem (Tell Balatah), some twenty-five miles north of Bethel. It would appear that the people of Shechem welcomed Israel, for there is no record of any opposition

31. Donald Redford, "Contact Between Egypt and Jordan: Some Comments on Sources," in *Studies in History and Archaeology*, ed. Hadidi, pp. 118–119; and Kenneth A. Kitchen, "Some New Light on the Asiatic Wars of Rameses II," *JEA* 50 (1964): 53, 63, as cited by Bimson and Livingston, *BAR*, p. 67, n. 20.

32. For a discussion of the technical phrase, "they put the city to the sword," or "smote the city with the edge of the sword," see Eugene H. Merrill, "Palestinian Archaeology," *GTJ* 3 (1982): 113–14.

there as well. It is of more than passing interest that the Canaanites of Shechem also cooperated with the ʿ*apiru* of the Amarna texts in a letter that was later by about thirty years from this 1406/07 B.C. date.[33]

Shechem is a site hallowed in the memory of the nation, for it was often associated with events in the lives of the patriarchs. Here Joshua would lead the people of Israel in a covenant ceremony at the altar he built on Mount Ebal, as the people antiphonally promised from Mount Ebal and Mount Gerizim—the two mountains cradling Shechem—to keep all the words of the law, even as Moses had commanded them to do (Josh. 8:30–35; Deut. 27:2–8). Years later, after Joshua had died, the people would return to Shechem in order to have the next generation pledge the same faithfulness to Yahweh (Josh. 23:1–24:28).

By now all the kings west of the Jordan River, including the kings of the Hittites, Amorites, Canaanites, Perrizites, Hivites, and Jebusites, had heard all that Joshua and Israel had been doing at Jericho, Ai, and Shechem. Something needed to be done. They gathered together to make war against Joshua and Israel (9:1–2).

But not the Gibeonites—whose four towns were listed as Gibeon (about seven miles south of Bethel), Chephirah, Beeroth, and Kiriath-jearim (Josh. 9:17)—all of which lived in a rather large area about ten by twelve without the benefit of a king, having only elders to rule them (Josh. 9:11). Gibeon may well be *el Gib*, Chephirah is modern *Tell Kefireh*, Beeroth is probably not *el Bireh*, and Kirath-jearim is *Deir el-Azhar*, near *el-Qiryeh* on the road from Jerusalem to Tel Aviv. The Gibeonites decided to use a ruse, pretending to be from a distant country, as borne out by their worn-out sacks, cracked and moldy old wineskins, worn and patched sandals, and moldy bread (Josh. 9:4–5). These Hivites (9:7) praised Joshua and Israel, telling them how far their fame had spread. They only wanted a nonaggression treaty.

This they got from Joshua and the elders only to find out, three days later, that the whole thing was a ruse and that the Gibeonites were neighbors (9:16). Their only recourse—for Israel could not break the oath they had taken before the Lord—was to make them servants forever as "woodcutters and water carriers for the house of . . . God" (9:23).

---

33. Historical and literary criticism is not happy with this peaceful acceptance by the Shechemites, for it proposes instead that Shechem fell after a series of savage attacks by the tribes of Simeon and Levi. But the basis for this unusual view is the story of the rape of Jacob's daughter Dinah by the son of Hamor of Shechem in Genesis 34, wherein Dinah's two brothers, Simeon and Levi, avenge the rape, after requiring every Shechemite to be circumcised, by killing off the whole city. Thus this story, some affirm, is an etiological story to tell how Israel happened to get Shechem under its control. See Robert G. Boling, *Joshua*, Anchor Bible (Garden City, N.Y.: Doubleday, 1982), 251–54 and T. Meek, *Hebrew Origins* (New York: Harper and Row), 124 -28.

Thus, we have another example of an Israelite settlement in Canaan without the force of arms or the destruction of a site.

The Southern Campaign

Because the Gibeonites had made a treaty with Israel, five Canaanite kings from the south decided to teach them a lesson and, apparently, to any others similarly disposed to sell out to these invaders. Thus, five Amorite kings joined together, at the instigation of King Adoni-Zedek of Jerusalem to go up against Gibeon. They were the kings of Jerusalem, Hebron, Jarmuth (*Khirbet Yarmuth*, about eighteen miles west-southwest of Jerusalem), Lachish (*Tell ed-Duweir*, about thirty miles southwest of Jerusalem), and Eglon (said to be *Tell el-Hesi*, about thirty-five miles southwest of Jerusalem). These five cities, whose locations formed a triangle-shaped consortium, must have been the most important Amorite enclaves in all of northern Judah at that time.

The Gibeonites, in turn, asked Joshua to defend them, for Israel was treaty-bound to do so. Joshua rallied his troops on a forced night march of some twenty miles, all the way up from Gilgal, where he had returned to camp after the fiasco of the ruse of extracting a treaty from him. Joshua sprang a surprise attack on the marauding five kings who had set siege to Gibeon. This threw Adoni-Zedek of Jerusalem, Hoham of Hebron, Piram of Jarmuth, Japhia of Lachish, and Debir of Eglon into a panic; they and their armies began to flee, taking the road over to Beth Horon and then south through Aijalon ("Deer[field]"), hoping to make it home before more damage was done. Joshua's military action was helped by the intervention of Yahweh, who threw down enormous hailstones from a storm front taking the same path as the fleeing enemy; more were dying from the hailstones than from the swords or weapons of the Israelites (10:11). On that same day, given the cover of the clouds during the hailstorm, the sun and the moon stood still (10:12–14) as Joshua finished the task.

The five kings fled to a cave in Makkedah, which Joshua stopped up with huge stones, posting a guard to make sure that is how things stayed while he finished pursuing his enemies (10:16–19). Thus ended the twenty-mile pursuit from Gibeon. Joshua gave specific instructions for the Israelites to attack the enemy from the rear of their fleeing lines before they reached their cities (10:19). Again, the point is so clear it is surprising so many have missed it: they were to preserve the cities intact and to take the enemy in the field if possible. The people were to be destroyed, or put under the ban (*ḥerem*), but not their physical structures.

Joshua reopened the mouth of the cave where the five kings had been stowed. These he brought out and hanged on five trees. Afterwards, he had their corpses taken down from the trees and thrown into the cave, sealing the mouth with stones. These were still there at the time this narrative was recorded (10:16–27).

Joshua then moved against Makkedah (*Khirbet el-Kheisum* [?]). Again, he merely "took" the city, a verb that always points to the capture and not the destruction or demolition of a town. He "put [it] to the sword," a metaphorical expression that means he took the lives of the people. All the inhabitants were "totally destroyed" (*heḥĕrim*; 10:28).

Next Joshua moved on to Libnah (perhaps *Tell es-Safi*), about eight miles southwest of Makkedah. This time the Lord "gave" Joshua the city and its king to Israel, so that there were no survivors there either. From Libnah, Joshua moved to Lachish, about ten miles south of Libnah. Even the assistance of Horam, king of Gezer, over twenty miles north of Lachish, was insufficient to spare Lachish and its people. Eight miles southwest of Lachish lay Eglon, and it too fell.

Hebron may have been the only exception to the policy of preserving the physical city. Here Joshua put both the city and the people under the ban (*ḥerem*), unless the "city" means, by virtue of the figure of speech called *synecdoche*, the population (10:37). Be that as it may, then Hebron and its environs were populated again within five years (14:6–5).

The final city listed in the southern campaign was Debir (which Albright identified as *Tell Beit Mirsim*), fifteen miles southwest of Hebron. It too suffered an overwhelming defeat. Thus, the whole southern campaign is summarized in Joshua 10:40–43. Israel had "subdued the whole region, including the hill country, the Negev, the western foothills and the mountain slopes, together with all their kings. He left no survivors." But the pointed absence of any mention of the taking of any of the towns must be insisted on, especially as the debate over the absence of any evidence of an Israelite destruction level for these towns increases in the archaeological and historical literature.

THE NORTHERN CAMPAIGN

Joshua returned with his troops to his base in Gilgal after the successful completion of the southern strategy.[34] The final phase of the Canaanite strategy was to invade the lands in the Jezreel Valley and those in Galilee.

Hazor was the "head of all these kingdoms" (Josh. 11:10). This is the only biblical text that mentions someone who is a king of Canaan, rather than merely or uniquely being a king of a town or city. King Jabin, then, must have been the leader of some kind of alliance as well as being the king of Hazor (*Tell el-Qedah*), the largest city of the north, and perhaps in all Canaan. Hazor covered some 110 acres, perhaps being home for some forty thousand people, located on a high mound, some twelve miles north of the Sea of Galilee and less than five miles from Lake Huleh ("the waters of Merom"). Jabin enlisted the support of Jobab, king of Madon (*Qarn Hattin*, five miles west of Tiberias), and the kings of Shimron (*Tell Semuniyeh*, on the northern edge of the Plain of Jezreel, some fifteen miles from the Mediterranean) and Acshaph (*Tell Keisan*, some six miles southwest of Acco on the Mediterranean). Others were part of this confederation, but their names are not listed here.

Jabin put his infantry and chariotry into formation and waited for Israel near the waters of Merom. But Joshua lit into these troops and overwhelmed them as they fled north some forty miles up to Sidon, to Misrephoth Maim (*Khirbet el-Musheirefeh*) on the seacoast between Mount Carmel and Tyre and to the Valley of Mizpah, just south of Mt. Hermon.

Joshua then took Hazor itself. In a major exception to his policy, he set the city on fire and leveled it to the ground. Joshua 11:12–13 specifically says that Joshua took all the cities tied together with Hazor, but he "did not burn any of the cities built on their mounds—except Hazor."

In the initial publications of the excavations at Hazor, its excavator, Yigael Yadin, specifically argued that Hazor underwent one of its several conflagrations about 1400 B.C., precisely the date suggested by the chronology advocated in this history.[35] Later, however, Yadin revised that date down by 150 years, thus allowing for a thirteenth-century

34. Note how strategic Gilgal was as a base of operations in Abraham Malamat, "How Inferior Israelite Forces Conquered Fortified Canaanite Cities," *BAR* 8 (1982): 31.

35. Yigael Yadin, "Further Light on Biblical Hazor," *BA* 20 (1957): 44; idem., "The Third Season of Excavating at Hazor, 1957," *BA* 21 (1958): 30–47.

date that was more acceptable to scholars. John Bimson of the University of Toronto, however, has carefully gone over all this evidence and has concluded that Yadin had no good reason for readjusting his original date from 1400 B.C.[36] Thus, Hazor is one of the better-attested archaeological sites for the Israelite destruction of Canaan.

The summary of all three phases of the Conquest is given in Joshua 11:16–20. Joshua took all the land, then, from Mount Halk (Jebel Halaq), far south in the Negev, to Baal Gad in the Bekaa Valley west of Mt. Hermon. Except for Jericho, Ai, and Hazor, not a word is said about destroying any other cities.

36. John Bimson, *Redating*, pp. 185–200.

11

The Occupation of Canaan

Our only source of information about the settlement of the land is the Book of Joshua. It was necessary to begin the occupation of the land as soon as possible, while the pyschological and strategic advantages were still with the victorious troops. The process of allotting the conquered land was, admittedly, quite complex and, at times, appeared to be contradictory. Joshua, however, cast lots and supervised the initial stages of the settlement of Canaan while the people were still encamped at Gilgal. Since the decision was to be determined by lot, as had been indicated while the people were still on the east side of the Jordan, the decision was to be left in the hands of God, not the wishes or the strategies of mortals (Num. 26:55–56; 33:54).

The Allotments East of the Jordan

Prior to Israel's crossing over the Jordan, Moses had supervised the allotting of the Transjordanian lands to the tribes of Reuben, Gad, and the half tribe of Manasseh (Num. 32:1–42; Deut. 3:13–17; Josh. 13:8–33). The tribes of Reuben and Gad had seen that the lands of Jazer and Gilead were ideal for raising stock. Thus they asked Moses for permission to settle in Transjordania with the understanding that they would take part with the other tribes in the Conquest of Canaan (Num. 32:1–22).

The Transjordanian territories occupied by the two and a half tribes extended from the Arnon River (which emptied into the Dead Sea almost at the midpoint on its east side) north to Mt. Hermon, though it is unknown just how much of this territory was actually occupied beyond the Yarmuk River (which flowed into the Jordan River just south of the south end of the Sea of Galilee). It is known that the states of Geshur and Maacah took up much of the territory north of the Yarmuk. Further, there is the express statement of Joshua 13:13 that neither Geshur nor Maacah came under the control of Manasseh.

Reuben was assigned the southern section, Gad the middle, and the half tribe of Manasseh had the eastern and northern-most parcels. The southern edge of Reuben was the Arnon River, while Reuben's northern border was just as distinctive: it was on a line running east about fifteen miles north of the Dead Sea, somewhere south of the city of Jazer.[1] The division between Gad and the half tribe of Manasseh is not as clear, however. Gad was given everything north of Jazer along the Jordan to the Sea of Galilee. His eastern border ran a few miles west of the Ammonite city of Rabbah and then on a northwesterly course to Mahanaim on the Jabbok River, and from there on up the Jordan Valley to the Sea of Galilee.

The territory of Manasseh[2] lay between the land of Ammon to the east and Gad to the west. The farthest south it got was Mahanaim, and it extended north well beyond the Yarmuk.

The allocations for the Transjordanian territories described in Joshua 13 appear to be at variance with those in Numbers 32. But it is not necessary to suppose that the two chapters contradict each other, as many have suggested; instead, it is only necessary to conclude that Joshua made some changes in the original distribution that Moses had made. Moses' distribution had left the possibility for Reuben and Gad to engage in hostile action toward each another over territory; thus, Joshua seems to reassign portions of it so as to avoid this potential.

The Allotments to Judah, Ephraim, and Manasseh

Joshua and Eleazar the priest began the distribution of territory in the conquered land of Canaan for the remaining nine and a half tribes. First in line was Judah, with their eighty-five-year-old Caleb reminding Joshua that Moses had promised him the Hebron region (Deut. 1:36);

1. Roland de Vaux, *The Early History of Israel*, pp. 576–81, thinks that Joshua 13:15–28 gives "a different geographical description" (p. 577) from that of Numbers 32. But it turns out that it is, as he himself says, only "more logical in [the Joshua] account."

2. According to de Vaux (*The Early History of Israel*, p. 584, n. 87), the only important study of the half tribe of Manasseh is A. Bergman, "The Israelite Tribe of Half Manasseh," *JPOS* 16 (1936): 224–256.

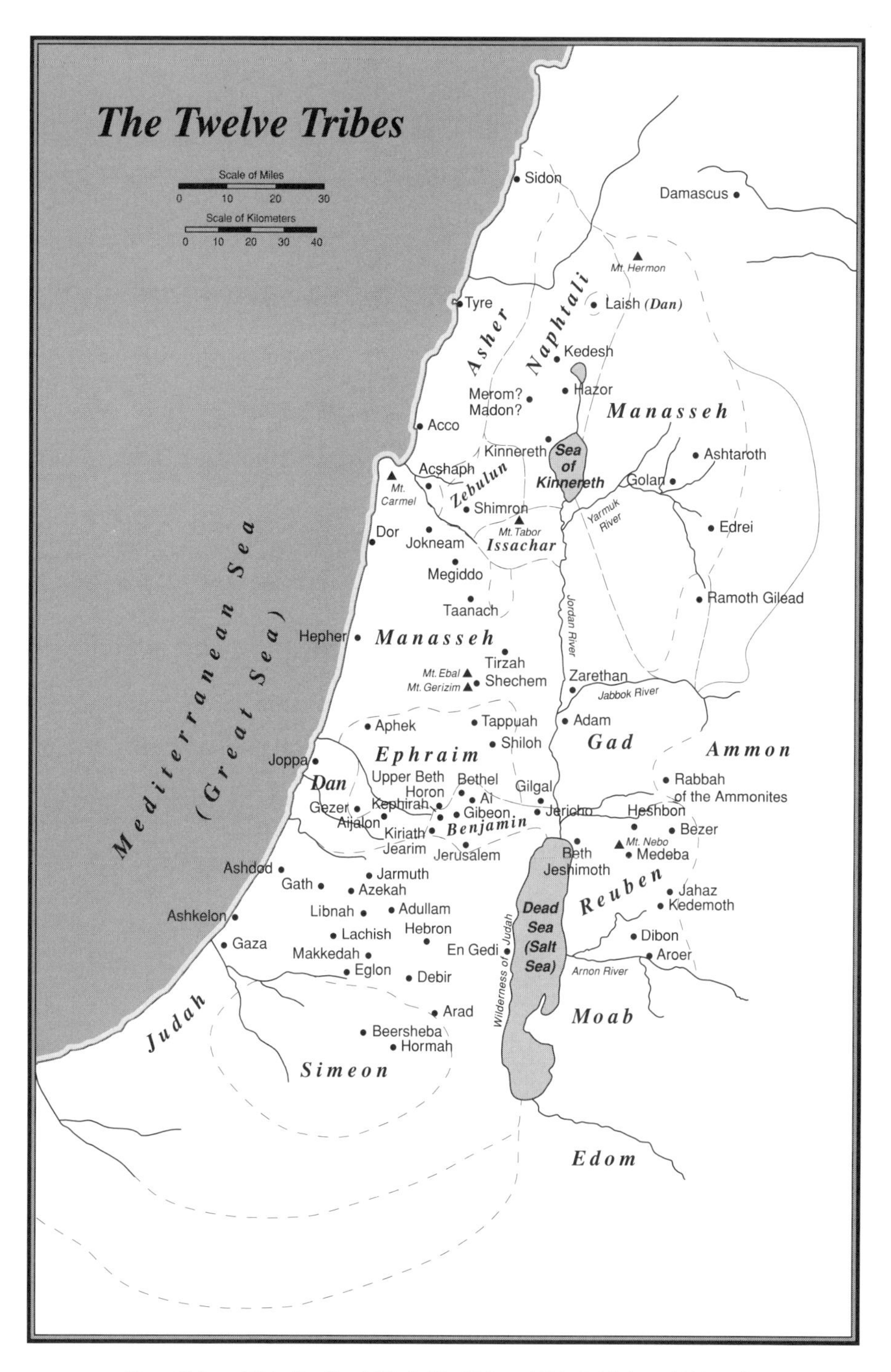

From *Holman Bible Handbook* (Nashville: Holman Bible Publishers, 1992), 169.

there the giant Anakim had previously frightened the other spies who went up to spy out the land in former days (Josh. 14:6–15). Even though Joshua's southern campaign had broken the strength of the Anakim, apparently some still remained to be conquered. Caleb wanted to complete this work and receive this area as he had been promised forty-five years previously when he was only forty years old. Therefore, if the scouting party had gone out in the second year after the Exodus (1445 B.C.), Caleb's request must have come to Joshua in 1400 B.C., or just seven years after the Conquest had begun in 1447 B.C. Caleb was given Hebron and the other cities of the Anakim. It would appear that the Conquest of Hebron came at this point around 1400 B.C. (Josh. 11:21–22; 15:13–19; Judg. 1:9–15).

After dislodging the Anakim from Hebron, Caleb offered his daughter as a bride to anyone who would take Debir, fifteen miles southwest of Hebron. Caleb's nephew Othniel accepted the challenge, later settling in Debir as well as becoming Israel's first judge.

The rest of the territory deeded to Judah was the vast area bounded by the Dead Sea on its eastern border and the Mediterranean Sea on its west. Its southern border ran from the south end of the Dead Sea in a southwesterly direction to Kadesh Barnea and then northwest to the mouth of the Wadi el-Arish. The northern border of Judah ran rather irregularly from the northern tip of the Dead Sea westward through Beth Hoglah to the waters of En Shemesh and En Rogel, at the juncture of the Kidron and Hinnom Valleys at Jerusalem; this implies that Jerusalem itself lay outside of and north of Judah. From just south of Jerusalem, it continued west to Kiriath Jearim and Beth Shemesh, finally arriving at the Mediterranean just north of Ekron, near Jabneel. Judah's land area included a long list of cities, including those actually taken in the Conquest and many others that were to be hers only by promise (Josh. 15:20–63).

The next lot was given to Ephraim (Josh. 16:1–10). Judah and Ephraim were the two most influential tribes and continued to be until the Exile. Ephraim, Joseph's son, was given prominence over his brother Manasseh when their grandfather Jacob blessed them (Gen. 48:1–22); Joshua was from the tribe of Ephraim, and Ephraim was given a smaller portion than Judah received; it was just north of Judah's inheritance, with room left for Benjamin between them.

Beginning eight miles due north of Jerusalem, at Ataroth Addar, Ephraim's southern border ran due west to Upper Beth Horon and then, apparently, in a southwesterly direction to join the border of

Judah somewhere near Shikkeron. The northern border began at Micmethah, some five miles south of Shechem. From there it went east to Taanath Shiloh, Janoah, then south to Jericho and east to the Jordan. The rest of the northern border went west from Micmethah to Tappuah to the Wadi Kanah and down its valley to the Mediterranean, coming to the sea at modern Tel Aviv.

The third lot that did not occupy Transjordania was given to the half tribe of Manasseh (Josh. 17:1–11). This portion bordered Ephraim on the north and all the way up to the Jezreel Valley and stretched like Judah and Ephraim from the Jordan to the Mediterranean Sea. A number of the cities given to Manasseh could not be possessed by this tribe; they were only gradually subdued as they put the Canaanites to slave labor. When both Ephraim and Manasseh complained to Joshua that he should give them more land due to the heavy Canaanite elements in the valleys and plains, Joshua answered that they should drive out the Canaanites who already lived in the wooded hills, thus making these two tribes strong enough to remove the Canaanites from places like Jezreel as well.

An Interruption in the Allotment of the Land

Despite the fact that there were seven more tribes that needed to have their portions allocated, that task was interrupted as Israel undertook the task of moving camp from Gilgal, which had been the base of operations all through the Conquest years (perhaps some seven or more years), to Shiloh, where they erected the tabernacle in the place it was to stay for many years (Josh. 18:1). Shiloh had just been allotted to Ephraim; thus it was now possible for the people to give a permanent place to the tabernacle in a central spot in the land.

The reason for moving so suddenly on this project of locating the tabernacle might be that the tribes were losing interest in receiving their portions after Ephraim and Manasseh's complaints about their territory being too wooded and too infested with remaining Canaanites. This brought Joshua's stern reply that it was up to them to finish the job of driving out the remaining undesirable elements. This change in activity would give the tribes an opportunity to reflect and to sense a new unity with the presence of God located in the center of the land—even in Ephraim, one of the complaining tribes.

THE SEVEN REMAINING ALLOTMENTS

After that task was completed, with all the people now at Shiloh, Joshua immediately gave orders for completing the allotment procedures (18:2–9). Three representatives from each of the remaining seven tribes were to form survey teams to reconnoiter the land left to be assigned. From the descriptions of the locations of the woods, the types of soil, and the density of the Canaanite population, the allotments were to be determined and then used as the basis for making the proper divisions of the land. The decision as to which portion was to be assigned to each tribe was still left to be revealed by lot. Thus, the allotting began once more.

The first tribe to receive its territory in this new allocation of sections of Canaan was Benjamin (Josh. 18:11–28). The small area between Judah and Ephraim, with the significant cities of Jericho, Bethel, Gibeah, Gibeon, and Jerusalem, were all part of her inheritance designated by lot for Benjamin. Whereas Judah and Ephraim's territories extended all the way to the Mediterranean Sea, Benjamin's allotment only went halfway to the sea.

The next assignment was made to the tribe of Simeon, which by now had suffered an enormous drop in its census count. In his case, no specific land area was mentioned, but only cities within the territory of Judah were indicated (Josh. 19:1–9). Seventeen cities (if Beersheba and Sheba in v. 2 are the same city) were mentioned, including Beersheba, Hormah, and Ziklag, with the small centers surrounding most of these cities. Several reasons could be mentioned as to why Simeon was given territory within the confines originally marked out for Judah. First of all, Judah had been given more land than it needed (Josh. 19:9). Also, as already indicated, Simeon's population had dropped to only 22,000 men by the time of the second census (Num. 26:14). And finally, Simeon had received from Jacob a prediction that it, like Levi, would be scattered in Israel as a consequence of the violent act the two brothers enacted against Shechem in the matter of the rape of their sister Dinah (Gen. 34:1–31).

Zebulun was third in line in the new distribution of land. Zebulun's southern border ran westward from a point not more than ten miles northeast of Meggido at Sarid and across the Jezreel Plain to Jokneam, and eastward from the same point to Japhia. From Japhia the border went north to Gath Hepher and Rimmon. A little north of Rimmon the boundary turned west through the Valley of Iphtah. Both this assignment and that of Issachar were relatively small, approximating the size of Benjamin.

The fourth tribe was Issachar, and it also received territory in the region of Galilee. On the west, the border went from Jezreel north through Shunem to Kesulloth. The southern border ran east from Jezreel to Remeth, some three miles from the Jordan and eight miles north of Beth Shean. From Remeth it went north along the Jordan, forming its eastern boundary, and then west to Mt. Tabor for the northern frontier. Issachar had some of the most fertile and level land of the Esdraelon Valley, but the Canaanites held most of the land, for neither Issachar nor Zebulun succeeded very well in completing the task of expelling the original inhabitants from the land.

Asher got the fifth allotment at Shiloh (Josh. 19:24–31): a section along the Mediterranean coast, a larger section than the two previous ones or the one given to Benjamin. Its border on the south touched Mt. Carmel and Shihor Libnah (Wadi Zerqa). It then went northeast along the border of Zebulon and the Iphtah El Valley. It went all the way north to Beth Emek, going through Neiel and Cabul and on north to Ebron, Kanah, and Hosah on the Mediterranean about four miles south of Tyre. Then the border followed the Mediterranean south to Ahzib and Acshaph and further south to Helkath on the Kishon River.

Asher's border descriptions present us with several problems. The most difficult was the tribe's loss of Mt. Carmel and the Mediterranean coast from Helkath to Acshaph and perhaps to Aczib. It would appear that the Canaanite population controlled this whole area. The other major problem is the location of Dor within Asher's territory when it seems it had been assigned to Manasseh. Some conclude that Manasseh, for reasons we do not know, actually possessed towns like Dor within the borders of Asher (Josh.17:11).

Naphtali was given the sixth allocation. Although all of her borders are not described in as much detail as were those of most of the other tribes, the southern border moved through Heleph east to Jabneel over to the Jordan. From Heleph the border went north, passing through Hukkok opposite the northwest corner of the Sea of Galilee. It would appear that this northern boundary continued up to Tyre on the west and as far east as the Jordan, for the list of fortified cities included En Hazor, Kedesh, and Hazor, all cities that were located north of Galilee.

Finally Dan was assigned a site west of Benjamin between Judah and Ephraim, just as Benjamin was located in the eastern part of this same small section. Dan also was unable to occupy this territory in the Shephelah and on the coastal plains; therefore, part of the tribe immigrated north to the small site of Leshem (Laish) north of Lake Huleh. Judges 18 indicates that originally only six hundred men went to Laish to seize the land. While others may have followed later, note that Samson's family, who were Danites, still lived in the territory originally allotted to them (Judg. 13:2).

The final allotment of the land (Josh. 19:49–50) was made to Joshua himself, just as the first on this side of Jordan had been made to that other spy who brought back a positive report: Caleb. The city Joshua requested and received was Timnath Serah in the hill country of Ephraim.

The Cities of Refuge

Moses had already designated three cities east of the Jordan as cities of refuge and three on the west side of Jordan (Num. 35:6–34; Deut. 4:41; 19:2). These sites were to provide a sanctuary for persons guilty of homicide until their guilt was established in a cooler and more relaxed atmosphere. Those guilty of murder would be executed, but where the death was accidental and unpremeditated, then the perpetrator could be safe within the confines of this city. The only disadvantage was that one guilty of the accidental death of another person had to remain in the city of refuge until the death of the high priest in office at the time of the deed.

The cities of refuge in Tranjordania were these: Bezer in Reuben, five miles east of Heshbon; Ramoth in Gad; and Golan in the half tribe of Manasseh in Transjordania, some twenty miles east of the Sea of Galilee. The cities of refuge on the west side of the Jordan were these: Hebron in Judah, Shechem in Ephraim, and Kedesh in Naphtali, about five miles from Lake Huleh. In no case would any citizen in Israel be so far from a place of refuge that he or she could not make it to this site in a short journey, hopefully before the relative of the one smitten attempted to bring blood revenge on the head of the guilty person.

The Levitical Cities

These six cities of refuge together with forty-two other cities were assigned to the Levites (Num. 35:1–8). The Levites were not assigned an allotment in the distribution of the land, for their tribe was given to the Lord in place of all the firstborn of Israel (Num. 3:41). Instead, these towns were to be their homes along with the outlying pasturelands.

It is unclear exactly what the Levites did in these towns, but they were to take their turns ministering at the central sanctuary on a set pattern. They were not, however, supposed to engage in any secular employment. But they could raise their own crops and raise a limited amount of livestock for their own domestic use.

The Merarite clan of Levites was settled in twelve cities in Reuben, Gad, and Zebulun. Those of the Gershonite clan of Levi were allotted thirteen cities in Issachar, Asher, Naphtali, and eastern Manasseh. The Kohathite segment of the Levites (i.e., all who were descended from the high priest Aaron), was assigned to thirteen cities in Judah, Benjamin, Ephraim, Dan, and western Manasseh. The Kohathites were the priests, therefore, and they had to be within close proximity to the capital and the future center of worship in this location. It is interesting to note that Hebron and Debir were two cities that were assigned to the Kohathites, but these were the ones that had been given to Caleb, from the tribe of Judah. Thus, what must have been intended was that Caleb got the general environs of these towns while the cities proper were inhabited by the priests. The priests also occupied Gibeon, which must mean that the Hivites were dispossessed after they had made the treaty with Joshua.

The Civil War That Almost Broke Out

Israel narrowly averted going to war with the two and a half tribes of Transjordania when the men of Reuben, Gad, and the half tribe of Manasseh returned home at the end of the Conquest. As these two and a half tribes had promised, they stayed in the main camp on the west side of the Jordan until the War of Conquest was over and the land had been allocated (Num. 32:16–32). Having done their duty, they could return.

On their way back home, they erected a memorial altar at the Jordan River. When the other tribes found out about this strange sight, they thought the altar had been erected as a place of worship and sacrifice, thereby substituting for the altar at Shiloh. This they were not going to stand for, so they prepared to punish the two and a half apparently renegade tribes.

Before declaring all-out war against Reuben, Gad, and the half tribe of Manasseh, the western tribes sent Phinehas, son of Eleazar the high priest, and ten other men to allow the offenders to offer some explanation for what they had done. The Transjordanian tribes denied, of course, that the altar had been erected with any intention of making it a substitute place of sacrifice. Rather, they had wanted it only to be a witness that they were part of the people who lived on the west side of the Jordan. The eastern tribes explained that they did not want anyone to think that they were not a part of Israel or any less a part of the nation to which God had given the land of Canaan. Phinehas and his delegation were satisfied with these answers, and they returned in time to relieve any troubled minds and to avert any precipitous military actions.

The Renewal of the Covenant at Shechem

As his final days on earth drew near, Joshua assembled the leaders of the tribes at Shechem to admonish them to be faithful to the covenant. He had led them in another ceremony of covenant reaffirmation some thirty years previously when they had entered the land (Joshua 8:30–35), just as Moses had commanded Joshua to do (Deut. 27:1–8). Now Israel would reaffirm it, for a new generation had come along and they also needed to be aware of all that God had done and required.

Joshua began by rehearsing all the works God had done on Israel's behalf (Josh. 23). Then they renewed the covenant (Josh. 24). A review of the historical relations between God and Israel formed the beginning of this process (24:2–13). Then, they were urged to reject all rival deities and to serve Yahweh alone (vv. 14–15). To this the people agreed (vv. 16–18), as Joshua continued to remind the people of all the judgments and curses that would follow if they disobeyed their pledge (vv. 19–20). Again, the people vowed to serve Yahweh alone and to reject all other gods (vv. 21–24). Finally, the ceremony concluded with the erection of a commemorative stele that would serve in the future as a reminder of the promises they had made that day (vv. 25–28). This ceremony also occurred at Shechem, the place where Abraham had been called into covenant by Yahweh many years before.

Joshua died not long after this ceremony and was buried in his city of Timnath Serah. In another act that seemed to emphasize the wrapping up of a segment of history, the writer of Joshua notes that the bones of Joseph, now preserved for some four centuries, were also buried at Shechem. It was almost from this same point (Dothan) that Joseph had left many years before as a slave bound for Egypt, but now he had made the round trip, even if somewhat belatedly, and the promises to him and to Israel had indeed come a long way. Eleazar also died, and he was buried in Ephraim. Truly, this was the close of one era and the beginning of another!

Part IV

The Period of the Judges

12

THE TWELVE-TRIBE SYSTEM

Now that the settlement of the land was accomplished, the common life of Israel in the land began in what is known as the period of the judges. But for some this posed a problem: How was this grouping of the nation formed? What bonds held the tribes together? How was their unity maintained?

THE THEORY OF AN ISRAELITE AMPHICTYONY

Beginning with Heinrich Ewald in 1864, it has been customary in some scholarly circles to gather all the references found to twelve tribes, cities, or peoples in the Bible or in Greek, Latin, or Semitic literatures to explain how such a similar group might have existed in Israel.[1] By 1923 Max Weber had described Israel as being in a cultic league that may have had "amphictyonic" rites.[2] After this first use of the term *amphictyony* in 1923, Albrecht Alt would use the term in 1929 in a similar context, talking about an "amphictyony of Mamre."[3] But

1. H. Ewald, *Geschichte des Volkes Israel*, I (Gottingen, 1864), 519 ff., as cited by R. de Vaux, *Early History of Israel*, p. 695, n. 1.
2. M. Weber, *Gesammelte Aufsätze zur Religionssoziologie*, III *Das antike Judentum* (Tübingen, 1923), 90 ff. and 98, as cited by R. de Vaux, ibid., n. 2
3. A. Alt, *Der Gott der Väter* (Stuttgart, 1929), p. 59. R. de Vaux, ibid., pp. 695–96, notes that after M. Noth published his book *Das System der zwölf Stämme Israels* (Stuttgart, 1930), Alt described the twelve tribes as a sacred league formed in the manner of the amphictyonies of Greece and Italy.

it was Martin Noth who gave this theory of the amphictyony its definitive form.

The Greek and Italian leagues and amphictyonies provided the analogies to explain why it was that the number of tribes, though often differing as to the precise names, was always kept at twelve. Moreover, they were always grouped around a central sanctuary, often gathering for religious purposes. For Noth, it was at Shechem where Israel was united in a pact of the covenant and where they acknowledged Yahweh to be their God. Noth's views influenced Old Testament studies, and his formulation of the theory on amphictyony became its classical definition and description. Today, however, there are serious objections to this theory.[4]

Roland de Vaux's conclusion on this whole matter was this: "The use of the word 'amphictyony' in connection with Israel can only cause confusion and give a wrong impression of the mutual relationships between the different tribes. It should be abandoned."[5] De Vaux argued that the two environments of the Greek and Israelite groups were so different that any similarities were most unlikely. Moreover, there never was anything remotely resembling a Greek amphictyony in the Semitic world, despite some scholars' failed attempts to speak of a Sumerian amphictyony. And while Noth at first placed a great deal of emphasis on the occurrence of the number "twelve," both he and his followers placed less and less importance on this number later on. The concept of an Israelite amphictyony eventually was dropped while the number *twelve* was retained as the number of the twelve sons of Jacob and two sons of Jacob with the Levites generally not being included (though there were different ways of calculating who was in the twelve).

The Connection between Joshua and Judges 1:1–2:9

To the casual reader, Judges 1:1–2:9 may appear either a contradiction or a conflation of some of the same material that appears in the Book of Joshua. For example, the death of Joshua is recorded three times: Joshua 24:29; Judges 1:1 and 2; 8. Why? Critical scholars, of course, use the ever-ready explanation that it was simply due to oppos-

4. Harry M. Orlinsky, "The Tribal System of Israel and Related Groups in the Period of the Judges," in *Oriens Antiquus* I (1962): 11–20 and G. W. Anderson, "Israel: Amphictyony: ʿAM; KAHAL; ʿEDAH," *Translating and Understanding the Old Testament: Essays in Honor of Herbert G. May* (Nashville: Abingdon, 1970): 135–151.

5. R. de Vaux, *The Early History of Israel*, p. 715.

ing source traditions which sloppy copyists failed to level out in their editorial redaction. But that would involve a most naive redactor, for the references are so close to each other (at least within the one collection of the Book of Judges) that it stretches the imagination to understand how any could have missed it.

A better attempt to understand the threefold reference to the death of Joshua in such short compass—and the different types of conquest found in the beginning of the Judges narrative from that described in Joshua—is that Judges 1:1 to 2:9 forms a literary transition from the Joshua story to the period of the judges. Apparently what the writer of Judges wished to avoid was beginning the book with the dreary record of the apostasy that took place in the times of the judges. But in order to show that the Conquest continued in the mopping-up exercises, to which Joshua had called all the tribes after the War of Conquest had ended and after the allotments of land had been made, the author began with the campaign by Judah and Simeon in the southern hill country against the Canaanites. Initially, Joshua had driven out the Amorites in this section. But there were the Canaanites, such as the king of Bezek, named Adoni Bezek, who ruled some three miles northeast of Gezer.

Adoni Bezek was taken prisoner to Jerusalem. Jerusalem? When did Israel take that city, since Jerusalem only came into Israel's hands in the early days of David's reign? Actually, Jerusalem had been taken by the men of Judah (and not all the tribes under Joshua) and set on fire. But as with most of these matters in times of war, the fortunes of war go back and forth, and so does the possession of towns and cities. Thus, the Jebusites must have regained control of Jerusalem once again; therefore, neither Judah (Josh. 15:63) nor Benjamin (Judg. 1:21) could finally shake them out of that strong position until the time of King David.

At this point in the record of the opening section of Judges, a flashback takes us back to Joshua's day and his allocating of Hebron and Debir to Caleb (1:9–15). But in verse 16 the author returns to the story begun in verses 1–7 with his interest in Judah and Simeon. After noting how the Kenites took up residence within the tribe of Judah, the writer showed how the Judahites and Simeonites captured Zephath, called Hormah during Israel's wilderness wanderings, and all the southern hill country, notably Hebron, and three of the Philistine cities in the Shephelah.

But more was going on than the mopping-up exercises of Judah and Simeon. The Joseph tribes were conquering Bethel as well (Judg. 1:22–26) through a bribery strategy. Since Joshua made no such mention of a capture of Bethel, again, this must be part of a later action.

Likewise, western Manasseh, Zebulun, Asher, Naphtali, and Dan made attempts to clear out more of their inheritances, but they were unsuccessful (Judg. 1:27–36). Almost as if in response to this increased frustration in their inability suddenly to expel the remaining elements in the land, the angel of Yahweh appeared to Israel in Bokim and rebuked the people for their failure to complete the task given to them. This, then, set the stage for what was to follow, for once again the death of Joshua is noted, functioning almost as one would draw a line underneath a particular stratum or segment of history to say thereby that it had now ended.

The Chronology of the Times of the Judges

If all the years mentioned in the Book of Judges (including the periods of oppression, rest, and deliverance by the judges) are calculated in a sequence, they total 410 years. But that number is already too high if we accept the time frame set in 1 Kings 6:1, where in Solomon's fourth year it was declared that 480 years had elapsed from the Exodus until that year of his reign. Added to the alleged 410 years of the judges are the following periods: 40 years of wilderness wanderings; possibly 15 years for Joshua's leadership during the Conquest and settlement, approximately another 30 years for the elders, 40 years for Saul's reign; 40 years for David's reign and the 4 years of Solomon to the point where this time summary was made: a total of another 169 years, making a grand total of 569 years. But there can only be 480![6] What is wrong here?

If the date that the Conquest began is set at 1407 B.C., forty years after the Exodus in 1447 B.C., then it ended about seven years later about 1400 B.C. (as determined from the testimony of Caleb, who said he was forty at the time he spied out the land, some two years after the Exodus, but eighty-five at the time of the completion of the Conquest, Josh. 14:7–10). The date of approximately 1400 B.C. would mark the beginning of this period.

6. For a survey of some of the solutions to this problem, see J. H. Peet, "The Chronology of the Judges—Some Thoughts," *Journal of Christian Reconstruction* 9 (1982–1983): 161–81 and Eugene H. Merrill, "Paul's Use of 'About 450 Years' in Acts 13:20," *Bib Sac* 138 (1981): 246–57.

The end of the period of the judges can also be set with some degree of accuracy. Starting from the 1407 B.C. date for the beginning of the Conquest, Judges 11:26 noted that Israel had occupied this portion of Transjordania for the three hundred years since the initial phase of the Conquest began. At that time Israel had defeated Sihon and Og in Transjordania. Why had Ammon not pressed its claim during that whole period if they thought they were the rightful heirs? Moreover, the territory had been won from the Amorites, not the Ammonites. Add to this 1407 the three hundred intervening years that had expired before the claim was pressed, and the three hundred total that had been given, yields a date of 1107 B.C.

If the Ammonite oppression ended in the same year that the judge Jephtah defeated Ammon in 1107 B.C., then it can also be observed that Judges 10:7–8 noted that the Ammonite oppression on the eastern side of the Jordan, that had begun eighteen years before the 1107 defeat of Ammon (i.e., in 1125 B.C.), coincided with the commencement of the Philistine oppression on the west side of the Jordan. After the historian of the judges has traced the course of events in the eastern side of the Jordan (Judg. 10:8b–12:7), he turned to the Philistine oppression and continued by carrying this line of the story so that we are able to match it up with the onset of the times of the monarchy.

The Philistines were a thorn in the sides of the Israelites for forty years (Judg. 13:1), i.e., from 1125 until 1085 B.C. During that time Samson was born, and he judged Israel for twenty years (Judg. 15:20), but he never was able to deliver the Israelites from the hand of the Philistines.

The final blow against the Philistines came in the "judgeship" of Samuel. Some twenty years after the ark of God had been taken in the battle of Aphek, in which Eli's sons Hophni and Phinehas died, and in which Eli himself broke his neck as he fell off his chair on hearing that the ark of God had been taken, Israel rallied to defeat the Philistines at Mizpah (1 Sam. 7:11, 13).

The next date that can be established with some certainty is the accession of Saul to the throne in 1051 B.C., for Saul, David, and Solomon each ruled for forty years prior to the division of the kingdom in 931 B.C. That would leave thirty-four years for Samuel to be judge and leader of Israel from 1085 to 1051 B.C.

The Years of the Oppressors, Judges, and Periods of Rest

Chronology of the Judges of Israel

Oppressor/No. Years	Judge	Deliverance and Rest	References	Total
98 years	Othniel	40 years	Judg. 3:8–11	48 years
Moab/18	Ehud	80 years	Judg. 3:14–30	98 years
	Shamgar	[Overlapping?]	Judg. 3:31	[?]
Canaanite/20	Deborah/Barak	40 years	Judg. 4:3–5:31	60 years
Midianite/7	Gideon	40 years	Judg. 6:1–8:28	47 years
	Abimelech	3 years	Judg. 9:22	3 years
	Tola	23 years	Judg. 10:1–2	23 years
	Jair	22 years	Judg. 10:3	22 years
Ammonite/18	Jephthah	6 years	Judg. 12:7	24 years
	Ibzan	7 years	Judg. 12:8–9	7 years
	Elon	10 years	Judg. 12:11	10 years
	Abdon	8 years	Judg 12:13–14	8 years
Philistine/40	Samson	[20 years]	Judg. 13:1–15:20	20 years
	Samuel	[34 years]	?	[34 years]
Total				409 years

Clearly some overlap occurs in the chronologies of the judges. The most important overlap is between the Ammonite and Philistine oppressions which took place simultaneously on both sides of the Jordan (Judg. 10:7–8). It would appear that following the Ammonite oppression are the names of the judges Ibzan, Elon, and Abdon. Likewise, Judges 3:31–4:1 implies that Shamgar judged during the eighty years of peace that followed Ehud's deliverance from the Moabites. Other lesser judges must also have "judged" simultaneously with some of the better-known judges, for their sphere of activity was severely limited. Accordingly, Tola judged in Issachar (Judg. 10:1–2), and Jair judged across the Jordan in Gilead (Judg. 10:3–5). Thus, the total number of years is not excessive for the time period into which these events must fit when one takes into account these explicitly stated overlaps and the fact that a number of the minor judges were operating simultaneously with other judges, but in very selected and restricted geographical areas.[7]

The Meaning of "Judge"

The Hebrew root of *špṭ* had a much wider meaning than the idea of simply "administering justice to," or "to pass sentence," "settle a case," "do justice," and "mete out justice."[8] Based on the usages of this same root in Ugaritic, Phoenician, and texts at Mari, the basic meaning could now successfully be established as meaning "to rule," or "to command." Especially significant was the Ugaritic cognate root *tpṭ*, with its meanings of "to do justice" and "to rule." The Ugaritic participle-noun had the meaning of "leader" or "ruler." But the Phoenician and Punic texts were no less significant. At Carthage, for example, the "suffetes," *špṭm*, were known as those who ruled. [9]

The word *špṭ* occurs outside the Book of Judges in the Bible with the meaning of "to rule," particularly in the Psalms. Thus, in Psalms 2:10 the *šōphēṭ* is parallel to the king, and in Psalm 148:11 the same designation appears alongside the king and the prince. In the kingship psalms of Psalm 96:13 and 98:9, the verb *špṭ* clearly means to rule rather than to judge.

Another clear example from the period of the judges is to be found in the description of the institution of the monarchy. There, in 1 Sam-

---

7. Some conservatives are more comfortable with the fact that there never was any intention of producing a complete chronology of the period. For example, Gleason L. Archer Jr. argued in *A Survey of Old Testament Introduction* (Chicago: Moody Press, 1964), 276–77, as we have here, that many of the judges' careers overlapped and several of them were contemporaneous. Samuel J. Schultz, *The Old Testament Speaks*, 3rd ed. (New York: Harper and Row, 1980), 104, argued that the writers had no intention of producing a complete chronology.

8. R. de Vaux, *The Early History of Israel*, pp. 766, shows how O. Grether attempted to limit the meaning of this term to this set of definitions in his article "Die Bezeichnung 'Richter' für die charismatischen Helden der vorstaatlichen Zeit," ZAW 57 (1939): 110–121. Even though A. Alt, M Noth, and J. Van der Ploeg accepted his conclusions, de Vaux argued that Grether's conclusions had to be reevaluated.

9. R. de Vaux, ibid., pp. 767–773.

uel 8:5, the people demand: "Appoint a king to lead [better: 'to rule over;' Hebrew *špṭ* us, such as all the other nations have." The same concept is found in verses 6 and 20. In fact, the difference between a judge and a king can be seen in the story of Gideon, who was invited to be the "master" (Hebrew: *māšal*) over the "men of Israel," but he refused, and his son Abimelech took up the right of kingship over the citizens of Shechem (Judg. 8:7, 22–23; 9:2).

13

The Judges of Israel

In keeping with the biblical practice, the expression *period of the judges* is used to designate the time between the settlement in the land of Canaan and the establishment of the monarchy. This habit of referring to this era is not limited to the Book of Judges, for the Book of Ruth took place "in the days when the judges ruled" (Ruth 1:1). Likewise, 2 Samuel 7:11 referred to a time when Yahweh "appointed leaders over [his] people Israel," just as 2 Kings 23:22 recalled the "days of the judges who led Israel."

Normally, judges were neither self-appointed nor elected leaders; rather, they were appointed by Yahweh, usually to deliver the people from some oppressor (Judg. 2:16–18). These deliverers were arranged in the Book of Judges in a chronological order interspersed by a period of apostasy and oppression. The apostasy usually was rooted in the issue of religious syncretism offered in the Canaanite religion that surrounded the newly arrived peoples from Egypt.

The Canaanite Religion

After the death of Joshua and the elders who had worked with him, it seemed as if Israel was constantly tempted to assimilate some or all of the religious culture that surrounded her. She was particularly vulnerable to the seductive forms of Canaanite religion with its offer of economic fertility and sexual enjoyment.

It has been possible for our generation to reconstruct much of the Canaanite religious ethos from the large number of epic and cultic texts that have been discovered at Ugarit.[1] According to this literature, El was the head of the pantheon of gods, a sort of fatherlike figure, but one who was also verging on senility and often the victim of plots from the younger and more ambitious and aspiring deities. Seated in remote and distant splendor on a mountain in the north, El and his wife, Asherah, the mother goddess, continually tried to maintain order among, and respect from, the younger gods. Asherah is the one by whom the fertility of the earth was maintained; her symbols were the "groves" or wooden poles often mentioned at the altar installations set up in her honor.

The real rising star among the Canaan deities of Ugarit, however, was Baal, the storm god who controlled the rain and dew, as well as the fertility of the land. Baal may well have been an epithet for the god Hadad, son of Dagon. Baal threatened El, as well as a number of other deities, such as Mot (god of death), Yamm (god of the sea), and Nahar (the river god).

According to the epics found in this literature, Yamm, Nahar, Mot, and others relentlessly waged war with Baal, jealously guarding their own spheres of influence. This struggle caused the various cycles of life to succeed one another: sowing, reaping, life, and death. For example, utilizing the dying-and-rising god motif, one of the epics related how Mot, god of death, killed Baal and held him captive in the netherworld, thereby causing the annual onset of the dry season, which lacked fecundity. But when the autumn rains began to revive the parched earth of Canaan, Anat, the goddess of war—Baal's sister and wife—was able to effect this restoration to new life by winning Baal's release from the underworld. The ritual that dramatized this myth centered on sexual activity: the rainfall that refreshed the ground was thought to represent Baal's semen falling to the earth to fertilize the ground with life, just as Baal impregnated Asherah herself.

Asherah, of course, was the wife of El, though she was also confusingly presented as the consort of Baal. Her carved poles were mentioned as standing by the pagan altar installations in Judges 6:25–28

1. See Walter C. Kaiser Jr., "The Ugaritic Pantheon," (Ph.D. dissertation, Brandeis University, 1973). Also Johannes C. de Moor, "The Semitic Pantheon of Ugarit," *UF* 2 (1970): 187–228; Cyrus H. Gordon, "Canaanite Mythology," in *Mythologies of the Ancient World*, ed. Samuel N. Kramer (Garden City, N.Y.: Doubleday, 1961), 183–218; P. D. Miller, "Ugarit and the History of Religions," *JNSL* 9 (1981): 119–28; and Ulf Oldenburg, *The Conflict Between El and Ba`al in Canaanite Religion* (Leiden: E. J. Brill, 1969).

and 1 Kings 15:13. Asherah was another goddess of love, fertility, and war, often linked with Baal in texts such as Judges 2:13; 10:16; 1 Samuel 7:3–4; 12:10.

The appeal of these myths and ritual dramatizations for Israel proved to be almost irresistible. Whether the appeal began as an economic one or some other alleged basis, it had the effect of causing Israel to apostatize repeatedly. Since Baal had no central sanctuary, altars and worship installations could be set up on virtually every hill, thus giving rise to the phenomenon of the "high places" in Israel, where each site was marked usually with a "pole" (*ʾăšērâ*) and a "pillar" (*maṣṣēbâ*). Thus, the Israelies "prostituted themselves to other gods . . . quickly turn[ing] from the way in which their fathers had walked" (Judg. 2:17).

That is how the cycle began, for when Israel turned away from Yahweh, he would hand them over to their enemies. The oppression would grow until it would become almost unbearable, and misery would finally cry out in its desperation to Yahweh. In time, a judge would be raised by Yahweh who would rescue Israel; and a time of peace and prosperity would settle in, only to be ruptured again by the people returning to the cultural ethos of their former way of life and to another oppressor and conqueror (Judg. 2:18–19).

The Mesopotamian Oppression and Othniel

One of the first of a number of apostasies came as the nation turned to serve "the Baals and the Asherahs" (Judg. 3:7–11). As a result, Yahweh had Cushan-Rishathaim of Aram Naharaim (literally: "Aram of the two rivers") invade the land. This Cushan-Rishathaim cannot be identified with any known historical figure from our present records,[2] but the second part of his name is surely a designation given to him by his enemies: Rishathaim = "double wickedness."

The area from which Cushan-Rishathaim came is in the Upper Euphrates, perhaps between the two rivers feeding into the Upper Euphrates called the Balikh and the Habur, where the patriarchs originally stayed on their journey from Ur of the Chaldees in Haran. Rame-

2. R. de Vaux, *The Early History of Israel*, p. 807, noted at least two unsuccessful attempts to identify this king. H. Hansler wanted to equate him with another king from this same region of Mitanni, named Tushratta (*Biblica* 11 (1930): 391–418; 12 (1931): 3–26; 271–296; 395–410), a king who reigned in the fourteenth century. But the name is not philologically related. A. Malamat suggested that Cushan-rishathaim was an Asiatic called Irsu, who seized power in Egypt and remained in power for eight years around the year 1200 B.C., but the chronology is contrary to our argument. Furthermore, the name is a Semitic name, possibly a nickname, meaning "the usurper," or "the self-made man." Said de Vaux, "This Irsu, then, is almost as enigmatic as Cushan-rishathaim" (p. 808).

ses II refers in his annals to a "Kushan-rom" and to a "Nhr(y)n."[3] If this episode is to be placed somewhere around 1350 B.C., there is nothing in the name *Aram Naharaim* to preclude this date since "Naharin" and "Nahrima" appear both in Egyptian and Akkadian texts as early as the fifteenth century B.C.[4]

There is no indication as to how extensive this conquest was or just how many tribes it affected. But since none of the other oppressors affected all the tribes, it is unlikely that this one did either. The duration of the oppression is given, however: it was eight years long (Judg. 3:8–11).

As the people cried out for relief to Yahweh, he sent a deliverer by the name of Othniel. Othniel was the younger brother of the more famous Caleb. But Othniel had also, by this time, distinguished himself by capturing Debir (*Kiriath-sepher*), for which he had been promised his uncle's daughter Achsah as wife if he was successful.[5] That reputation may have played a part in his being called on once again to rid a segment of the land of a foreign element.

It is clear in Othniel's case, as with the other "judges," that the term *judge* did not suggest a juridical function, especially since at the beginning of this time that function fell to the elders. Instead, it signified the office of a military leader and protector. Some have pointed to the Ebla Tablets where judges coexisted with kings and elders.[6] But in Israel, these leaders served as liberators of the oppressed and governors of those whom they freed for the rest of the days that the judge lived. Thus, Othniel drove out the Mesopotamian Arameans and the land had rest until Othniel, son of Kenaz, died somewhere around 1310 B.C.

THE MOABITE OPPRESSION AND EHUD

With the help of the Ammonites and the Amalekites, Eglon, king of Moab, became the second great oppressor as Israel once again did

3. See Merrill F. Unger, *Israel and the Arameans of Damascus* (Grand Rapids: Baker, 1980), 40–41, 134–35. Unger also noted that "Aram," contrary to the denials of many scholars, did exist as a name as early as 2300 B.C. in a text of Naram-Sin, ibid., pp. 161–162.

4. As noted in Abraham Malamat, "The Arameans," in *Peoples of Old Testament Times*, ed. D. J. Wiseman (Oxford: Clarendon, 1973), 140, as cited by Eugene H. Merrill, *Kingdom of Priests*, p. 161, n. 47.

5. R. de Vaux, *Early History of Israel*, p. 807, does not think that this Othniel is the same one mentioned in Joshua 15:16–19; Judges 1:12–15, but he gives no evidence. He also incorrectly argued on p. 808 that "Aram was an error for "Edom," to which "Naharaim" had been added in the text when "Aram" erroneously slipped in for the correct "Edom." But no evidence is given for this "hypothesis" either.

6. Giovanni Pettinato, "Ebla and the Bible—Observations of the New Epigrapher's Analysis," *BAR* 6 (1980): 40.

evil in the eyes of Yahweh (Judg. 3:12–31). Moab, of course, lay just to the east of Judah across the Dead Sea, south of the two-and-a-half Transjordanian tribes of Reuben, Gad, and Manasseh, usually located between the wadis Arnon and Zered, but in other periods Moab extended well north of the Arnon.

The provocative act of hostilities was Moab's attacking Israel and taking possession of the "City of Palms" (Judg. 3:13). This site must be identified with Jericho, for so it was equated in Deuteronomy 34:3 and 2 Chronicles 28:15. This identification is further enforced by references to the enemy's actions affecting the Benjamites, and references to Gilgal and the fords of the Jordan in Judges 3:15, 19, 28. A few have argued for a town south of the Dead Sea called Tamar,[7] which means "palm tree," but that would have involved an expedition against Judah and not against the tribe of Benjamin.

If Jericho, then, is the correct site, as argued here, it must be recognized that Jericho remained in a state of ruin from Joshua's day (Josh. 6) until the time of Ahab (1 Kings 16:34). Furthermore, we have no archaeological evidence that the site was reoccupied until the seventh century B.C., approximately around the time of Ahab.[8] But even if the site remained unoccupied, the oasis and the surrounding area continued to be inhabited. Perhaps that is why the name *City of Palms* was used rather than Jericho: it pointed instead to the oasis.

To alleviate the oppression, Yahweh raised up a Benjamite named Ehud, from the clan of Gera, who devised a daring plan of entering the presence of Eglon, king of Moab, on the pretext of offering tribute. However, after he had presented the tribute to Eglon, an exceedingly heavy and fat man, Ehud requested a private audience with the king, saying he had a secret message for him. Unknown to Eglon, Ehud was, like most Benjamites, left-handed, and he had therefore strapped on his right thigh a foot-and-a-half-long double-edged sword (Judg. 3:16). When the room was cleared, Ehud stabbed the king in his belly and escaped by some unusual exit (the meaning of the Hebrew word is uncertain), leaving the door to the king's chambers locked with his attendants waiting in the hallways and his dagger implanted in the fat king's belly.

The unsolved question is where Ehud brought the tribute to Eglon: Was Eglon in Jericho at the time, as most have supposed? If so, why

7. E. Auerbach, "Ehud," *ZAW* 51(1933): 47–51. On the story of Ehud, also see A. H. Van Zyl, *The Moabites* (Leiden: Brill, 1960): 125–130; and E. G. Kraeling, "Difficulties in the Story of Ehud," *JBL* 54 (1935): 205–210.

8. Kathleen M. Kenyon, *Jericho*, II (London, 1965), 482–489.

does the text not say that was the place of Eglon's residence and the place where Ehud brought the tribute? Moreover, why would the Israelites cut off the Moabites' retreat by occupying the fords of the Jordan (Judg. 3:28)? Unless it was an act of retaliation and an opportunity to easily kill some of the key leaders in the military, thereby reducing Benjamin's exposure should there be any reprisals for their treasonous actions. Ehud, meanwhile, escaped to the hill country of Ephraim. Eighty years of rest ensued—the longest such period in the times of the judges. If our suggested chronology is correct, this is the period that directly coincides with the strong rule of the Nineteenth Dynasty of Egypt, when Egypt once again asserted its prowess and power in Palestine and southern Syria, especially under the reigns of Seti I (1316–1304 B.C.) and Rameses II (1304–1238 B.C.). With such displays of power, small nations and people groups in the area would have been unlikely to stir up the wrath and unwanted attention from Egypt during this period from about 1300 to 1220 B.C.

A third judge in this same period was Shamgar, who delivered Israel from the Philistines. In addition to the almost passing reference to him in Judges 3:31, he is also mentioned in the Song of Deborah, the next judge:

> "In the days of Shamgar son of Anath,
> in the days of Jael, the roads were abandoned;
> travelers took to winding paths" (Judg. 5:6).

Shamgar is called the son of Anat, which could refer to the Canaanite goddess Anath, or as others prefer, to the town of Beth-anath in southern Judah (Josh. 15:59; not a similarly named town in northern Naphtali, Judg.1:33, since he fought the Philistines who lived in the south). Shamgar's victory was a heroic personal feat of strength, for he cut down six hundred Philistines with an oxgoad, the long stick, usually tipped with a bronze point, used to prod oxen that lagged behind in their work. The feat brought deliverance to Israel.

THE CANAANITE OPPRESSION: DEBORAH AND BARAK

This time the problem arose in the north. Jabin, king of Hazor,[9] with his general Sisera of Harosheth (*Tell el `Amr*), a town just eleven miles

9. Many critical theories note the close relationship between Joshua 11 and Judges 4–5. They include: (1) the battle of the waters of Merom (Josh. 11) and the battle of the waters of Megiddo (Judg. 4–5); (2) Jabin, king of Hazor, was the main adversary in both cases. The fact that both involve waters should be nothing more than a coincidence. But that both kings are called Jabin is more serious. The fact that both kings could have the same name is usually rejected flat out without any comment (e.g., R. de Vaux, *The Early History of Israel*, p. 657, says "[it] is not worthy of serious consideration"). But the Phoenicican kings were known to alternate every other generation with the same name. It also has not been proven as yet that the so-called name of Jabin may not instead be a title, much as *pharaoh* is in Egypt or Abimelech may well be among the Philistines.

northwest of Megiddo on the Kishon River, held the northern tribes under oppression for twenty long years because of his superior military advantage of nine hundred iron chariots, not to mention Israel's dabbling in evil once again (Judg. 4:3).

The deliverer, this time, was a woman named Deborah from Ephraim. Before her victory over the Canaanites, she was a sitting judge and a prophetess, wife of Lappidoth (Judg. 4:4–5), holding forth under a palm tree between Ramath and Bethel. But the call of Yahweh was to take her some sixty miles north to battle with Sisera, in and around the Jezreel Valley.

At first she urged Barak of Kedesh in Naphtali, a site not more than ten miles north of Hazor, to lead the troops in battle against Jabin, but Barak steadfastly refused. Barak would go into battle only on the condition that Deborah would also go with him. With that agreement, they gathered an army of ten thousand men from Zebulun and Naphtali, presumably the two tribes most affected by the Canaanite oppression.

Barak and Deborah came around the south side of Mt. Tabor to meet Sisera's heavily equipped army, but the battle soon was maneuvered to the banks of the Kishon River. There Sisera's vaunted nine hundred iron chariots got mired down in mud and Sisera himself was forced to escape to Zaanannim, a town near Kedesh in Issachar, taking refuge in the tent of one called Heber, the Kenite. The Kenites were related to the Midianites, for Moses' father-in-law, Jethro, was called a Midianite and a Kenite (Exod. 18:1; Judg. 1:16). Many have argued that Kenite means "smith"; thus, their abode in tents referred not so much to their being nomads who were herdsmen, but to the fact that their occupation required that they travel about (as more recent tinkers did) in order to practice their work as smiths.

Sisera fled to Heber's tent, where his wife Jael offered hospitality for the exhausted and battle-fatigued general. But as he slept, she pounded a tent peg through his temple and thus, the defeat of Sisera and the end of Jabin's oppression in the north. This resounding victory was celebrated in the Song of Deborah and Barak (Judg. 5). What took place at the Kishon was as decisive, they sang, as that which happened in the Conquest of Transjordania and in the Conquest of Canaan. But despite this spectacular feat, Deborah was unable to gain a united front from all the tribes against this northern foe. Besides Zebulun and Naphtali, she mentioned the help of some Amalekite Ephraimites, Benjamin, Issachar, and Makir. Asher remained at home, Gilead (presumably Gad) did not even consider participating, while that is all Reuben did, and

Dan "linger[ed] by the ships." Judah and Simeon were omitted, not because they were not part of the Israelite confederation, as some have supposed, but only because the distance was greater for them and probably because some provincial rivalries were already beginning to appear.

The Midianite Oppression and Gideon

Forty years of peace and rest followed Deborah and Barak's triumph.

Each year, for six years, the Midianites, joined by the Amalekites and the "sons of the East" (Judg. 6:3), came into Israel with their tents, camels, and flocks, going into the fields that the Israelites had just sown. During this time, the land was stripped of its livestock and grain in what would appear to be an unopposed takeover of territory from the Jordan River all the way southwest to Gaza.

In response to the outcry of the populace, Yahweh at first sent an unnamed prophet to warn the people of their sin (Judg. 6:7–10). Whether this preaching had the desired effect of the people's repentance is not stated, but God did send a deliverer named Gideon.

Gideon was from the town of Ophrah (perhaps modern `*Affuleh* in the Esdraelon or Jezreel Valley) in Manasseh, the center of the Midianite attacks. The fact an Israelite settlement was there speaks well for Deborah and Barak's campaign, for prior to this it had been under Canaanite control. Nevertheless, the people of Ophrah had acceded to the Baal worship of the land to such an extent that they built their own altar to Baal with its Asherah symbol. Gideon's first task, therefore, was to destroy this Baal installation, which he did, even if it was done under the cover of darkness.

The apostate community, however, was incensed that such sacrilege should take place in their area. Gideon's father, Joash, defended his son when the people wanted Gideon put to death, noting that if Baal were a god, then he could do the job of punishing his son without the help of any mortals! Thus, Gideon was spared; in fact, having experienced no harm from Baal (Judg. 6:31), he emerged as the conqueror of Baal; thus, he was given the name of Jerub-Baal, for just as his father said, the name meant "Let Baal contend [for himself]" (Judg. 6:32).

Now that the clan of Abiezer was won over, along with other clans in Manasseh, and the tribes of Asher, Zebulun, and Naphtali, a confrontation was now possible. Some thirty-two thousand men responded, but Gideon was up against an enemy of over one hundred and twenty thousand (Judg. 8:10). He still felt he had too few men.

Gideon was assured of divine success through a series of signs (involving a fleece placed on the threshing floor, and the hearing of an interpretation of a dream from a Midianite warrior while stealing into the camp for purposes of reconnaissance and further confirmation of the divine purpose).

Amazingly, Yahweh informed Gideon that he had too many warriors, so he reduced his army to three hundred men (Judg. 7:7). On the eve of the battle, the enemy was encamped in the Jezreel Valley between Mt. Gilboa on the south and Mt. Moreh to the north. Gideon's men were nearby at the well or spring of Herod, at the foot of Mt. Gilboa, armed only with trumpets and pitchers containing torches. The small regiment of three hundred men was divided into three sections and deployed around the edge of the Midianite camp. On signal, the three hundred trumpets blared all at once and three hundred torches lit up the countryside. The resulting panic in the enemy camp set off a pandemonium that never subsided as each hostile opponent headed off in the direction of the Jordan River, hoping to reach neutral territory and head south through Transjordania for home.

Gideon sent out word that the Ephraimites were to cut off the enemy's escape at the Jordan. They did so, capturing two of their leaders named Oreb and Zeeb (Judg. 7:25). Many of the Israelite tribes that had been sent home returned for active duty, giving chase with Gideon all the way back to the land of Midian. Gideon overtook the Midianites at Karkar, far south in the Arabian Desert, some sixty miles east of the Dead Sea. Zebah and Zalmunna, the two hostile leaders, were captured by Gideon as he routed the enemy.

En route to this rout, Gideon had requested food and provisions from the people of Succoth, south of the Jabbok River and from nearby Peniel, but each had haughtily refused help because they feared reprisals by the enemy (Judg. 8:6–8). These people were Israelites, from the tribe of Gad. Apparently, the sense of belonging to the nation of Israel had given way to regionalism, the very things Moses and Joshua had warned the people about before they settled east of the Jordan (Num. 32:6–15, 20–27; Josh. 22:13–20). On his return, Gideon punished both cities severely.

After his return home, the people wanted to make Gideon their king, but he refused, deferring to Yahweh as their king. He did, however, accede to their urgings to receive earrings taken as spoil in the battle. With this gold he made an ephod, perhaps like one worn by the high priest. From this we gather that he took upon himself the prerogative of the priesthood. The ephod became an object worshiped by the people as they lived in quietness for forty years (Judg. 8:24–27).

The Abortive Attempt at Kingship and Abimelech

The trouble during the next three years did not come from outside the land of Palestine; but it came from treachery and bloodshed at the hands of Abimelech, the son of Gideon (Jerub-Babel) by a concubine who lived in Shechem (Judg. 8:31).

Up to this point, there had been no king in Shechem, but the leaders or "lords of Shechem" are mentioned several times in Judges 9. These lords of Shechem fell in with Abimelech, presumably because of his close maternal connections with them. At first they gave him money from the temple of Baal-Berith "to hire reckless adventurers, who became his [Abimelech's] followers" (Judg. 9:4). These "reckless adventurers" or "worthless scoundrels" probably were some of the 'Apiru/Habiru who were mercenaries. Then the lords proclaimed Abimelech king over Shechem. Abimelech, however, never took up residence in Shechem, but he appointed a sort of personal representative, Zebul, as his *pāqîd*, "deputy" (Judg. 9:28) or *śar*, "governor." Never was the area of his reign very large, for all of it was confined to the area around Shechem in territory belonging to the western half tribe of Manasseh.

Here in the central part of the land was a pagan installation for the deity of Shechem, Baal-Berith, "Baal of the covenant." Shechem had a rich heritage and long association with some of the great historical markers in Israel's spiritual background. Abraham had built his first altar in Shechem. Jacob bought property there and dug a well. Joseph's grave was at that site as well. And at Shechem Joshua had led the nation in reaffirming the covenant Yahweh had pledged to the patriarchs. It would appear from the compound name of Baal-Berith that the forces of Canaanite religion had taken the Yahwhistic elements of their history and cleverly joined them to the popular Baal theology of the land, making a new compounded theology.[10]

Whereas Abimelech's father, Gideon, had declined the offer of kingship, his son jumped at the chance and assumed the office with a vengeance. In order to make sure there would be no contesting his

10. Ronald E. Clements, "Baal-Berith of Shechem," *JSS* 13 (1968): 31–32. Note that our interpretation (following that of Eugene H. Merrill, *Kingdom of Priests*, p. 169, n. 70) runs counter to that of most scholars, who argue that a Canaanite cult was taken with a Yahwhistic overlay for Israelite worship.

position, Abimeleck had all but one of his seventy brothers murdered. Jotham, the youngest, escaped and shouted a parable from the ridge above Schechem, predicting that the city which had appointed this murderer as king would soon be consumed by him (Judg. 9:7–21). Indeed, within three years, Shechem had had enough.

The Shechemites sought relief from Abimelech under the leadership of one named Gaal, the leader of a roving band. Abimelech was able to crush Gaal's forces at Shechem and to slaughter a great number of the population, including those who had taken refuge in the tower of El-Berith (Judg. 9:46–49).

Abimelech then went on to Thebez, some nine miles north of Shechem, where he attempted to crush any further resistance once again by burning the people out of the tower of the inner city where they had gone for refuge. However, he was killed by a woman who dropped a millstone on his head (Judg. 9:50–57). This was not the kind of king or kingship that Israel needed or was ready to receive.

The Judgeships of Tola and Jair

During the days of Abimelech, a man from the tribe of Issachar judged in Shamir (Samaria?), Ephraim, for twenty-three years. His judgeship came without the prompting of the presence of an outside oppressor, although the turbulence being created by Abimelech's ill-fated kingship must have raised more than a little concern.

With little more than the statement that he arose to save Israel, Tola led Israel for twenty-three years, died, and was buried in Shamir (Judg. 10:1–2), thereby covering the entirety of his life.

Meanwhile, across the Jordan in thirty towns of Gilead, a judge by the name of Jair led the people for twenty-two years (Judg. 10:3–5). Apparently, he was a wealthy man, for his thirty sons rode on thirty donkeys. His city, Kamon (*Qamm*), was about twelve miles southeast of the Sea of Galilee. The area of Gilead that he had the oversight for was a district just south and east of the Sea of Galilee.

The Ammonite Oppression and Jephthah

Religious affairs appeared to go from bad to worse Israel, for the people of Israel not only worshiped the various Baals and Ashtoreths as before, but they added to these pagan deities the gods of Aram, Sidon, Moab, Ammon, and Philistia. Accordingly, Yahweh "sold them into the hands of the Philistines and Ammonites" (Judg. 10:7). This is a key statement, for it meant that the next oppression would come from two quarters simultaneously: from the Ammonites in the east and the Philistines in the far west. The narrative line actually will continue through the Philistine oppression and its relief under the final judge, Samuel, but what took place mainly in Transjordania must be investigated first.

The Ammonite oppression lasted eighteen years on the east side of the Jordan (Judg. 10:8). But it did not stop there. The Ammonites crossed the Jordan and harassed Judah, Benjamin, and Ephraim, causing great distress for Israel.

A frantic search for a leader turned up an outlaw, Jephthah, the son of a man named Gilead and his harlot. Jephthah had been driven from his home by his older half brothers because he was illegitimate. Thus, he had been leading a roving band of adventurerers in the land of Tob, an area east of the Sea of Galilee, north of Gilead, deep in the Hauran wilderness.

When the Ammonites invaded what had been Jephthah's home territory, the desperate elders begged him to return and lead the attack against the enemy. He agreed to do so on the condition that he would be made their leader after the defeat of Ammon.

At first Jephthah tried negotiating with the Ammonites on the basis that Israel had now held the land for three hundred years, but this was to no avail (Judg. 11:26). Therefore, Jephthah raised an army from Manasseh and Gilead with his headquarters at Mizpah in Gilead. His victory was overwhelming. He seized twenty cities between Minnith and Aroer, an area originally allotted to Reuben.[11]

All was not well that ended well, however. The Ephraimites reacted to Jephthah's success by chiding him for not inviting them to share in Ammon's defeat, especially since they had suffered at the hands of the Ammonites when the raiders crossed over the Jordan into their territory. Jephthah's protestations were in vain (Judg. 12:2), and the latent hostilities and old regional suspicions sprang up again as the Ephraimites charged that the Gileadites were disloyal renegades from Ephraim and Manasseh.

---

11. Jephthah's infamous "vow" that he would sacrifice to Yahweh whatever was first out of his house as he returned from a victory over Ammon is not treated in this history, but it has been the subject of a large literature. Did Jephthah sacrifice his daughter, or did she live? He did sacrifice her, which is only another indication both of his character and the times of the judges when all the people did what was right in their own eyes. See Walter C. Kaiser Jr., *Hard Sayings of the Old Testament* (Downers Grove, Ill.: InterVarsity, 1988), 101–105 = idem., *Hard Sayings of the Bible*, coauthored with Peter H. Davids, F. F. Bruce, and Manfred T. Brauch (Downers Grove, Ill.: InterVarsity Press, 1966), 193–95.

Jephthah was not a man to fool with, for he launched an attack against the Ephraimites after they threatened to burn down his house. Furthermore, after the battle with Ephraim, Jephthah had the Gileadites man the fords of the Jordan, demanding that those suspected of escaping from the troops of Ephraim should pronounce the word *Shibboleth* (meaning "flowing stream," a reference no doubt to the Jordan to which the interrogators must have pointed), but the Ephraimites were unable to do so. They used the *s* sound in place of the *sh* sound (i.e., pronouncing the Hebrew *shin* as if it were a *samek*). That was enough to condemn themselves. Accordingly, forty-two thousand Ephraimites were killed either in battle or at the fords of the Jordan.

Jephthah served as a judge for six years, in keeping with the promise made by the Gilead elders. But the split that had previously existed between the tribes on the two sides of the Jordan only increased as a result of the massacre that had taken place over a misunderstanding.

Three minor judges followed Jephthah's judgeship, or ruled simultaneously with him (Judg. 12:8–15). Ibzan of Bethlehem judged Judah (?) for seven years. Elon of Aijalon in Zebulun judged for ten years in the north, and Abdon of Pirathon in Ephraim judged for eight years. Abdon's wealth also is signified by the fact that he had forty sons and thirty grandsons who rode on seventy donkeys.

The Philistine Oppression: Samson and Samuel

While the Ammonites were oppressing Israel, mainly east of the Jordan, the Philistines were encroaching on the hill country from the west. Those who were most directly and immediately affected were from the tribe of Dan. For forty years, this harassment continued until at last Yahweh raised up Samson, who began to deliver the Israelites for the twenty years of his judgeship (Judg. 15:20). But it fell to Samuel, finally, to extricate Israel from the Philistine menace.

Samson

Samson was the son of godly parents in Zorah, a town in the Sorek Valley. He was a Nazirite from his birth (meaning, among other things, that his hair was not to be cut) and one on whom the Spirit of God had fallen, just as many of the other judges had experienced, and one whose birth had been heralded by the appearance of an angel of Yahweh.

Samson's approach to the Philistine oppression was quite different from the other judges. Rather than engaging the enemy in battle by means of an army, Samson used his personal strength to take on the enemy. His acts of mayhem were enough to disrupt the sense of tranquility in Philistia. Such feats of individual prowess are viewed suspiciously by critical scholars who prefer to treat these descriptions as legends or sagas. But this is to foist a new literary category on the text without the proper indicators within the text.[12]

Some of the feats of Samson include: the wedding riddle used at his marriage to the Philistine girl from Timnah, only four miles southwest of Zorah, where Samson slew thirty Philistines in Ashkelon to pay off the Philistine men who bribed his wife to obtain the answer to the riddle; setting on fire the tails of three hundred foxes he caught and released in the wheat fields of the Philistines just before harvest as revenge for his wife-to-be being given away in marriage to his best man at the canceled wedding; and his final escapades with the harlot Delilah, who deceived him to learn the secret of his strength.

When the Philistines learned the secret of his strength, they captured Samson and put out his eyes. He was led into the temple of Dagon and made sport of as part of the entertainment. By now his hair had begun to grow. Thus, in one last effort, he pulled the two supporting pillars of the temple down and destroyed up to three thousand Philistines as it collapsed.

SAMUEL

It was left to Samuel to finish the job that Samson began. Samuel was also dedicated as a Nazirite. He was born to Elkanah and his wife Hannah as a direct result of her prayers in the city of Ramathaim Zuphim in Ephraim, some eighteen miles west of where the tabernacle was located in Shiloh. As a Levite in the line of Kohath, Samuel was able to function at the tabernacle and altars of Yahweh worship throughout the land.

Samuel was raised at the tabernacle in Shiloh under the mentorship of the high priest Eli, descendant of Ithamar. But the high priesthood line would be taken from Eli because of his failure to deal with his sons, Hophni and Phinehas, and their continual sin as officiating priests. The priesthood was given instead to Zadok, descendant of Eleazar.

In Samuel's early years, the forty-year Philistine domination of Israel continued. Israel had suffered a major defeat at Aphek, with some four thousand men killed. Israel, thinking they could force Yahweh into

12. Eugene H. Merrill, *Kingdom of Priests*, p. 175, n. 82, refers to clarifications on this subject by John J. Scullion, "Marcehen, Sage, Legende: Towards a Clarification of Some Literary Terms Used by Old Testament Scholars," *VT* 34 (1984): 324–31.

granting them victory by the presence of the ark of the covenant in battle, brought out this most sacred of all pieces of furniture in the tabernacle as a return engagement for the loss suffered at Aphek. But to the horror of all Israelites, even this symbol of the presence of Yahweh was lost in the next battle with the Philistines as thirty thousand Israelites fell in battle, along with Hophni and Phinehas. Eli himself fell off his chair and died on learning the tragic news of the battle and especially about the ark.

But the ark was not the prize that the Philistines thought it to be at first. Placed in a subordinate position in the temple of Dagon, the idol of Dagon twice keeled over in obeisance before the ark of the covenant, and bubonic plague broke out wherever the ark went in the Philistine Pentapolis. In exasperation the Philistines determined to send the ark back to Israel, but in an experiment that clearly went directly against nature. They built a new cart, hooked it up to two cows that had just given birth to calves, put the ark, five golden rats, and five golden swellings (one for each of the five cities in the Pentapolis and to imitate the swellings that came from the disease spread by rats in the cities where the ark had visited) and watched to see if the cows, contrary to every instinct of nature, would go toward Israel with its cargo. They did!

The ark remained in Kiriath Jearim, a village nine miles west of Jerusalem. Samuel, who had not been heard from in the biblical text since the days of Eli and the battle at Aphek, led the populace in a revival at Mizpah. What followed was the final overthrow of the Philistine oppression. The enemy was chased and routed all the way back to Beth Car (1 Sam. 7:10–13).

Thus, Samuel was the last judge in a long succession of charismatic leaders raised up to answer the series of oppressions that hit Israel at one time, one place, or another. Though Samuel's circuit of priestly ministry was rather small—an area of some twenty miles from Bethel to Gilgal to Mizpah—yet the impact he had, at least on the west side of the Jordan, was enough to mark the end of an era and the times of the judges.

The Bethlehem Trilogy[13]

The Book of Judges has, as it were, three appendixes that center around the town of Bethlehem. In a way, all three mirror the desperate

13. This label is given by Eugene H. Merrill, *Kingdom of Priests*, p. 178.

state of the times in which the judges were serving. The first concerned the movement of the Danites from their allotted territory to an area north of Naphtali (Judg.17–18). The second detailed the gruesome rape of a Levite's concubine that resulted in a war that almost annihilated the tribe of Benjamin (Judg. 19–21). The third was the Book of Ruth, which related how David's line happened to include a mother from Moab.

THE DANITE MIGRATION

A wealthy man of Ephraim named Micah built a house for his idols and installed his son as priest of this shrine. It all began with a hastily uttered curse announced by Micah's mother in the presence of her son Micah over the theft of eleven hundred shekels of silver. Quickly trying to counter the curse she had just uttered, she dedicated a portion of the returned shekels by having a silversmith construct a silver idol for their household. Such was the nature of religious devotion in those days.

In the meantime, a Levite from Bethlehem, who was searching for a ministry position, stayed at Micah's house and was offered employment at this new shrine. He accepted. Therefore, when a search party from the tribe of Dan stopped overnight at Micah's house on their way north to scout out new territory for some of the tribe, they saw Micah's idols and his Levite, who gave them counsel regarding their venture.

Later, when six hundred Danites returned on their way to conquer Laish, some twelve miles north of Lake Huleh, the new site chosen for Dan, they stole Micah's idols and the newly employed Levite for themselves. This Levite was none other than Jonathan, son of Gershom, Moses' son.[14] Micah in his frustration pursued the six hundred idol-mongering thieves, but they sarcastically told him to be quiet, lest something bad suddenly happen to him. Indeed, everyone was doing precisely what they thought was right in their own eyes.

THE LEVITE AND HIS CONCUBINE

Another Bethlehemite connection concerned the Ephraimite Levite who had taken a concubine from Bethlehem (Judg. 19–21). For some reason the concubine had fled back home, and the Levite went to retrieve her. As he returned to Ephraim with her via Gibeah in Ben-

14. Judges 18:30 has a *nun suspensum* in the Hebrew text in order to make it appear as if it should not be read "Moses," but "Manasseh." But there was such a strong respect for the text that those who tampered with it would not add it to the body of the text, but left it suspended above the line as if it were an inserted correction.

jamin, the only lodging he was offered for the night was with an old man in Gibeah. The men of this Benjamite city wanted to have sexual relations with this man, but the Levite offered them his concubine instead. She was taken and abused by the men of the city that night. In the morning, the Levite found her dead on the doorstep.

Shocked and angered by such an outrage, the Levite chopped up the corpse of his concubine and sent a part of her to each of the twelve tribes, urging them to take some sort of reprisal for what had been done in this city of Benjamin.

When the Benjamites refused to hand over the offenders, a civil war ensued. Twice the small tribe of Benjamin beat back the other eleven tribes with severe losses. The third time, however, after consulting with the high priest Phinehas, the grandson of Aaron, Gibeah was leveled; all the Benjamite men were killed except the six hundred men who had fled to the rock of Rimmon. Four months later, the other tribes suddenly realized what they had done and the oath they had previously taken not to give any of their number in marriage to Benjamin. The measures they took to remedy this situation testified further that the times called for divine judgment.

Both of these narratives tended to reflect badly on Benjamin, and by implication on the dynasty of Saul, since the wife of the Benjamite survivor—who became an ancestor of the first king of Israel, Saul—was probably either from Shiloh or Jabesh Gilead. In fact, no sooner had Saul become king than Jabesh Gilead came under a siege from the Ammonites (1 Sam. 11:1–11). Thus, it was likely that he traced the maternal side of his line to that city. Later, the men of Jabesh Gilead retrieved Saul's body and buried it in their town (1 Sam. 31:11–13).

The events narrated in these two appendixes to the Book of Judges probably fell early in the period of the judges, since a grandson of Moses, in one case, and a grandson of Aaron, in the other, would need to be contemporaneous with the generation that came after the Conquest.

Ruth and the Line of David

Ruth was a Moabite maiden, who had been married to Mahlon, one of the two sons of Elimelech and Naomi, a couple who fled from the famine in Bethlehem-Judah probably during the days of the Midianite oppression. The couple's other son, Chilion, had married another Moabite woman named Orpah. The father, Elimelech, and both sons had died, leaving three widows. Naomi determined to return to Bethlehem after her family had lived as resident aliens in Moab for ten years, but Ruth clung to her mother-in-law, despite all of her efforts to dissuade her.

In so doing, Ruth encountered Boaz, a close relative of the family, who performed the duty of a levirate and married Ruth. From this union came the son Obed, who was the father of Jesse, who in turn was the father of the one who would become King David. Thus, a descendant from Lot's older daughter entered into not only the Davidic line, but also the line of Israel's Messiah.

Part V

The Monarchy

14

THE PEOPLE'S CALL FOR A KING

W. A. Irwin concluded in 1941 that historians were "in the disturbing position of possessing not a single narrative of Samuel's activity that merits respect as good source material."[1] Even though W. F. Albright gave a much brighter picture on the historiographical value of the early Samuel narratives in general,[2] the mood of scholars remained by and large extremely pessimistic through the rest of the twentieth century. J. M. Miller and J. H. Hayes concluded in 1986 that Samuel "remains a very elusive figure as far as tangible historical information is concerned."[3]

So wary were historians of following any "text-based history" that originates from sources in the Bible that they usually stigmatized such approaches as "fundamentalist" approaches.[4] Long called Miller a "fundamentalist," and Miller returned the compliment by calling Long a "fundamentalist" as well.[5] The point is not who is the greater fundamentalist, but, as Robert P. Gordon sanely commented with a bit of irony, "perhaps we must add to Long's 'holy books' the category of 'holy

1. W. A. Irwin, "Samuel and the Rise of the Monarchy," *AJSL* 58 (1941): 134.
2. W. F. Albright, *Samuel and the Beginnings of the Prophetic Movement* (Cincinnati: Hebrew Union College Press, 1961). Albright excavated Tell el-Ful, the Benjamite village believed to be Gibeah, in 1922 and again briefly in 1933, which he reported on in *AASOR* 4 (1924) and *BASOR* 52 (1933): 6–12.
3. J. M. Miller and J. H. Hayes, *A History of Ancient Israel and Judah* (Philadelphia: Westminster, 1986), 134.
4. B. O. Long, "On Finding the Hidden Premises," *JSOT* 39 (1987): 11.
5. J. M. Miller, "In Defense of Writing a History of Israel," *JSOT* 39 (1987): 54.

stelae' to take in such hitherto respectable historical sources as the Mesha Stele and the Zakir Inscription, which [also] mix in a little divine activity with their historical reminiscences. That the Old Testament historical books are theologically motivated is an argument against simplisms, but not against their entire historical quest."[6]

Behind some of the evaluations of the appropriateness of the sources used for constructing a history of the times like those of Samuel is the deep reaction against event-laden, personality-oriented, or what is stigmatized as "Flavian" history writing. Knowing that such ventures that center around events or persons will be labeled precritical, scholars have gone off into the safer fields of writing about the social structures and the movements of peoples and family units of the day rather than using political constructs with events that impacted the masses through the leaders of the times. Unfortunately for this new definition of history, however, is the open fact that much of the Bible is precisely what most moderns have described history not to be: event-laden and oriented around personalities.[7] If this is to be a history of Israel, it must follow this lead to the extent that it exhibits the criteria used in all other inductive forms of learning and writing. This is not to say that additional profit may not be gained from sociological studies of settlement patterns and the like; indeed, they do contribute substantially. But our point is that history must not be reduced to sociology or mere statistics; there are also events, personalities, and claims of an ancient text; claims that often can be submitted to tests for validation to the degree that similar claims can be tested in our own world.

The Philistines and the Rise of the Monarchy

While no attempt is made at being "monocausal"[8] by centering on the Philistine oppression in the west and the Ammonite oppression in the east as the sole strong cause for the people's sudden passion for the monarchy, the ominous nature of these pressures could not but have influenced and hastened whatever sentiment was already present. There were other factors as well, to be sure, such as the failure of Samuel's sons to administer in a way that would instill confidence among

6. Robert P. Gordon, "Who Made the Kingmaker? Reflections on Samuel and the Institution of the Monarchy," in *Faith, Tradition, and History: Old Testament Historiography in Its Near Eastern Context*, eds. A. R. Millard, James K Hoffmeier, and David W. Baker (Winona Lake, Ind.: Eisenbrauns, 1994), p. 256.

7. This point is also made by Robert P. Gordon, "Who Made the Kingmaker?" p. 258.

8. A complaint registered by K. W. Whitelam, "Recreating the History of Israel," *JSOT* 35 (1986): 62, as pointed out by R. P. Gordon, ibid., p. 257.

the populace (1 Sam. 8:1–5). But there is no doubt that from the standpoint of the biblical text, the straw that seems to have broken the camel's back was the long oppression of the Philistines and Samson's inability, despite his heroic efforts, to deliver the nation from the grip of the Philistines.

The battle of Aphek (probably modern Tell *el-mukhar* near *Ras el-ʿen*) had a dramatic effect on Israel. This site is on the river that flows into the Mediterranean north of Joppa. It was a strategic point of departure for an attack on the central hill country. After the Israelites had lost their initial skirmish to the Philistines, they brought the ark of the covenant from Shiloh with the hope that Yahweh's presence, as symbolized by the ark, would guarantee them victory in their next offensive. Unhappily, they suffered the loss of the priests Hophni and Phineas, sons of Eli who carried the ark, as well as the loss of the ark itself, for the Philistines captured it and took it back to the Philistine Pentapolis as a trophy of war. As the Philistines captured and occupied the land, Shiloh itself was destroyed—the site of the taberncle and the ark!

The results of this defeat for Israel were still being talked about four centuries later by the prophet Jeremiah (Jer. 7:12, 14; 26:6, 9) for it would appear that Shiloh (*Selun*), where the tabernacle had been set up after the wilderness wanderings, was left in ruins, probably at the same time that the Philistines won the battles of Aphek and its follow-up battle of Eben-Ezer. After the ark of the covenant had fallen into Philistine hands, the Philistines also destroyed the tabernacle that housed it, reducing to ashes what had been the central place of worship for the twelve tribes.

To compound this depressing turn of events, the Philistines installed garrisons in Israelite territory, such as the garrison we hear of in Benjamite Gibeah (1 Sam. 10:5; 13:3; modern Tell *el-Ful*), a mere ten miles north of Jerusalem. The Philistines had forbidden the Israelites to work with metal, forcing them to take their plowshares and other agricultural tools to the Philistines (1 Sam. 13:19–22).[9] Israel's humiliation was almost total.

The victory that Israel finally realized at Mizpah in 1 Samuel 7 must not be detached or isolated from the actions that come in 1 Samuel 8

---

9. The most intriguing iron discovery was an iron plow point from the time of Saul at what was believed to be his citadel at Gibeah. See Lawrence A. Sinclair, "An Archaeological Study of Gibeah [Tell el-Ful]," *BA* 27 (1964): 55–57. Also see James D. Muhly, "How Iron Technology Changed the Ancient World—And Gave the Philistines a Military Edge," *BAR* 8. 6 (1982): 40–54.

with the desire to "be like all the other nations, with a king to lead us and to go out before us and fight our battles" (1 Sam. 8:20). However, recent studies using an anthropological approach that deals with issues such as social stratification, population increase, social conflicts, and administrative needs have cast serious doubts on the claim that the Philistines were a major factor in explaining why Israel became a monarchy. But as Robert P. Gordon countered:

> There is nothing improbable about the Samuel storyline as far as it goes. . . . [T]o claim that the anthropological approach flies in the face of the literature and archaeology of the period would be an inappropriate response, and one that might be contested at either level. A more likely way forward is to consider why, from an internal Old Testament point of view, the Philistines are given such prominence as they are in 1 Samuel. Also involved . . . is the question what constitutes history-writing.[10]

The early chapters of 1 Samuel revolve around Eli and his sons, the ark of the covenant, Samuel, and the Philistines. If the complaint is that to make the Philistines the sole cause for the crisis that precipitated the Israelite monarchy, in a type of mono-causality, then it can be agreed that there were other factors as well. But there can be little doubt from the literary and military standpoints that the Philistines presented the largest share of the impetus as they began to expand territorially about the same time that Israel's population needs were likewise needing a similar expansion. Israel Finkelstein concluded in his work on "settlement patterns" in the central hill country of Palestine that settlement in the western area, especially in the Shephelah, developed friction between the Philistines from the Gaza strip coastal region and their neighbors to the east, primarily Judah, Benjamin, and Ephraim. Consequently, Finkelstein thought that the pressure of Philistine expansion and constant encroachments on the hill country contributed to Israel's desire for a monarchy.[11]

Israel's defeats not only shattered their morale but also caused other problems as well. It encouraged her neighbors to expand into territory that Israel had previously held. The Ammonites renewed their attempts to regain territory they had been frustrated from gaining by Jephthah's victory. They appear to have seized the land of Gilead south

10. Robert P. Gordon, "Who Made the Kingmaker?" p. 257.

11. I. Finkelstein, "The Emergence of the Monarchy in Israel: The Environmental and Socio-Economic Aspects," *JSOT* 44 (1989): 43–74.

to the Jabbok River. At least that is where we find them, in the city of Jabesh,[12] as Saul is called upon to relieve them from the horrible terms of surrender offered by the Ammonites.

THE RISE OF SAUL

At the middle of this century there was general agreement among scholars that Saul's career marked the beginning of the actual events in the Bible and the history of Israel.[13] But today the matter has again reversed itself because there is so little archaeological evidence and so much controversy about the whole era of the monarchy, much less about Saul.

Even the limited archaeological remains of the Iron I tower at Tell el-Ful, which W. F. Albright thought was the "citadel of Saul," is now held with much more tentativeness than when Albright first set it forth as evidence of a Saulide construction.[14]

But as V. Philips Long has demonstrated in several masterful studies, most of these pessimistic verdicts about Saul are prompted by one or two lines of reasoning. First, ever since the Enlightenment, writings which purport to be historical events, but which also make explicit or implicit reference to God or gods as participants are automatically disqualified as "history." Secondly, the ancient Near East provides so very few examples of history writing from the times of Saul, David, and Solomon that we would not be led to expect that a genuine historiographical tradition could be found in those times. But there is a third and much more pervasive assumption for all the historical agnosticism surrounding Saul: the biblical narrative just does not make sense as a unified, coherent, sequential story.[15] This objection needs to be faced if

---

12. Contrary to some modern atlases, Eusebius placed Jabesh on the later Roman road from Pella to Gerasa, i.e., on the upper end of the Wadi Yabis in the mountain region. Nelson Glueck, *AASOR* 25–28 (1951): 211 ff., placed the site on the ruins of Tell el-maklub on the northern side of the valley.

13. For example, V. Philips Long, in his article "How Did Saul Become King? Literary Reading and Historical Reconstruction," in *Faith, Tradition, and History*, p. 272, pointed to W. E. Evans, "An Historical Reconstruction of the Emergence of Israelites Kingship and the Reign of Saul," in *Scripture in Context II: More Essays on the Comparative Method* (eds. W. W. Hallo, J. C. Moyer, and L. G. Perdue; Winona Lake, Ind.: Eisenbrauns, 1983), 61.

14. See now the criticism of P. J. Arnold, *Gibeah: The Search for a Biblical City* (*JSOTSup* 79; Sheffield: JSOT Press, 1990): 51–52.

15. V. Philips Long has argued this whole issue in a compact volume entitled *The Art of Biblical History* (Grand Rapids: Zondervan, 1994), especially the chapter, "An Extended Example: The Rise of Saul," on pp. 210–223. The shorter version of this chapter appears in the article already quoted, "How Did Saul Become a King?" in *Faith, Tradition, and History*.

any kind of history of Saul's rise and reign are to made part of history writing.[16]

The perceived roadblocks to a coherent reading of Saul's rise to power begin usually with Julius Wellhausen, who distinguished between at least two originally independent narratives based on his detecting discrepant attitudes to kingship itself in the text. John Bright explained it best:

> The account of Saul's election comes to us in two (probably originally three) parallel narratives, one tacitly favorable to the monarchy, and the other bitterly hostile. The first (1 Sam. 9:1 to 10:16) tells how Saul was privately anointed by Samuel in Ramah; it is continued in 13:3b, 4b-15. Woven with this narrative is the originally separate account (chap. 11) of Saul's victory over Ammon and his subsequent acclamation by the people at Gilgal. The other strand (chap. 8; 10:17–27; 12) has Samuel, having yielded with angry protests to popular demand, presiding over Saul's election at Mizpah.[17]

The complaint is that Saul appears to have come to power through several different routes: (1) by distinguishing himself in his victory over the Ammonites (the route most favored by modern scholars, if any is preferred); (2) or by Samuel's anointing him first, followed by a battle (as a pro-monarchical source apparently would have it); or (3) by the casting of lots (as the antimonarchical source preferred to tell it). And there was the rub: especially the promonarchical and anti-monarchical accounts contradicted each other; it was simply impossible for Saul to have become king by so many different routes![18]

But there is one other difficulty that has occasioned a huge literature in itself. After anointing Saul and giving him his charge, Samuel instructed him to go down to Gilgal and wait for him there, where Samuel would offer sacrifices and tell him what to do (1 Sam. 10:8). That was all good and well, but the preceding complicates the matter; Samuel had just told him, "Do whatever your hand finds to do, for God is with you" (v. 7). The assumption is that verse 7 is an unqualified authorization for Saul to act on his own as the situation may demand. If so,

16. The first two objections are treated in V. Philips Long, "History and Modern Scholarship," in *The Art of Biblical History*, pp. 120–168 and in A. R. Millard, "The Old Testament and History: Some Considerations," *Faith and Thought* 110 (1983): 34–53, especially pp. 39–40.

17. John Bright, *A History of Israel* (3rd ed.; Philadelphia: Westminster, 1981), p. 188.

18. The consensus of modern historical studies is this sentiment expressed by H. Donner, "Basic Elements of Old Testament Historiography Illustrated by the Saul Traditions," *Die Ou-Testamentiese werkgemeenskap in Suid-Afrika* 24 (1981): 43, as pointed out by V. Philips Long, "How Did Saul Become King?" p. 274.

then verse 8 is an outright contradiction, if not an intrusion into the text; especially since verse 8 is not fulfilled until chapter 13. The conclusion that many draw from this apparent debacle is that verse 8 is a secondary addition to chapter 10, acting perhaps as a "theological correction" for those who were unhappy with the kind of freedom Saul was given to act on his own in verse 7.[19] And if verse 8 in chapter 10 is secondary, then scholars have unsurprisingly assumed that chapter 13 (vv. 4b, 7b-15a) must likewise be intrusive to the text as well.

Is there any way to sort out this tangle of routes to the throne with its subsidiary distractions? V. Philips Long thought there was. He began with Baruch Halpern's recent works,[20] from both biblical and extrabiblical sources, showing that leaders in early Israel came to power in the three stages, which he labeled: (1) designation, (2) demonstration, and (3) confirmation. The process appeared to work this way: first an individual was *designated* in some manner as God's chosen instrument. This new appointee was expected to *demonstrate* the appropriateness of his new appointment by some military feat, whether real or merely ceremonial, that would distinguish him as a leader in the public's eye. With this feat accomplished, he was then set to be *confirmed* publicly as that leader of the people of God.

Halpern isolated two separate examples of such an accession pattern from 1 Samuel 9–14, on the basis of his commitment to a theory of sources and doublets.[21] However, Diana Edelman improved on Halpern's analysis by finding but one example of the accession pattern in 1 Samuel 9–11.[22] Her analysis had the divine *designation* represented by Saul's anointing in 9:1–10:16, the *demonstration* by Saul's victory over the Ammonites in 11:1–11, and the *confirmation* by the renewal of the kingdom in 11:14–15.

While Edelman has advanced the discussion beyond Halpern, she has failed to explain the lot-casting episode in 10:17–27, which falls

19. The term *theological correction* is used by V. Phillips Long, "How Did Saul Become King?" p. 275 from J. Kegeler's characterization of 1 Samuel 10:8 as a "theologische Korrektur" in *Politisches geschehen und theologiches Versten: Zum Geschichtsverständnis in der frühen israelitischen Königszeit* (Calwer Theologische Monographien 8; Stuttgard: Calwer, 1977), p. 264.

20. Baruch Halpern, *The Constitution of the Monarchy in Israel* (*HSM* 25; Chico, Calif.: Scholars Press, 1981; idem., "The Uneasy Compromise: Israel between League and Monarchy," *Traditions in Transformation: Turning Points in Biblical Faith*, B. Halpern and J. D. Levenson; F. M. Cross Festschrift, eds. (Winona Lake, Ind.: Eisenbrauns, 1981): 59–96, as cited by V. Philips Long, ibid, p. 276.

21. V. Philips Long critiqued Halpern's two-source theory in his *Reign and Rejection of King Saul: A Case for Literary and Theological Coherence* (*SBLDS* 118; Atlanta: Scholars Press, 1989): 191–93.

22. Diana Edelman, "Saul's Rescue of Jabesh-Gilead (1 Sam. 11:1–11): Sorting Story from History," *ZAW* 96 (1984): 195–209.

between the anointing of Saul and his victory over Ammon. Furthermore, she has linked 1 Samuel 10:7, "Do whatever your hand finds to do," with the military engagement of the Ammonites. However, the problem is that the context of 10:7 suggested that it was not the Ammonites, but the Philistine presence in Gibeah that was the real problem. Thus, Edelman leaves this aspect unsolved. In order to solve this dilemma, scholars have tended to argue that chapter 13 followed close on 10:7 originally, but that only raises again the problem of the literary coherence of the whole narrative.

Long's way of straightening all this out is to argue that 10:7–8 are not contradictory, but complementary instructions, with the second being contingent on Saul's acting on the first. In the context of chapter ten, three signs would serve as evidences to Saul that he was Yahweh's designate to lead the people. The third sign was to occur at Gibeah, where there was a Philistine outpost, as Samuel noted (10:5). Most scholars feel a reference to the Philistines at this point is unnecessary or just plain out of place. But Saul had been appointed in 1 Samuel 9:16 to deal with the Philistines, so neither the command nor the sign was out of place.

What, then, is the solution? It is this: a military challenge from Saul against the Philistine garrison at Gibeah would surely demonstrate his divine designation, but it would only be the beginning of troubles for Israel. Therefore, Samuel issues a second command: "Go down ahead of me to Gilgal. I will surely come down to you to sacrifice burnt offerings and fellowship offerings, but you must wait seven days until I come to you and tell you what you are to do." Thus, Long thinks that as soon as Saul has done what his hand found to do (that is, in attacking the Philistine garrison), Saul was to go immediately to Gilgal where Samuel joined him to offer sacrifices, consecrated him to the conflict that must surely take place, and gave him further instructions. Thus, what had appeared to be contradictory is really sequential and complementary.

But then why is the prescribed rendezvous in Gilgal not mentioned until chapter 13? Surely the seven days mentioned in 13:8 are the same seven days prescribed in 10:8. Long counters by observing that the delay is no worse than the delay between Saul's charge in 10:7 and Jonathan's attack on the Philistine outpost in 13:3. After Jonathan carries out what Saul's hand was to find, Saul immediately went down to Gilgal to wait for Samuel (1 Sam. 13:8). Thus, the same two-part pattern proposed in chapter 10 (Philistine provocation with the Gilgal meeting) actually takes place in chapter 13.

Even if the above answers all the problems, one more remains: why is there such a large gap between the instructions given in 10:7–8 and its fulfillment in the three chapters that follow? Long answers this problem by pointing to Meir Sternberg's principle that all literary works have a "system of gaps that must be filled in by the reader in the process of reading."[23] These links the reader usually fills in automatically, but some must be figured out rather laboriously, always with modifications in light of the additional material disclosed in the subsequent context.

Presuming the proper key to unlocking the puzzles mentioned has been found, how does this make sense out of Saul's rise to power? It argues that Saul failed in his first charge as he hesitated to tell his uncle about his being anointed by Samuel, reporting only that the lost donkeys had been found (1 Sam. 10:14–16). His inaction after his designation as king has the result that there has been nothing worthy of public attention that would demonstrate that he was suited to be their leader. It was necessary for Samuel to convene an assembly at Mizpah (10:17–27). Thus, the process of designation followed by demonstration has been stalled, according to Long. Now Samuel must bring Saul to public notice along a different route than was originally planned. This would mean that Saul's hiding among the baggage when he was selected was not a sign of his humility, but rather the result of timidity (10:22) and reticence to take up the task he was being called to do by God.

Finally, the demonstration that was sought came in chapter 11 with the Ammonite victory. Accordingly, the kingship was "renewed" (1 Sam. 11:14) and the derailed process of designation, demonstration, and confirmation was put back on track again. But it does mean that the conquest of the Ammonites served as a substitute for the original demonstration of routing the Philistine garrison that was envisaged by Samuel in 1 Samuel 10:7.

In the very next chapter, however, Jonathan attacks the Philistine garrison in Geba (1 Sam. 13:3), which was to have been the program for Saul's first charge in 10:7. The immediate sequel of Jonathan's attack was that Saul went immediately to Gilgal to wait for Samuel (13:4–5), which had been the plan in 10:8. But once again, Saul failed

23. Meir Sternberg, *The Poetics of Biblical Narrative: Ideological Literature and the Drama of Reading* (Bloomington: Indiana University Press, 1985), 186.

in executing the second phase, thereby earning a stiff rebuke from Samuel (13:8–14).

This discussion has been excessively long, but it is foundational not only for understanding Saul's rise to power, but for grasping some of the newer literary techniques for reading the text vis-à-vis the former critical treatments that found that Saul's story simply could not be read as a coherent sequential account. This is why the Samuel narrative often has figured prominently in debates over the nature of history writing in the Old Testament.[24]

---

24. Again, see H. Donner's "Basic Elements of Old Testament Historiography Illustrated by the Saul Traditions," pp. 40–54 as a prime example along with W. E. Evans, "An Historical Reconstruction of the Emergence of Israelite Kingship and the Reign of Saul," *Scripture in Context II: More Essays on the Comparative Method*, eds. W. W. Hallo, J. C. Moyer, and L. G. Perdue (Winona Lake, Ind.: Eisenbrauns, 1983).

15

King Saul

No evidence requires us to distinguish between sections in Samuel that present Saul in a favorable light from supposed anti-Saulide and anti-monarchical sources. The story is best read as a whole, for no evidence substantiates the existence of these alleged sources or editings of the text (see arguments in the previous chapter). Histories of Israel by scholars such as Miller and Hayes[1] focus first on passages they regard as favorable to Saul (1 Sam. 9:1 – 10:16; 10:26 – 11:15; 13:2 – 14:46). But our previous chapter has shown that such a division is indebted more to special theories of historical criticism than to a patient listening to a fair literary analysis of the passage.

The Structure of the 1 Samuel Account

The Books of 1 and 2 Samuel are part of the continued story line that began in the Books of Genesis to Judges. But the section dealing with Saul (1 Sam. 9 – 31) has its own distinctive characteristics, as W. Lee Humphries pointed out in 1978.[2] Humphries divided the Saul material as follows:

1. J. Maxwell Miller and John H. Hayes, *A History of Ancient Israel and Judah* (Philadelphia: Westminster, 1986), 127.

2. W. Lee Humphries, "The Tragedy of King Saul: A Study of the Structure of 1 Samuel 9–31," *JSOT* 6 (1978): 18–27; idem., "The Rise and Fall of King Saul: A Study of an Ancient Narrative Stratum in 1 Samuel," *JSOT* 18 (1980): 74–90.

Introduction (9:1–2)
Part I (chaps. 9–14)
Part II (chaps. 15–27)
Finale (chaps. 28–31)

These two parts follow a common pattern: Saul and Samuel meet privately (9:3–10:15; 5:1–35). Samuel announces Saul's destiny. This is followed by two scenes: in the first Saul is presented positively (10:17–11:15; 16:14–19:10), but the second is unfavorable, and Saul's doom is realized (13:1–14:46; 19:11–28:2). The finale follows the same pattern: at a meeting of Saul and Samuel, Saul's defeat and death are foretold (28:3–25), followed by a climax that had both constructive and destructive aspects as Saul committed suicide (31:1–13).

Humphries's 1978 analysis is helpful as a general assessment of the structure and movement of ideas in chapters 9–31. But in a 1980 article, Humphries tries to isolate two sources of tradition: (1) an older layer of pro-Saul material in which Saul dominated the scene; (2) later and secondary elements that present Saul as an illustration of all that was perverse in kingship or as a foil for Yahweh's elect future king, David. Humphries' 1980 proposal turns the text on its head and arbitrarily separates elements in keeping with *ab extra* criteria that cannot be demonstrated from the text.

The Man Saul

Saul was the son Kish, a wealthy Benjamite whose ancestral home was the village of Zela in southern Benjamin (2 Sam. 21:14; cf. Josh. 18:28, also called Zelzah in 1 Sam. 10:2, perhaps a variant on the same name). Saul was "an impressive young man without equal among the Israelites—a head taller than any of the others" (1 Sam. 9:2).

The first incident that the Samuel account records is Saul's search for his father's lost donkeys. After searching through the hill country of Ephraim and the area around Shalisha, Saul and one of his father's servants went on to the district of Shaalim and on to the territory of Benjamin, but the donkeys were not to be found anywhere. So when Saul and his servant reached the land of Zuph, the servant urged him to inquire of Samuel, the man of God who resided in the nearby town. Samuel was offering sacrifices in that village that day, and Saul first met Samuel as Samuel was on his way up to the high place to sacrifice.

Yahweh had revealed to Samuel that Saul would be coming that day and that he was to anoint him as prince, or leader (*nāgîd*), over Israel. Samuel ate a meal with Saul, a meal in which Saul was the guest of honor. The next morning Samuel sent Saul on his way with the disclosure that his father's donkeys had been found. Saul was given three signs to confirm Samuel's predictions that he would be a leader over Israel:

1. Two men would meet Saul upon his return to the land of Benjamin, informing him that the donkeys had been found.
2. Saul was to proceed to the oak of Tabor, where he would meet three men going up to worship God at Bethel, one carrying three young goats, another three loaves of bread, and the other a skin of wine. Saul would receive a greeting from them and two loaves of bread.
3. Saul was to go on to Gibeah of God, a Philistine garrison (*nĕṣîb*, meaning uncertain). As he would approach this town, a procession of prophets coming down from the high place with lyres, tambourines, flutes, and harps would meet him, and would prophesy, as the Spirit of God would fall on Saul (1 Sam. 10:2–8).

Once these signs were fulfilled, Saul was to "do whatever [his] hand found to do, for God [would be] with [him]" (v. 7). Then, as we argued in the previous chapter, Saul was to repair immediately to the old military staging grounds in Gilgal and wait for Samuel to come to him after seven days.

When Saul left Samuel, "God changed Saul's heart" (10:9), and each of the predicted events occurred as Samuel had foretold them. The Spirit of God fell on Saul, and he too began to prophesy so mightily that the people inquired: "What is this that has happened to the son of Kish? Is Saul also among the prophets?" (10:11). Then it was that Saul ascended the high place—apparently to worship.

In his conversation with his uncle, where we next find him in the text (10:14–16), Saul related how he and his father's servant had gone to Samuel to inquire about the donkeys, but he said not a word about any anointing or any of Samuel's words about kingship. If the uncle here is the same person as Abner, the military strategist, then it becomes all the more significant that Saul did not mention this biggest news of the day to him. We can only speculate why Saul failed to do so: Was he intimidated by his uncle's military prowess and knowledge, or was he merely choking on the brink of undertaking so large a task that he knew his uncle would immediately set in motion for him? The text specifically noted that "[Saul] did not tell his uncle what Samuel had said about the kingship" (10:16b). That may have been a crucial mistake in the life of this leader, for he was to do whatever his hand found to do, namely, to take on the Philistines who had wrought such havoc in their central hill country around Benjamin. No doubt Abner could have been the encouragement and the needed strategist that God had provided for him; otherwise, why record this conversation with his uncle at this tense moment when Saul has been singularly attested by three signs and given such a changed heart?

SAUL'S MILITARY CAREER

Saul failed his first test of his leadership by failing to initiate a conflict with the Philistines. But soon a second opportunity came from another direction. The people of Jabesh in Gilead were under attack by king Nahash of the Ammonites. When the inhabitants of Jabesh Gilead appealed to Nahash for a peace settlement, he offered outrageous terms: "I will make a treaty with you only on the condition that I gouge out the right eye of every one of you and so bring disgrace on all Israel" (1 Sam. 11:2). As a last ditch stand, the people of Jabesh Gilead sent messengers across the Jordan to Saul with an appeal for help.

Saul's reaction was instantaneous: he butchered the oxen with which he had been plowing when the message was received and sent messengers to all the tribes with a sample of the butchered oxen and a call to arms, adding the threat that their oxen would look like the specimen that Saul had sent to each tribe if they failed to respond (1 Sam. 11:7). So startled, apparently, were all the tributes that this shy, retiring, and most unlikely person would be so blatantly aggressive that many must have come out of sheer wonderment and curiosity to see what had come over the man who had so recently, but so unimpressively, been appointed as their leader. Saul exhibited some of the same charismatic gifts that the judges who preceded him had demonstrated. The news of the plight of the besieged Jabesh Gileadites affected him much as it would have impacted a typical charismatic: "When Saul heard their words, the Spirit of God came upon him in power, and he burned with anger" (1 Sam. 11:6).

Three hundred and thirty thousand men turned out, a most impressive mustering of troops since the good old days of Joshua. Saul divided his troops into three divisions and fell upon the Ammonites during the last watch of the night with such resounding results that "no two [Ammonites] were left together" (11:11). It was a momentous victory that served to confirm Saul as their new leader and king. The men of

Jabesh Gilead would never forget Saul's response in their time of need, for they would be the only ones to haul Saul's body off the wall where the Philistines would later hang it after the king's defeat at the battle of Mt. Gilboa.

Throughout Saul's reign, Israel experienced continual warfare. It is all summarized in a small notice given in 1 Samuel 14:47–48.

> After Saul had assumed rule over Israel, he fought against their enemies on every side: Moab, the Ammonites, Edom, the kings of Zobah, and the Philistines. Wherever he turned, he inflicted punishment on them. He fought valiantly and defeated the Amalekites, delivering Israel from the hands of those who had plundered them.

This is hardly an anti-Saulide assessment of Saul's military career. After Saul had rescued the people of Jabesh Gilead from the Ammonites, he took on the Philistines—that is after a fashion—for actually it was Jonathan who finally carried out that which should have taken precedence in his father's confirmation program (as outlined in our previous chapter).

The battle shaped up in this manner: "Saul chose three thousand men from Israel; two thousand were with him at Micmash and in the hill country of Bethel, and a thousand were with Jonathan at Gibeah of Benjamin. The rest of the men he sent back to their homes" (1 Sam. 13:2). Now Micmash and Gibeah were situated on opposite sides of a steep valley today called *Wadi es-Suweinit*, a valley that comes up from the Jordan Valley near Jericho into the hill country just north of Jerusalem near Bethel. Micmash, on the northern bank, afforded easy access to the territory north of the wadi, while Gibeah gave one access to all the territory south of the valley: it was a strategic place from which to begin the opening wedge to pry the Philistines from their stronghold over the hill country of Israel. Both Jonathan and Saul's army were in visual contact with each other, so the spot was in every way advantageous.

Jonathan opened the fray by attacking the Philistine outpost at Geba and the news rang out all over the land of Israel: "Saul has attacked the Philistine outpost, and now Israel has become a stench to the Philistines" (1 Sam. 13:4). The Israelites were summoned to join Saul at Gilgal. The Philistine response was overwhelming: three thousand chariots and six thousand charioteers and soldiers without number came up from Philistia and camped at Micmash, east of Beth Aven, that is Bethel. When Saul's potential army saw these overwhelming odds, they hid in caves, woods, behind rocks, in pits, cisterns. Some even crossed over the Jordan to the land of Gad and Gilead (13:6–7).

Meanwhile, Saul waited seven days for Samuel to appear as he had been instructed (1 Sam. 10:8). Saul, now desperate, after watching his army dwindle before his eyes, decided he had waited long enough for Samuel, so he offered up the burnt and fellowship offerings. Just as he was finishing these ritual tasks, Samuel appeared and rebuked him for doing so. Samuel's rebuke included the charge that Saul had not kept the command that God had given him, for if he had, Saul's kingdom would have been established over Israel for all time (13:13–14). Samuel then departed for Gibeah, leaving Saul at Gilgal with a mere six hundred men. Saul and Jonathan went up to Geba of Benjamin, over against the Philistine encampment at Micmash.

While the Philistines continued to harass Israel by sending out three raiding parties, Jonathan and his armor bearer decided to test the waters by climbing up the steep ascent of the wadi to Micmash. After arriving at the top of the cliff in the Philistine camp, in short order they killed some twenty men. Then God struck the enemy with panic and the rout was on (14:13–15). Saul belatedly joined in the fray to find the superior and well-equipped Philistine forces in total confusion. Those Israelites who had melted away from fear suddenly came out of hiding and joined the other Israelite forces as God sent deliverance that day as the battle moved beyond Bethel, here stigmatized as Beth Aven, "house of iniquity" (14:23).

This was not the last time that Saul would face the Philistines; conflicts with these descendants of one of the Sea Peoples, who held the monopoly over the forging and use of iron, would reappear throughout Saul's reign (1 Sam. 17:1–2; 18:20–30; 19:8). In fact, Saul and Jonathan would die in their final battle fighting the Philistines.

Another evidence of the demise of Saul and his kingship came in his refusal to devote everything that belonged to the Amalekites to destruction (1 Sam. 15). Instead of obeying God, Saul thought it best to save some of the sheep and cattle from destruction and use them as an offering to Yahweh. He also saved King Agag, the Amalekite. Evidence was mounting that the Spirit of God had been removed from Saul and that he no longer demonstrated the gift of government that had been given to him when the charisma of the Spirit fell on him years earlier. Samuel reminded him that God does not delight in sacrifices so much as in obedience. Samuel himself put Agag to death as the prophet warned once again that "because [Saul had] rejected the word of the

LORD, he [had] rejected [Saul] as king" (1 Sam. 15:23b). The die was set; Saul was finished as king in God's eyes.

But Saul also had great success as he fought other battles throughout his lifetime with Zobah, Ammon, Moab, and Edom. Zobah dominated the southern part of Aram during Saul's days, probably extending its influence over the northern part of Transjordania. Moab and Ammon bordered on Gilead to the east and the south. Saul also confronted Edom, probably in the Judean wilderness and in the Negeb. On almost every front, Saul was beleaguered by raiding parties desperately trying to take away territory or produce from Israel. On balance, Saul managed to turn in a rather impressive set of victories over a formidable range of enemies and armies, but this was probably during the earlier days of his reign.

SAUL'S ADMINISTRATION

Most of the leadership within Saul's government came from within his own family. Saul's son Jonathan and his uncle Abner took leading roles in the affairs of state. Abner was given the title "commander" of the army (1 Sam. 14:50; 26:5; 2 Sa m. 2:8), though Saul himself is generally depicted as leading the army. There are also several references to Saul's "servants," a designation for his "officials," but few specific tasks of state are delegated to any of them apart from military involvements (1 Sam. 18:5, 22, 30; 22:6; etc.). One title does survive, "Doeg the Edomite," who was "chief of Saul's herdsmen" (1 Sam. 21:7; 22:9). This does not mean, however, that Doeg had the oversight of raising Saul's cattle, for the name of the office appears often in antiquity, but it did not correspond to the function the name seemed to signify.

There is no mention of taxes during Saul's reign, but Samuel warned that kingship would involve the confiscation of some of their properties by the crown, and other forms of taxation (1 Sam. 8:10–18). A fair inference from Saul's words in 1 Samuel 22:7 ("Listen, men of Benjamin! Will the son of Jesse give all of you fields and vineyards?") suggests that Saul did redistribute some of the lands to his commanders in the army by taking it away from those who owned it. A later insight into the methods by which the nation was financed may be seen from the two "leaders of raiding bands" (2 Sam. 4:2–3), who were employed by Ish-Bosheth. Taken at face value, they appear to be captains of hit-and-run squads that gathered spoil and pillage in order to run the government.

SAUL'S SPIRITUAL LIFE

Saul is depicted as a man who was set apart by Yahweh for greatness and for a special work. As he began his reign, the "Spirit of the LORD" came upon him "in power" (1 Sam. 10:6) and "God [was] with [him]" (10:7).

But in a tragic turn of events, Saul appeared to set himself on a course of destruction. As life went on, God became ominously silent (1 Sam. 14:18, 27; 28:6) and even hostile to him (1 Sam. 15; 16:14; 19:9; 28:16, 19). As relationships with his family deteriorated, this isolation was made even more dramatic by a divine silence that in the end drove him to the witch of Endor to seek some guidance from the netherworld (1 Sam. 28), if indeed guidance from God was now unavailable.

We do read of Saul's erecting an altar to Yahweh in the time of battle (1 Sam. 14:31–35) in his earnest but misguided zeal to have the men of his army ceremonially pure for battle with the Philistines. But this act, along with his direct disobedience of divine revelation on several occasions, make him an opponent to the plan of God being given to him through Samuel.

SAUL'S LAST BATTLE

Saul concluded his work exactly as he began it: fighting the Philistines (1 Sam. 28–31). David, of course, was not there; fortunately, in light of later developments, he had been prevented by the Philistine's suspicions of his loyalities from having any part in this battle. The site for the battle was at the southeastern end of the Jezreel Valley, at the base of Mt. Gilboa where it protrudes out into the valley (1 Sam. 31:1). Whether the battle was fought for control of the valley, or was an effort to drive the Philistines from the whole Esdraelon Plain is difficult to judge. But it was clear that the tribe of Manasseh was given this section of the valley, but they lived mostly in the hill country with a few settlements spilling over into this valley which the Philistines controlled at that point.

The Philistine camp was at Shunem on Mt. Moreh, opposite Mt. Gilboa and also at Aphek. But the battle itself turned out to be a disaster for Saul and for the people he led. The Philistines overwhelmed the Israelites, forcing them to run for cover in Mt. Gilboa. Saul himself was mortally wounded (31:3–6), finally falling on his own sword when his armor bearer refused to finish him off. It is true that an Amalekite tried to take credit for the act of killing Saul in order to curry the favor of

David (2 Sam. 1:1–16), but David did not take kindly either to his lying or to any defaming of Saul, the nation's slain leader.

Three of Saul's sons also were killed: Jonathan, Abinadab, and Malchishua. The bodies of all three, along with that of King Saul, fell into the hands of the Philistines, who publicaly displayed their bodies on the walls of Beth Shan. They would have been left there to rot, it seems, had not some brave men from Jabesh Gilead, remembering how Saul came to their aid in their desperate time of need, stole the bodies from their disgraceful exposure on the walls and took them back to Jabesh for a proper burial (1 Sam. 31:11–13).

David's lament for Saul and Jonathan (2 Sam. 1:17–27) is one of the most touching pieces in Hebrew literature. This lament expressed respect for Saul and Jonathan's heroic accomplishments, and celebrates David's deep fondness for Jonathan (1:22–26). No doubt this lament helped heal some of the rifts that had developed in the nation as polarizations had gathered around David and Saul.

Abner and Ish-Bosheth

Saul's defeat left the country in almost total disarray. The Philistines were as much a threat to an Israelite occupation and progress in the land they had begun to occupy years ago. David might have been an available leader, but he had acted in ways that could have been interpreted as opposing Saul and as being antimonarchical. In addition, David had at times gone over to offer help to the Philistines in order to secure some respite from Saul's frantic attacks on David and his men.

Thus, it turned out that Abner, Saul's uncle, took matters into his own hands and arranged for the transfer of the administration of the kingdom from Gibeah to Mahanaim in Transjordania. This move may not have been as wise as it seemed at the time, for it put the government far out of the reach of the Philistines (as well as out of the reach of David). It symbolically tended to abdicate the rule over the west side of the Jordan. In all of these moves, Abner remained the power behind the throne.

Ish-Bosheth, also called Esh-Baal in 1 Chronicles 8:33 and 9:39, is called the son of Saul in 2 Samuel 2:8, 12, but he is never mentioned as one of Saul's sons in 1 Samuel 14:49; 31:2 (= 1 Chron 10:2); or in 2 Samuel 21:7–8. In these passages, Saul's sons are identified as Jonathan, Ishvi, Malchishua, and Abinadab. This may indicate that *son* may mean something like *grandson*, or that he was very young at the time of Saul's death, for he is not mentioned in connection with Saul's last battle.

Ish-Bosheth, at any rate, was forty years old when he began to reign over Israel from Mahanaim; but his reign lasted only two years (2 Sam. 2:10). He claimed authority over all the areas Saul had ruled, but Saul's empire was in disarray, and little of Saul's empire was left. Things had turned so bad that Ish-Bosheth could even hold on to Gibeah, from which Saul began his rule. Mahanaim was more secure among the Gileadites who, for historical reasons, had remained loyal to Saul's house.

But there were other troubles besides the Philistines and the shambles in which the nation found itself: David's house troubled Ish-Bosheth's greatly. Second Samuel 3:1 noted, "The war between the house of Saul and the house of David lasted a long time. David grew stronger and stronger, while the house of Saul grew weaker and weaker." But the only contest between the two houses after Saul had died was the strange contest of champions that took place at the pool of Gibeon between the Israelite troops under Abner and David's troops under the command of Joab (2 Sam. 2:12–32). Before it was all over, nineteen of David's men, three hundred from Benjamin, and sixty of Abner's men had been slain. The fact that it took place in Gibeon suggests that David had authorized Joab to encroach on the territory controlled by Ish-Bosheth. More and more this contest between the two ruling houses was taking on the dimensions of a family feud, for Abner was Saul's uncle (or some say his cousin; 1 Sam. 14:50) while those prominent in David's house were sons of his sister Zeruiah and therefore nephews of David: Joab, Abishai and Asahel (1 Sam. 26:6; 2 Sam. 2:18; 1 Chron. 2:13–6). Abner killed Asahel in this contest, a fact that later would have great consequences. It is a question as to why the account makes a distinction between the Benjaminites that fell to the sword and those from Abner's men who died. Presumably, the Benjaminites were loyalists to Saul's house who fought alongside Abner and his men.

Ish-Bosheth had reason to fear his general, Abner, for in addition to being the power behind the throne, Ish-Bosheth found it necessary to accuse Abner of having relations with one of Saul's concubines (2 Sam. 3:7–11). Usually the successor to the throne inherited the harem that went with the throne, but other aspirants, after a manner, staked their rival claims to the throne often by having relations or by seeking to marry one of the women of the former king's harem. Abner denied nothing but expressed his deep anger and resentment for being interrogated about the matter. This event led Abner to slowly shift his allegiance from Ish-Bosheth to David. Perhaps Abner could see the handwriting on the wall: David would eventually triumph in his quest to rule over all Israel. Abner arranged to talk with David while he could negotiate from a position of strength.

David demanded that two rather difficult matters be arranged as a condition to his further bargaining with Abner: (1) Michal, the daughter of Saul, to whom David had been married while he was still in favor with the court of Saul, must be returned to him (cf. 1 Sam. 18:17–27; 2 Sam. 3:13); and (2) Abner must convince the Benjamites, who had already suffered heavy losses to David's men, that David was the man they should trust.

David's request to Ish-Bosheth for the return of Michal (now married to Paltiel; 2 Sam. 3:14–16) surprisingly was granted, probably on the advice of Abner. On the second matter, as Abner conferred with the elders, he wisely gave special attention to the Benjamites and thus won over their allegiance. As Abner returned to David at Hebron with everything requested of him signed and sealed as completed agreements, Joab assassinated Abner as a vendetta for Abner's killing of Joab's brother Asahel (2 Sam. 3:20–30). But it may have been motivated just as much by the fact that Joab feared that his own job as commander of the troops may have been in jeopardy if Abner continued to win the favor of David.

With Abner out of the way, it would appear that Ish-Bosheth stood a better chance to get on with governing Israel, but the momentum was against him, for the sympathies of the council of the elders was already beginning to swing against Ish-Bosheth. What finally concluded the whole matter was the brutal assassination of Ish-Bosheth by Baanah and Recah, the brothers from Beeroth (2 Sam. 4:1–6). Hoping to reap a reward from David for quickly delivering the head of Ish-Bosheth, they hastened through the night to reach David at Hebron. David instead ordered that both men be killed, their hands and feet be cut off, and their bodies hung by the pool in Hebron (2 Sam. 4:12). Meanwhile, David ordered the head of Ish-Bosheth be taken and buried in Abner's tomb at Hebron.

Abner and Ish-Bosheth were gone. The elders of Israel went to David in Hebron and arranged to recognize him as king over Israel as well as the tribe of Judah where he had been ruling. It would be a lot less costly in lives to turn over the country voluntarily than to suffer a large loss of life if David took it forcibly, which they probably felt he was capable of doing. So David ruled over both Judah and Israel, and the united kingdom and monarchy became a reality for the first time.

16

The Rise of King David

Until the recently discovered inscription found at Dan containing the *bet David*, "house/dynasty of David," with its epigraphical evidence from archaeology,[1] McCarter's 1986 assessment was correct: "The Bible is our only source of information about David."[2] But that judgment is now passé, for this inscription has enormous significance in light of the grave doubts that had been cast on the actual existence of either David or his dynasty.

Now, a second reference to the "house of David" has been detected in the restored Moabite Mesha Stele, wherein the ninth century B.C. Moabite king Mesha claimed victory over the Israelites.[3] Andre Lemaire reexamined this stele, discovered in A.D. 1868, which still remains the longest monumental inscription found anywhere in Palestine, in order to publish its first *editio princeps*, which has never been published in all this time.

Previously it had been noted that lines 5, 10, and 18 of the Mesha Stele contained a reference to the "king of Israel," but no one had noticed up until now that the broken line 31 also contained a reference to the "house of David," (*bt [d]wd*; the text was broken where the *d* had

1. A recently discovered Aramaic inscription found at Tell Dan, dating from the ninth century B.C., is published by A. Biran and J. Naveh, "An Aramaic Stele Fragment from Tel Dan," *IEJ* 43 (1993):81–98. Also see idem, "'David' Found at Dan," *BAR* 20.2 (1994): 26–39.

2. P. Kyle McCarter Jr., "The Historical David," *Interpretation* 40 (1986): 117.

3. Andre Lemaire, "'House of David': Restored in Moabite Inscription," *BAR* 20.3 (1994): 30–37.

appeared). Also, the final *t* on *bt* had eluded scholars until the German scholar Mark Lidzbarski tentatively identified it in 1900. Professor Lemaire has confirmed this reading and also restored the missing *d* which followed it on the basis of a squeeze that was made of the stele just before it was broken apart by the Bedouins by heating the stone and pouring cold water on it to keep the Turks from buying it. Thus, while many current scholars are denying that David ever existed, much less had a dynasty, now there are two archaeological, external references to the "house of David," both coming from the ninthcentury B.C.

But these inscriptions, significant as they are, cannot pretend to help us assess the meaning and significance of David, a man who played a vital role in Israel's national existence. It is certain that David founded a dynasty that maintained a rule from the capital city of Jerusalem, a dynasty that lasted for more than four centuries. Even after David's kingdom fell in 586 B.C., his line was still visible when the Jews returned from Babylon, and the promise that one would still come from his throne to rule, as in the former days, was one of the mainstays of Israel's theology and national life.

David in the Biblical Sources

To show the value and importance placed on David's life and works, one need only note that some seventy-five chapters of the Bible are devoted to David. There are forty-two such chapters in 1 and 2 Samuel and 1 Kings alone. First and 2 Chronicles add another twenty chapters, while thirteen of the superscriptions in the Book of Psalms are directly related to significant events in his life and career.

Prior to 1970, most scholars were impressed by the rather frank and clear style in which the events and personalities of David and his reign were recorded. It was thought that such an achievement must be due to a "Solomonic Enlightenment," which produced Israel's earliest example of history writing. But in the 1970s this all began to change: gradually a reappraisal of the historical value of the two previously highly acclaimed components of the Davidic biography, the "History of David's Rise" (hereafter HDR) and the "Succession Narrative" (hereafter SN), were downgraded due to what scholars now described as "apologetical" and "propaganda" materials. Thus, the vivid portrayal of persons and events that had been explained as being possible only because of the writer's proximity to the material he was recounting, now was attributed to the writer's imaginative and descriptive powers. The "History of David's Rise" (1 Sam. 16 to 2 Sam. 5 and 2 Sam.

8:1–15), was regarded as an extraordinary example of artistic skill, according to many writers. Until recent times, the "Court History of David" or the "Succession Narrative" (2 Sam. 9–20 and 1 Kings 1–2), was considered one of the finest pieces of historical storytelling from the ancient world.

Hayes and Miller, writing in 1977, list four reasons to reject the Succession Narrative as a historical record:

1. The presence of anecdotal episodes, such as David's liaison with Bathsheba (2 Sam. 11:2–21) or the death of Absalom (2 Sam. 18:9–19:8);
2. The psychological feelings of Amnon for his half sister Tamar (2 Sam. 13:1–17);
3. The scenes and conversations from the bedroom witnessed by no one else (2 Sam. 13:1–17; 1 Kings 1:15–31);
4. The emphasis on the presence of God who knows all, judges all, and rewards all (2 Sam. 11:27b; 12:7–12; 17:14; etc.).[4]

In 1986, Miller and Hayes reduced to three their list of objections to considering as historical the Samuel-Kings descriptions of the events of David's reign:

1. The composite nature of the record;
2. The selection and tone of the materials; and
3. The arrangement of material governed in large measure by the theological interests of the late Judean compilers.[5]

Each of the points raised in the two sets of objections is worthy of criticism and rejection. Already in our introductory chapter, we have critiqued the view that excludes any divine intervention as a proper subject for historical reporting. The issue of the composite nature of the documents was different, however. For example, the Goliath story was said to include three contradictory claims:

1. David was already in Saul's employ, yet Saul did not recognize him;
2. Goliath's head, it was claimed, was taken to Jerusalem (1 Sam. 17:54), though David had not yet conquered Jerusalem (2 Sam. 5:6–10);
3. Elhanan the Bethlehemite, son of Jaareoregin, it was claimed, killed Goliath, though Goliath's death was attributed already in the text to David (2 Sam. 21:19).

---

4. John H. Hayes and J. Maxwell Miller, *Israelite and Judean History* (Philadelphia: Westminster, 1977), 337–38.
5. J. Maxwell Miller and John H. Hayes, *A History of Ancient Israel and Judah* (Philadelphia: Westminster, 1986), 152–56.

Each of these complaints will be considered later in our discussion of the history of David.

Nevertheless, the candor of SN seriously suggested what it had achieved with an earlier generation of scholars: its utter frankness, refusal to gloss over the king's sins or weaknesses, the family disruptions, the bitterness, the revolt, and the ignominious deeds in David's life all promoted the idea that realistic life and events were being presented. One event after another told the story of David, warts and all: his sin with Bathsheba, the rape of Tamar, the murder of Amnon, the rebellion of Absalom, and the rebellion of Sheba.

Despite all these acknowledgments, recent scholarship feels that the reason the literary history of 1 and 2 Samuel and 1 Kings was composed was to serve as a court apology or a royal justification of David against charges and suspicions of wrongdoing in his bid for the throne from Saul and Saul's family.[6]

Of even a lower usefulness in constructing a history of David was the Book of 1 Chronicles. Indeed, the chronicler's intent was clear from the start in that he made no mention of David's youth, his anointing by Samuel, or the like. His narrative commenced with the Israelite delegation coming to Hebron to talk with him about being king over all Israel. The seven years of David's reign in Hebron and his rule over Judah are never mentioned. What is emphasized is that Yahweh had put Saul to death and had now turned the kingdom over to David (1 Chron. 10:14).

The chronicler also omits references to David's affair with Bathsheba, his struggles with Saul, his service with the Philistines at the time of the battle on Mt. Gilboa, his previous crowning by the elders of Judah, or what happened to Ish-Bosheth and Abner. Such omissions appear to be a tendentious use of the Samuel-Kings material, if that was one of the chronicler's sources.

However, it is also clear that part of the chronicler's purpose was to show that even during David's exile there were those outside of Judah who clearly recognized his election as king. Some of Saul's own kinsmen joined David while he was in Ziklag (1 Chron. 12:1–2). Some non-Saulide Benjamites also came over to David along with those from Gad in Transjordania (1 Chron. 12:16–17). David himself at first sus-

6. P. Kyle McCarter Jr., "'Plots, True or False': The Succession Narrative as Court Apologetic," *Interpretation* 35 (1980): 355–67; J. W. Flanagan, "Court History or Succession Document? A Study of II Samuel 9–20 and 1 Kings 1–2," *JBL* 91 (1972): 172–81; and L. G. Perdue, "The Testament of David and Egyptian Royal Instructions," in *Scripture in Context II: More Essays on the Comparative Method*, ed. W. W. Hallo et al. (Winona Lake, Ind.: Eisenbrauns, 1983), 79–96.

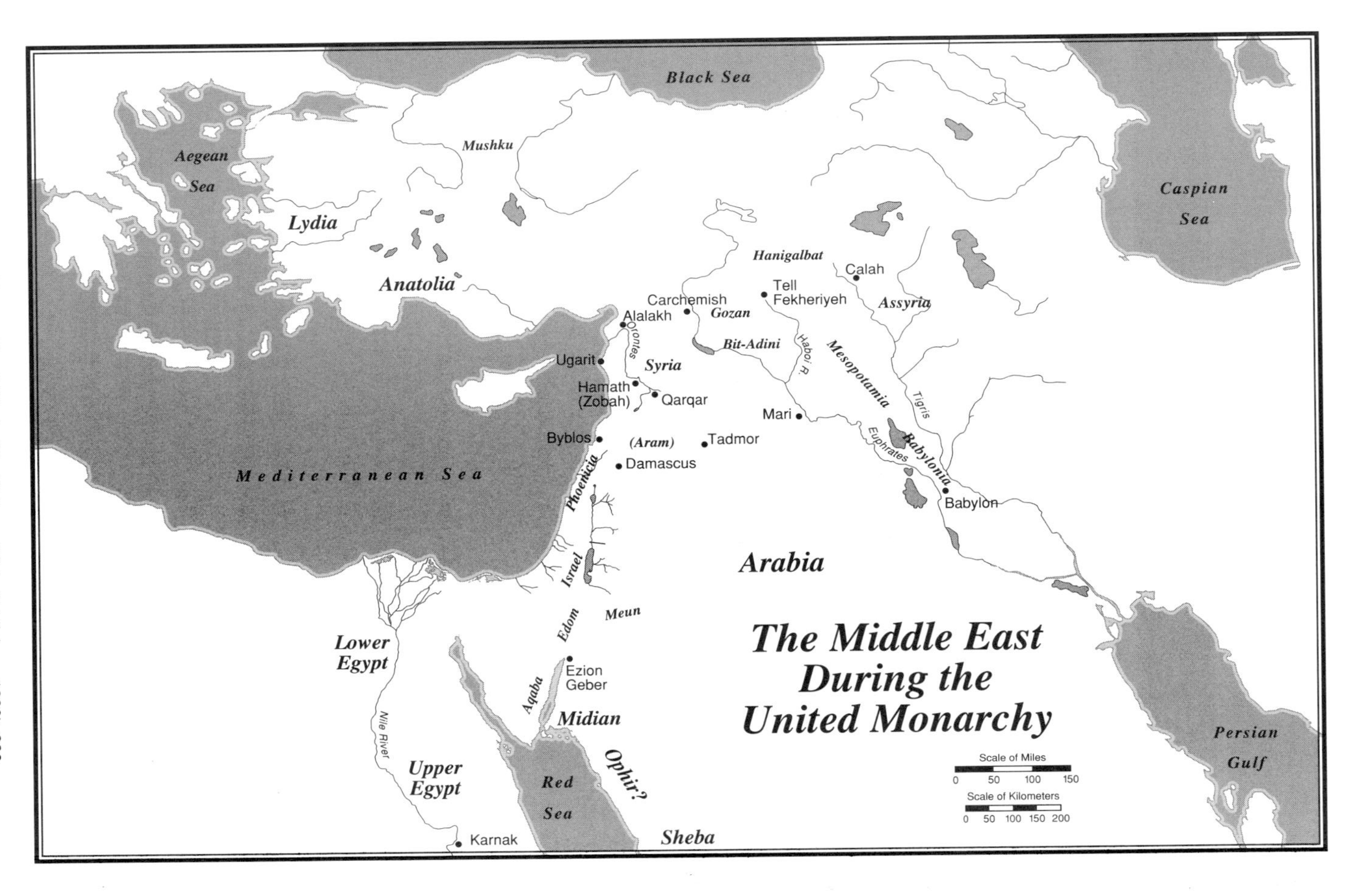

From *Holman Bible Handbook* (Nashville: Holman Bible Publishers, 1992), 232.

pected these joiners, but when they pledged their loyalty to David and not to Saul, he welcomed them. Other defectors from Saul from the tribe of Manasseh joined David when he went to fight with the Philistines at Mt. Gilboa (1 Chron. 12:19–22). Finally, the chronicler lists each tribe by name, and not just the general statement that all the tribes came to make him king at Hebron, as 2 Samuel 5:1–3 had it (1 Chron. 12:23–40).

Most characteristic of all was the chronicler's portrayal of David as the real organizer of the plans, materials, and rituals for the temple (1 Chron. 15–16; 23–26; 28–29). The chronicler includes much that parallels Samuel-Kings, but he also introduces new material, including a heavy emphasis on the theological aspects of the kingdom of David and Solomon. The chronicler includes none of the troubles of David's reign: his struggles with Absalom, Sheba, or the later struggle of Solomon with Adonijah.

But is even this admittedly tendentious use of the Samuel-Kings materials sufficient reason for us to question the trustworthiness of those materials without parallels in Samuel-Kings? What is demonstrated by his use of Samuel-Kings is a selectivity that focused on certain elements in the reign. What rule prevents him from doing so? How could that reflect on the writer's credibility unless it was decided in advance, based on one's hermeneutical circle, that such things were disallowed or that they even reflected poorly on the writer?

Two separate trends may be seen with regard to the use of the materials from Chronicles, according to Sara Japhet:

> One was the attempt to sift from the book maximum historical data through a cautious, critical method. . . . and exploit as far as possible the material peculiar to Chronicles. The other was the treatment of the book as a specific section of biblical historiography with interest focused on questions of a literary and religious nature and with the question of historical reliability losing its centrality.[7]

When all is said and done, the biblical sources remain our best sources on David and his times. Had the same materials been available from an external source, which nevertheless named a number of pagan deities, it would have been accorded much more serious treatment compared to the usual reception given to biblical materials. A certain

7. Sara Japhet, "The Historical Reliability of Chronicles," *JSOT* 33 (1985): 97. R. North, "Does Archaeology Prove Chronicles Sources?" *Light Unto My Path: Old Testament Studies in Honor of J. M. Myers*. ed. H. N. Bream et al. (Philadelphia: Temple University Press, 1974), 375–401.

selectivity guided by rather defined purposes must be agreed on, but it is not clear, by any means, that such an admission has as yet disqualified most or all of the material from SN, HDR, the "appendix" of 2 Samuel 21–24, all of which are said to be intrusive to the SN, or the Chronicles.

David's Early Life

David was born in the town of Ephrath or Ephrata (1 Sam. 17:12), later known as the town of Bethlehem (1 Sam. 16:1, 18; cf. Mic. 5:2), the eighth[8] and youngest son of Jesse (1 Sam. 16:10–13). The name *Ephrath* might have come from a group of Ephraimite Ephrathites who migrated south at some time in history, for the northerners of 2 Samuel 5:1 speak of David as his own "flesh and blood." That, however, could have been a reference to their kinship as Jews and not to themselves as northerners. Still, there is the additional reference in Genesis 35:19 and 48:7 that appears to assume that the Ephrath of Ephraim, associated with Rachel's burial place, is also connected with Ephrathah/Bethlehem.

David, the shepherd boy of his father's sheep and goats, was anointed by Samuel after the prophet/judge had passed each of David's seven older brothers before Yahweh. When Samuel anointed him, the Spirit of God fell on him just as the Spirit had fallen on the judges in an earlier day (1 Sam. 16:1–13).

First Samuel 16:14–23 described how David was called to Saul's court to help soothe the king's frayed nerves. Here began the tradition of David's connection with the music of Israel. As the Spirit of God had fallen on David, an evil spirit (perhaps a demonic oppression) had overcome Saul. David's music was to counter the monarch's fits of moodiness and rage. In the meantime, David became acquainted with court life in preparation for a role he would later fill. Saul approved of David, making him his armor bearer and his musician. The next time

8. 1 Samuel 16:10–11 and 17:12–14 claim Jesse had eight sons while 1 Chronicles 2:13–15 says seven. Which is correct? First Samuel names only four of Jesse's sons: Eliab, Abinadab, Shammah, who is called Shimea in 1 Chronicles, and David. First Chronicles names three other sons, Nethanel, Raddai, and Ozem, but specifies that David is the seventh.What happened to this unnamed son is not known, but some suggest that he may have died without posterity; thus, he was not included in the list. But the Syriac lists Elihu as the seventh son in 1 Chronicles 2:15, then it makes David the eighth son, thus bringing it into harmony with the Samuel list. The Syriac reading is based on the Hebrew reading of 1 Chronicles 27:18, where the Septuagint had Eliab instead of Elihu (apparently going with the known name from the list of 1 Samuel. If the Syriac preserves an accurate Hebrew text, then Elihu is the missing son in the 1 Chronicles 2:15 list.

we meet David, however, he is back in Bethlehem. Whether finances got tight, or something happened, we are not told.[9]

When the story continued in 1 Samuel 17, David was instructed by his father to visit the site of a battle with the Philistines where his three older brothers were serving at Ephes Dammim, which lay between Socoh (*Khirbet `Abbad*) and Azekah (*Tell Zakariyeh*) in the Valley of Elah, about twenty miles southwest of Jerusalem. David took bread and cheeses for his three oldest bothers, Eliab, Abinadab, and Shammah, as well as for the commander of the unit. When David arrived at the camp of Saul's men, he learned that the Philistines had selected a champion named Goliath of Gath, a nine-foot giant, perhaps descended from the legendary Anakim, to represent their side. The challenge was for someone from Israel to fight Goliath, but no one had applied for the job for some forty days.

David became so incensed at the defiance of the Philistine that he volunteered to fight Goliath himself. With only a slingshot and some stones in his hand, David slew the giant and won the duel for Israel. David's reward was that he was to be married to Saul's daughter and that his father's family would be exempt from paying taxes in Israel (1 Sam. 17:25).

If David came to the throne in Judah in 1011 B.C. at age thirty (2 Sam. 5:4), then he was born in 1041 B.C., about ten years before Saul began to reign. Certainly he could have been tending sheep at the age of twelve or fourteen, about the time Yahweh rejected Saul, and Samuel anointed David (early in the 1020s B.C.). Given the fact that Saul's son Jonathan was already a leader in his father's army in the 1050s, Jonathan must have been David's senior by some twenty to thirty years.

But what of the conflicting explanations of 1 Samuel 16, where David is known by Saul, plays music for Saul, and serves as his personal bodyguard? What of 1 Samuel 17:55–58, where Saul ordered Abner to "find out whose son this young man [was]"? Is this a sure sign that these two accounts stem from two independent but conflicting traditions? If not, how could Saul—and Abner too—be ignorant about this lad who had been Saul's personal armor bearer and musician?

While some have tried to blame the discrepancy on Saul's diseased and failing mental health, others argued it was due to the hustle and bustle of court life and the multiplicity of servants and attendants. A

9. Many consider the narrative about David's anointing to be historically unreliable and a late addition to the text, but Martin Kessler has shown on rhetorical analysis that it is an integral part of the David narrative: "Narrative Technique in 1 Sam. 16:1–13," *CBQ* 32 (1970): 552–53.

third attempt even tried to claim that Saul was not asking for David's identity, which he knew well enough, but only about his father's social position, for he had promised to grant the one who would defeat the Philistine the hand of his daughter in marriage. But how does that explain Abner's amnesia? No, the most plausible explanation, instead, is the one favored by most of the older commentators: The events of 1 Samuel 16–18 are not given in chronological order but are transposed by a figure of speech known as *hysterologia*,[10] where something is put last, that in its usual order should be put first. This rearrangement was for the special purpose of bringing certain facts together, especially those relating to the Spirit of God. As David was anointed in 1 Samuel 16:1–13, the Spirit of God came upon him. But that is contrasted with the removal of the Spirit of God from Saul (1 Sam. 16:14–23), an episode brought forward from later history to make the theological point. In the actual order of events, 1 Samuel 16:14–23 should have followed 1 Samuel 18:9. In this way the narrative alternates between David and Saul and contrasts the work of the Spirit in both:

A. 16:1–13—David anointed. The Spirit comes on him.
B. 16:14–23—Saul rejected. The Spirit departs from him.
A. 17:1–18:9, David—An earlier incident in his life.
B. 18:10–30, Saul—The Spirit departs from him.

The fact that such a rearrangement did occur is suggested in the fact that the Vaticanus Manuscript of the Septuagint deletes twenty-nine verses in all (1 Sam. 17:12–31 and 17:55–18:5).

But there is another alleged indication of the presence of conflicting episodes: Goliath's death is not only attributed to David in 1 Samuel 17, but also to a certain Elhanan in 2 Samuel 21:19. How can both be right? Many say that must be a sign of composite, but conflicting, and independent sources.

The solution to this dilemma cannot be, as is sometimes suggested, that Elhanan is the throne name for David. Instead, 1 Chronicles 20:5 noted that it was "in another battle" that Elhanan killed "Lahmi, the brother of Goliath the Gittite." The problem, then, is with the text of 2 Samuel 21:19, which we can trace through the correctly preserved text of 1 Chronicles 20:5.

The copyist of 2 Samuel 21:19 made three mistakes: (1) he read the direct object sign (*ʾet*) that came just in front of the name of the giant

10. See E. W. Bullinger, *Figures of Speech* (1898; reprint ed., Grand Rapids: Baker, 1968), 706–707. Also see Walter C. Kaiser Jr., *More Hard Sayings of the Old Testament* (Downers Grove, Ill.: InterVarsity, 1992), 154–57.

Elhanan killed, named Lahmi, as if it were the word "*beth*," thereby getting "the Bethlehemite," when the "Beth" was put with "Lahmi." (2) The copyist also misread the word for "brother" (Hebrew *ʾaḥ*) as the direct object sign before Goliath, thus making Goliath the one that was killed, instead of what it should have been—"the brother of Goliath." (3) The copyist misplaced the word *Oregim*, meaning "weavers," so that it yielded "Elhanan son of Jaare-Oregim," a most improbable reading for anyone: "Elhanan the son of the forests of weavers!" Instead, the word for "weavers" should have come as it does in 1 Chronicles 20:5 as the spear being "a beam/shaft like a weaver's rod."[11]

There was one other troubling feature in the Samuel story that betrayed the fact that a good number of the episodes in David's life were invented. This one is found in 1 Samuel 17:54, where David took Goliath's head to Jerusalem. But this is a "hopeless anachronism" according to Simon J. DeVries.[12] First, the text informs us that David put Goliath's weapons in "his" own tent, but it is unlikely that David had a tent, since he had just arrived at the battlefield. Hoffmeier, however, made a strong case that the text referred to Goliath's tent and not David's, for Goliath's tent and weapons were part of the plunder that belonged to David.

As a common sign of humiliating the enemy, the chopping off of the vanquished person's head and putting it on public display were all part of ancient Near Eastern practice.[13] In like manner, David proceeded to deal with the vanquished Goliath. Indeed, the Philistines themselves would later treat Saul's vanquished head in just this manner by attaching it to the wall of Beth Shan (1 Sam. 31:10).

But, it is objected, Jerusalem was not yet under Israelite control (cf. 2 Sam. 5:6–10). But that may have been the very point David was making: just as the Philistine had fallen victim to David's sword, so would the Jebusites in Jerusalem soon feel the edge of David's sword. All David would need to have done was to sneak up to the Jerusalem wall under the cover of darkness and attach Goliath's head to the outside.

---

11. See J. Barton Payne, "1 Chronicles," in *The Expositor's Bible Commentary*, vol. 4, ed. Frank E. Gaebelein (Grand Rapids: Zondervan, 1988), 403–404. Also, Gleason L. Archer Jr., *Encyclopedia of Bible Difficulties* (Grand Rapids: Zondervan, 1982), 178–79.

12. Simon J. DeVries, "David's Victory over the Philistine as Saga and as a Legend," *JBL* 92 (1973): 24, n. 3. See, however, James K. Hoffmeier, "The Aftermath of David's Triumph over Goliath: 1 Samuel 17:54 in Light of Near Eastern Parallels," *Archaeology in the Biblical World* I, 1 (1991): 18–19.

13. For a pictorial representation of such beheading and placing on public display, see James Pritchard, *ANEP*, no. 236.

Thus, on close investigation, every one of the commonly used signs of the composite nature of the Samuel stories evaporates under a close reading of the text. They betray signs of neither anachronism nor of contradiction. Accordingly, the objections against using them as pieces of evidence in reconstructing the history of the period must be removed.

DAVID THE FUGITIVE

David's rise to fame and success appeared meteoric and unabated. His military prowess was celebrated by the women in the streets as the soldiers were welcomed home. The women sang:

> "Saul has slain his thousands,
> and David his tens of thousands" (1 Sam. 18:7).

The comparisons and competition from this young upstart grated on Saul's mind and well-being. The king had by this time been ostracized from Samuel. Now he faced a challenge to his throne and to the line of his family on the throne. In his jealousy and rage, Saul attempted to kill David, but David averted the thrust of his spear. Saul reneged on his promise to give his daughter Merab as wife to the slayer of Goliath, giving instead his younger daughter Michal, when he learned she loved David. But an additional price of one hundred foreskins of the Philistines was required, which David cheerfully doubled, thereby thwarting another royal plan that may have intended for David to be killed in carrying out such an operation. All attempts by Saul's son Jonathan to assuage the hostilities and bad feeling of his father against his friend David were to no avail. David had to flee from Saul's court if he wanted to live.

David's escape from Saul's court and Saul's plots to kill him are recorded in 1 Samuel 19:11–21:9. There are four main narratives in these escape stories that feature David's wife Michal, the prophet/judge Samuel, Saul's son Jonathan, and the high priest Ahimelech and his family at Nob. The first tells how Michal stalled Saul's soldiers while David made a hasty exit through a window: Michal pretended that David was too sick to answer Saul's summons to the palace (1 Sam. 19:11–17).

The second related how David went to Ramah, Samuel's home, on the hill opposite from Gibeah, where Samuel had a camp or a conference grounds (the text has *Naioth*) of some sort. But when Saul sent men to capture David there, the Spirit of God fell on each of the three detachments, including, finally, Saul himself, thus preventing David's capture (1 Sam. 19:18–24).

Even Jonathan was not able to help David or explain his father's passionate desire to get rid of David. It had become clear that David must totally break off serving and living in Saul's court (1 Sam. 20:1– 42).

David immediately sought refuge at Nob, probably to be identified with Mt. Scopus, northeast of Jerusalem, the extension of the Mount of Olives, some five to six miles south southwest of Jerusalem. Innocently, Ahimelech gave David the five loaves of consecrated bread and the captured sword of the Philistine, Goliath, that David must have donated to the tabernacle. Later, when Doeg the Edomite, who had been detained at the house of God for some matter, reported that the priests had given this assistance to David, Saul murdered the eighty-five priests of Nob, including Ahimelech, the high priest. Only Abiathar, son of Ahimelech, managed to escape this massacre and escape to David's camp (1 Sam. 21:1–9; 22:6–23).

David's plight was now desperate and he fled to Achish, the Philistine king of Gath (1 Sam. 21:10–15; cf. Ps. 34). But the Philistines became suspicious and started to say, "Isn't this David, . . . the one they sing about in their dances:

> 'Saul has slain his thousands,
> and David his tens of thousands.'"

In order to escape, David pretended that he had gone mad and began to scratch on the city gate and to let his saliva run down his beard. Achish, frightened by the whole display, ordered: "Am I so short of madmen that you have to bring this fellow here to carry on like this in front of me? Must this man come into my house?" So they let David and his brigade go.

Saul did not immediately pursue David. David left Gath of the Philistines in favor of a hideout near the cave at Adullum in the Shephelah, some fifteen miles southwest of Bethlehem. David was now the leader of a band of four hundred debtors, fugitives, and political malcontents like himself. He and his band of outlaws would maintain themselves by selling protection to wealthy landowners in the vicinity or by raiding certain outposts for booty. Meanwhile, he moved his parents to Mizpah in Moab (unknown location), where he requested and received permission to leave his family for protection. This was natural in one way, since his great-grandmother Ruth came from Moab, and Saul had already made war on Moab (1 Sam. 14:47). The rift between

Saul and David could be used to Moab's advantage as they offered help to David's family.

At this time, two important religious figures joined David: Abiathar, the sole survivor of Doeg and Saul's massacre at Nob, and the prophet Gad (1 Sam. 22:5). Both remained with David throughout his career (2 Sam. 24:11). Gad convinced the fleeing David that he and his men would best leave Adullam and camp instead in the forest of Hereth (location uncertain). If this site is the present-day Kharas, some five miles southeast of Adullam, it had a twofold advantage: (1) it was in the territory of Judah, and (2) the forest offered better cover than a known fortification.

David was in the vicinity of Adullam, where he had gone in attempting to the rescue of the town of Keilah (*Khirbet Qila*) from the Philistines (1 Sam. 23:1–5). Saul learned of David's whereabouts and came to capture him. David inquired of the Lord through the ephod that Abiathar the priest had brought down to him. From the ephod David learned that the ungrateful residents of Keilah, a village of Judah just south of Adullam, would hand David over to Saul, even though he had just delivered them; and that Saul would come down to end this now prolonged hostility by capturing David. The local populace wanted relief from the Philistines, but that engendered no particular loyalty to David; they were loyal to the throne of Saul!

Abandoning Keilah, David and his men sought refuge in the southern hills of Judah, near the village of Ziph (*Tell Zif*). But the Ziphites turned out to be loyalists to Saul and twice reported to him on David's movements and whereabouts (1 Sam. 23:19–29). David came close to losing everything as Saul was closing in on him from one side of the mountain and David was hurrying along the other side of the same mountain. Just as Saul had David squeezed into a trap, word providentially came that the Philistines were attacking the land, and Saul had to break off at the very moment when victory seemed to be within his grasp (1 Sam. 23:26–27).

When Saul returned from chasing the Philistines, he was told that David had gone over to En Gedi (near the Dead Sea), but this time Saul almost lost his life in the cave where David and his men had previously hidden. But David refused to take advantage of what seemed to be an opportunity handed to him on a silver platter (1 Sam. 24:1–22). He was divinely preserved from exercising what every human instinct must have told him was the thing to do: kill Saul!

David left En Gedi and went into the Desert of Paran to Carmel (*Khirbet el-Kirmil*), a mile or so from Maon (*Khirbet Ma`in*). Saul had set up a monument to himself and his own deeds in Carmel (1 Sam. 15:12), and large landowners such as Nabal of Maon recognized no other authority than that of Saul. David entered there with a brigade now numbering six hundred. When the time of sheepshearing came around, a time traditionally appropriate for sharing with others in need, David sent some of his men to request some food supplies since he and his men had voluntarily been providing protection for Nabal's shepherds and flocks, as the men themselves were willing to affirm. But Nabal did not take kindly to the request and handled the matter so poorly that an exasperated David was now ready to seek vengeance for such brusque treatment (1 Sam. 25:21–22). Nabal's wife, Abigail, decided to take matters into her own hands and personally conducted a caravan of supplies, meeting David, who was much aroused and bent on destruction. David recanted of his planned mission of revenge and, instead, learned that the pompous Nabal suffered a sudden medical condition that took his life in a short ten days (25:37–38). Eventually, David married Nabal's widow Abigail, also taking another wife from the area, Ahinoam from Jezreel, a town a little to the southwest of Hebron. Meanwhile, Saul had taken Michal away from David and given her to another man, Paltiel. After David became king, Ahinoam bore to him his first son, Amnon, and Abigail bore his second son, Kileab (2 Sam. 3:2–3). The fact that Ahinoam is the same name as one of Saul's wives (1 Sam. 14:50) and that her village had the same name as the Jezreel in the famous Jezreel Valley are only coincidences; they are not to be equated or confused.

David and the Philistine Exile

The exhausted David must have realized by now that he could not elude the desperate Saul forever. He and his brigade took the drastic step of entering the service of Achish, the Philistine king of Gath (1 Sam. 27:1–4). Achish, like the Moabites, recognized a political moment for gaining advantage over the Saul-David split and took David on as a vassal.

David was given the city of Ziklag (perhaps *Tell esh-Shari`ah*), a city in the southern Shephelah and western Negev, no doubt on the Philistine frontier. David would protect Achish's frontier, join any general mobilization of the Philistines against her enemies (such as Saul), and raid the Philistine enemies, particularly Jerahmeelite and Kenite villages in the surrounding hill country and the Negev.

David remained in the service of Achish for sixteen months, all the while deceiving Achish by raiding farther south against the Amalekites down to Shur, near the border of Egypt, thereby avoiding preying on his own people of Judah. David conducted sorties also against the Geshurites and the Girzites, always taking the spoil back to Achish, saying it came from Judah (1 Sam. 27:10)! This increased Achish's estimate that David was now fully at odds with his own people, but the whole scheme was only that: a scheme to keep Achish thinking otherwise.

In the most critical moment for the nation of Israel, David and his men accompanied Achish in the general mobilization at Aphek to fight the Israelites. The other Philistine rulers, however, were wary of "these Hebrews," fearing that they would bolt from their professed allegiances to the Philistines and join up with the Israelites just as the Hebrews had suddenly changed sides in the battle of Micmash (1 Sam. 29:1–10, cf. 14:21). Fortunately, David was relieved of his obligation to join the Philistines as they fought what would be Saul's last battle: Saul gave his life on Mt. Gilboa (*Jebel Fuqu`ah*), about eight miles south of Shunem (*Solem*), the city close by Endor, where Saul resorted to contacting a medium to learn what would happen in the battle the next day with the Philistines. Samuel was resurrected long enough to inform Saul that Saul and his sons would be with him in death the next day.

The Philistines moved from their staging area at Aphek to Shunem and the battle was joined from Mt. Moreh, where Shunem and Endor were located, to Mt. Gilboa. That day Israel was thoroughly defeated and, just as Samuel had predicted, Saul and his three sons died in the battle. David's long years of running from Saul were now over.

David returned to Ziklag to find it in ruins and all the people, including his family, taken captives by the Amalekites. Abiathar consulted the ephod, to see if David and his six hundred men should pursue the Amalekites: yes, they should: it was in the will of God to do so! Two hundred of David's party of six hundred were exhausted after a four-day march back from Aphek. Unable to go on, they stayed by the stuff at the Besor Ravine (*Wadi Ghazzeh*), some fifteen miles south of Ziklag. The others went on and found an Egyptian who had fallen sick and was very willing to show which way the Amalekites had gone. David overtook the Amalekites, destroyed them, and recovered his loved ones and the spoils the enemy had removed. The other spoils were divided among all six hundred of David's men, with the rest being sent to the elders of Judah for further distribution. The last city to receive something from David's largess was Hebron. Such an action further ingratiated David with the people of Judah.

Three days after David had returned from the Amalekite battle, an Amalekite runner came to him from the Gilboa battlefield, claiming personally to have killed Saul. The runner presented David with Saul's crown and bracelet (2 Sam. 1:1–10), but he lied about his being the one who killed Saul. David ordered the runner executed. Saul and Jonathan's death was not an occasion for rejoicing, but one of sadness.

David could not go up to Gibeah and simply take over the kingdom, despite his divine anointing. Saul's surviving son Ish-Bosheth was ruling by then. Only the tribe of Judah was ready for the Davidic kingship. The year was 1011 B.C. David went to Hebron, and there he was crowned king of Judah (2 Sam. 2:4).

17

The Reign of King David

David set the standard and high-water mark for kingship among his people for all time. His kingship fell into two distinct periods. After the death of Saul, he reigned for seven and one-half years in Hebron, most of that time over Judah alone (2 Sam. 2:10). The longest period came after the transfer of his capital to Jerusalem, where he reigned over all Israel and Judah for some thirty-three years (2 Sam. 5:5). It was during this same period that Israel came to be recognized as the nation holding the greatest political power in the ancient Near East.

David's Reign in Hebron

It was natural, of course, that David should have become king over the tribe of Judah first, for had he not protected the outlying areas of Judah during the days when he was a fugitive from Saul? And was not David himself a Judean, a native of Bethlehem? Hence, with the tragedy on Mt. Gilboa, where Saul and Jonathan lost their lives in the battle with the Philistines, Judah independently acclaimed David king in Hebron, the chief city of Judah. Judah had always been noted for being one of the largest tribes and, therefore, it had a tendency to go its own way. This independent action gradually gained support from other places and persons outside of Judah.

David's early years on the throne were characterized by a masterful demonstration of statesmanship and diplomacy. He brought swift retribution to the person who had brought the news of Saul's death, for he would have no part of appearing to rejoice over the removal of his chief rival. He also sent a note of gratitude to those of Jabesh Gilead who had rescued Saul's body from the walls of Beth Shean and given him a decent burial in their city (2 Sam. 2:4–7). Nor did he get involved in events that were being played out between the army of Abner and King Ish-Bosheth, the heir apparent of what was left of Saul's dynasty. David chose to wait out the situation and to bide his time. Then when David's army captain, Joab, murdered Abner, who was actually in the process of coming over to David's side, and in line possibly as a candidate for Joab's job, David publicly reprimanded Joab. Moreover, David ordered the execution of the two officers who murdered Ish-Bosheth.

All of these events, as narrated by the Scriptures, appear to many scholars to be overly apologetic and defensive of David. Indeed, there must have been widespread public suspicion that David had arranged some or all of these deaths. The principle of *cui bono* ("to whose benefit") naturally focused on David, for each event appeared to clear the way to the throne for David while removing another possible contender from Saul's line. But the text made it clear that David did not murder his way to the throne of Israel; after all, he had been promised that throne and that kingdom by God himself! Furthermore, events were already swiftly moving in David's favor. Abner had worked on David's behalf to have his former wife Michal, Saul's younger daughter, returned to him, and Abner had also convinced the elders of Israel to join up with David. Thus the war with the house of Saul was going David's way (2 Sam. 3:1).

Abner had engineered the solid backing of the elders of Israel for David. But when Joab murdered Abner, David faced a potentially nasty problem. It could have been interpreted that he had plotted against Abner to remove the last obstacle that stood in his way to seizing power. To offset such an interpretation, David proclaimed a public mourning for Abner, then gave him a burial at Hebron with full state honors.

David's actions and lament for Saul and Jonathan were so sincere that all Israel and Judah took them at face value and exonerated David of any charges of complicity in what had taken place (2 Sam. 3:36–39). David appeared to be anxious to make the point that divine election had placed him where he was, not personal ambition or political maneuvering.

Ultimately, every possible contender to the throne by virtue of association with Saul was removed, and David was left as the sole candidate to everything that Saul had controlled. The elders of Israel made the journey to Hebron to ask David to rule over the north just as he had been ruling over Judah in the south. The result was that "the king made a compact with them at Hebron before the LORD, and they anointed David king over Israel" (2 Sam. 5:3). Albrecht Alt observed:

> The inevitable result is that the king whom they have in common never fully belongs to either of the kingdoms, and from his mediating position gains a superiority over both, which it would be far more difficult for him to acquire as a ruler of a single kingdom. This effect was strengthened in David's case by the fact . . . that he possessed in his mercenaries a domestic bodyguard owing allegiance to himself alone.[1]

This became one of David's most important achievements: the uniting of Israel and Judah under one monarch. Added to this was the fact that he established Israelite hegemony in Palestine while extending his influence into Phoenicia, Egypt, Syria, and Anatolia. It was one of the grandest moments in the history of Israel.

David's Reign in Jerusalem

One of the most determinative moves of David for the future was his conquest of Jerusalem and the choice of this city as the capital of his domain. While Judges 1:8 noted that the men of Judah had taken Jerusalem temporarily at some earlier stage of the Conquests, like most of the fortunes of war, the control of such key sites tended to go back and forth in the battle for possession. This is what happened with the city of Jerusalem: David must now win it back.

The Jebusites, who held Jerusalem up to the time when David captured the city, were one of the population groups that inhabited the hill country, probably gaining their name from Jebus, a place in that vicinity. The Jerusalem of that day would have been confined to Ophel, the hill projecting south of the present-day Temple Mount. The city occupied no more than eleven acres, but it was supplied with water from the Gihon Spring. Ophel was easily fortified, for it was surrounded on three sides by three valleys: Hinnom Valley on the south, the Kidron Valley to the east, and the Tyropean Valley to the west; only the north had no pronounced natural defense.

1. Albrecht Alt, "The Formation of the Israelite State in Palestine," in *Essays on Old Testament History and Religion*, tr. R. A. Wilson (Garden City, N.Y.: Doubleday, 1968), 282–83.

David's capture of Jerusalem is shrouded in some obscurity by our inability to interpret firmly the term *ṣinnôr* in 2 Samuel 5:8. David had said, "Anyone who conquers the Jebusites will have to use the [*ṣinnôr*] to reach those 'lame and blind' who are David's enemies" (v. 8). The reference to the lame and blind came from the cynical saying that the Jebusites hurled at David and his men; "You will not get in here; even the blind and the lame can ward you off" (v. 6). The word *ṣinnôr* means either "scaling hooks" that were used to scale the city walls, or probably the "water shaft" through which the city water supply was carried from the Gihon Spring.[2] If it were, as we think most likely, the water shaft, then the city was taken when the men of David discovered access to the tunnel cut through the rock beneath the city wall to the spring or well inside the city where the buckets were dropped to draw water during the siege of the city. David's men would have shimmied up that shaft, thus scaling the walls of that well, to gain access to the city, without damaging the property inside the city, in a surprise move that suddenly opened the gates to the rest of David's army waiting outside the city walls.

Recent studies, however, claim that the water shaft, called Warren's Shaft, was built at a later period, perhaps at the end of the reign of King Solomon or later. While *ṣinnôr* may also mean a utensil similar to a pitchfork, it is also used as a musical instrument in Psalm 42:7. If this interpretation is followed, then the conquest of Jersualem was carried out in a manner similar to the capture of Jericho; for just as Jericho was taken by blowing on the *shofars* on the seventh day, so the Jebusite city was taken with trumpets.[3]

Another word in this same context, *millôʾ*, may refer to the system of retaining walls that allowed David to expand the city down the terraces of Ophel (2 Sam. 5:9).[4] Later, with the help of the Phoenicians, David would construct his palace there as well.

Jerusalem was an ideal capital for David in many ways. It was situated on the central hill country watershed. Its capture meant that one of the last alien towns of any note that had separated the northern Israelites' territory from the southern Judean realm now was in Jewish

---

2. See Kathleen M. Kenyon, *The Bible and Recent Archaeology*, rev. ed. (Atlanta: John Knox, 1987), 92; also Philip J. King's review of Harry Thomas Frank, *Discovering the Biblical World*, ed. James F. Strange; rev. ed., (Maplewood: Hammond, 1988) in *BAR* 15 (1989): 13.

3. See Dan Bahat and Chaim T. Rubinstein, *The Illustrated Atlas of Jerusalem*, tr. Shlomo Ketko (New York: Simon and Schuster, 1990), 16, 24. Also see N. Avigad, *Discovering Jerusalem* (New York, 1983) and Y. Shiloh, *Excavations at the City of David. QEDEM* 19 (Jerusalem: 1984).

4. W. Harold Mare, *The Archaeology of the Jerusalem Area* (Grand Rapids: Baker, 1987), p. 65; also Kathleen Kenyon, *Royal Cities of the Old Testament* (New York: Schocken, 1971), pp. 33–35.

hands. Thus, it served as an administrative center, poised as it was between the two geographical divisions that had grown up during the final and subsequent years of Saul. Moreover, it represented a sort of neutral territory since it had belonged to neither Judah nor Israel previously.

DAVID AND THE PHILISTINES

The Philistines were not happy over David's accession to the throne over all Israel (2 Sam. 5:17). It is a real possibility that David still served as a vassal under Achish even while he ruled over Judah, but now they must have thought that he was growing too big for his own boots. They could have tolerated his being king over Judah, for he still represented the antithesis of all that Saul stood for in their minds. But now he was their enemy as well.

The Philistines launched a preemptive strike against David in the Valley of Rephaim, a valley just southwest of Jerusalem. They were determined to nip in the bud any sort of Israel-Judah reunification before David could build a power base against them. The battle is described in 2 Samuel 23:13–17 in connection with the listing of David's mighty/valiant men. But all of this must have taken place before the capture of Jerusalem, but just after the coronation of David as king over both Israel and Judah. That would explain why David had taken up his position at the cave of Adullam, while the Philistines were dug in at Bethlehem, some fifteen miles up the valley toward the northeast. Three of David's mighty men risked their lives to infiltrate enemy lines in order to get water from a Bethlehem well after hearing their leader say he wished he might have a drink from there. Just why the Philistines were in Bethlehem, how they got there, and how they were dislodged, the text does not say, but David won a victory over them at Baal Perazim (2 Sam. 5:20). As a result, the Philistines abandoned their idols and left the battlefield (2 Sam. 5:21). A second time, David inquired of Yahweh whether he should go out to the Valley of Rephaim, but he was told not to proceed against them until he heard the sound of marching in the tops of the balsam trees (v. 24). Then he was to move out quickly, which he did, and David smote the Philistines all the way from Gibeon to Gezer (v. 25).

The political significance of David's victory over the Philistines was important for this young monarchy. The Philistines had become heirs to the Egyptian Empire in Palestine following their battle with Rameses III. Now that David had defeated the victors over the Egyptians and pushed them back from occupying the hill country, the inheritance was transferred to Israel. This became, no doubt, the basis on which David built his empire. It also may have been the reason why David suddenly found himself in conflict with neighboring states as far removed as southern Syria.

DAVID, THE ARK, AND THE TABERNACLE

David wisely understood the importance of tying in the tribes to the new capital by means of their commitment to Yahweh. The ark of the covenant had been captured by the Philistines but returned after seven devastating months. Presumably Shiloh had been destroyed about the same time, for while the ark remained at Kiriath Jearim after its return, the tabernacle seems to have been located, at least for some of that time, at Nob (1 Sam. 22:11), where a descendant of Eli, Ahimelech, was high priest.

The tabernacle, or tent of meeting as it was also called, had remained at Shiloh until the Philistines destroyed Shiloh sometime between 1050 and 1104 B.C., either immediately after or sometime later than the famous battle of Ebenezer.[5] The ark of the covenant had been taken from the tabernacle all to no avail, for it had been captured in that battle and went to reside for seven months among the Philistines until they returned it under the duress of the afflictions breaking out in each of the cities that took charge of the ark. The Philistines marched on Shiloh after their victory at Ebenezer, ultimately destroying the tabernacle (1 Sam. 4; Jer. 7:12–14; Ps. 78:60).

Sir Charles William Wilson (1836–1905) was the first to suggest that the Shiloh tabernacle was located about 160 yards north of the summit of the *Tell Seilun*, identified with ancient Shiloh.[6] The tabernacle and its court would have needed a flat place of 140 feet long by 70 feet wide (using the cubit standard of that time—16.9 inches or 42.8 centimeters). The tent of meeting had become by that time a "house"

5. Usually the date given for the destruction of Shiloh is 1050 B.C. (e.g., John Bright, *A History of Israel*, 3rd ed. (Philadelphia: Westminster, 1981), 185–86. But Eugene H. Merrill, *Kingdom of Priests*, p. 176, notes that the Bible does not say that Shiloh was destroyed at the same time that the ark was lost to the Philistines. He argues that the destruction referred to in Jeremiah 7:12, 14; 26:6, 9 may have taken place as much as fifty years after the tabernacle had long been removed from that city to Nob and Gibeon. It is difficult to say, for the evidence is not clear one way or the other.

6. See the definitive article by Asher S. Kaufman, "Fixing the Site of the Tabernacle at Shiloh," *BAR* 14.6 (1988): 46–52. This identification some will find tentative at best, with some justification. On Ebenezer, see Moshekochav and Aaron Demsky, "An Israelite Village from the Days of the Judges," *BAR* 4 (1978): 18–21.

(Hebrew *bayit*, 1 Sam. 1:24), the same word used of Solomon's temple in 1 Kings 6:1 and elsewhere.

The site just north of the tell where Wilson placed the tabernacle allows for a complex of just this size. It is on a hewn-out terrace from the rock, just fifty feet lower than the summit of the tell, thereby also avoiding placement on a high place. This flat terrace can be divided into three areas: the middle area (Wilson called it *A*), which was 180 x 78 feet, more than adequate to fit the tabernacle with a general orientation towards the east as God had commanded Moses to set it up, and two other areas (*B* and *C*) on either side, lower than area *A*, thereby giving prominence, as it should, to the site of the tabernacle.

This site also fits a careful reading of 1 Samuel 4:12–14. The messenger who brought the bad news from the Ebenezer battlefield about Israel's defeat and the loss of the ark had to pass through the town, whose entrance then as now was on the south side. He went to the place where Eli was sitting on a chair by the wayside on the north side of town on the spur leading over to the terrace where the tabernacle stood. The terrace was protected by steep slopes on all sides, except the south, the side facing the tell of Shiloh.

The ark remained at Kiriath Jearim, of course, after it was returned by the Philistines, but the tabernacle at that time appears to have been located at Nob, where the descendant of Eli, Ahimelech, was high priest. It was at Nob, after all, that David and his men were provisioned from the consecrated bread (1 Sam. 21:4), a town known as "the town of the priests" (1 Sam. 22:19).

From Kiriath Jearim David had the ark of the covenant removed and brought to Jerusalem, where he placed it in a special tent that he had pitched for it (2 Sam. 6:17; 2 Chron. 1:4). The symbolism was clear: David was the protector of that which stood most directly for the essence of their faith in God. But it is also clear from 2 Chronicles 1:5 that the "bronze altar that Bezalel . . . had made was [by that time] in Gibeon in front of the tabernacle of the LORD." That is why Solomon went to Gibeon to worship rather than to Jerusalem (1 Kings 3:4–5; 2 Chron. 1:3–6). Thus the site of the tabernacle must have moved from Shiloh to Nob and then to Gibeon before it came to Jerusalem.

But the startling fact is that David did not remove the ark of the covenant until late in his reign. First Chronicles 15:1 clearly states that David pitched a tent for the ark only "after [he] had constructed buildings for himself in the City of David." David had accomplished his building projects with the direct assistance of Hiram (also Ahiram), the son of Abibaal, who reigned as king of Tyre from approximately 980–947 B.C. Accordingly, he was a contemporary of both David (1011–971 B.C.) and Solomon (971–931 B.C.), but only in David's last decade. If that is so, David's building program must have come late in his reign, not while he was finished fighting all the wars in the earlier part of his kingship. Since the tent for the ark was not put up until "after" the building projects, David hesitated to bring the ark into Jerusalem until late in his reign. Why?

David's rise to power was not all that simple; it was filled with opposition and difficulty, at which the text hints, but without explanation. Furthermore, it is one thing to lead as a political and military genius, but it is another thing to be perceived as tampering with religious traditions that were so firmly set by Moses. The lines between these two spheres of crown and cult had been rather sharply defined and distinguished. And the lessons of Saul's meddling in the cult had brought drastic and severe reprimands from Samuel and Yahweh. Thus it behooved David to proceed slowly in this area.

There were other more pressing needs, anyway. God had not yet given David rest from all his enemies round about (2 Sam. 7:1; 1 Chron. 17:1), so how could he devote his efforts to anything else at the time? But when Philistia, Moab, Zobah, Damascus, Ammon, Amalek, and Edom had been vanquished, David could turn his hand to establishing the center of worship in Jerusalem.

The Problems in the Chronology of David's Life

Starting from what is certain, we can say that David died in 971 B.C. (forty years before Solomon reigned for his forty years ending with the kingdom being split in 931 B.C.).[7] And since David ruled in Jerusalem for thirty-three years, Jerusalem was captured by David in 1004 B.C., seven years after he began his reign in Hebron in 1011 B.C. All of this follows from the thesis of Edwin Thiele's 931 B.C. date for the division of the kingdom, which will be discussed and defended below, but the rest of David's dates cannot be given with the same confidence.

The best place to begin our estimating the relative sequence of the dates for the rest of the events in David's life is with the birth of Solomon. Solomon must have been fairly young when he began to rule, for he called himself a "little child" in 1 Kings 3:7 when he prayed in

7. This section is indebted to the careful suggestions made by Eugene H. Merrill, *Kingdom of Priests*, pp. 243–48.

Gibeon for wisdom. If this means that he was not much over twenty years old when he came to the throne in 971 B.C., he must have been born no more than thirteen years after David captured Jerusalem, i.e, about 991 B.C.

Solomon was born a year or two after David's adulterous affair with Bathsheba, an event marked by Joab's leading the troops in the field against the Ammonites at Rabbah, about 993 B.C. Since this is the last narrated military adventure of David (except for 2 Sam. 8, a catalogue of all David's foreign conquests and not a part of the sequential narrative), it must be just prior to David's flight from Absalom. Absalom was the son of David's wife Maacah, a princess of Talmai, king of Geshur, born to him in Hebron. Depending on when he was born during that seven-year period, Absalom was anywhere from twenty to thirteen years older than Solomon (born in 991 B.C.). Soon after Solomon's birth, Absalom led a rebellion against his father. In some ways this was logical, for he could claim he was the only son who had royal blood in his line.

With Hiram's accession to the throne in Tyre in 980 B.C., the moving of the ark can be placed any time after that—perhaps 977 B.C. Thus Absalom's rebellion cannot be put any earlier than 976 B.C. The rebellion ended in 975 B.C., about four years before David's death. Then David conducted the ill-advised census of the nation. After the end of the plague—a punishment for David's census—he spent his remaining days in a renewed desire to gather all the materials for building the house of God. It was somewhere in this period that David made his son Solomon coregent with him (1 Chron. 23:1). Together both David and Solomon laid plans for the temple and the appointing of the priests and Levites to serve in the house of God.

First Chronicles 29:22b gives clear evidence that Solomon had been made coregent some two years before Adonijah's plot to preempt Solomon's succession to the throne (1 Kings 1:5–10; 1 Chron. 23:1), for when Solomon was finally anointed as king, 1 Chronicles 29:22b claimed, "Then they acknowledged Solomon son of David as king *a second time*, anointing him before the LORD to be ruler and Zadok to be priest" (emphasis ours). Adonijah's attempted usurping of the throne had been supported by the high priest Abiathar and by Joab, captain of the army. But Zadok was not made high priest in Abiathar's place until after David's death (1 Kings 2:35).[8] Thus, the coronation mentioned

8. Eugene H. Merrill, *Kingdom of Priests*, p. 248, n. 37, calls attention to the fact that "if one fails to recognize a time interval between 1 Chronicles 29:22 a and b . . . [one must] see H. G. M. Williams, *I and II Chronicles*, New Century Bible Commentary (Grand Rapids: Eerdmans, 1982), 186–87" for the problems thus incurred.

here was in answer to Adonijah's forcing David's hand to announce the changing of administrations, aided, of course, by the prophet Nathan and David's wife Bathsheba.

DAVID'S WARS

EGYPT

During the whole time of the united monarchy in Israel, Egypt posed not one threat. The Third Intermediate Period (ca. 1100 to 650 B.C.)[9] was a time when Egypt had either pharaohs who were not interested in foreign military adventures or monarchs who were more interested in domestic affairs. Psusennes I (1039–931 B.C.), of the Twenty-first Dynasty, a contemporary of Saul and David, listed no military campaigns in Palestine.[10] His successor, Amenemope (991–978 B.C.), was even less motivated to involve himself in foreign affairs, although he did offer asylum for Hadad, the prince of Edom, whom David drove into exile (1 Kings 11:14–22), for the Davidic conquest of Edom must be dated somewhere around 980 B.C. Queen Tahpenes, whose sister married Hadad (1 Kings 11:19), must have been the wife either of Amenemope or more likely Siamun (978–959 B.C.).

It was probably this pharaoh, Siamun, who gave his daughter in marriage to Solomon after Solomon's third year (1 Kings 2:39; 3:1) and provided the city of Gezer as her dowry (1 Kings 9:16). This means that at some point he or one of his predecessors had taken Gezer out of the hands of the Philistines. But how could any of the pharaohs of this weak period have been capable of such a feat unless they had help from outside? The answer is probably to be found in David, who may have helped Siamun in his first year (978) accomplish the wresting of Gezer from the Philistines, thus making possible David's free movement of the ark into Jerusalem. It also would explain why there is no record of any Israelite opposition to an Egyptian contingent moving so deeply into Israel's territory.

9. See Kenneth A. Kitchen, *The Third Intermediate Period in Egypt (1100–650 B.C.)* (Warminster: Aris and Phillips, 1973) and Pierre Montet, *Egypt and the Bible* (Philadelphia: Fortress, 1968), 38–39.

10. This spelling of the pharaoh's name is found in Sir Alan Gardiner, *Egypt of the Pharaohs. An Introduction* (Oxford: At the Clarendon Press, 1961), 318, 447.

AMMON

Egypt presented no problem to David, but the Ammonites[11] did—shortly after he conquered Jerusalem. This is described in 2 Samuel 9–20 and 1 Kings 1–2, a section known in scholarly circles as the Succession Narrative—presumably because one of its main themes is the preparation for the successor to David's throne. Until recently, this was almost universally regarded as the finest example of history writing from the ancient Near Eastern world. Now that estimate has changed, as we have already pointed out above. Nevertheless, the weaving of plot, counterplot, intrigue, and suspense gave it more than a casual ring of authenticity.

After having been anointed king by the elders of Israel, David found himself once again at war with the Philistines. Now, rather than being a vassal of Achish and the Philistines, he was the protector of Judah and Israel against the Philistines. These wars are summarily presented in 2 Samuel 5:17–25, and referred to again in 2 Samuel 23. No doubt there were other border skirmishes as well, especially on the frontier of the Shephelah.

But it was the Ammonites who gave David the greatest amount of grief. These conflicts must have started just after he acquired Jerusalem in 1004 B.C., for Hanun, son of Nahash, came to power in Ammon just about that time. Moreover, as Eugene H. Merrill has pointed out, 2 Samuel 9 immediately precedes the account of the Ammonite war and probably is an integral part of the Succession Narrative (SN). In that chapter, David inquires if there are not some survivors from the house of Saul to whom he might show favor for the sake of his late friend Jonathan. Whether this search was motivated by political expediencies—as some cynically suggest—or by real compassion cannot be determined precisely, but the search turned up a servant of Saul, Ziba, who informed David that Jonathan's son Mephibosheth was living at Lo Debar, some ten miles south of the Sea of Kinnereth (Galilee). David sent for Mephibosheth and put him on a permanent state pension, instructing Ziba and his family to care for everything he would need. David restored the estate of Mephibosheth, which he placed in the custody of Ziba, the former servant of Saul. Ziba was to till the land

---

11. The only major study on the Ammonites in English is George M. Landes, *A History of the Ammonites* (Ph.D. dissertation, Johns Hopkins University, 1956). More recently, Randall W. Younker, "Ammonites," in *Peoples of the Old Testament*, ed. Alfred J. Hoerth, Gerald L. Mattingly, and Edwin M. Yamauchi (Grand Rapids: Baker, 1994), 293–316; Daniel I. Block, "*Bny ʿmwn*: The Sons of Ammon," *AUSS* 22 (1984): 197–212; Larry G. Herr, *The Archaeology of the Transjordan in the Bronze and Iron Ages* (Milwaukee: Milwaukee Public Museum, 1983).

and to "bring in the crops, so that your master's grandson may be provided for" (2 Sam. 9:10).

Now in a parenthetical note we are told that Mephibosheth was five years old when Jonathan died at Gilboa, at which time his nurse picked him up to flee, but dropped him, leaving him crippled in both legs (2 Sam. 4:4). If Mephibosheth was five years old in 1011 when David began his reign in Hebron, right after the battle of Gilboa, then in 1004, when David captured Jerusalem, he was twelve, meaning, of course, that he was born in 1016 B.C. But when he came to Jerusalem as a result of David's largess, Mephibosheth already had a young son (2 Sam. 9:12). Assuming that Mephibosheth was somewhere around twenty when he married, his return to Jerusalem could be dated about 996 B.C.

It would appear that 993 B.C. is the best estimate as to when the Ammonite wars began. A series of campaigns against the Ammonites had been provoked by the disgraceful treatment accorded David's ambassadors, who were bringing congratulatory messages from King David to King Hanun of Ammon, just as Hanun's father Nahash had sent such a message to David when he ascended the throne of Saul (2 Sam. 10:2). Since there was real animosity between Saul and Nahash, the assumption is that Nahash would have welcomed anyone other than a relative of Saul's on the throne, presuming that this could mean a period of peace between the two nations.

Things had not always been well between Ammon and Israel. Going back to the judgeship of Jephthah (1106–1100 B.C.), the Ammonites laid claim to everything Israel had occupied for three hundred years. Jephthah soundly defeated the Ammonites, driving them into the eastern deserts. When Nahash declared that he would settle for peace with the inhabitants of Jabesh Gilead if each would submit to having his or her right eye gouged out, Saul rallied the troops of Israel and again trounced the Ammonites.

It is little wonder that an official delegation from David was viewed somewhat suspiciously by Hanun, hence the insult to the delegation. But such a breach of protocol could not be regarded lightly, so David sent Joab to Rabbah to avenge the indignity foisted on the crown and people of Israel.

Aram

Suddenly Hanun realized the seriousness of the situation that he had caused by his ill-advised shaving off one half of each man's beard

(2 Sam. 10:1–5). He appealed to the Arameans[12] of Beth Rehob and Zobah and the kingdoms of Maacah and Tob to come to his aid, lest he be annihilated. Beth Rehob lay in the Bekaa Valley between the Lebanon and Anti-Lebanon mountains, reaching from the resettled city of Dan to the realm of Zobah in the north.

Zobah itself was a major player in the Aramean kingdom, for Saul had already faced its kings (1 Sam. 14:47), but later it really came into its own in David's day under the leadership of Hadadezer, son of Rehob. Its territorial holdings were large, stretching from Damascus in the south to Hamath in the north. Maacah was east of Lake Huleh, and Tob was southeast of the Sea of Kinnereth (Galilee).

David's two generals, Joab and Abishai, beat the Ammonites, but they did not take the city. The strategy had to be brilliant, for the Ammonite troops guarded the gates to the city while another thirty-three thousand Aramean troops assembled in the nearby fields, thus enclosing Joab's troops. The only way Joab got out of that precarious situation was by dividing his troops into two groups and assigning his brother Abishai the task of attacking the Ammonites while he, Joab, took on the Arameans. The strategy worked. Therefore, the Arameans fled, temporarily reforming and augmenting their troops for another assault, this time at Helam in the desert east of the Sea of Kinnereth.

David, however, gathered all Israel and crossed the Jordan and went to Helam (2 Sam. 10:17; 1 Chron. 19:16–19), where he faced Hadadezer's troops under the generalship of Shobach. The slaughter of the Aramean troops and its commander was overwhelming. Hadadezer and his vassal states, therefore, came under the realm of David. Damascus was placed under tribute to David; the gold shields of Hadadezer's officers and the bronze tribute given to Hadadezer by his vassals all came to David to use in making vessels for the temple (1 Chron. 18:7–8). Tou, king of Hamath, likewise submitted to David by sending to him, under the aegis of his son Joram, lavish gifts of gold, silver, and bronze. By now David was in control of most of Aram, but the Ammonites still continued to be nettlesome.

At the turn of the year, another siege of Rabbah took place. It was during this time that David, having stayed at home, entered into his

12. See for a good overview Wayne T. Pitard, "Arameans," *Peoples of the Old Testament World*, pp. 207–230; idem., *Ancient Damascus: A Historical Study of the Syrian City-State from Earliest Times Until Its Fall to the Assyrians in 732* B.C.E. (Winona Lake, Ind.: Eisenbrauns, 1987); A. Malamat, "The Aramaeans," in *Peoples of Old Testament Times*, ed. Donald J. Wiseman (Oxford: At the Clarendon Press, 1973), 134–155; Merrill F. Unger, *Israel and the Aramaeans of Damascus* (London, 1957). The older study was by Andre Dupont-Sommer, *Les Arameens* (Paris: Maisonneuve, 1949).

affair with Bathsheba (2 Sam. 11:1). He spied his neighbor's wife bathing in full view of the palace rooftop. Bathsheba was summoned, and thus began one of the most painful experiences in David's life. A plot was hatched to bring Bathsheba's husband from the front at Rabbah so that he might have relations with his wife. If any children came from the adulterous affair, perhaps Uriah would think the child was his. But Uriah was loyal to the core, refusing to indulge himself while the king's men were in the field. Thus, a second plot was hatched in which Uriah would be put up front and Joab's men would fall back suddenly, without alerting Uriah, leaving him to face the death-dealing arrows from the walls of Rabbah alone and perhaps die, which is what happened. A child was born from this clandestine affair, but the child died. Later, Solomon was born to David and Bathsheba.

MOAB

Once more Joab took the field against the Ammonites, putting Rabbah under siege (2 Sam. 12:26–31). Since Joab had to go across territory nominally under the control of the Moabites[13] to get from Jerusalem to Rabbah, it is likely that David took control of Moabite territory during this time in a most brutal way (2 Sam. 8:2). How David could justify this, given his Moabite grandmother and the refuge Moab gave to his parents during the time Saul was a threat to the whole Davidic family, is hard to say.

Finally, Rabbah fell, and David made all the Ammonite towns subject to hard labor, consigning them to working with saws, iron picks, and axes (2 Sam. 12:31). This may have been in retaliation for the difficult time he had in subduing them.

EDOM

Meanwhile, David had already subdued Edom[14] earlier in his reign. The date for that could probably be set by the flight of the Edomite prince, Hadad, to Egypt (1 Kings 11:14–22) as mentioned already. The

13. See Gerald L. Mattingly, "Moabites," in *Peoples of the Old Testament World*, pp. 317–333; John R. Bartlett, "The Moabites and Edomites," in *Peoples of Old Testament Times*, pp. 229–258; James R. Kautz, "Tracking the Ancient Moabites," *BA* 44 (1981): 27–35; James A. Sauer, "Transjordan in the Bronze and Iron Ages: A Critique of Glueck's Synthesis," *BASOR* 263 (1986): 1–26; and A. H. Van Zyl, *The Moabites* (Leiden: Brill, 1960).

14. See Kenneth G. Hoglund, "Edomites," in *Peoples of the Old Testament World*, pp. 335–347; Stephen Hart, *The Archaeology of the the Land of Edom* (Ph.D. Dissertation, Macquarie University, 1989); John R. Bartlett, *Edom and the Edomites*. *JSOT Sup* 77 (Sheffield: Sheffield Academic Press, 1989); and Jacob M. Myers, "Edom and Judah in the Sixth-Fifth Centuries B.C.," in *Near Eastern Studies in Honor of William Foxwell Albright*, ed. Hans Goedicke (Baltimore: Johns Hopkins University Press, 1971), 377–392.

battle in the Valley of Salt (*Wadi el-Milh*), in the Negev near Beersheba and Arad, was the site for the decisive victory, for at that place David slew eighteen thousand Edomites. Since Edom was so far into Israelite territory, it may indicate that they had launched an offensive strike first. It was Abishai who won this victory. He also went against the garrisons in Edom and made Edom a vassal to Israel (1 Chron. 18:12–13). This same Hadad would return during Solomon's day and be a real contributing cause in Solomon's decline.

Some argue that the account in 1 Kings 11:14–22 is at variance with the account given in 1 Chronicles, but the accounts are complementary. When Edom had been subdued, David and Joab went to the Valley of Salt to bury the dead and mop up any further opposition. The prince Hadad and some of the royal family escaped and went eventually to Egypt, where they were warmly received. The text stresses that Hadad was "still only a boy" (1 Kings 11:17) when he went into exile in Egypt, but when he returned to Edom after the death of David and Joab, he had married the sister of pharaoh's queen and had fathered a son (1 Kings 11:20). Hadad's return, then, was some time after 971, perhaps about 969 B.C.; that would make Merrill's proposed date of 993 B.C. for the Ammonite wars very likely, for he would have been somewhere around thirty-four to thirty-five years old by then.

David's wars had finally come to an end, the Edomite war perhaps being the final one in the long string of Ammonite and Aramean wars. David could at last rest. But alas, it was at this period that all his family troubles began.

The Extent of David's Kingdom

David expanded the kingdom far beyond what Saul had controlled. One of the best sources for determining the limits of David's kingdom was David's census in 2 Samuel 24 and 1 Chronicles 21:1–27.

The geographical extent of the kingdom is described as beginning at the Arnon River in Transjordania, proceeding to a point near Dan at the foot of Mt. Hermon in the north, then crossing Upper Galilee westward almost to the cities of Sidon and Tyre. Another survey covered the Negev of Judah to Beersheba. Accordingly, the entire western side of the Jordan except for the Gaza strip, or Philisitia, and all of Transjordania possibly including most of Moab and Edom. It also became clear that the territory of Aram was also included in the realm over which David exercised authority, meaning that his control reached up to Damascus and into the Lebanon and Anti-Lebanon ranges.

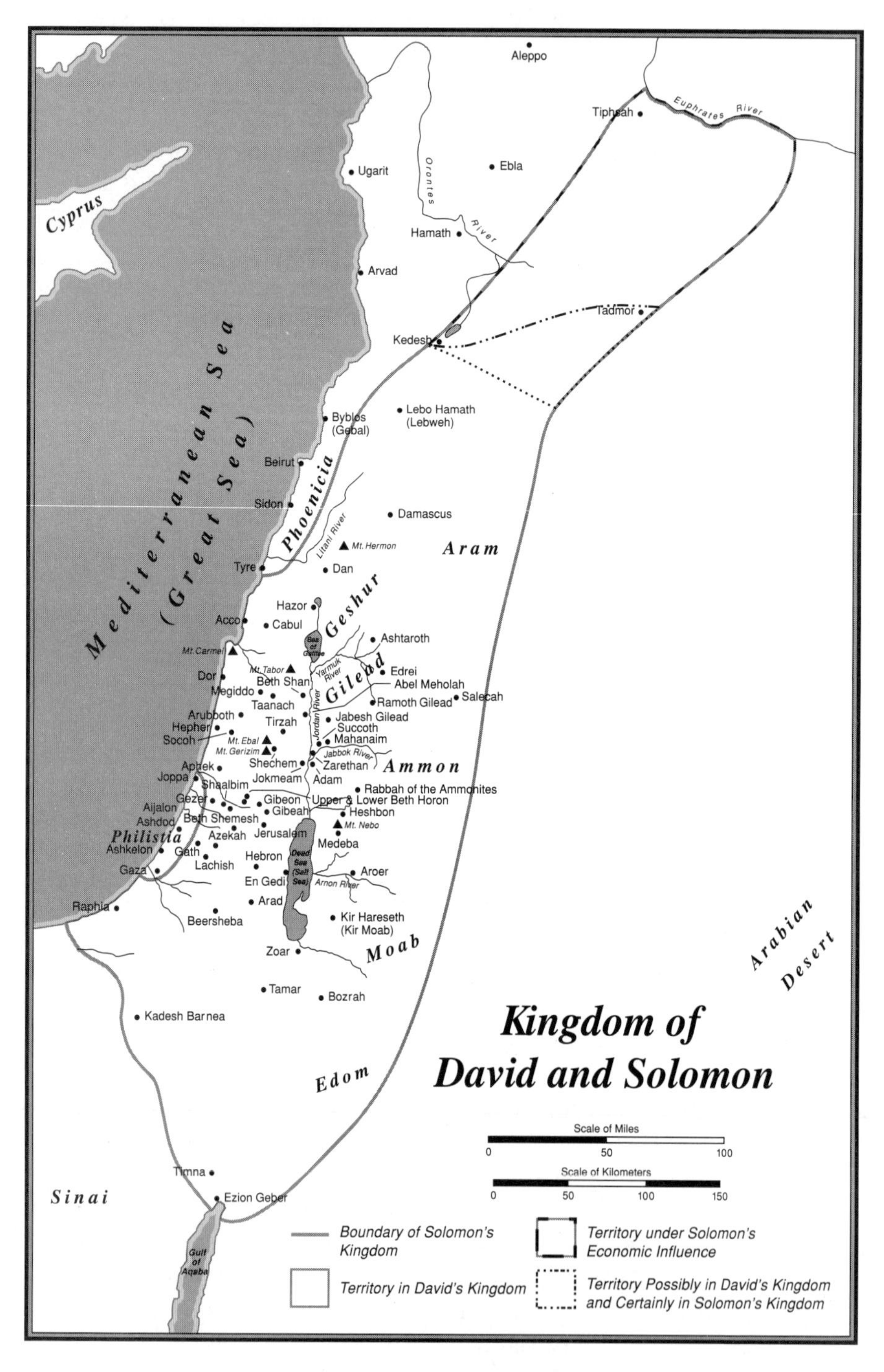

From *Holman Bible Handbook* (Nashville: Holman Bible Publishers, 1992), 259.

18

David and His Domestic Troubles

After David had finished almost all of his foreign conquests and had given both his realm and himself rest from the almost incessant fighting of one enemy or another, his family met many troubles. These ranged from rape and murder to sedition and outright rebellion! The whole set of problems almost cost David everything he had fought to win.

The Beginning of David's Troubles

There is little doubt that all David's grief came following his affair with Bathsheba. If Solomon was about twenty years old (at most) when he began to reign in 971 B.C., he must have been born about 991 B.C. About this time David was finishing the Ammonite and Aramean wars. Second Samuel 12:10–12 directly attributes David's troubles to his earlier adultery with Bathsheba. In that text the prophet Nathan had predicted:

> "Now, therefore, the sword will never depart from your house, because you despised me and took the wife of Uriah the Hittite to be your own.
>
> " This is what the LORD says: 'Out of your own household I am going to bring calamity upon you. Before your very eyes I will take your wives and give them to one who is close to you, and he will lie with your wives in broad daylight. You did it in secret, but I will do this thing in broad daylight before all Israel.'"

Therefore, just as the first twenty years of David's reign were marked by blessing and one success after another, the last twenty years, by and large, would be marked with trouble, heartache, and mischief.

The Rape of Tamar

The first fulfillment of the prophetic word delivered by Nathan was Amnon's rape of his half sister Tamar. Tamar was Absalom's full sister, born to David and the Aramean princess from Geshur in Jerusalem (1 Chron. 3:4–9). Since Absalom was noted for his beauty and charm among the people (2 Sam. 3:3; 15:6), it is fair to suppose that Tamar must have had some of that same beauty and personality flowing from the same royal blood from their mother's line.

Amnon was David's oldest son, born to Ahinoam, the Jezreelitess (2 Sam. 3:2) in Hebron. Amnon must have been about twenty years old at the time, but Tamar was obviously younger. Amnon trapped her into coming to his house by feigning sickness and the need for Tamar to cook a special dish in order to help him get well. But while she unsuspectingly prepared a meal for him in his presence, he attacked and raped her. In the same instant, however, what had been a burning, lustful passion for her turned into such hatred that Amnon refused her request to marry her and take away her shame, as the law required in such circumstances. Severely wounded physically and psychologically, Tamar left Amnon's presence and sought comfort from her full brother Absalom.

The Murder of Amnon by Absalom

Absalom was outraged at his half brother Amnon and began to plan his revenge. Unfortunately, he felt it would do no good to raise the matter with his father David, for David was in a somewhat delicate position, having been compromised by his adulterous affair with Bathsheba and implicitly involved in the murder of her husband Uriah; David would do nothing, for it would be a condemnation on himself as well. Amnon was his oldest son and heir apparent to the throne. Surely David would not want to spoil that prospect. David, no doubt, would grant Amnon some kind of executive immunity from prosecution and punishment.

Consequently, Absalom would have to bide his time until he could find an opportunity to get revenge for his sister Tamar. Besides, if he were successful on behalf of his sister, his own chances for being next in line to the throne would instantly be increased! (There was another older brother, Chileab [2 Sam. 3:3], but he nowhere figures in the biblical narratives. The assumption is that Chileab probably died at an early age: that would make Absalom next in line to the throne.) David eventually found out about Amnon's rape of his half sister. Though he was outraged, he appeared to be powerless to make any other response than his anger. How can a father punish a son for doing what he himself has done?

For two full years Absalom plotted and schemed until he finally felt he had discovered the best way to even the score. He would invite his father David to the yearly sheepshearing festival at Baal Hazor (*Tell `Asur*), a site between Bethel and Shiloh. When David declined the invitation, which Absalom must have expected, he begged his father to send Amnon in his place. Amnon came and proceeded to get drunk at the festivities. Then, in the middle of the feast, Absalom's assassins rose up and murdered the drunken Amnon in front of all the guests.

Absalom wisely decided he had better flee to his grandfather, Talmai king of Geshur, until this whole affair blew over. He stayed for three years in Geshur and did not see the face of King David during that whole time—estimated to be somewhere around 985–982 B.C.

Finally, Joab, David's general, intervened for the exiled son and went to David to plead his case. Meanwhile, Absalom had fathered three sons and a daughter also named Tamar. Joab was able to get David to allow Absalom to return home, at least to keep up appearances in the palace. But the rebellion in Absalom's heart was not yet extinguished: in four years he would openly oppose his father in all-out revolution.

In order to put himself on the fast track to the throne of David, Absalom began to make a concerted effort at winning the hearts of the people away from his father over to himself, as 2 Samuel 15:1–6 details:

> In the course of time, Absalom provided himself with a chariot and horses and with fifty men to run ahead of him. He would get up early and stand by the side of the road leading to the city gate. Whenever anyone came with a complaint to be placed before the king for a decision, Absalom would call out to him, "What town are you from?" He would answer, "Your servant is from one of the tribes of Israel." Then Absalom would say to him, "Look, your claims are valid and proper, but there is no representative of the king to hear you." And Absalom would add, "If only I were appointed judge in the land! Then everyone who has a complaint or case could come to me and I would see

> that he gets justice."
>
> Also, whenever anyone approached him to bow down before him, Absalom would reach out his hand, take hold of him and kiss him. Absalom behaved in this way toward all the Israelites who came to the king asking for justice, and so he stole the hearts of the men of Israel.

The fact that many were coming with grievances may have been a clue to the fact that things in David's reign were not so rosy as they appeared.

The Revolt of Absalom

Absalom began his coup by begging his father's permission to go to Hebron, his birthplace, to offer sacrifices in fulfillment of a vow he had sworn to the Lord in Geshur. Once he was in Hebron, the site of David's earlier capital and David's proclamation of his own kingship some thirty-five years earlier in one of the most important cities in Judah, Absalom proclaimed himself king. This announcement in Hebron was coordinated with similar proclamations in other centers, particularly in Ephraim and northern Israel (2 Sam. 15:7–12).

So well contrived was Absalom's conspiracy against his father that, by the time David learned what was going on, there was little to do but get out of Jerusalem before he was caught in a pincer movement (2 Sam. 15:13–31). However, prior to leaving the capital of Jerusalem, David made arrangements that the priests Abiathar and Zadok should stay behind and gather what information they could on developments in Absalom's government. He also sent back his counselor Hushai as a deliberate plant and pretended-supporter of Absalom, an attempt to sabotage any advice that his unusually wise and gifted adviser Ahithophel might give to Absalom (2 Sam. 15:32–37; 17:15–22).

Apparently, Absalom had correctly seen that his father neglected some key areas in matters of state while he busied himself with finishing up his wars and making preparations to build the temple. He must have been so preoccupied that many citizens who sought to see him were unable to get redress for their complaints. Absalom, the astute politician, seized this weakness as the very area he would use for his own cause. Whether David's meddling in the affairs of religious authority provided another cause for discontent among the populace cannot be determined, but it is clear that he had lost some of his support. Even important members of his own administration were abandoning him, such as Ahithophel, who had gone to join Absalom, and David's nephew, Amasa, whom Absalom made commander of the forces of the rebellion.

Now it was David's turn to go into exile. He voluntarily left Jerusalem with some of his closest friends. Ziba, the custodian of the royal lands that had belonged to Saul, and now were being worked by Ziba for the benefit of Jonathan's son Mephibosheth, rushed to David's side and accused his master of hoping to be restored to the former throne of Saul. David declared Ziba the new owner of the former Saulide royal estate (2 Sam. 16:1–4). It would turn out that this information was untrue and slanderous, but it tended to play on the anti-Saulide sentiment that still was present in the kingdom.

A Benjamite from the house of Saul, Shimei, threw stones at the king as he was fleeing along the southern flank of the Mount of Olives, all the while denouncing him as the one who shed the blood of Saul's family (2 Sam. 16:5–14; 21:1–6). The old wounds of the conflict between Saul and David appeared still to be open and festering. Sectionalism and regionalism still needed to be attended to, even at this late stage in the Davidic kingdom.

Once David was in Transjordania, east of Mahanaim on the upper Jabbok River, he was joined by other prominent persons from that region, including: Shobi, a son of Nahash the Ammonite king, and possibly a brother of Hanun, who came perhaps hoping to undo what his brother had done; Machir of Lo Debar, who had previously given shelter to a younger Mephibosheth, came with supplies; and Barzillai, a man of Rogelim in Gilead (a village twelve miles southeast of Lo Debar), who had great wealth, also extended his benefactions to the king, an act that was later to be rewarded by the king as he invited Barzillai to return to Jerusalem with him.

David placed his forces under three field commanders: Joab and Abishai, his sister's sons, and Ittai, a Gittite, who seems to have headed up a brigade of six hundred Philistine mercenaries. The Gittites had recently arrived along with their families from the city of Gath (2 Sam. 15:18–22) and formed a sort of foreign legion, loyal to the crown of David.

On the advice of Ahithophel, Absalom made a public show of taking over the women in the harem of David. This act, no doubt, was meant to demonstrate that he had made an irrevocable break with his father—there would be no turning back now. Ahithophel also counseled Absalom to pursue his father immediately before he had time to regroup and recover from the staggering blow that he had been dealt by his son. But the infiltrator Hushai countered Ahithophel's better advice by devising some sort of razzle-dazzle story about waiting until David went into a city. Then Amasa could capture it even if he had to get ropes and literally pull the city into the valley. It was only bravado, but Absalom fell for it. Ahithophel, who had put his very life on the line in rebellion, did not stay to witness the conclusion to this scenario. In his God-given wisdom, he knew what would eventuate. Even if Absalom were reconciled with his father, as had happened previously, he would be on the outs, for blood was thicker than water. So Ahithophel put his affairs in order and then committed suicide (2 Sam. 17:23). Absalom had wasted his chance to take David by waiting until he could get a large force together to pursue David. The astute politician was not so astute a military strategist, nor was he able to sort out the difference between the advice given to him by Ahithophel and that given by Hushai.

Finally, the two forces met in the forest of Ephraim (2 Sam. 18:6). Absalom's forces, led by Amasa, suffered a staggering defeat, even though Joab spared them from a virtual slaughter. Absalom was caught in some low-lying branches of an oak while attempting to flee, but despite David's strict orders that his son was to be dealt with gently, Joab decided here was one character who had to be dealt with immediately and directly, or history no doubt would repeat itself. Thus, while Absalom was suspended between heaven and earth, Joab cruelly murdered him (2 Sam 18:4–5).

David's grief and mourning was so intense and so open that it affected the troops and began to undermine the morale of all. They had risked their lives for the king, and now the king appeared to be more grieved over the loss of the one who had begun the rebellion in the first place than he was concerned for those who had followed him faithfully with their very lives. Joab was infuriated: why all this public weeping for the one who was a rebel and a competitor to the kingdom—in effect making Joab out to be the bad guy when it was David's own son who had brought all the grief on the nation. And, in some ways, it was David's own fault in that he could not even manage his own family well. Joab rebuked his boss saying, "You love those who hate you and hate those who love you" (2 Sam. 19:6). If David did not straighten out soon, he would be in worse trouble than he had just survived with Absalom, cautioned Joab.

David's Return to Jerusalem

For the moment, then, Israel and Judah were left without a monarch. In this vacuum there must have been the possibility of anointing another person as king over Israel and Judah. In the meantime, the Israelites had returned to their homes and were arguing among themselves as to whether they should invite King David back to power again (2 Sam. 19:8b-10). Suddenly David came to his senses and decided he had better act swiftly, or Joab would be right—the kingdom would be lost forever! He sent a message to Zadok and Abiathar with the instructions that they should encourage the elders of Judah to take the lead in restoring him to his throne, for he was one of their kinsmen.

David, ever the political tactician and strategist, immediately promised to retain Amasa, the defeated general of Absalom's army. Surely this move was to serve as an olive branch and a sign that all who had supported Absalom would receive clemency. Anyway, Joab had disobeyed David's orders and had acted insolently, so he must be taught a lesson by the king. This news was warmly welcomed by the people of Judah, so they sent a delegation to Gilgal to meet the king and to reaffirm their allegiance to him (2 Sam. 19:15).

As Judah was deciding to support once again David, Shimei and Ziba led a delegation from Benjamin to seek reconciliation with David. Despite Abishai's desire to avenge Shimei's cursing of the king while he was fleeing Jerusalem by killing Shimei, David again took the high road of reconciliation, perhaps seeing in this situation an opportunity to heal the breach between Benjamin and Judah, so he ordered that Shimei should live. Likewise, Mephibosheth came and denied Ziba's accusations that this son of Jonathan had planned to profit from David's troubles. Mephibosheth's explanation was that he was prevented from joining David by his lameness. Of course, David also forgave him and his lying servant, Ziba, as well.

But once again some of the old canards resurfaced as a fight broke out between the Judean and the Israelite delegations. It seems that the main part of the Israelite contingent arrived late, just after David had been escorted over the Jordan, mainly by the Judeans. The Israelites charged the Judeans with acting unilaterally and precipitously, again being favored because of their superior numbers. Since when were two tribes more significant than ten tribes? they queried. Unfortunately for future events, the men of Judah retorted in words even more harsh than those of the Israelites (2 Sam. 19:41–43).

THE REVOLT OF SHEBA

This internecine acrimony played right into the hands of any who were of a mind to use it for their own purposes. One such adventurer was a certain Sheba, a Benjaminite. Sheba called for a clean break with the house of David, claiming:

> "We have no share in David,
> no part in Jesse's son!
> Every man to his tent, O Israel!" (2 Sam. 20:1).

The text says, "So all the men of Israel deserted David to follow Sheba, son of Bicri" (2 Sam. 20:2). This is a hyperbole, as is 2 Samuel 19:41, which states that "all the men of Israel" went to Gilgal to welcome David back. Of course, many in Israel did not buy Sheba's line of reasoning or acting, as 2 Samuel 20:14 demonstrates.

After his return to Jerusalem, David moved swiftly to stop Sheba's rebellion, fearing that if he did not, things would surely get out of hand—and quickly (2 Sam. 20:6). Amasa was to assemble the troops and to pursue Sheba, but for one reason or another Amasa dillydallied beyond the time David had set for the start of the campaign. Thus, David was forced to turn the matter over to Joab, Abishar, and his foreign legion of Cherethites and Pelethites. Joab killed Amasa, who had been his temporary replacement as leader of the forces, and then pursued Sheba to Abel Beth Maacah in the far north near Dan, where the sources of the Jordan River are found.

Joab put the city under siege. But a wise woman who lived in the city arranged for Sheba's head to be cut off and thrown over the wall, thus sparing the city from destruction by Joab (2 Sam. 20:14–22). Thus ended the rebellion and revolution.

DAVID'S UNAUTHORIZED CENSUS

Whether David ordered the census to reassess his military situation in the event of similar uprisings like those of Absalom and Sheba, or as a prelude to going out to conquer more territory—perhaps to demonstrate that he really was still capable of leading this people despite signs of deterioration—cannot be known for sure. The Lord permitted him to do so (2 Sam. 24:1). First Chronicles 21:1 attributes the census to the more immediate cause: Satan incited David to do so. The problem, however, was that a census usually meant much more in that day than it does in our day: it meant a call to arms and a mobilization of the troops. But that raises a question: Why should David be taking a census when God had not commanded him to move against any other targets. Not even David could conquer whomever he pleased: that right and prerogative belonged exclusively to Yahweh.

Joab had enough sense to protest the census, but he was assigned the task, nevertheless; therefore, he began the task in a counterclockwise direction from Transjordania to Dan, over to the environs of Tyre and Sidon and then down to Beersheba. The total came to eight hundred thousand men in Israel and five hundred thousand in Judah, excluding the tribes of Levi and Benjamin.

All too late, unfortunately, David realized the error of his ways. Yahweh announced that as a result of David's disobedience he was going to punish David and the nation in one of three ways, from which David would be able to choose: three years of famine, three months of flight from his enemy, or three days of plague. David cast himself on God's mercy, and as a result the Lord brought a plague that took the lives of seventy thousand people from all over the land. The plague stopped at the threshing floor of Araunah. David bought this spot from Araunah and erected an altar there on which he sacrificed offerings to Yahweh. The temple would later be built on this spot (1 Chron. 21:28–22:1). Here the plague was arrested, and the suffering ended.

The Davidic Covenant

David began to be consumed with the desire to build a temple for God. The idea became most prominent in his thinking after Hiram, the king of Tyre, had finished building a palace for David. In his view, it was not proper for him as a human monarch to live in such a prestigious cedar palace while Yahweh continued to reside in a tent (2 Sam. 7:1–2).

When David broached this subject with the prophet Nathan, Nathan urged him to proceed at once. That night, however, the Lord told Nathan to inform David that he could not undertake the building of a house for Yahweh because his hands were stained with blood from the wars of the Lord that he had fought. Instead, his son would build a house for Yahweh. David could assemble the materials and make certain other preparations, but that was all. The name of this house in Hebrew would be *hêkāl*, "temple," coming presumably as a loan word from the Sumerian *E.GAL*, meaning "great house," just as Akkadian *ekallu(m)* meant the same thing and acted as the probable means by which the Sumerian word got into Hebrew.

Nathan, however, had something better for David. Instead of his making a "house" for Yahweh, God would make a "house" (i.e., a dynasty) out of him and his subsequent seed (2 Sam. 7:11–13). And this dynasty would serve as a "law/charter for humanity" (Hebrew: *tôrat hāʾādām*; 2 Sam. 7:19). In other words, everything that Yahweh had promised to the patriarchs and Moses was now being invested in the house of David, in order that the whole world might profit spiritually and participate by faith in that kingdom now being established (2 Sam. 7:16).[1]

This gift to David would henceforth be known as the Covenant of David. It came in the form of a royal grant[2] in which the great King (in this case, Yahweh) graciously bestowed his blessing on the vassal (David and his succeeding line). But what was here promised was a continuation of the unilateral, unconditional covenant given to the patriarchs, only now it also involved an eternal perpetuation of David's throne, his dynasty, and his kingdom! As such, the Davidic Covenant (2 Sam. 7:8–16) resembled the Abrahamic Covenant (Gen. 12:1–3; 17:3–8) in much of its language and content. Without stipulating any conditions, David was promised that he and his line would continue to enjoy the blessings of the land, progeny, and transferable benefits for all the Gentile nations. Even though Yahweh reserved the right to punish disobedient descendants in David's line, he nonetheless swore on an oath that he would never permanently withdraw his gifts from David's dynasty. Therefore, while the Northern Kingdom of Israel was periodically wracked by violent changes in ruling dynasties, a remarkable stability continued for the most part in Judah until her collpase in 586 B.C.

---

1. For a justification of this rendering of *tôrat hāʾādām*, see Walter C. Kaiser Jr., "The Blessing of David: The Charter for Humanity," in *The Law and the Prophets: Oswald T. Allis Festschrift*, ed. J. Skilton (Philadelphia: Presbyterian and Reformed, 1974): 290–318 and the bibliography mentioned there. Also see on the covenant Delbert R. Hillers, *Covenant: The History of a Biblical Idea* (Baltimore: Johns Hopkins Press, 1969); and Roland Clements, *Abraham and David: Studies in Biblical Theology*, 2nd series (Naperville, Ill.: Allenson, 1967).

2. Whether David's Covenant was a vassal or grant type has been discussed by M. Weinfeld, "The Covenant of Grant in the Old Testament and in the Ancient Near East," *JAOS* 90.2 (1970), especially pp. 184–85. Contrast Ron Youngblood, "The Abrahamic Covenant: Conditional or Unconditional?" in *The Living and Active Word of God: Essays in Honor of Samuel J. Schultz*, eds. Morris Inch and Ronald Youngblood (Winona Lake, Ind.: Eisenbrauns, 1983), 31–46. Also see William J. Dumbrell, "The Prospect of Unconditionality in the Sinaitic Covenant," in *Israel's Apostasy and Restoration: Essays in Honor of Roland K. Harrison*, ed. Avraham Gileadi (Grand Rapids: Baker, 1988), 154 ff; Avraham Gileadi, "The Davidic Covenant: A Theological Basis for Corporate Protection," in *Israel's Apostasy and Restoration*, p. 159 ff; and Bruce K. Waltke, "The Phenomenon of Conditionality within Unconditional Covenants," in *Israel's Apostasy and Restoration*, pp. 130 ff.

DAVID'S ADMINISTRATION

We are given a more detailed look at the administrative setup of David's government than we had from Saul's reign. Clearly, David's must have been much more developed and nuanced. The list of his officers was as follows:)

David's Cabinet
(2 Sam. 8:16–18; 1 Chron. 18:15–17)

Over the army	Joab, son of Zeruiah
Recorder	Jehoshaphat, son of Ahilud
Priests	Zadok, son of Ahitub Ahimelech, son of Abiathar
Secretary	Seriah (or Shavsha in 1 Chron.)
Over the (foreign legion): Cherethites and Pelethites	Benaiah, son of Jehoiada
Royal advisors/"Chief officials in the service of the King" (1 Chron.)	David's sons

Later, another office would be added in 2 Samuel 20:23–26, "over the forced labor/or corvee," a position held by Adoniram, or Hebrew Adoram. This same passage also mysteriously adds, "Ira the Jairite was David's priest."

The recorder would care for state documents and records presumably. The secretary would handle the day-to-day operations, such as the diplomatic correspondence. Joab would serve as the commander-in-chief of the armed forces, while the Cherethites and Pelethites would function much as the Swiss guard functions at the Vatican: it was a foreign legion devoted to looking out for the king and his protection—a sort of secret service branch of the government assigned to protect the life of the monarch. This list does not mention a place for prophets such as Gad and Nathan, but clearly, they played a major part in all that took place in the court. The king also had advisors such as Ahithophel and Hushai. So good was Ahithophel's counsel that it was like "consult[ing] the oracle of God" (2 Sam. 16:23, my own translation).

David died in 971 B.C. and passed on quite a legacy to his son Solomon. Israel had become, in a greater sense than ever before, a leading nation in the ancient Near East; and such a tranquility fell over the area that little, if any, hostilities broke out during Solomon's reign.

19

THE REIGN OF SOLOMON

About two years before the death of David, Solomon had been installed as vice-regent with his father David. It should have been clear which way David thought the line of descent ought to go in his dynasty. But both Joab and Abiathar the priest disagreed with David's choice and risked backing Adonijah.

THE ILL-FATED INSTALLATION OF ADONIJAH

Adonijah, the fourth-eldest son of David, was now his oldest surviving son. But David had made clear his preference for Solomon as his successor by associating himself with Solomon rather than Adonijah. With this decision, some of David's closest and most loyal friends were in deep disagreement. Apparently, they just thought that the dynastic succession ought to go to the oldest surviving son, or so it would seem. Of course, other circumstances may have motivated them to favor Adonijah.

Joab, David's extremely successful commander of the army, had been one of David's closest advisors. But it is also true that time and again David would take the opposite course of action that Joab had either proposed or executed: say in Joab's assassinations of Abner, Absalom, or even an Amasa. In fact, Amasa had been appointed by David to be Joab's replacement. Could it be then, that Joab feared that, in the transfer of power to Solomon, he had more to lose from one who was closer to David, as Solomon was, than from someone he could help install in the reins of government? Possibly.

Likewise, the high priest Abiathar had been with David since the days when David was a fugitive, going back to the time when Abiathar's whole family at Nob had been wiped out by Saul and his herdsman, Doeg, in a jealous rage over the priestly family's alleged disloyalty to David. Surely Abiathar also knew that he was a direct descendant of Eli, the priest in the Aaronic line of Ithamar, against whom the man of God and Samuel had pronounced a word of judgment, saying that line was to come to an end (2 Sam. 2:30–36; 3:12–14). Abiathar must have been on his guard against the possibility that Samuel's prophecy would be fulfilled in his lifetime. However, there was a new priest on the block, Zadok; and Zadok's presence must have threatened Abiathar. It had been Zadok who was the priest connected with the removal of the ark from the house of Obed-Edom (1 Chron. 15:11). The next thing we notice is that Zadok is serving with Abiathar as copriest, first at Gibeon (1 Chron. 16:39) and then with the ark on Mt. Zion (2 Sam. 15:24). Toward the end of David's life, Zadok's name starts appearing in front of Abiathar's, though it had always been the reverse of that up to that point. Zadok did not descend from the cursed house of Eli and Ithamar, but from Eleazar, son of Aaron. It would make sense for Abiathar to join a pro-Adonijah party, just as Joab had and for the same reasons. Clearly David, and now his protégé Solomon, were favoring Zadok over Abiathar.

First Kings 1 and 2 are connected to the Succession Narrative of 2 Samuel 9–20, because it is incomplete without it, say most scholars. It details how Adonijah gathered a military contingent without arousing David's suspicions and then proceeded to go to En Rogel, where the Kidron and Hinnom Valleys meet in the southeast corner outside the walls of Jerusalem. Invited to this clandestine gathering were Joab, Abiathar, Adonijah's brothers, the king's sons, and royal officials of Judah. There they proclaimed Adonijah king in place of David (1 Kings 1:9, 11, 18).

Nathan the prophet, Shimei, Zadok the priest, and David's special guard of the foreign legion had not been invited to the ceremonies. However, when Nathan learned what was transpiring, he immediately went to Bathsheba and said they must both go immediately to David to get him to declare Solomon king over Israel and Judah.

David was persuaded to act. He called Zadok the priest and ordered him to arrange for the orderly, but hasty, transfer of the government to

Solomon, before Adonijah usurped the throne. Immediately Zadok went to set up a coronation ceremony at Gihon, also in the Kidron Valley, just north of En Rogel, where the rival coronation was already underway. Consequently, Solomon was escorted on David's own mule to Gihon, where Zadok formally anointed him as king. A hastily gathered crowd hailed the succession of Solomon to David's throne (1 Kings 1:39–40; 1 Chron. 29:22).

As the jubilant sound of Solomon's coronation reached the competing coronation celebration just down the valley from them, a messenger arrived in Adonijah's celebration with the news that their attempted coup had failed. That party suddenly broke up as everyone made a hasty retreat and a quick disassociation from Adonijah. Adonijah himself rushed for sanctuary to the great altar on Mt. Zion, hoping to avoid any retaliatory responses from Solomon, but Solomon pardoned Adonijah and all his accomplices.

When David died at the age of seventy, having served thirty-three years in Jerusalem and another seven years previous to that in Hebron, he carefully instructed Solomon as to how he was to deal with those who had caused him grief during his reign—it was quite a hit list!

THE ESTABLISHMENT OF THE KINGDOM IN SOLOMON'S HANDS

Adonijah approached Bathsheba, now the queen mother, to ask her if she might intervene on his behalf with her son Solomon for a small request. He would like to have David's nurse-maid, Abishag the Shunammite, as his wife. Innocently Bathsheba took this request to her son, but it infuriated Solomon: "You might as well request the kingdom for him—after all, he is my older brother—yes, for him and for Abiathar the priest and Joab's son Zeruiah!" (1 Kings 2:22). Solomon understood what his mother apparently did not: Adonijah's intent was to use this marriage as a basis for his attempt once more to take over the reins of the kingdom. This move was not so subtle as Adonijah thought it might be, for what may have gone over the head of Bathsheba was not missed by Solomon. This action made it clear to Solomon that Adonijah was so fixed on undermining his government that there was no use in trying to placate him and extend to him any more mercy. Instead, Solomon ordered Benaiah to execute him. Adonijah had invited his own demise, as had his brother Absalom.

Things moved rather rapidly after Adonijah's death. The priest Abiathar, Solomon declared, deserved to die but would not be put to death because he had carried the ark of God and had shared all sorts of hardships with his father David. Instead, Abiathar must be confined to his home in Anathoth under what was a virtual house arrest. The priestly line, in accordance with Samuel's prediction, was removed from the house of Eli, which Abiathar represented, and transferred to the descendants of Aaron's son Eleazar (1 Kings 2:26–27).

Joab, whose murderous brutality had caused David much trouble, fled to the tent of the Lord and took hold of the horns of the altar as a sanctuary. Repeated orders and requests for Joab to quit the altar went unheeded. "No," he insisted, "I will die here" (1 Kings 2:28–30). "Do as he says," ordered Solomon (1 Kings 2:31–34); therefore Banaiah killed him right at the altar where he had hoped for sanctuary. Benaiah was then awarded the position that Joab had once held, commander in chief of Solomon's army.

But Solomon was not yet finished with setting right what had long festered in the kingdom. He summoned Shimei, who had cast derision on David when he had been forced into exile by his son Absalom (2 Sam. 16:5–8), and placed him under house arrest; if Shimei left Jerusalem, he would surely be put to death. As it happened, three years later, Shimei did leave the city to catch two runaway slaves and Solomon remained true to his word (1 Kings 2:36–46a).

Only after all of this had been dealt with could the narrator say: "The kingdom was now firmly established in Solomon's hands" (1 Kings 2:46b). But in the midst of all this carnage, Solomon's posture was to remain passive and to let others carry out his instructions.

SOLOMON'S DREAM AT GIBEON

Early in Solomon's reign, Pharaoh Siamun of the Twenty-first Dynasty (who reigned from 978–959 B.C.) proposed that his daughter be given to Solomon as a wife, thereby securing peaceful relations between the two nations through such a marriage alliance (1 Kings 3:1–3). Apparently, Egypt had no interest in challenging Israel, even though he had attacked the Philistines. The so-called Tanis Relief in Egypt pictures the pharaoh in a victory pose over a group of prisoners that can easily be identified as Philistines by the double axe, commonly used by the Philistines and peoples of the Aegean and Anatolian regions.[1] This may have been the same time when Siamun captured

1. Pierre Montet, *Egypt and the Bible* (Philadelphia: Fortress, 1968), 36–39. As Eugene H. Merrill, *Kingdom of Priests*, p. 292, n. 9, points out, some objected to this interpretation: Alberto R. Green, "Solomon and Siamun: A Synchronism between Dynastic Israel and the Twenty-first Dynasty of Egypt," *JBL* 97 (1978): 363–64, even though Green conceded that Siamun was Solomon's father-in-law.

Gezer, set it on fire and killed all its Canaanite inhabitants (1 Kings 9:16). This is the town he would give to his daughter as a dowry for her wedding to Solomon.

The king went to the "great high place" at Gibeon to make his inaugural sacrifice (1 Kings 3:4). The writer is at pains to be fair in this matter: "Solomon showed his love for the LORD by walking according to the statutes of his father David, except he offered sacrifices and burned incense on the high places" (1 Kings 3:3). But the writer hedged, explaining: "The people, however, were still sacrificing at the high places, because a temple had not yet been built for the Name of the LORD" (1 Kings 3:2).

It is not clear why Solomon assembled the people at Gibeon rather than on Mt. Zion. But since his interest was in sacrificing, and not in the ark itself, the great bronze altar that Moses had built was at Gibeon, not at Mt. Zion. Solomon offered a thousand burnt offerings at Gibeon on that altar.

That night God appeared to Solomon in a dream and invited him to ask for anything he wanted (1 Kings 3:5). Solomon's request was this: "a discerning heart" (1 Kings 3:9). In fact, he saw his own position as a fulfillment of the promise that God had given to his father David (1 Kings 3:6; 2 Sam. 7; 1 Chron. 17). This request pleased Yahweh, who gave him—in addition to the requested wisdom—riches and honor similar to nothing ever before witnessed (1 Kings 3:10–12).

Solomon displayed God's gift of wisdom when he solved the puzzle of the two harlots who both claimed the same baby (1 Kings 3:14–28). While flatterers compared David's wisdom to that of "an angel of God" (2 Sam. 14:17; 19:28), Baruch Halpern observed that the puzzle Solomon solved in his wisdom was the kind that "consistently confounded David (2 Sam. 16:1–4; 19:18, 25–31)."[2] But in Solomon's case, this episode of the two women forever settled the fact that Yahweh had granted what he had promised in the dream at Gibeon. Solomon's administration would be different.

Solomon's wisdom is reflected in the fact that he is credited with writing parts or the whole of the books of Proverbs, Ecclesiastes, and Song of Songs. He composed three thousand proverbs and over one thousand songs, dealing with matters ranging from animals, birds, and fish to human relationships (1 Kings 4:32–33). His wisdom became so legendary in his own time that it drew Queen Sheba from the south-

2. Baruch Halpern, "Dr. Faustus or Mr. Hyde (?): The Problem of Solomon ben-David," chapter 7 in *The First Historians: The Hebrew Bible and History* (San Francisco: Harper & Row, 1988), 146.

west corner of Arabia to test that wisdom and to experience it for herself.

Solomon's Administration

Solomon's administration evidenced an increase in bureaucracy over David's model. First Kings 4:7–19 lists twelve officers (*nissabim*) who were "over all Israel," entrusted with providing food for the king and his household. The list of high officials in 1 Kings 4:1–6 was indeed similar to that of David, though it, too, had increases. They were:

Solomon's Chief Officials (1 Kings 4:1–6)

The Priest	Azariah, son of Zadok
Secretaries	Elihoreph and Ahijah, sons of Shisha
Recorder	Jehoshaphat, son of Ahilud
Commander in chief	Benaiah, son of Jehoida
Priests	Zadok (and Abiathar?)
Over the district officers	Azariah, son of Nathan
Priest and the king's personal advisor	Zabud, son of Nathan
Over the palace	Ahishar
Over the forced labor	Adoniram, son of Abda

Two priests are listed, probably because both were functioning at the beginning of Solomon's reign; this must be a list from the early days of his reign. Benaiah and Nathan were both rewarded because each helped Solomon in getting his reign established; Benaiah took Joab's place, and Nathan's two sons were given cabinet positions.

The functions of the twelve officers who provided for the King (1 Kings 4:7–19) is not altogether clear: they appear to have managed the king's estates, much as Ziba had managed Saul's estate; but these twelve also appear to have collected taxes, for they gathered food for the court and barley and straw for the horses in Solomon's chariotry.

Each district was responsible for an entire month every year; thus the twelve districts matched the twelve months. A distinction seems to be made between the Israelites who were conscripted for temporary service and the non-Israelites who were reduced to permanent slave labor (1 Kings 9:15–22). The twelve districts approximately matched the twelve tribes, though Dan and Zebulun have disappeared as independent entities. Dan may have been incorporated into Naphtali to counteract their penchant for paganism. Also, coastal Asher was given to Hiram's Phoenicia for 120 talents of gold; this may suggest that Solomon was desperate to finance his building projects. Even more surprisingly, Judah and Jerusalem were omitted from the districting, making them a sort of federal district exempt from the obligations that the rest of the nation faced. This exemption from taxation, the forced labor and similar burdens of state, must have been one of the sorest points of contention between the tribes, ultimately forcing the division between the kingdoms of the north and the south.

The office of forced labor would continue to be a sticky point for Solomon, even though it had been inaugurated under David (2 Sam. 20:24). Under David's wars, much of the labor force came from foreign prisoners whom David captured and brought back to Jerusalem to aid in his projects. But now in peacetime, Solomon had to rely on conscription of his own people. First Kings 5:13–16 indicated that a levy of thirty thousand men, ten thousand each month, were sent to Lebanon in relays, working one month in Lebanon and two months at home. Adoniram was in charge of what must have been a very unpopular job. In addition to these, Solomon had seventy thousand burden bearers and eighty thousand hewers of stone in the hill country, not to mention the thirty-three hundred chief officers who were over the work and in charge of these conscripts. First Kings 9:15–23 explains that the labor gangs were made up solely of foreigners: Amorites, Hittites, Perrizites, Hivities, and Jebusites. The Israelites were Solomon's soldiers, officials, chariot commanders, and the like, but not his slaves (1 Kings 9:20–22). But by the time of the split of the kingdom at the end of Solomon's reign, the Israelites were being forced to do labor, and this was an issue for separation of the tribes when the united monarchy divided (1 Kings 1:26–40).

The Construction of the Temple

Pride of place is given to Solomon's construction of the temple, for it extends from chapter 5 to chapter 8 in 1 Kings. The site for the temple had already been purchased by David from Araunah his threshing floor on Mt. Zion. David had prepared the site, gathered the building materials, including the precious metals and stones, and had already gotten an agreement from Hiram, king of Tyre, that he would supply the cedar timber as well as the workers needed to erect the temple.

The basic pattern of the temple, though no specifications or descriptions are given, appears to be identical to that of the Mosaic tabernacle and other ancient Near Eastern temples from that time.[3] This structure, whatever its final appearance, was seven years in the making under the supervision of Huram-Abi. The description of its gold and other appointments have been so breathtaking that many have seriously doubted anyone, much less a monarch like Solomon, could have had access to this much wealth.

Solomon's temple exhibited the general forms of Phoenician architecture (note the use of Phoenician craftsmen in 1 Kings 5:10, 18; 7:13, 14) with many of the traditional symbols of Hebrew worship. It is not surprising therefore to find parallels in the design and decoration of the temple with such similar floor plans as those exhibited in the small shrine from the eighth century B.C. at Tell Tainat on the Orontes River with its three rooms, an altar in the innermost room, and two columns on the porch. The same tripartite division was found at the Late Bronze Tell Munbaqa temples (on the east bank of the middle of the Euphrates River). An Akkadian term, *bit-hilani*, was used to describe a type of architecture that used a colonnaded entrance porch, usually with a long hall, rather than a wide hall footprint for the building. The plan for these types of buildings often included these three parts: a porch (*ʾûlām*), a sanctuary or holy place (*hêkāl*) and a holy of holies (*dĕbîr*). Detailed descriptions of the Solomonic temple appear in 1 Kings 5:16–7:38 and 2 Chronicles 4.

The Phoenician masons dressed the stone ashlars (consisting of headers and stretchers) and worked as experts in bronze casting such temple ceremonial vessels as a "basin on wheels," a bronze laver on a stand (similar to presumably pagan lavers found at Megiddo and Cyprus), and a great "molten sea," containing 2,000 baths of water for

---

3. Volkmar Fritz, "Temple Architecture: What Can Archaeology Tell Us about Solomon's Temple?" BAR 13.4 (1987): 38–49; Carol L. Myers, "The Elusive Temple," *BA* 45 (1982): 33–41; for an older work on ancient Near Eastern temples, William F. Albright, *Archaeology and the Religion of Israel* (Garden City, N.Y.: Doubleday, 1969), 138–50. Also D. Ussishkin, "King Solomon's Palaces," *BA* 36 (1973): 78–105; and J. Ouellette, "The Basic Structure of the Solomonic Temple and Archaeological Research," in *The Temple of Solomon and Medieval Tradition in Christian, Islamic and Jewish Art*. ed. J. Gutmann, *Religion and the Arts*, 3 (Missoula, Mont.: Scholars Press, 1976). Also Th. A. Busink, *Der Tempel von Jerusalem* I (Leiden: Brill, 1970); Kathleen M. Kenyon, "New Evidence on Solomon's Temple," *Melanges de l'Universite Saint-Joseph* 46.9 (1970): 139–49 and D. Ussishkin, "Building IV in Hamath and the Temples of Solomon and Tell Tayanat," *IEJ* 16 (1966): 104–10.

use by the priests in their presacrificial lustrations, which stood on twelve bronze oxen.[4] Two bronze pillars, named Boaz and Jachin, each standing nearly forty feet high, stood on the porch of the temple. The walls and floor were covered with Phoenician cedar.

Solomon's construction of the Jerusalem temple tended to consolidate relationships between Israel's political and economic forms and the centrality of the sanctuary. Yahweh was the real monarch, and the king was Yahweh's vice-regent. The ornateness of the temple, matching the exquisite decoration and attention of the other royal buildings, set the values for the state and for the people.

Solomon's Seaport

First Kings 9:26–28 described how Solomon, with the help of Phoenician King Hiram, built a fleet of ships that sailed from Ezion-Geber, near Elath, on the shore of the Red Sea.[5] Hiram's men had the knowledge and skills to serve as mariners with Solomon's men. These ships went as far as Ophir, where they obtained 420 talents of gold (2 Chron. 8:17–18 had 450 talents of gold) for Solomon.

But where was this site of Ezion-Geber? Israel had few, if any, good seaports on the Mediterranean coast; but the Phoenicians had Tyre, Sidon, and Arwad. This gave the Phoenicians access to the Mediterranean coastline and perhaps even further afield, but they had little or no access to southern Africa, India, and similar destinations. Solomon, however, did have a sliver of the Red Sea, known today as the Gulf of Eilat in Israel or the Gulf of Aqabah in Jordan. This port was the gateway to the very places that Hiram lacked. Both Solomon and Hiram must have known of the Egyptian ventures to the legendary land of Punt, where the Egyptians obtained gold, silver, ivory, apes, and the like that were described in hieroglyphic texts of Queen Hatshepsut's mausoleum near Thebes. With Hiram's expertise, perhaps Solomon could emulate what the Egyptians had accomplished in the fifteenth century.

Philo of Byblos (30 B.C.-A.D. 40) quoted the Phoenician historian Sanchuniathon to the effect that Hiram sent 800 camels loaded with timber to Ezion-Geber for building ten ships.[6] So where did they build these ships?

---

4. See Lamoine F. DeVries, "Cult Stands: A Bewildering Variety of Shapes and Sizes," *BAR* 13.4 (1987): 26–37, and Mervyn Fowler, "Excavated Incense Burners," *BA* 47 (1984): 183–86.

5. I am beholden to Alexander Flinder, "Is This Solomon's Seaport?" *BAR* 15.4 (1989): 30–43 for much of the factual data in this section.

6. Philo of Byblos, *The Phoenician History*.

Nelson Glueck was certain in 1959 that:

> The whereabouts of Solomon's long-lost port of Ezion-Geber was for centuries an unfathomable mystery, because no one paid attention to the Biblical statement that it was located "beside Elath on the shore of the Red Sea in the land of Edom" [1Kings 9:26]. And that is exactly where we found it, in the form of a small, sanded-over mound of Tell el-Kheleifeh on the shore of the Gulf of Aqabah, which is the eastern arm of the Red Sea.[7]

Glueck thought that Tell el-Kheleifeh was the elusive port "beyond all question of doubt . . . Tell el-Kheleifeh had to be Ezion-Geber: Eloth!"[8] Glueck nicknamed the site the "Pittsburgh of Palestine" because of what he believed to be the evidence of copper slag, extensive sulfuric discoloration of the walls of what he called a copper smelting room with flues positioned exactly to take advantage of the north winds from the Arabah. The pottery and the casemate wall (two parallel walls with intermittent crosswalls creating rooms within the walls) pointed, he claimed, to the Solomonic period. Thus, Solomon, in Glueck's mind, was the copper magnate of the Near East, trading copper ingots for all the fancy products that had formerly flowed into Egypt, but were now coming into his coffers.

In 1962, however, Beno Rothenberg, exploded this whole description by disputing almost every point that Glueck had made. Glueck's furnace room was in fact a large storage room; the sulphuric discloration was not from industrial processes but from the final destruction of the building by fire; there were no large quantities of copper slag; the flues were holes left from the burned-out joice of the building consumed by fire; and the windiest site was further to the west, not where Glueck had placed it.[9]

In 1965 Glueck published a graceful *mea culpa*, saying:

> It had been our thought, which we now abandon, that the apertures served as flue-holes . . . These apertures resulted from the decay and/or burning of wooden beams laid across the width of the walls for bonding or anchoring purposes . . . Obviously then, this structure could not have functioned as a smelter. . . . We believe now, as Roth-

7. Nelson Glueck, *Rivers in the Desert* (London: Weidenfeld and Nicholson, 1959), 31–32.
8. Nelson Glueck, *Rivers in the Desert*, pp. 159, 161.
9. Beno Rothenberg, "Ancient Copper Industries in the Western Arabah," Part II, " Tell El-Kheleifeh; Ezion-Geber; Eilath," PEQ 94 (1962): 5–71.

> enberg has suggested, that this structure with its purposely high floors was also designed and used as a storehouse and/or granary . . . [a] coarse, handmade type of pottery was found that at the time was new to us, and that for a brief while appeared to us to be utilized for crucibles. We soon abandoned this idea when it became apparent how common this pottery was at contemporary sites in the Negev.[10]

However, a massive reevaluation of Glueck's excavation materials from Tell el-Kheleifeh was completed by my colleague Gary Pratico. Pratico was able to demonstrate that the earliest occupation of the site was post-Solomonic.[11]

If Ezion-Geber is not to be identified with Tell el-Kheleifeh, then where is it? As early as the nineteeth century (A.D. 1837), the traveler Friedrich Von Schubert had pointed to the offshore island of Jezirat Faraun ("pharaoh's island") as a candidate. This island is some seven miles south of modern Eilat and nine hundred feet from the Sinai shore. It is only one thousand feet from north to south and two hundred feet from east to west, consisting of three hills. The northernmost hill occupies over half of the island and is today surmounted by a Moslem fortress dating back to the twelfth century A.D. The two southern hills have Byzantine ruins on them.

This island has the most naturally protected anchorage available in that part of the Red Sea between the island and the mainland. About a mile south of the island the Wadi Jereya empties into the Red Sea. During the times when this otherwise dry wadi is flooded, it carries sand and debris out into the Gulf forming a one-half-mile-long submerged breakwater that further breaks up the turbulent storms and waves from the prevaling southern winds. Thus the area between the island and the mainland of Sinai was the best anchorage available.

Jezirat Faraun's perimeter was encased in a casemate wall (double walls divided into small rooms by short perpendicular walls) and nine towers that appear to date to Phoenician/Solomonic times in the tenth century B.C. There is also a small harbor basin measuring 180 feet by 90 feet, now heavily silted, but it was obviously used in another day as a spot for unloading ships. Submerged just outside the harbor are the remains of two artificially built dolphins; these are mooring piers where

10. Nelson Glueck, "Ezion-Geber," *BA* 28 (1965): 73.

11. Gary Pratico, "Tell el-Kheleifeh," *AASOR* (1995); also idem., "Where is Ezion-Geber? A Reappraisal of the Site Nelson Glueck Identified as King Solomon's Red Sea Port," *BAR* (September/October 1986).

ships coming from the open sea could fasten on the dophin[12] while waiting to enter the harbor to unload their cargo. In ancient times, goods were apparently unloaded, then transferred to caravans for the long journey north to Israel and Phoenicia. There is every indication, therefore, that this island is the long-sought-after site of Ezion-Geber and the area from which much of Solomon's wealth flowed into his kingdom.

The Wealth of Solomon

The Old Testament is the only ancient document to report the annual income of one of its mighty monarchs.[13] The figure given in 1 Kings 10:14 for Solomon is 666 talents of gold (almost 25 U.S. tons). In addition to that, another 420 talents of gold (15.75 U.S. tons) came from Ophir (1 Kings 10:11).[14] The expression "gold of Ophir" itself was thought to be mythological until it was found at Tell Qasile in Israel on an eighth-century ostracon (a potsherd with an inscription on it). While the location of Ophir is still unknown, it is now known that this was a destination from which gold could be obtained.

According to Allan Millard, only two other figures in the ancient world approach that amount: Pharaoh Osorkon I's (in 921 B.C.) gift to his gods included an astonishing 383 tons of gold and silver, as indicated on a pillar in a temple at Bubastis, and Alexander the Great found 1,180 tons of gold in Susa for a total of 7,000 tons in the whole of Persia, according to Greek sources.

Writers in antiquity did not always distinguish between gold as "pure" gold and "red" gold (i.e., "alloyed" gold). It is not always possible to tell which is meant. Furthermore, as Millard pointed out, the weights of golden objects did not always distinguish between the core of wood, ivory, or base metal and the weight of the gold that covered them. But occasionally they did, for Solomon's tableware was of "pure gold" (1 Kings 10:21).

When Solomon built the temple, the interior stone walls and cedar boards were completely plated with gold (1 Kings 6:15, 18); the floors of both the inner and outer rooms were entirely overlaid with gold (1 Kings 6:20–22, 30; 2 Chron. 3:4–7). The typical response of mod-

12. This is a sailing term for mooring piers just outside the harbor where ships coming from the open sea could "fasten on the dophin" while waiting to enter the harbor to unload their cargo.

13. Allan R. Millard, "Does the Bible Exaggerate King Solomon's Golden Wealth?" *BAR* 15.3 (1989): 21–29, 3, 34, has provided some of my best material for this section.

14. Allan R. Millard, "Does the Bible Exaggerate King Solomon's Golden Wealth?" pp. 21–29, 31, 34.

ern commentators has been to discount such descriptions as the result of "exuberant imaginations," or the result of some type of sprayed gold paint—as if from a power sprayer or an aerosol can! (Talk about anachronistic explanations!)[15]

Millard's response was this: "It is impossible to prove that Solomon did build a temple overlaid with gold as described in 1 Kings and 2 Chronicles. But the evidence assembled here shows it would be foolish to deny the possibility."[16] Moreover the amount of gold that came to Solomon was staggering. Already it had been noted that Hiram gave him 120 talents of gold for the city of Cabul on the Phoenician coast (i.e., about 9,000 lbs.—some four and one-half tons of gold 1 Kings 9:14)! The queen of Sheba brought to him a similar gift of 120 talents of gold. No wonder Solomon could claim that his golden shields weighed 4,000 pounds, more than two tons (1 Kings 10:16, 17).

But if these figures appear easy to dismiss, how much more confidence should we have in reports that the tribute Assyrian king Tiglath Pileser III received, when he subjugated Tyre in 730 B.C., was 150 talents of gold? Or that Sargon II gave a gift of 154 talents of gold to the gods of Babylon, as part of his booty taken in his Babylonian campaign?[17]

Another question is this: Where did all Solomon's gold go if he had so much? The answer Kenneth Kitchen gave was that in the summer of 925 B.C., under the reign of Solomon's reckless son Rehoboam, Shishak—otherwise also known as Pharaoh Shoshenq I—stripped all the gold from the temple, including the gold shields, and carried them off to Egypt. Within a year Shoshenq I was dead, but he was followed to the throne by his son Pharaoh Osorkon I. The new pharaoh proudly recorded that he had donated an astonishing 383 tons of gold and silver to a temple at Bubastis.[18] Nor did that exhaust Osorkon I's treasury, for he had to bury his coregent son before the end of his reign. Pierre Montet found Shoshenq II in 1939 entombed in a solid silver coffin at Tanis. Certainly, most, if not all of this treasure, came from Solomon's

15. Millard points to two such examples in Joseph Robinson, *The First Book of Kings*, Cambridge Bible (Cambridge: Cambridge University Press, 1972), 79; and John Gray, *I and II Kings* (London: SCM Press, 1964), 160.

16. Allan R. Millard, "Does the Bible Exaggerate," p. 31.

17. D. D. Luckenbill, *Ancient Records of Assyria*, 2 vols. (Chicago: University of Chicago Press, 1927) I: para. 803; II: para 70; also James B. Pritchard, ANET, 3rd ed. (Princeton, N.J.: Princeton University Press, 1969), 282b, as cited by Millard, "Does the Bible Exaggerate?" pp. 31, 34, nn. 18, 19.

18. Kenneth A. Kitchen, "Where Did Solomon's Gold Go?" *BAR* 15.3 (1989): 30.

hoard of silver and gold in Jerusalem taken in 925 B.C. by Shishak/Shoshenq I.

Solomon's Building Projects

When Solomon had finished building the temple, he turned to other projects. First he built his own magnificent palace. While the temple took seven years to build, Solomon's own palace took thirteen (1 Kings 6:38; 7:1), meaning that both projects consumed twenty years (1 Kings 9:10). Thus, the temple was completed by 959 B.C. and the palace in 946 B.C.

Solomon constructed his Palace of the Forest of Lebanon even larger than the temple. It had wings or semidetached structures such as the hall of justice and Solomon's private quarters. David Ussishkin identified at least six separate structures, some of which were joined together into complexes in Solomon's palace.[19] In addition, Pharaoh Siamun's daughter, who was married to Solomon, was given her own palace, for she had resided in temporary facilities on Mt. Zion all this time. She was transferred from the sacred precincts of Zion, in order not to continue to offend the holiness of God (2 Chron. 8:11).

In other projects, the king built a wall around the original town of Jebus on Ophel, enclosing the area of the temple and the public buildings on the north of Ophel for the first time. Even though the total area enclosed was only about one thousand yards from north to south and two hundred yards from east to west, it was quite a city by ancient standards.[20] Solomon also worked on the terraces of Ophel, a word meaning "filling," or the terraces built on the sides of the hill. This provided more space for other buildings and for defensive structures such as the walls of the city.

Construction was not limited to Jerusalem, for Solomon fortified other cities: Hazor, Megiddo, and Gezer (1 Kings 9:15). Each city was strategically located on a trade route and served as a military facility. Excavations of all three sites have yielded evidence of Solomon's presence and his military prowess.

Most interesting, yet the most debated in recent years, are the installations of Solomon's stables. At Megiddo, for instance, the Oriental

19. David Ussishkin, "King Solomon's Palaces," *BA* 36 (1973): 78–105; idem, "Solomon's Palace and Megiddo 1723," *IEJ* 16 (1966): 179–86; and G. R. H. Wright, *Ancient Buildings in South Syria and Palestine*, vols. 1–2 (Leiden: Brill, 1985).

20. Eugene H. Merrill, *Kingdom of Priests*, p. 297; and Kathleen Kenyon, *Jerusalem* (New York: McGraw-Hill, 1967), 56–58.

Institute thought they had found his stables in two areas of the mound: northeastern and southwestern. On the basis of 1 Kings 9:19 ("[Solomon] built . . . towns for his chariots and for his horses") P. L. O. Guy named the two sets of buildings at Megiddo "the stables of Solomon." The stables consisted of rows of long narrow rooms separated by a solid wall, with each group of three rooms divided only by a monolithic pillar that had holes, presumably for tethering the horses, with stone containers identified as mangers between the pillars.[21] These accommodations could provide for three squadrons of chariot horses, each squadron consisting of fifty chariot-teams of three horses each, making a total of 450 horses.

But as early as 1970, University of Pennsylvania's James B. Pritchard began questioning whether these buildings were stables.[22] Pritchard thought they were storehouses instead, but that view has declined and the fact that they are stables is now affirmed by Finkelstein and Ussishkin as well as by the Israeli archaeologist Yigael Yadin, who undertook a modest excavation at Megiddo to correct several stratigraphical errors. But what became obvious was that the stables, that had been identified as belonging to Solomon's tenth century, actually belonged to Kings Omri and Ahab in the ninth century. The current supposition of Graham Davies, with some supporting evidence, is that the Solomonic stables lie under those of Omri and Ahab, just as another set of these pillared buildings lies one on top of the other from the tenth and ninth centuries at Beer-Sheba.

Solomon appeared to refortify the sites of Beth Horon, northwest of Gibeon, and Baalath, southwest of Gezer, probably against Philistine invasion. Likewise Tamer, some 25 miles south of the Dead Sea, was set up as a guard for the frontier to the south. But there were even towns rebuilt as far away as Hamath Zobah on the Orontes River. Also Tadmor, some 140 miles northeast of Damascus, became another in the defensive chain of locations "in Lebanon and throughout all the territory [Solomon] ruled" (1 Kings 9:19). He was the master builder, indeed.

---

21. Graham I. Davies, "King Solomon's Stables Still at Megiddo?" *BAR* 20.1 (1994): 45–49. In that same issue of *BAR*, see Israel Finkelstein and David Ussishkin, "Are They Solomon's? Are They Stables?" on p. 38 for photographs and models of the stables.

22. James B. Pritchard, "The Megiddo Stables: A Reassessment," in *Near Eastern Archaeology in the Twentieth Century*, Nelson Glueck volume, ed. J. A. Sanders (Garden City, N.Y.: Doubleday, 1970), 268–76.

Solomon's International Trade

Israel was located on the maritime and overland crossroads. Solomon took advantage of this situation and acted as the middleman par excellence in the ancient Near East. Everything passing through his borders was assessed custom taxes, which helped build the national treasury.

One thriving example of such brokering can be seen in the role Israel played in the horse-and-chariot sales. Of course, Solomon himself had fourteen hundred chariots and twelve thousand horses stationed in his chariot cities. These ensembles had been introduced under King David, but Solomon developed the horse-and-chariot collection to a fine art.

But his acting as the conduit for buying and selling these animals provided an even more specialized trading opportunity. Egypt produced the best horses and chariots (1 Kings 10:28–29). Each horse brought 150 shekels of silver, and a chariot sold for 600 shekels. Solomon bought them from Egypt and sold them to the Hittites and those in the Aramean city-states, no doubt at a good profit.

Other treaties called for Israel to provide wheat and oil in exchange for building materials from Hiram of Tyre. But when the building projects were completed, those treaties had to be renegotiated. Later, Hiram provided sailors to man Israel's merchant marine from the port of the Gulf of Aqabah (1 Kings 9:26–28). This fleet sailed to Lower Arabia, Lower Africa, and out the Mediterranean to Spain (Tarshish), returning with gold, sandalwood, precious stones, ivory, apes, and baboons (1 Kings 10:11–12, 22). Clearly, Solomon was the international tycoon of that day.

The Decline of Solomon

Solomon's last years were not at all like his earliest days: the empire began to fall apart right before his eyes. The ultimate reason was spiritual: "The LORD became angry with Solomon because his heart had turned away from the LORD, the God of Israel" (1 Kings 11:9). At the root of his problems was his multiple marriage alliances with other nations, alliances that required him to provide for their foreign pantheons right in the heart of the land to pacify his wives.

As a result of this departure from Yahweh, "the LORD raised up against Solomon adversar[ies]" (1 Kings 11:14). The first such was Hadad the Edomite. It was perhaps the height of irony that Pharaoh gave his daughter to Solomon as a wife, who was the sister-in-law to Solomon's most resolute enemy, Hadad.

Hadad returned to Edom after the news of David and Joab's death (1 Kings 11:21). To what extent Hadad was able to reassert his independence of Solomon is not known. When the Edomites will be mentioned again, some seventy-five years later, they are loosely under the control of Jehoshaphat, king of Judah (1 Kings 22:47).

A second adversary arose in the person of Rezon of Damascus, who had been a vassal of Hadadezer when David defeated the king of Zobah; but now Rezon had established his own base of power in Damascus. While Damascus was still theoretically under Israel's rule, Rezon became a constant thorn in Solomon's side.

A third adversary was Jeroboam the son of Nebat, who was a former trusted member of Solomon's cabinet. He had been promoted to the position of overseer of the labor force in the district of Ephraim (1 Kings 11:27–28), after Solomon noticed his industry and abilities while he was building the Millo at Jerusalem. But when the prophet Ahijah met Jeroboam one day and informed him that he would be given the ten northern tribes to rule over as a result of Solomon's apostate ways, then Jeroboam found it necessary to flee to Egypt to save his life when word about this prophecy leaked out. Pharaoh Shoshenq (945–924 B.C.) of the Twenty-second Dynasty gave him sanctuary, and there Jeroboam waited until the death of Solomon to become the first king of the Northern Kingdom of Israel.

For forty years Solomon ruled his people, but the seeds of defection from the union had been well established in his own day. Though he would die before the fruit of some of his own disastrous policies would come to fruition, the division of the kingdom was now beyond repair or remediation.

Part VI

The Divided Monarchy: The Independent Kingdoms of Israel and Judah

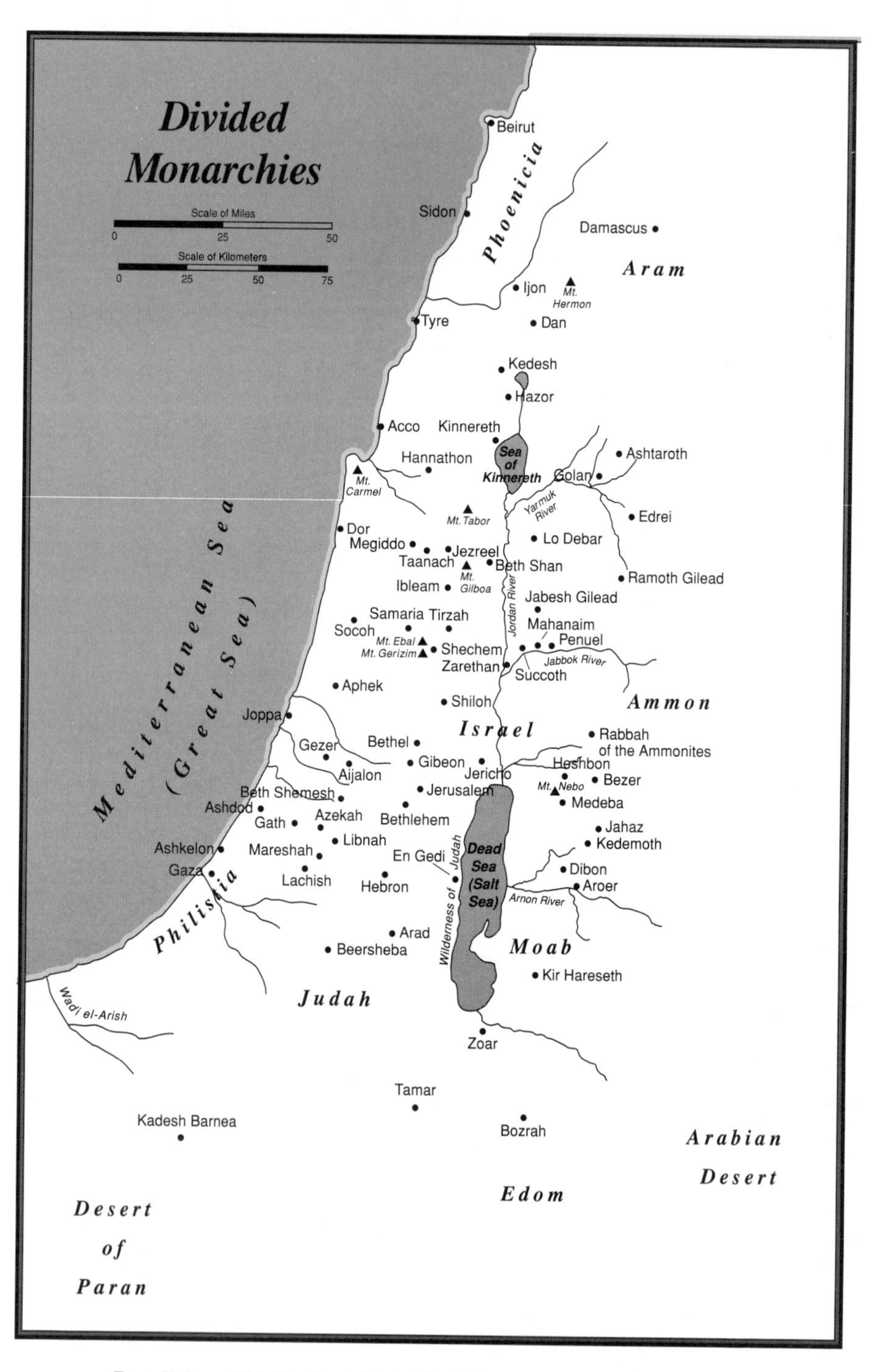

From *Holman Bible Handbook* (Nashville: Holman Bible Publishers, 1992), 292.

20

THE DIVISION OF THE MONARCHY (931/930 B.C.)

The united kingdom of Israel and Judah of the days of David and Solomon suddenly divided in 931/930 B.C. The ten tribes in the north would henceforth be known as Israel or Ephraim, after its most assertive and most influential tribe. The two tribes in the south, Judah and Benjamin, would be known as Judah.

THE SEEDS OF ALIENATION

As far back as the times of the judges, it could be foreseen that the fragile unity among the twelve tribes was headed for trouble. In the days of Gideon, for example, the Ephraimites complained that they had been omitted from the muster of Gideon's army (Judg. 8:1–3). Gideon, with great difficulty, was able to assuage their indignant spirit over being neglected and left out of the draft call-up by pointing out that the greater glory was theirs for having slain the Midianite leaders themselves. But the chip-on-the-shoulder attitude continued to evidence itself throughout the days that followed.

Again during the leadership of the judge Jephthah, Ephraim again complained that it had not been consulted or called to the battlefield to share in the victory (Judg. 12:1–6). Ephraim could not base her demands on the fact that she was the largest tribe in Israel, for her census fell from 40,500 to 32,500 during the wilderness journey (Num.

1:33; 26:37). This made Ephraim second smallest, only Simeon having a lower census. Meanwhile Judah grew from 74,600 to 76,500 for the same period of traveling in the wilderness (Num. 1:27; 26:22). Often, then, Judah and Ephraim had acted independently of each other, as well as from the other tribes. This antagonism became a major contributing factor in the division of the monarchy.

Even earlier in Joshua's time, factionalism appeared in the allotment of tribal territories. Part of this had to do with geography: the Jordan River sealed off those in Transjordania from the western tribes; similarly, the Galilean tribes were sealed off from Manasseh and Ephraim by the Esdraelon and Jezreel Valleys, just as Judah and Benjamin were set off physically and psychologically from Manasseh and Ephraim by the deep and broad Sorek Valley.

By the time of Samuel, it was noteworthy that Saul's army was composed of the men of Israel and the men of Judah (1 Sam. 11:8; 15:4; 17:52). Even in the Philistine perception of things, the sphere of Saul was always equated with Israel, while Judah was the sphere of David, a more neutral place from the Philistine point of view in the earlier days of David's reign in Hebron.

The heavy taxes of Solomon and the forced periods of labor imposed on the citizenry under Solomon and Rehoboam brought this sore to a head.

One particular name can be associated with the development of the seeds of sedition: Jeroboam. Jeroboam, son of Nebat, had come to the attention of Solomon for his industry and abilities during the building of Millo in Jerusalem. For his outstanding work at Millo, Solomon promoted him to the rank of supervisor of civilian labor in the district of Ephraim (1 Kings 11:27–28). But things changed drastically when the prophet Ahijah from Shiloh met Jeroboam. With the symbolic action of ripping Jeroboam's garment into twelve pieces and handing him back ten of those pieces, the prophet predicted that he would become the ruler of the tribes in Israel (1 Kings 11:31). One tribe would be left in the hands of the Davidic dynasty, though surprisingly Saul's tribe of Benjamin affiliated with Judah and became known as the one tribe of Judah (1 Kings 12:21; 2 Chron. 11:1, 10; 15:2, 9). The rumor of the Shilohite prophet's prediction spread rapidly. Jeroboam was forced to resign and even flee for his life to Egypt. There he found refuge with Pharaoh Shishak, who was anxious to gain whatever political advantage he could milk out of the situation.

For the moment, the potential rebellion was squelched, but discontent continued to reappear after Solomon's death. The union so tenuously achieved by David, was now in serious danger of being dissolved. A man of David's sensitivity would possibly have been able to stem the tide of resentment and open rebellion, but Solomon's son Rehoboam was not made of the same stuff.

The Sources of Information

The primary source for recounting what took place during this period of the divided kingdom from 931 B.C. to 722 B.C. is 1 Kings 12 to 2 Kings 17. This section covers everything from the death of Solomon to the fall of Samaria in 722 B.C. It is paralleled and duplicated in part by 2 Chronicles 10–28 as well as the eighth-century prophets Isaiah, Amos, Hosea, and Jonah.

The account in 1 Kings 12–2 Kings 17 is usually entitled the deuteronomic interpretation of Hebrew history because of the large impact that the informing theology of Deuteronomy had on the later books. History, from this perspective, was viewed either favorably (if they walked in the law of God) or unfavorably (if it evidenced apostasy from the will of God). The norm for all kings was King David and the theology that centered around the everlasting covenant/promise that God had made with David and the city of Zion/Jerusalem.

The following is a stylized pattern for introducing each king in Israel:

1. The name of the king and the name of his father;
2. The dating of the king's reign in terms of the reigning monarch in Judah;
3. The name of the capital city;
4. The length of the reign; and
5. A brief characterization of the reign of the king (usually in negative terms).

Likewise, a definite style emerged for introducing the kings of Judah:

1. The name of the king and the name of his father;
2. The date of the king's accession in terms of the king in Israel;
3. The age at which the king came to the throne;
4. The name of the queen mother; and
5. A comparison of this king's reign with that of David.

Epigraphical materials from archaeological digs have also contributed to our understanding of this era. Some of the more outstanding finds include the report of Pharaoh Shishak, better known in Egypt as Pharaoh Sheshonq. On a pylon in the Egyptian temple of Aton at Karnak, ancient Thebes, is a record of his campaign in the fifth year of Rehoboam, king of Judah (1 Kings 14:25–27; 2 Chron. 12:1–12). Another Moabite memorial inscription from ancient Dibon recounts the deeds of king Mesha, a ninth-century ruler in Moab, also mentioned in 2 Kings 3:4–27. This inscription also makes mention of Omri, king of Israel. Scores of royal Assyrian Akkadian cuneiform inscriptions parallel the biblical account from numerous sites in the ancient Near East.

A limited number of inscriptions, ostraca (inscribed potsherds), seals, and seal impressions have come from Palestine itself. Some of the more famous are the Siloam Tunnel Inscription from Jerusalem (2 Kings 20:20; 2 Chron. 32:30), the Samaritan Ostraca, the Arad and Lachish Ostraca, and other seals and seal impressions.[1]

Added to this list of epigraphical materials must be the long list of results that have come from Iron Age II sites.[2] These evidences from the material culture often indicate the size and layout of a town, its domestic and military architecture, its pottery types, and some indication of the nature of the times, whether they were experiencing prosperity or scarcity. Thus, the ninth-century heyday of the Omride period corresponded to the prosperity of tenth century Solomonic times. Less impressive structures were built, on the whole, in the eighth, seventh, and sixth centuries, thereby indicating a general economic downturn and periods of national instability.

THE CHRONOLOGY OF THE KINGS OF ISRAEL AND JUDAH

Chronology, it is rightly said, is the backbone of history. But it also has been the bane of the historian of the kings of Israel and Judah. Indeed, the Book of Kings is filled with chronological material of the Hebrew kings: when their reigns began, when the king came to the throne in terms of the parallel kingdom of Judah or Israel, the total number of years that the king reigned, and other occasional correlations of events in the history of these divided nations. But the tangle of dates and systems used for determining these dates is so complex that the remark attributed to Jerome in the fourth century A.D. appears to be correct: "Read all the books of the Old Testament, and you will find

1. See on many of these, James Pritchard, *ANET*, pp. 320–22. For seals and other inscriptions, see references below to the chapter 26 (*BAR* 13.5 [1987]: 58–65 and Nahum Avignad's 1986 work.

2. Y. Shiloh, "Elements in the Development of Town Planning in the Israelite City," *IEJ* 28 (1978): 36–51, and Amihai Mazar. *Archaeology of the Land of the Bible: 10,000 to 586 B.C.E.* (New York: Doubleday, 1992), 463–530.

such discord as to the number of the years of the kings of Judah and Israel, that to attempt to clear up this question will appear rather the occupation of a man of leisure than of a scholar."[3]

Modern scholarship has been even more vigorous in its denunciations of the unwieldy nature of this material. But one scholar did devote his life to untangling this Gordian knot: Edwin R. Thiele. Despite that fact of scholarly dedication, neither Thiele's carefully argued University of Chicago dissertation, nor anyone else's, has achieved as yet universal acceptance. Nevertheless, Thiele's evidence and argumentation has never been successfully refuted. His case has stood now for well over forty years. It is his argument that we will trace here.

ESTABLISHING AN ABSOLUTE DATE

Thiele began by appealing to the Assyrian Eponym Lists, a list that named a "man of the year" (hence: *eponym*) from 892 B.C. to 648 B.C. In the course of registering the designee as the man of the year, they also noted significant events that had taken place during that year, including any notable astronomical occurrences.

For the year of Bur-Sagale, a governor of Guzana, it was noted that there was a "revolt in the city of Assur," and an eclipse of the sun took place in the month of Simanu. This event can be located on our Julian calendars as June 15, 763 B.C. by astronomical computations. If this date is secure, then we are able to move on either side of this solar eclipse in June 15, 763 B.C., in the eponym list and correlate each year to our present-day calendars.

It becomes extremely significant then, that in the eponym of Daian-Assur, 853 B.C., the sixth year of Shalmaneser III, that the battle of Qarqar was fought in which the Israelite king Ahab opposed him. Twelve years later, in the eponym of Adad-rimani, or 841 B.C., Shalmaneser III received tribute from a king "*ia-a-u*," a ruler of Israel. This could be none other than the Israelite King Jehu.

Now it so happens that there were twelve actual years between the death of King Ahab and the accession of King Jehu, two official years, but one actual year for King Ahaziah (1 Kings 22:51) and twelve official, but eleven actual years for King Joram (2 Kings 3:1). Accordingly, 853 B.C. is the year of Ahab's death and 841 B.C. is the year of King

3. As cited by Edwin R. Thiele, A *Chronology of the Hebrew Kings* (Grand Rapids: Zondervan, 1977), p. 12. No citation is given there as to its source.

Jehu's accession. Here then is the toehold on linking Israel and Judah's history with an absolute chronology and other world events.

Three Chronological Procedures

Thiele set forth three important chronological procedures that were operative in ancient Israel and Judah. The first related to the separate calendars that were used in the two nations: Israel began its year on the month of Nisan in the spring (our March/April) while Judah reckoned its year as starting in Tishri in the fall (our September/October). When compared to our year that begins in January, both the Nisan and Tishri years bridged parts of two of our calendar years. And even more confusing is the fact that a regnal year in Israel would overlap two regnal years in Judah.

The second chronological peculiarity was the use of "accession year" and "nonaccession year" reckoning. When the country divided in 931/930 B.C., the nations used opposite methods of counting up the regnal years. For example, on the nonaccession-year principle, the first year counted as year number one, but the accession-year method would not count that first year as regnal year one until the monarch had passed the month starting the respective calendar that was in use in that country (Nisan or Tishri).

As a matter of fact, Judah used the accession-year principle from Rehoboam until Jehoshaphat, but Israel used the nonaccession year-principle from Jeroboam to Ahab. When relations between the north and the south thawed during the days of Ahab and Jehoshaphat, being sealed by the marriage of Athaliah, Ahab and Jezebel's daughter, to Jehoshaphat's son: prince Jehoram—Jehoram and Athaliah introduced the nonaccession-year system into Judah. This remained in place until the snub of King Jehoash of Israel to King Amaziah of Judah over the proposal of marriage of the royal daughter to Amaziah's son (2 Kings 14:8–10). Prior to this rupture in diplomatic relations, however, both nations had continued to resort to the accession-year principle. For some reason that now eludes us, both nations used the accession-year principle from that time on to the end of their respective histories.

The third principle Thiele discovered was that each nation used its own system in determining the years of a ruler in the other nation. Accordingly, Rehoboam of Judah had a seventeen-year reign as judged by Judah's accession-year principle, but according to Israel's nonaccession-year principle it was eighteen years.

Each of these three principles is necessary if one is to untangle what otherwise would be an unsolvable disarray of numbers.

THE DATE FOR THE DIVISION OF THE UNITED KINGDOM

Thiele argued for a 931/930 B.C. date for the division of the kingdom at the death of King Solomon. This date, however, has not been widely accepted by the larger academic community. The scholarly fashion has been (until just recently) to accept William Foxwell Albright's date of 922 B.C., but his date involved an almost outright rejection of some of the biblical data. Albright argued that in view of the data found in 2 Chronicles 15:19 and 16:1, it was necessary to "reduce the reign of Rehoboam by at least eight, probably nine years"[4] from that required by the biblical text. But such a reduction is not necessary when the principles as set forth by Thiele are employed.

More recently the figure of 927/926 B.C., a date that seems to be drawing closer to Thiele's date, has been proposed as the first regnal year of Rehoboam in Judah and Jeroboam I in northern Israel by John Hayes and Paul Hooker.[5] Hayes and Hooker deny all three of Thiele's principles but arrive at this date by readjusting any of the biblical dates they considered inaccurate for one reason or another.

Nevertheless, Thiele's dates of 931/930 B.C. can be shown to be accurate. The following chart will demonstrate this claim:

JUDAH		ISRAEL		
	Official Year		Official Year	Actual Years
Rehoboam	17	Jeroboam	22	21
Abiajm	3	Nadab	2	1
Asa	41	Baasha	24	23
Jehoshaphat	18	Elah	2	1
	79	Omri	12	11
		Ahab	22	21

4. William Foxwell Albright, "The Chronology of the Divided Monarchy of Israel," *BASOR* 100 (1945): 20, n. 14.

5. John H. Hayes and Paul K. Hooker, A *New Chronology for the Kings of Israel and Judah and Its Implications for Biblical History and Literature* (Atlanta: John Knox, 1988), 18.

JUDAH		ISRAEL		
	Official Year		Official Year	Actual Years
		Ahaziah	2	1
			86	79

This chart demonstrates two rather significant points: (1) the 86 years of Israel's nonaccession year reckoning equal the 79 actual calendar years; and (2) that from Ahab's death in 853 B.C., as determined by the astronomical observations in the eponym lists, and the 12 actual years separating Jehu from Ahab, there are 78 actual years to the beginning of the division of the monarchy. Therefore, 78 plus 853 equals 931/930 B.C. for the division of the kingdom.

The Principle of Overlapping Reigns or Coregencies

In the entirety of the two nations, there were nine overlapping reigns or coregencies. This makes a fourth important principle that must be recognized and factored into any arrangement of chronologies for the kings of Israel and Judah.

The first overlapping reign was that of Tibni and Omri in Israel. First Kings 16:21 reads: "Then the people of Israel were split into two factions; half supported Tibni son of Ginath for [or, to make him] king , . . . and the other half supported Omri." Therefore, there were three kingdoms in the land at this time: two in the north under Tibni and Omri and one in the south, Judah.

This identical phenomenon of *three* kingdoms occurred later on, for Menahem ruled in one kingdom in the north and Pekah ruled the other, probably in Gilead. Hosea 5:5 witnessed this fact as it warned: "Therefore Israel and Ephraim [*they*] will stumble [or fall] in *their* iniquity, Judah also will stumble [or fall] with *them*" (my own translation, emphasis added). Note the three Hebrew plurals, for once again there were two kingdoms in the north.

A third overlapping of reigns occurred during the twelve years of Jehoash and Jeroboam II in Israel, as noted by 2 Kings 13:10 and 14:23. Thus, the otherwise sixteen years of Jehoash and the forty-one years of Jeroboam II would add up to fifty-seven years, but with the coregency, it actually was only forty-five years.

Another coregency had twenty-four of Azariah's years overlapping the twenty-nine years of Amaziah. Again, this reduced an otherwise total of eighty-one years to fifty-seven instead.

The fifth was the coregency of Jotham and Azariah as mentioned in 2 Kings 15:5. Azariah became a leper, and his son ruled in his stead. The sixth overlap took place between Ahaz and Jotham in Judah, for the attack of Pekah and Rezin were not only aimed at Ahaz in Judah (2 Kings 16:5–9), but also against Jotham as well (2 Kings 15:37).

King Jehoram was coregent with his father Jehoshaphat as recorded in 2 Kings 8:16: "In the fifth year of Joram son of Ahab king of Israel, when Jehoshaphat was king of Judah, Jehoram son of Jehoshaphat began his reign as king of Judah." Further confirmation of this synchronism is given in 2 Kings 3:1, where Joram began in "the eighteenth year of Jehoshaphat king of Judah," but according to 2 Kings 1:17, he began "in the second year of Jehoram son of Jehoshaphat." Thus, the eighteenth year of Jehoshaphat was the second year of Jehoram's coregency. This would mean that Jehoram became coregent with his father in the seventeenth year of his father's reign, the year when, it turns out, he joined forces with Ahab against Syria. It was in this battle that Ahab lost his life (1 Kings 22:29–37); thus, prudence had dictated that Jehoshaphat place Jehoram on the throne prior to his undertaking this joint venture with Ahab—a venture in which Jehoshaphat narrowly escaped losing his own life.

The eighth coregency was between Jehoshaphat and his elderly father Asa. In the thirty-ninth year of Asa's reign, Asa became seriously ill by being diseased in his feet. This event, coming at the end of Asa's forty-one-year reign caused him to make Jehoshaphat regent with him to help him govern the people (2 Chron. 16:12).

The final coregency was between Manasseh and Hezekiah. Once again illness was a factor (2 Kings 20:1, 6). Since Hezekiah knew that he had only fifteen years to live, it would seem most natural that he would place his son Manasseh on the throne early enough to train him in the ways of government.

Thiele was able to solve every one of the chronological synchronisms except one—the dates surrounding Hezekiah. He called it "the single greatest problem in the chronology of the kings."[6] One of the solutions suggested for this problem was to conclude that it was a textual error, e.g., removing the plural ending on the Hebrew word for *ten*

6. Edwin R. Thiele, *The Mysterious Numbers of the Hebrew Kings: A Reconstruction of the Chronology of the Kingdoms of Israel and Judah*, rev. ed. (Grand Rapids: Eerdmans, 1965), 10.

in 2 Kings 18:1, which otherwise would read "twenty" and "five" (i.e., "twenty-five"), into "ten" and "five" (i.e., "fifteen") instead, for the age of Hezekiah when he became king of Judah.

Be that as it may, Thiele's overall thesis and work will stand the test of time as one of the great contributions of scholarship in the twentieth century. His work has been tested time and again and has tended to gain more credibility than any other solution and to withstand any attack to which it has been subjected.

An Overview of the Kings of Judah and Israel

JUDAH	ISRAEL	ISRAEL DYNASTY	FEATURES
Rehoboam (931–913)	Jeroboam (931–910)	Fifty years of hostilities between Israel and Judah	Two weak kingdoms fighting each other and draining their mutual resources
Abijam (913–911)	Nadab (910–909)		
Asa (911–870)	Elah (886–885)		
	Zimri (885)		
Jehoshaphat (873–848)	Omri (885–874)	OMRIDE DYNASTY (885–841)	A strong Northern Kingdom that enjoys international prestige emerges in this era
Jehoram (848–841	Ahab (874–853)		
Ahaziah (841)	Ahaziah(853–852)		
	Joram (852–841)		
Athaliah(841–835)	Jehu (841–814)	JEHU DYNASTY (841–753)	Twin palace coups bring new rulers to the thrones of Israel and Judah
Joash (835–796)	Jehoahaz (814–798)		
Amaziah (796–767)	Jehoash (798–782)		

JUDAH	ISRAEL	ISRAEL DYNASTY	FEATURES
Uzziah (792–740)	Jeroboam II (793–753)		
Jotham (750–731)	Zechariah (753)		
	Shallum (752)		
	Menahem (752–742)	THE ASSYRIAN DOMINATION (745–627)	The Assyrians dominated Israel while Judah survived by being a vassal of Assyria
Ahaz (735–715)	Pekahiah(742–740)		
Hezekiah (729–642)	Pekah (752–732)		
	Hoshea (732–722)		
	Fall of Samaria (722)		
Manasseh (696–642)			
Amon (642–640)			
Josiah (640–609)			
Jehoahaz (609)			Babylonian Domination of Judah (605–586)
Jehoiakim (608–598)			
Jehoiachin (598–597)			
Zedekiah (597–586)			
Fall of Jerusalem (586)			

The Northern Kingdom survived for 210 years after Solomon's death (931 to 722 B.C.), while the Southern Kingdom of Judah went on for another 135 years, for a total of 345 years, until its capital, Jerusalem, was destroyed in 586 B.C.

The Shechem Convocation

The Bible does not report that the citizens of Judah confirmed Rehoboam as the monarch who would succeed Solomon, but this seems the most likely scenario. After all, Jerusalem was the domain of the Davidic dynasty.

But matters were not going to be that easy in the north. Instead of reading that the northern tribes sent delegates to Jerusalem to help confirm Rehoboam as king, as they did in the case of David, we read of Rehoboam traveling north to Shechem to obtain the northern support. There the Davidic descendant appeared at "the whole assembly of Israel" (1 Kings 12:3).

Shechem was selected as the spot for this assembly for several reasons: (1) The nation had gathered there under Joshua to repeat antiphonally to each other the curses and blessings Moses had warned the nation about (Josh. 8:30–35); (2) Shechem was a central meeting place for the discontented tribes; and (3) Shechem had had an association in the past with Israel's spiritual ministries as Joshua gathered all Israel at Shechem for his farewell speech (chap. 24).

Rehoboam's confirmation by the north was not an automatic matter, of course, since it was necessary for him, not them, to take the effort to travel the distance and to submit to their questioning and evaluation. Previously the elders of Israel had come to Hebron for this very purpose (2 Sam. 5:1–3), but that would not happen this time. Rehoboam knew matters were serious enough for him to take the initiative and to try to negotiate his way into kingship over the same realm his father Solomon had held. When no representatives from the north showed up at Jerusalem for his crowning, it became necessary for him to go to meet them.

Jerusalem had eclipsed Shiloh as the center for all worship to Yahweh. True, the northern prophet Samuel had anointed David as king over all Israel, thereby also eclipsing the house of the Benjaminite Saul, whose kingdom had been centered in Ephraim/Israel, but too much seemed to be moving south in the view of some. Besides, there were other more tangible evidences that things were not as they should be, which only exacerbated the deep feelings that already existed.

Rehoboam was immediately confronted by the demand that he alter his father's harsh policies: "Your father put a heavy yoke on us, but now lighten the harsh labor and the heavy yoke he put on us, and we will serve you" (1 Kings 12:4). In other words, the load of labor conscription and the heavy burden of taxation had to be changed immediately as a condition for Israel's cooperation and confirmation of Rehoboam as king up north. The demand, apparently, was voiced by Jeroboam the son of Nebat, for the assembly gave the candidate Rehoboam three days to respond to their demands before "Jeroboam and all the people returned to Rehoboam" (1 Kings 12:12).

In order to render his decision, Rehoboam turned first to his older advisors, presumably those who had had experience under his father's administration. Since they had lived through Solomon's harsh years, they urged the king to respond favorably to the demands of the northerners. But his youthful counselors' advice prevailed with Rehoboam, perhaps out of a desire to continue enjoying the lavish benefits of court life. Rehoboam responded with much bravado: "My father made your yoke heavy; I will make it even heavier. My father scourged you with whips; I will scourge you with scorpions" (1 Kings 12:14). The negotiations had broken down completely and recalcitrant attitudes had set in on both sides. Thus, the old cry of 2 Samuel 20:1 was taken up again:

> "What share do we have in David,
> what part in Jesse's son?
> To your tents, O Israel!
> Look after your own house,
> O David!" (1 Kings 12:16).

Rehoboam was still not convinced that the power once held by the Davidic house had slipped away. Therefore, he delegated Adoram, who was no doubt the same person as Adoniram, the taskmaster who had begun his service under David as state supervisor of the compulsory labor (2 Sam. 20:24; 1 Kings 4:6; 12:17–18) to deal with this insubordination. Instead, the people saw him as the symbol of all that they had hated and hoped that Rehoboam would reject and rectify. Adoram was stoned to death, and Rehoboam adroitly made a hasty exit for Jerusalem in his chariot (1 Kings 12:17–18).

Once in Jerusalem, Rehoboam still had not grasped the significance of what he had done or what had happened to him. He raised an army of 180,000 from the two tribes of Judah and Benjamin (though few of these would have come from Benjamin, that had aligned itself more with northern policies and only gradually must have come under Rehoboam's control). However, the prophet Shemaiah (1 Kings 12:21–24) intervened and ordered the Davidite to desist and send the draftees home without fighting their brethren up north.

Thus began a period of instability and insecurity for both nations that lasted almost half a century (931 to 885 B.C.).

Comparisons between the Two Kingdoms

It might appear that the Southern Kingdom retained more of the strength, power, and wealth of the once united kingdom, but the reverse was true. Pharaoh Shishak invaded Judah in Rehoboam's fifth year. He carted off literally tons of gold (see chap. 19). With this leveling and humbling action of Shishak, everything tilted in favor of Israel's ten northern tribes, who were larger in size, military strength, geographical position, and potential for international exposure and interchange.

Judah was more than insulated and isolated from the outside world. The Dead Sea formed a barrier on her eastern flank, the Negev to the south, and the Philistines to the west in the Gaza strip. Only to the north did Judah have any openness for access, but there is where Israel put up her strongest defenses and forced Judah to erect more fortresses to make the isolation even more complete. Meanwhile, Israel enjoyed the advantages of trade and commerce from her coastal route, the Way of the Sea, which could bypass Judah altogether and cross through the Esdraelon and Jezreel Valleys on their way across the Fertile Crescent. Thus, close communication was opened up to Egypt, Philistia, Phoenicia, Syria, Assyria, and other countries.

Israel enjoyed these advantages but also suffered from greater exposure to pagan and secular concepts and compromises. With spiritual instability came political instability as well, for eight of Israel's kings would be assassinated, resulting each time in a dynastic change. Meanwhile, Judah retained the Davidic dynasty for all her history and some twenty monarchs.

21

The First Fifty Years of the Divided Kingdom (931–885 B.C.)

Very little exists for the construction of the history of the early years of the new kingdom of the north in 1 Kings 12:25–16:20. With even less attention given to this period is the writer of Chronicles, for he ignored the first four Israelite kings, except for where their lives intersected with the Judean kings.

Jeroboam and the New Kingdom

"Jeroboam, the son of Nebat" became a refrain and a stereotype for evil in the Northern Kingdom for most of the kings of the northern ten tribes. This bad press resulted from the new forms of worship that Jeroboam inaugurated and because of the apostasy that he introduced in Israel.

The Bible does not record how Jeroboam went about establishing a new kingdom, with all its organization and the services needed almost at once. He did manage to field a working government in fairly short order, showing he did have more than just a few talents. It is no wonder that he was a threatening challenge to Solomon. The supposition is that Jeroboam drew heavily from the Davidic organization patterns he had observed while working under Solomon and from the experience that he had gained while living in Egypt and associating with Pharaoh Shishak (= Shoshenq).

Jeroboam's Construction Projects

One would think that he immediately avoided any heavy taxation of the people or labor conscription that Rehoboam had demanded if he had continued as king over the united kingdom. Where he got his capital to erect the buildings and cities he put up is not known. But Jeroboam did manage to establish his capital, initially at Shechem, the place where the ill-fated convocation with Rehoboam had taken place (1 Kings 12:25). Soon after Jeroboam had established Shechem as his capital, he apparently began building activities across the Jordan River at Penuel on the Jabbok River. The association of Shechem and Peniel with Jacob was too obvious to miss: Jeroboam was a master statesman, and the choice of these sites was a deliberate calculation on his part to establish his own credibility and his claims for legitimacy . Whether he built Penuel also as an alternative capital or as a symbol of identification with the people in Transjordania cannot be determined. However, Jeroboam eventually established his capital at Tirzah (1 Kings 14:17; 15:21, 33; 16:6, 8, 9), a site about six miles northeast of Shechem.[1]

Jeroboam's reign lasted twenty-two years (931–910 B.C.), even though he had been promised an unending dynasty (just as Saul had been promised in 2 Sam. 13:13), if he would walk faithfully with God (1 Kings 11:38). Instead, Jeroboam became the paradigm for evil, the model against which all subsequent kings of Israel were measured (1 Kings 13:34; 15:30, etc.). Instead of setting the standard of stability for the Northern Kingdom and the generations to come, Jeroboam set the tone of evil and the basis for instability; indeed, in the brief 210–year history of the Northern Kingdom, it would have no less than five different dynasties.

Jeroboam's Cultic Reformation

The northern rejection of the Davidic house of Rehoboam brought in its wake a rejection of the royal Zion theology as it was institutionalized in Jerusalem. In order to prevent the ten tribes from eventually drifting back into the Davidic sphere of influence by their attending the temple services in Jerusalem, Jeroboam set up rival places of worship at Dan, in the far north, and Bethel, just north of the Benjamite border (1 Kings 12:26–33). Bethel, of course, had figured in Israel's ear-

1. The excavation of this site is described by Roland de Vaux in a series of articles on Tirzah in *RB* (1947–1952).

lier history during the age of the patriarchs (Gen. 12:8; 28:18–22; 35:1–15) as well as the time of Samuel (1 Sam. 7:16). Dan, on the other hand, could make claims of a priestly ancestry that went back to Moses (Judg. 18:30). This move demonstrated Jeroboam's political astuteness.

In order to make up for the loss of religious symbols retained at Jerusalem, Jeroboam had two golden calves fashioned for the two sites of Dan and Bethel. The ritual center at Dan, which was uncovered on the northern edge of the mound near the spring, is presently the only structure mentioned in the Bible that has been positively connected with an archaeological excavation. Jeroboam's sanctuary is a unique example of an Iron Age temenos: a sacred enclosure used in formal cultic practices. There were three parts to the temenos: a podium that had a nineteen-meter-long facade of large ashlars; a square open area where the main sacrificial altar was located; and side chambers for other rituals and administration.[2] Thus far, no trace of the famed golden calf erected by Jeroboam at Dan (1 Kings 12:29) has come to light.[3]

Scholars are deeply divided as to the full significance of Jeroboam's religious intentions: some saying that the two calves were indeed idols;[4] others contending that they were merely pedestals on which the invisible Yahweh was presumed to stand, much as his shekinah glory dwelt in the temple. For example, Albright thought that the calves were not intended to be the representations of Yahweh, but were only animals on which people in that day thought the deity stood, albeit in an invisible form for Yahweh, much as the Canaanites depicted Baal and Hadad visibly (in their case) riding on the backs of animals.[5]

The whole action was reminiscent of Aaron's building of the golden calf during Moses' absence on Mt. Sinai. In fact, the words of presentation were actually the same in both instances: "These/Here are your gods, O Israel, who brought you up out of Egypt" (Exod. 32:4; 1 Kings 12:28). Likewise, in both cases this installation of the golden calves was followed by a festival that substituted for the more traditional and authorized festivals. Jeroboam made this an annual feast that substi-

2. Ahimai Mazar. *Archaeology of the Land of the Bible*, pp. 492–95.

3. See the interview article and drawings of the temenos area, "Avraham Biran: Twenty Years of Digging at Tel Dan," *BAR* 13.4 (1987): 12–37; also Avraham Biran, "Tel Dan Scapter Head: Prize Find," *BAR* 15.1 (1989): 29–31.

4. John N. Oswalt, "The Golden Calves and the Egyptian Concept of Deity," *EQ* 45 (1973): 13–20, argued that the calves were indeed idols.

5. William Foxwell Albright, *Yahweh and the Gods of Israel* (Garden City, N.Y.: Doubleday, 1969), pp. 197–98; idem, *From Stone Age to Christianity*, 2nd ed. (Garden City, N.Y.: Doubleday, 1957), 203, 229. For pictures of Canaanite deities standing on the backs of animals, see *ANEP*, figs. 500, 501, 522, 534, and 537.

tuted for the legal Feast of Tabernacles, but set just one month later than the authorized feast—once again to set a different pattern from what was happening in the south so that there would be no links or possible bridges by which to unite the people once again.

And just as Aaron functioned as the priest, now Jeroboam installed himself as the head of this new cult, for he appeared at the altar at Bethel as the officiant and offerer of the sacrifice there. He also appointed non-Levites (1 Kings 12:31) as priests of the new cults, perhaps sensing that the Levites might have been loyal to the house of David. No doubt, by this time, most of the Levites had left the ten northern tribes for Judah, perhaps in protest over these innovations (2 Chron. 11:13–14). Several scholars have pointed out parallels between Aaron in Exodus 32 and Leviticus 10 with Jeroboam in 1 Kings 12. Both Aaron and Jeroboam constructed golden calves on the advice of the people (Exod. 32:1–4; 1 Kings 12:28a); both used the same presentation formula; both Aaron and Jeroboam had two sons with essentially the same names: Nadab and Abihu/Abijah (Lev. 10; 1 Kings 14:1, 20); and both used the occasion for the celebration of a festival.

Jeroboam's Demise

The religious innovations introduced into the north by the new kings directly violated the Mosaic Covenant, providing at the very least an opportunity for syncretistic amalgamations with the fertility cult of Baal, a potential that became a reality under Ahab and Jezebel. Indeed, the Canaanite gods of Baal and Hadad rode on the backs of bull calves.

Thus it had to happen: "A man of God" from Judah came to Bethel and declared God's judgment on this installation. In a move of political incorrectness, the unnamed man of God from Judah predicted that a prince from the rival house of Judah, specifically named "Josiah" in his prophecy, would one day come and burn the bones of Jeroboam's false priests on the very altar the king had set up (1 Kings 13:1–3; cf. 2 Kings 23:15 -16). The enraged King Jeroboam ordered, with an outstretched hand, that his bodyguards seize this impudent prophet who had dared to make such impertinent remarks. But when the king's outstretched hand "shriveled up," Jeroboam quickly canceled the order of arrest and begged instead that the prophet restore his hand—which he did. Nevertheless, Jeroboam continued on the course he had set.

Later, the prophet Ahijah, who had acted favorably toward Jeroboam by predicting that he would rule over the ten tribes taken from the Davidic line, was approached by the disguised queen to see if her son would recover from his serious illness. However, the prophet was forewarned by God that the queen was coming; he was to announce to her that her son would die and that the entire household of Jeroboam would be destroyed (1 Kings 14:1–18). The king would learn the hard way that even though he had been favored once, it would not necessarily be so a second time, for God's prophets did not exist to court royal favor, or any other particular group of human cause. The child died as predicted, and the entire family was destroyed later by a successor, Baasha, as Ahijah had announced.

Rehoboam and the Judean Kingdom

Rehoboam now ruled in Jerusalem, but the Judean kingdom was a shadow of the kingdom his father Solomon had left him. Rehoboam and Jeroboam engaged in constant border skirmishes, but there was little semblance of the former glory of Israel when she was in her prime during the heydays of David and Solomon.

> Rehoboam became king at the age of forty-one, and he continued to rule for seventeen years (931–913 B.C.). This meant that he had been born to Solomon and his wife Naamah of Ammon during Solomon's brief coregency with his father David. Solomon's marriage to Naamath from Ammon (1 Kings 14:21) may have been deliberately arranged so as to give more prestige to any children they might have and their claim on the throne as the heirs apparent. But it would also have disastrous implications for his religious affections and the spiritual direction in which he would lead the nation.

Rehoboam's Fortifications

The earliest days of his reign were taken up with fortifying Judah against their big brother to the north. Benjamin was incorporated into Judah, but there is no record as to how this was accomplished. Nevertheless, Benjamin functioned as a buffer zone against Israel. Citadels were built throughout the Judean kingdom (2 Chron. 11:5–12) with copious supplies of food, wine, and olive oil stashed in all of them. In the fifteen "cities of defense" Rehoboam "dispers[ed] some of his sons throughout the districts of Judah and Benjamin, . . . giv[ing] them abundant provisions and [procuring] . . . many wives for them" (2 Chron. 11:23). It is clear that Rehoboam was more than a little fearful. The way in which all these cities were scattered and the Davidic family was dispersed throughout indicated also that the move was meant to strengthen the continuity of the Davidic family, not merely to provide against possible invasion from the north.

Rehoboam's Defeat by Shishak

Pharaoh Shishak (Shoshenq I, ca. 945–924 B.C.)[6] was a native of Libya and founder of the Twenty-second Dynasty in Egypt. He had given asylum to Jeroboam when Jeroboam fled from Solomon (1 Kings 11:40). Suddenly, Shishak decided to reassert Egypt's presence and control over Palestine. Thus, in Rehoboam's fifth year, Shishak came into Judean territory. In fact, Shishak listed some 150 cities in Palestine that he had conquered on the south wall of the Amon temple at Karnak.[7] Shishak moved quickly through southern Judah and came to the very walls of Jerusalem in the spring of 925/926 B.C. No further moves on any cities in central Judah were made, but Shishak did take vast treasures from Jerusalem itself. He returned to Egypt with enormous amounts of gold, for it may be that Rehoboam simply gave him all the treasure Solomon had acquired to keep him from destroying the rest of Judah (1 Kings 14:26; 2 Chron. 12:9). Shishak was deterred from destroying and controlling the land only because Rehoboam belatedly listened to the prophet Shemiah with a repentant heart and was given some measure of deliverance (2 Chron. 12:6–7).

Shishak moved north into Israel, which in itself was all the more surprising given his close relationship with Jeroboam. This move must have shocked Jeroboam, but Shishak must have extended his conquest once he saw how easy it was to take Judah. Quite a few of the cities listed at Karnak are from the area of the northern ten tribes. A fragment of a victory stele bearing Shishak's name was found in the Megiddo ruins. The Egyptian forces also invaded Gilead across the Jordan and entered Edom as well. However, Shishak never returned to follow up on any of his victories. His own situation at home must have been too tenuous for him to maintain a permanent stranglehold on Palestine or the neighboring countries that he had overrun.

---

6. The dates for Pharaoh Shoshenq are quite secure. See Kenneth A. Kitchen, "Late-Egyptian Chronology and the Hebrew Monarchy," *JANES* 5 (1973): 231–33.

7. A picture of Shishak smiting the Asiatics, as the god Amon, appears in *ANEP*, fig. 349. A translation and discussion of this inscription is found in J. Simons, *Handbook for the Study of Egyptian Topographical Lists Relating to Western Asia* (Leiden: Brill, 1937), pp. 99–101, 178–86. Also see Kenneth Kitchen, *The Third Intermedicate Period in Egypt* (Warminster: Aris and Phillips, 1973), pp. 293–94, 300, 432–47. Again, see Alan R. Millard, "Does the Bible Exaggerate King Solomon's Golden Wealth?" *BAR* 15.3 (1989): 21–29, 31, 34.

Shishak died the very next year. He never returned to Palestine, nor did his son, Osorkon I (924–889 B.C.), who followed him on the throne. Osorkon occupied himself with building the lavish temple of Atum, using the tons of gold plundered from Solomon's temple.

The Biblical Evaluation of Rehoboam's Reign

The first part of Rehoboam's reign was heavily influenced, it would appear, by his father's apostasy. He built "high places" (*bāmôt*), "pillars," or "sacred stones" (*maṣṣēbôt*), and "Asherah poles" (*ʾăšērîm*); he allowed "male prostitutes" (*qādēš*) to remain in the land (1 Kings 14:23–24). What with the influence of Solomon's syncretistic introductions into the land, his pagan wives, and his own upbringing by Naamah, a woman from Ammon, it is not an altogether surprising turn of events.

However, the final twelve years of Rehoboam's reign, after his run-in with Shishak and his encounter with the prophet Shemiah, are viewed more favorably by the Chronicler. "Rehoboam humbled himself;" accordingly, "the Lord's anger turned from him and he was not totally destroyed" (2 Chron. 12:12). Nevertheless, Israel and Judah fought each other periodically (1 Kings 14:30), with no indication that either one ever gained the upper hand or the final advantage.

Abijah/Abijam of Judah[8]

The coronation of Rehoboam's son, Abijah, also called Abijam, did not signal a drastic reversal in the steady deterioration of the nation's spiritual life. Abijah ruled from 913–911 B.C. (1 Kings 15:1–8; 2 Chron. 13:1–22). Even though Abijah did not follow in the ways of David spiritually, yet "for David's sake the LORD his God gave [Rehoboam] a lamp in Jerusalem by raising up a son to succeed him and by making Jerusalem strong" (1 Kings 15:4). This is because the promise made to David was based on an unconditional covenant and was unilateral; it did not depend on how faithfully the house of David lived their lives. Abijah had twenty-two sons and sixteen daughters from fourteen wives.

Eventually, Abijah faced Jeroboam on Mt. Zemaraim, about a mile or so east of Bethel.[9] Jeroboam's army clearly outnumbered his by a

8. Second Chronicles 13:1–2 called him "Abijah," meaning "My father is Yahweh," but he was also known as "Abijam," meaning "father of the sea," or the like. He must have used both names.

9. Why there is no parallel to this battle in Kings is not known. It is for this reason, as well as the theologizing propensities of the Chronicler, that many scholars dismiss this battle as being unhistorical. For example, Ralph W. Klein, "Abijah's Campaign against the North (2 Chron. 13)—What Were the Chronicler's Sources?" *ZAW* 95 (1983): 210–17.

wide margin. Abijah wanted to win back Israel into the Davidic kingdom (2 Chron. 13:4–12), for he believed that the kingdom of Jeroboam was an illegitimate kingdom. Abijah thought Rehoboam had been naive and intimidated by Jeroboam, and he was acting to correct what his father lacked the courage to effect when this rupture took place. Moreover, Abijah argued that Jeroboam's golden calves were idolatrous and antithetical to the will of God. Jeroboam and his breakaway kingdom were therefore ordered forthwith to return to the kingdom of David without further loss of time.

Jeroboam paid no attention to such talk and promptly surrounded Abijah's army in front and around back. Abijah was miraculously rescued and delivered from a follow-through blow to Jeroboam by capturing the Israelite cities of Bethel, Jeshanah, and Ephron. Jeroboam never quite recovered from this blow, for it undermined him both politically and religiously. But the territorial advance was short-lived. Abijah's son, Asa, lost these sites to Baasha, who moved for a time as far south as Ramah, just four miles from Jerusalem with his occupation forces.

Asa of Judah

Abijah's son Asa ruled Judah for forty-one years (911–870 B.C.; 1 Kings 15:9–24; 2 Chron. 14–16) and was the first of eight kings who were thought by the writers of Kings and Chronicles to have acted in a way that was pleasing to God. Asa is called the "son" of Maacah in 1 Kings 15:10; therefore, some scholars have argued that Abijah and Asa were brothers and not father and son, as 1 Kings 15:8 and 2 Chronicles 14:1 indicated. But Maacah was his grandmother who had authorized the erection of the Asherah pole in Jerusalem, which Asa cut down as part of his reforms.

Asa took steps to stem the steady drift into spiritual deterioration. He put the male prostitutes and the idols out of the land. Furthermore, he removed his grandmother from being queen mother because of her association with the pole set up to Asherah. In the fifteenth year of his reign, about 896 B.C., following his victory over the Egyptian army, encouraged by the prophet Azariah (2 Chron. 15:1–7), he convened an assembly of the people of his two tribes, and some from Ephraim, Manasseh, and Simeon, to renew their covenant with God. Sacrifices and offerings, ranging in the hundreds and thousands of animals, were made to God. He also contributed additional furniture to the temple and renewed the altar of God. Despite all of this religious reform, however, Asa did not remove the old high places that the people found so attractive.

Toward the end of his life, Asa did not achieve such a remarkable record with Yahweh. Prompted in part by his own successes, he became proud and haughty, treating the prophet of God, Hanani, roughly by imprisoning him for rebuking him. He also developed a disease in his "feet" (perhaps a euphemism for genitals, as it sometimes is in other parts of the Bible; 1 Kings 15:23; 2 Chron. 16:12); he entrusted this disease entirely to his physicians, who in this case may have been more of a combination of magic and medicine.

During the years of Asa's reign, he had two major wars to fight. During the first fifteen years of his reign, Judah was at peace (2 Chron. 14:6), but suddenly he found himself embroiled in a war with Egypt, led by a certain Zerah from Ethiopia, most likely a commander under Pharaoh Osarkon I (ca. 914–874 B.C.).

The date of this war is a perplexing problem. According to 2 Chronicles 15:19, it began in Asa's thirty-fifth year, which would be 876 B.C. The very next verse, 2 Chronicles 16:1, however, claims that Asa went up in his thirty-sixth year to fortify Ramah against Baasha, king of Israel, which would be the year 875. Unfortunately for this chronology, Baasha of Israel died in 886 B.C., some eleven years earlier!

While some have suggested emending the text from "thirty-fifth" and "thirty-sixth" to "fifteen" and "sixteen" respectively, no Hebrew manuscripts support such a move. Edwin Thiele gave what is perhaps the best solution when he argued that the "thirty-fifth" and "thirty-sixth" referred not to Asa's years of ruling, but the number of years that had transpired since the division of the kingdom in 931 B.C.; i.e., the thirty-fifth year would be 897 and the thirty-sixth year would be 896 B.C.[10] While this is indeed a most unusual method of indicating the length of a king's reign, it is not altogether impossible. Moreover, as Merrill suggests, when the seventeen years of Rehoboam, the three years of Abijah, and the fifteen years of Asa are added up, they total thirty-five, precisely what the narrator claimed in this case. Thus Asa met the Egyptian force in his fifteenth year and Baasha in his sixteenth year.

---

10. Edwin Thiele, *The Mysterious Number of the Hebrew Kings* (Grand Rapids: Eerdmans, 1957), 60, as cited by Eugene H. Merrill, *Kingdom of Priests*, p. 333–34, and n. 40. Merrill noted that Raymond B. Dillard assumed that the Chronicles must have been working with a textual tradition that had an error, or was at least at variance with the Samuel/Kings record, "The Reign of Asa [2 Chronicles 14–16]: An Example of the Chronicler's Theological Method," *JETS* 23 (1980): 217.

Some thirty years had elapsed since Shishak's invasion of Judah. Zerah's attack was launched in the area near Sharuhen, and especially Mareshah, near Lachish in Judah. Perhaps Sharuhen had been left as an Egyptian outpost since the days of Shishak's invasion, for 2 Chronicles 14:12–15 depicted the losses as those suffered in an enemy territory. Zerah suffered enormous losses despite the overwhelming size of his army.

The challenge that came from Baasha, king of Israel, in the very next year seems almost incomprehensible given the action taken by Asa. Baasha had fortified Ramah, which was only four miles north of Jerusalem, so that he might control any traffic from his kingdom into Judah on the north-south axis in the central mountains. But Asa considered a fortified Ramah as a threat to his security; thus he took steps to seek relief by appealing to Ben-Hadad, king of Damascus. Now Ben-Hadad did have a treaty with Israel, but with the inducements from Asa, he was willing to break it—especially with the gold and silver offered him by Asa from the temple and royal treasuries. Ben-Hadad attacked northern Israel and took the cities of Ijon, Dan, Abel Beth Maacah, and much of Naphtali, including the region just west of the Sea of Kinnereth, or Sea of Galilee. King Baasha in turn was forced to drop his project at Ramah and return to the capital at Tirzah. This allowed King Asa to dismantle the fortifications at Ramah and to construct an alternative defense line to the east of Ramah at Geba and Mizpah (*Tell en-Nasbeh*) to the west of Ramah. This latter site of Tell en-Nasbeh has a twenty-foot-thick wall that excavators have uncovered. On the lower part of the wall is a heavy coat of plaster that made it almost impossible to scale. All in all, the formidable appearance of these fortifications is more than an eloquent testimony to the lack of trust and ill-feelings that existed between Israel and Judah at this time.[11]

Despite what appeared to be a wise decision for the moment on Asa's part, it ended up placing not only Israel under the heel of Damascus and the power of Ben-Hadad; it likewise was a tacit acknowledgment on Judah's part that Damascus was greater and more powerful than Judah, for she had to appeal to outside help for deliverance. Amazingly, this came right on the heels of the most astounding victory and deliverance of Judah from Zera and the Egyptians by just one year. Furthermore,

11. See Jeffrey R. Zorn, "Tel en-Nasbeh," in Ephraim Stern, et al., eds., *The New Encyclopedia of Archaeological Excavations in the Holy Land*, vol. IV (Jerusalem: Israel Exploration Society, 1993), 1098–1102.

Ben-Hadad had virtually full control over all of the northern Galilee area. It is no wonder that the prophet Hanani rebuked Asa so sternly for obligating himself to a foreign power rather than depending on Yahweh, as he had in the previous year (2 Chron. 16:8–9).

NADAB AND BAASHA OF ISRAEL

Not long after Asa began to rule in Judah, Jeroboam died, and his son Nadab took the throne in Tirzah for two years (910–909 B.C.; 1 Kings 15:25–31). The only deed recorded about his short reign was his siege of Gibbethon, a Philistine fortress three miles east of `Aqir and three miles west of Gezer. This site must have been small in size, yet it appears to have had some major significance, for twenty-six years later Omri, then general for King Elah, also besieged it (1 Kings 16:15–17).

However, in the midst of the siege, Nadab was assassinated by Baasha (1 Kings 15:27–28), who went on to destroy the entire house of Jeroboam, thereby fulfilling Ahijah's prediction and ending Jeroboam's dynasty after the duration of a mere two generations! The reason the theological historians of Kings gave for the sudden demise of this monarch and the Jeroboam dynasty was "because of the sins Jeroboam had committed and had caused Israel to commit" (1 Kings 15:30). This analysis will be used for eighteen successors of Jeroboam.

Baasha the son of Ahijah of Issachar, an Israelite officer, took the throne following his act of assassination, and he ruled for twenty-four years (909–886; 1 Kings 15:32–16:7; 2 Chron. 16:1–6). As founder of Israel's second dynasty, Baasha quickly fell into the ways and practices for which the previous dynasty had been judged. Therefore, God sent the prophet Jehu, son of Hanani, to pronounce on Baasha the very same judgment that had been pronounced on Jeroboam: his house would be utterly destroyed despite the fact that Yahweh had allowed him to come to power (1 Kings 16:1–4). Little more is known of Baasha's rule in Israel except that he had constant struggles with Judah's King Asa. As already noted, the treaty Baasha had concluded with Ben-Hadad of Damascus was not very effective when the gold and silver was put in front of Ben-Hadad by Asa.

ELAH AND ZIMRI OF ISRAEL

Elah succeeded his father Baasha for a mere two years (886–885 B.C.; 1 Kings 16:8–22). Just as his father Baasha had found Gibbethon attractive for some reason, he too sent his general, Omri, to lay siege to the city once again. History repeated itself, however, for while Elah was there, another military figure, named Zimri, rose up and assassinated Elah. Zimri proceeded to destroy all the house of Baasha, in keeping with the word of Jehu the prophet.

When Omri learned of the assassination, he left off besieging Gibbethon and had himself declared as king. He hastened to Tirzah, the capital, and subdued the rebellion of Zimri, forcing Zimri to commit suicide by burning the palace down over himself. Zimri's rule was a mere seven days in duration!

But the grasping for power was not yet at an end, for another man by the name of Tibni, the son of Ginath, also set himself up as king; thus a divided rule existed for the next four years. Finally, Omri was able to vanquish Tibni and establish the new dynasty of Omri. The stage was now set for one of the more enduring dynasties that Israel had in her whole history.

22

The Fifty Years of the Omrides and Alliances (885–835 B.C.)

The era of fighting that had characterized the first fifty years of relations between northern Israel and southern Judah ceased and was replaced by a period of another fifty years of relative peace between the two countries. The house of Omri (hence, the Omrides) appeared clearly to have the upper hand in wealth, power, and initiative over that evidenced in Judah. Nevertheless, a treaty was enacted between the two countries and eventually sealed with the marriage of Athaliah, daughter of northern Israel's King Ahab, to the Judean prince in the south. While this alliance was able to effect peace between the two nations, it also worked enormous religious ill for Judah as time passed, by importing syncretistic allegiances with Baalistic tendencies that already were at work in the north.

Israel had about all the political instability that she could bear during those first fifty years, from 931 to 885 B.C. After Jeroboam I, there were only abbreviated reigns, frequent bloody coups, and assassinations. Hardly any of the first five kings and two dynasties in northern Israel had been able to maintain a memorable charismatic leadership or give the people any sort of political stability.

But there were new emerging factors as well: by about 825 B.C. new powers were emerging in at least two new realms: Syria and Assyria. If Israel was going to survive, she must drop her petty scrapping and her fraternal feuds by rearranging her priorities so that she could face the much more challenging situations she was exposed to—a degree of exposure that Judah did not share—at least for the time being. Israel had the advantage of being on the international trade routes of the way of the Sea and the interstate connection in the Esdraelon and Jezreel Valleys to the Mesopotamian and Syrian economies. Israel's advantage in trade and communication brought power and wealth (as contrasted with Judah's rather isolated and landlocked position) but it also brought Israel maximal exposure to the armies of the Levant. The times were destined to change.

THE HISTORICAL SOURCES FOR THE OMRIDE ERA

Most scholars acknowledge four main sources for the Omride era: (1) 1 Kings 16:15 to 2 Kings 8:27; (2) 2 Chronicles 17–20; (3) epigraphical materials, such as the Mesha Inscription from Moab and Shalmaneser III's Monolith Inscription, the Bull Inscription, the Black Obelisk; and (4) the archaeological record from key sites in this era.

The Kings source is unusual in that it not only includes the usual summation of the kings' reigns, but also embraces a large number of prophetical narratives. One of the reasons for such a large introduction of the prophetical element is that the Omrides were, at best, syncretistic in their worship of Yahweh, but downright hostile to Yahweh and partial to various forms of Baal worship, at worst. Therefore, few achievements of the Omrides are noted in the text except for the fact that Omri founded the city of Samaria (1 Kings 16:24), along with the fact that his son Ahab built a "palace . . . inlaid with ivory, and the cities he fortified" (1 Kings 22:39). For this cause, the Yahwistic prophets' stories blanket the text. They included:

- the Elijah Narratives—1 Kings 17–19; 21; 2 Kings 1:1–2:14;
- the narrative of an unnamed "man of God" and "one of the sons of the prophets"—1 Kings 20;
- the Micaiah Son of Imlah Narrative—1 Kings 22; and
- the Elisha Narratives—2 Kings 2:15–8:15; 13:14–21.

Historians generally have great difficulty accepting the themes and miraculous deeds recorded in these narratives: jars of flour and cruses of oil that never run dry; fire that falls from heaven at the behest of a mortal's prayer and consumes not only the sacrifice but the dust and water around the altar as well; leprosy that is cured by dipping in the muddy Jordan River seven times; and persons who spring back to life when they are tossed on the grave of a deceased prophet. These, some complain, are not the stuff out of which history is made! Moreover, some object that these same prophetic narratives rarely mention the king or kings of Israel that were in office during the occurrence of these miracles, which is, of course, true.[1]

The archaeological evidence comes from a number of sites, but chief among them are the cities of Samaria,[2] Megiddo,[3] Hazor,[4] and Dor. [5] Much of the extensive building, incorrectly attributed to Solomon in the past, must now be dated approximately to the Omride period.

ALLEGED CONFLICTS IN THE SOURCES

Miller and Hayes conclude that the four sources listed above present some basic conflicts, both in detail and in general.[6] For example, to cite a general conflict, while all the sources presuppose Baalistic leanings or religious preferences of the Omrides, they differ over whether the Omrides were strong rulers over an independent kingdom or international weaklings bullied about by the Syrian kings of Damascus. The answer resides, of course, in distinguishing precisely what period of time we are talking about during the fifty years they monopolized the throne of Israel, and for a time, the throne of Judah.

A more serious problem that Miller and Hayes raise is that of conflicting chronologies between the Hebrew Masoretic text and the Lucianic recension of the Greek Septuagint. This is not a new problem by any means, for a summary of these same variations is given as early as the beginning of this century in C. F. Burney's 1903 commentary.

---

1. J. Maxwell Miller and John H. Hayes, *A History of Ancient Israel and Judah* (Philadelphia: Westminster, 1986), 252–55, unnecessarily argue that these prophetic narratives show evidence of being modified and having gone through "three stages in the process of their transmission." Every one of the evidences they suggest, however, can be met on other grounds than hypothecating, which is all they are doing in the absence of any real textual data, modifications, or stages in composition.
2. See G. Ernest Wright, "Samaria," vol 2 of *The Biblical Archaeologist Reader*, eds. Edward F. Campbell Jr., and David Noel Freedman (Garden City, N.Y.: Doubleday, 1964), 248–57.
3. Yigael Yadin, "Megiddo of the Kings of Israel," *BA* 33 (1970): 66–78.
4. Yigael Yadin, "Hazor," in Ephraim Stern, et al., eds., *The New Encyclopedia of Archaeological Excavations in the Holy Land*, I-IV (Jerusalem: Israel Exploration Society, 1993), II, pp. 594–606.
5. Ephraim Stern, "How Bad Was Ahab? The Many Masters of Dor, part 2," *BAR* 19.2 (1993): 18–29; and Andrew Stewart, "A Death at Dor," *BAR* 19.2 (1993): 31–36, 84.
6. Miller and Hayes, *A History of Ancient Israel and Judah*, pp. 259–65.

The variant Greek numbers, as compared with the Hebrew text, are as follows:

1 Kings	Masoretic text	Septuagint	Lucian
15:9 Asa	20th of Jeroboam	24th of Jeroboam	24th of Jeroboam
16:8 Elah	26th of Asa	20th of Asa	20th of Asa
16:15 Zimri	27th of Asa	[unavailable]	22nd of Asa
16:29 Ahab	38th of Asa	2nd of Jehoshaph	2nd of Jehoshaph
22:41 Jehoshaphat	4th of Ahab	11th of Omri	11th of Omri
22:52 Ahaziah	17th of Jehosha	17th of Jehosha	24th of Jehosha
2 Kings	Masoretic	Septuagint	Lucian
1:17 Joram	2nd of Jehoram	18th of Jehosha	2nd of Jehoram
31: Joram	18th of Jehosha	18th of Jehosha	[unavailable]
8:16 Jehoram	8 years	40 years	8 years
8:25 Ahaziah	12th of Joram	12th of Joram	11th of Joram
9:29 Ahaziah	11th of Joram	11th of Joram	11th of Joram
15:23 Pekahiah	2 years	years	10 years

But as Edwin Thiele pointed out in 1951 and again in 1965:

> A careful study of these variations reveals the fact that they are not the result of scribal errors but constitute editorial changes made with the object of correcting what were regarded as errors in the early Hebrew text. . . . It will not be our province here to provide a detailed explanation of just how each of the above variations in the Greek texts arose,[7] but it is interesting to note the specific details of the struggles early students of the Old Testament were having with the data of the Hebrew kings only a few centuries after the kingdoms had ended and very shortly after the Old Testament canon had been brought into being. In no instance is a Greek variation an improvement over the Hebrew. The fallacies of the Greek innovations may

7. A detailed explanation of each of these variations is given in the first edition of Edwin R. Thiele, *The Mysterious Numbers of the Hebrew Kings* (Chicago: University of Chicago Press, 1951, 1955), chap. 9, "The Variant Figures of the Greek Texts," pp. 167–203.

> be proved by the wide divergence of the pattern of reigns they call for from the years of contemporary chronology.[8]

The Omride period is a most interesting period of history. It is marked by both success in the domestic cultural level and failure in the religious and international level.

THE EMERGENCE OF SYRIA AND THE REEMERGENCE OF ASSYRIA

The century from 931 to 841 B.C. was one of extraordinary growth and vitality for Damascus. The city emerged from the embarrassment of being an occupied territory during the times of David's kingdom to initiating a rebellion under Rezon. By the time that the ninth century rolled around, Damascus was a real factor in Israelite and Judean politics.[9]

Solomon had already confronted Rezon of Damascus. While Rezon had been a vassal to Hadadezer, the king of Zobah whom King David had defeated, Rezon broke from his overlord and established his own base of power at Damascus. By about 850 B.C., Damascus was the capital of the most powerful state in the Levant, a state called "Aram" by its inhabitants.

The most difficult historical problem is that of royal succession in Damascus during this period. The biblical pattern is found in 1 Kings 11:23–24; 15:18:

- Rezon son of Eliada [presuming Rezon is = to Hezion];
- Tabrimmon [Aramaic Tab-Ramman] son of Hezion; and
- Ben-Hadad [Hebrew for Bir-Hadad] son of Tabrimmon.

This order of succession raises the problem of whether the Rezon of 1 Kings 11 is the same person as Hezion, the grandfather of Bir-Hadad I. This connection of the two names may have come about because of the Lucianic Greek Septuagintal reading of the ruler's name in 1 Kings 11:23–25 as an "*`Esron*," or '*Esrom*," reflecting perhaps a Hebrew *Hezron*. Merrill Unger thought the equation likely or even feasible, even though the Hebrew names of Rezon and Rezin came from two

8. Edwin R. Thiele, *The Mysterious Numbers of the Hebrew Kings*, rev. ed. (Grand Rapids: Eerdmans, 1965), 197–99.

9. For full details, see Wayne T. Pitard, *Ancient Damascus: A Historical Study of the Syrian City-State from Earliest Times until its Fall to the Syrians in 732 B.C.E.* (Winona Lake, Ind.: Eisenbrauns, 1987), Chapter Five, "Aram-Damascus: From Rezon to the Usurpation of Hazael (ca. 931–844/42 B.C.E.," pp. 99–144. Also see the older Merrill F. Unger, *Israel and the Aramaeans of Damascus* (Grand Rapids: Baker, 1980 reprint).

very different roots .[10] Others suggested that the one name was merely a corruption of the other name, with Hezion being the ruler's real name and Rezon being related to a Hebrew root that meant "ruler," perhaps his throne name. Others, like Dupont-Sommer and William F. Albright assumed Rezon and Hezion were two different individuals.[11]

One of the most important pieces of information used in constructing the history of Aram-Damascus, it has often been affirmed, is the Bir-Hadad or Melqart Stela found in the late 1930s in the village of Bureij. It is a basalt monument, slightly more than a meter in height and carved with a relief representation of the god Melqart. The four-line Aramaic inscription identifies the donor as a certain Bir-Hadad. Unfortunately it was not found *in situ*, for it had been incorporated in the remains of some Roman period walls at Bureij, perhaps even removed from its original site at Aleppo. It reads:

> The stela which Bir-Hadad, the son of [ ],
> the king of Aram, set up for his lord, Melqart, to
> whom he made a vow and who heard his voice.

However, the name of Bir-Hadad's father, along with the identification of Bir-Hadad with the I, II, and III, has finally led to Pitard's conclusion, based on a direct examination of the stela and not photographs of its inscription, that "the name of Bir-Hadad's father now seems to have no relation to any known king of Damascus."[12] Therefore, Pitard's reconstruction of the Syrian kings reads like this:

Rezon	mid tenth century
Hazyon (Hezion)	late tenth century
Tab-Ramman	late tenth/early ninth century
Bir-Hadad I	early ninth century
Hadad-`idr	mid ninth century
(Bir-Hadad II)?	ca. 844/842 B.C.
Hazael	ca. 844/842 B.C.

10. Merrill F. Unger, *Israel and the Arameans of Damascus*, 1957, pp. 56–57. The two Hebrew roots are *rzon* and *rsyn*. E. G. H. Kraeling, *Aram and Israel* (New York: Columbia University Press, 1918), 48, n. 2, took the same position as Unger did later on.

11. A. Dupont-Sommer, *Les Arameens* (Paris: Maisonneuve, 1949), pp. 29, 33; William Foxwell Albright, "Syria, the Philistines, and Phoenicia," in CAA II/2 ed. I. E. S. Edwards, et al. (Cambridge: Cambridge University Press, 1975), 534–35.

12. Wayne T. Pitard, *Ancient Damascus*, p. 143.

Meanwhile, the Assyrian giant that had left the Mediterranean world free for over a century since the days of Tiglath-pileser I was reawakening to the potential of reentering this realm of influence once again. Beginning, therefore, sometime around 900 B.C., the Levant began to feel the pressure from Assyria.

The Neo-Assyrian King List	
Adad-nirari II	911–891
Tukulti-Ninurta II	890–884
Assur-nasirpal II	883–859
Shalmaneser III	858–824
Shamshi-Adad V	823–811
Adad-Nirari III	810–783
Shalmaneser IV	782–773
Assur-dan III	772–755
Assur-nirari V	754–745
Tiglath-pileser III	745–727
Shalmaneser V	727–722
Sargon II	722–705
Sennacherib	705–681
Esarhaddon	681–669
Ashurbanipal	668–627
Ashur-etil-ilani	627–623
Sin-sum-lisir	623
Sin-sar-iskun	623–612
Assur-ubalit II	612–609

Assyria's new advance came under Adad-nirari II. After he had secured himself against attacks from Babylonia to his south, he began his westward thrust into metal-rich deposits in Asia Minor. In a long annalistic inscription at the conclusion of his account of the restoration of the Gula temple, he bragged: "I built palaces throughout my country. Ploughs I caused to be made in all my country. The piles of corn I allowed to grow far more than those of the old days, I stored them. Throughout the country I provided draught-horses."[13] It was from this secure agricultural base that Adad-nirari II began his conquests of the neighboring lands.

In Adad-nirari II's fourth campaign he assaulted the old kingdom of Hanigalbat on the Upper Euphrates. This was the Assyrian name for the state of Mitanni, whose rulers had Indo-European names and gods. The population of Mitanni, however, was Hurrian, with its capital of Washshukkanni, near Tell Halaf. Adad-nirari II, in his sixth campaign, captured the capital city of Mitanni itself.

Adad-nirari II's son, Tukulti-ninurta II, continued his father's assertion of Assyrian power in the area to the northeast of the Hanigalbat area as well as to the southwest of Lake Van. He moved against the cities under Aramean rule along the River Habur and its tributary Balih.

Tukulti-ninurta II's son, Ashur-nasirpal II, was well situated when he came to the throne, because of the tribute accruing to the throne from his predecessors' conquests. He secured the areas already won and added new ones to the list in the east, north, and west. However, he avoided the strong Aramean city of Damascus.

As Shalmaneser III came to the throne in 858 B.C., a new power had arisen—the state of Urartu, on the other side of Lake Van in the Armenian highlands, with a Hurrian base. Shalmaneser III made several campaigns against Urartu, including storming the important city of Arzashkun in 856 B.C. Having secured his northern flank, he turned to the west in an attempt to reduce the Aramean power, especially that of Damascus. Damascus survived, but the whole Palestine coast of the Mediterranean was put under tribute. A Babylonian insurrection, with Aramean armed bands also making devastating raids, was quelled, and Mesopotamia was once again under one ruler. On the Black Obelisk and the famous bronze reliefs of Balawat, decorating the gate of his newly built palace southeast of Mosul, Shalmaneser III enumerated his victories. Even though his last years were filled with a three-year civil war, Assyria was now set for her final and most brilliant period (745–627 B.C.).

13. Svend Aage Pallis, *The Antiquity of Iraq: A Handbook of Assyriology* (Copenhagen: Ejnar Munksgaard, 1956), 621–22.

The Reign of Omri

Omri initiated the third ruling family in the north in three years: the Omrides. Elah's reign had lasted but two years. Zimri's rule was shorter still—only seven days; and now Omri was struggling with one named Tibni, son of Ginath, for four years to see who would emerge as the ruler over all ten tribes in the north.

Omri finally won—and none too soon—for the Aramean state centered in Damascus was making a rapid rise in power. When Omri finally did stabilize the kingdom under his rule, he initiated a dynasty that lasted for three generations. He ruled Israel for only twelve years, but in that time he set such a mark that Assyrian rulers would refer to Israel as the "land of Omri" (*Bit Humri*) for a century after he had died.[14] Omri was not favored by the biblical writers, however, for Kings devotes a mere eight verses to his otherwise spectacular reign. From this source, however, three accomplishments can be noted here.

Omri's Erection of the New Capital of Samaria

First Kings 16:23–24 briefly observed that Omri resided in Tirzah for six years after his accession to the throne. Then "he bought the hill of Samaria from Shemer for two talents [about 150 pounds] of silver and built a city on the hill, calling it Samaria, after Shemer, the name of the former owner of the hill." This is the site of one of the greatest ruins in the land of Israel, especially in the well-preserved architecture of the Omrides. The royal acropolis occupied a huge leveled rectangular enclosure covering some four acres.[15]

It is to be carefully noted that Omri bought a place where a city had not existed previously, a site seven miles northwest of Shechem. Shemer, the owner of the land, may well have been a Canaanite who was able to retain and sell his property in the hill country of Ephraim, just as Abraham purchased the cave of Machpelah as a burial place (Gen. 23) and as David bought the threshing floor of Araunah (2 Sam. 24). The site would be Omri's own residence and property that he owned, not that of the kingdom of Israel. Since he began something new, he was able to give his own shape and form to his concepts and dreams for this new capital without having to fight with any inherited traditions from the past. But by naming the city not after himself, but

14. For example, Adad-nirari III in *ANET*, pp. 281–82; Tiglath-pileser III in *ANET*, 283–84; and Sargon II in *ANET*, pp. 284–85 as cited by Leon Wood, *A Survey of Israel's History*, rev. and enlarged ed. by David O'Brien (Grand Rapids: Zondervan, 1986), 262, n. 19.

15. Ahimai Mazar, *Archaeology of the Land of the Bible*, pp. 406–09. Also Kathleen Kenyon, *Royal Cities of the Old Testament* (New York: Schocken Books, 1971), 71–89.

after its former owner, who might well have been a Canaanite, since it had to be purchased from him, he might also have had an eye to improving relations with the Canaanites who still inhabited the land.

The site of Samaria had a dominant position on almost every side, especially the west side, where it towered over a broad valley. Samaria was called in Isaiah 28:1 a "glorious beauty, set on the head of a fertile valley." It stood some three hundred feet high, though ringed by other mountains. But most important of all, it had a strategic location on the north-south trade routes.

Omri's successor, Ahab, built an "ivory house" (1 Kings 22:39), meaning that the house was decorated with carved ivory and inlaid ivory furniture. Ahab also built a temple to Baal in the city, thereby cementing his relationships with Baal worship and the Canaanite populace.

The city of Samaria continued as Israel's capital until it fell to the Assyrians in 722 B.C. Following its capture, it became a provincial seat for both the Assyrians and the Persians. Later still, Herod the Great rebuilt it and renamed it Sebaste in honor of Augustus Caesar, his patron; *Sebastos* is the Greek word for "Augustus." The name remains to this day, for an adjacent village is known as Sebastiyeh.

Omri's Conquest of Moab

Omri's second accomplishment is known from the Moabite Stone,[16] a stone slab, or stela, measuring three feet high and two feet wide and discovered near the Arnon River by F. A. Klein, a French Anglican medical missionary. The inscription was commissioned by King Mesha of Moab. Its text states that "Omri, king of Israel" "had taken possession of the land of Medeba. And he dwelt in it in his days and half the days of his son: 40 years; but Chemosh restored it in my days" (lines 7–9 of the Moabite Stone).

Medeba was the disputed Transjordanian territory north of the Arnon Gorge, nicknamed by some the "Grand Canyon" of the Near East. Mesha claimed that he had captured some one hundred towns in this area that Omri had held for forty years. Of course, Omri only reigned for twelve years—twenty-two years for his son Ahab, two years for Ahaziah, Ahab's son, and six of the years of Ahaziah's brother (i.e., Joram's reign), in whose day this inscription and claim was being made. The total of these reigns comes to 42 years, or given the sharing of com-

16. See James Pritchard, *ANET*, pp. 320–21.

mon years in two cases, it comes to the forty years that Mesha claimed Omri's house held this territory. Thiele gives the absolute years for this period of forty, from the beginning of Omri's reign in 885 B.C. to the sixth year of Joram's reign, about 846 B.C. Twelve of the one hundred cities in Medeba are mentioned in the Moabite Stone, but are also known from the Old Testament: Dibon, Baal Meon, Ataroth, Kerioth, Nebo, Jahaz, Aroer, Beth Bamoth, Bezer, Medeba, Diblaten, and Horanaim.[17]

Mesha's point was that he was enabled by his god Chemosh to get out from under the tribute that Omri had imposed by his rebellion in King Joram's day (2 Kings 3:4–27). The impressive fact is that Omri was able to raise an army adequate to defeat that of Moab, even though Israel had recently been weakened by insurrection and serious instability.

Omri's Phoenician Alliance

Omri's third accomplishment was much more dubious, for he is given a negative mark by the biblical historian for his arranging the marriage of his son to the Phoenician princess Jezebel. The evil Omri did against Yahweh in this regard, and in actions similar to it, surpassed that of all his predecessors (1 Kings 16:25), argued the biblical writer.

It is likely that Omri made a treaty with Ethbaal, king of the Sidonians, as he is called in 1 Kings 16:31. Josephus speaks of an *ithobalos*, "King of Tyre," but not of Sidon (*Antiquities* VIII, 13, 2). Sidon is about twenty-two miles north of Tyre on the Phoenician coast, its nearest city. Thus, "Sidonia" may have been used as a generic term for the Phoenicians, for Ethbaal is best known as the king of Tyre and Sidon (887–856 B.C.).

Ahab's marriage to this Phoenician princess had major consequences for Israel's domestic policy and for her worship practices. Ahab and Jezebel were devoted to the worship of Baal, the deity the Phoenicians revered in different local manifestations as the supreme god of their city-states. Jezebel was clear as to where her loyalties lay, for she exterminated those prophets of Yahweh known to her. The Tyrian form of Baal was the cult of Baal-Melqart, a fertility god. It was in these days and under such influences as these that the "Molech" sacrifices reappeared in Israel. Molech worship was linked with "mak[ing one's]

17. Bryant G. Wood, "Mesha, King of Moab," *Bible and Spade* 9.2 (1996): 58–65.

sons pass through fire," which was generally understood to mean human sacrifice.[18]

While this pact with the Phoenicians was disastrous to the spiritual health of Israel, it worked out to the mutual benefit of both Israel and Phoenicia. Israel imported Lebanon cedar wood and other merchandise garnered from the ends of the known world of that day; Israel enjoyed revenue from valuable trade routes to a larger clientele further south and east, and from supplying Phoenicia with grain and olive oil. Tyre also welcomed, as did Samaria, an ally with the growing power of Damascus on the east. Thus, just as Tyre had been David's link with the world of trade and international ports, so it was for the house of Omri as well.

The Reign of Ahab

The two most infamous names in the history of northern Israel are probably King Ahab and Queen Jezebel (874–853 B.C.; 1 Kings 16:28–34; 20:1–22:40). Jezebel is portrayed as a domineering and resourceful woman who was not content with coexistence with Yahwehism: she wanted to supplant Yahweh with her Baal-Melqart. In fact, she came close to accomplishing just that (1 Kings 18:4). Thus Israel had moved far beyond the introduction of the two golden calves to the outright substitution of Baal for Yahweh.

Ahab's Administrative Abilities

Despite his religious shortcomings, Ahab governed Israel for twenty-two years with more than a modicum of success. He resumed the building programs of his father Omri. As the excavations at Samaria revealed, he surrounded the acropolis of the royal quarter of the capital with an impressive casemate wall (a double wall with partitions between the two walls forming rooms inside the walls). On the north side, the wall was six feet thick on the outer wall and four feet thick on the inner wall, with twenty-three feet of space in between the two. A large number of ivory plaques and fragments were found throughout the city, suggesting that the ivory palace criticized by the prophet Amos (3:15; 6:4) did in fact exist. The ivories were used as inlays in paneling and furniture, reflecting the artistic conventions of Egypt and Mesopo-

18. See B. Levine, "Excursus 7: The Cult of Molech in Biblical Israel," in *The JPS Torah Commentary* (Philadelphia: Jewish Publication Society, 1989), 258–60; and Roland de Vaux, *Studies in Old Testament Sacrifice* (Cardiff: University of Wales Press, 1964), 52–90, against Moshe Weinfeld, "On Burning Babies," *UF* 4 (1972): 135–54. Weinfeld argued that the Molech cult did not actually involve child sacrifice in Israel, but the evidence seems to be against him.

tamia. In addition to this activity on the capital, Ahab built other cities for the populace as well (1 Kings 22:39), including Hazor, Megiddo, and Dor.

Ahab built the "pool of Samaria" (1 Kings 22:38), as well as the famed stables at Megiddo previously attributed to Solomon. His building projects reached into Transjordania as well, for Ahab also stretched his influence across the Jordan.

Ahab's Confrontation with the Prophet Elijah

Among the prophets of Yahweh, one towers above the rest: the prophet Elijah. First Kings 17–19, 21 and 2 Kings 1:1–2:14 records a whole series of Elijah stories.[19] In the midst of Israel's greatest apostasy, Elijah stood as a determined fighter in the cause of Yahweh for a ministry of approximately one decade, ending in the year of 852 B.C. In open defiance of all the foreign trappings that went with the infusion of foreign cults, this intrepid inhabitant from Tishbe of Transjordania (exact location unknown) dared to buck the rising tide and popularity of this foreign fertility cult of Baal.

While Elijah appeared at a number of places in Israel, he never once was located in Judah. He appeared at the summer palace of Ahab and Jezebel in Jezreel, in the Phoenician suburb of Sidon, Zarephath, and on Mt. Carmel, not to mention his long pilgrimage and despondent journey to Sinai in the south. His greatest triumph was the day he called down fire on Mt. Carmel to the despair of the empty-handed 850 prophets of Baal and Asherah from Jezebel's personal roster of approved state prophets (1 Kings 18). The challenge of Elijah was for the people to stop wavering between two opinions: between serving Yahweh and serving Baal (1 Kings 18:21). The failure of the prophets of Baal to produce anything, much less the dew and rain, for which Baal was said to be responsible, did much to ruin Baal's credibility in the eyes of the people.

The chronology of the Elijah stories is difficult to reconstruct, since they are arranged in topical rather than with an eye to any chronological pattern. However, there are references to Jehu and Hazael in his stories. Elijah's commissioning as a prophet must have come at least four years before Ahab's death, for it took place before Ben-Hadad's siege of Samaria, an event that occurred four years prior to Ahab's

19. See Lelia Bronner, *The Stories of Elijah and Elisha as Polemics against Baal Worship* (Leiden: Brill, 1968). Also, see John C. Whitcomb Jr., *Solomon to the Exile* (Grand Rapids: Baker, 1971), 50–59 on Elijah; on Elisha, pp. 76–83.

death at the battle of Ramoth-Gilead in 853 B.C. (1 Kings 20:1, 26; 22:1). Accordingly, Elijah's first encounter with Ahab must have come some time around 860 B.C., fourteen years after Ahab had come to the throne—an adequate time for the serious decline in Yahweh worship described in the Elijah stories.

AHAB'S BATTLES

Besides being an usual leader and an aggressive builder, Ahab comes off as an effective military leader as well. On two occasions he defeated the Aramean forces of considerable strength, just as "a prophet" of Yahweh had predicted (1 Kings 20:1–34). Ben-Hadad, accompanied by thirty-two kings with their horses and chariots, besieged Samaria, boasting, "This is what Ben-Hadad says: 'Your silver and gold are mine, and the best of your wives and children are mine.'" He continued, "About this time tomorrow I am going to send my officials to search your palace and the houses of your officials. They will seize everything you value and carry it away" (1 Kings 20:3, 6). The bravado and the speeches went back and forth until "a prophet" of Yahweh came and announced that Yahweh promised, "I will give [this vast army] into your hand today, and then you will know that I am the LORD" (20:13). Ben-Hadad ended up fleeing on horseback for his life as Ahab and his men inflicted heavy losses on the Arameans (20:20–21).

Ben-Hadad's handlers and advisors had another plan for the attack on Ahab the following spring: attack Israel in the valley, because Israel's gods are the gods of the hills and mountains, they rationalized. But Ben-Hadad suffered an even more humiliating defeat as the Arameans were forced to sue for peace (1 Kings 20:26–43). Ahab showed such leniency to the captured Aramean king Ben-Hadad that it drew the criticisms of the prophet of Yahweh. Ahab's motive for showing such leniency must have been the threat posed now by the emerging Assyrian Empire under Shalmaneser III (859–824 B.C.). Under the terms of the treaty made with Ben-Hadad, the Aramean king returned the cities that had been taken from Baasha forty years previously (1 Kings 15:20), along with those lost to Hezion and Tabrimmon.

Significantly, in that same year[20] Ahab fought Damascus to recover Ramoth Gilead in Transjordania (1 Kings 22). The Judean King Jehoshaphat joined with Ahab in this battle, due, no doubt, to an alli-

---

20. Edwin R. Thiele, *Mysterious Numbers*, p. 66, n. 7, for the argument that both battles took place in the same year.

ance that existed between the two nations. However, Jehoshaphat requested that inquiry be made of the prophets as to the success of this mission after he had agreed to join it. Ahab dutifully supplied Jehoshaphat with four hundred prophets who all chorused that they should "go." Jehoshaphat, a little more conservative than that, asked if a prophet of Yahweh might not be available as well as these four hundred prophets. In fact, Ahab had one in jail at the time, so this prophet was summoned with the wise side-advice that the score presently stood at four hundred to zero in favor of going on with the mission. The Yahweh prophet was Micaiah, son of Imlah. At first he sarcastically joined the crowd, but the edge and irony in his voice (presumably) prompted Ahab to rebuke him and demand a straight word from Yahweh, which he then gave. The battle would be lost, and Ahab would lose his life in the attempt. Micaiah was hauled off to jail again, but he repeated his warning.

Stung by this prediction, Ahab dressed down for the battle by taking off his kingly robes and designating Jehoshaphat as king for the day. However, the word had gone out to get the king. Jehoshaphat almost lost his life as he went screaming out of the battle, disclaiming that he was Ahab. But an archer with an aimless and haphazard shot let an arrow fly which found and pierced Ahab so that he was mortally wounded. He was propped up in the chariot as the battle raged, but he died before he got back to Samaria; dogs licked up his blood from the washed out war chariot as Micaiah had predicted.

Ahab's Alliances

Jehoshaphat must have been involved in the battle of Ramoth Gilead due to the obligations of an alliance with Ahab. Ahab's daughter Athaliah had been married off to Jehoshaphat's son Jehoram, another sign of such an alliance, for this was the normal seal of such a pact (cf. 2 Kings 8:26).

Ahab was a statesman of the first order, but he lacked judgment when it came to his faith and to the compromises he was willing to make in order to gain short-term goals and objectives for the sake of the Northern Kingdom and for his own interests.

The Reign of Jehoshaphat of Judah

Already we have been introduced to Jehoshaphat, king of Judah, who ruled from 873 to 848 B. C. (1 Kings 22:41–50; 2 Chron. 17–20). Jehoshaphat began his twenty-five-year reign when he was thirty-five years old with a three-year coregency with his father Asa. King Asa had developed a disease in his feet (2 Chron. 16:12) in the thirty-ninth year of his reign (ca. 873 B.C.), perhaps incapacitating him somewhat; thus the necessity of his son joining with him on the throne. This was the first instance of a corule of a father and son except for the brief coregency of David and Solomon before the division of the nation. The coregency system was used, all told, nine times in Israel and Judah.

Jehoshaphat's Character

The biblical writers were kind to Jehoshaphat, saying that he walked in the ways of Yahweh, particularly during his early years. However, there was a certain form of naiveté that characterized this king that is befuddling: how could he be caught so frequently in associations, alliances, and ventures he had no business being involved in, much less that were not approved by Yahweh? On three specific occasions, he aided the kings of Israel almost to the point of his own death. He was nearly killed in the battle at Ramoth Gilead, as already noted (1 Kings 22:29–33; 2 Chron. 18:29–34). Later, he joined Ahab's eldest son Ahaziah in a ship-building venture at Ezion-Geber in the Gulf of Aqabah, but every vessel was lost before the project ever took off (1 Kings 22:48–49; 2 Chron. 20:35–37). Finally, he allied himself with Ahab's second son, Jehoram, in a military offensive against Moab to restore Moab's tributary status, but nearly perished once again for lack of water (2 Kings 3:4–27). Each time, however, he was gently rebuked and guided by a prophet of Yahweh: Micaiah, in the Ramoth Gilead episode; Eliezer, in the shipbuilding venture; and Elisha, in the southwesterly attack on Moab. Jehoshaphat was a slow learner, but Yahweh graciously spared him and warned him time after time.

Jehoshaphat's Spiritual State and Activities

This king walked in his father's footsteps and thus he was the second good king Judah had. However, he failed to remove the high places in Judah even though he took away many of the other vestiges of the false cults around him (1 Kings 22:43; 2 Chron. 17:3–6).[21]

21. Both 1 Kings 22:43 and 2 Chronicles 20:33 declare that the high places were not removed, but 2 Chronicles 17:6 affirms that they were. It is not, as some commentators have infrequently alleged, that the Chronicler deliberately altered the facts at this point because in his zeal for Jehoshaphat's character, he must have thought the statement in Kings to be in error. However, both are correct, for the Chronicler (20:33) did acknowledge the very point made in Kings (22:43). Thus, while the official policy and action was to remove the high places, that did not keep the people from reerecting them in less conspicuous places throughout the land.

Jehoshaphat also gave orders for Levites and others to go throughout the land teaching the people the "Book of the Law" (2 Chron17:7–9). Following the alliance with Ahab, some of these same teachers penetrated the hill country of Ephraim with a call to be reconciled to Yahweh (2 Chron. 19:4). How could the people obey God's Law if they had not been instructed in it?

Jehoshaphat also took steps to revise and upgrade the judicial procedures and system in the land. Apparently the Mosaic Law was not being followed, so he reinstated these provisions by appointing judges in the larger cities. Provision was also made for certain priests, Levites, and outstanding leaders to serve in a sort of central court in Jerusalem, as Deuteronomy 17:8–13 had specified. Amariah, the high priest, was to act as chair in matters involving religious questions of the Law, and Zebadiah, a civic leader, was to officiate in matters of civil law. In all of these actions, Jehoshaphat demonstrated that his heart was tender towards Yahweh and discerning in the area of statesmanship.

Jehoshaphat's Leadership Abilities

Despite a certain naiveté, this ruler emerged as a strong leader. In an overwhelming attack on Judah by a coalition of Moab, Ammon, and Meunites (2 Chron. 20:1–30), Jehoshaphat did not despair, but he called for a time of fasting and prayer in Jerusalem. A strong army of five divisions, two from Benjamin and three from Judah, went into battle singing Yahweh's praises. When they finally came upon a host that clearly outnumbered them, they found that the opposing army had turned on itself with armed conflict breaking out among the nations arrayed against Judah. It only remained for Jehoshaphat's army to collect the booty of the slain enemy.

Jehoshaphat must have had a strong reputation, for the nations felt it necessary to band together to face him. Both the Philistines and the Arabs sought his good will by bringing to him significant gifts. His penchant for compromising himself by uniting with ungodly colleagues in the north remained his Achilles' heel.

Ahab's Successors

Ahab's two sons succeeded him: first Ahaziah, the eldest, and then Jehoram.

The Reign of Ahaziah

Ahaziah died after a two-year reign (853–852 B.C.; 2 Kings 1:2–18) without a son to follow him on the throne. His death was caused by wounds he received from falling through an upper lattice in the palace. In an attempt to learn if his wounds were fatal, he sent messengers to the Philistine city of Ekron to inquire of Baal-zebub. But these messengers were intercepted by Elijah and returned with a rebuke for the king and a message that he would not recover.

Only two items are known from this short reign. He entered into a joint maritime venture with Jehoshaphat, which failed almost immediately. This failure was in accordance with the word uttered by the Yahweh prophet Eliezer. The other event was that Mesha, king of Moab, revolted against the heavy tribute that had been imposed by Omri. Thus, amid the turmoil of Ahab's death and Ahaziah's fatal accident, Mesha took advantage of the situation to break away from the north and to assert his independence. Probably Edom did the same thing at this time.

The Reign of Joram/Jehoram

Ahab's second son, Joram or Jehoram, ruled for a total of twelve years (852–841 B.C.; 2 Kings 3). He too was as evil as his brother and his father, according to the biblical estimate. Joram faced a most active Aramean city-state from Damascus and a most active prophet Elisha, Elijah's protégé. Elisha had a ministry that lasted approximately fifty-five years, about 850 to 795 B.C.

One Elisha episode records how the Aramean general Naaman, who served under Ben-Hadad, came to the prophet, on the advice of a young, captured maid from Israel, seeking to be healed of his leprosy (2 Kings 5). In yet another narrative, so distraught was the Aramean king over Elisha's ability to reveal to Israel's King Jehoram even what the Damascus king was thinking and planning (2 Kings 6:10), that he sent a military contingent to capture Elisha. But the military squadron was struck with blindness and led by the prophet into the city of Samaria, ten miles south of the site of Dothan, where they had originally accosted him. They were treated kindly by Jehoram, however, on the prophet's instructions, and they returned home with supplies. Several months later the Arameans returned in an even larger force to lay siege to Samaria, bringing the city to its knees and close to starvation (2 Kings 6:24–7:20). Elisha again called for the king and nation to turn back to Yahweh, promising that the very next day the siege would be lifted and that food would be plentiful—which it was. The Arameans, for some unexplained reason, had fled in the night, imagining that the Egyptians had been summoned to help the besieged city of Samaria. In a final conflict with the Arameans, once against Ramoth Gilead, Jehoram was seriously wounded, even though he once again had help from Ahaziah, king of Judah (2 Kings 8:28–29). While Jehoram was attempting to recover from his wounds at the summer palace of Jezreel, Ahaziah paid a visit to him at Jezreel to see how he was recovering, when Jehu's insurrection caught both kings off guard and led to the death of both of them.

Jehoram's attitude towards the Baal cult of his father and mother is difficult to determine. At first he removed the image of Baal that his father had made (2 Kings 3:2), leaving the impression that he was not sympathetic to Baal worship. But that could hardly be the case, since he was ironically urged by the prophet Elisha to seek help from the prophets of his father and mother, an obvious reference to Baal prophets. Did this not signify that such was his normal practice anyway (2 Kings 3:13)? In fact, when Jehoram's successor—the usurper Jehu—came to the throne of Israel, it was necessary for him to slay the prophets of Baal (2 Kings 9:30–33).

Joram attempted to put down the revolt of Mesha, king of Moab. The heavy tribute that Omri had imposed on Moab was thrown off in the days of Joram's brother, Ahaziah. Joram was determined to restore this lucrative source of income; Joram, aided by King Jehoshaphat of Judah and the king of Edom attempted a surprise attack from a novel approach—around the southern end of the Dead Sea (2 Kings 3:9). But all three armies found themselves in an arid land without water. Fortunately, the prophet Elisha had attached himself to the three armies and intervened with divine instructions that rescued them.

Mesha rebounded in time to save Moab from complete destruction. His story is recorded on the Mesha Stone.[22] The Mesha Stone has about thirty-four lines, written in Moabite, a language that is very similar to Hebrew. It is the longest monumental inscription ever found to date in Palestine. Even though it was broken into pieces by the local Bedouin tribes, two-thirds of the pieces were recovered and a squeeze impression was made of it prior to its being broken apart.

---

22. For some of the more recent studies on the Mesha Stone, see J. A. Dearman, ed., *Studies in the Mesha Inscription and Moab* (Atlanta: Scholars Press, 1989); A. Lemaire, "House of David Restored in Moabite Inscription," *BAR* 20.3 (1994): 30–37; Baruch Margalit, "Why King Mesha of Moab Sacrificed His Oldest Son," *BAR* 12.6 (1986): 62–63, 76; Bryant G. Wood, "Mesha, King of Moab," *Bible and Spade* 9.2 (1996): 55–65.

Mesha turned defeat into victory by sacrificing his son atop the city wall in full view of the enemy troops (2 Kings 3:26–27). But a question arises: Why was Mesha's revolting act so decisive? Baruch Margalit has convincingly argued that Mesha's act, though morally outrageous, was not so unprecedented as it might at first appear.[23] He noted a recently discovered Ugaritic text from 1250–1200 B.C., four centuries before Mesha of Moab, that read in part:

> We shall sacrifice a bull [to thee], O Baal,
> A votive-pledge we shall fulfill [viz.]:
> A firstborn, Baal, we shall sacrifice,
> a child we shall fulfill [as votive-pledge].
> . . . .
> Then shall Baal hearken to your prayers,
> He shall drive the [enemy] from your gates,
> The aggressor from your walls.[24]

The practice of child sacrifice continued on into Punic and Roman times. The biblical account simply says that "the fury against Israel was great; they withdrew and returned to their own land" (2 Kings 3:27). The Hebrew word translated "fury" is *qeṣep*, but in light of the context it cannot be understood as "fury," "anger," or "indignation" of the Moabite national god Chemosh. Instead, the word must signify a psychological breakdown and a trauma that affected the Israelite, Judean, and Edomite troops as they watched the sight of a human sacrifice atop the walls of Kir-Hareseth. Likewise, the Ugaritic text anticipated a similar mass hysteria when this Ugaritic text also predicted that attacking forces would withdraw in a sort of conditioned reflex at such a ghastly sight. The sacrifice of Moab's firstborn son of the king virtually guaranteed the deliverance of the entire population that was under siege. Mesha went on to boldly capture one hundred cities in the land of Medeba, formerly held by Israel.

The Reigns of Jehoram and Ahaziah of Judah

Jehoshaphat of Judah appointed his son Jehoram as coregent for his last four years of reign. This appointment coincided with the time that Jehoshaphat was going to Ahab's assistance; thus, Jehoshaphat must

23. Baruch Margalit, ibid.
24. As cited by Baruch Margalit, ibid., p. 62, 76, citing A. Herdner, "Nouveaux Textes Alphabetiques de Ras Shamra," *Ugaritica* VII (Paris, 1978) , 31–38; text facsimile on p. 33.

have worried that something could go wrong while he was helping someone of whom the prophets of Yahweh disapproved.

Jehoram's reign (853–841 B.C.; 2 Kings 8:16–24; 2 Chron. 21) was not characterized by his devotion to Yahweh as his father's reign was. What contributed to this spiritual demise was his marriage to Ahab and Jezebel's daughter, the wicked Athaliah (2 Kings 8:18). His eight years of rule after his father's death were marked by a series of tragedies. He slaughtered his six brothers, all of whom his father Jehoshaphat had given gold and fortified cities to in Judah (2 Chron. 21:2–4). This was buying insurance for his reign at a high price. Athaliah continued this practice of murder by massacring her own grandchildren after she seized the throne on the death of her husband Jehoram and her son Ahaziah (2 Chron. 22:10–12).

Edom revolted against Judah (2 Kings 8:20–22; 2 Chron. 21:8–9) and then the city of Libnah did so as well (2 Kings 8:22). This was followed by an invasion by the Philistines and the Arabs, with almost all of Jehoram's wives and sons being captured except the youngest Ahaziah (also called Jehoahaz in 2 Chron. 21:17, which is the same name as "Ahaziah," with the compound elements of "Ahaz" and" Yah" simply transposed). Finally, in accordance with a warning given by Elijah, Jehoram died of a gruesome disease of the intestines (2 Chron. 21:12–15, 18–20).

Ahaziah succeeded his father to the throne of David in Judah in 841 B.C. (2 Kings 8:25–29; 9:27–29; 2 Chron. 22:1–9) and ruled for only one year. Encouraged by his mother Athaliah in doing wrong (2 Chron. 22:3), he met his end at the hand of Jehu, even though as the youngest son of the family he had survived the Philistine-Arabian raid. This raid came as he visited his ailing uncle, Jehoram, king of Israel, who was recovering from wounds inflicted at the battle of Ramoth Gilead. Ahaziah died at Megiddo; and his servants carried his body back to Jerusalem for burial.

The demise of this dynasty carried enormous political, religious, and cultural consequences for the northern state. The economic and cultural growth were leveraged off against corresponding losses in religious health. When the moral, ethical, and religious nerve of the nation was cut, the people of the northern ten tribes began their decline and eventual disappearance as a state in 722 B.C.

THE REIGN OF ATHALIAH

The six-year rule (841–835 B.C.; 2 Kings 11:1–16; 2 Chron. 22:10–23:15) of this daughter of Jezebel is unrivaled for the brutality of her reign. One would think that the unprecedented catastrophes that she had faced would have softened her, but they appear to have had the reverse effect. Her mother had been trampled by horses and eaten by dogs; her brother, Jehoram of Israel, had been killed in the coup of Jehu; her husband, Jehoram of Judah, had just died of a gruesome disease of the bowels; her son Ahaziah had been killed by Jehu's men; and her other sons had been captured by the raiding Philistines and Arabians—more than enough trouble to make one stop and ask if Yahweh was trying to say something. Instead, she plunged on, installing the Baal cult in Judah as her mother had done in Israel, though with somewhat less success (2 Kings 8:18, 27; 11:18).

In an attempt to give herself absolute and uncontested power, as her son Ahaziah had committed fratricide (no doubt at her instigation), she murdered her own grandchildren. Unbeknown to her, however, a baby, Joash, escaped, thus saving the Davidic line (and Christians as well).

Nevertheless, when Joash was seven years of age, he was brought out of hiding by Ahaziah's sister and crowned king. Athaliah could do little more than yell "Treason, treason;" but she was summarily assassinated. Thus, the Omride Dynasty in Israel and, for a moment, in Judah, came to an end.

THE PROPHETS OF THE NINTH CENTURY

Both Elijah and Elisha were the two great nonwriting prophets of this era (860 to 795 B.C.). Some of their deeds and involvements in the politics of the day have been alluded to already in the description of the history of the Omride line. Both ministered exclusively to the Northern Kingdom.

The first of the writing prophets probably appeared at this time in the ninth century as well: Joel and Obadiah. Though there is no absolute certainty on the point, nor is any point of orthodoxy at stake if they are both dated as late as the fall of Jerusalem, as many currently favor, it seems that the conditions noted in the locust plague of Joel and the time when the Edomites stood by, refusing to help their brother Judah when the Philistines and Arabs attacked, fits this era best. Both prophets focused on the "day of Yahweh." So seminal was Joel's message, that twenty-seven of his seventy-three verses are found as direct or indirect quotes in other prophets, presumably prophets who followed him (since his use of almost 50 percent of what others had to say hardly sounds original).

The tentative date for Obadiah would be approximately 845 B.C. It had to be one of four occasions when Jerusalem was under attack and her blood brother Edom stood aloof, refusing to come to her aid: (1) Shishak's attack around 926 B.C. in Rehoboam's fifth year (1 Kings 14:25); (2) the attack on Jerusalem by the Philistines and Arabs (2 Kings 8:20–22; 2 Chron. 21:16–17); (3) Jehoash's attack against Amaziah of Judah (2 Kings 14:8–14); or (4) Nebuchadnezzar's destruction of Jerusalem in 586 B.C. (2 Kings 25). When the location of Edom is noted in Obadiah 3, and the calamity mentioned in verses 11 and following of Obadiah are noted, along with the literary parallels found in other parts of the Bible—such as Jeremiah 49:7–16—it seems best to adopt the time when the Philistines and Arabs were attacking Jerusalem.

Ninth-Century Prophets

Joel	Obadiah
A locust plague triggers a series of apocalyptic visions that signal the coming Day of the LORD. Joel calls for repentance and foresees the outpouring of the Holy Spirit.	Shortest of Old Testament prophetic books. Edom stood aloof when Judah needed her help. Her unbrotherly conduct will be repaid in kind while Judah's exiles inhabit Mount Zion.

Israel's classical prophets were not primarily foretellers or prognosticators of future history; their function was to receive God's revelation and then to announce Yahweh's will in the immediate circumstance. Thus, their message often had a now and not-yet aspect to it: The here and now was integrally related to the not-yet, because Yahweh was Lord of all history and all nations.

23

The Century of the Jehu Dynasty (841–753 B.C.)

The year 841 B.C. is one of the great "benchmarks" in Israelite and Judean history, for Jehu effectively ended the Omride Dynasty and influence in both kingdoms simultaneously by assassinating both monarchs: Jehoram of Israel and his nephew, Ahaziah, king of Judah, Jehoram's sister's son. Intoxicated by his spectacular victory over Ahab's son, Jehoram, Ahab's widow, and Ahab's grandson, Jehu proceeded to take on the rulers and elders of Samaria. If these nobles of Samaria were to surrender, they should immediately murder the seventy sons of Ahab and bring their heads in baskets to Jezreel. This they did, so Jehu placed the heads in two piles at the entrance of the city gate for all who passed by to see—thereby mimicking some of the terror tactics for which the Assyrians were notorious.[1] The year 841 B.C. was a time when Israelite and Judean history came to a halt for a moment and waited to see what would take place next.

1. Shalmaneser III used a similar method, for he said: "I slew with the sword 300 of their warriors. Pillars of skulls I erected in front of the town . . . In the moat of the town I piled them up. I covered the wide plain with the corpses of their fighting men, I dyed the mountains with their blood like red wool. I erected pillars of skulls in front of his town." James Pritchard, ed., *ANET*, p. 277.

The Historical Sources for the Period

Less than half the space in Kings is devoted to the Jehu Dynasty than that given to the Omri Dynasty, even though Jehu's line of five generations ruled for eighty-nine years while Omri's three generations held the throne only for forty-four years. Given the impressiveness of this century with its high prosperity and the extent of the kingdom practically matching the extent it achieved in the days of David and Solomon, it is all the more puzzling why so little attention is given to it. From the coup narrated in 2 Kings 9:1 to 10:27, and the rest of the events of the dynasty through 2 Kings 15, the account is very succinct and brief. More space is given to events, such as the survival of the Davidic baby Joash and the coronation of this seven-year-old boy king, along with his repair of the Jerusalem temple (2 Kings 11:1–12:16), and events such as the sacking of Jerusalem by Joash, king of Israel (2 Kings 14:8–14), than to the events that took place during the reigns of Jehu, Jehoahaz, Jehoash, or Jehoram, all kings of Israel.

The Chronicler is likewise, as usual, stingy in his treatment of the Israelite kings in the Jehu era (2 Chron. 22:10–27:9). They appear only where they touch on affairs in Judah. For the most part, the material replicates that found in Kings with some modifications and expansions in order to reflect the emphasis of the Chronicler.

What is of more help at times for this era are the eighth-century prophetical books of Amos, Hosea, Micah, Jonah, and Isaiah. Amos and Hosea composed their books, according to their own internal claims, during the prosperous reigns of Jeroboam II and Uzziah, while Isaiah places his writings in the days of Uzziah and Jotham of Judah. Hosea 1 begins by alluding to Jehu's bloody massacre of the Omrides and prophesies that Jehu's dynasty would come to its own destruction.

Another helpful source of information in this period is the royal records of Assyria and Syrian inscriptions. Shalmaneser III's last campaign in 838 B.C. is reported on the Black Obelisk,[2] an inscription already described in the previous chapter. Four inscriptions described Adad-nirari's western campaigns, in two of which he reached southern Syria-Palestine. The first of these two is known as the Saba'a Stela,[3] discovered in present-day Iraq in 1905, in which Abad-nirari claimed that in the fifth year of his reign, "I gave the order to advance against

2. D. D. Luckenbill. *Ancient Records of Assyria and Babylonia*, 2 vols. (Chicago: University of Chicago Press, 1926–1927), vol. I, sections 555–93. See excerpts in J. Maxwell Miller and John H. Hayes, *A History of Ancient Israel and Judah* (Philadelphia: Westminster, 1986), pp. 286–87.

3. D. D. Luckenbill, op. cit., I, sections 734–35.

Palasht [Palestine]." The second was the Rimah Stela discovered in 1967 in the excavations of al-Rimnah, Iraq,[4] in which the Assyrian monarch claims to have conquered "the land of Amurru and the Hatti Land" all in one year. In this same inscription, he claimed to have received tribute from the rulers of Tyre, Sidon, Mari' of Damascus and from *Ia'asu* [= Joash] of Samaria.

Also of interest for this period is the Melqart Stela, found north of Aleppo in 1939, mentioning a "Bar-Hadad son of [ ], king of Aram."[5] Even more helpful is the Zakir Inscription found some twenty-five miles southeast of Aleppo in 1904, which identifies Ben-Hadad as the son of Hazael.[6]

A wide variety of archaeological sites bear on the Jehu era. Included are levels: III-IV of Samaria, IV-A of Megiddo, Tirzah/Tell el-Far`ah, VII-V of Hazor, VIII-VII of Shechem, VI of Gezer/Tell Jezer, IV of Lachish/Tell ed-Duweir, X-IX of Arad and II of Beersheba/Tell es-Seba`. Many of the remains of the building structures from the Omride era were discovered, though many of them showed evidence of being expanded and repaired.

A few inscriptions came from the Palestinian excavations, such as the sixty inscribed potsherds from Samaria called the Samaria Ostraca.[7] These, however, were mostly records of shipments of wine and oil. More interesting are the many seals and seal impressions from this era. The most famous is the one reading "Shema the servant of Jeroboam."[8] "Servant" in this context probably refers to a royal official who served under Jeroboam II.

Chronological Difficulties in the Jehu Era

If Jehu came to the throne in Israel in 841 B.C. and the dynasty came to an end in 753 B.C., the years of Jehu's Dynasty add up to 102 1/2 years instead of the 89 years that fit into the parameters of the Assyrian

4. Conveniently pictured and found in J. Maxwell Miller and John H. Hayes, op. cit., pp. 288, 299. H. Tadmor, "The Historical Inscriptions of Adad-nirari III," *Iraq* 35 (1973): 141–50; especially p. 143.

5. J. A. Dearman and J. M. Miller, "The Melqart Stele and the Ben Hadads of Damascus: Two Studies," *PEQ* 115 (1983): 95–101.

6. James Pritchard, *ANET*, 3rd ed. (Princeton: Princeton University Press, 19 69), pp. 655–56.

7. James Pritchard. *ANET*, p. 321.

8. For a photograph and brief discussion, see J. M. Miller and J. H. Hayes, op. cit., pp. 294–95.

records. The Judean years add up to 137 years of the 95 years between 835–740 B.C. The following chart displays these differences:

The Kings of Israel		The Kings of Judah	
Jehu	28 years	Joash/Jehoash	40 years
Jehoahaz	17 years	Amaziah	29 years
Joash	16 years	Uzziah/Azariah	29 years
	102 ½ years		137 years

But there are other problems as well. The deaths and successions of both Judean kings named Jehoash and Amaziah raise difficult chronological problems. Joash died in 782 B.C., at which time his son Jeroboam II began his reign. Jeroboam II himself died in 753 B.C. with a total reign of forty-one years, according to 2 Kings 14:23. Moreover, in 2 Kings 14:23, Jeroboam II came to the throne in the fifteenth year of Amaziah of Judah, 782 B.C., while 2 Kings 15:1 indicated that Azariah, successor of Amaziah in Judah, began to reign in Jeroboam's twenty-seventh year, a year which is known to be 767 B.C.

Thiele explained that there is an excess of twelve years, meaning that there was a twelve-year coregency between Joash and Jeroboam II, thereby making the forty-one years begin in 793.[9]

Likewise, there was a twenty-five-year coregency between Amaziah of Judah and his son Uzziah. Scholars are virtually united in their acceptance of the 740 B.C. date for the death of Uzziah/Azariah: his fifty-two years of reign would require a 792 B.C. accession date for the commencement of the coregency, coming only four years after Amaziah's coronation. Thus, father and son shared the throne for twenty-five years. Amaziah would have been about twenty-nine or thirty years of age; Uzziah was sixteen years old in 792 B.C., making Amaziah about fourteen years of age when his son Uzziah was born.

Another instance of overlapping of reigns came between King Uzziah and Jotham. Jotham's first 12 years were as coregent with his father Uzziah (2 Kings 15:30, 33; 2 Chron. 27:1).[10] Therefore, the 12 + 25 = 37 years that must be deducted for coregencies from the 137–year total

9. See Edwin R. Thiele, "Coregencies and Overlapping Reigns among the Hebrew Kings," *JBL* 93 (1974): 192–93.

10. Harold G. Stigers, "The Interphased Chronology of Jotham, Ahaz, Hezekiah, and Hoshea," *BETS* 8 (1966): 86–88.

of 100 years between 841–740 B.C. to give the correct total for the calendar years that had expired in the interim.

Similarly, the total years for the northern kings is found to reconcile when it is noted that there was a twelve-year coregency between Jehoash and Jeroboam II, leaving twenty-nine years of sole reign. Once again, as in the case of Judah, there is a synchronism for Jeroboam's accession, the fifteenth year of Amaziah, the year also when Jehoash died and Jeroboam began his sole reign. This is what Edwin Thiele referred to as examples of "dual dating." He explained:

> The fact that dual dating for both Jeroboam and Azariah have in the past not been understood has been responsible for many vexatious perplexities regarding the regnal data for the lengths of period. When once it is understood that the data for the lengths of reign of Jeroboam and Azariah include both their years of overlap with their fathers and their years of sole reign and that the synchronisms of their accessions mark the years when their fathers died and their sole reigns began, all the data involved are found to be in perfect harmony with each other, and the reconstruction of the chronological pattern becomes a matter of comparative simplicity.[11]

One other fact must be noted: both Israel and Judah used the nonaccession year system at this time, thus one year must be deducted from the official length of reign for each ruler to obtain the actual years of reign from the official years listed in the text.

The Reign of Jehu of Israel

Jehu founded the longest-lasting dynasty the Northern Kingdom was ever to experience—five generations of father-to-son succession (841–753 B.C.). He was the first king of the fifth and final dynasty of Israel. He is best known as the scourge of God, for he wiped out the Omrides who preceded him as Elijah had foretold some twenty years before (1 Kings 19:15–17; 21:21–24).

While Elisha personally fulfilled the commission God had given to Elijah to anoint Hazael king of Syria (1 Kings 19:15; 2 Kings 8:8–15), he delegated one of the "sons of the prophets" the task of anointing Jehu as the king of Israel—almost as if he wanted to avoid giving the impression that he approved of all means Jehu used or that he was personally responsible for the blood bath that followed Jehu's savage insur-

11. Edwin R. Thiele, *A Chronology of the Hebrew Kings* (Grand Rapids: Zondervan, 1977), p. 43.

rection against the king of Israel and Judah, In fact, with Jehu's assassination of King Ahaziah of Judah, and his systematic purging of all the Judean royal family, the messianic line of David hung by the slenderest thread it ever was suspended on in the whole history of the Davidic messianic line.

Thus, one of the sons of the prophets ignited the flame that Jehu fanned into a forest fire, when he broke into a group of army captains and asked to see Jehu privately. Quickly the delegated prophet anointed Jehu and commissioned him to fulfill the prophecy about Omri's house. With that he left and Jehu at first dismissed the encounter with an off-hand remark about everyone knowing how crazy such people as these prophets were. But Jehu's fellow captains eventually wormed out of him the fact that he had been crowned as king of Israel, to which they greeted the news with a shout, "Jehu is king!" They spread their garments to form a processional aisle in this hastily devised and crudely arranged extemporaneous coronation ceremony.

Jehu now had to race back to Jezreel, where the ailing and wounded king was recuperating, before news leaked out of what had happened. His riding was as "maddening" and "furious" as the qualities he had just attributed to the "mad" son of the prophets (2 Kings 9:11). The ailing king's messengers had gone to intercept the furious rider, but they failed to return to the summer palace at Jezreel with news of what all the haste and fury was about. King Jehoram of Israel, along with the allied Ahaziah, king of Judah, went out to investigate for themselves. But it was too late, for Jehu turned on both of them, and both lives suddenly ended at Jehu's hands (2 Kings 9:20–28).

Jezebel must have sensed what was coming. She painted her eyes, set her hair, and waited for the inevitable. As Jehu approached, she defiantly mocked Jehu saying, "Have you come in peace, Zimri, you murderer of your master?" (2 Kings 9:31). Her point was that just as Zimri had destroyed Baasha's dynasty by murder, but paid for his act of defiance seven days later by having to burn down the palace at Tirzah over his own head (1 Kings 16:9–20), so Jehu would no doubt have to pay with his life. Jehu was unimpressed, for in response to his request for help from those within this summer palace at Jezreel, two palace eunuchs threw Jezebel out the upper story window and Jehu drove the horses over her body. Her corpse was left for the dogs to consume (as Elijah had predicted in 1 Kings 21:23), while Jehu went into the palace to enjoy a kingly meal.

Nor was Jehu finished with all of this. He would intimidate the nobles of Samaria to polish off all seventy sons of Ahab from Ahab's various wives and concubines. Jehu ghoulishly placed these seventy trophies on display in the gates of Jezreel in two piles of skulls. He then left for Samaria, where he met and killed forty-two more relatives of Ahaziah who were on their way to visit the two kings. All forty-two had been unaware of what had just taken place.

Following his stumbling on Ahaziah's relatives, Jehu also met Jehonadab, son of Rechab (the Recabites were strict followers of Yahweh, an ascetic group that the prophet Jeremiah later admired, Jer. 35:1–19). Jehu invited Jehonadab into his chariot, after Johonadab professed sympathy and support for Jehu. When Jehu arrived with Jehonadab at the capital of Samaria, he murdered all the officials, possibly including those who had murdered the sons of Ahab for Jehu as well. Then Jehu called all the prophets and priests of Baal together to their temple in Samaria, pretending to extend royal favor to them. Amidst an apparent sacrifice to Baal, Jehu had eighty of his men enter the Baal temple to kill every priest and prophet of Baal. The sacred stone inside was brought outside and burned, the temple of Baal was torn down; and the place was designated as a latrine from that time on (2 Kings 10:18–29).

If all this sounds like Jehu favored Yahweh instead of Baal, that was not so. The writer of Kings noted immediately after relating all that had happened, "Jehu destroyed Baal worship in Israel. However, he did not turn away from the sins of Jeroboam son of Nebat, which he had caused Israel to commit—the worship of the golden calves at Bethel and Dan" (2 Kings 10:28–29). Nevertheless, because Jehu had accomplished all that Yahweh had ordered against the house of Ahab, Yahweh was promised that his descendants would sit on the throne of Israel until the fourth generation (2 Kings 10:30).

Jehu's Administrative Abilities

Jehu ruled for twenty-eight years (841–814 B.C.; 2 Kings 10:29–36), in a reign that was marked by turmoil and general unrest, despite the spectacular speed and dispatch with which he pulled off his coup. For one thing, Jehu's overthrow of the Omri line meant the end of Israel's favorable relations with Phoenicia. This Phoenician connection had been one of the main sources of economic prosperity for the Northern Kingdom. But when he assassinated Queen Jezebel and her daughter

Athaliah, Israel never again could look to that source for help and assistance.

One of the reasons for Jehu's weak responses to the attacks that were constantly being made on his country was that he had slaughtered most of the able leaders in his overzealous response to purging Israel of the house of Omri. Jehu went beyond Yahweh's instructions, particularly in his killing of the court officials of Jezreel, Samaria, and those who came from Judah. Replacing and training new leaders would take time. Since Jehu served as a captain of the army under King Jehoram, he must have had some military expertise, but it did not appear that he used good judgment or diplomatic skills.

Jehu's Trials with Foreign Powers

Just as Jehu was coming into power, Shalmaneser III swept through Syria and Palestine, destroying towns and exacting heavy tribute as the price for further concessions. Shalmaneser returned in 838 B.C., with the only merciful aspect being that it delayed Hazael, king of Damascus, from beginning his rampage of Syria-Palestine. It happened in those days, that

> the LORD began to reduce the size of Israel. Hazael overpowered the Israelites throughout their territory east of the Jordan in all the land of Gilead (the region of Gad, Reuben and Manasseh), from Aroer by the Arnon Gorge through Gilead to Bashan (2 Kings 10:32–33).

Thus, Shalmaneser III's scourging of northern Transjordania may be the event that Hosea referred to in Hosea 10:14:

> The roar of battle will arise against your people,
> so that all your fortresses will be devastated—
> as Shalman devastated Beth Arbel on the day of battle,
> when mothers were dashed to the ground with their children.

Shalmaneser III is the same Assyrian who had humiliated Ahab and Benhadad. The Black Obelisk depicted his humiliation of King Ahab and described his severe oppression in Israel. But then the Assyrian attacks all stopped as the Assyrians attended to more pressing civil wars and economic matters at home. This permitted Hazael to recoup his losses from Shalmaneser's devastation of Damascus and the area and to inflict his own will on Israel, as the Assyrians had inflicted their will on the Arameans.

But Shalmaneser's (and later Hazael's) invasion of the Transjordan was only the beginning. Later in Jehu's Dynasty, the Syrian armies would extend their conquests right into the center of the hill country on the west side of the Jordan. In the days of Jehu's son Jehoahaz, they took cities as far south as Gath (part of the Philistine Pentapolis) and extorted from the temple as well as the temple coffers and treasury in Jerusalem itself (2 Kings 12:17–18). Hazael himself became the main irritant in Jehu's life, just as Elijah had predicted (1 Kings 19:15–17). Elisha wept as he anointed Hazael as king, for he could foresee the havoc that this monarch would bring on Israel (2 Kings 8:7–15). Eventually, Hazael seized all Transjordan, including territories that the two-and-a-half tribes had held since the time of Moses.

Jehu did reduce the influence of Baal in the land, but King Jehoram had already taken measures earlier to do the same. Nevertheless, Jehu did not replace Baalism with Yahwistic worship, but he turned, instead, to the golden calves that Jeroboam I had set up as the kingdom broke away from Solomon. The fact that the Baal influence remained strong can be attested in Baal-compounded names on the Samaria Ostraca.

The Reign of Jehoahaz of Israel

The Syrian menace continued into the reign of Jehoahaz, Jehu's son, who ruled for the next seventeen years (814–798 B.C.; 2 Kings 13:1–9). Very little is recorded about his reign other than the fact that Israel continued to be subject to Syrian domination and harassment (2 Kings 13:3).

In the days of Jehoahaz's reign, things got so bad that Israel's once-glorious power was reduced to "fifty horsemen, ten chariots and ten thousand foot soldiers, for the king of Aram had destroyed the rest and made them like the dust at threshing time" (2 Kings 13:7).

Toward the end of Jehoahaz's reign, in desperation he temporarily abandoned his worship of the golden calf that Jeroboam had set up at Bethel and turned to Yahweh in prayer. Graciously he was given a "deliverer" (2 Kings 13:5) to bring them out from the "power of Aram." That "deliverer" was no doubt the Assyrian king Adad-nirari III (810–783), who began to launch his campaigns to the west in 805 B.C., an event that resulted in the subjugation of Hazael and relief for Israel. Israel was forced to pay tribute to Adad-nirari III, along with Tyre, Sidon, Edom, and Philistia. But they were spared the crushing blow that the Assyrian delivered to Damascus. So wounded was Damascus that it gave Israel an opportunity to rebuild.

Many of the stories about the prophet Elisha took place during the days of Jehoahaz. The Syrians' constant raids were taking away all levels of the Israelite population, such as the young Israelite maid who was captured and forced to serve the Syrian general Naaman. The unexpected letter from Damascus demanding that the Israelite king favor King Hazael of Damascus by healing his general of his skin disease (leprosy) sent the capital of Israel into convulsions until Elisha restored calm with his assurance from Yahweh that such was possible. The siege of Samaria grew severe. Then, Elisha predicted that the siege would be lifted the next day, and grain prices would fall precipitously, to the astonishment of all who heard the prediction. Time after time, Elisha helped Jehoahaz by informing him of secret strategies and places where the Syrian king would be hiding, much to the disgust of Hazael.

The Reign of Joash of Israel

When Jehoahaz died, his son Joash/Jehoash came to the throne and immediately the prophet Elisha promised him victory over the Arameans of Damascus. Elisha instructed the king to smite the ground with arrows, which he did for only three times—to the dismay of the prophet. Nevertheless, Elisha predicted that Joash would be victorious over Damascus three times. In those conquests, he regained the Israelite cities that Hazael had seized.[12]

Jehoash had become strong enough by this time to win the battle that Amaziah, king of Judah, the "thistle king," provoked against him (2 Kings 14:8–14). Jehoash reigned from 798 to 782 B.C. (2 Kings 13:10–25; 14:15–6). According to the Rimah Stela, Joash was among those who paid tribute to Adad-nirari III, probably in the Assyrian's 796 B.C. campaign. But like his father and grandfather before him, he persisted in the same sins of Jeroboam and that of their forebears had done.

The Reign of Joash of Judah

Judah had to endure six years of Athaliah's reign before another descendant of David's line came to the throne. So hated was Athaliah that the usual datelines and synchronisms are missing for her years in

12. J. Maxwell Miller and John H. Hayes, *A History of Ancient Israel and Judah*, pp. 299–301, argue unpersuasively that the three battles that Joash fought against Benhadad are misplaced in Ahab's reign (1 Kings 20; 22:1–38). In fact, the supposition is that the three battles in both narratives are the same cannot be sustained. But just as the authors themselves admit, "All of this is highly speculative, and there are counterarguments that cannot be ignored" (p. 300).

the biblical text. Athaliah single-handedly would have wiped out the Davidic dynasty had it not been for Jehosheba, a daughter of Jehoram and sister of King Ahaziah (and later wife of high priest Jehoiada). She rescued young Joash, the sole survivor, and hid him for the six years of Athaliah's reign.

When Joash was seven years old, the high priest Jehoiada presented him in public under heavy guard as the royal heir and claimant to the throne in Judah. The day set was the Sabbath, when the temple workers would be present. Jehoiada divided the incoming shift of priests into three groups, each with an assignment to guard a strategic point, while the outgoing shift remained to function as security for the boy king. Together the Levites placed a crown on Joash's head and presented him with a copy of God's Law. Then they shouted, "Long live the king!" Athaliah suddenly became aware of what was happening. Her plaintive cry was "treason, treason," but it was too late. She was executed a short distance from the house of God on orders from Jehoiada.

Thus, Joash began his forty-year reign (835–796 B.C.; 2 Kings 11:4–12: 2 Chron. 23:1–24:27). As long as Jehoiada the priest, his spiritual mentor, lived, Joash did what was right in the eyes of Yahweh. But while he was under such great influences for good, he had the temple repaired. He destroyed the religious articles that Athaliah had imported into Judah, including the Baal-Melqart temple, its altars and images. He also killed the Baal priest Mattan, while restoring the personnel and ritual prescribed by the Mosaic Law. This was all under the direct influence of Jehoiada the priest.

When Jehoiada died at the age of 130 years (2 Chron. 24:15), King Joash entered a new but tragic phase of his life. With the death of the high priest, Joash fell under the influence of nobles who were more sympathetic to the deposed cult of Baal-Melqart. These advisors misled him so that he ended up commanding his men to stone Zechariah, the son of the high priest Jehoiada, for his daring to speak against the king. As the prophet of Yahweh lay dying in the temple court as a result of the wounds inflicted on him under Joash's direction, he cried out, "May the LORD see this and call you to account" (2 Chron. 24:22). And indeed God did. Before the year was out, Hazael's army approached Jerusalem and defeated Judah, being finally bought off with the temple treasures (2 Kings 12:18; 2 Chron. 24:23–24). What is more, Joash had the greatest indignity attached to his life when he was assassinated by conspirators and then refused burial among the sepulchers of the kings, while Jehoiada was given just that honor (2 Chron. 24:15, 16).

THE REIGN OF AMAZIAH OF JUDAH

Fortunately, the assassination of Joash did not bring to an end the Davidic line, for Joash's son Amaziah ruled for twenty-nine years, though the last twenty-four years of Amaziah's reign were in a coregency with his son Uzziah. The years he ruled were from 796 to 767 B.C. (2 Kings 14:1–20; 2 Chron. 25). One of his first actions as king was to punish the assassins of his father, but he did not wipe out the entire family of the assassins as most ancient kings would have done to prevent further retaliation.

AMAZIAH'S CAMPAIGN AGAINST EDOM

Edom had revolted against her overlords in Judah during the days of Jehoram. Now, however, Amaziah looked favorably on the possibility of restoring the southern trade routes once again for Judah. Thus the Judean king made ambitious plans, in the meantime hiring mercenary soldiers from northern Israel for one hundred talents of silver to add to his own troop strength. But when he was rebuked by a man of God for hiring these soldiers, Amaziah sent them back home. In the rejected mercenaries' displeasure, they plundered some of the cities around Beth Horon, killing some three thousand people and taking much loot (2 Chron. 25:13). This would seem to imply that Judean subcultures existed throughout this section of the Northern Kingdom, perhaps some of the very towns that Asa had captured in Israel or towns where Jehoshaphat had sent priests and Levites to instruct them in the way of Yahweh (2 Chron. 15:8; 17:2; 19:4–5).

Finally, the Judean army entered into battle with Edom in the Valley of Salt (*Wadi el-Milh*), between Beersheba and Arad. With savage brutality, Amaziah slew ten thousand Edomites and cast another ten thousand to their deaths from the top of a cliff. Then he went on to the capital city of Sela and forced it into submission to Judah once again (2 Kings 14:7; 2 Chron. 25:11–12).

AMAZIAH'S CAMPAIGN AGAINST ISRAEL

Amaziah, fresh and flush from this victory over Edom, immediately confronted the king of Israel. His excuse or basis for war is not known. Could it have been that he thought the king of Israel encouraged or at least tolerated the outbursts of the frustrated troops that Amaziah had released?

This whole affair was headed for no good. Jehoash's response showed that he had little time or respect for Amaziah when he replied to Amaziah's challenge with a proverb that compared himself to a mighty cedar of Lebanon and the king of Judah to a mere thistle that was arrogantly demanding the cedar to provide the thistle with his daughter as wife (2 Chron. 25:18–19). The proverb ended with a mighty beast stamping on the thistle. The implication was clear: Amaziah had better not fool with Jehoash, or he would merely step on him.

Amaziah was no wiser, but only more determined, so the armies met at Beth Shemesh. The Chronicler saw Amaziah's stubborn persistence as from Yahweh to punish him for his idolatry (2 Chron. 25:20). Amaziah just about escaped with his life due to Jehoash's merciful treatment of him. He took Amaziah captive to Samaria as a prisoner, disgraced and humbled in every way.

Fortunately, Amaziah outlived Jehoash by fifteen years (2 Kings 14:17; 2 Chron. 25:25); thus his release from captivity must have been tied to the death of the one who triumphed over him. But if Amaziah thought Jehoash was a strong king to deal with, Jeroboam II was an even more formidable leader.

In 767 B.C. a conspiracy against Amaziah forced the king of Judah to flee Jerusalem to Lachish, where he was found and killed. Once again, a son had been placed as a coregent with his father. This time the son was Azariah/Uzziah. They ruled together for twenty years.

The Reign of Jeroboam II of Israel

Jeroboam II was the greatest of all the kings of northern Israel, for he "restored the boundaries of Israel from Lebo [or: from the entrance to] Hamath to the Sea of the Arabah, in accordance with the word of the LORD, the God of Israel, spoken through his servant Jonah son of Amittai, the prophet from Gath "Hepher" (2 Kings 14:25). "Lebo Hamath" refers to the Bekaa Valley, a valley between the Lebanon and Anti-Lebanon mountains, the southern portion of which corridor was approximately at the city of Dan. The Sea of Arabah is the Dead Sea. In addition to this, Jeroboam II also regained control of much of Transjordania.

This third descendant of Jehu's dynasty ruled from 793–753 B.C. (2 Kings 14:23–29) for forty-one years. While no description of his battles is extant today, he achieved a remarkable kingdom by extending the eastern and northern borders to about where they were under the empires of David and Solomon. Jeroboam II also recovered Damascus (along with Hamath) that had belonged "to Judah" (2 Kings 14:28), a reference to David and Solomon, for those cities had not belonged to

Israel since that day. Thus, in less than twenty-five years Jeroboam II was able to take a nation that was just about ready to die and turn it into one of the great powers of his day. The wealth and economic turnaround were so dramatic that it became a matter of concern for the prophets as they inveighed against those who "adorned [their] houses with ivory," both "winter house" and "summer house" (Amos 3:15). In fact, so prosperous had they become that their wives were said to "lie on beds inlaid with ivory and lounge on [their] couches . . . din[ing] on choice lambs . . . strum[ing] away on [their] harps like David and improvis[ing] on musical instruments, . . . drink[ing] wine by the bowlful and us[ing] the finest lotions, but . . . not [being] griev[ed] over the ruin of Joseph" (Amos 6:4–6). Hosea had warned as well (12:8) that "Ephraim boasts,/ 'I am rich; I have become wealthy./ With all my wealth they will not find in me/ any iniquity or sin.'" But Samaria, unknown to its inhabitants, was a "fading flower," whose "glorious beauty" was about to be "laid low" (Isa. 28:1).

The lull in the Assyrian campaigns permitted Jeroboam II to move into Syria with virtually no challenges. When things were good, they were very, very good. Damascus fell to Benhadad's successor, whose name we do not know. The next ruler of Damascus, Resin, did not come to the throne until 750 B.C., making him the final king of Damascus, since he would still be in power when the capital Damascus fell in 732 B.C.

The death of Jeroboam II in 753 B.C. was the beginning of the end of the Northern Kingdom. Jeroboam II was followed to the throne by his son Zechariah, the fifth and final king in the Jehu Dynasty. He had ruled only six months (753 B.C.; 2 Kings 15:8–12) when he was assassinated by his successor Shallum. The only fact noted about King Zechariah is that he continued in the worship of the calves at Bethel and Dan. Thus, four generations of Jehu came to a halt. Assassins and instability continued to be hallmarks of the few remaining days of a nation that had persisted in departing from its Yahwistic roots.

The Reign of Uzziah/Azariah of Judah

Amaziah's successor in the south was his son Uzziah (also called Azariah). He ruled fifty-two years, longer than any previous king in Israel or Judah (792–740 B.C.; 2 Kings 14:21–22; 15:1–7; 2 Chron. 26). Judah, like her neighbor to the north, was also experiencing unprecedented prosperity and economic recovery during this long reign of Uzziah.

Uzziah shared the first twenty-four years of his reign as a coregent with his father; his last twelve were likewise shared with his son Jotham; thus, of his fifty-two years of reign, he only had sixteen years of solitary rule. He would have been sixteen years of age when his father Amaziah was taken captive by Jehoash, leaving him the sole head of the government for the nine years or so that his father remained as a prisoner in Samaria.

Like Kings Asa, Joash, and Amaziah before him, Uzziah, too, began well, but he failed to finish in the same style. King Asa was guided by the prophets Azariah, son of Oded and Hanani the seer. Joash was guided by Jehoiada the high priest. Uzziah had the prophet Zechariah as a real moral influence and counselor during his earlier years. It was said of Uzziah that "he sought the LORD God during the days of Zechariah, who instructed him in the fear of God. As long as he sought the LORD, God gave him success" (2 Chron. 26:5). But that too would change.

During this early period of his reign, Uzziah accomplished all his outstanding achievements: construction of cities, towers, cisterns, cattle raising, planting fruit trees, and equipping his army with some of the most advanced weapons of the day. In fact, he installed some rather unique engines that were capable of shooting arrows and catapulting stones from the walls. He also had siege engines that allowed his men to scale enemy walls and platforms from which his army could rain destruction on those within the city.

Uzziah attacked the Philistines and broke into Gath, Jabneh, and Ashdod. He overtook the Arabs in the region of Beersheba and Arad. He also subdued the Meunites, who lived in the Arabah near the Dead Sea. Finally, he also overcame the Ammonites and made them subject to Judah.

The last twelve years of his reign were no doubt shared with his son Jotham because of Uzziah's sudden leprous condition just about that time. The problem was that he had intruded into the priestly office (2 Chron. 26:16–21)—attempting to offer incense in the temple, though he had been cautioned not to do so by the eighty-one members of the priestly staff of the temple. It became necessary for Azariah the high priest and the eighty-one priests to confront Uzziah for this breach of protocol. Uzziah angrily responded and as a result leprosy broke out on his forehead. In horror Uzziah rushed out of the temple and spent the final decade of his life crying out, "Unclean, unclean" to all who passed by (Lev. 13:45–46). A more tragic end to one who had begun so well is hardly imaginable.

THE EIGHTH-CENTURY PROPHETS

The writing prophets and nonwriting prophets played a prominent role in eighth-century Israel and Judah. Among the writing prophets are Amos, Hosea, Jonah, Micah, and Isaiah. Each played a key role in calling both nations back to Yahweh, especially the Northern Kingdom that was so close to self-destructing. Alas, there was little visible response in the north. The five prophets of this century were as follows.

AMOS (CA. 750 B.C.)

Amos was a Judean prophet who ministered in the Northern Kingdom, vigorously denouncing the luxurious living of the upper classes that were getting rich by exploiting the poor. Instead of the day of Lord being a panacea for all the nation's ills, it would bring disaster, as perverted religion and empty ritual must lead to political and economic crashes.

HOSEA (CA. 745–735 B.C.)

Hosea fathered three children, who were symbolically named "Scattering/Sowing," "No Mercy," and "Not-My-People." His wife Gomer left the prophet for her lovers, only to be taken back again later by Hosea—an act that symbolized God's graciousness and faithfulness to his spiritually adulterous people. Israel's economic and social corruption spelled certain disaster for a people who had no knowledge of God, no loving devotion to God, and no truth. But the love of God would finally triumph, despite such reprehensible sins.

MICAH (CA. 725 B.C.)

Micah was a Judean prophet who condemned the rich and religiously careless alike. But history would not rest with these defectors, but the "Breaker" would come from Bethlehem as conquerer and ruler over all. He was so forgiving that none pardoned sins so completely and freely as he.

JONAH (CA. 780–765 B.C.)

Jonah was a disobedient prophet who would rather preach about the expansion of his own people's boundaries than be the bearer of any news (whether it was good or bad) to such hated and brutal enemies as the Assyrians in Nineveh. He finally reached his audience, under some extraordinary duress, only to learn that he was effective and that the people had repented, much to his personal disgust and disappointment.

ISAIAH (CA. 740–690 B.C.)

Isaiah was the greatest theologian of the classical prophets. His sixty-six chapters cover both the holiness (Isa. 1–39) and coming glory (Isa. 40–66) of God, following the very pattern of his inaugural call (Isa. 6). Isaiah was intimately connected with the Jerusalem sanctuary and the Davidic royal family, and he focused on the future son of David who would redeem the sins of the world by his own life and work.

The eighth century was a period of extraordinary utterances from the prophets. In many ways their revelations form the center of the prophetic message, for many of their themes recur in the later prophets. But they also were the radicals of their day. However, instead of being revolutionaries who fixed the blame on institutions as such, they took a different approach: they wanted individuals to change so that society and a national existence could be preserved. If there were no evidences of turning back to God, the prophets threatened that judgment was so certain that kings and citizens could begin to count on it immediately!

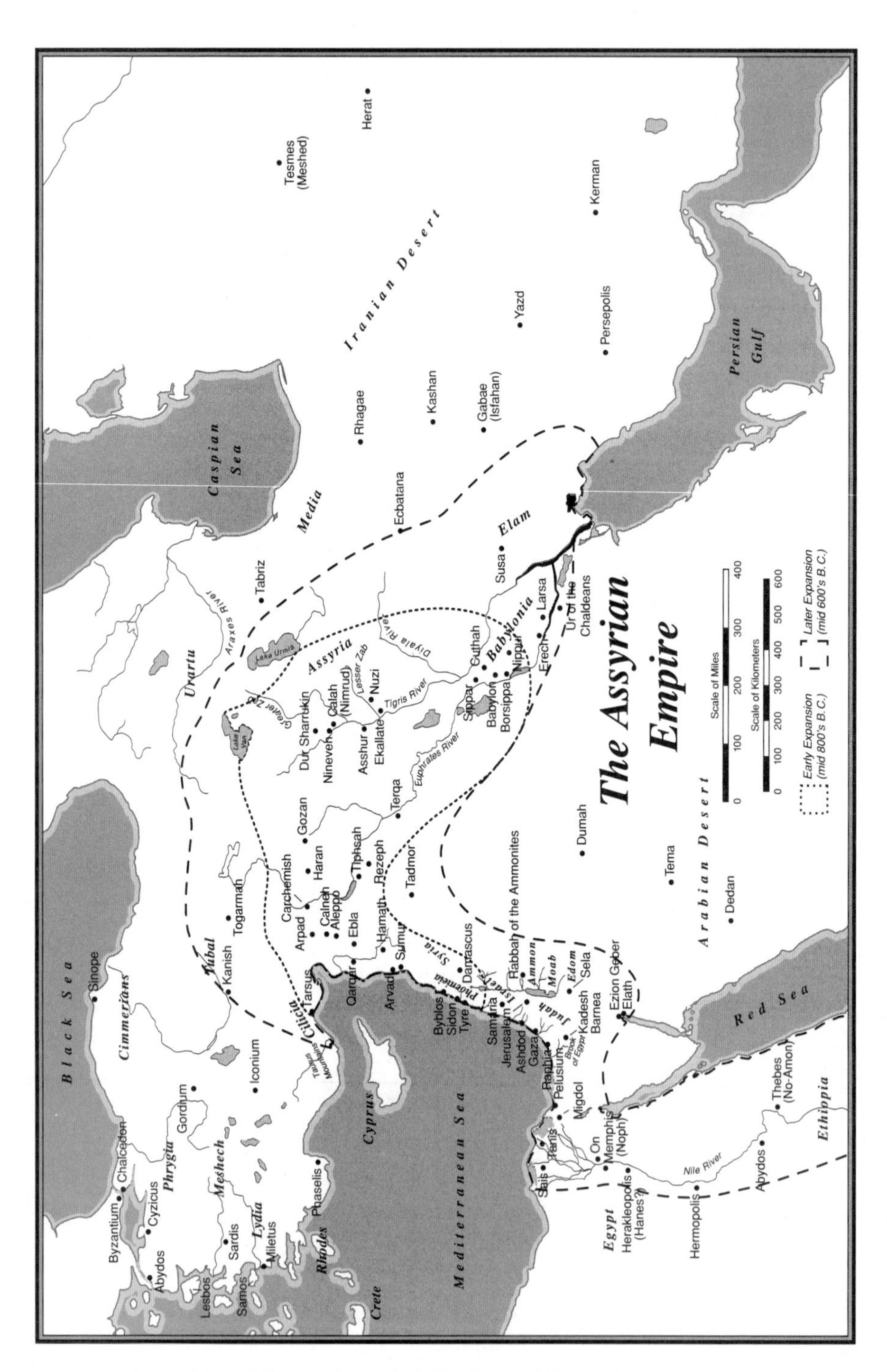

From *Holman Bible Handbook* (Nashville: Holman Bible Publishers, 1992), 360.

24

The Era of Assyrian Expansion and the Fall of Samaria

The last brilliant period of Assyria was the 130 years of the neo-Assyrian empire from 745–612 B.C. Before 745, Assyria had faced so many internal upheavals and pressures from powerful states such as Urartu and the Aramean states after the reign of Adad-nirari III (810–783 B.C.) that she had her hands full without taking on new conquests in the west.

The Neo-Assyrian Era (745–612 B.C.)

Tiglath-Pileser III (also known in the Bible as "Pul") usurped the throne and reigned from 745–727 B.C. Simultaneously he set out to achieve three goals: defending the borders against Urartu to the north, regaining control of Syria to the west, and stabilizing the restlessness of Babylonia to the south. To accomplish this, he developed an efficient and competent standing Assyrian army with equipment, technique, and tactics superior to those used up to that time by Assyria's enemies. Smaller nations did not have a standing army at their disposal, relying instead on conscription and draft call-ups for each and every emergency. Thus, every freeman had to drop his agricultural pursuits and go fight while the economic and food-producing economy of the nation either came to a halt or was carried out by women.

One of the first actions of Tiglath-Pileser III was to put down the Aramean nuisance in Babylonia. Babylon had a long-standing tradition of harassing Assyria, but newly arrived Aramean immigrants in Babylonia created an additional crisis that had to be addressed by Tiglath-Pileser. Strong Assyrian defenses had to be built in Babylonia and Assyrian governors placed in control with only a nominal king left in residence as a formality.

To the north, Urartu was finally reduced at least to a fear of the Assyrian threat, even though the capital of Turushpa at Lake Van was not breached, even after a siege. Tiglath-Pileser III was more successful in the northwestern Aramean states of Arpad (*Tell Erfad*), north of Aleppo, and Unki, near the present-day Antiochia. These became Assyrian provinces, thus securing control over northern Syria and the northern Palestinian coast of the Mediterranean. Finally, Damascus in the southwest was treated in the same way, making the domain of the Assyrian king extend from Lake Van in Armenia to the Mediterranean, and down to the Persian Gulf. All this was accomplished in the early years of Tiglath-Pileser III.

The Assyrians developed a systematic method for extending and consolidating their empire. It involved using three levels or degrees of dependency, rather than immediately depriving each conquered nation of all of its freedoms and forcing it to give up its independence. For states on the fringes of the empire, Assyria was content with a declaration of loyalty; rulers in these distant regions needed only to continue to pay tribute and assume the status of a tributary state.

If a tributary state rebelled and refused to pay tribute, or planned and joined anti-Assyrian coalitions, that nation was moved to the second level or degree of affiliation. The state was stripped of its former degree of independence and was incorporated into one of Assyria's provinces; a vassal-leader who was sympathetic to Assyria and its policies was appointed to govern a very small area around its capital. Many of the ruling and aristocratic classes were deported to distant parts of the empire, leaving mainly the peasants. Simultaneously, deportees from the opposite side of the empire were moved in to replace those who had been removed. This mixing of nationalities and religions minimized the chances for rebellion or the formation of coalitions against Assyria.

When a vassal state conspired against the Assyrian throne and directly entered into opposition against it, the Assyrian Empire imposed the third level of dependency: national extermination. Assyria exterminated the remnants of the state, leaving it only a shadow of its former size by incorporating it, too, into the province.

There are no historical inscriptions or archival records for Shalmaneser V's reign (727–722 B.C.), but it is known that Hoshea paid tribute to this successor of Tiglath-Pileser III (2 Kings 17:3; "Shalmaneser king of Assyria came up to attack Hoshea, who had been Shalmaneser's vassal and had paid him tribute"). Shalmaneser discovered that Hoshea "had sent envoys to So king of Egypt, and he no longer paid tribute to the king of Assyria, as he had done year by year" (2 Kings 17:4). Thus, Hoshea's attempt to pay the tribute when he met the Assyrian king must have come too late. It was for this reason that Shalmaneser imprisoned Hoshea and laid siege to Samaria for the next three years, which was the beginning of the end.

Hoshea's revolt must have been part of a larger anti-Assyrian movement at that time. This is suggested by several lines of evidence. Josephus (*Antiquities* IX. 283–84),[1] citing the Greek author Menander as his source, who claimed that he in turn was relying on Tyrian archives, reported that "all Phoenicia" was in revolt during the days of Shalmaneser. Shalmaneser's successor, Sargon II (722–705 B.C.) had to finish the job of suppressing the revolt in Syria-Palestine. Moreover, it makes very little sense for a tiny Ephraimite state ruled by Hoshea to declare a revolt on its own with little more than some promised aid from Egypt as its basis for doing so.

THE EGYPTIAN HELP FROM "SO"

The reference to "So king of Egypt" is puzzling since no pharaoh is known by this name. At least two major ways have been suggested for handling this anomaly. One rather ingenious suggestion is that the name *So* may refer to the delta city of "Sais." In Egyptian *S'w* (Sa'u) and in Assyrian *Sa-a-a* could phonetically produce "So" in Hebrew rather than "Sa." This view generally requires another textual move—one that says that the Hebrew *ʾel sôʾ melek miṣrayim* "to So/Sais, king of Egypt" had another *ʾel* in the Hebrew text just before the "king of Egypt," that has dropped out by way of haplography. The reading therefore would be *ʾel sôʾ [ʾel] melek miṣrayim*, "to Sais, to the king of Egypt." This would mean that "So" was indeed the name of a city and not the name of a Pharaoh.[2] The interesting fact is that an independent

1. This reference and the other lines of evidence that follow were suggested by J. Maxwell Miller and John H. Hayes, *A History of Ancient Israel and Judah*, pp. 334–35.

2. H. Goedicke, "The End of 'So, King of Egypt,'" *BASOR* 171 (1963): 64–66; R. Borger, "Das Ende des agyptischen Feldherren Sib'e = *Ysw'*," *JNES* 19 (1960): 49–53, as cited by Siegfried Hermann, *A History of Israel in Old Testament Times*, 2nd rev. ed. (Philadelphia: Fortress, 1981), 250.

dynasty was raised up about this time in Egypt. The residence of the ruler was at Sais in the eastern delta. Pharaoh Tefnakhte founded the Twenty-fourth Dynasty and reigned from 727–720 B.C. He may well have been the one in Egypt whom Hoshea called upon in his revolt from Assyria. Pharaoh Tefnakht I tried to unify both Upper and Lower Egypt by marching south to bring the Nubian dynasty of Pharaoh Piankhy (737–716 B.C.) of the so-called Twenty-fifth Dynasty under his reign; but in a decisive battle at Memphis, Piankhy won and assumed rulership over the whole of Egypt. When Pharaoh Piankhy returned south without having set up any sort of administrative structure in the delta, Tefnakht reasserted his rule over the delta and its princes once again.

The other view is to assume that "So" is an abbreviation for Osorkon IV (ca. 730–715 B.C.), the last ruler of the Twenty-second Dynasty.[3] At present, the former view appears to have the edge. Regardless of which is the correct identity of "So," Hoshea's appeal for help was in vain; Shalmaneser's siege of Samaria came off without any interference from Egypt.

THE REIGNS OF SHALLUM AND MENAHEM OF ISRAEL

Shallum, assassin of King Zechariah and usurper of the throne of Israel in 752 B.C. (2 Kings 15:13–15) was hardly able to get the sixth dynasty of Israel going when he too was murdered by Menahem, perhaps a military leader at the time.

Since Menahem (752–742 B.C.; 2 Kings 15:16–22) came from Tirzah, the old capital of Israel, he may have represented the pro-Assyrian "peaceniks" of his time. The chief event recorded in Kings is about his tribute to Tiglath-Pileser (2 Kings 15:19–20) . He imposed a poll tax on each of the "mighty men of wealth" (*gibbôrê haḥayil*) for fifty shekels of silver, totaling a thousand talents of silver.[4] Menahem must have maintained his rule over the land by stern measures and marked brutality. Paying the tribute to Tiglath-Pileser enabled him "to strengthen his own hold on the kingdom" (2 Kings 15:19). The upper classes must have felt the pinch, but Menahem stayed on the throne because of the Assyrian policy to leave those monarchs in power, especially those most distant from the Assyrian capital who raised the tribute money. Menahem may have thought of himself as someone of

3. Kenneth A. Kitchen, *The Third Intermediate Period in Egypt (1100–650 B.C.)* (Warminster: Aris and Phillips, 1973), p. 374.

4. One talent equals 3,000 shekels; thus, the total must have been 66,000 pounds of silver, which at current market averages of $4.00 an ounce would be worth $4,244,000 per year!

major importance, but from the perspective of the Assyrian monarch he was small indeed. Tiglath-Pileser III had this written about him in his inscriptions:

> As for Menahem, I overwhelmed him like a snowstorm and he . . . fled like a bird, alone and bowed at my feet."[5]

The Reigns of Pekah and Hoshea in Israel

Menahem's son Pekahiah reigned two more years in the Menahem Dynasty (742–740 B.C.; 2 Kings 15:23–26) after his father's death. But he too was assassinated by one of his military leaders, Pekah, son of Remaliah. This may indicate that his father's voluntary submission to Tiglath-Pileser III was an attempt to defuse a conspiracy that had been brewing against him at the end of his reign. But an anti-Assyrian party must have formed in reaction against Menahem's head-tax program, thus paving the way for Pekah's rebellion.[6]

The fact that such a rebellion had an anti-Assyrian flavor to it and that it had begun during Menahem's rule is attested by the fact that Pekah began his twenty-year rule (752–732 B.C.; 2 Kings 15:27) in 752 B.C., the very year of Menahem's accession, which meant that Pekah had only eight years of sole reign (740–732 B.C.). Once again, however, there is evidence of "dual dating," for 2 Kings 15:27 also claimed that Pekah, son of Remaliah, became king in Israel in the "fifty-second year of Azariah king of Judah" (740 B.C.) and that he "reigned twenty years." But if he ruled for twenty years and this reign began in 740 B.C., this would mean he ended his reign and died in 720 B.C., a clear impossibility since Samaria fell in 722 B.C. King Hoshea followed him in a nine-year reign, all this coming a decade before the 722 B.C. collapse of the Northern Kingdom.

Edwin Thiele suggests that Pekah ruled across the Jordan River in Gilead as a rival during the entire reign of Menahem and Pekahiah.[7] It is known, for instance, that Pekah took "fifty men of Gilead with him" (2 Kings 15:25) when he assassinated Pekahiah. Since he probably ruled over an area that bordered on Syria, Pekah embarked on a policy of friendship with Syria, her northern neighbor, in what became known as the Syro-Ephraimitic league. This association with King Rezin of Damascus aligned Pekah and Rezin against King Ahaz of Judah for his

5. James Pritchard, *ANET*, pp. 283–84.
6. Merrill Unger, *Israel and the Arameans of Damascus* (Grand Rapids: Baker, 1980 reprint), 99.
7. Edwin Thiele, *Mysterious Numbers of the Hebrew Kings*, 1965, pp. 124–25.

unwillingness to join their rebellion against the Assyrians. The purpose of the Syro-Ephraimite alliance was to replace King Ahaz in Judah with the "son of Tabeel" (Isa. 7:6), but more will be mentioned on this in the next chapter.

So the first twelve years[8] of Pekah's twenty-year reign were merely over Gilead, ruling simultaneously with first Menahem and then Pekahiah. This explains not only the "dual dating" given in the text but also the mention of Pekah as "one of [Pekahiah's] chief officers" (2 Kings 15:25), while also maintaining a distant base of sovereignty as a rebel movement against the crown in Samaria. Some scholars use the term *partisan dating* to describe the practice of including within a king's tenure those years wherein he was supported by a small but significant minority. Clearly, despite the failure of Menahem and Pekahiah to recognize Pekah's rival claims, some segments of the Transjordanian population did recognize his claim and supported his anti-Assyrian stance. When Menahem, the man from the former capital of Tirzah (representing perhaps an anti-Samaritan policy) was removed from the scene, Pekah felt free to make his move and reassert a pro-Samaritan policy with a strong nationalistic basis in 740 B.C.

Tiglath-Pileser did not undertake another western campaign after 738 B.C. until 734 B.C. Then this renewed campaign brought him "to Philistia," the Pentapolis of the Philistines. This fact, recorded in the Assyrian Eponym List, has now been confirmed and further elaborated on by the find of a tablet fragment in the northwest palace of Asshurnasir-pal (883–859 B.C.) in Nimrud.[9] In the year 734 B.C., Tiglath-Pileser reached the "brook of Egypt" (*wadi el-ᶜArish*), after having crossed Syrian and Israelite territory. The king of Gath, Hanun, fled to Egypt to avoid becoming a vassal as the city of Gath fell into Assyrian hands. The point of the Assyrian advance into the Philistine territory must have been to control the trade routes from Egypt and to cut off contacts between Israel/Syria and any possible Egyptian help. This campaign is not recorded in the Old Testament.

The following year, 733 B.C., an alliance of small states in Aram, along with Pekah from Israel, sought to assert their independence from Assyria. This was an alliance that the King of Judah, Ahaz, refused to join, and thus incurred the wrath of Rezin of Damascus and Pekah of Samaria. Whether the attack of Tiglath-Pileser was directly motivated

---

8. Many simply reject the "twenty years" of Pekah. For example, T. R. Hobbs, *2 Kings: Word Biblical Commentary* (Waco, Tex.: Word, 1985), 201.

9. The tablet was published by Donald Wiseman in *Iraq* 13 (1951): 21–23, pl. XI. See also the inscription of Tiglath-Pileser in James Pritchard, ed., *ANET*, pp. 283–84.

by King Ahaz of Judah's requests cannot be determined, but he apparently moved against the Northern Kingdom of Israel first in 733, for Damascus hung on until 732 B.C. Tiglath-Pileser reported the steps he had taken against Israel in an inscription from his annals. He claimed this: "In my former campaigns I had all the cities of Bit-Humri [="House of Omri," Assyria's designation for Israel years after Omri's reign] to my land . . . and . . . only left Samaria (?), they cast down *Pa-qa-ha* [=Pekah of Israel] their king."[10] This would have involved Assyria's second step in her policy of reducing a king's domain to a very small area around the capital after the king had allied himself with another in rebellion against Assyria. In yet another Assyrian text, we learn "Bit-Humria . . . all its inhabitants [and] their possession I led to Assyria. They overthrew their king *Pa-qa-ha* and I placed *A-u-si-'* [=Hoshea, the last king of Israel] as king over them. I received from them 10 talents of gold, [?] talents of silver as their tribute."[11] Thus the deportation of the population, the fall of King Pekah, and the appointment of a new king Hoshea are all attested in this text as part of the events in 732 B.C.

Tiglath-Pileser moved against Damascus, executed its king, Rezin, in 732 B.C., and incorporated the territory that Damascus had controlled into the Assyrian provincial system (2 Kings 15:29). This area became the provinces of Damascus, Karnaim (approximately the Golan Heights area), Gilead (mid Transjordania), Megiddo, and perhaps Dor. Much of the same territory had once been under the domain of Israel and then under Hazael of Damascus.

Israel had, by now, been reduced by Rezin to the central hill area of Mount Ephraim. Tiglath-Pileser III somehow had the Israelites overthrow King Pekah (2 Kings 15:30), with the result that Tiglath-Pileser recognized Hoshea in his stead. According to the Assyrian annals, the people "overthrew their king Pekah and I placed Hoshea as king over them."[12] Second Kings 15:30 placed the responsibility for the overthrow of Pekah on Hoshea's head, but it is clear that a pro-Assyrian party was in charge once again. Israel had its nineteenth—and final—monarch, Hoshea son of Elah.

Hoshea ruled Israel for her final nine years (732–722 B.C.; 2 Kings 17:1–6), making him the ninth royal family line in just two centuries of the kingdom's existence. Hoshea began to reign at some point during

10. The lines in the annals are 227–28; James Pritchard, ed., *ANET*, p. 283
11. James Pritchar ed., *ANET*, pp. 283–84.
12. James Pritchard, ed., *ANET*, p. 284.

the 733–32 campaigns of Tiglath-Pileser III against Damascus. He ruled little more than the city of Samaria and the surrounding Ephraimite hillsides as the remnants of the former Israelite kingdom. He paid tribute to Tiglath-Pileser III's successor, Shalmaneser V (727–722 B.C.), either voluntarily or under coercion (2 Kings 17:3). Eventually, Hoshea decided to stop paying tribute to Shalmaneser V and appealed instead to So/Sais of Egypt for relief and assistance (2 Kings 17:4). Since there are no records from the reign of Shalmaneser, it is impossible to determine why Hoshea decided to quit paying tribute. It may have been nothing more than residual anti-Assyrian sentiment in Israel or it could be that Hoshea erred in overestimating the strength, willingness, and abilities of Egypt to counteract the massive strength of Assyria.

Shalmaneser V had had more than enough of Israel's rebelling by this time. He took Hoshea by force and "put him in prison" (2 Kings 17:4). He then besieged Samaria for the next three years (2 Kings 17:5; 18:9–10) before finally capturing it. The capture of Samaria is attributed to Shalmaneser in the Book of Kings and by the Babylonian Chronicles.[13] Shalmaneser V died shortly after the capture of Samaria. When Sargon II (722–705 B.C.) came to the throne, he too claimed to have been the ruler when Samaria fell.[14] But this may have been just so much propaganda because (1) Sargon's claims to have taken Samaria only appear in the Khorsabad Texts from his fifteenth and sixteenth years; (2) Sargon did not begin his reign until December 722 B.C., too late to qualify as Hoshea's ninth year, which would have ended nine months earlier; and (3) 2 Kings 17:1–6 and the Babylonian Chronicles state clearly that Shalmaneser was the king who conquered Samaria.[15]

The siege of Samaria lasted from 724 to 722 B.C. When it fell, Sargon II claims that 27,290 were taken captive. Many others already had been deported by Tiglath-Pileser and Shalmaneser. According to 2 Kings 17:6, the deportees were settled in Halah, in Gozan [=Tell Halaf] on the Habor River, sixty miles southeast of Haran (the place where Abraham stopped on his way to Canaan and whence the relatives of the patriarchs had come!), and in the city of the Medes, present-day Iran. Alternatively, foreign populations were resettled in Samaria,

---

13. A. K. Grayson, *Assyrian and Babylonian Chronicles* (Locust Valley, N.Y.: J. J. Augustin, 1975), 73.

14. James Pritchard, ed., *ANET*, pp. 284–85.

15. The arguments used here are suggested by Leon J. Wood, *A Survey of Israel's History*, p. 282, n. 94. See also A. T. Olmstead, "The Fall of Samaria," *AJSL* 21 (1904–1905): 179–82; Edwin Thiele, *Mysterious Numbers of the Hebrew Kings*, pp. 141–47; and H. Tadmor, "The Campaigns of Sargon II of Assur: A Chronological-Historical Study," *JCS* 12 (1958): 39.

according to 2 Kings 17:24, from Babylon, Cuthah, Avva, Hamath, and Sepharvaim.

The Impact of the Fall of Samaria

The shock and tragedy of the collapse of the Northern Kingdom was so severe that the writer(s) of Kings had to explain how such a devastating blow could have come to the people who had such a firm covenant from God. Therefore, in the midst of recording the narrative of the kingdoms of Israel and Judah, the text paused to list about twenty reasons why God's judgment was necessary and deserved by Samaria (2 Kings 17:7–18). It was not that Yahweh had been helpless or unable to come to the rescue of Israel, but that they had been so disloyal to Yahweh's sovereignty that the threatened judgment known from the days of the Law of Moses had finally to be fulfilled, or else Yahweh himself would no longer be trustworthy in any of His promises. While some of that generation failed to enter into the benefits of the covenant, the covenant itself continued to be transmitted to succeeding generations and to remain intact. Indeed, some of the remnant of the northern tribes had long since fled the north for refuge in Judah (2 Chron. 11:16).

The prophet Isaiah had predicted that the process of deportation would take place over a sixty-five-year period beginning in 734 B.C. (7:8). That is what happened, for the task of moving the people continued from 734 to 669 B.C., exactly sixty-five years as Isaiah had promised. The Assyrian king Esarhaddon (681–669 B.C.) , grandson of Sargon II, completed the task. This fact can be noted in Ezra 4:2, where the Samaritan population (a mixed race with the Jewish people because of the policy of deportation) attempted to hinder the work of Governor Zerubbabel and High Priest Joshua in rebuilding the Jerusalem temple. They did so because they were unable to participate in its building, persisting in their claim by saying, "We . . . have been sacrificing to [Yahweh] since the time of Esarhaddon king of Assyria, who brought us here."

So sparse did the population become in Israel in those days that the lions began to multiply out of control. This, too, was in accordance with the predicted judgment threatened in Leviticus 26:21–22. In order to cope with this crisis of wild animals attacking the populace, the Assyrians called for "one of the priests [they] took captive from Samaria [to] go back to live there and teach the people what the god of the land requires" (2 Kings 17:27). Whether this was a genuine believer in Yahweh, which seems doubtful, or one of the Yahweh calf-priests who had ministered at the golden calves at Bethel and Dan is an open question. "Nevertheless," verse 29 goes on to assert, "each national group made its own gods in the several towns where they settled, and set them up in the shrines the people of Samaria had made at the high places."

25

The Era of Assyrian Domination: Judah from Jotham to Amon

The life of Judah was closely linked with the dominant Assyrian Empire in the century from 740 to 640 B.C. Previously, the Assyrians had left Judah pretty much to herself, usually limiting their campaigns to Damascus and Israel as terminating goals. But things began to change after 740 B.C.

King Ahaz reversed this state of affairs. From the beginning of his reign he voluntarily adopted a pro-Assyrian policy. This enabled Ahaz to assume power over his father, King Jotham, while Jotham still was alive. The position of the Jerusalem nobility must have been that it would have been better for the health and welfare of the nation of Judah to submit to Tiglath-Pileser III than to be forced eventually to oppose him and suffer the devastating consequences.

While Judah generally offered no major resistance to the Assyrian imperial powers throughout this century, King Hezekiah did join in at least one Syria-Palestine revolt against Assyrian rule, although the Assyrians suppressed the short-lived revolt in 701 B.C.

The Assyrians ruled their vast empire almost unchallenged in this century under rulers such as Tiglath-Pileser III (745–727 B.C.), Shalmaneser V (727–722 B.C.), Sargon II (722–705 B.C.), Sennacherib (705–681 B.C.), Esarhaddon (681–669 B.C.), and Ashurbanipal (668–627 B.C.). Only Sennacherib faced a rather well-orchestrated revolt, but he was able to suppress Hezekiah's challenge, which led to Judah's lengthy submission to Assyria throughout the long reign of Manasseh (696–642 B.C.) and his immediate successors.

Understanding the political situation of this century requires some knowledge of what was happening in Egypt. The prophet Isaiah made much of Egypt's involvement in Judah's national life at this time. Isaiah was correct, of course, for this same century demonstrates the fact that the intertwining of Assyria and Egypt was highly significant for Judah—indeed, for the whole of southern Syria-Palestine.[1]

Three dynasties struggled to control Egypt: the Twenty-third, the Twenty-fourth, and the Twenty-fifth. The Twenty-second and Twenty-third Dynasties had ruled over very limited areas in the delta region. Simultaneously, Dynasty Twenty-four was setting up its house in the north at Sais while Dynasty Twenty-five, an Ethiopian or Nubian dynasty, was coming into prominence in the far south.

By the year 737 B.C. Pharaoh Piankhy, the Nubian of Dynasty Twenty-five, controlled all of southern Egypt. In a crucial battle at Memphis, Piankhy won control over Lower Egypt (in the north) as well. But when he returned south to Upper Egypt, Pharaoh Tefnakht of the Twenty-fourth Dynasty returned and reasserted his headship over Lower Egypt once again. The nonnative family of the Twenty-fifth Dynasty sought to run direct competition with Assyria in order to gain control over the commerce on the eastern Mediterranean seaboard.

Piankhy died and was succeeded by Shabako, who again moved to unify Egypt, especially in light of a threatened invasion of Egypt by Sargon II. Oddly enough, the only way he was able to effect the unification he desired, and also to stave off the threatened attack of Sargon, was to extradite a Philistine prince he was holding to Sargon. But Piankhy's rule from that point on seemed to be only by Assyrian permission until he died in 702 B.C.

A son of Piankhy, Shebitku, followed Pharaoh Shabako to the throne. Along with the general rebellion that was taking place in 705 B.C., following Sargon II's death, Shebitku also resisted the Assyrian domination by coming to the defense of King Hezekiah, whom Sennacherib had put under siege in Jerusalem. However, Shebitku arrived too late in 701 B.C., for already Sennacherib had divided his army, leaving half to face the Egyptians and Judeans at Eltekeh, and the other half

1. The following material is developed in Kenneth A. Kitchen, *Third Intermediate Period*, pp. 356–87.

to go to Jerusalem to retaliate against Hezekiah for his act of insubordination in collaborating with the enemy.

A second contingent of troops from Egypt was led by crown prince Tirhakah and was now making its way to join in the battle against Sennacherib. Sennacherib warned Hezekiah not to take any solace in the fact that the Egyptians were coming, for the Assyrian record of success over all previous enemies was too overwhelming to expect that they would be the answer to Hezekiah's problems. In the end, Egypt proved to be nothing Judah could lean on; it was no more than "a splintered reed," which "pierces a man's hand and wounds him if he leans on it!" (2 Kings 18:21). Shebitku and Tirhakah both retreated, inflicting little if any harm on the Assyrians.

The Historical Sources for This Century

The materials that document the life and times of kings Jotham, Ahaz, Hezekiah, Manasseh, and Amon of Judah are fairly extensive in the biblical texts: 2 Kings 16–21, paralleled by Isaiah 36–39, and 2 Chronicles 28–33, are all replete commentaries on these times, as is Isaiah 1–35 and portions of Hosea and Micah.

There are also the extensive historical inscriptions from the six Assyrian kings who ruled the Assyrian Empire during this time. Records are available from every one of the six rulers except Shalmaneser V.[2] Although the records of Sargon II and Sennacherib are not as full as those of Tiglath-Pileser, or even those of Esarhaddon and Ashurbanipal, they are still very helpful. Some of this material is not presented in a chronological framework; nevertheless, they are still helpful in providing information on aspects of this period.

The Egyptian materials are very sparse for this era, given the internal confusions and rivalries. They are represented best by references to them in the Assyrian or biblical materials. The Egyptian involvements are attested elsewhere, though in the later classical period, such as Herodotus and other authors of that time.

The Reign of Jotham

Judah, as already argued, weathered the storm that was brewing all around her by becoming a loyal vassal of Assyria. In so doing, Judah was left as a lonely outpost along with few other semiautonomous states in Palestine. However, Judah would narrowly escape experiencing the

2. James B. Pritchard, ed., *ANET*, pp. 283–301.

disastrous results that would befall her less fortunate neighbors as she flirted on these two occasions with an anti-Assyrian league.

Jotham (750–731 B.C.; 2 Kings 15:32–38; 2 Chron. 27) was coregent, ruling in his father Uzziah's stead from 750 to 740 B.C. due to his father's contracting leprosy by his rash intrusion into the priestly office by offering a sacrifice in the temple. After this, Jotham ruled on his own until 731 B.C.

Jotham's kingdom of Judah reached as far south as the Egyptian border and the Red Sea. Reaching across the Jordan River, Jotham made Ammon a tributary nation while continuing to exercise control over Edom. This was made possible by Tiglath-Pileser's forced retirement to Assyria in 738 B.C. Jotham's action ended good relations with Pekah in Israel. Previously, they had been comrades in rebelling against Jeroboam. Now, however, Judah's action in Transjordania infringed on Israel's sphere of interest.

But after three years the Ammonites stopped paying tribute (2 Chron. 27:5). This bold revolt by Ammon betrayed the hand and the schemes of Rezin in Damascus. Rezin would do everything he could to thwart the formation of a strong Judean bloc around the Dead Sea. Thus he took the offensive, joined by his protégé Pekah son of Remaliah, to launch in about 735 B.C. a direct attack on Judah (2 Kings 15:37). Now Jotham had installed his son Ahaz as coregent about twelve years before his death.[3] In retaliation against Jotham and Ahaz for their unwillingness to join in the growing anti-Assyrian sentiment that was brewing in the area in anticipation of a second major offensive of Tiglath-Pileser extending from 734 to 732 B.C., Rezin would continue to apply the pressure on Judah over the next years, pushing Judah to the brink of disaster. But Ahaz not only refused to cooperate; he wholeheartedly collaborated with the Assyrians, thus bringing Judah under Assyria's heel without any coercion from Assyria.

Rezin was playing a high-stakes game, defiantly creating a Syro-Palestinian bloc. But he faced two annoying obstacles to his plan: the nations of Israel and Judah. He would neutralize Israel by having his puppet, Pekah, assassinate Pekahiah, king of Israel, while Pekahiah's protector, Tiglath-Pileser, was busily occupied in Media. Pekah had

3. The year of Ahaz's accession to the throne was 743 B.C., the same year that King Uzziah of Judah went north to lead the coalition. Jotham, now left alone in charge of the government in Jerusalem, fearful about the possible retaliation that Tiglath-pileser could take on Judah for his father's participation in the battle against him, made his son Ahaz his coruler. Apparently he did not believe his father would return alive. It also gave an opportunity to present Ahaz as heading up a pro-Assyrian policy, backed no doubt by a pro-Assyrian group of influential backers in Judah.

never been recognized as an equal with the kings of Israel, whom they referred to as a *shalish*, an adjutant, or a viceroy in the provinces under his rule in Transjordania.

But it would be a more difficult task to get Judah to join Rezin and Pekah, now that Ahaz had insisted on neutrality with regard to the plan. The king of Judah had been warned by the prophet Isaiah (8:6–8) that to rejoice "over Rezin and the son of Remaliah [Pekah of Israel]" would be to risk "the mighty floodwaters of the River [Euphrates]—the king of Assyria with all his pomp" who would "sweep on into Judah, swirling over it, passing through it [until it] . . . reach[ed] . . . up to the neck." The whole venture would prove disastrous for everyone involved: Pekah and Rezin would not win against Assyria, and Judah would be beholden to Assyria by virtue of their appeal to that nation for help.

Jotham was the fourth consecutive monarch in Judah who had earned the approval of God. Among the pleasing things that he did were building an important temple gate in Jerusalem, adding the wall of Ophel to the city, enlarging other cities, and establishing forts and towers to strengthen Judah's fortifications.

The Reign of Ahaz

Ahaz chose not to follow in the godly steps of his father or grandfather in his twenty-eight-year reign from 743 to 715 B.C., although only sixteen of those years was he the head ruler (2 Kings 16; 2 Chron. 28). This son of Jotham, also known as Jehoahaz in one of Tiglath-Pileser III's inscriptions,[4] was unusual in that—contrary to Judean custom—his mother's name was not given.[5] Ahaz's wife and the mother of King Hezekiah, who was to follow him, interestingly enough was Abi, the "daughter of Zechariah" (2 Kings 18:2), who may be the same Zechariah who was king of Israel. If so, here was a second case of intermarriage between the Northern and Southern Kingdoms. It could also explain why Ahaz was dissuaded from following Yahweh, despite the example of four previous generations of godly ancestors, preferring, instead, to "walk . . . in the ways of the kings of Israel" (2 Kings 16:3).

Ahaz does not receive friendly treatment from the biblical sources. He made images of Baal, sacrificed (presumably his oldest son) to Molech in the Valley of Hinnom, had the pagan altar he saw in

4. James Pritchard, ed., *ANET*, p. 282.
5. The only other exception to a long line of Judean kings is King Jehoram (2 Kings 8:17).

Damascus copied by Uriah the priest in Jerusalem, which he then placed instead of the brazen altar prescribed by the Mosaic law. Later, he even closed the temple doors, forcing the people to worship just where and how he wanted them. It was as if Ahab and Jezebel, with all their Canaanite syncretism, had been brought back to life again, only this time in Judah!

Ahaz and the Syro-Ephraimite Crisis[6]

Ahaz was hard pressed on all sides for his steadfast resistance to joining the anti-Assyrian coalition. Rezin of Damascus and Pekah of Samaria had been encroaching on Judean territory for some time now. In one battle with Pekah, 120,000 Judeans had been killed (2 Chron. 28:6) and another 200,000 had been taken captive. Had it not been for the intervention of the prophet Oded (2 Chron. 28:9), this staggering loss would have left the south with little future, but the prophet Oded demanded that Pekah send the captives back home, which he did. Likewise, the Arameans of Damascus had taken many Judeans captive and carried them off to Damascus (2 Chron. 28:5). Meanwhile, the Philistines were raiding the Shephelah and the Negev, taking and occupying "Beth Shemesh, Aijalon and Gederoth, as well as Soco, Timnah, and Gimzo, with their surrounding villages" (2 Chron. 28:18). Moreover, the Edomites, apparently with Rezin's help and instigation, took the Negev and occupied Elath, the seaport city, which now gave Damascus control of the trade route and all of the king's highway from Elath to Damascus. Ahaz was being hammered from all sides.

But his greatest contest came in the form of the Syro-Ephraimite alliance. Kings Rezin and Pekah were determined either to get Ahaz's cooperation in their anti-Assyrian venture or to replace him on the throne with the unnamed son of Tabeel (Isa 7:6). Tabeel may well have been a son or relative of King Tubail (=Tabeel), king of Tyre, for Tyre was a strong advocate of the anti-Assyrian forces. This was more than an empty threat, for the dynasty of Menahem/Pekahiah had been removed by Pekah just as he now threatened to remove Ahaz. More was at stake than the mere removal of King Ahaz—the entire reigning line of the house of David was now threatened with extinction as well as the liquidation of the eternal covenant given to David by Nathan (2 Sam. 7; 1 Chron. 17). No wonder, then, that "the hearts of Ahaz and his people were shaken, as the trees of the forest are shaken by the wind" when

6. This section will be more detailed than most due to the central role it played in the prophet Isaiah's view of history and the way events shaped up for the divine plan in history (Isa. 7–12).

they were told that "Aram has allied itself with Ephraim" (Isa. 7:2). If successful, this action could have removed more than the political fortunes of the house of David; it could have removed the divine promises embodied in the Davidic covenant—Messiah and the coming kingdom of God!

The prophet Isaiah urged Ahaz to follow a course of independence, regardless of the threats and boasts of these two kings; for if he did, both of these kings would be removed within the time limits set by the sign of an (as yet) unborn son in the Davidic line. Indeed, before he would be mature enough to know right from wrong (Isa. 7:10–16), the threat from these two kings would be gone.

Ahaz's response was to avoid the prophet's fine words of the promised intervention of God and to appeal instead to Tiglath-Pileser III for help. However, it had hardly been necessary to call Tiglath-Pileser III's attention to what was happening in Syria-Palestine. There is a strong possibility that his armies were already on the march when Ahaz's letter was received and the "gift" (which was really a bribe) from Ahaz was placed in his hands. He was, no doubt, delighted to have one isolated spot of support in the middle of a seething sea of anti-Assyrian sentiment from Philistia, Edom, Ammon, Moab, Israel, and Damascus. Thus Judah provided a needed foothold and a base of operations against the insurgents. However, contrary to Ahaz's hopes, "Tiglath-Pileser king of Assyria came to him, but he gave him trouble instead of help" (2 Chron. 28:20). This must have been a most bitter pill for Ahaz to swallow! Edom was not restored to Judah's control, nor was the seaport of Elath; in fact, even Judah's title to Ammon, won by Ahaz's father Jotham, was not recognized by the Assyrian tyrant. Instead, what had begun as a "gift" from Ahaz for certain pressures that Tiglath-Pileser was to place on Rezin and Pekah turned out to be a requirement for an annual tribute laid on Judah. The Assyrian king simply interpreted the "gift" as the first installment on an annual tribute; thus Ahaz, in his attempt to bypass the divine promise offered by Isaiah the prophet, ran headlong into the arms of Assyrian domination and taxation.

Even more autocratic and frustrating to Ahaz was the fact that Tiglath-Pileser boldly bypassed Damascus and Samaria, directing instead his first blow against Philistia, presumably in order to secure his southern flank from exposure to Egypt. Hanno of Gaza, another ringleader in the anti-Assyrian caucus, was defeated as he fled to Egypt. But when his city fell, Hanno submitted and was reinstalled as a vassal to the Assyrian crown. It was at this point, one would assume, that the Syro-Ephraimite armies withdrew their siege of Jerusalem.

In order to get to Philistia, Tiglath-Pileser had to march through the northern districts of Pekah's kingdom and his coastal plain. The populations of these areas Tiglath-Pileser began to deport to other areas as he transformed these territories into Assyrian provinces in 734 B.C. In 733 B.C., Tiglath-Pileser set out to crush Damascus while isolating it from Samaria. First, he conquered the Transjordanian area of Gilead from Israel's rule. Then he turned north and defeated the Syrian armies. Rezin was able to hold out in Damascus until the next year, 732 B.C., but he was then soundly defeated and more Assyrian provinces were established in its place.

Pekah had so little left around Samaria by this time that it was not worth the effort of an expedition. Instead, he was left to his own fate: Hoshea slew him and seized the throne and kingdom of Israel—such as was left!

Ahaz under Shalmaneser V and Sargon II

Ahaz maintained his servility to Assyria for the rest of his life. When Tiglath-Pileser died in 727 B.C., Kings Elulaeus of Tyre and Hoshea of Samaria rebelled and withheld their tribute. But the son and successor of the Assyrian throne, Shalmaneser V, reacted with unexpected speed. He dispatched his troops, while he was detained at home, to the critical areas that had rebelled. Stunned by this prompt and efficient response to their withdrawal of tribute, both the Tyrian and Israelite kings hastily agreed to pay the tribute laid on them.

A temporary lull settled over the area for the next two years. However, Egypt (involving the "So" of the Bible), relying on Hoshea and Elulaeus, once again withheld tribute in 724 B.C., counting on their enhanced chances of success this time by the revolt in at least one north Syrian state, Que (Cilicia), which had previously been reduced to the status of an Assyrian province. About this same time, Mita of Muski (the Midas of Phrygia) pushed from central Asia Minor (Anatolia) to invade the province of the Cilician coast.

Shalmaneser V decided that it was time to deal with these pestering trouble spots once and for all. The approach of the Assyrian armies brought about the defection of Sidon and other cities under Tyrian control. The troops pushed on relentlessly and forced Hoshea into his capital of Samaria, where a siege began in the winter of 724 B.C. After less than two and one-half years, the capital of Israel capitulated without any Egyptian help being in evidence. King Hoshea and 27,290 Israelites were deported. Shalmaneser died shortly after this, leaving Sargon II, who also listed Samaria as one of his conquests, though he clearly was too late to have conducted and ended the siege. The northern ten tribes had disappeared from history as a national entity, never to be heard from again; their land was intermingled with settlers from distant lands to replace the deportees.

One would have thought that Ahaz would have been sobered by the events that Shalmaneser V precipitated in capturing the city of Samaria in 722 B.C., but there is no evidence of change in his lifestyle or religious affections. However, while Sargon's accession occasioned numerous uprisings in all the Assyrian Empire, Ahaz made no such moves.

Sargon, a usurper, was faced with challenges from the alliance of the Elamites and Babylonians at Dor, some eighty miles northeast of Babylon. The leader of the Babylonian forces in this contest was none other than Marduk-apla-iddina (otherwise known in the Bible as Merodach-Baladan). For a full year Sargon II appeared to be unable to take any direct action against this new Babylonian usurper. He had to stabilize his throne and cope with critical emergencies in the west. Sargon left a skeleton army in Syria while he fell upon the king of Elam before Merodach-Baladan could come to his support. Both sides claimed victory, but Babylonia remained lost to the Assyrian Empire.

Meanwhile Syria was aflame with revolt. The king of Hamath, previously loyal to Tiglath-Pileser, had been overthrown by a certain Ilubidi (or: Iaubidi). Other provinces were now following his lead as the Assyrians no longer seemed invincible. At Qarqar, just as in the time of Ahab, another battle was fought and Iaubidi lost his life and his throne. Hamath was made an Assyrian province.

Now Sargon II followed the classic pattern set by Tiglath-Pileser as he marched down the coast, aiming his first blows at the king of Gaza and his Egyptian ally, whose pharaoh was in the field at the battle of Raphia on the Egyptian border. Sargon captured Hanno, king of Gaza, deported him, and gave Gaza a new vassal status. Tyre was never conquered, but it was "pacified" under a formula in which both sides saved face. Sargon once again returned to Palestine in 711 B.C. to stop a revolt in the Philistine city of Ashdod.

The Reign of Hezekiah

Hezekiah began his reign as a coregent with his father Ahaz for thirteen years of his forty-two total years of reign from 729 to 686 B.C. (2 Kings 18–20; 2 Chron. 29–32). Hezekiah was only eleven years old when he began his coregency with his father Ahaz in the third year of Hoshea king of Israel (2 Kings 18:1) in 729 B.C; he was twenty-five years of age (2 Kings 18:2) when he began his sole reign in 715 B.C. As a veritable youngster, he had little or no positive impact on the spiritual conditions that existed while his father ruled. But by the time he became sole ruler, he had seen and witnessed enough to have determined that things would definitely change when he came to power.

Hezekiah's Reformation

Hezekiah reversed all of the spiritual bankruptcy that he had observed in 715 B.C. when he began to rule independently of his father. He initiated a return to Yahweh and severed all ties with Assyria (2 Kings 18:3–7). Hezekiah reopened and repaired the temple his father had closed. He destroyed all the foreign cults that had been installed since the time of Ahaz's subservience to his Assyrian overlords.

Hezekiah's Reform Measures

Reform Measure	Text
"He [re]opened the doors of the temple."	2 Chron. 29:3
"They brought out to the courtyard . . . everything unclean . . . and carried it out to the Kidron Valley"	2 Chron. 29:16
"Purified the entire temple of the LORD."	2 Chron. 29:18a
"Purified . . . the altar of burnt offering with all its utensils."	2 Chron. 29:18b
"Purified . . . the table for setting out the consecrated bread, with all its articles."	2 Chron. 29:18c
"Consecrated [the priests]."	2 Chron. 29:5, 15

In an attempt to appeal to what remained of any northern Jewish people, Hezekiah made the temple the center of attention and worship. He also adopted the Israelite calendar, which began in the spring; this had the advantage of being in tune with the Assyrian calendar, which also began in the spring, rather than the older Judean calendar that began in the fall.

Hezekiah also reinaugurated the celebration of the Passover, commemorating both the kingdoms' liberation from Egyptian bondage when they had been one united people. This was another move to reconcile the disparate peoples of Israel into a united nation once again. In fact, when the month of Passover arrived, it was impossible to observe it at the proper time, for too few priests were ceremonially qualified (2 Chron. 30:1–9). Because there was insufficient time to advertise the event in both kingdoms, Hezekiah postponed the festival until the second month as messengers went out from Dan to Beersheba to extend the invitation. Few of the northerners chose to attend, but a great crowd did gather, though some worshippers were still ceremonially unclean—another evidence of the spiritual laxity of the times. Hezekiah interceded for those so unqualified that Yahweh would look instead to their devoted hearts and not to their unclean hands (2 Chron. 30:18–19). The celebration continued past the seven days into fourteen days in an event unmatched since the days of Solomon.

Among the vestiges of the pagan cults that had to be dealt with by this reformation was the bronze serpent that Moses had made and raised up in the wilderness. What Moses had intended only as a symbol had become, instead, the object of veneration (2 Kings 18:3–4; 2 Chron. 31:1).

The Passover celebration included a covenant renewal followed by a reorganization of all religious personnel in accordance with the Law of Moses. To meet the needs of the revamped priesthood and Levitical staff, a tithe was brought that so exceeded expectations that new storage facilities had to be erected to contain all the goods. Some were appointed to oversee the allotment of these goods.

Hezekiah's Rebellion against Sargon

While these movements for spiritual reform were underway, negotiations were simultaneously going on with Egypt and other Palestinian kingdoms in preparation for what would be known as the Ashdod revolt, which came in 712 B.C. Neither Kings nor Chronicles makes any reference to this revolt, or its outcome. But the focus of the action seemed to be on King Azuri of Ashdod, who withheld his tribute to Assyria; accordingly, Sargon sent his field marshal (*tartān*) to Ashdod

(Isa 20:1). Azuri was replaced by his brother Ahimiti, and presumably Hezekiah and the others quickly paid up the withheld tribute.[7]

Having secured allegiance from the western states, Sargon turned to deal once again with Merodach-Baladan of the Sealands Dynasty in Babylon. He also had to attend to matters on the northwestern flank, coming to terms with King Mita in 709 B.C. Finally, in 706 B.C. Sargon had to face the Cimmerians in the north, losing his life in 705 B.C., possibly as a result of fighting with the Cimmerians.

Hezekiah's Revolt against Sennacherib

Sennacherib, Sargon's son, came to the throne in 705 B.C. and ruled until 681 B.C. He moved the capital from Dur-Sharrukin back to Nineveh. But he too was immediately faced with the rebellion of the same Merodach-Baladan, who had just returned from exile. Sennacherib took the city of Babylon and completed a systematic subjugation of the entire Sealands area. But Merodach-Baladan amazingly bounced back once again in 700 B.C., being put down once more, with Assur-nadin-sumi, Sennacherib's son, installed as regent over Babylon. Hezekiah took advantage of this preoccupation of Sennacherib with Babylon and revolted once more.

Hezekiah had made enormous preparations for the expected Assyrian retaliation. He had constructed further fortifications, made new weapons, reinforced his military, and built stables and storehouses in the city (2 Chron. 32:5, 28–30; Isa. 22:8–11). Especially significant was the "broad wall" that Hezekiah built outside the city (2 Chron. 32:5). This massive wall (sometimes up to seven meters wide), sixty-five meters of which have been found in the Old City of Jerusalem by N. Avignad, must have been built after the 701 offensive by Sennacherib, for the pottery sherds found in connection with this wall belong to the eighth and seventh centuries B.C.[8]

---

7. The best overview of this campaign is Gerald L. Mattingly, "An Archaeological Analysis of Sargon's 712 Campaign against Ashdod," *NEASB* 17 (1981): 47–64.

8. See N. Avigad, "Excavations in the Jewish Quarter of the Old City of Jerusalem 1969/1970," *IEJ* 20 (1970): 1–8, 129–40; idem., "Excavations in the Jewish Quarter of the Old City of Jerusalem," *IEJ* 22 (1972): 193–200 and idem, *Discovering Jerusalem* (Nashville: Thomas Nelson, 1980), 46–57. Due to the influx of refugees from Israel and later from the part of Judah Sennacherib had given over to the Philistines in 701 B.C., Jerusalem expanded to the western hill, thus forming the *mishneh*, "second city" mentioned in 2 Kings 22:14 and being the possible justification for the dual form indicated in the Hebrew writing of the name *Yerushalayim*. See M. Broshi, "The Expansion of Jerusalem in the Reign of Hezekiah and Manasseh," *IEJ* 24 (1974): 21–26. Also A. D. Tushingham, "The Western Wall under the Monarchy," *ZDPV* 95 (1979): 39–55; idem., "The Western Boundary of Jerusalem at the End of the Monarchy," *IEJ* 29 (1979): 84–91.

Hezekiah also gave special attention to stopping up the water supplies at the Gihon Spring outside the city that the enemy might use. Then he built the famous Siloam Tunnel from the concealed Gihon Spring. In an amazing engineering feat, workers cut an aqueduct from both ends of the course it was to take, meeting in the middle—all this for almost a third of a mile (about 534 meters long) through solid rock beneath Jerusalem (2 Kings 20:20; 2 Chron. 32:3–4, 30). Excavators coming from opposite directions finally joined their respective courses with only a slight miscalculation of a few inches, possibly because they followed the natural fissures in the limestone. An inscription in Hebrew, found near the Siloam end of the tunnel, is one of the most important monumental pieces of writing from this period of Judah's history.[9]

It was no surprise to learn that Sennacherib marched west in 701 B.C. to engage Judah and Egypt at Eltekeh (*Tell esh-Shallaf*), west of Gezer. First, Sennacherib dealt with Tyre, the leading city in that coastal region. Tyre's king Luli fled to Cyprus, disheartening the kings of Byblos, Arvad, Moab, Edom, and Ammon into submission. Then the Assyrian monarch moved against the other leading city of Ashdod, deporting its king Sidqia to Assyria.

Next Sennacherib moved up to Jerusalem. On the way he laid siege to Lachish. Although the Assyrian texts do not mention Lachish, Sennacherib pictured this siege with graphic and lavish detail on his palace walls in Nineveh.[10] The archaeology of the 701 campaign of Sennacherib is one of the richest moments in the archaeology of the Iron Age in Israel. In addition to the biblical record, there are the archaeological excavations of Lachish and Jerusalem and the Nineveh reliefs. The combination of these four sources is one of the most significant moments in the historiography of the ancient Near East and of biblical archaeology. Especially revealing are the Assyrian reliefs that come from the southwest palace of Nineveh depicting the capture of Lachish. There Sennacherib is presented as sitting on his throne (*nimedu*) while the people of Lachish pass in front of him with their carts and belongings. The scene is filled with pathos, for the people are leaving the city as a spoil for the Assyrians as the populace heads out for deportation. Likewise, the graphic depiction of the capture of the city itself is one

---

9. V. Sasson, "The Siloam Tunnel Inscription," *PEQ* 114 (1982): 111–17; also James Pritchard, ed., *ANET*, p. 321. The Hebrew inscription was discovered in 1880.

10. See James Pritchard, *ANEP*, figs. 371–74. For a description of a pit where as many as fifteen hundred people were buried en masse, see G. Ernest Wright, *Biblical Archaeology*, rev. ed. (Philadelphia: Westminster, 1962), 167–72.

filled with violence and enormous energy as the walls are breached and many lives are lost. It is the closest that we come to a photograph of a historical event from antiquity.[11]

While this battle was being waged, Hezekiah indicated that he would now pay the tribute (2 Kings 18:14–16). He also released Padi, the former king of Ekron, who had been deposed by the coalition for his refusal to cooperate in the revolt. But Sennacherib was not satisfied with this show of submission. Instead, he sent three lieutenants with the titles of Tartan (*turtannu*, meaning "second in rank"), Rabsaris (*rabushareshi*, meaning "chief eunuch") and Rabshakeh (*rab shaqu*, meaning "chief officer") to exercise some psychological warfare on Hezekiah. They appealed to every trick in the books in order to frighten Hezekiah into full submission. For example, reading their declamation of Hezekiah aloud so that all the Judeans on the wall could hear for themselves in Hebrew, they urged that resistance was useless against someone who was irresistible. Certainly an invincible conqueror would not be stopped by such an insignificant kingdom as Judah. Furthermore, appeal to their God Yahweh was useless as well since Hezekiah had instituted so many reforms that Yahweh probably was angry with him and therefore would not come to his aid!

The results of Hezekiah's submission were disastrous for Judah, for he had to pay an exorbitant tribute which left the temple and palace treasuries practically empty. Sennacherib must have still been smarting from Hezekiah's vacillation of loyalty, for he surrounded the city and would have forced it into total submission had not Yahweh intervened and forced him to abandon the siege immediately. Sennacherib lost 185,000 troops as a result of some divine intervention, according to the Bible. Herodotus[12] explained this loss as a result of mice devouring the quivers, bows, and shield handles of the warriors. Whether that is a garbled reflection of a sudden attack of the bubonic plague, which Yahweh may have used as his instrument of judgment, cannot be determined. Naturally, Sennacherib mentions nothing of this enormous loss in keeping with the general Assyrian policy that reports only the successes and not the losses. Sennacherib satisfied himself with noting that he

---

11. See R. D. Barnett, *Assyrian Palace Reliefs and their Influence on the Sculptures of Babylonia and Persia*_(London, 1960), plates 44–46; cf. D. D. Luckenbill, *ARAB*, II, paragraph 489; James Pritchard, ed., *ANET*, p. 288; also, Anson F. Rainey, "The Fate of Lachish during the Campaigns of Sennacherib and Nebuchadnezzar," *Lachish* V. *Investigations at Lachish*;ed. Y. Ahoroni, et al. (Tell Aviv, 1975), 51–52; I Eph`al, "The Assyrian Siege Ramp at Lachish: Military and Lexical Aspects," *Tel Aviv* 11 (1984): 64.

12. Herodotus, 2.141. See also Jack Finegan, *Light from the Ancient Past*, 2nd ed. (Princeton: Princeton University Press, 1959), 213–14.

took forty-six of Hezekiah's cities and shut him up in Jerusalem "like a bird in a cage."[13] There was little use in resisting any further, for large areas of Judah had been stripped from his control and the treasuries had been depleted to the point of being negligible.[14]

Two other events are significant for Hezekiah's life, both related to the Assyrian campaign just mentioned. The first was the severe illness of Hezekiah, from which he recovered due to divine intervention. This happened right at, just after, the time when Sennacherib invaded the land. Hezekiah prayed that he might recover from his sickness and through the prophet Isaiah, Yahweh granted him fifteen more years of life.

Shortly after Hezekiah's recovery, the second event took place: a state visit from the messengers of Merodoch-Baladan of Babylon (Isa. 39:1). While the ostensible purpose of their visit was to wish Hezekiah well on his recovery, there can be little doubt that the real purpose was to gain a comrade who would make common cause with them in their power struggle with Assyria. The lavish gifts that this diplomatic mission brought to Hezekiah was matched by the Judean king's candor and openness as he showed them all the wealth that Judah owned. But for this act, Hezekiah was soundly rebuked by Isaiah, who prophesied that one day the nation these men represented would come and seize the treasury that Hezekiah had so nonchalantly exposed for all to view.

The Reign of Manasseh

Hezekiah's son, Manasseh, holds the record for the longest reign of any monarch in Israel or Judah: fifty-five years (696–642 B.C.; 2 Kings 21:1–18; 2 Chron. 33:1–20). For the fifth time in a row, this Judean king began as a coregent with his father during the eleven years of

13. See the text of the Cylinder of Sennacherib in James Pritchard, *ANET*, pp. 287–89. The Cylinder of Sennacherib is a hexagon prism containing an account of his westward expedition that enlarges on the biblical account given of his invasion into Palestine in 701 B.C.

14. The argument that Sennacherib undertook two campaigns against Jerusalem, fifteen years apart, argued by Albright and Bright (William F. Albright, *BASOR* 130 (1953): 8–11; 141 (1956): 23–27; John Bright, *History of Israel*, pp. 298–309), has not won general support. The argument rests on the fact that Tirhakah of Nubia (2 Kings 19:9), who led the Egyptian army against Sennacherib, was only fourteen to eighteen years old in 701 B.C. He could not have been a military commander at that age; thus he must have led another campaign fifteen years later in 686 B.C. The claim that Tirhakah was a teenager in 701 B.C. rests on a miscalculation of the chronology of the Twenty-fifth Dynasty of Egypt and stelae 4 and 5 from Kawa. Kenneth Kitchen has shown that Tirhakah was twenty or twenty-one in 701 B.C. and was able to be at the very least the "titular head of the expedition," who was probably called "the Cushite king" in 2 Kings 19:9 in proleptic anticipation of his kingship that began in 690 B.C. See Kenneth Kitchen, *Third Intermediate Period*, pp. 157–61.

696–686 B.C., perhaps prompted by his father's near fatal disease sometime around 701 B.C.

What is most puzzling about Manasseh's reign is his total lack of godliness, the direct opposite of his father. Why had Hezekiah left no imprint on his son's life? Manasseh embraced and zealously promoted the Canaanite cults and their trappings. Altars to Baal were erected and the image of Asherah was everywhere, even within the holy temple of Yahweh itself. The arts and practices of sorcery, divination, witchcraft, spiritists, and necromancers all reappeared in Israel in the days of Ahab and Jezebel. Manasseh even offered his own sons in the Valley of Hinnom to Molech as human sacrifices![15] His was a deliberate, but total, abandonment of righteousness as set forth in the law and in prophets such as Isaiah and Hosea. Now the criteria that had brought judgment to Samaria would apply to Judah's capital Jerusalem.

Eventually, Manasseh was carried off to Babylon (2 Chron. 33:11), probably by Asshurbanipal (668–627 B.C.), the son and successor of Esarhaddon. Some scholars argue that the deportation site of "Babylon" is an error for Nineveh, but that is not necessary. Esarhaddon had rebuilt Babylon after his father Sennacherib had destroyed it and made it once again a part of the Assyrian Empire around 648 B.C. The Assyrian texts show that Manasseh was a vassal of Ashurbanipal as early as 667 B.C. Accordingly, he must have violated his agreements with Ashurbanipal to merit being deported to Babylon by the Assyrians in 648 B.C. He was taken into captivity in hooks and fetters (2 Chron. 33:11), a most humiliating posture for one who was a king.

There is no way to determine how long Manasseh stayed in Babylon, but it is clear that he did return to Jerusalem a changed person. He tore

15. In recent years, renewed work at Carthage and other sites of the Punic Empire in the west, such as Sardinia, have added to our cumulative knowledge of child sacrifice in antiquity. Reference to the cult of Molech appears in the Torah in Leviticus 18:21, 20:1–5, and Deuteronomy 18:10. King Josiah, Manasseh's grandson, put an end to this practice in 2 Kings 23:10 by "desecrat[ing] Topheth, which was in the Valley of Ben Hinnom, so no one could use it to sacrifice his son or daughter in the fire of Molech." Topheth, located in the environs of Jerusalem, recalls Isaiah 30:33, where the prophet depicts the destruction of the enemy in a firepit, in the same way that human sacrifices were being consumed in the fire of Topheth. See L. E. Stager, "The Rite of Child Sacrifice at Carthage," in *New Light on Ancient Carthage*, ed. J. G. Pedley (Ann Arbor: University of Michigan Press, 1980), 1–11; L. E. Stager and S. R. Wolf, "Child Sacrifice at Carthage: Religious Rite or Population Control?" *BAR* 10 (1984): 30–51. Also P. G. Mosca, *Child Sacrifice in Canaanite and Israelite Religion: A Study in Mulk and MLK*. (Ph.D. dissertation, Harvard University, 1975); G. C. Heider, *The Cult of Molek: A Reassessment*. *JSOT Sup*. 43 (Sheffield: JSOT Press, 1985); Frank Moore Cross, "A Phoenician Inscription from Idalion: Some Old and New Texts Relating to Child Sacrifice," in *Scripture and Other Artifacts: Essays on Bible and Archaeology in Honor of Philip J. King* (Louisville, Ky.: Westminster/John Knox, 1994), 93–107; and J. Day, *Molech: A God of Human Sacrifice in the Old Testament*, University of Cambridge Oriental Publications, 41 (Cambridge: Cambridge University Press, 1989).

down all the vestiges of pagan worship and restored the worship of Yahweh. In addition to these expressions of his repentance and faith, he also refortified Jerusalem and several other cities. No doubt the fortification work was done in cooperation with the Assyrians, for they still regarded him as a vassal.

What happened in the remainder of Manasseh's rule after his return back to Jerusalem is unattested anywhere, but he must have reigned for some four or five years after that event.

The Reign of Amon

The spiritual change in Manasseh must have had little to no effect on his son, for Amon reverted to his father's previous style of life as he revived the old paganism that Manasseh had inaugurated and then attempted to destroy towards the end of his life. Apparently the impressions made on Amon's life during his earlier years were not eradicated by the late conversion of Manasseh, for Amon was born some sixteen years before his father's conversion. Even Amon's name is another indication of the former symbiotic relationship that existed between paganism and Manasseh's Judah: Amon is most frequently associated with the Egyptian sun-god, Amon.

Amon ruled only for two years, from 642 to 640 B.C. (2 Kings 21:19–26; 2 Chron. 33:21–25), coming to the throne when he was twenty-two years of age. Amon would have been born, interestingly enough, in the very year (664 B.C.) that Ashurbanipal and the western allies defeated the Egyptians.

After his two-year reign, Amon was killed in a palace conspiracy by his "servants," i.e., the officials of the court. His death was requited in a sense, for "the people of the land" rose up to execute those who had conspired against their king, and they placed his eight-year-old son, Josiah, on the throne in his place.

The century of Assyrian dominance was coming to a close. Already the ominous head of Babylon was being raised with such frequency that some could have guessed where the power of the empire would move next. But it was just as clear that Judah also was in her final moments as a nation. Manasseh's repentance had come in time for his own personal deliverance, but it had come too late for the deliverance of the nation, just as Amon's lifestyle evidenced.

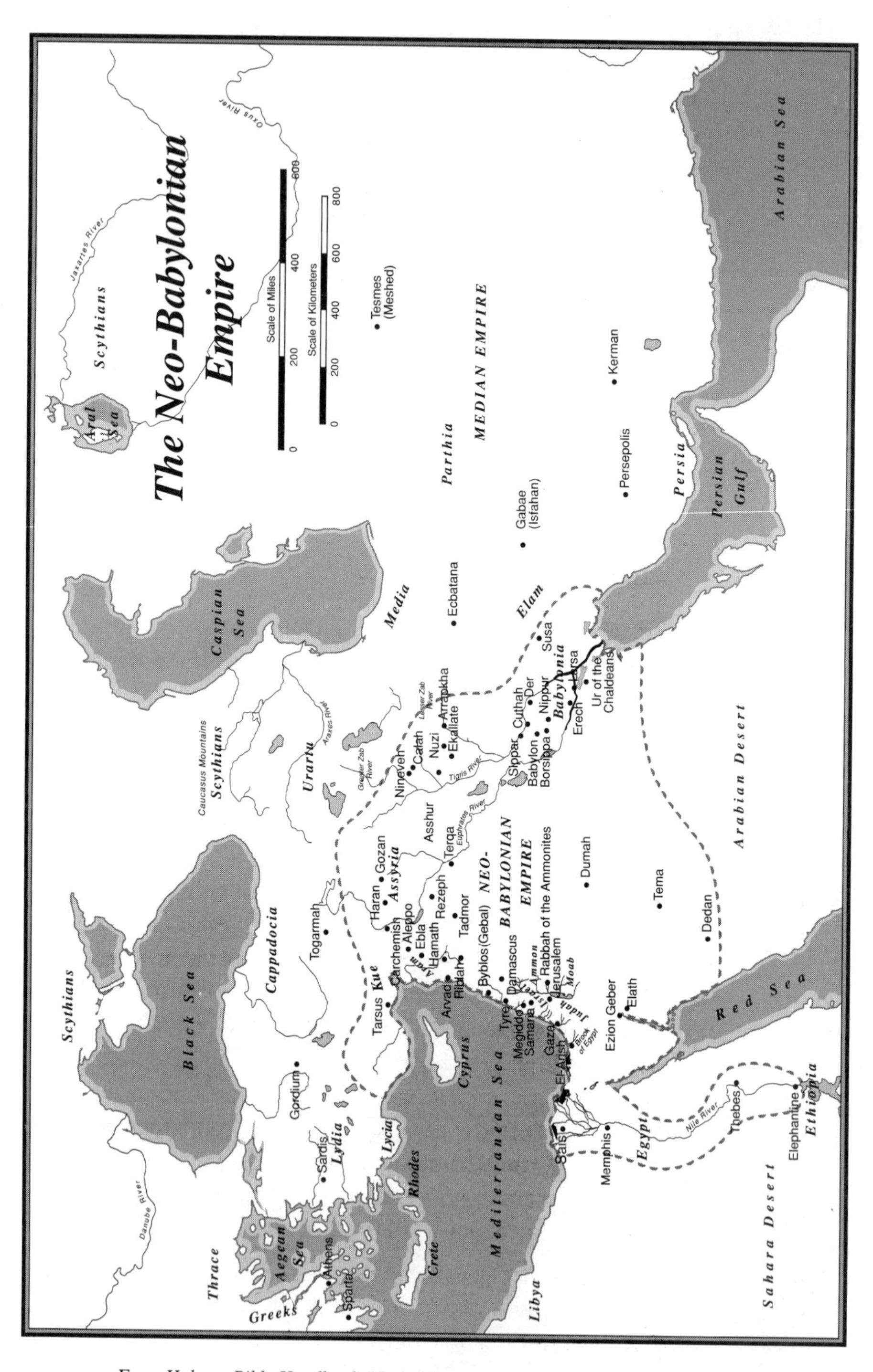

From *Holman Bible Handbook* (Nashville: Holman Bible Publishers, 1992), 388.

26

THE ERA OF BABYLONIAN HEGEMONY (640–539 B.C.)

The era from 640 to 539 B.C. is one of the best-documented periods in Hebrew history. Not only does 2 Kings 21–25 and 2 Chronicles 33–36 devote a large amount of space to the events of this time (though Josiah's reform occupied the greater portion of those texts), but this material is supplemented by the extensive references found in the prophets—especially the writings of Jeremiah, along with his colleagues of this same period: Ezekiel, Nahum, Zephaniah, and Habakkuk. In addition, the Babylonian Chronicle[1] supplies a rather detailed commentary for the decades surrounding the fall of Jerusalem.

Archaeological excavations at many Judean sites evidence the destructive presence of Nebuchadnezzar's campaigns. This path of havoc extends from *Tell ed-Duweir* (Lachish) in the west, to Arad in the south, and to En-gedi in the east. Some cities, especially those north of Jerusalem in the territory of Benjamin, escaped much of this destruction.

Another source for reconstructing the history of the period is the more than two hundred Hebrew and Aramaic ostraca, i.e., inscribed potsherds. Many of these are letters dating to the last years of Judah.

1. The *Babylonian Chronicle* is not a single document, but a genre of texts giving selective summaries of Babylonian reigns, including year-by-year records covering 626–623, and 616–595 B.C. See Donald J. Wiseman, *Chronicles of Chaldaean Kings (626–556 B.C.) in the British Museum* (London: British Museum, 1956).

Some, such as the twenty-two Lachish letters,[2] describe the conditions under the relentless hammering that Nebuchadnezzar gave to Judah. They refer to the preparations for battle, the use of signal fires from town to town as a means of communication during their sieges, and their concerns for the harvest, and the division of opinion among the people over the proper strategy in those days of Babylonian oppression.

The drama of the final years of Judah and the Davidic line of kings involved the three major international powers of the day: Assyria, Babylon, and Egypt. Of course, there were minor roles given to the Cimmerians, the Scythians, Medes, and other people groups who longed to fill the vacuums as Assyria began to show signs of weakening.

Three of the final four decades of the seventh century (640–609 B.C.) provided a glimmer of hope and the prospect for the revival of a restored and even a reunited nation as a result of Josiah's reform in 621 B.C. Alas, however, the maelstrom of international unrest proved too much for the last five Davidic kings of Judah in the last decade of the seventh century and the first decade and a half of the sixth century (600–587 B.C.). Two of the last five Davidic kings met their deaths as a direct result of involvement in these international struggles, while the other three died in exile.

Babylon's Rise to Power[3]

Assyria's superiority over the Near East declined rapidly and dramatically with the death of Asshurbanipal in 627 B.C. Already in 630 B.C. he had either abdicated the throne or made his son Ashur-etil-ilani coregent, perhaps fearing a dispute over succession or in recognizing that he was no longer effective in administering so large an empire. But his son inherited a real mess, both internally and externally. It is impossible to indicate just what the state of affairs was since Ashurbanipal's annals break off in 639 B.C.; thus his last years of reign are largely unknown to us.

---

2. For the collection of Lachish and Arad Letters, see D. Pardee, *Handbook of Ancient Hebrew Letter: A Study Edition* (Chico, Calif.: Scholars Press, 1982), 84–100; 31–64.

3. Among the vast bibliographical items, one should consult Seton Lloyd, *Foundations in the Dust: The Story of Mesopotamian Exploration* (Hammondsworth: Penguin Books, 1955); Peter R. Ackroyd. *Israel under Babylon and Persia* (London: Oxford University Press, 1970); H. W. F. Sagga. *The Greatness That Was Babylon: A Sketch of the Ancient Civilization of the Tigris-Euphrates Valley* (New York: Mentor Books, 1962).

The Death of Ashurbanipal

When Ashurbanipal died in 627 B.C., an Assyrian commander named Sin-shum-lishir had himself proclaimed king in Babylon. However, he was quickly defeated and Sin-shar-ishkun, a brother of Ashur-etil-ilani, another son of Ashurbanipal, became king of Babylon instead of the aspiring commander. This in turn led to four years of civil strife (627–623 B.C.) which, when combined with the external pressures on the kingdom, were enough to trouble the Assyrian house and eventually rock it to its foundations.

The external pressures on the Assyrian empire were coming from three seminomadic groups: the Cimmerians, the Scythians and the Medes. The Cimmerians had invaded Urartu in the eighth century and defeated the Urartians. Sargon II apparently had lost his life fighting with the Cimmerians in the province of Tabal in 706/05 B.C. The Cimmerians continued to challenge Assyria until the Scythians defeated them.

The Scythians were Indo-Europeans from the region of Crimea who moved into the areas of Asia Minor and eastward to the Iranian Plateau. The Medes were settled in northwestern Iran, consisting of a number of associated tribes. When they united under King Phraortes (ca. 647–624 B.C.), they became a rather formidable enemy for Assyria. Phraortes's son and successor, Cyaxares (ca. 623–584 B.C.) defeated the Scythians, but they rebounded enough to become a rather significant factor in the fall of Assyria.

Egypt and Babylon

The Twenty-sixth Dynasty of Egypt (Saite) enjoyed good relations with Assyria under its first two kings, Pharaohs Necho I and Psammetichus I. But Psammetichus decided to dispute Assyria's claim to Syria and Palestine, invaded Philistia, and set siege to Ashdod; Herodotus said the siege lasted twenty-nine years (Herodotus II.157), but he may have mistaken the year of the king's reign for the length of the siege. This was right about the time that Ashdod was seeking to free itself from the Assyrian subjugation. It was also the same time when the Scythians had moved down the eastern Mediterranean seaboard only to encounter the Egyptians. Herodotus reported that the Scythians were dissuaded from engaging in a military contest by gifts and prayers to come no farther (Herodotus I.105), even though the Scythians plundered the temple of the "heavenly Aphrodite" at Ashkelon. Thus Egypt was able to assert a position of strength that had not been seen in Palestine since the days of Rameses III in the twelfth century B.C. (1198–1166 B.C.) .

The Egyptians appeared to control the Via Maris, the highway running along the eastern Mediterranean seaboard from the late 630s to 620s B.C. This is demonstrated by the statuary and artifacts found among the possessions of the early Saite pharaohs from as far north as Arvad and from inscriptional evidence such as the Babylonian Chronicle or Wadi Brisa inscriptions, which suggest that portions of the Phoenician, Palestinian and Syrian areas were subjugated by Egypt. Thus Assyrian control over Judah during the previous century was now giving way to Egyptian dominance.

Egyptian policy changed after the fall of Nineveh in 611 B.C. No longer was Assyria painted as the villain Egypt had experienced in days past. The emergence of Babylon as the new power demanded that Egypt side with Assyria. One of the first acts of Pharaoh Necho II (609–593 B.C.) in 609 B.C. was to march his army to Carchemish to help the Assyrian Ashur-uballit retake Haran from the Babylonians. It was as Necho marched through the Megiddo Pass that he killed the disguised King Josiah in 609 B.C. Josiah was seeking to prevent the Egyptians from coming to the aid of the Assyrians. While Necho was unsuccessful at Haran, he managed to take Kadesh on the Orontes. Thus he was still able to claim control over much of Syria and Palestine. On his way home, Necho took Jehoahaz, Josiah's son, who had reigned a mere three months after his father's death in the battle at Megiddo, in chains to Egypt. In his place, Necho installed as Judean king another son of Josiah, a puppet named Eliakim, renamed Jehoiakim. Judah had to pay a heavy tribute to Necho of one hundred talents of silver and one talent of gold.

Necho would not be left alone and unchallenged by Babylon, however. The young Babylonian prince named Nebuchadnezzar, eventual heir to the throne in Babylon, gained a decisive victory over Necho at Carchemish in 605 B.C. Nebuchadnezzar would have chased Necho all the way back into Egypt, but he was called back to Babylon suddenly with the news that his father had died. The result was that "the king of Egypt did not march out from his own country again, because the king of Babylon had taken all his territory, from the Wadi of Egypt to the Euphrates River" (2 Kings 24:7). Accordingly, when the puppet whom Necho had placed on the Judean throne—Jehoiakim—rebelled against Nebuchadnezzar (597 B.C.), Necho did not even bother to come to his aid. Instead, Necho turned his attention to constructing a canal from the eastern arm of the Nile River to the Red Sea. But even this project was halted when an oracle warned that his canal would benefit the foreigner[4] or, as his engineers were alleged to have warned,[5] that the Red Sea was higher than the entire delta region and thus the entire delta would be flooded. In the meantime, Necho had built an impressive fleet that sailed both the Red Sea and the Mediterranean. In fact, he is most famous for commissioning a crew of Phoenician sailors to navigate around the southern tip of the African continent, a feat that took three years to complete.

Psammetichus II succeeded his father Necho II in 593 B.C. In 591 B.C. he led a retinue of priests to visit Phoenicia, where he laid a votive wreath on an Egyptian shrine at Byblos, but he made no attempt to challenge the Babylonians in Syria. Psammetichus was best known for his heavy dependence on Greek culture and Greek mercenaries.

In 588 B.C. Pharaoh Apries (Hebrew Pharaoh Hophra) came to the throne and immediately, but unwisely, contested Nebuchadnezzar's control over Syria. Joined by allies in Moab, Ammon, and the Judean king Zedekiah, Apries attacked the Phoenician cities of Tyre and Sidon. Nebuchadnezzar, camped at Riblah on the Orontes River, did not immediately respond to Apries but turned instead to besiege Jerusalem. But when Judah looked for help from Egypt, there was not much help there. Egypt did march to challenge Nebuchadnezzar in the summer of 588 B.C., causing the siege to be momentarily lifted from Jerusalem. However, Apries was outclassed by the Babylonians; thus Apries was driven back to Egypt and the siege of Jerusalem was again set in place.

During Apries's rule in Egypt, many Jews settled in Elephantine at the first cataract on the Nile River. Apries's army was composed of many mercenaries from Libya, Greece, and Syria. When trouble broke out among the Greek settlers at Cyrene, who had encroached on the territory of the Libyans, Apries sent a force of Egyptians to aid the Libyans, for he could not use Greek mercenaries against Greeks. But the Egyptian forces were annihilated by the Greeks of Cyrene. Apries sent a member of the royal household named Ahmose, or Amasis as Herodotus called him, to bring the rebels into submission. Amasis betrayed Apries, however, and was declared king by the disaffected Egyptian soldiers; thus Apries was forced to recognize a coregency. Nevertheless, war broke out among the Greek mercenaries who supported Apries and the native Egyptians who supported Amasis. Apries died while resting

4. Herodotus, *Histories*, II, 1.58
5. Diodorus, I, 33.9

in one of his few remaining vessels, where he was a virtual fugitive. Amasis occupied the throne until 525 B.C. in a forty-four-year reign in which the drift toward a Greek-oriented society continued. Greek merchants were permitted to trade only in one city in the western delta—Naucratis.

Nebuchadnezzar marched against Egypt in Nebuchadnezzar's thirty-seventh year. He did not conquer Egypt, but he did force Amasis to give up any plans he might have had to reconquer Syria and Palestine.

The Neo-Babylonian Emergence

In the eighteenth century B.C., Babylon had been the center of power in the Tigris-Euphrates Valley, but the power of the Old Babylonian Empire had declined as the political center shifted northward. Now after decades of troubling Assyria in the seventh century, the Babylonians had moved to reassert their independence and to become entangled in a struggle to dominate the Assyrian throne and the empire of the Assyrians.

The future of Babylon lay with Nabopolassar, the king of the Sealands, who had proclaimed himself king in 626 B.C. This meant that three armies were destined to fight it out: Nabopolassar, claimant to the throne of Babylon; Sin-shar-ishkun, who had been designated king of Babylon by his brother Ashur-etil-ilani, but who wanted to have his brother's job as king of Nineveh; and Ashur-etil-ilani, the successor to the Assyrian throne left vacant by Ashurbanipal. Nabopolassar emerged the victor after defeating the Assyrian army sent to subdue him in 626 B.C.

Sin-shar-ishkun also gained the throne of Assyria in 623 B.C. with Ashur-etil-ilani having fallen, apparently, in battle. But Sin-shar-ishkun's agreement with Nabopolassar expired, and the two fought for dominance in Mesopotamia.

What happened between 623 and 616 B.C. is unknown, for the Babylonian Chronicle has a gap for this period of time. Nabopolassar advanced up the Euphrates in 616 B.C., but had to withdraw before combined Assyrian and Egyptian forces. In 615 B.C. Nabopolassar attacked Ashur, the old Assyrian capital, where he was forced to flee to Takrit. Amazingly, the Assyrians continued the siege for only ten days, and Nabopolassar escaped.

In 612 B.C.[6] Nabopolassar joined forces with Cyaxeres the Mede to capture Assyria's capital of Nineveh. The Assyrians retreated westward to the city of Haran, but it too fell to the Babylonians and their allies

6. This date and event are most important for the history of this period. It was one of the major turning points in the history of the ancient Near East.

(e.g., the Scythians) in 610 B.C. The effort of the Egyptians and the Assyrians to retake Haran failed and the Assyrians never regained power.

Nabopolassar died in 605 B.C., just as his son Nebuchadnezzar was defeating the Egyptians at Carchemish and at Hamath. He returned to Babylon to claim the throne while he sent his troops to Syria and Palestine. It may have been at this time that Daniel and his three friends were taken with the other exiles noted in Daniel 1 during Jehoiakim's reign.

The effects of the Babylonian conquest of Carchemish and Hamath were impressive indeed. According to the Chronicle, all the kings of Hatti-land (the geographical term *Hatti* included at this time both Syria and Palestine) came before Nebuchadnezzar with heavy tribute in the first year of his reign. Egypt's control over the area must have been minimal, for all resistance suddenly collapsed.

The Reign of Josiah

After the assassination of Amon, "the people of the land" placed the eight-year-old son of Amon on the throne. He ruled for thirty-one years (640 to 609 B.C.), three of the best decades in Judah's latter years (2 Kings 22:1–23:30; 2 Chron. 34–35). During these years, Judah experienced no war from outside enemies and concentrated on rebuilding her land and her spiritual resources.

Josiah was a youngster when he was crowned. Idolatry was rampant in the land, but the effects of Josiah's godly advisors was more formative in his life than either that of his grandfather Manasseh or his father Amon. When he was sixteen years old, Josiah began to seek the God of his father David (2 Chron. 34:3), and at age twenty (628 B.C.) he began to cleanse the land of Judah and its capital of Jerusalem of all idolatrous objects that his immediate predecessors had introduced. Not only did he pursue this activity in Judah, but he also carried his campaign for cleansing and removal of false deities into northern Israel as well. His reforms reached "Manasseh, Ephraim and Simeon, as far as Naphtali, and in the ruins around them" (2 Chron. 34:6).

Josiah's Reformation

The reforms of Josiah's great grandfather, Hezekiah, had been undone by Josiah's grandfather, Manasseh. A reversal of this religious syncretism and idolatry came late in Manasseh's life, but too late to affect Josiah's father Amon, who in two brief years was able to reinstate the Canaanite cults and the abominations that had been removed on two earlier occasions in this brief chronology listed here. But Josiah plunged ahead, instituting reforms in his eighth regnal year (632 B.C.), when he was only sixteen years old (2 Chron. 34:3), his twelfth year (628), and his eighteenth regnal year (622 B.C.).

The reform that came in 622 B.C. was one of the most important episodes in Judah's history. Josiah purged the land of idolatry; then he moved to cleanse, renovate, and repair the temple at Jerusalem. The Levites collected money "from the people of Manasseh, Ephraim and the entire remnant of Israel and from the people of Judah and Benjamin and the inhabitants of Jerusalem" (2 Chron. 34:9). In the sixty years since Hezekiah had repaired the temple, it had, apparently, greatly deteriorated (2 Kings 22:5–6).

After the stone and timber had been purchased and after work on the temple restoration had commenced, Hilkiah the priest announced to Shaphan the secretary, "I have found the Book of the Law in the temple of the LORD" (2 Chron. 34:15). Shaphan took the Book of the Law to King Josiah at once and began reading it to him. So shocked was Josiah by the words he was hearing that he tore his clothes in deep contrition and fear for the imminent wrath and judgment that lay over the nation of Judah.

Scholars have argued over the precise contents of this scroll found by Hilkiah. Most will agree that it contained most of Deuteronomy, but it is even more likely that it contained the whole corpus of the Torah, given the frequent designation used for the first five books of the Bible and the identical expression used here.[7] What is most amazing is that the people of the Book could have so neglected it that it was entirely lost to that generation.

Josiah immediately wanted further confirmation and instruction in what he was understanding from the first reading of this Mosaic word. Hilkiah and the priests went to Huldah, a prophetess living in Jerusalem, to inquire just what the texts meant. She confirmed Josiah's worst fears: God was going to bring disaster upon that place: all the curses written in the scroll of the Law would be realized if the people did not repent. The populace was loath to respond in any heartfelt way. But because Josiah had humbled himself before Yahweh when he first heard

7. Nothing in the record indicates, either, that the book had just been written, as critical scholarship has contended. Since Manasseh had ordered all copies of the Law to be destroyed, someone may have been prompted to hide the copy in the temple as well.

this Book of the Law read, his eyes would not see this imminent disaster; instead he would be buried in peace (2 Chron. 34:23–28).

The radical contrast between the syncretistic emphases of the Canaanite cults and trappings with the lofty ideal announced in the Mosaic faith (2 Kings 22:11–20) was enough to set off one of the most epochal religious reformations in the history of Judah and Israel, even though it flared only for a decade or two. The prophets had at last found energetic leadership in one at the head of the government. Josiah set out to establish in the nation the norms established in the Book of the Law.

The king assembled his elders and all the people of Judah and Jerusalem to hear the reading of all the words of the Book of the Covenant (2 Kings 23:2). There, he led the people in renewing the covenant and in directing that every high place be broken down, the idolatrous priests be deposed, and all that smacked of sympathetic magic in the fertility cult be disposed of immediately. This included the pulling down of the altar built by Jeroboam I for the golden calf at Bethel (2 Kings 23:15). Josiah defiled this altar at Bethel by offering the dug-up bones of the priests that had been buried around this installation; his actions thereby fulfilled the prophecy of the unnamed prophet from Judah during the days of Jeroboam I (2 Kings 23:16; 1 Kings 13) that one named "Josiah" would come and would burn the very bones of the officiating priests at the altar of the golden calf on that very altar. Houses of religious prostitution were destroyed and child sacrifice to Molech in the Valley of Hinnom was also abolished.

The ceremony of covenant renewal was followed by a celebration of one of the greatest Passover feasts observed in Israel since the days of Samuel (2 Chron. 34:1–19), just as it was prescribed to be observed in the newly discovered scroll of the Law. The kings and other leaders offered a lavish number of sheep and goats as the temple musicians helped the nation to praise Yahweh.

While the Josianic reforms were most successful outwardly, there is little evidence that any significant inward change took place among the people. The populace had come to treat the temple and God himself as a good luck charm; this led to the deceptive sloganeering that announced: "The temple of Yahweh, the temple of Yahweh, the temple of Yahweh" (Jer. 7:3–4 author's translation). But, as Jeremiah the prophet warned, to claim that Judah was immune to disaster and destruction because God had given David and Jerusalem an everlasting covenant was as dangerous as saying that Shiloh would never be destroyed, for Shiloh too had once been the place where the tabernacle stood. History had shown that too was a lie, for Shiloh had long since been reduced to ashes. So the fallacy of such irresponsible claptrap was all the more alarming to a nation that was almost impervious to genuine repentance before Yahweh .

The Debacle at Megiddo

Little is known of Josiah's reign from 622 until 609 B.C. During these thirteen years, Assyria's power had diminished while Egypt's fortunes appeared to rise once again. Assyria's two main cities, Ashur and Nineveh, had already fallen in 614 and 612 B.C., respectively. In 610 B.C. Haran fell to Nabopolassar of Babylon, which just about finished Assyria. However, a desperate call from Asshur-uballit II of Assyria went out to Pharaoh Necho II in 609 B.C. to come to his aid and join him in fighting off the Babylonians.

Pharaoh Necho II succeeded his father Psammetichus as king of Egypt in 609 B.C. This appeared to Necho as a moment for Egypt to step back into the limelight as a leader of the Near East. King Josiah, however, had already declared his allegiance to Babylon. Therefore, he took steps to intercept Necho II at Megiddo, either to prevent or to impede Egypt's ability to rescue a nation that had brought such grief to Judah and Israel. The result was a tragic defeat for Judah and the untimely death of Josiah at thirty-nine years of age.

Pharaoh had warned Josiah to cease and desist from his opposition, for Necho declared that his mission was from God (2 Chron. 35:21–22), but Josiah refused this counsel. Instead, he disguised himself and fought Necho on the plain of Megiddo, where he was shot by the archers. He was removed from the battle and taken back to Jerusalem to be buried and mourned. This tragedy so impacted the nation that the postexilic chronicler reports that the laments Jeremiah composed for Josiah continued to be sung down to his own day (2 Chron. 35:25).[8]

The Prophets of Judah's Decline

During the last half of the seventh century, four prophets warned of Judah's potential disaster, the waning power of Assyria, and the rise of Babylonian hegemony. The best documented life and ministry is that of Jeremiah, who not only ministered during the last three decades of

8. S. B. Frost, "The Death of Josiah: A Conspiracy of Silence," *JBL* 87 (1966): 369–82.

the seventh century but continued beyond the destruction of Jerusalem in 587 B.C. The other three were Zephaniah, Habakkuk, and Nahum.

ZEPHANIAH (CA. 640–609 B.C.)

Zephaniah described himself as a descendant of Hezekiah, but whether this was the King Hezekiah or not is unknown; it is just strange that he went back for four generations if he was not trying to make a link with the godly king Hezekiah (Zeph. 1:1). Nor can it be precisely determined if his preaching came before or after Josiah's reform in 622 B.C. What he does describe, however, is precisely the same state of affairs that King Josiah addressed in his reform: the adoption of foreign customs (Zeph. 1:4–9), the worship of the Canaanite Baal, the Ammonite Milcom, and the Assyrian astral deities. He decried as strenuously as any prophet the violence, fraud, idolatry, and pride evidenced in the nation. So corrupt was Judah that:

> Her officials are roaring lions,
> her rulers are evening wolves,
> who leave nothing for the morning.
> Her prophets are arrogant;
> they are treacherous men.
> Her priests profane the sanctuary
> and do violence to the law (Zeph. 3:3–4).

The "day of Yahweh" would fall on all "those who turn back from following the LORD and neither seek the LORD nor inquire of him" (Zeph. 1:6). Judah could therefore expect distress, anguish, ruin, darkness, and devastation. The other nations likewise stood under the sovereign judgment of Yahweh (Zeph. 2:4–15). Yahweh's purpose, however, was not to bring judgment, but to bring redemption to both the nations and Judah if only they would turn back to Yahweh.

NAHUM (CA. 663–612 B.C.)

Nahum urged Assyria and her capital of Nineveh to repent. Writing some time after the sack of Thebes in 663 B.C., Nahum used Thebes as a model and example for Nineveh that felt she too was impervious (Nah. 3:8–10). Assyria's brutality was legendary—flaying the skins of its captives, impaling its victims on stakes outside besieged cites, and massacring, and decimating whole quarters of cities. Still, the unscrupulous Assyrians refused to heed any of Nahum's warnings and rushed headlong into the destined destruction of Nineveh in 612 B.C.

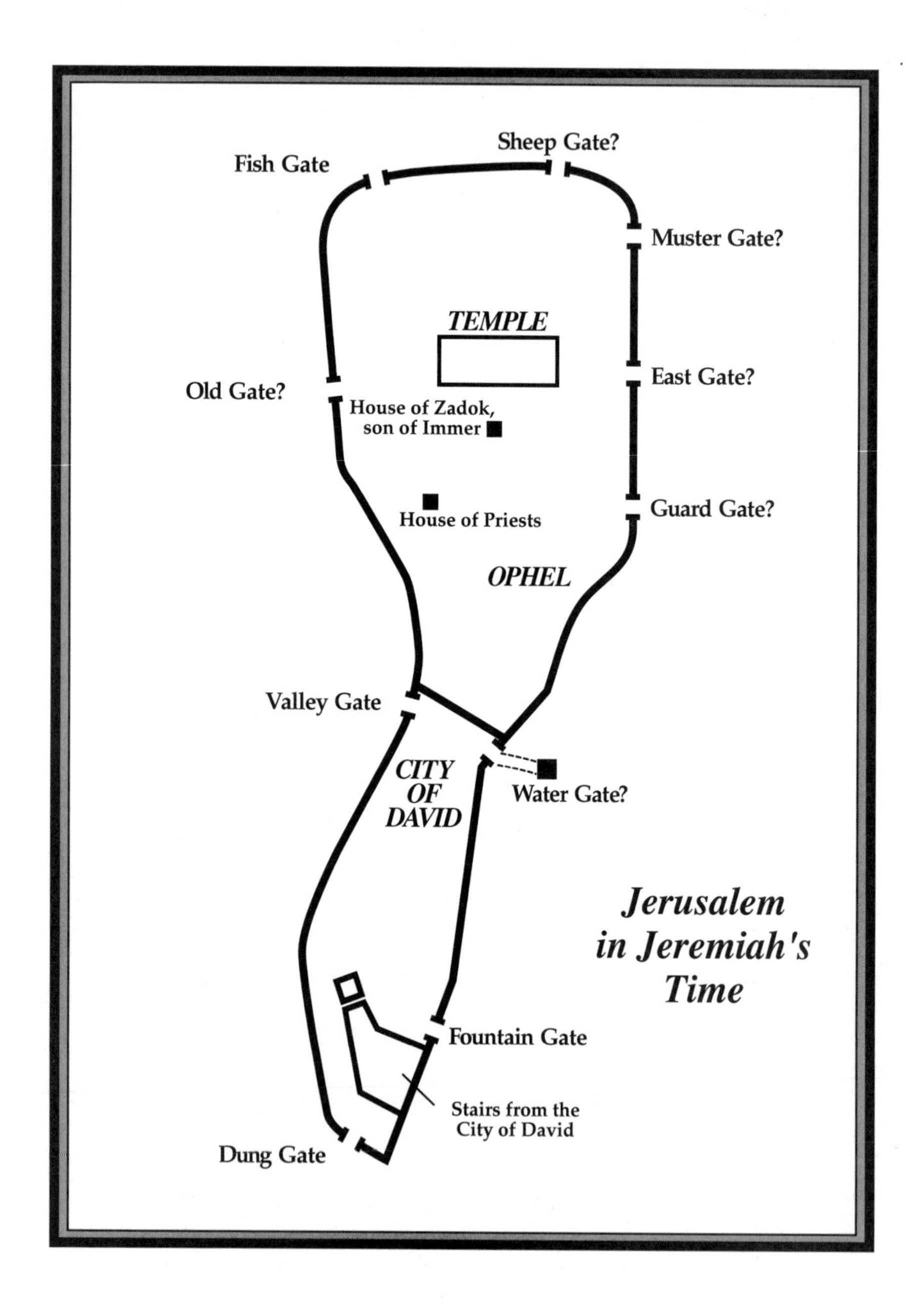

From *Holman Bible Handbook* (Nashville: Holman Bible Publishers, 1992), 400.

HABAKKUK (CA. 615–598 B.C.)

Habakkuk also interpreted the events of the end of the seventh century in light of Yahweh's sovereignty over history. He predicted that Babylon would accomplish such a work on Judah that it would be unbelievable in the day when he made his announcement. But his point was that a righteous God could not forever tolerate an unrighteous people, even if they had an everlasting covenant: Yahweh could carry out the promises of the covenant without involving most of the nation of Judah. Thus God answered the prophet's two questions: (1) Why has the Lord made me so sensitive to my own people's sin and yet he seems to do nothing about their sin? God's answer was that he was going to use Babylon to severely rebuke Judah for her sin. (2) Why would God use a people more wicked than we are to judge us for our sin? Answer: Silence! Consequently, Habakkuk would take his stand on his watchtower and wait to see what God would do, for just people really live, but they live by faith (Hab. 2:4). Then it was that the word came to Habakkuk that God would also judge Babylon for the brutal way in which they carried out the divine order to chastise Judah.

JEREMIAH

Jeremiah's call to minister (627–562 B.C.) came in the thirteenth year of Josiah's reign (627 B.C.) and continued through the reigns of Jehoahaz, Jehoiakim, Jehoiachin, and Zedekiah, even beyond the fall of Jerusalem. He remained in Jerusalem after 587 B.C., but then was taken to Egypt against his will. The last recorded message in his book is the release of Jehoiachin from prison by Evil-Murodach of Babylon in 562 B.C., which would have meant that Jeremiah was between eighty-five and ninety years old at the time. Thus he lived to see this rise in the fortunes of Jehoiachin.

Even though Jeremiah witnessed the revival and reformation under Josiah in 622 B.C., he also witnessed a most intransigent and rebellious people as they played into the hands of their own destruction more and more. Judah had abandoned Yahweh and pursued other gods instead. As he graphically put it:

> "My people have committed two sins:
> They have forsaken me,
> the spring of living water,
> and have dug their own cisterns,
> broken cisterns that cannot hold water"(Jer. 2:13).

Jeremiah came from the small village of Anathoth, two or three miles north of Jerusalem. He was from the family of priests in the line of Abiathar, whom Solomon had removed from authority (1 Kings 1:28–2:26). From such small and humble origins he was called to be a prophet to the nations.

In the fourth year of King Jehoiakim (ca. 605 B.C.), Yahweh instructed Jeremiah to write his prophecies on a scroll (36:1–2). Jeremiah was told by Yahweh, "Perhaps when the people of Judah hear about every disaster I plan to inflict on them, each of them will turn from his wicked way; then I will forgive their wickedness and their sin" (36:3). So Jeremiah called Baruch, son of Neriah, as his scribe, and had him write down the prophet's words as he dictated them to him. Baruch was then to take the words and read them in the house of the LORD (36:8). But when he carried out this act, the king ordered "Yerahmeel, a son of the king," to "arrest Baruch the scribe and Jeremiah the prophet" (36:26). A hoard of over 250 inscribed Hebrew bullae have recently come on the antiquities market containing the names of "Baruch the son of Neriah" and "Yerahmeel son of the king."[9] These bullae are small lumps of clay impressed with a seal that acted as a kind of signature and were attached to ancient documents to secure them and to identify the sender. In these bullae, Baruch's full name is revealed for the first time as Berekyahu, with the *-yahu* suffix referring to Yahweh, and the full name meaning "blessed of Yahweh." The fact that both Jeremiah's scribe and the "son of the king," Yerahmeel, who was sent to arrest Jeremiah, appear in these bullae serves to fill out the biblical story. A third person from the narrative in Jeremiah 36:11, "Elishama the secretary" is also attested in this same collection of seal impressions. It reads: "Elisahama, servant of the king." Another unique seal has the title "governor of the city" on it with two figures dressed in pseudo-Assyrian style. The larger figure, presumably the king, holds a bow with three arrows in it, and the smaller figure lifts his hand indicating submission and loyalty to the king. The seal may indeed have been used by successive governors of the city as a sort of seal of the office. The title "governor of the city" is known from Judges 9:30; 1 Kings 22:26; 2 Kings 23:8; and 2 Chronicles 34:8. In these instances, they appear as titles held by the rulers of capital cities.

9. Shanks, "Jeremiah's Scribe and Confidant Speaks from a Hoard of Clay Bullae," *BAR* 13.5 (1987): 58–65. Also N. Avigad, *Hebrew Bullae from the Time of Jeremiah* (Jerusalem: Israel Exploration Society, 1986).

During the catastrophic days when Judah was being bounced back and forth between Assyria and Egypt, Jeremiah consistently announced Yahweh's word to the people. He also advised Judah to yield without rebellion to the new Babylonian power, just emerging from the east. But his advice went unheeded and Judah as well as Jeremiah himself felt the crushing weight of Babylon as it descended on Judah in three campaigns from Nabopolassar and Nebuchadnezzar in 598, 606, and 587 B.C.

THE REIGNS OF JOSIAH'S THREE SONS AND ONE GRANDSON

Few events in the life of the nation would leave a blow as devastating as the death of Josiah in 609 B.C. The religious and political question was this: why would God allow a tragedy this drastic to befall so righteous and God-fearing a king as Josiah? The writer of 2 Kings 23:25–26 would attempt to explain it this way:

> Neither before nor after Josiah was there a king like him who turned to the LORD as [Josiah] did—with all his heart and with all his soul and with all his strength, in accordance with all the Law of Moses.
>
> Nevertheless, the LORD did not turn away from the heat of his fierce anger, which burned against Judah because of all that Manasseh had done to provoke him to anger.

Other texts would explain that Josiah was spared witnessing the tragedy that had to come on unrepentant Judah; thus he went to his grave in peace just before the first Babylonian incursion in 606–605 B.C.

JEHOAHAZ'S REIGN

Josiah's successor was his son Jehoahaz.[10] His evil reign lasted only three months (609 B.C.; 2 Kings 23:31–33; 2 Chron. 36:1–3) as Necho II was returning from the same campaign in which Jehoahaz's father, Josiah, had lost his life trying to prevent Necho's aiding Assyria. The Babylonians proved to be too much for Necho. As the Egyptians and Assyrians tried to retake Haran, the Egyptians were forced back to the

10. Josiah had the distinction of having three of his sons each rule one at a time over Judah. The only other king in either Israel or Judah to have a close second was Ahab, who had his two sons rule: Ahaziah and Jehoram.

south and west of the Euphrates River, leaving intact most of their claim on western Asia.

The Babylonians were preoccupied with the Assyrians for the moment, enabling Egypt to maintain a token hegemony over lower Palestine and Syria. Pharaoh Necho removed Jehoahaz from the throne and sent him to Riblah to be kept under Egyptian detention. In his place, Necho set on the Judean throne Jehoahaz's brother Jehoiakim, while requiring that Egypt receive one hundred talents of silver and one talent of gold.

Jehoahaz, Josiah's middle son, came to the throne at age twenty-three. The people bypassed the eldest son apparently for political reasons, which may have become clear when Necho deposed him. Apparently he had an anti-Egyptian and/or an anti-Assyrian proclivity that Necho disliked; therefore, Necho favored having the eldest son reign in his stead.

Eliakim/Jehoiakim's Reign

Jehoahaz was replaced by his older brother, Eliakim. Necho, however, changed his name to Jehoiakim, apparently for no reason other than to show his authority, for the name *Eliakim* means "God has established," which has basically the same meaning as Jehoiakim, "Yahweh has established."

Jehoiakim ruled for twelve years (609–597 B.C.; 2 Kings 23:34–24:7; 2 Chron. 36:4–8). His was the horrific burden of raising the enormously heavy tribute laid on Judah by Egypt. Since the nation's wealth had long since been exhausted, there was little to do but to resort to heavy taxation of the populace.

Jeremiah had nothing but disdain for Jehoiakim, declaring that he would "have the burial of a donkey" (22:19). One act singled out Jehoiakim for criticism: construction of a new palace in the midst of such an oppressive tax burden and the unstable international situation. Mocked Jeremiah in as severe tones as he could muster for Jehoiakim:

> "Does this make you a king
> to have more and more cedar?
> Did not your father have food and drink?
> He did what was right and just,
> so all went well with him.
> He defended the cause of the poor and needy,
> and so all went well.
> Is that not what it means to know me?"

declares the Lord.
"But your eyes and your heart
are set only on dishonest gain,
on shedding innocent blood
and on oppression and extortion" (Jer. 22:15–17).

"Woe to him who builds his palace by unrighteousness,
his upper rooms by injustice,
making his countrymen work for nothing,
not paying them for their labor.
He says, 'I will build myself a great palace
with spacious upper rooms.'
So he makes large windows in it,
panels it with cedar
and decorates it in red" (Jer. 22:13–14).

This same Jehoiakim put his infamous penknife to the scroll of Jeremiah as each section was read to him in his winter apartment in the fifth year of his reign and tossed each severed sheet into the nearby firepot (chap. 36).

Liberation from Egyptian bondage came in 605 B.C. when Nebuchadnezzar drove the Egyptians out of Palestine, but little changed for Judah. Extradition from one form of slavery only meant its replacement with another form of slavery under Babylon.

Jehoiachin's Reign

Babylon had not yet achieved dominance over the eastern Mediterranean countries in 609 B.C. Necho had been repulsed, but he still dominated much of Syria-Palestine for the next three years. But in 605 B.C. things began to change drastically. Babylon confronted Egypt and Assyria in the Battle of Carchemish on the Euphrates. The Babylonian forces were now led by the young Nebuchadnezzar, for the ailing Nabopolassar was confined to his home. Babylon won the battle of Carchemish and forced Necho to retreat to Hamath. The young Babylonian commander was not content with that, but relentlessly pursued Necho, who had hoped to regroup at the Orontes River. Necho's army was annihilated and Babylon emerged the new world leader over "the whole of the land of Hatti," as the Babylonians referred to all of Syria and Palestine.

In the summer of 604 B.C., Nebuchadnezzar fought against the Philistine city of Ashkelon and again in 601 he attacked Egypt. Nebuchadnezzar was repulsed by Necho and therefore had to return to Babylon, thereby giving Jehoiakim a brief respite from the constant Babylonian incursions. Nebuchadnezzar returned in 597 B.C., in part because Jehoiakim had rebelled, hoping once again that Egypt would come to Judah's rescue. At first, the Babylonian monarch sent only contingents of his army, reinforced by Aramean, Moabite, and Ammonite troops. But in December of 598 B.C., Nebuchadnezzar himself left Babylon, the same month that Jehoiakim died in Jerusalem. Whether Jehoiakim was assassinated by his own people or was killed in a battle by one of the marauding bands, which in turn prevented his burial in an honorable and stately way, is unknown.

Jehoiakim's eighteen-year-old son, Jehoiachin, was placed on the throne in late 598 (December) to 597 B.C. (2 Kings 24:8–16; 2 Chron. 36:9–10) for only three months. The Babylonian blow came in March 597 B.C. without any help from Egypt materializing. Jehoiachin, the queen mother, the princes, and ten thousand leading citizens, smiths, and craftsmen were taken along with servants and booty into captivity to Babylon. It was in this group that the prophet Ezekiel was taken off to Babylon as well (Ezek. 1:1–3).

Zedekiah's Reign

Nebuchadnezzar installed Jehoiachin's uncle, Mattaniah, Josiah's third son, on the throne in 597 B.C. He ruled until the fall of Jerusalem in 587 B.C. (2 Kings 24:17–25:21; 2 Chron. 36:11–21; Jer 39:1–10).[11] Nebuchadnezzar changed Mattaniah's name to Zedekiah just as Pharaoh Necho had changed Eliakim's name to Jehoiakim.

The populace never seemed to have accepted Zedekiah as their real king, for they persisted in ascribing that honor to Jehoiachin. This is evidenced in the collection of cuneiform tablets published in 1939 by Ernst F. Weidner of Berlin, containing a list of payments in oil and grain to the captives and workers in Babylon between 595 and 570 B.C.

11. Recent archaeology is shedding great light on these Babylonian campaigns, especially at Tel Miqne-Ekron and Ashkelon, but unfortunately nothing substantive has yet been published to date except various news releases and news articles. For example, *The Jerusalem Post International Edition*, October 12, 1996, no. 1875, tells of a five-line inscription found at Tel Miqne, one of which read: "Achich, the son of Padi built a temple." Padi is not mentioned in the Bible, but he is mentioned in the Assyrian annals as the King of Ekron when the Assyrians under Sennacherib went up against Jerusalem and Hezekiah, king of Jerusalem. Hezekiah had taken Padi as a hostage when Padi refused to enter into the alliance against the Assyrians. Sennacherib demanded and obtained the release of Padi. Ekron went on to become the olive oil-producing center of the Middle East—over one hundred olive oil-processing installations have been found so far at Ekron. The Babylonian hegemony ended this boom that lasted more than seventy years; it also meant the end for the Philistines.

Among the captives listed is one named King Yaukin (=Jehoiachin) of Judah. The fact that Yaukin was considered to be the king of Judah by the Babylonians suggests that Zedekiah was only a regent. Likewise, Ezekiel regarded Jehoiachin as his king, for he dated his vision in Ezekiel 1:2 "on the fifth day of the month—it was the fifth year of the exile of King Jehoiachin."[12]

Three jar handles found in Palestine bear this inscription: "Belonging to Eliakim, steward of Jehoiachin." Two were found at Debir, southern Judah, and the third one at Beth-shemesh. The conclusion derived from these three finds is that Eliakim remained Jehoiachin's personal crown property in Judah while the king was in captivity. Neither did Zedekiah appropriate Eliakim for himself or his government.[13]

Zedekiah wavered on whether to listen to the pro-Egyptian and anti-Babylonian forces within the government and nation or to side with the pro-Babylonian sentiments. Zedekiah feared both his ministers and his people (Jer. 38:14). Moreover, he continued to be ambivalent about the revolt.

In the fourth year of his reign, Zedekiah personally went, or sent a delegation, to Babylon to underscore his loyalty to Babylon (Jer. 29:3; 51:59). Ultimately, however, he gave in to the anti-Babylonian side and formed a new coalition with Edom, Moab, Ammon, and Phoenicia. False prophets added to the confusion by boldly announcing that the yoke of Babylon would soon be lifted, and within two years the captives would return from Babylon (Jer. 28:2–4). Jeremiah, however, counseled the captives in Babylon in just the opposite way:

> This is what the LORD Almighty, the God of Israel, says to all those I carried into exile from Jerusalem to Babylon: "Build houses and settle down; plant gardens and eat what they produce. Marry and have sons and daughters; find wives for your sons and give your daughters in marriage, so that they too may have sons and daughters. Increase in number there; do not decrease. Also, seek the peace and prosperity of the city to which I carried you into exile. Pray to the LORD for it, because if it prospers, you too will prosper. . . . Do not let the prophets and diviners among you deceive you" (29:4–8a).

12. Albright, "King Jehoiachin in Exile," *BA* 5 (1942): 49–5; idem., "King Jehoiachin in Exile," *The Biblical Archaeologist Reader*, I, eds. G. E. Wright and D. N. Freedman (Garden City, N.Y.: Doubleday, 1961), 106–12.

13. Albright, "The Seal of Eliakim and the Latest Pre-Exilic History of Judah," *JBL* 51 (1932): 91–92.

Jeremiah did believe the captives would return, but not before seventy years had expired (29:10). Meanwhile, the false prophets filled the air with promises of "peace, peace."

Zedekiah had decided to rebel against Babylon some time around the ninth year of his reign. Pharaohs Psammetichus II (593–599 B.C.) and Apries (=Hophra; 588–569 B.C.) were still intent on having an empire that extended into western Asia (Syria and Palestine). As Apries (Hophra) came to the throne in 588, Nebuchadnezzar advanced against Jerusalem and began a siege that finally led to the downfall of the city and the end of the Judean monarchy in July 586 B.C. (2 Kings 25:1–7).[14]

The Fall of Jerusalem

Jeremiah suffered at the hands of his countrymen severely as the final days of the Judean nation approached. Zedekiah respected Jeremiah, but he had no backbone to stand up against his own counselors. Even during the siege, Jeremiah counseled submission to Babylon, but for this he was imprisoned.

When rumors of the approach of Egypt forced Nebuchadnezzar to temporarily lift the siege on Jerusalem, Jeremiah counseled that the Babylonians would return. Despite the inevitability of the city's collapse, Jeremiah was instructed by Yahweh to buy a field near Anathoth and place the deed in a sealed jar for safekeeping against the day when the nation would be restored as promised by Yahweh.

Meanwhile, Judah's fortresses were being overrun. When only two fortresses—Lachish and Azekah—remained, Jeremiah informed Zedekiah that he could still save his life if he would surrender. Events of these times are documented in what are now known as the Lachish Letters, a collection of eighteen broken pieces of pottery with hastily written letters and lists discovered mainly in 1935 in the burned debris of the guardroom of the city gate of Lachish. Three more letters were found in 1938. Only a third of the letters are legible. Most of these let-

14. It is impossible to date with certainty the precise date for the fall of the city of Jerusalem in the closing days of the Judean monarchy since we are uncertain as to which chronological system was being used in Judah. Was it the system employing the month of Nisan (March/April) as the beginning of the calendar year, or was it Tishri (September/October)? It is also uncertain whether the years were reckoned by postdating or antedating methods. See, e.g., K. S. Freedy and D. B. Redford, "The Dates in Ezekiel in Relation to Biblical, Babylonian and Egyptian Sources," *JAOS* 90 (1970): 464–70. This is why both July 586 (E. Thiele, *Mysterious Numbers*, 1965, p. 169; H. Tadmor, "Chronology of the Last Kings of Judah," *JNES* 15 (1956): 226–30) and July 587 B.C. (Bright, *A History of Israel*, 1972, p. 329; E. Kutsch, "Das Jahr der Katastrophe: 587 v. Chr.," *Biblica* 55 [1974]: 520) appear as the dates for the fall of Jerusalem.

ters are addressed to Yoash, commander of the Judean forces at Lachish from a man named Hoshaiah. Hoshaiah appears to be in charge of an outpost north of Lachish where he could see the smoke signals from Azekah. Ostacon IV read, "And let [my lord] know that we are watching for the signals of Lachish, according to all indications which my lord has given, for we cannot see Azekah."[15] Jeremiah 34:7 noted that Lachish and Azekah were the last cities to fall to Nebuchadnezzar before he finally took Jerusalem. Apparently Azekah too had fallen according to the letter IV when no more signals came, just before Lachish and then Jerusalem fell.[16]

Zedekiah was forced to flee for his life as the city fell, but he was captured near Jericho and brought to Nebuchadnezzar's headquarters near Riblah. There Zedekiah's sons were slain before his eyes and his own eyes were then put out. Zedekiah was then taken to Babylon along with many other captives while Nebuzaradan, Nebuchadnezzar's officer, demolished the temple built by Solomon, as he also devastated the city and its walls.

Archaeological finds indicate that many Judean and nearby cities were destroyed in this Babylonian campaign. Among them were Bethel, Ramat Rahel, Beth Zur, Ein Gedi, Arad, Beth-shemesh, Tell el-Ful, Tell Beit Mirsim, Lachish, and Azekah and more.[17]

The Babylonians deported the rest of the people left in the city along with the deserters who had gone over to the king of Babylon (2 Kings 25:11). But the Babylonian system of deportation had two major differences from that of the Assyrians: (1) The Babylonians did not resettle new groups of peoples in the areas from which they deported their people as did the Assyrians; it was a one-way deportation. (2) The Babylonians appointed a local governor to oversee the poor populace still left in the devastated area rather than appointing a Babylonian to govern.

Thus it happened that Gedaliah, the son of Ahikam, who came surprisingly enough from a family with some nobility in it, was appointed to govern the "poorest people of the land" (2 Kings 25:12; Jer. 26:24; 40; 41; 52:16). Gedaliah was put in charge of Jeremiah after his release from prison (39:14). Indeed, a clay seal-impression found at Lachish reads: "Belonging to Gedaliah, who is over the house." The title "who is over the house" was reserved for the highest office at the royal court

15. Pritchard, ed., *ANET*, p. 322.

16. Thomas, *DOTT*, pp. 212–17, and James Pritchard, *ANET*, p. 322, for the Lachish Letters.

17. See Amihai Mazar, *Archaeology of the Land of the Bible*, pp. 458–60, 548. He concluded, "Most of the Judean towns and fortresses excavated in the Shephelah, the Negev, and the Judean Desert were destroyed during the Babylonian invasion" (p. 459).

next to the king. In the Bible, this title was held by Shebna, under King Hezekiah until Shebna was reduced in rank to a scribe (Isa. 22:15–7; 36:3; 2 Kings 18:18).

Zedekiah died shortly after being taken to Babylon. The few people left in the land set up headquarters for Judah in Mizpah, some eight miles north of Jerusalem, under the governorship of Gedaliah. Some of the Judeans who had fled to Edom, Moab, or Ammon trickled back to form a center around Mizpah and their governor Gedaliah. Gedaliah counseled loyalty to Nebuchadnezzar (Jer. 40:12), but not everyone agreed with that philosophy: the Judeans apparently were as divided as ever.

In the ruins of Mizpah, if *Tell en Nasbeh* is ancient Mizpah, a seal was found with this inscription: "Belonging to Jaazaniah, servant of the king." Jaazaniah was one of those mentioned in 2 Kings 25:23 and Jeremiah 40:8 as being associated with Governor Gedaliah. Gedaliah's grandfather, Shaphan, had served King Josiah as scribe, perhaps a title reflecting something like our present secretary of state.

The effective rule of Gedaliah in Mizpah came to a violent end when he was murdered by Ishmael, a man of royal blood who had ambitions on the throne for himself (2 Kings 25:25; Jer. 41:1–2). But that is part of the story from the days of the Exile treated in the next chapter.

Part VII

The Babylonian Exile (605–536 B.C.)

27

The Exile and the First Return

The events surrounding the trauma of 586 B.C. created a crisis of unbelievable proportions for both the exiled community and the ragtag band of survivors left at Mizpah. Everything seemed to be in shambles, not the least of which was the Davidic theology—a theology that had been interpreted as promising the inviolability and invincibility of Zion under any and all conditions. But not only had enemy soldiers crossed the lines of Judah's borders once again; they appeared to have demolished the whole superstructure of faith when they dethroned the last of the Davidic line and sacked the temple of God. It appeared that all had been lost; no remediation was left!

Life in what was left of Judah and in Babylon was at a low ebb, socially, politically, and religiously. All hope for any future seemed to have been evacuated. And how could the new Babylonian appointee, Governor Gedaliah, pose any hope for the future, for he certainly was not from the Davidic line, no matter what else he did or represented. The future seemed bleak. But it would grow even darker before it got better.

The Assassination of Gedaliah

Gedaliah had been governor for only two months when he was suddenly murdered by Ishmael. Ishmael had returned to Judah along with other refugees promising loyalty to the new regime. But his intentions were under suspicion from the beginning, for Johanan son of Kareah,

Gedaliah's military aide and a Jewish army officer, had warned Gedaliah to be cautious of Ishmael, for his profession of loyalty was false (Jer. 40:13–15). Gedaliah refused to believe Johanan and paid for doing so with his life.

As Gedaliah was entertaining a group of his comrades at Mizpah, Ishmael and a group of conspirators rose up and murdered Gedaliah and the small garrison of Babylonian soldiers stationed there (Jer. 41:1–3). Ishmael, son of Nethaniah, had both the backing and the prompting of Baalis, king of Ammon (Jer. 40:14),[1] who was the son of the King Amminadab mentioned in the Tell Siran inscription.[2] Some have argued that the Ammonite king must have feared that an emerging state of Judah would once again pose a problem for his country, or it would attract Jewish refugees from his country back to their own land. Others assume that Ishmael and his cohorts were nationalistic patriots, backed by Baalis, the Ammonite king, who wanted to reestablish an independent Judean state under a Davidic king with the support of a foreign monarch such as Baalis. Why Baalis would be interested in such a prospect is difficult to imagine, however. It is clear that he was somehow involved in the plot to murder Gedaliah and to rebel against Babylon.

So secret and so sudden was the takeover that nothing leaked out for two days. But everything changed when Ishmael and his men found it necessary to kill a visiting group of pilgrims. Ishmael was now forced to flee, taking a number of Judeans as hostages, including the daughters of the now-exiled King Zedekiah, who had been entrusted to Gedaliah's care.

Johanan intercepted Ishmael before he was able to go beyond Gibeon and freed the prisoners. However, Ishmael and eight other men were able to escape to Ammon and to King Baalis (Jer. 41:4–11). Meanwhile, Johanan, now fearing stiff reprisals by the Babylonians for this civil unrest, asked the prophet Jeremiah to inquire of God whether the remaining populace ought not take shelter in Egypt before any Babylonian reprisals resulted from this melee. Jeremiah had taken up residence in Mizpah after he had been given a choice by the Babylonian monarch to decide whether he wanted to stay in Judah or to go to Babylon. He chose to stay and to move to Mizpah to be of assistance to Gedaliah. The word from the Lord was that all would be well with the

---

1. Confirmation of the name *Baalis* was reported in Larry G. Herr, "The Servant of Baalis," BA 48 (1985): 169–72.

2. Henry O. Thompson and Fawzi Zayadine, "The Works of Amminadab," *BA* 37 (1974): 13–19.

people if they remained in the land, but contrary to the promise of the people, they decided to go to Egypt anyway—forcibly taking Jeremiah with them as surety and for good measure (chap. 42).

The migrants came to Tahpanhes (*Tell Dafanneh*) in the northeastern delta of Egypt (Jer. 43:1–7).[3] There Jeremiah took stones, at Yahweh's instruction, and hid them at the entry to a royal palace, predicting that God would one day bring Nebuchadnezzar to conquer this place and set his pavilion on that very spot (Jer. 43:8–13). The same refugees from Judah who had sought asylum there would experience the same destruction that the Egyptians would feel. In fact, none of the refugees who had deserted Judah in disobedience to the word of God would be allowed to return to Judah (Jer. 44:12–14). In a message prepared for the Jewish diaspora living in Egypt, who had by now adopted the Egyptian lifestyle and syncretistically adopted many features of Egyptian religious life, Jeremiah reminded them that they would be the same ones who would suffer the judgment of God. Pharaoh Hophra (= Apries; 589–570 B.C.) would be handed over to his enemies and the shelter the Judeans had sought would no longer exist.

Information about life in Judah following Gedaliah's assassination is almost nonexistent, except for a brief report in Jeremiah 52:30 that another Babylonian deportation involved 745 Judeans who were exiled in the twenty-third year of Nebuchadnezzar (581 B.C.). The cause of this deportation is unknown. Many scholars link it with the Gedaliah affair, but 2 Kings 25:25 and Jeremiah 41:1 imply that Gedaliah was killed shortly after the fall of Jerusalem in 586; the deportation came some five years later. The best explanation seems to reside in Josephus's description that Nebuchadnezzar was back in Syria-Palestine in 582/1 B.C.[4] It would appear that Josephus conflated two events, the exiling of more Jews to Babylon in 581 B.C., and the killing of Pharaoh Hophra (Apries), which did not occur until 570 B.C. In the meantime, Egypt seemed to be open to receiving Judeans fleeing Palestine for fear of the Babylonians. Also, at this same time Nebuchadnezzar continued his

3. This site is twenty-seven miles southwest of Port Said. Sir Flinders Petrie excavated this site in 1883–84 and discovered the foundations of a castle there—perhaps the one mentioned in Jeremiah's symbolic action. A Phoenician letter from the sixth century mentions this site with the same consonantal spelling, *thpnhs*, A. Dupont-Sommer, *PEQ* 81 (1949): 52–57. Also see Eliezer D. Oren, "Migdol: A New Fortress on the Edge of the Eastern Nile Delta," *BASOR* 256 (1984): 31–32.

4. "And so it happened; for in the fifth year after the sacking of Jerusalem, which was the twenty-third year of the reign of Nebuchadnezzar, Nebuchadnezzar marched against Coele-Syria and, having killed the king who was then reigning and appointed another, he again took captive the Jews who were in the country and carried them to Babylon." Josephus, *Antiquities*, X. 181–82.

siege of Tyre on the coast of Canaan for thirteen years (586–573 B.C.). The fact that Tyre was able to withstand Babylon's siege for so long a period of time, and that it ended in a virtual stalemate, may have provided the impetus for the other nations to conclude that Babylon was not as invincible as she had once appeared to be.

LIFE AMONG THE EXILES IN BABYLON

The first group of captives taken to Babylon came in 605 B.C., when Daniel and his three friends, Hananiah, Mishael, and Azariah, went along with other captives from the royal family and the nobility. The "seventy years" (Dan. 9:2) captivity that the prophet Jeremiah had predicted in Jeremiah 25:12 and 29:10 lasted, then, from 605/6 B.C. until some time after the famous decree of Cyrus in 538 B.C.—perhaps to 536 B.C. There is no evidence that the first return took place immediately with the issuing of Cyrus's decree in 538 B.C., as some suppose, thereby concluding that the "seventy year" reference in Jeremiah must be a "round number" which is close enough to some sixty-six years (605–539 B.C., the fall of Babylon).[5] But it could just as well have been a full seventy years since the exact year of the first return is not known.

Jeremiah urged the exiles to plan for a long stay. They should plant gardens, build houses and enter into the life of the community there (29:1–3). This was difficult for many Jews as they remembered Zion. Their state of mind is vividly cast in Psalm 137:1–4:

> By the rivers of Babylon we sat and wept
>   when we remembered Zion.
> There on the poplars we hung our harps,
>   for there our captors . . . demanded songs of joy:
> they said, "Sing us one of the songs of Zion!"
>
> How can we sing the songs of the LORD
>   while in a foreign land?

While in Babylon, the Jews adopted a calendar which, despite some refinements in the fourth century A.D., remains the basis for the Jewish calendar today. The Babylonians had a twelve-month lunar calendar of

---

5. Eugene H. Merrill, *Kingdom of Priests*, p. 469, n. 1, quotes John Bright, *Jeremiah*, Anchor Bible (Garden City, Doubleday, 1965), 160–61. The "seventy years" in Zechariah 1:12; 7:5 are thought to refer to a different period of time, namely the time from the destruction of the temple in 586 B.C. until the commencement of its rebuilding in 516 B.C. See David L. Petersen, *Haggai and Zechariah 1–8* (Philadelphia: Westminster, 1984), 149, though Peterson prefers the dates of 590–520 B.C. for this seventy-year period in Zechariah.

thirty days, each with an intercalary month (a second Adar) every six years. The twelve months and their corresponding names in Hebrew and in our present calendar are as follows:

Hebrew Name	Babylonian Name	Current Calendar
Nisan	Nisannu	March-April
Iyyar	Ayaru	April-May
Sivan	Simanu	May-June
Tammuz	Du'uzu	June-July
Av	Abu	July-August
Elul	Ululu	August-September
Tishri	Tashretu	September-October
Marsheshvan	Arakshamna	October-November
Kislev	Kislimu	November-December
Tevet	Tabetu	December-January
Shevat	Shabatu	January-February
Adar	Addaru	February-March

This Babylonian revision of calendar names appears in the postexilic books (Nisan in Neh. 2:1; Esther 3:7; and Adar in Ezra 6:15). The reckoning of the day from sunset to sunset was the same for the Babylonians as it was for the Hebrews.

Life changed for the exiles in more ways than their calendar and living space. A major change took place in their speech as well. The exiles switched from speaking Hebrew to the diplomatic and commercial *lingua franca* of the day: Aramaic. The Aramaic letters back and forth to Artaxerxes and Darius (Ezra 4:11–22; 5:7–17; 6:3–12; 7:11–26) may preserve an authentic transcript of the originals kept in the Persian archives. Hebrew was not lost altogether, for the prophets Haggai, Zechariah, and Malachi continued to use Hebrew as if it were a living language, as did the Books of Chronicles, large portions of Ezra and Nehemiah, and Esther. Likewise, the Qumran community continued to copy the Hebrew manuscripts in their possession; thus Hebrew had a continued usage until the Arab conquest in the seventh century A.D.

One exilic settlement is known to us as Tel-abib, the community where the prophet Ezekiel ministered along the river Chebar (Ezek. 3:15). The Chebar (*nari Kabari*, "great river") was probably a canal that flowed out of the Euphrates north of Babylon, passed Nippur, and then entered the Euphrates once again. Israelite pottery was found near modern Tilabub, which no doubt marks approximately where Tel-abib was. In towns such as these the captives settled in for the duration of the judgment placed on them. Many knew that they would never again see the land they had been forced to leave.

Nevertheless, the Jews experienced economic well-being, and some found opportunities to rise high in the government, just as Daniel did. There is evidence that they were able to form their own council of elders and to have the advantage of prophets and priests in their midst as well, for Jeremiah addressed all three groups when he wrote to the captives (Jer. 29:1).

The captive artisans and craftsmen found work in the skilled trades. One particular fifth-century B.C. business house, the Murashu Sons, known from tablets that come from Nippur on the Canal Kabari, shows that many Jews were active in renting, buying, and selling, judging from the large number of Hebrew names that occur in these tablets.[6] In comparison with those who had remained in the land of Judah, the exiles had the better deal. Life in Babylon was so comfortable that most of the exiles were unwilling to return to Palestine when the opportunity arose.

The Glory of Babylon[7]

"Is this not the great Babylon I have built as the royal residence, by my mighty power and for the glory of my majesty?" (Dan. 4:30) boasted the proud Nebuchadnezzar as he walked on the roof of his royal palace

6. For examples of these Murashu documents, see Hermann V. Hilprecht and Albert T. Clay, *Business Documents of Murashu Sons of Nippur Dated in the Reign of Artaxerxes I (464–425 B.C.)*, Babylonian Expedition 9 (Philadelphia: University of Pennsylvania, 1898). For these same documents along with other materials, see Michael D. Coogan, "Life in the Diaspora: Jews at Nippur in the Fifth Century B.C.," *BA* 37(1974): 6–12.

7. Note S. Smith, *Babylonian Historical Texts Relating to the Capture and Downfall of Babylon* (London, 1924); H. W. F. Saggs, *The Greatness that Was Babylon*, 146–57; George Roux, *Ancient Iraq*, 3rd ed. (Baltimore: Penguin, 1992); Donald J. Wiseman, *Nebuchadnezzar and Babylon*. Schweich Lectures 1983 (Oxford: Oxford University Press, 1985); and Paul-Alain Beaulieu, "King Nabonidus and the Neo-Babylonian Empire," in *Civilizations of the Ancient Near East*. 4 vols., ed. Jack M. Sasson, *et al.* (London: Charles Scribner's Sons, 1995), II: 969–79; and Raymon P. Dougherty, *Nabonidus and Belshazzar: A Study of the Closing Event of the Neo-Babylonian Empire*. Yale Oriental Series, 15 (New Haven: Yale University Press, 1929); and Bill T. Arnold, "Babylonians," in *Peoples of the Old Testament World*, pp. 43–77.

in Babylon. The Greek historian Herodotus, writing a century and a half after Nebuchadnezzar, described the city of Babylon in glowing terms. It was a huge square, 480 stadia (55 1/4 miles) in circumference, surrounded by a series of walls that made it virtually impregnable. Robert Koldewey, who excavated Babylon for eighteen years, verified how security-conscious Nebuchadnezzar was. The city ruins were surrounded, according to Koldewey, with a brick wall 22 1/3 feet thick, with a space outside that wall some 38 1/3 feet wide, then another brick wall 25 feet thick. In the event that this outer wall was breached, the invader would be trapped between two walls. Inside the inner wall was still another wall 12 feet thick. Every 160 feet the walls were topped by watchtowers, 360 towers in all, reaching the height probably of some 90 feet, not 300 feet mentioned by Herodotus, and wide enough to accommodate two chariots riding side by side.

Nebuchadnezzar completely rebuilt the palace of his father Napolassar with cedar beams brought from Lebanon. He also constructed the city gates of cedar wood covered with strips of bronze. Numerous gates, but hardly the one hundred that Herodotus mentioned,[8] were installed in the walls. The most famous of these, the Ishtar Gate, was fifteen feet wide and its arched passageway was thirty-five feet above the level of the street. This gate led directly into the Procession Way, which was used primarily for the great annual New Year's Festival. The pavement was 73 1/2 feet wide and was lined with a series of 120 lions in enameled relief at 64–foot intervals.

Along this Processional Way was the famous ziggurat or staged tower known as E-temen-anki, "The House of the Foundation of Heaven and Earth," which rose 300 feet high and could be seen for miles around the city. It is estimated that some 58,000,000 bricks were used in the construction of this ziggurat. Atop this seven-staged or terraced tower was a temple to Marduk, the god of Babylon. The temple atop this tower was reached by a triple staircase and was made of bricks enameled in bright blue to represent the heavens. Other lesser temples and architectural marvels lined this Procession Way, such as the shrine known as E-Kur, "Temple Mountain," which towered some 470 feet into the air.

On a mound called Kasr, Nebuchadnezzar built one of his most impressive palaces. Its walls were made of yellow brick and the floors were of white and mottled sandstone. Near this palace were the famed hanging gardens, considered one of the Seven Wonders of the World,

8. Herodotus, *Histories*, I, 178–87.

built by Nebuchadnezzar for his wife, who is said to have missed the hills of her homeland in Media.

Babylon was a marvel in city planning. It was laid out in rectangles, with wide roads named after the gods of Babylon. A bridge connected the eastern or new city with the western city across the river that flowed through the city. It had stone piers on both shores some 600 feet across the river, with a wooden footpath thirty feet wide that reached from shore to shore. The dwellings in the city often reached three or four stories high with the familiar eastern central courtyard.

The accomplishments of Babylon were staggering and spectacular for their times. The Neo-Babylonian Empire reached its zenith under Nebuchadnezzar. He left the nation with enormous gains on the battlefield and in architectural accomplishments, but with little political stability. It was an empire that was held together by his own charisma and personality, but it quickly fell apart after his time.

Babylon's Last Kings

Twenty-three years after the death of Nebuchadnezzar, the capital city of Babylon fell to Cyrus of Anshan, founder of the Medo-Persian Empire. The whole Neo-Babylonian kingdom saw only six or seven monarchs.

Nabopolassar	626–605
Nebuchadnezzar II	605–562
Evil-Merodach	562–560
Neriglissar	560–556
Labashi-Marduk	556
Nabonidus	555–539
Belshazzar	552–359

When Nebuchadnezzar died, Amel Marduk, "Man of Marduk," or Evil-Merodach as he was also known, and son of Nebuchadnezzar, took the throne for two years. While he is best known for his kind treatment in releasing King Jehoiachin from prison, thirty-seven years after his being taken captive (2 Kings 25:27–30), he was generally depicted as a tyrannical ruler by a fragment preserved from Berossus. The French archaeologist De Morgan discovered a vase when he was excavating

Susa with the inscription: "Palace of Amel-Marduk, king of Babylon, son of Nebuchadnezzar, king of Babylon."[9] In the second year of his reign he was assassinated by his sister's husband, Neriglissar.

Neriglissar (the Nergal-sharezer of Jer. 39:3), son-in-law of Nebuchadnezzar, previously had held the post of *rab-mugi* (meaning unknown) with the occupying armies. It was he who sat in the middle of the gate of Jerusalem serving as the center of the government of the Babylonians before they destroyed the city. His reign (560–556 B.C.) witnessed a Babylonian campaign into southwestern Asia Minor against a certain King Appuashu of Pirindu, who had invaded Syria. On his way home to Babylon, he suffered a mysterious death, leaving his son Labashi-marduk, a minor, to take over. But he too was quickly replaced after only a nine-month reign by a rebellion of the officers of the kingdom.

The new ruler, Nabonidus (555–539 B.C.), was a Babylonian military commander from Haran in northern Syria, the son of a nobleman and of a high priestess of the moon god Sin in his native city of Haran. It was no surprise, then, that Nabonidus attempted to reform Babylonian religion by using the worship of the moon god Sin as the unifying force in the Babylonian kingdom. Already, of course, the moon god was worshiped by many in the empire, including the Arabs and the Arameans, but Babylon long before had committed itself to the sun deity Marduk. Nabonidus restored the Sin sanctuary in Haran, where his mother was a high priestess.

Nabonidus rebuilt many temples and shrines in Babylon, but only after he had located the original foundation stone and recorded the name of the king who first constructed the temple. In this antiquarian interest, Nabonidus was distinct among his predecessors. But these antiquarian interests led to Nabonidus's abandonment of the affairs of state. In fact, he chose to live at Tema, an oasis in the Hejaz region of the Arabian peninsula. To deal with the more mundane matters of government, Nabonidus appointed his son Belshazzar as coregent. The account of this transfer of government and his assuming of a new residence in Tema goes as follows:

> He entrusted the "Camp" to his oldest son, the first-born
> The troops everywhere in the country he ordered under his command.
> He let everything go, entrusted the kingship to him.

9. Charles F. Pfeiffer, *Old Testament History* (Grand Rapids: Baker, 1973), 454.

. . . .

He turned towards Tema, deep in the west,

. . . .

He killed in battle the prince of Tema. . . .
And he, himself, took his residence in Tema. . . .
He made the town beautiful, built there his palace
Like the palace in Babylon, he also built walls. . . .
He surrounded the town with sentinels. [10]

Also, among the Dead Sea Scrolls is a document known as the Prayer of Nabonidus which tells of a "dread disease by the decree of the Most High God" that befell Nabonidus.[11] This event is so similar to the account of what befell Nebuchadnezzar in Daniel 4 that many think the text is mislabeled in the Dead Sea Scrolls. But there is strong evidence supporting the fact that Nabonidus was ailing while he remained for over a decade in Tema, Arabia. What the disease was is unknown.

Belshazzar ruled as coregent with his father Nabonidus from the third year of his reign, even though Nabonidus had for all intents and purposes practically abdicated the throne. Belshazzar[12] was not that strong a ruler either. He is best known for the infamous feast in which he brought out the sacred vessels taken from the temple of Yahweh in Jerusalem to toast Marduk (Dan. 5). It was during these festivities that the handwriting appeared on the wall and the doom of the Babylonian Empire was predicted by Daniel and immediately enacted as the Medes and Persians entered the city through the diverted Euphrates that flowed through the city.

All during this decade while Nabonidus was doing whatever he was doing in the desert at Tema, Cyrus was busily amassing his own empire. Then it came time to set his sights on the realm that Babylon had acquired during the seventy years of the Nabopolassar dynasty (626–556 B.C.), but which Nabonidus was unable to manage during the fourteen years of his reign.

The decisive battle for the empire was not fought in Babylon but at Opis on the Tigris River. Cyrus emerged victorious. Babylon itself fell

10. James Pritchard, *ANET*, pp. 313–14.

11. J. T. Milik, "Priere de Nabonide et autres ecrits d'un cycle de Daniel," *RB* 63 (1956): 407–15.

12. The limited but helpful documentation for this coregency is found in R. P. Dougherty, *Nabonidus and Belshazzar* (New Haven: Yale, 1929), 96–97, 133. Also see Gerhard F. Hasel, "The Book of Daniel: Evidences Relating to Persons and Chronology," *AUSS* 19 (1981): 42–5; Alan R. Millard, "Daniel 1–6 and History," *EQ* 49 (1977): 71–72; and William L. Reed, "Nabonidus, Babylonian Reformer or Renegade?" *LQ* 12 (1977): 24.

to Cyrus's general Ugbaru On October 12, 539 B.C. without a fight. Nabonidus had just returned from Tema in time to see the capture of Babylon by Ugbaru, the governor of Gutium and commander of the Persian army. Cyrus subsequently made Gubaru the satrap of Babylon. Whether this Gubaru (also known as Gobryas) was Darius the Mede or not, as John Whitcomb has long contended, is difficult to affirm or deny.[13] That search still continues for definitive evidence.

The very night, as already mentioned, during the infamous feast mentioned in Daniel 5, in which the handwriting, "Mene, Mene, Tekel, and Parsin," appeared on the wall, the Babylonian kingdom came to a sudden end. Belshazzar was slain but the city was spared by order of Cyrus. Entry to this impregnable city had been gained by diverting the waters of the Euphrates upstream and then marching into town down the reduced waterbeds to take the city virtually unopposed. Nabonidus fled, but he was subsequently imprisoned.

The First Return[14] from the Babylonian Exile

Cyrus II, from the Persian province of Anshan, had energetically pursued a course of conquest that had already won him Media and Asia Minor. The fabulously rich Croesus, who ruled the Lydian Empire, had been conquered by Cyrus as well. Even the Babylonian governor of Elam (Gutium) had deserted Nabonidus and gone over to Cyrus. Gobryas, whom we have identified as Darius the Mede with John Whitcomb, had been enormously successful. As the end for Babylon drew to a close, Gobryas took Opis on the Tigris, then Sippar, and, finally, without any resistance, he took Babylon itself.

While experiencing these earth-shattering events, the captives from Judah in Babylon could not help but be concerned as to what their plight might be next. The three deportations of exiles in 605, 597, and 586 B.C. hung in the balances as the world waited to see what would emerge from this cataclysmic turn of events.

13. John C. Whitcomb, *Darius the Mede* (Grand Rapids: Eerdmans, 1959). Many scholars equate Ugbaru, who in the Nabonidus Inscription took Babylon for Cyrus, with Gubaru, whom Cyrus appointed governor of Babylon some time later. Whitcomb points out that they cannot be the same person, for Ugbaru is said to have died on the eleventh day of the month of Arakshamna, which is only a matter of days after the fall of Babylon, but Gubaru, under the general name of Gobryas, is mentioned for several years after the fall of Babylon. Therefore for Whitcomb, Darius is Gubaru (Gobryas). Donald J. Wiseman, "The Last Days of Babylon," *CT* 2 (November 1957): 7–10, suggests that Darius may be nothing more than another name for Cyrus himself.

14. There would be three returns in all: this first one under Joshua and Zerubbabel in 537/6 B.C; the second under Ezra in 458/7 B.C. and the third under Nehemiah in 445 B.C.

Cyrus personally entered Babylon and was welcomed by the populace as a hero. Gobryas was made a satrap of the new province of Babirush (i.e. Babylon) and many of the former officials retained their government posts. One new policy of Cyrus would have a major effect on subsequent history. Cyrus set aside Nabonidus's replacement-of-deities policy, which had so antagonized the Babylonians, by returning the captive gods that Nabonidus had removed in favor of his own deities. This would have a direct effect on the Judeans as well.

In the first year of his reign in Babylon, Cyrus issued a decree authorizing the rebuilding of all the temples of the gods that had been conquered by the Babylonians and an order to restore whatever vessels of gold and silver that had been taken and stored in Babylon. All expenses for such rebuilding of the various temples was to be borne by the royal treasury of Medo-Persia (Ezra 6:3–5).

The Edict of Cyrus, as recorded in Ezra 1:2–4 stated the following:

> "This is what Cyrus king of Persia says:
> 'The LORD, the God of heaven, has given me all the kingdoms of the earth and he has appointed me to build a temple for him at Jerusalem in Judah. Anyone of his people among you—may his God be with him, and let him go up to Jerusalem in Judah and build the temple of the LORD, the God of Israel, the God who is in Jerusalem. And the people of any place where survivors may now be living are to provide him with silver and gold, with goods and livestock, and with freewill offerings for the temple of God in Jerusalem.'"[15]

In Judah's case, the sacred vessels and the leadership of the Jews who wished to return to help in rebuilding the temple was entrusted to a "prince of Judah" named Sheshbazzar (Ezra 1:8). This name appears as Sanabassar in 1 Esdras and in Josephus, probably from the Babylonian name *Sin-ab-usur*. Others think that Sheshbazzar was the same as Shenazzar (1 Chron. 3:18), a son of Jehoiachin.

But the relationship between Sheshbazzar and Zerubbabel is even more enigmatic. Zerubbabel is never called a "prince," and he is not said to be a son of Jehoiachin, but from Shealtiel (Ezra 3:8). However, it is known that the line of Jehoiachin was declared to be at an end when Jeremiah 22:30 announced that he would be "childless." His sons

15. See the Cyrus Cylinder in James Pritchard. *ANET*, pp. 315–16, where Cyrus claimed that the "entire population . . . bowed to him and kissed his feet. They were glad that he was king. Their faces lighted up. The master by whose aid the mortally sick had been made alive, all had been preserved from ruin." Despite overstatement of his popularity, there was no doubt some basis for fact in his claims.

would, according to Isaiah 39:6–7, be "carried off to Babylon" and "become eunuchs in the palace of the king of Babylon." This is indeed what did happen. Accordingly, the Davidic line switched at this point from descending from David's son Solomon to David's son Nathan as Jehoiachin adopted a descendant of Nathan's named Shealtiel, and then Pedaiah, to continue the line by virtue of fulfilling the levirate relationship. It was from such a union that Zerubbabel came. Therefore, even though he is not called a "prince" in the prophetic books, he may well be the same person as Sheshbazzar. If not, Sheshbazzar must have died shortly after his leading the first return back to Jerusalem, for he is not mentioned again in the text.

The total number who returned under Sheshbazzar/Zerubbabel was just short of 50,000: 49,897. It included 42,360 returnees, 7,337 slaves, and 200 singers (Ezra 2:64–65). Since it is estimated that only 25,000 went into the Babylonian captivity, and that Jerusalem herself took most of the brunt of the devastation and attacks in 605, 597, and 586 B.C., it is no wonder that so few Jerusalemites were among this first 50,000 who returned. In fact, one hundred years later, Nehemiah found Jerusalem so sparsely populated that he had to search the genealogical lists to determine if any of the early returnees should have taken up residence in Jerusalem by virtue of their lineage (Neh. 7:4–5).

As the people settled in, under the leadership of Joshua the high priest and Zerubbabel the governor, they built the altar in the seventh month of that year on the ruins of the old one on the temple mount and immediately celebrated the first Feast of Tabernacles. Again the exact year is not known, but it was either 537 or 536 B.C., depending on how soon the returnees were able to take advantage of Cyrus's decree made in 538 B.C. The materials for the construction of the temple were ordered from Tyre and Sidon, and the foundations for the rebuilt temple were laid in the second month of the year, usually given as 536 B.C.

When this stage in the rebuilding process was reached, the returnees broke out into jubilant song of thanksgiving and praise to Yahweh. But the joy was not without its detractors. Many of the older generation, who had seen and remembered the size of the Solomonic temple, wept when they realized how this new temple paled in proportion to what they had before. Thus, it was difficult to distinguish whether the people were rejoicing or weeping, for the two commingled so that eventually all were demoralized, and the project ground to a halt (Ezra 3:12–13).

This was not the only problem that Joshua and Zerubbabel faced. The Samaritans, now a mixture of transplanted peoples resettled and intermarried with the nonexiled northern Israelites, demanded to be a part of the temple project as well. But their religious affinities by now were so syncretistic, with so little of the former exclusive Yahweh faith remaining, that such cooperation would be impossible. All of this was enough to bring the whole project to a halt for sixteen years between 536 and 520 B.C.

The Judeans were back in the land once again, but there would be very little celebrating, for it would be a long time before they would recover and again have anything like they had known just before the crash came in 586 B.C. Nevertheless, God had brought them back to start all over again—and start again they did!

Most of our information about the Judeans during this period focuses on the exiles, leaving an occupational vacuum as to what was happening back in the land of Judah during this time. However, it can be said that conditions were far inferior to those the exiles had left in Babylon. The province or district of Judah consisted of the territory that stretched from just north of Bethel to south of Beth-zur and from the Jordan River to just west of Emmaus and Azekah—an area about twenty-five miles north to south and about thirty miles east to west. It was only a shadow of what Judah had been in days past! Life would be bleak for many years to come!

Part VIII

The Persian Hegemony

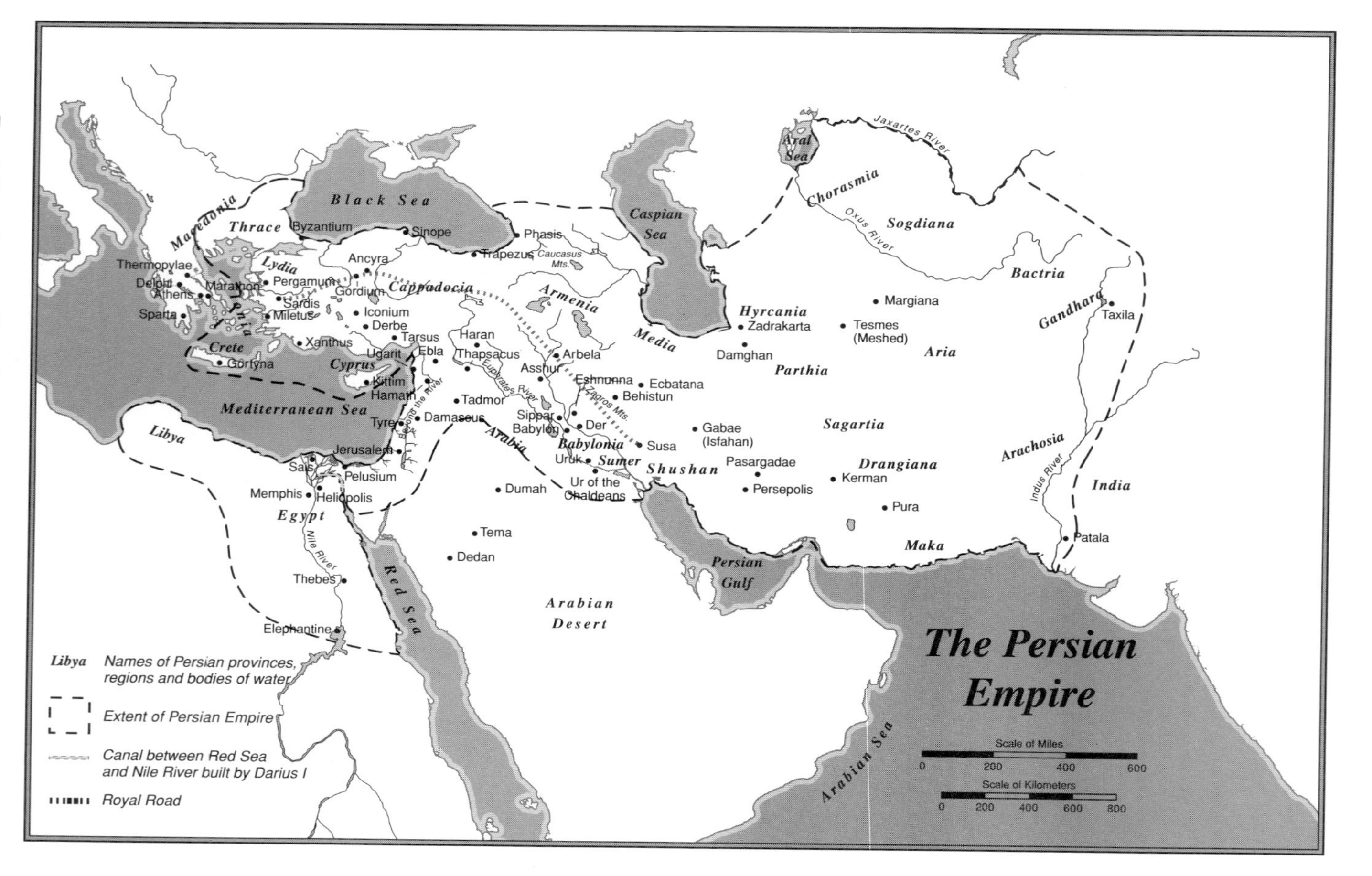

From *Holman Bible Handbook* (Nashville: Holman Bible Publishers, 1992), 424.

28

The Returns under Ezra and Nehemiah

Babylon became the ongoing center of activity for the people of the covenant during the seventy years of the Exile. Although a remnant remained in the land of Israel, the spiritual and intellectual center shifted to Babylon for the most part. A thriving community, both in its religious achievements and economic strengths, would continue in this land of exile even into the Christian era, generating its own scholarly tradition that was separate from the Jewish centers of study in Alexandria and Jerusalem.

It was from Babylon, for example, that the Babylonian Talmud emanated. Babylon also was the center of separate families of biblical texts and manuscripts. Nor did matters change much with the Persian takeover of the Babylonian government. Life in the Jewish community resumed without any apparent evidence of disruption.

The Medo-Persian Origins and Leadership[1]

The Medes and the Persians were descendants of Aryan tribal groups which had moved south into Urartu from the plains of Russia, settling around Lake Urmia in the extreme northwestern part of what is today

1. The best sources on this period are still A. T. Olmstead, *History of the Persian Empire* (Chicago: University of Chicago, 1948) and Roman Ghirshman, *Iran* (Hammondsworth: Penguin, 1954), especially for these early movements through Cyrus II, pp. 90–126.

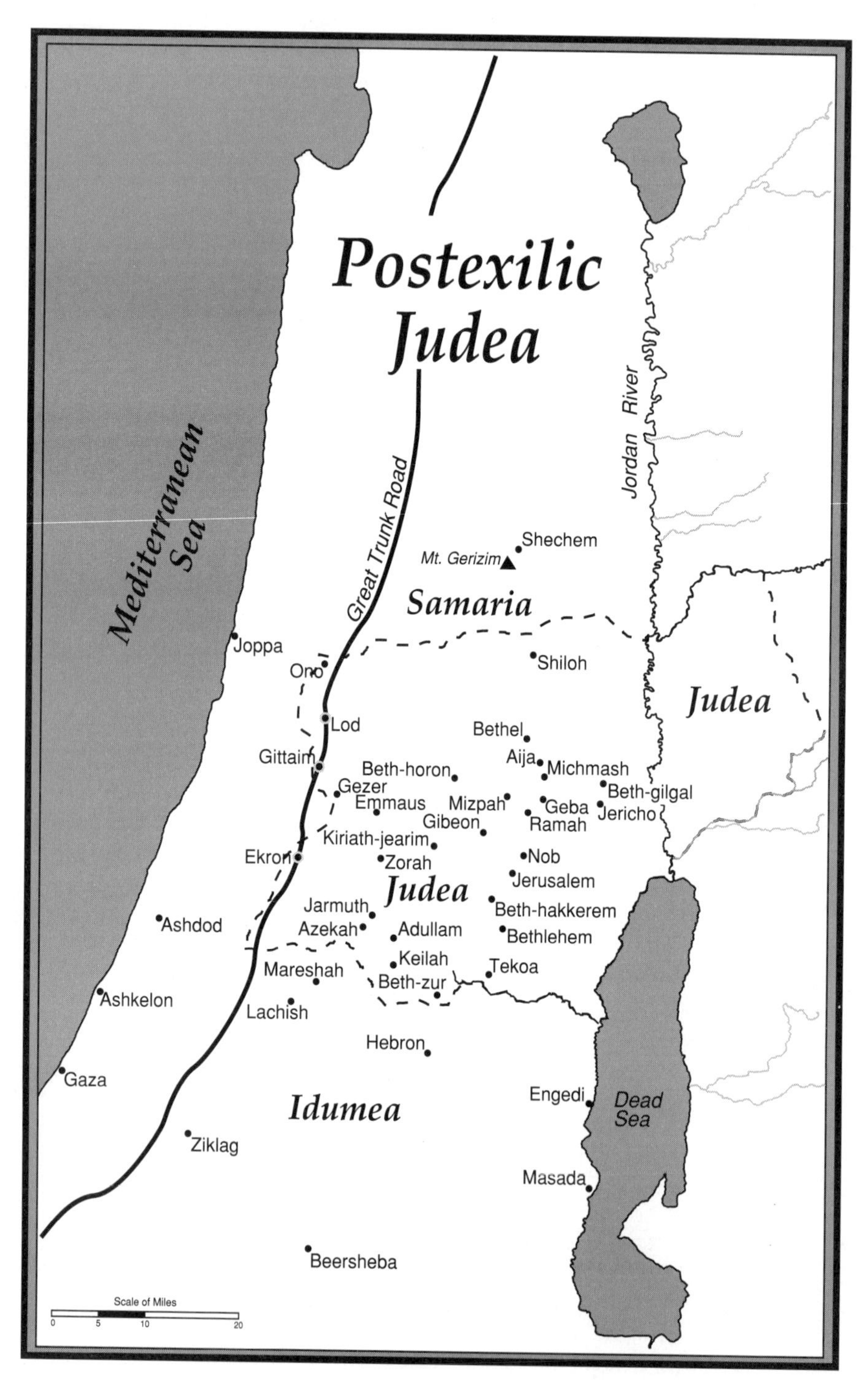

From *Holman Bible Handbook* (Nashville: Holman Bible Publishers, 1992), 428.

called Iran. Apparently the Medes moved east and took up the territory south of the Caspian Sea, while the Persians migrated far south to the southeastern corner of present-day Iran near the Persian Gulf.

The royal line from which Cyrus II descended was founded by Achaemenes (700–675 B.C.) and is known as the Achaemenid Dynasty. Achaemenes's son Teispes (675–640 B.C.) extended the land of Parsa (Persia) as far south as Pasargadae, but he feared that his realm was becoming too large for one person to manage. After regaining his independence from the Medes (who had forced Parsa into vassalage around 670 B.C.), Teispes divided Parsa between his two sons, Ariaramnes (640–615 B.C.) in the south and Cyrus I (640–600 B.C.) in the north. Among those who were in the line of Ariaramnes were Arsames, Hystaspes, and Darius Hystaspes. But the line of Cyrus I produced Cambyses I (600–559 B.C.) and Cyrus II (559–530 B.C.). This Cyrus II created the Medo-Persian Empire.

Meanwhile, the Median contemporary of the Persian Achaemenes was Deioces, who is virtually unknown. It was Deioces's son, Phraortes (675–653 B.C.) who made Parsa a vassal in 670 B.C. as already mentioned. But Phraortes lost his life fighting the Assyrians in 653 as he helped Teispes regain independence. Thus from 653 to 625 B.C. the Median throne remained vacant while the Scythians dominated all of northwestern Iran. However, Cyaxeres (625–585 B.C.) arose and overthrew both the Scythians and the Assyrians, asserting Median domination over most of that area. He also reduced Persia to submission and set up Cambyses as governor over the province. After Cyaxeres came his son Astyages (585–550 B.C.). Governor Cambyses married Astyages's daughter, who in turn became the parents of Cyrus II.

In time Cyrus II, as vassal to his grandfather Astyages, ruled an area known as Anshan, locating his capital in Pasargadae. Cyrus II began the task of unifying the Persian tribes, a feat that had not been successfully carried out. Gradually Cyrus built up his area of influence and power; first by forging an alliance with Nabonidus of Babylon, but then by going on the offensive in other areas to enlarge his fortunes. But this alliance with Nabonidus did not sit well with his grandfather, for the Babylonians were by now the feared enemy of Media. When Cyrus II refused to obey a summons to come to the capital in Ecbatana, Astyages launched an attack against his wayward grandson. Astyages's army defected on him and Cyrus took Ecbatana and made his grandfather a prisoner as Media and all her territories were added to the Persian province.

Croesus, the famed leader of Lydia on the Aegean Sea in Asia Minor, marched east against Cyrus II to block any aspirations that he might have on the Hellenic world. But Cyrus backed him up to his capital in Sardis and there defeated him in 547 B.C. Croesus's kingdom was immediately incorporated into the growing Persian Empire as the new Persian satrapy of Saparda. This gave Cyrus access and friendly relationships with the Greeks in that region, an asset that he would later use as allies and mercenaries were needed for the Persian empire.

The Persian Kings

Cyrus II	559–530 B.C.
Cambyses II	530–522
Gaumata	522
Darius Hystaspes	522–486
Xerxes	486–465
Artaxerxes I	464–424
Darius II	423–404
Artaxerxes II	404–358

Cyrus II ruled for another nine years after his impressive conquest of Babyon in 539 B.C. He mixed, in almost perfect balance, a knack for knowing when to be firm and when to be charitable, eventually gaining the admiration of both friend and foe. In 530 B.C., he was wounded and died while fighting in the far north. His body was returned to the Persian capital of Pasargadae for burial.

Cyrus's son, Cambyses II, succeeded his father. He had often acted in his father's absence as his deputy, but now he was in control alone. Cambyses did away with his brother Bardiya, for he wished no rivals to the throne. But he continued his father's prowess and gifts in conquest by extending the reach of the empire into Egypt in 525 B.C. He engaged the Egyptian army at Pelusium, some twenty miles east of the modern port Said, at the most eastern branch of the Nile known as the Pelusiac branch, which today is silted in. His was a clear victory over the Egyptian army, a victory helped in no small part by the defection of the commander of the Greek mercenaries whom Pharaoh Amasis had hired.

When Pharaoh Amasis died and Psammetichus III took over, Cambyses extended his reach into the delta region; he then held control over the entire land of Egypt, organizing it into another satrapy of the empire.

Cambyses went even farther afield as he attempted to reach westward into Carthage and southward into Nubia and Ethiopia. In these ventures he was not successful.

While Cambyses was en route home in 522 B.C., word came to his encampment at Mt. Carmel in Palestine that one named Gaumata had usurped the Persian throne, masquerading as Bardiya, the brother of Cambyses whom Cambyses had secretly assassinated. How Cambyses lost his life in 522 B.C. is unknown, but the most frequently told story indicates that he committed suicide.

It was one of Cambyses's officers who took control of the army and marched them home to deal with the insurrection. His name was Darius I or Darius Hystaspes (522–486 B.C.). He put down the revolt and seized the throne for himself, putting Gaumata to death. He recorded his triumph on a mountain cliff, 350 feet above the road leading to Ecbatana, later known as the Behistun Inscription. Because the Behistun Inscription was written in three languages (Persian, Elamite, and Akkadian), it proved invaluable in unlocking the decipherment of the Akkadian cuneiform writing.[2]

Darius was every bit as capable a leader as Cyrus II had been. In fact, where Cyrus had added kingdoms without changing the boundaries, Darius sought to deal with the effects of the serious revolts that had attended his taking over the reins of leadership by changing the boundaries so that the satrapies were arranged in new boundary lines.

To all of these achievements, Darius added a system of judges with fixed circuits and an intricate postal system that provided a much-improved system of communication throughout the Persian Empire. He also revised the fiscal policies of the empire and standardized the coinage, along with making uniform weights and measurements a reality. All of this had the effect of stimulating trade and commerce. Unfor-

2. The heroic efforts of H. C. Rawlinson in 1835, who scaled the cliff to make copies and squeezes of this inscription, finally made it available to scholars. George C. Cameron, *JNES* 2 (1943): 115–16; also idem, *National Geographic Magazine* 98 (1950): 825–44. Samuel Noah Kramer has a good discussion of the Behistun Stone in the first chapter of his *The Sumerians: Their History, Culture and Character* (Chicago: University of Chicago Press, 1963).

tunately for Darius and the economy, all of these changes also had the effect of producing a drastic inflationary spiral which demanded further governmental intervention and controls in what had traditionally been the private sector of the economy. Naturally, this did not win any friends for Darius, bringing him in the end to ruin.

Massive building projects were undertaken during Darius's time as well. Sometime around 521 B.C., Darius made plans to build another palace beside Parsargadae, some three hundred miles to the northwest to Susa (called Shushan in the Bible). It was in this palace that both Esther and Nehemiah lived and served. Later, Darius constructed a new city called Persepolis, where he had hoped to move the capital to its permanent location, but he only saw the beginning of this project. His son and successor, Xerxes, finished the task of building Persepolis.

Peace was restored in all the empire in 520 B.C. except for one satrapy, Mudraya, which is Egypt. Darius launched a campaign in 519 B.C. to rectify that situation, passing through Syria-Palestine, as he must, to get to Egypt. This was the precise time when the dispute broke out in Jerusalem with the Samaritans and Tattenai, the satrap of that province, over whether the Jews were authorized to rebuild their temple, which had been destroyed in 586 B.C. The Judeans claimed that Cyrus had indeed authorized this project, but the Samaritans and Tattenai contested the point. Darius had the records searched, found that the authorization did exist, and ordered that all hostilities against this project cease. Since he was in the area right around the time that the problem arose, passing through on his way to Egypt, he was able to bring a swift and decisive resolution to the problem. Darius entered Egypt in 519 B.C. and marched all the way to Memphis with hardly any resistance.

After he returned to Susa, Darius remained there until 516 B.C. when he began to press east as far as India and to the west as far as Libya. When he went north, the Scythians resisted his advances, so he was forced to retreat. Dissatisfied with this rebuff, Darius set his sights on Europe. His invasion of the Aegean states was hampered by the Ionian states breaking free of their Persian loyalty to assist the Aegeans. Eventually Darius did prevail, and all of Asia Minor was brought into the Persian Empire.

Darius was so elated over his success that he attempted to cross the Aegean Sea in 490 B.C., hoping to conquer Athens and other city-states of that area. He did take the city of Eretria, but the Athenians met Darius in a decisive battle at Marathon, where the Persians suffered a most humiliating defeat, being forced to retreat to the Asian mainland. Darius longed for revenge and resolved to return once more to Greece to do what he had been denied in 490 B.C., but a revolt in Egypt preempted his resolve. But even before he completed attending to this problem, much less completing his European designs, he died and all was left to his son Xerxes (486–465 B.C.) to complete.

Xerxes I is the same as the biblical Ahasuerus.[3] Some years before his death, Darius had designated Xerxes as the heir to his throne. Since there was no contesting of the throne, as often happened in situations such as this, Xerxes's early years as king were occupied with quelling revolutions, especially in that old trouble spot—Babylon. He also had to deal with the problem in Egypt. Unfortunately for the peace of that satrapy, he resolved it in two years, but he did so by suppressing the Egyptian religion. This alienated the priests of Egypt, who had to be relied on to support Persia if Egypt was to remain a loyal part of the empire.

But Xerxes's main interest appeared to lie in completing the palace at Susa and enhancing and completing the work of building at Persepolis. This latter project would occupy his interests on and off for most of the twenty-one years of his reign.

The other part of this monarch's agenda was to avenge his father's defeat at the hands of the Greeks. He moved his armies and navies west in 481 B.C., where he was at first successful due to the badly divided Greek city-states. Even the mighty Spartans were defeated at Thermopylae, fighting down to the last man. But at Salamis, Xerxes met his match, for after he had trapped thousands of Greek warriors, he did not count on how ferociously they would fight. As a result, Xerxes lost two hundred Persian ships. When Xerxes blamed this loss on the cowardice of his Phoenician and Egyptian mercenaries, these mercenaries responded by abandoning Xerxes.

Xerxes placed his general Mardonius in charge of the troops that still remained in Greece as he left for Persia. That proved to be a disaster. Mardonius committed some tactical errors and suffered a series of setbacks, before losing his life in the battle of Plataea. Finally in 479 B.C., the Greeks delivered the decisive blow at Mycale.

The Persians had lost two of their armies to the Greeks, and the third ignominiously returned to Asia. By now the Greeks were learning that some unification was necessary if they were to face such threats and

---

3. Robert Dick Wilson, *A Scientific Investigation of the Old Testament* (Chicago: Moody, 1959), 69, n. 25, has shown that "Ahasuerus" is the proper Hebrew rendering of the Greek "Xerxes."

military challenges in the future. They formed the Delian League in 478 B.C., making Athens the leading partner in the league.

There was little left for Xerxes to do but to turn to a life of indulgence that included numerous sexual encounters with all of the more beautiful women of his court and even with the wives of his chief officials. This too became his undoing. For this dalliance he paid with his life at the hands of a jealous husband or an enraged court official—perhaps Artabanus, commander of the palace guard.

The last important Persian official was Artaxerxes I (464–424 B.C.), also known as Artaxerxes Longimanus. He was not Xerxes's oldest son, since Artaxerxes murdered him, but encouraged by Artabanus, captian of the guard, he took the king's place on the throne.

Artaxerxes's task was not easy. Despite his reduction in the taxes his father had imposed along with some reorganization of the central government, more and more lands began to default on their taxes, falling therefore into the hands of the crown. This created havoc throughout the empire. In 460 B.C. Egypt refused to pay any further tribute and appealed instead to the Delian League for support in this act of defiance. In turn, Artaxerxes bribed Sparta to attack Athens, thereby compromising the league and removing the threat from Egypt.

This was the age of the famous orator Pericles, who gave to Athens a sense of destiny to lead all the other Greek states. Athens emerged from Sparta's challenge in good enough shape to form its own power base, thereby provoking Persian wrath. From 450 B.C. until the start of the Peloponnesian Wars in 431 B.C., control of the Hellenic and Aegean areas seesawed back and forth with no clear victor on either side. Fortunately for Persia, civil wars in the western Asian provinces had the effect of keeping everything in that part of the world in a permanent state of turmoil, thereby allowing Artaxerxes to attend to other matters close at hand. His death came in 424 B.C., just about the time the Old Testament was concluding its story and records.

The Completion of Rebuilding the Temple

During the early years of Darius's reign, the stalled work of reconstructing the temple finally was resumed. The project, which had begun sixteen years previously in 536 B.C. (Ezra 3:8), would now be reinstated as two prophets of Yahweh, Haggai and Zechariah, were sent to urge God's people into action under Zerubbabel the governor and Joshua the high priest. In no more than twenty-four days, from the first message from Yahweh through Haggai (1:1, 15), the people picked up where they had left off sixteen years before and resumed the work on the temple in earnest. This was the second year of King Darius.

Clearly, Zerubbabel was depicted by Ezra-Nehemiah as a returnee from exile (Ezra 2:1–2; Neh. 7:6–7), while the Chronicler also traced his lineage to the Davidic family (1Chron. 3:17–24). We have already treated doubts as to whether he was the same individual as Sheshbazzar in a previous chapter. Besides, Haggai unabashedly presented Zerubbabel as a messianic figure (Hag. 2:2–9, 20–23). Likewise, Zechariah called him one of the "anointeds" (Zech. 4) and may even have linked him with the political-messianic title of "branch" in its present manifestations in Zechariah 6:12–13.

Associated with Zerubbabel in this task of leading the rebuilding of the temple was Joshua, the son of Jehozadak, the high priest. He was designated as the "high priest" in Haggai 1:1, 12, 14; 2:2, 4 and in Zechariah 3:1, 8; 6:11. Indeed, 1 Chronicles 6:1–15 provided a genealogy for Joshua that went back to Aaron, for there were twelve priests from Aaron to the building of the temple and twelve more, if one counts Joshua, from Solomon's temple until the rebuilding of this temple. Surely the genealogy is schematized, as so often happens in other biblical genealogies, for if there were no collpasing of the lineage to these main figures, it would mean an approximate forty-year term for each of the twenty-four priests.

Second Kings 25:18–21 reported that Seriah was the high priest at the time of the fall of Jerusalem. First Chronicles 6:14 declared that Seriah was the father of Jehozadak. Thus Joshua was in the family descended from Zadok the high priest, the official family of priests in Jerusalem previously.

The widespread international turmoil at the time of Cambyses's death and the early years of Darius's reign serve as the background for the renewed prophetic activity of Haggai and Zechariah. These two prophets announced a new, radical, impending action of God that would directly connect the fortunes of the present community, desperate though they were at the time, with the final conquest and victory of Yahweh over every obstacle. Yahweh would shake both the heavens and the earth in a cataclysmic reordering of all things (Hag. 2:1–9).

Opposition to the rebuilding of the temple, however, arose from the Samaritans. This people group had been left in the northern part of the land at the time of the fall of Samaria; they had intermarried with numerous Gentiles who had been repopulated in the area, according to the Assyrian policy of redistribution of their subjugated peoples. The satrap of Abar Nahara itself, Tattenai, joined in the opposition. At first it was not that serious: they merely inquired as to who gave authority to undertake this building project. Then Tattenai wrote directly to Darius, asking if confirmation could be given. When word was received that official Persian approval had been given long ago by Cyrus II (Ezra 5:3; 6:14), the Samaritans ceased their opposition and even lent assistance as they were informed by Persia that they had to do so (Ezra 6:6–12). A copy of Cyrus's decree turned up at the palace of Ecbatana, the old Median capital, where Cyrus must have been in residence when the decree was made.

Four years later, in March 515 B.C., the sixth year of Darius, the temple was completed. This was some twenty years after the foundations had been laid when the people had first returned from exile (Ezra 6:15)—a date that marked the end of the threatened "seventy years" of captivity in a cultic sense.

Haggai warned that the people were not to treat this small accomplishment with contempt, for the day would come when God would fill this humble structure with the glory of his climactic triumph (Hag. 2:6–9).

Esther and the Persian Court

Almost all critical scholars deny the historicity of the Book of Esther,[4] which is our only Book of the Bible that describes life in the Jewish diaspora and the only witness to the reign of Xerxes. But the fact remains that the author of Esther does not contradict anything that is known from all the sources from this period that are available to us. The objections are basically arguments from silence.

4. For example, Otto Eissfeldt, *The Old Testament: An Introduction*, tr. Peter R. Ackroyd (New York: Harper and Row, 1965), 507, claims that "the book contains a whole series of historical inaccuracies and inexactitudes." Eissfeldt (p. 512) quotes with approval a remark attributed to Martin Luther: "For Christianity Luther's remark should be determinative, a remark made with reference to II Maccabees and Esther in his Table Talk: 'I am so hostile to this book and to Esther that I could wish that they did not exist at all, for they Judaize too greatly and have much pagan impropriety.'" (From the Weimar Edition, *Tischreden*, vol. 1, 1912, p. 208, or W. Hazlitt, *Table Talk* [1919], p. 11). The same negative judgment can be found in B. Davie Napier, *Song of the Vineyard: A Theological Introduction to the Old Testament* (New York: Harper and Brothers, 1962), 364: "It is a good story; but it isn't history, and it certainly isn't theology." A more positive appraisal can be found in Gleason L. Archer, *A Survey of Old Testament Introduction* (Chicago: Moody, 1964), 404–06 and R. K. Harrison, *Introduction to the Old Testament* (Grand Rapids: Eerdmans, 1969), 1085–1102. Harrison concludes by agreeing with the judgment of B. W. Anderson in *The Interpreter's Bible*, vol. III, p. 827, that "historians and archaeologists have already confirmed the fact that the author possessed an amazingly accurate knowledge of Persian palaces and manners. Further light on this dark period of Jewish history may reveal that the author's claim for the historicity of this story is not totally erroneous."

The Book of Esther began in Susa, the winter palace of the Persian kings. It was the third year of Xerxes[5] (483 B.C.), who is here called "Ahasuerus" in Hebrew or *Khshayarsha* in Old Persian, the Persian ruler from 486 to 465 B.C. All commentators agree that Xerxes's empire stretched from India to Ethiopia (Esther 1:1) and that the lavish banquet at the opening of the Book of Esther in Xerxes's third year corresponded to the great council to plan the invasion of Greece (Esther 1:3; Herodotus, vii. 8). Moreover, the strange gap of four years between 1:3 and 2:16 can be satisfactorily explained as the time from 483 to 480 B.C., when Xerxes was pursuing his ill-fated invasion of Greece.

At the end of a seven-day banquet, Xerxes ordered his queen Vashti to pose before the drunken revelers. When she refused, the king had her deposed. A search for a new queen was inaugurated, but apparently it was interrupted by the Grecian campaign from 483 to 480 B.C. before the new queen could be installed.

The contest winner was Esther, a young Jewish orphan, who lived in Susa with her older cousin Mordecai. "Mordecai" is a Hebrew transliteration of the Babylonian name of the god Marduk. What a pious Jew was doing with a pagan name like this can only be surmised! "Esther" is likewise a form of the goddess "Ishtar." Apparently neither revealed their national identity up to this point.

Cyrus H. Gordon[6] has drawn attention to a distinctively Iranian institution, which survives into modern times, known as *kitman* or *taqiyya*, which may be rendered as "dissimulation." According to this procedure, an individual is permitted to deny his or her own religion while posing as a member of some other faith if confronted with acute personal danger. Professor Gordon illustrated this from modern Iranian life by showing how Shiites of Iran are permitted to pose with impunity as Sunnites when going on the pilgrimage to Mecca, which is in the hands of the Arab Sunnites, who on occasion have been known to display violent hostility towards Shiites. Thus Mordecai forbade his cousin Esther to disclose her identity. This may explain her use of her non-Hebrew name, even though her Hebrew name was Hadassah (Esther 2:7), meaning "myrtle."

---

5. Even though Xerxes is the correct equivalent for Ahasuerus, it is not without note that the Septuagint and Josephus regard him as Artaxerxes I (464–424 B.C.). In recent years two authors have made a case for his being Artaxerxes II (404–358 B.C.), viz., Jacob Hoschander, *The Book of Esther in Light of History* (Philadelphia: 1923) and Arthur T. Olmstead, *History of Palestine and Syria* (New York: Scribner, 1931), 612–14. But the etymological equation is against both of these suggestions.
6. Cyrus H. Gordon, *Riddles in History* (New York: Crown Publishing, 1974), 88–89.

J. Stafford Wright[7] argued rather convincingly that Vashti refused to pose before the drunken banquet when ordered to do so by Xerxes because she was pregnant with Artaxerxes I. This Wright deduced from the fact that Artaxerxes I was eighteen when he came to the throne in 464/5 B.C. That would mean he was born in 483 B.C., presumably sometime shortly after the lavish banquet described in Esther. This would mean that Vashti is the Hebrew rendering of the Greek "Amestris," a case that Wright presses with more than a little care. Amestris/Vashti exerted her power until her death in 424 B.C.

Herodotus recorded a particularly unpleasant episode in Amestris's past.[8] Amestris, despite her being deposed, was taken along with the king's other women on the Grecian campaign. Amestris tried to win Xerxes back by making an especially fine robe which she wove herself. Meanwhile Xerxes, continued Herodotus, was having an affair with his brother's wife and her daughter, a daughter who could have whatever she requested from Xerxes. She chose the robe that Amestris had woven for Xerxes. Amestris was furious and, as a result, had her mutilated and her tongue torn out. Apparently one does not easily get rid of the mother of the royal children as easily as a mere statement of deposition. Xerxes had to wait, therefore, for things to cool down before a new queen could be announced. Perhaps this is why Esther 2:1 implied a lapse of time when it said, "Later when the anger of King Xerxes had subsided, he remembered Vashti and what she had done and what he had decreed about her."

However, after the lapse of time, Esther was made queen in Xerxes's seventh year, 479 B.C. He had returned from the Grecian campaign, leaving Mardonius in charge and to his fate at Plataea.

It was about this same time that a conspiracy was brewing in the palace. Esther's cousin, Mordecai, was "sitting at the king's gate" (Esther 2:19, 21; 5:13; 6:10), not as a sort of unemployed vagabond who frequented the palace entrance, hoping for a free handout from some of the persons going in and out of the palace on business. The king's gate was not a simple architectural unit; it was the center of auxiliary buildings belonging to the palace and included all the management offices of the palace. "To sit" means, in this context, as in modern Hebrew, "to

7. J. Stafford Wright, "The Historicity of Esther," in *New Perspectives of the Old Testament*, ed. by J. Barton Payne (Waco, Tex.: Word, 1970), 37–47.

8. Herodotus, *History of the Persian Wars*, ix. 108 f. Also see Ctesias' *History of Persia*, xiiii. 59. Herodotus was a contemporary of Xerxes (ca. 484–424 B.C.), and Ctesias completed his *History* about 398 B.C. Both had access to original sources, and Ctesias was a physician at the Persian court from 412 B.C. onwards. He claims to have used written records and the testimony of eyewitnesses for this part of his history.

be stationed, to have an office at a particular place." It was in this capacity as a royal employee working in the palace offices that Mordecai learned of the plot of two bodyguards to kill King Xerxes. Mordecai may have been the head of what amounted to the king's secret service (note that Esther 4:1 claimed that Mordecai knew everything that was going on in the court).[9] The king's ill fortune in the Greek campaign may have signaled to some that the king could be replaced and that he was losing his grip on things. Anyway, Mordecai reported the plot to the king through Esther and the incident was made a matter of record. As such, Mordecai may have received the title of *orosanges* (benefactor of the king), as Herodotus described it.[10] This benefactor had the privilege of not prostrating himself to anyone other than the king. This may have been the reason why Mordecai did not prostrate himself to Haman. Angered by Mordecai's refusal, Haman somehow learned that Mordecai was Jewish and thus he persuaded Xerxes to sign a decree that on the thirteenth of Adar (the twelfth month), all Jews would be attacked and killed and their property confiscated. Mordecai informed Esther that she had to go at the risk of her life to Xerxes and disclose that she too was Jewish and what this meant to her people.

At a special banquet at which Haman was present, Esther revealed to the king what Haman was about to do. Xerxes ordered Haman's immediate execution. He also authorized the Jews to defend themselves. In the fighting that ensued on that date, some eleven months from when "they cast the *pur*," that is the "lot" (Esther 3:7), to choose the date for the murder of the Jews, 75,000 would-be executioners died. The *pur* is known from other contexts as a one-inch cube of clay with writing on it. These cubes were used as dice to determine matters that needed to be arbitrated or which were believed to be in the hands of the gods. It was for this reason—when the Jews successfully defended themselves—that the festival called the Feast of Purim was instituted to mark the turning of this sorrowful day into one of joy (Esther 9:26–28).[11]

---

9. See Michael Heltzer, "The Book of Esther," *BA* 8.1 (1992), 25–30, 41, for this and other interesting background information from archaeology on this book. For example, he pointed to a number of Old Persian terms that had gone out of use by hellenistic times: *parthĕmîm*, the Hebrew word for "aristocrats" is from *fratama* in Old Persian; *achashdarpan* is the word for "satrap" or "provincial governor;" *bitan*, a Western Semitic word, is the word for "garden house" or "pavilion." All these words were no longer in use in the Hellenistic periods; and thus the book could not have come from that late period, said Heltzer, pp. 26–27. It had to come sometime in the reign of Xerxes or between 465 and 325 B.C.

10. Herodotus, *History* iii. 138, 140; v: 11; viii. 88; ix. 109.

11. See the Glossary in the appendix for a list of all the festivals with a brief definition of each.

THE RETURNS OF EZRA AND NEHEMIAH

When Cyrus the Great had conquered Babylon and became the titular head of the Medo-Persian Empire, he issued his famous decree in 538 B.C. that allowed deported peoples like the Judeans to return to their homes. Sheshbazzar led that first return, which ultimately led to the rebuilding of the temple. Two more returns were to follow under Ezra and Nehemiah.

THE CHRONOLOGICAL PROBLEM[12]

Both Ezra and Nehemiah date the year of their returns in the reign of Artaxerxes: Ezra to "the fifth month of the seventh year of the king" [Artaxerxes in Ezra 7:8) and Nehemiah to "the month of Nisan in the twentieth year of King Artaxerxes" (Neh. 2:1). But which Artaxerxes did they mean: Artaxerxes I or Artaxerxes II? Thus, if both labored under the reign of Artaxerxes I, then Ezra returned to Jerusalem in 458 B.C., just sixteen years after the institution of the Feast of Purim in 474 B.C.; and Nehemiah returned in 445 B.C. Those are the traditional dates favored for the returns of both under the rule of Artaxerxes I.

The alternative view, favored by many scholars, has Nehemiah's return in 445 B.C., but would have Ezra *follow* Nehemiah either in the seventh year of Artaxerxes II, i.e., in 398 B.C.,[13] or by gratuitously assuming a mistake in the manuscript reading of the "seventh year" that should have read instead the "thirty-seventh year" of Artaxerxes I, i.e. 428 B.C.[14] There is no manuscript evidence for this last position. Hence, the options are between the 458 and 398 B.C. views.[15]

Of all the arguments used to place Nehemiah before Ezra, contrary to the traditional reversal of this order, two are most telling: (1) Ezra's work in Jerusalem seems to presuppose a restored, reconstructed, and repopulated city; and (2) the high priest at the time of Nehemiah was Eliashib (Neh. 3:20; 13:4), whereas the high priest at the time of Ezra

12. For a discussion of this problem, see H. H. Rowley, "The Chronological Order of Ezra and Nehemiah," in *The Servant of the Lord and Other Essays on the Old Testament* (London: Lutterworth, 1952), 131–59, and for an evangelical view, J. Stafford Wright, *The Date of Ezra's Coming to Jerusalem*, 2nd ed. (London, Tyndale, 1958).

13. This view is held, e.g., by Otto Eissfeldt, *The Old Testament: An Introduction*, p. 554.

14. This last view is espoused by John Bright, *History*, p. 400.

15. Recently Aaron Demsky, "Who Returned First: Ezra or Nehemiah?" *BR* 12.2 (1996): 28–33, 46, has argued that Ezra arrived in Jerusalem the "fifth month of the seventh year" was Ab (August) 443 B.C., just two and one-half years after Nehemiah arrived. The reference to "King Artaxerxes" in Ezra 7:7, he would argue, was added by a redactor or copyist as a gloss; but there is no support for this supposition. He would make the seventh year the seventh year of the Sabbatical cycle. Indeed, a Sabbatical cycle would fall in the year 444/443 B.C., but there still is the problem of the text to contend with.

was Jehohanan the son of Eliashib (Ezra 10:6). Are these arguments adequate to sustain a Nehemiah-Ezra chronology?

There is every reason to believe that some kind of wall and a settlement of Jerusalem did exist when Ezra arrived in Jerusalem before Nehemiah's return; for why would Nehemiah be surprised that the wall of Jerusalem had been destroyed some 140 years after the event if he meant the 586 B.C. destruction of Jerusalem (Neh. 1:2–4)? Neither is Ezra's failure to mention Nehemiah's name significant, for Nehemiah does in fact mention Ezra (Neh. 8:9; 12:26, 36), and many other contemporaries in the Bible fail to mention each other (e.g., Haggai and Zechariah or Isaiah and Micah).

The line of the high priests is not the problem some believe it to be, for the line, as given in Nehemiah 12:10–11, 22 is: Jeshua, Joiakim, Eliashib, Joiada, Jonathan [a variant of Jehohanan], and Jaddua. Thus, Jehohanan is actually the grandson of Eliashib, not the son. *Son* can be used as the legitimate word for "grandson," for both render the same Hebrew word. Moreover, Johanan appears in the Elephantine Papyri as the high priest of Jerusalem in the seventeenth year of Darius II (407 B.C.), almost fifty years after the traditional date of 458 B.C. for Ezra's return—a date suiting the 398 B.C. date. However, note that the "Eliashib" of Ezra 10:6 is not called a priest, so linking him with the Eliashib in Nehemiah's time is speculative. The names and the order of the high priests in the Persian period is a most complex matter, especially since they often alternated generations, using the same name over again in a phenomenon known as patronymics. When this is coupled with a tendency to record only the more important persons in the line, it becomes extremely complex and is probably not to be used as a basis for making any sure chronological conclusions.

The Return under Ezra

Like Sheshbazzar almost eighty years before him, Ezra also received from the Persian monarch permission to return to Jerusalem. Perhaps Artaxerxes's reasoning was that this was the way to secure Judean loyalty in a key area that was a link between Mesopotamia and Egypt: have a highly popular and recognized Jewish leader reestablish Jewish life in this area that was a land bridge to all of the Fertile Crescent. Regardless of his motives, Artaxerxes graciously allowed Ezra to lead a second return back to Jerusalem.

Artaxerxes had neutralized the Delian League by 460 B.C. He had also had an official named Megabyzus bribe Sparta to attack Athens, thus denying Egypt her anticipated help against Persia. Then Megabyzus went south and brought Egypt into line in 456 B.C., thus the period around 458 B.C., when Ezra returned home, provided an opportune window for such an event.

Ezra assembled the small group of some 1,500 men at the Ahava Canal, a number smaller by far than the almost 50,000 people in the first return. When Ezra discovered that no Levites were among this small number, he delayed his return until he had persuaded 38 Levites and some 220 Nethinim (meaning "given ones," descendants of the foreign prisoners who had been made "hewers of wood and drawers of water" for the temple) to join in this return to Jerusalem. Finally they departed on the twelfth day of the first month (458 B.C.) and arrived three and one-half months later in Jerusalem (Ezra 7:9; 8:31).

Ezra had won a number of important concessions from Artaxerxes, including the return of the gold and silver that had been taken from the Jerusalem temple; permission to draw on the royal treasury of the satrap of Abar-nahara for any additional needs that might arise; exemption of temple personnel from Persian taxation; and the right to appoint civil magistrates in the land of Judah and to enforce the Torah with power of life and death over the guilty. Even with all of these inducements, the prospects of returning to the Jewish homeland were not all that tempting to most Judeans who had by now settled down to life in exile.

Over fifty years of silence pass between the dedication of the second temple in 515 B.C. and Ezra's arrival in the land in the seventh year of Artaxerxes in 458 B.C. As the delegated representative of the Persian crown, Ezra bore the title of "scribe of the law of God of heaven" (Ezra 7:12), which was roughly equivalent to making him minister of Jewish affairs.[16] Typical of the Persians' tolerance of all religions, Ezra was recognized by the government as the responsible authority for Jewish affairs in the province of Abar-nahara, Syria, and Palestine (Ezra 7:25).

The populace left in the land did not receive Ezra enthusiastically, for there were a number of matters that needed attention from a spiritual standpoint. Chief among them was the matter of marriage outside the faith, which included a number of priests and Levites as well (Ezra 9:1). Moses had warned that the Israelites were not to marry or give in marriage any of their sons and daughters to those who did not confess Yahweh as their Lord (Deut. 7:3). Such disobedience had always been the prelude to apostasy, as was true, for example, in the case of Solomon (1 Kings 11:1–8). Ezra was stunned by such disregard for the Law of

16. See John Bright, *A History of Israel*, p. 370.

God as he poured out his heart and soul to God in confession and penitence (Ezra 9:6–15). He ripped his clothes, tore out his hair, and sat appalled and confounded until evening.

Slowly the populace gathered around the grieving scribe. A certain Shechaniah, a descendant of Elam (Iran) no less, suggested that they all put away their foreign wives and children (Ezra 10:2–3). This was agreed on, but when the people came together in the public square to carry out this affirmation, they found that it was too large a task to accomplish in a short time, especially during a cold rainstorm (Ezra 10:9–15). A divorce court was set up (Ezra 10:16–17) for the next three months to adjudicate these matters. There is no doubt that such separations caused enormous hardship and heartbreak, but Ezra was determined to be zealous for the purity of the community's life and faith as taught in the Law of God.

The Return under Nehemiah

Nehemiah had risen in the court to be the cupbearer of Artaxerxes I (Neh. 2:1), a position that put him in personal contact with the monarch himself.[17] What got Nehemiah involved in the Jerusalem affair was word that came to him from a small delegation of persons that included his brother. Their description of the state of affairs in Jerusalem was disheartening. Surprisingly, this small delegation had deliberately bypassed the uncooperative adminstrators of the satrapy "Beyond the River" (Ezra 4:7–23) and had gone directly to the king's cupbearer, hoping for some clout from Nehemiah and personal attention of Artaxerxes. The report was that "the wall of Jerusalem is broken down, and its gates have been burned with fire" (Neh. 1:3).

Once again it would appear that the times had been arranged providentially for this third return to Jerusalem to take place. It happened in this manner. After Megabyzus, now governor of Syria, had subdued Egypt, he took some Greek and Egyptian commanders with him to Susa with the promise that they would be under Persian protection. This promise was kept for several years until Amestris, Xerxes's widow, demanded and obtained their execution in 449 B.C. This action so infuriated Megabyzus that he left Susa and returned to Syria, where he announced his independence from Persia of the whole of the trans-Euphratean satrapy. Twice he was able to repel two Persian campaigns against him; but, now that he had demonstrated what he wanted to say

17. The position of "cupbearer" in the Persian court was a very exalted position, as A. T. Olmstead, *History*, p. 217 noted: "Behind Xerxes stands the cupbearer, who in later Achaemenid times was to exercise even more influence than the commander-in-chief."

and had made his point, or matters had changed in Susa, Megabyzus returned to Susa, announcing his loyalty once again to the crown sometime around 447 B.C., just two years before Nehemiah would ask Artaxerxes for permission to return to Israel.

These incidents are enough to provide us with a window into what was going on in Syria and perhaps in Palestine at this time. Things were not going well in Syria-Palestine for Artaxerxes I. After Nehemiah had spent four months praying about the devastating report of conditions back in the city of Jerusalem, he was ready to verbalize his request one day when the king noticed his downcast countenance, inquiring why he was so disheartened. Nehemiah then told of the distressing news he had heard some four months previously. Artaxerxes was more than prepared to grant such a request, providing him royal letters guaranteeing safe conduct and whatever materials Nehemiah would need for the task of rebuilding the walls (Neh. 2:7–8).

When Nehemiah arrived in Jerusalem, things were as bad or worse than he had imagined. The city and its walls lay in ruins, and opposition to any restoration to what things had been previously was strong. After all, it was to Samaria's advantage to keep her former partner in the country weak so that her own prosperity could be enjoyed. In order to keep any news about Nehemiah's intentions from leaking out, he made a secret noctural survey of the ruins and began to form a plan for their restoration. Nehemiah then gathered the leaders of Jerusalem and presented his plan in which every segment of society—including the priesthood, Levites, the landed gentry, goldsmiths, and merchants—each would work on a specified section of the wall (Neh. 3). Workers also came from the outside villages: Jericho, Gibeon, Mizpah, Beth-haccherem, Zanoah, Beth-zur, Keilah, and Tekoa.

Opposition to this refortification work came almost immediately from the neighboring leaders of provinces. Leading the opposition was Sanballat the Horonite (from Bethhoron in Samaria; Neh. 2:10). His daughter later married into the family of Eliashib, high priest in Jerusalem (Neh. 13:28). He is also known from the Aramaic Papyri from Elephantine as the governor of Samaria in the seventeenth year of Darius III (i.e., 407 B.C.). It is likely that he had been governor some forty years earlier during this time of Nehemiah since he had grown sons by the time we meet him in the Elephantine Papyri.[18] Sanballat was aided by Tobiah, called "the Ammonite official" (Neh. 2:10), but is known

18. James Pritchard, ed., *ANET*, 2nd ed., p. 492. For more on the Sanballat family, see Frank M. Cross, "Papyri of the Fourth Century B.C. from Daliyeh," in *New Directions in Biblical Archaeology*, ed. David Noel Freedman and Jonas C. Greenfield (Garden City, N.Y.: Doubleday, 1971), pp. 47–48, 59–63.

elsewhere as the governor of Ammon.[19] The third opponent was Geshem the Arab (Neh. 2:19; 6:6), a chief of sorts from a tribe in northwestern Arabia, whose name was discovered in 1947 at *Tell el-Maskhutah* in Lower Egypt on a silver bowl inscription along with three other similarly inscribed bowls dedicated to the goddess *Han-'ilat.* It read: "That which Qaynu, son of Gashmu, king of Qedar, brought in offering to *Han-'Ilat.*" This inscription is dated around 400 B.C., based on the style of the Aramaic script, the type of bowl, and the Athenian coins found along with the bowls at this site.[20] There was more than enough opposition to discourage Nehemiah and make him give up the idea of restoring the walls.

After Sanballat and his allies found out that mockery would not stop the work on the walls, they determined to take more drastic action. By now the walls had grown to half their height (Neh. 4:6). Sanballat sent guerilla bands against Jerusalem. The Ammonites, Arabians, and Ashdodites all harassed the workers and Nehemiah (4:7). Then there came a sneak attack, but Nehemiah had stationed armed guards to protect the vulnerable spots in the wall (4:13). Seeing that the Jews were now armed, the opposition resorted to other means.

A trumpeter stood beside Nehemiah at all times to summon the people to respond to an attack, for all builders now carried a sword girded to their side as they wielded the trowel (4:18). Those outside of Jerusalem were instructed to remain in the city and sleep with their weapons close at hand (4:22–23). But there were new problems for Nehemiah to face: loss of income for the workers, who had left farms and homes, was forcing some of them into debt as they mortgaged their fields and vineyards to pay their taxes and provide for food. Some had even sold their children into slavery to raise the capital necessary to meet these obligations (5:5).

Nehemiah was angered by the way the wealthy class was using this national crisis to make an inordinate amount of money for themselves. The nobles and officials promised Nehemiah that they would cease to exploit the poor and restore what they had taken unfairly (5:12–19).

Nehemiah's enemies resorted to new tactics: they would take him by intrigue. Four times they tried to get him to come to confer with them

19. Benjamin Mazar, "The Tobiads," *IEJ* 7 (1957): 137–45. It is almost certain that he was an ancestor of the Tobiads, who governed Ammon for generations, as indicated by the Zenon Papyri (third century) and from their tomb remains and the palace near present-day Amman, Jordan (*Araq el-Emir*). There is an inscription at the tomb containing the name *Tobiah.* See C. C. McCown, *BA* 20 (1957): 63–76.

20. William J. Dumbrell, "The Tell el-Maskhuta Bowls and the 'Kingdom' of Qedar in the Persian Period," *BASOR* 203 (1971): 33–44.

in the Valley of Ono in Benjamin, but he refused to stop his work to go (6:1–4). In a fifth attempt, they sent a letter accusing Nehemiah of a conspiracy to rebel against Persia and make himself king in Judah (6:5–7). The charge was utterly false and unworthy of a dignified response (6:8). Finally, Sanballat and Tobiah took the extreme measure of hiring a prophet to advise Nehemiah, as from God, that he ought to take sanctuary in the temple (an act prohibited by the Law) to avoid assassination (6:10–13), but Nehemiah remained unmovable, to the consternation of his enemies.

In less than two months, fifty-two days in all, the wall was finished (6:15). In the next two years and four months, the gates and battlements were further strengthened, according to Josephus.[21] Nehemiah appointed his brother Hanani and a man named Hananiah, governor of the castle, to assume responsibility for the welfare of Jerusalem. They were to keep the city gates locked until the sun was well up in the sky and to post a guard at all times (7:2–3). Judah itself was much smaller in these postexilic times than previously. The whole of it was a rough rectangle extending north and south about twenty-five miles; bounded on the north by Gibeon and Mizpah (Neh 3:7, 15, 19), on the east by Jericho, and on the south near Hebron; its western boundaries are unknown to us. South of Judah, the province of the Idumaeans had been established; it included the cities of Hebron in the north and Beersheba in the south, without the coastal plain.

The dedication ceremonies were full of celebration and personal dedication to Yahweh (12:30). Two processions circled the rebuilt walls in opposite directions, Ezra at the head of one and Nehemiah at the head of the other, meeting at the temple area (12:31–43).

Nehemiah took leave of Jerusalem for a short time to return to the court at Susa under Artaxerxes I, but when he returned, after being granted a second leave of absence from the court, he found that the enemy was now the people themselves within the gates rather than the old opposition on the outside. There was internal dissension, infidelity, intermarriage with nonbelievers, operations of the wine presses on the Sabbath, and Tyrian merchants bringing fish and merchandise into the city on the Sabbath contrary to the Law of God (13:15–16). Israelite men had once again married women from Ashdod, Ammon, and Moab; thus, their children spoke no Hebrew but the language of their mothers. Even Nehemiah's inveterate enemy, Tobiah, the Ammonite,

21. Josephus, *Antiquities*, XI. 179.

had been befriended by Eliashib the high priest and had been given housing in the temple chambers (13:4–5).

Nehemiah chased off Tobiah and appealed to the leaders of the city to close the gates on the Sabbath (13:17–18). When some tried to circumvent this law by selling their wares outside the city, Nehemiah threatened to remove them forcibly (13:20–21). As for the intermarriages, Nehemiah made the people swear that they would not permit their children to marry into the families of the neighboring nations. Even Eliashib's grandson had married the daughter of Sanballat; the grandson was banished from Jerusalem (Neh. 13:28).

How long Nehemiah remained in Judah this time is unknown. It is not known if he ever went back to the Persian capital. What is known is that he was not governor of Judah in 407 B.C., for the Elephantine Papyri give the governor's name as Bagoas.

The Prophet Malachi

Malachi, the last writing prophet of the Old Testament, probably ministered during the time of Nehemiah. Even though Nehemiah does not refer to him, he probably wrote sometime around 433 to 425 B.C., while Nehemiah was back in Susa.

Malachi, just like Ezra and Nehemiah, called the people to repent, for the people had grossly violated the covenant of God. They had failed to understand the fact that God loved them. Instead, they had treated God with mere lip service, offered maimed and diseased sacrifices and gifts that cost them very little (1:6–14). They had also violated their marriage vows, divorcing their legitimate wives and marrying any they pleased (2:10–16). God would send his messenger of the covenant to deal with such abuses and violations so that a purified remnant would emerge. In that final day, the Sun of Righteousness would rise with healing in his wings (Mal. 4:2) and the hearts of the fathers would turn to their children and the hearts of the children would turn to their fathers (Mal. 4:6).

Late Developments in This Period

The trail of the history of Israel grows cold from the days of Ezra-Nehemiah until the times of Alexander the Great. What effect such events as the Persian-Egyptian wars, the revolt of the satraps, or Tennes's Phoenician rebellion had on Judah is unknown.

One account from Josephus's *Antiquities* (XI. 297–301) during the reign of Artaxerxes III (if this location of the events is correct) gives us some insight into the turmoil that was affecting Judah in these years of silence. According to Josephus's account, the Jewish high priest Johanan slew his brother Jeshua in the temple of God. Jeshua had hoped to acquire the position of high priest with the help of his friend, the Persian general Bagoas.

This Bagoas was a close friend of Artaxerxes III, according to the historian Diodorus,[22] who must have entered the temple on behalf of Jeshua. Because the Jews protested so loudly his entry into the temple and also as a consequence of the murder, Bagoas "made the Jews suffer seven years" by placing on them a special tribute tax for every sacrifice made in the temple.[23]

Bagoas was described as the real master of the kingdom and the one who advised Artaxerxes so frequently that the monarch did nothing without checking with Bagoas. But Bagoas was very powerful, for after the Persian troops had plundered the temples of the Egyptians, Bagoas returned the inscribed records to the Egyptian priests when they paid huge sums as ransom.[24]

All of this shows that members of the high priestly family such as Jeshua were able to work their way into the upper echelons of the Persian administration. And it also demonstrates, by Bagoas's intervention into the life of the temple, just how much control Persia was able to exercise in the satrapies. Moreover, the struggle between Johanan and Jeshua shows the importance of a political post such as the high priest's office.[25]

The Persian Empire would shortly come crashing down just as had the Israelite, the Aramean, the Assyrian, and the Babylonian Empires before it. The lessons of the previous empires were experienced, only to be repeated by those who learned very little from their predecessors.

---

22. Diodorus, XVI.
23. Josephus, *Antiquities*, XI. 297, 301.
24. Diodorus XVI. 51. 2.
25. These observations follow closely those made by J. Maxwell Miller and John H. Hayes, *A History of Ancient Israel and Judah* (Philadelphia: Westminster, 1986), 474-75.

Part IX

The Intertestamental Period

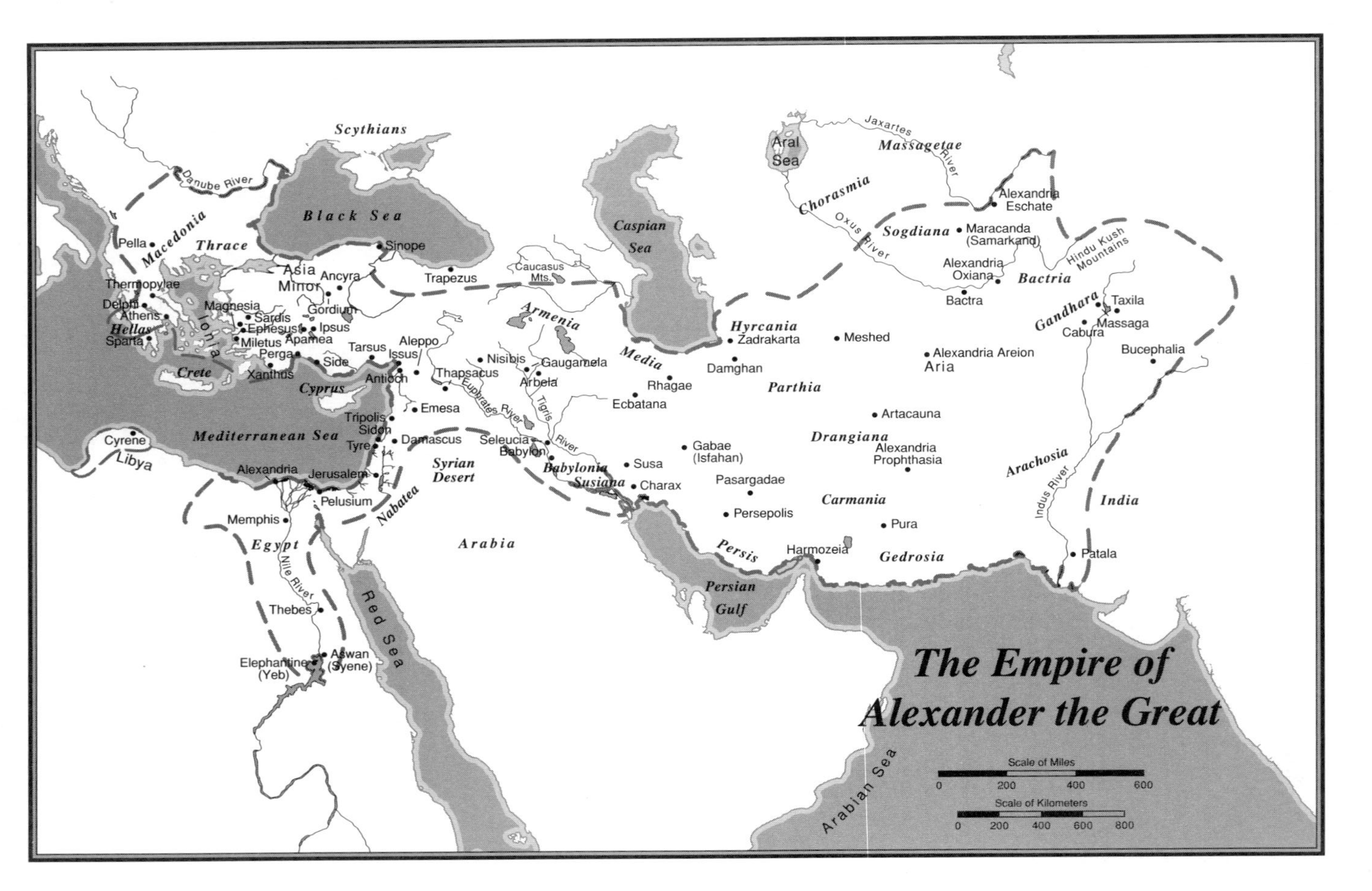

From *Holman Bible Handbook* (Nashville: Holman Bible Publishers, 1992), 452.

29

THE HELLENISTIC AGE (332–167 B.C.)

The period of Persia's greatness extended from about 550 B.C. to about 330 B.C. The latter days of the Achemenians (a name derived from a not-too-well-known ruler from the mountainous area in southwestern modern Iran) was filled with intrigue and corruption at every level. But other forces were at work as well, namely, the Greeks.

THE LATTER ACHEMENIANS

At first, the Persians used their horde of gold to incite Athens against Sparta in the Peloponnesian Wars. This strengthened the Persian influence over the Greek cities in Asia Minor while the Greeks on the mainland attacked each other instead of coming to the rescue of those who lived in ancient Asia Minor or Anatolia.

Family intrigues in the Persian court further weakened their empire. For example, Artaxerxes II barely missed being killed by his brother Cyrus during his coronation ceremony at Persepolis. Because his mother intervened, Artaxerxes pardoned Cyrus, but Cyrus would not halt his plots of rebellion. Cyrus raised an army and almost won a battle near Babylon. But Cyrus was killed in battle; thus, the threat passed.

Xenophon made the Greek contingent of Cyrus's army famous by telling the story of how, after the disastrous battle of Cunaxa in 401 B.C., the "ten thousand," as the Greeks were called, fought their way back home as they passed through hostile territory controlled by the Persians and led by Tissaphernes. After the Persians killed the Greek's generals, Xenophon was chosen as one of the leaders of the retreat. Xenophon's account of how he led the troops up the Tigris, past ruined Nineveh, to the Black Sea and on to Byzantium is recorded in his *Anabasis*, now regarded as one of the best books on military science from the ancient world.

The Persian Empire, however, was beginning to fall apart. A number of the satrapies had already become powerful and continued as hereditary offices. Egypt had also revolted at the accession of Artaxerxes II and was never reconquered during his whole reign. Cyprus, Phoenicia, and Syria followed suit. Disintegration continued except for a moment of glory under Artaxerxes III, who ruled momentarily with the strength of a former Darius the Great. He began his reign by murdering all his brothers and sisters—several dozen. He retaliated against the revolters by burning Sidon to the ground for its sympathizing with rebellious Egypt. He then reconquered the land of Egypt and stood poised to take on the Greeks.

The Latter Achemenians

Artaxerxes II	404–358 B.C.
Artaxerxes III	358–338 B.C.
Arses	338–336 B.C.
Darius III	336–331 B.C.

By this time, Hellenism had become a major cultural and, increasingly, a political force that the Persians had to deal with. This Greek culture became the bond and rallying cry that would unite otherwise disparate peoples against the Persians. While the Greeks on the mainland lacked the unity necessary to overthrow the Persians, such a leader—named Philip—was emerging in the north at Macedonia.

Athens timidly had concluded an alliance with Persia, strongly influenced by the oratory of Demosthenes. But Philip of Macedonia did not agree with this action. Thus in 338 B.C., Philip and his son Alexander won a major victory over Athens, placing the Persian threat on notice. Artaxerxes was poisoned that same year, probably by one named Bogoas, a eunuch in the court with his own political ambitions.

Bogoas spared the life of Artaxerxes's youngest son, Arses, hoping to use him as a puppet king. But when Arses showed that he, too, had a mind of his own, Bogoas poisoned him as well. Bogoas chose the cousin of Artaxerxes III as someone he could use, a man who had proved himself in previous battles and had been appointed satrap in Armenia. This cousin took the name of Darius III. Since he did not trust Bogoas, Darius III had him poisoned. Darius III is probably the same "Darius the Persian" mentioned in Nehemiah 12:22. This same verse also mentions the priest Jaddua, whom Josephus[1] identifies as a contemporary of Alexander the Great.

Just as Darius III was ascending the throne as king of Persia in 336 B.C., the twenty-year-old Alexander was ascending the throne in Macedonia with his father Philip's commission to make war on Persia. It did not take long for the tide of history to change, for by 333 B.C. Alexander opened a new chapter in the history of the Near East by defeating Darius III at the crucial battle of Issus.

Two years later, Alexander had carried the battle all the way to the center of the Persian Empire with his victories at Gaugemela or Arbela. Darius III fled, first to Ecbatana, then to Bactria, where he was murdered by his cousin Bessus. Bessus then took command, but he was unsuccessful in opposing Alexandria in Bactria. And so the last hurrah was heard from the mighty Persians.

The Elephantine Jews

Very little information exists about the Jews in Israel during this period. Some data about Jews in Egypt during the close of the Persian period, however, did become available as a result of the excavations of 1907 and 1908.[2] These excavations were carried out on the island of Elephantine, ancient Yeb, opposite Assuan (called Syene in Ezek. 29:10; 30:6), at the first cataract of the Nile River. A number of Aramaic papyri were discovered; these described the life of Jews who were living there between 494 and 400 B.C.

Most of the Elephantine documents were business contracts involving loans, conveyance of property, and the like. But two documents help explain Jewish religious life in Egypt in the fifth century B.C. One letter written in 407 B.C. contained a petition addressed to Bagohi (Bagoas), the Persian governor of Judah, asking him to order the rebuilding of their recently destroyed temple at Elephantine. This same petition was sent jointly to Bagohi and to Delaiah in Samaria. Another

1. Josephus, *Antiquities* xi. 8. 4
2. The most useful summary of the Elephantine finds is to be found in Emil G. Kraeling, "New Light on the Elephantine Colony," in *Biblical Archaeologist Reader*, eds. G. E. Wright and D. N. Freedman (Garden City, N.Y.: Doubleday, 1961), I: 128–44.

petition was also addressed to Delaiah and Shelemiah in Samaria, the sons of Sanballat, the old enemy of Nehemiah.

How this community began in Egypt is a puzzle to most. The scraps of evidence include the following: a Jewish colony antedated the Persian invasion of Egypt by Cambyses, Cyrus's son and successor, for Cambyses found a temple built in Egypt when he arrived; and the *Letter of Aristeas* stated that some Jews had entered Egypt before the time of Cambyses to fight as mercenaries in the army of Pharaoh Psammeticus when Psammeticus II waged war with the Ethiopians. Thereafter they were stationed at Elephantine, near the Egyptian-Ethiopian border.

But such a theory of their origins in Elephantine raises other problems, for they would have been speaking Hebrew, it would seem, rather than Aramaic, the language of the papyri that have been found. Psammeticus II was on the throne in the years immediately preceding the fall of Jerusalem, thus making it hard to imagine why Jews would be forsaking their homeland to volunteer as mercenaries in Egypt at that time. W. O. E. Oesterley thought that the Elephantine colony was made up of Jews whom Ashurbanipal had deported from northern Israel after Ashurbanipal's conquest of Egypt. The group represented by the Elephantine Papyri would have been second generation of the captives who stayed on long after the days of the Assyrian Empire's control of Egypt. Such a theory has one major advantage: it explains why these writers would be appealing simultaneously both to Judah and to Samaria—even on the very sensitive topic of building another temple!

The number of those in this colony of mercenaries was not large, for the papyri speak of a *degel*, a company of one hundred men (Old Persian: *drafsha*, "banner"). The razed temple that these Jews wished to have restored was one that worshiped *Yahu*, a form of the name *Yahweh*. But there were also clear signs of syncretism as well, for they also worshiped Ishumbethel, Herembethel, Anathbethel, and most amazingly of all, Anatyahu. Anat was the Canaanite goddess of fertility and war, sister and consort of Baal. At Elephantine she appears to have been regarded as a consort of Yahweh! Bethel appears to have been another such deity for them.

From the year of 419 B.C., there is a papyrus[3] relating to the celebration of the Festival of Unleavened Bread. In it, a certain Hananiah claims that Darius II had written to Arshan, the satrap of Egypt, ordering him to see to it that the Jews were left free to celebrate the feast.

---

3. V. B. Porten, "Aramaic Papyri and Parchments: A New Look" BA 42 (1979): 74–104, especially 90–92.

However, during the absence of Arshan, satrap of Egypt, the Jewish temple (ʾ*egora*) at Elephantine was sacked and destroyed by the Egyptian priests of the god Khnum, presumably because the Jews offered rams as sacrifices. The ram was the symbolic animal of Khnum. The Jews were in the service of Persia, a foreign oppressor as far as the Egyptians were concerned.

The petitionary papyrus read in part:

> Now your servants Yedoniah and his colleagues and the Jews, the citizens of Elephantine, all say thus: If it please our Lord, take thought of this temple to rebuild it, since they do not let us rebuild it. Look to your well-wishers and friends here in Egypt. Let a letter be sent from you to them concerning the temple of the God Yahu, to build it in the fortress of Elephantine as it was built before; and the meal offering, incense, and burnt offering will be offered in your name and we shall pray for you at all times, we, and our wives, and our children. . . We have set the whole matter forth in a letter in our name to Delaiah and Shelemiah, the sons of Sanballat, the governor of Samaria. Also, Arsames [satrap of Egypt] knew nothing of all that was done to us. On the twentieth of Marheshwan, year 17 of King Darius [407 B.C.].

Elephantine exhibits what can happen to the community of God that allows religious syncretism to creep in and reshape its foundational concepts. The pantheon of deities found here confirm the worst fears of the Hebrew prophets.

The Samaritans

Another group that emerged just outside of the normative Judaism of the postexilic period was the Samaritans, a people that came into being after the fall of Samaria in 722 B.C. The fall of this northern capital and the consequent mixing of peoples widened the gap between north and south that existed since the days of the divided empire that resulted from the division of the kingdom in 931 B.C. after Solomon's death.

The strict measures of Ezra and Nehemiah left little, if any, room for a Samaritan identification with a restored temple in Jerusalem in the Persian period. The Samaritans had by now hardened their position as well. They recognized only the Pentateuch as their Scriptures, rejecting the prophetic and wisdom writings as being nonauthoritative for their movement.

Sometime prior to the early second century B.C., the Samaritans built their own temple to rival the Jerusalem sanctuary. We do not have any facts on how this came about,[4] but it is clear that by the time of Jesus, things had hardened so that the Samaritan woman in John 4:9 could say, "Jews do not associate with Samaritans." The question this woman thought was the burning religious question of the day was this: Should we worship on Mt. Gerizim (alongside Samaria) or in Jerusalem? (John 4:20–24). No wonder the stories that Jesus told about the good Samaritan (Luke 10:25–37) and the sole thankful leper, who returned to thank God for his healing, was also a Samaritan (Luke 17:11–19), were regarded as being politically incorrect as far as the Jews of Jesus' day were concerned.

The Synagogue

Renan called the synagogue[5] "the most original and fruitful creation of the Jewish people." The word *synagogue* is Greek in origin and means "a gathering of people" or "a congregation." The Hebrew word for such an assembly is *keneset*, the very same name that is used for the parliament in the modern state of Israel. Thus the name *synagogue* came to be used for the local congregation of Jews and also the building in which they met. In Hebrew the building would be called *bet hakkeneset*, "the house of assembly."

With so many Jews remaining in "the dispersion" throughout the former Babylonian and Persian empire cities, it became necessary for places to be established where Moses' law could be read and taught (Acts 15:21). Therefore, the synagogue came to be a place of prayer and Bible study in most of the major cities where the Jews were exiled.

In the larger towns, a body of twenty-three elders formed what was called the "sanhedrin," or governing body of the synagogue community. In smaller towns, the number was a seven-member sanhedrin. These *presbuteroi*, "elders," or sometimes called *archontes*, "rulers," had over them one who was called the *gerousiarches*, i.e., the "chief ruler." In this way the Sanhedrin served as a court in Judea, taking up civil as well as religious matters. They had the power to punish by scourging ("forty lashes minus one," 2 Cor. 11:24), excommunicating, and death

---

4. The best discussion of this problem is found in H. H. Rowley, "Sanballat and the Samaritan Temple," *BJRL* 38 (1955): 166–98.

5. For a summary of the archaeological data regarding the synagogue, see Itzhak Magen, "Synagogues," in Ephraim Stern, et al., eds., *The New Encyclopedia of Archaeological Excavations in the Holy Land*, 4 vols. (Jerusalem: Israel Exploration Society, 1993) IV: 1421–27

(but this required confirmation from the Roman procurator). While each community had its own sanhedrin, the Sanhedrin in Jerusalem attained eminence as the highest Jewish judicatory, becoming known eventually as the "Great Sanhedrin." It was presided over by the high priest and met in a hall connected with the temple.

Worship in the synagogue was simple, allowing any Israelite to officiate, just as the apostle Paul illustrated as he visited city after city in the Roman world. The ruler of the synagogue (*archisunagogos*) supervised the services and oversaw the care and upkeep of the building. The *hazzan*, "minister" of the synagogue, brought the Scriptures to the reader and then returned the scrolls back into the ark after the lesson had been read by the reader for the day.

The synagogue service likewise was simple and consisted mainly of prayers, the reading of the Scriptures, and an explanation of a section of the biblical text. Later, in the times of the Mishna (about the second and third centuries of the Christian era) the service had grown to five distinctive parts: The Shema (meaning "hear," from the famous passage in Deut. 6:4–9, and in Deut. 11:13–21); prayer; the reading of the Law from the Torah; the reading of the Prophets with the benediction; and the explanation of the Scripture lesson.

The chief prayer of the synagogue, dating back traditionally to the time of Ezra, with a final redaction around A.D. 110, was the *Shemoneh ʿesreh*, the "eighteen (benedictions)." This prayer exists in a Babylonian and Palestinian recension, with its present form dating to a time just after the fall of Jerusalem in A.D. 70.

At the center of the synagogue service was the reading of the Law of God from the five Books of Moses. There were four patterns for accomplishing this: an annual cycle for completing the reading of the whole five books, a two-year cycle, a three-year cycle, and a three-and-one-half-year cycle. Additional special readings were selected for the four Sabbaths before Passover, the festivals, the new moons, and the fast days. Every Sabbath, at least seven readers were selected with priests being given priority, followed by any Levites that might be present, and then lay readers from the congregation. The first and the last readers got to pronounce a special benediction. Later, a parallel portion of the prophets was added to the synagogue reading. Whether these prophetical portions had been standardized by New Testament times, when Jesus made his selection from the prophets when he read in the synagogue of Nazareth (Luke 4:16), is not known. Along with the readings came the interpretation of the passages, a form of address to the audience that was the forerunner of the sermon today.

The central focus of attention in the synagogue was the "ark," which held the scrolls of the Law, and those of the Prophets and the Writings of the sacred Scriptures. The ark stood near the wall at the farthest end of the synagogue from the entrance. In the center of the building was a raised platform called the *bēma*, on which the lectern was located. Wooden seats faced the lectern with the chief seats being those nearest the ark. From at least the Middle Ages on, the women viewed and participated in the service from the balcony in orthodox synagogues, but this appears to be a late innovation, for evidence exists to show that women could occupy even the chief seats in earlier times.

Alexander, the Apostle of Hellenism

"Alexander of Macedon cracked the Persian Empire like a rotten egg"[6] beginning sometime around 332 B.C. Prior to this time the Greek states had never achieved a united government, but it was the genius of Philip of Macedon, Alexander's father, who brought into existence a Hellenic League that was made up of all the Greek states except Sparta. It would be this instrument that would deal the death blow to the Persian Empire.

Unfortunately, Philip was murdered in 336 B.C. and Alexander took up where his father left off. While he was Macedonian by nationality, culturally he was Greek, educated by Aristotle himself. The bible he carried with him on his campaigns was none other than the Greek *Iliad* and the *Odyssey*.

The Greeks were producing a surplus population that continued to plant colonies around the Mediterranean, pushing into Asia and Africa, thereby carving trading and cultural islands in the sprawling kingdoms of Ptolemy's Egypt, in the Seleucid's Syria and Mesopotamia, and the Jews' Judea. Soon the coastlands were completely Hellenized, and Greek rulers gave ample freedom and privileges to *polis*-style sites such as Tyre, Sidon, Gaza, Straton's Tower, Byblos, and Tripoli. Shortly after this, these same conditions and culture were seen far into the interior such as at Shechem, Marissa in the south, and Philadelphia (Amman) and Gamal in Transjordania. All of these factors provided an excellent base for Alexander's great moment in the sun.

6. Paul Johnson, *A History of the Jews* (New York: Harper Perennial, 1988), 97.

This transmitter of Hellenism took a small army that consisted mainly of Macedonians, along with historians, geographers, and botanists, across the Dardanelles by boat, the very spot where Xerxes had crossed on a hastily constructed bridge. Alexander took Troy and announced that a new era of conquest had begun.

Darius III failed to take this sortie with the degree of seriousness he should have and ordered that an army of Persian cavalry, Greek mercenaries, and some native troops seize Alexander and bring him to Susa. The battle took place at the river Granicus. Alexander almost lost his life, but the Persians were narrowly defeated. Alexander left the Persians alone in their retreat, but he massacred the Greek mercenaries for their acting as traitors to what was Greek. This victory opened up Asia Minor to Alexander and became the beginning of his march into history.

Alexander continued his conquests across Asia Minor, "liberating" the Greek cities from Persia's grip, and organizing them into districts as they fell before his eastward advance. The decisive battle with the Persians was at Issus at the Cilician Gates in 333 B.C. The Persians retreated before Alexander as he took Damascus, captured Darius III's family, ambassadors from Thebes, Sparta, and Athens, and huge amounts of booty. Alexander was writing a whole new chapter in the history of the Near East.

He left the Persians for the moment and went to securing his flanks, viz., the cities on the coast of Phoenicia, which all capitulated to him; all, that is, except Tyre. Meanwhile, Darius twice offered favorable terms to Alexander with offers of huge amounts of money, territory, and the hand of his daughter in marriage if he would return his family to him. But none of these petty offers interested one who was by now bent on conquering the world. Only Tyre held Alexander up for seven months. Finally, in desperation, Alexander scraped up the ruins of the old mainland city of Tyre and dumped them into the Mediterranean Sea, creating a causeway from the mainland city out to the island, where the Tyrians had moved. Alexander then marched his troops out the causeway and finally took the island fortress of Tyre. With the fall of this great mistress of the sea, the maritime and commercial corner on the markets of the Mediterranean that the Phoenicians had held for so long crumpled without returning to their previous position of dominance.

Alexander marched on to Gaza, where the city fell after a two-month siege. He then turned to Egypt, where he was welcomed because the Egyptians had come to hate the Persians. Alexander was declared to be the son of the god Ammon, given a chapel at the temple of Karnak, and announced as the legitimate pharaoh. In a reorganization of Egypt's affairs, Egyptians were placed in charge of the country, but Macedonians were put in charge of the army. The most durable of all of Alexander's work in Egypt was the new city of Alexandria, a Macedonian metropolis that took over the position that had been held in the Mediterranean by Tyre.

Retracing his steps northward, the victorious monarch was depicted by Josephus as a friend of Judea. Josephus described Alexander as one who offered a sacrifice in the temple under the high priest's direction. Most doubt the veracity of this story.[7] Samaria fared differently than Jerusalem. Josephus described the Samaritans as initially being granted permission to build a temple on Mt. Gerizim by Alexander.[8] But when they rebelled against Andromachus, the governor Alexander had appointed, Alexander changed the status of the city into a Macedonian military colony; this status continued until the Seleucids came. The discovery of the Aramaic Papyri at the Wadi Daliyeh further attest the grim circumstances that befell the Samaritans.[9]

By 331 B.C., Alexander felt ready to confront the Persian army, now that his flank and rear guard had been secured on the coast and in Egypt. The battle took place on Mesopotamian homeground at Gaugamela. The Persians were outmaneuvered and roundly defeated. Darius escaped, but Alexander easily took the entire Persian territory, including the capitals of Persia: Babylon,

Susa, Persepolis, and Ecbatana. As he went from city to city, Alexander was more often greeted as a liberator than as a conqueror. The wealth of the former Persian Empire was at the feet of Alexander as he plundered Susa and then Persepolis, reputed to be the wealthiest city in the world. He treated Persepolis with particular harshness, slaying all the men and enslaving the women, no doubt in retaliation for all the grief the Persians had brought to the Greek realm in former days and as a symbol of his final conquest of the Persian Empire.

After assuming the title of *Basileus*, the "Great King," Alexander adopted Persian dress and assumed the role of an oriental despot. He

---

7. Josephus, *Antiquities*, xi. 336–39. Most felt that Alexander did not visit Jerusalem, but he was satisfied that the high priest recognized Greek overlordship in his role as representative of the people.

8. Josephus, *Antiquities*, xi. 322–24.

9. Frank M. Cross, "Papyri of the Fourth Century BC from Daliyeh: A Preliminary Report on Their Discovery and Significance," in *New Directions in Biblical Archaeology*, eds. David N. Freedman and J. C. Greenfield (Garden City, N.Y.: Doubleday, 1969), 494–95, 548.

continued eastward to Bactria and Sogdiana (Russian Turkestan) in three more years of bitter fighting. To resolve the long contest as peacefully as possible after such protracted fighting, Alexander married Roxana, a Bactrian princess. He continued his conquests all the way into the Punjab area of India.

After this, Alexander released his army to return home, half by ship in a newly built navy that sailed from the Indus delta into the Persian Gulf, the other half by land. When Alexander returned to Susa in 324 B.C., he found much resentment to his rule because the officials he had left in charge had not handled things properly. His men deeply resented his orders that the Macedonians were to take Persian wives and to mingle culturally with the Persians, along with Alexander's own orientalizing ways. His men mutinied against him, but the revolt was put down quickly.

As Alexander was planning a voyage around Arabia in 323 B.C., he died of a fever before the voyage could begin; he had only reached the age of thirty-three. His only son was born to his wife Roxana after his death. But in Alexander's brief thirteen years of ruling and commanding the troops, he clearly changed the world that he inherited from his father Philip. The one who began as the emissary of Greek culture actually ended up personally adopting much of the oriental culture. But the impact of Greek culture by this time was irreversible: the Orient had experienced and frequently adopted Hellenistic ways of thinking and acting. Not only had his conquests changed the face of the ancient Orient and marked a new era in history; he had erased the old cultural and political boundaries. The rise of the Hellenistic gymnasium, stadium, theater, odeum, lyceum, and agora were to be seen not only in the Greek colonies but also in many other cities of the ancient Near East as well. Sculptors, poets, musicians, playwrights, philosophers, and debaters were appearing as part of the regular landscape. Greek was destined to become the official language, and Greek thought forms were providing new formats for grappling with old ideas.

Judah was not insulated from all these developments. She, too, would drink deeply of these new waters of Hellenism as her land fell first to the Ptolemies of Egypt and, after a century of Ptolemaic rule, to the Seleucids of Syria.

Life in Judah under the Ptolemies

When Alexander died in 323 B.C. at the height of his military success, no logical successor had been designated or naturally emerged from all the others. After seven years of struggle, four generals emerged in 315 B.C.: Antigonus, who ruled from the Mediterranean to central Asia; Cassander, ruler of Macedonia; Ptolemy Lagi, ruler of Egypt; and Lysimachus, ruler of Thrace. Ptolemy's general was Seleucus, a man whose house was destined to shape Palestinian history in a major way. In that same year of 315 B.C., the other three generals formed an alliance against Antigonus, who apparently had designs on succeeding Alexander the Great. Ptolemy demanded that Antigonus hand over the Asian territory so that Seleucus could receive Babylon, from which he had been driven out. Antigonus refused the demand; therefore, Ptolemy and Seleucus defeated his army at Gaza in 312 B.C., an army led by Antigonus's son, Demetrius.

The two co-belligerents pressed on into Antigonus's territory and took a number of Syrian cities, including Sidon. Ptolemy chose to enter Jerusalem on the Sabbath, when he knew that the Law enjoined the Jews not to fight. Thus began a century of hardships for Judah under the hand of a cruel master. The *Letter of Aristeas* further detailed what happened when Ptolemy entered the country.

> He had overrun the whole of Coele-Syria and Phoenicia, exploiting his good fortune and prowess, and had transplanted some and made others captive, reducing all to subjection by terror; it was on this occasion that he transported a hundred thousand persons from the country of the Jews to Egypt. Of these he armed some thirty thousand chosen men and settled them in garrisons in the country.[10]

Egyptian inscriptions and papyri confirm that many Jews were living in Ptolemaic Egypt.

The story of the Ptolemaic and Seleucid influences and control over Palestine is a seesaw battle that tells of an extended struggle between the two houses. The principal leaders and their dates are as shown in the chart on the next page.[11]

Coele-Syria changed hands several times between 315 B.C. and the decisive Battle of Ipsus in 301 B.C. At first, Antigonus Monophtalmos, Alexander's most powerful general, conquered Syria and Palestine, but lost them to Ptolemy in 312 B.C. When Ptolemy Lagi pulled back, Syria-Palestine fell again without a fight to Antigonus and his son Demetrius Poliorketes. This was repeated again in 302 B.C., as Ptolemy

10. *Aristeas to Philocrates*, 12–13. Translation of Moses Hadas as cited by Charles F. Pfeiffer, *Old Testament History* (Grand Rapids: Baker, 1973), 556.

11. This chart is modeled largely (with some revisions) after the one in Henry J. Flanders Jr., Robert W. Crapps, and David A. Smith, *People of the Covenant: An Introduction to the Hebrew Bible*, 4th ed. (New York: Oxford, 1996), 467, fig. 15.3.

Egypt	Judah	Syria
Ptolemy I (323–285 B.C.) (Lagi)	315–198 Judah under the Ptolemies	Seleucus I (323–281 B.C.
Ptolemy II (283–246) (Philadelphus)		Antiochus I (281–261)
Ptolemy III (246–221)		Antiochus II (261–246)
		Seleucus II (246–226)
Ptolemy IV (221–203) (Philopater)		Seleucus III (226–223)
	Battle of Paneion, 198 Seleucids gain control of Palestine	Antiochus III (223–187) (the Great)
Ptolemy V (203–181		Seleucus IV (187–175)
Ptolemy VI (181–146)	Maccabean Revolt 167 B.C.	Antiochus IV (175–163) (Epiphanes)
	Jewish Independence 142–163 until Pompey establishes Roman rule over Jerusalem	Antiochus V (163–162)

conquered Coele-Syria for the third time, and once again withdrew. Why Ptolemy did not participate in the decisive battle waged by Seleucus, Cassander, and Lysimachus against Antigonus at Ipsus in 301 B.C. is unknown. Antigonus died on the battlefield and his Asian empire came to an end, although his son Demetrius Poliorketes managed to hang on to Macedonia and the Phoenician coast of Syria. It had been agreed that Ptolemy should be assigned Coele-Syria if the generals were successful over Antigonus, but since he stayed on the sidelines, the other three generals decided that the territory should be assigned to Seleucus. Ptolemy beat them to the punch, however, and took possession of the land. Though Seleucus protested that this takeover was not fair, since Ptolemy had not fought Antigonus, there was little more to do than to protest.[12] Thus, Syria was now part of three domains after the battle of Ipsus: Demetrius, Antigonus's son, occupied the Phoenician coast; Seleucus took northern Syria, building a capital in Antioch; and all of Syria south of Arvad was kept by Ptolemy. However, while Demetrius was away tending to other matters, Ptolemy quietly occu-

12. Seleucus's protest is recorded, purportedly, in Diodorus's *Histories*, xxi. 5.

pied Phoenicia, thus Ptolemy emerged as the *de facto* ruler of Coele-Syria (i.e., of Palestine).

Three great powers now shared Alexander's empire: the house of the Antigonids in Macedonia, the Ptolemies in Egypt, and the Seleucids of Syria with the Seleucids and Antigonids either by themselves or together at war with the Ptolemies for most of the third century B.C.

It took until 286 B.C. before the Ptolemaic kingdom had effective control over most of Syria and Palestine. In contrast to the Seleucid kingdom, the Ptolemaic was a tightly run, well-organized, and internally unified government. Its leader was, in the tradition of the oriental idea, endowed with divine honors and had the final authority in every detail. Serving along with the king was the *dioiketes*, "minister of finance and economic affairs," an example of which is seen in the person of Apollonius under Ptolemy II in the Zenon Papyri.[13]

Though the Ptolemies controlled Palestine and much of Syria for most of the third century B.C., the Ptolemies were in continual war with the Seleucids over this territory. The first Syrian war was between Ptolemy II (Philadelphus) and Antiochus I in 274–271 B.C. Ptolemy was able to hang on to his territories in Coele-Syria, and with his *dioiketes*, Apollonius, to open up Syria-Palestine economically. The story of how this was accomplished is found in the Zenon Papyri, as already mentioned. They tell of how during the journey of a certain Zenon, undertaken in 259–258 B.C. at the direction of Apollonius, Zenon went through all Palestine. He came to the military colony in Transjordan of a Jewish "local prince" named Tobias (probably a descendant of the Tobiah in Neh. 6:17–19; 13:4–9), where Apollonius owned a large wine-growing estate in Beth-Anath in Galilee. No doubt Zenon undertook this journey at Apollonius's instigation as an inspection tour and in an effort to improve economic relations and the financial administration between the Egyptian mother country and these northern provinces. The Zenon Papyri preserve two letters from Tobias to Apollonius that refer to gifts sent to Ptolemy and to Apollonius. This demonstrates the pro-Ptolemaic attitude of the Tobiad family that also worked to protect their economic and commercial interests.

A second and third Syrian war saw Ptolemy II emerge as the victor over a Seleucid-Macedonian coalition in 260–253 B.C. and again in 246–241 B.C. Jerusalem seems to have resisted Ptolemaic rule in this struggle when the high priest Onias II refused to pay the regular tribute.

---

13. The Zenon Papyri can be found in V. Tcherikover and A. Fuks, *Corpus Papyorum Judicarum* I (Cambridge: Harvard University Press, 1957).

This presented a dangerous situation for the Tobiad family, whose home was east of the Jordan; but Tobias's son, Joseph, who also was a nephew of the high priest Onias II, had by this time moved to Jerusalem. Joseph arose as spokesman for the opposition and demanded that Onias II cease his opposition to the Ptolemaic policies and be reconciled to the king. Onias yielded to this pressure from the opposition, but he thereby lost his power as it was transferred to Joseph in the office of *prostasia*, the political representative of the people before the king. Joseph then borrowed the money "from his friends in Samaria," according to Josephus,[14] in order to make a personal visit to Ptolemy in Alexandria. Once there, he outbid all his competitors by promising to double the amount of taxes sent to Egypt. For this he was given a contingent of two thousand soldiers to help him carry out his duties, an office he held for twenty-two years (ca. 240–218 B.C.).

After Ptolemy III died in 221 B.C., the fourth Syrian war (221–217 B.C.) broke out between Prolemy IV (Philopater) and Antiochus III ("the Great"). This time Antiochus III was able to gain a large part of Coele-Syria back until the battle at Raphia in southern Palestine in 217 B.C., where he was forced to retreat from Palestine. The third Book of Maccabees tells how Ptolemy visited all the cities of Syria after his victory at Raphia. The Jews were supposed to have sent a delegation to congratulate him, whereupon Ptolemy insisted on entering the Holy of Holies, only to flee in terror after reaching only the Holy Place (3 Macc. 1:9–11, 24).

But fortunes of the Ptolemaic Empire were dwindling as evidenced by a split in the Tobiad family, which was by now, for all intents and purposes, the ruling family in Judea. According to the Tobiad novel used by Josephus, Joseph sent his youngest son Hyrcanus to Egypt to celebrate the birth of a crown prince (ca. 210 B.C.). He too took advantage of this occasion to buy the favor of the king.[15] Joseph may have by this time been flirting with changing his loyalties to the Seleucids, for Hyrcanus may have been named by Ptolemy as *prostasia* in place of Joseph. Enmity broke out between father and son and the brothers in the Tobiad family. Hyrcanus was unable to assume his office; but he was forced instead to retreat to the family estate at `*Araq el-Emir* in Transjordania, where he remained loyal to the Ptolemies even after the Seleucids took over Palestine under Antiochus IV (Epiphanes). With

14. Josephus, *Antiquities*, xii. 160–80.
15. Josephus, *Antiquities*, xii. 221–22.

the full realization of what had happened, Hyrcanus committed suicide sometime around 169–168 B.C.

While Antiochus III was still hurting from his defeat at Raphia, he turned his attention to the eastern part of his domain and expanded his holdings all through Asia to India. After the death of Ptolemy IV, Antiochus again invaded Syria-Palestine in 201 B.C. and was victorious. Ptolemy's commander, named Scopas, was momentarily successful, but Scopas was soundly defeated in 200 B.C. at Paneion, near the sources of the Jordan River, unable to save the province for his sovereign, Ptolemy V, still only a minor at the time. With this victory at Paneion by Antiochus III, the Ptolemaic sovereignty over Palestine came to an end. The long century of Ptolemaic rule over Judea had been terminated and life under the Seleucids had begun.

Life in Judah under the Seleucids

Antiochus III had come to the throne at age eighteen in 223 B.C. He had, however, already served as a ruler of Babylonia under his brother Seleucus III. With his decisive victory at Paneion, the tables turned in Syria-Palestine and the Seleucids took over Palestine, ruling from about 200 to 135 B.C. After the harsh measures of the Ptolemies, the Jews enjoyed the relaxed rule of Antiochus III, for he recognized the Torah as the "national law," and gave the people a measure of internal autonomy. The entire population of Jerusalem was exempted from taxes for three years and given a one-third reduction for all future taxes. All temple personnel were granted complete exemption from taxes and generous aid was given for rebuilding Jerusalem and the temple. Even though pro-Ptolemaic factions remained in the country, the majority was pro-Seleucid.

Antiochus was interested in taking on Rome, which was emerging as a new force to be reckoned with. The Carthaginian, Hannibal, had been defeated by the Romans at Zama in 202 B.C., thus ending the Second Punic War. However, Hannibal fled eastward and joined up with Antiochus. With Antiochus's prompting, Antiochus and Hannibal invaded Greece, much to Rome's discomfort. Roman forces moved into Greece and defeated Antiochus, forcing him back into Asia Minor. There at Magnesia in 190 B.C., the Romans defeated Antiochus and required that he surrender his war elephants, his navy, and his younger son, Antiochus, later to be called Epiphanes. The younger Antiochus was taken as captive to Rome, where he spent twelve years learning Roman ways and power.

When Antiochus returned to take his father's place, he took the surname *Epiphanes*, "the manifest [one]," but the Jews, ever the masters of innuendo, nicknamed him *Epimanes*, "the madman." Antiochus determined to Hellenize his domain and instituted changes to accomplish these ends. At the time Jerusalem was ruled by the high priest Onias III, a most orthodox Jew who was a descendant of Simon the Just. Onias's brother, Jason, succeeded in having himself appointed high priest by Antiochus, promising a larger tribute to the Seleucids. Jason adopted a friendly attitude toward the Hellenists. He encouraged the building of a gymnasium in Jerusalem where Jewish athletes would exercise in the nude. These newly persuaded Jewish Hellenists were dubbed "Antiochites" by Antiochus in 170 B.C., when he saw what was taking place in Jerusalem during his visit there in that year. Meanwhile, the Hasidim, "the holy/pious ones," were scandalized by what was happening and formed a resistance movement in an attempt to defend orthodox Jewish institutions. Antiochus IV looked upon this Jewish orthodoxy as a divisive force within his kingdom. He needed an occasion to implement his full program of Hellenizing the masses or, in his terms, "civilizing" the people.

That occasion came when a dispute broke out between Jason and his close associate Menelaus, a man from the tribe of Benjamin. Menelaus offered an even higher tribute rate to Antiochus than that paid by Jason, so this non-Levitical person was nominated to the office of high priest. Now the Hasidim were outraged when Jason was replaced by Menelaus, a thoroughgoing Hellenist.

Jason would not go down quietly. He raised an army and waited until Antiochus was busy fighting in Egypt. Immediately Jason moved his army from Transjordania to attack Jerusalem. Menelaus beat off the raid, but Antiochus now knew that neither he nor his Hellenistic policies were favored by many in the land.

Menelaus placed all the temple treasury at the disposal of Antiochus IV when he returned. But once more Antiochus left for another campaign in Egypt, for he was determined to overrun the empire of the Ptolemies. Rome, however, would not hear a word of this ambition; they were determined that Antiochus would not strengthen his position by annexing Egypt. Thus in the Battle of Pydna (168 B.C.), the Romans defeated the Macedonians in a battle of epic and history-making proportions. Rome had served notice that she, not the Macedonians, would be the inheritor of the spoils of the previous empires. In one of the most famous, but oft-repeated scenes outside the city of

Alexandria, the Roman envoy drew a circle around Antiochus in the dirt, demanding that he promise to evacuate Egypt before he left that circle. Antiochus sadly capitulated.

Palestine must now be held more than ever, so Antiochus sent his general Apollonius to occupy Jerusalem. In a Sabbath attack, when he knew there would be no resistance from the orthodox Jews, he slaughtered large numbers of Menelaus's opponents, destroyed the city walls, and built a new fortress on the citadel called Akra, which then housed a large garrison.

There followed a systematic attempt to Hellenize the country by force. Greek deities were to be worshiped by all. An Athenian philosopher was sent to Jerusalem to supervise the reprogramming of the people; he identified Jupiter as the god of Israel, who was then set upon the temple altar. The Jews called this "the abomination of desolation." Swine were sacrificed on the altar in the temple, and Greek soldiers and their paramours performed licentious acts in the courts of the temple itself. Under penalty of death, the Jews were forbidden to practice circumcision, Sabbath observance, or any of their feast days. Copies of the Hebrew Bible were destroyed and drunken orgies associated with Bacchus were made compulsory. These were Judah's darkest days: an elderly scribe named Eleazar was beaten to death for refusing to eat pig's meat, and a mother single-handedly cheered and encouraged her seven sons not to capitulate as each was routinely butchered in her presence before the governor for rejecting the pagan image and failing to pay homage to it.

Menelaus and his hellenistic sympathizers had for the moment triumphed, but the Hellenists had overreached themselves as later events would prove. It is the excessiveness and the brutality with which the Hellenists forced their views on the Jews that worked to bring about their immediate downfall.

THE SEPTUAGINT

The most enduring monument to the hellenizing tendencies of this era was the translation of the Hebrew Old Testament into the Greek vernacular.[16] The exact origins of this translation are unknown. Around 100 B.C. a letter known as the *Letter of Aristeas* purported to know that the Septuagint was written at the official instigation of

16. S. P. Brock, et. al., *A Classified Bibliography of the Septuagint* (1973); and S. Jellicoe, *The Septuagint and Modern Study* (1968).

Ptolemy II Philadelphus, 283–246 B.C., to provide a copy of the Hebrew Scriptures for the library at Alexandria, Egypt. Philadelphus wanted to be known as the great patron of the arts. Indeed, it was under his reign that the great library at Alexandria was inaugurated.

According to the *Letter of Aristeas*, Ptolemy's librarian, Demetrius of Phalerum, called the Jewish Law to the king's attention. He suggested that the king send a delegation to the high priest in Jerusalem, Eleazar, to obtain his help in this project. Eleazar chose six elders from each of the twelve tribes to translate the Law into Greek. These seventy-two elders, with an accurate and beautiful copy of the Law, were sent to Alexandria. From there they were sent to the Island of Pharos, also famous for its lighthouse, where, the tradition assures us, the seventy-two translators finished in seventy-two days a Greek version of the text, one in which everyone's translation agreed with everyone else's translation! The translation is remembered as the Bible of the Seventy, or Septuagint.

No doubt some features of this story are overdrawn, but there can be little doubt that the Law was translated in Philadelphus's time since Greek quotations from Genesis and Exodus appear in Greek literature before 200 B.C. The language of the Septuagint is more like Egyptian Greek than it is like Jerusalemite Greek, according to some.

The point of the *Letter of Aristeas* seemed to be to show that the Greek translation had the same inspiration as did the Hebrew originals. Whether it was first copied in order to provide a copy for the Alexandrian library or simply under the pressure of Alexandrian Jews who wanted their Greek-speaking children to be able to read the Scriptures is a question that must remain unanswered. Thus we conclude that the Torah was translated as early as 250 B.C., but that the rest of the canonical books of the Old Testament along with the apocryphal books were subsequently translated by the time of the church father Origin in the third century A.D.

30

THE MACCABEAN INSURRECTION (167–134 B.C.)

What really provoked the persecution by Antiochus Epiphanes remains an enigma despite the studied attempt of scholars to identify what triggered such inflammatory and repressive measures against the Jews and their religion. But this much is clear: the Maccabean insurrection began as a struggle for religious liberty. So strong was the reaction of the Jews that it must have stunned Antiochus as well as many of the hellenized Jews themselves.[1]

THE OBSCURE VILLAGE OF MODIN[2]

At the most unlikely place, an obscure village of Modin (also, Modein), located between Beth-Horon and Lydda to the northwest of Jerusalem, the battle against the hellenizing tendencies of the Seleucids began. Antiochus's emissaries demanded that a pagan installation be set up in Modin to show respect to Seleucid government. The citizens of that village were expected to present themselves before this pagan altar with a sacrifice.

1. The sources for this period are: 1 Maccabees 2:1–9: 22; 2 Maccabees 8–15; Josephus, *War* 1.1.3–6, paragraphs 36–47; idem., *Antiquities* 12.6. 1–11.2, paragraphs 265–434.
2. See Lester L. Grabbe, *Judaism from Cyrus to Hadrian: Volume One: The Persian and Greek Periods* (Minneapolis: Fortress, 1992), 285–299.

To ensure that the populace would comply, the aged priest of the village, one named Mattathias, was approached and issued a command to present the first sacrifice on this pagan altar. Now Mattathias was one of the "sons of Jaarib" (1 Macc. 2:1); therefore, he was a member of the priestly order named after Joarib, the first of such orders described in 1 Chronicles 24:7 ff. His grandfather (or great-grandfather) bore the name of Hasmon;[3] thus the whole family was also known as the Hasmoneans. However, many used the name *Hasmonean* to refer to the members of the family that came after Simon, to distinguish them from the Maccabees, the sons of Mattathias. The Maccabees were joined by the *Ḥāsîdîm*, "the pious," who had previously formed a party independent of the Maccabean insurrection (1 Macc. 2:42).

Mattathias promptly refused to commit such an act of sacrilege. But a more timid soul, fearing the wrath of Antiochus against the village, stepped forward to do what Mattathias was refusing to do. Enraged at the effrontery of this Jew, Mattathias immediately slew the apostate, along with the emissary of Antiochus (1 Macc. 2:15–28). Thus began the clash between the Maccabeans and the Seleucids.

Mattathias, joined by his five sons, destroyed the heathen installation, then fled to the hills, hoping to avoid the almost certain wrath of the government of Antiochus. There on the eastern slopes of the hill country of Judea, others quickly joined his renegade camp. From this fairly secure position, the insurrectionists made forays into the countryside to destroy other pagan altars that had been set up by the Seleucids to propagate the new Hellenistic culture and the absolute rule and reign of Antiochus Epiphanes. Guerrilla warfare broke out as a rugged band of outlaws murdered many of the royal officers and Hellenistic Jews who supported the Syrians.

At first the Maccabeans refused to fight on the Sabbath. On one Sabbath, a band of Maccabeans was surrounded and massacred when they refused to fight on this holy day of the week. Recognizing their disadvantage, Mattathias adopted a new principle that allowed fighting in self-defense on the Sabbath day.

All of this trouble began, as 1 Maccabees 1:11 described it:

> In those days lawless men came forth from Israel, and misled many, saying, "Let us go and make a covenant with the Gentiles round about us, for since we separated from them many evils have come upon us."

---

3. For further details, see Josephus, *Antiquities* xii. 6. 1.

The measures imposed on the Judeans were nothing short of breathtaking—when the teaching of the Torah was taken into consideration. It began with Antiochus's sending Apollonius as the "chief collector of tribute" (1 Macc. 1:29; 2 Macc. 5:24). Apparently he was ordered to completely hellenize the city of Jerusalem and to provide for its military defense. Thus, Apollonius either expanded, or completely rebuilt, the fortress citadel in Jerusalem named the "Acra." This guaranteed a permanent Seleucid presence in the holy city but rescinded the special privileges which Antiochus III had granted to Jerusalem. The Acra was populated with a Syrian garrison and with hellenized Jews, both of which the Maccabeans referred to as a "godless/lawless people."

But this was not the end of Syria's repressive measures. Antiochus stopped all temple sacrifices to Yahweh, banned circumcision, banned the observance of the Sabbath and all other festivals in the Jewish calendar, and prohibited the study of the Torah. But most noxious of all these measures was the institution of the cult of the Olympian Zeus in Jerusalem itself in 167 B.C. This notorious act of insolence was what Daniel the prophet had anticipated as the "abomination of desolation" (Dan. 9:27; 12:11).

Royal permission was granted for Hellenistic Jews to build a gymnasium, where the Jews, following the Greek practice, could exercise in the nude. All sporting events were held under the aegis of the gods, especially the cult of Heracles or Hermes, and were meant to honor these gods. For a significant number of Jews, this posed an enormous theological and cultural problem, even for those who might be receptive to some aspects of Greek culture. Second Maccabees 4:18–20 relates, for example, how a group of Hellenistic Jews traveled to Tyre as a Jerusalem delegation. The high priest, Jason, gave the delegation money to offer a sacrifice to Heracles, but these Jews requested permission to use the money for other purposes since they felt it "inappropriate" to use the money for a sacrifice to Heracles!

Judas the Maccabee

Mattathias was killed early on in the revolt, dying in 166 B.C. His third son Judas, surnamed "the Maccabee," would go down in history as "Judas the Maccabee." (This title is usually interpreted to mean "the hammerer.") As a result, the revolt of those who wished to remain faithful to the Law of God would be remembered as the Maccabean revolt or insurrection.

At first the Syrians refused to take this uprising with any degree of seriousness, underestimating the religious furor that lay behind the movement. They sent inferior generals and small detachments of soldiers to quell the rebellion. Surprisingly, the Maccabeans held their own and whipped one detachment after another. Finally it dawned on Antiochus that he had a full-sized rebellion on his hands. Judas won his first battles in the area around Modin, Beth-Horon, and Emmaus, facing such opponents as Seron, the supreme commander of Coele-Syria, and Gorgias, a general in the service of Lysias.

Alarmed by these setbacks, Antiochus ordered that the governor, Lysias, march against the rebels. The ensuing battle took place at Beth-zur, some eighteen miles south of Jerusalem. Nicanor and Gorgias, Lysias's subordinates, were in charge of the attack. But once again, Judas and his brigand were victorious (1 Macc. 4:26–35).

Judas carried his attack to the city of Jerusalem itself. Menelaus and his cohorts fled as the Maccabees entered the city and took over everything except the fortress of Acra. Judas entered the temple and removed all trappings of paganism, including the altar dedicated to Jupiter. The statue erected in honor of Zeus/Antiochus was ground to dust and a new altar was erected to Yahweh. Thus the three-year period in which the temple had been descrated ended on the twenty-fifth day of Kislev (December) 164 B.C. (1 Macc. 4:36–61; 2 Macc. 10:1–8). This period became known as the Feast of "Dedication" or *Hanakkak*, the Feast of Lights, an eight-day festival that would be observed annually thereafter (see 1 Macc. 4:50).

This peace did not last long, however. Lysias besieged Jerusalem, hoping to starve the Maccabees into submission. Instead, he broke off this engagement to return to Syria after learning that a rival was marching toward Antioch. In an effort to get on the road to block that action, Lysias offered terms of peace to the Jews.

The terms of the peace were that Syria would not interfere in the internal affairs of Judea. The laws prohibiting Jewish observances would be rescinded and Menelaus would be removed from the high priesthood and a man named Jakim or Eliakim (also known by his Greek name of Alcimus) would be his replacement. There would be no punishments for the military action of the Maccabees, but the walls of Jerusalem were destroyed.

These terms for peace were considered by a provisional council in Jerusalem, which included Maccabean army officers, scribes, and elders connected with the *Hasidim*, the orthodox party that had supported

Judas. Judas was not pleased with these terms, for he wanted political as well as religious liberty; however, the combination of peace and religious liberty appealed to most, so the terms were accepted. The *Hasidim* had reached their goal, but the Maccabees were not happy. Alcimus was installed as high priest and Menelaus was executed. Judas and a few of his followers left Jerusalem, deeply unhappy with this turn of events.

Time proved that Judas had had every reason to be cautious and dubious. Alcimus seized a number of the *Hasidim* and had them put to death. This caused the old war spirit to reopen, but now Judas's band was severely depleted—only eight hundred men were left to face a massive Syrian army. Judas died in the battle and another chapter in the Maccabean struggles came to an end.

Jonathan Maccabees

Jonathan, the youngest of the five sons of Mattathias, took over after the death of Judas. Simon, Jonathan, and Johanan, along with several hundred men, fled across the Jordan despite the peace that had been offered by Alcimus. All Syrian attempts to destroy this patriot band of Maccabean followers failed. Finally, Alcimus died in 159 B.C., but his office remained vacant. In 157 B.C., an offer of peace allowed Jonathan to return to the western side of the Jordan and settle at Michmash, just eight miles outside Jerusalem, where he acted as a sort of judge or local administrator.

Another peace treaty was made with Jonathan by Demetrius I in 153 B.C. and a certain Alexander Balas, who claimed to be a son of Antiochus IV and the rightful heir to the throne. Jonathan went with both men to Jerusalem, secured the temple mount, and forced the Syrian garrison back to the fortress of Acra. But Alexander Balas went further and offered Jonathan the high priesthood office in 152 B.C. Jonathan now moved his total loyalties to Alexander Balas and assumed the office of high priest. Demetrius fell to Alexander on the battlefield, and Alexander showed his appreciation for Jonathan's help by inviting him to his wedding to Cleopatra, the daughter of Ptolemy VI (Philometor) in Ptolemais (Akko). Jonathan was made *strategos* and *meridarches* ("general" and "part-governor") of Coele-Syria, thus giving to him the status of a provincial governor. But along with these military and civil rights, he also had the responsibility of going to war on behalf of the Syrians. Thus, Jonathan met Demetrius II's troops in the coastal plain between Joppa and Ashkelon, for Demetrius II had his heart set on being a rival king. For this deed, Alexander granted to Jonathan the city of Ekron with its surrounding territory as a gift.

Events became even more turbulent. Ptolemy VI (Philometor; 181–145 B.C.) forced Alexander Balas to flee for refuge to Arabia. Ptolemy was supporting Demetrius II Necantor with a contingent of troops in Syria. But then Ptolemy died, leaving Demetrius to take over the power slot he vacated (145–139 B.C.). Demetrius II was particularly unhappy about Jonathan Maccabees's brashness in laying siege to the Acra in Jerusalem. Apparently, Jonathan was able to pacify the king in this incident and to secure additional requests from Demetrius II.

Jonathan overstepped the bounds of Syrian propriety when he decided to support the son of Alexander Balas, still a minor, who had been set up as a rival king by the one named Diodorus Trypho for Apamea. Jonathan and his brother prepared to fight for Trypho in south and central Syria in order to give this new rival a territorial base from which to operate. But the power and success of these Maccabean brothers worried Trypho, for Jonathan now had contacts in Rome and Sparta (1 Macc. 12:1–23). Therefore, Trypho lured Jonathan to come to Ptolemais with only a small escort. When Jonathan arrived, Trypho gave him a ceremonial reception, but then took him as his prisoner. Jonathan's bother Simon rushed to Jerusalem to enlist a large number of recruits to continue the struggle and to free his brother.

Simon Maccabees

Simon was an old man, but he took over where his brother Jonathan had left off. Simon forced Trypho to retreat in his advance against Judea, but he was unable to free Jonathan from Trypho, even though Jonathan was with Trypho as a captive during the fighting.

In Trypho's retreat through Gilead, Trypho had Jonathan murdered at Baskama (an as-yet-unidentified site). Simon carried Jonathan's bones back to Modin for an honorable burial.

Now Trypho was the first Syrian king who was not from the Seleucid line. Simon's response to Trypho was to ignore him and to recognize Demetrius as the rightful king of Syria. In return, Demetrius granted the Jews full immunity from taxes, an act widely interpreted as a recognition of the Jews' independence. As a result, Simon was able to starve out the Syrian garrison at Acra and to occupy the cities of Joppa and Beth-zur. A new era began with Simon, for he had succeeded in doing what none of the men of his family had achieved.

A period of peace marked the days of Simon's reign in which he also was recognized as high priest. Accordingly, the question of the legitimacy of the Maccabean priests was also settled. In recognition of Simon's wise rule, the leaders in Israel named Simon "leader and high priest for ever, until there should arise a faithful prophet" (1 Macc.14:25–49). In doing this, the Hasidic party justified this action by pointing out that the family of Onias had gone to Egypt during the Maccabean fighting, even though they were the legitimate heirs of the Aaronic line of high priests. But since the Onias family had gone to Egypt, all future claims to the priesthood were thereby forfeited and revoked. Simon would now claim that title of high priest alone!

This act of legitimizing Simon and his offices begins a new chapter in the history of the Judeans known as the time of the Hasmoneans. The name, as already mentioned in this chapter, came from their ancestor Hasmon. Thus the last son of Mattathias became the first to begin a new line of legitimized hereditary high priests.

Simon and his two sons were murdered in 134 B.C. by a son-in-law who also was somewhat ambitious for the power to rule. But a third son of Simon named John Hyrcanus managed to escape. It was John Hyrcanus who succeeded his father and became the hereditary head of the newly recognized independence of the Jews.

31

THE HASMONEAN KINGDOM (135–63 B.C.)

The rise of the Hasmoneans[1] was made possible in part by the gradual collapse of the Seleucid and Ptolemaic power structures. Both of these powers were finally defeated because of their own internal conflicts. Moreover, both lived in mortal fear of Rome's steadily growing power. Yet Rome itself was also in a period of internal wars that began in 133 B.C., caused by the Gracchi; this strife continued until Augustus established the principate in 31 B.C. Thus Rome fought against Jugurtha of Numidia (111–105 B.C.), the Cimbri (113–101 B.C.) and the Italian Confederation (91–88 B.C.), in addition to the wars against Mithridates of Pontus. This gave Rome little time to worry about intervening in the eastern lands of Syria and Palestine.

THE GENESIS OF THE HASMONEAN KINGDOM

Demetrius had given to Simon Maccabees, in the 170th year of the Seleucid reign (142/1 B.C.),[2] independence and freedom from tribute to

1. I am indebted for much of the general argument and outline of events to the discussion by Siegfried Herrmann, *A History of Israel in Old Testament Times*, Revised and Enlarged edition, tr. By John Bowden (Philadelphia: Fortress, 1981), pp. 368–92. See also T. Rajak, "Roman Intervention in a Seleucid Siege of Jerusalem?" *Greek, Roman and Byzantine Studies* 22 (1981): 65–81; and Lester L. Grabbe, *Judaism from Cyrus to Hadrian: Volume One: The Persian and Greek Periods*, pp. 299–307.

2. Lester L. Grabbe, *Judaism from Cyrus to Hadrian: The Persian and Greek Periods* (Minneapolis: Fortress, 1992), 1:298. Grabbe dates this 170th year of the Seleucid era as 143–142 B.C., when according to 1 Macc. 13:41–42, "the yoke of the Gentiles was lifted from Israel."

Judea. Thus the year 142/1 was the first year of this new era. Simon had extended his territory by capturing the port of Joppa, thereby gaining direct access to the sea. He had also taken over the former Samaritan territory southeast of Shechem, in the area around Akraba. Beth-zur and Gazara (Gezer) had been conquered and added to his territory as well (1 Macc. 14:6–15).

But when Antiochus VII Sidetes ascended the throne in 139 B.C., after his brother Demetrius II had been taken prisoner by the Parthians, Sidetes besieged Trypho in Dora (Dor), the older port city just south of Mt. Carmel. Trypho managed to escape by way of the sea, but he was later killed at Apamea in central Syria. Antiochus VII, while at first accepting Judean help, ended up rejecting it in his siege of Dora. He also demanded the restoration of the territories Simon had taken, namely Joppa and Gezer and the Acra in Jerusalem. Simon refused to budge.

Antiochus VII sent his general, Cendebaeus, to attack Simon's forces near Jamnia, but Simon's sons, Judas and John, defeated him near Modein and drove Cendebaeus back to the plain, thereby securing once again the freedom and independence of Judea (1 Macc. 15:25–16:10).

But not everything was yet settled within this newly won state that Simon had been so instrumental in establishing. Simon's son-in-law, Ptolemy, a provincial governor in the area of Jericho, made an attack on Simon and his sons, Mattathias and Judas, in 134 B.C. Simon had gone to the small fortress of Dok (where the spring *`en duk*, northwest of Jericho still preserves the name), on an inspection tour. Ptolemy had built the fortress for himself, obviously hoping one day to extend his control. After he had succeeded in this triple murder, he desperately tried to do away with Simon's other son John, who lived in Gazara (Gezer); but John was warned in time, and he escaped to Jerusalem, where the people received him in the name of his father, giving him the rights that had belonged to his father. Ptolemy was turned back by the gates of the city and returned to his fortress near Jericho, the very fortress where Simon and his sons had been murdered. John's own mother also lived in the same fortress; nevertheless, John laid siege to the fortress, but he hesitated to take it out of concern for the safety of his mother. Ptolemy managed to escape despite all these efforts, killing John's mother and other relatives in the process.

The Hasmonean Line Included:

Simon	142/1–134 B.C.
John Hyrcanus I	134–104
Aristobulus I	104–103
Alexander Jannai	103–76
Salome Alexandra	76–67
Aristobulus II	67–63
Hyrcanus II	63–40

John Hyrcanus I

John adopted the ruling name of John Hyrcanus as he led Judea from 134 to 104 B.C. He is somewhat of a survivor, for he had troubles almost from the very beginning of his rule. Ptolemy had fled to Transjordania, where he persuaded Antiochus VII Sidetes to lay siege to this new Hasmonean state. Antiochus VII was only too happy to accede to this request since he too was smarting over the failure of his general Cendebaeus to match Simon's skills.

Thus, Antiochus VII laid siege to Jerusalem, but then relaxed it as he reaffirmed the autonomy of Judea. Nevertheless, he razed the walls of Jerusalem and laid a tax on the Judeans once again. The port of Joppa was to be handed back, all weapons were to be turned in, and hostages were to be taken, including John Hyrcanus's brother. Once more Judea was under the heel of a foreign power.

But that, too, changed, for Antiochus VII died in a battle with the Parthians in 129 B.C. Demetrius, who had himself been a prisoner of the Parthians (139/8 B.C.) but had been freed to fight against his brother, now ascended the Seleucid throne (129–125 B.C.). In the midst of all these changes, this Hasmonean named Hyrcanus once more became an independent ruler. Meanwhile, the Seleucid throne was riddled with disputes, reducing Seleucid strength and effectiveness. In this hiatus, Hyrcanus rebuilt fortifications on the north side of Jerusalem and raised a fortification on the northwestern side of the temple platform called "Baris," the forerunner of the later citadel of "Antonia."

In response to the hellenistic spirit of the day that had continued to encroach on the Judean culture, various groups continued to polarize because of Hellenism and related topics. The Hasidim, "the pious," were the most conservative Jews. They insisted on their religious liberty, strict adherence to the law, and rejection of all forms of Hellenism. The Maccabean struggle vindicated the Hasidim, even though the Hasidim were not totally aligned with the Maccabeans. The Hasidim eventually became the party of the Pharisees.

The hellenistic party, on the other hand, was best seen in the Sadducees. The name *Sadducee* may be connected with the high priest of King David's time, Zadok. The Sadducees recognized the written Torah, but they did not want it to be applied to all the circumstances of their times for fear it would limit their ability to move freely in society. Both the Pharisees and Sadducees were mentioned as parties for the first time during the days of Hyrcanus.

John Hyrcanus's foreign policy attemped to keep on the best side of the Romans. Therefore, he renewed the earlier declarations of the Roman senate for their protection. In the decree of Fannius, Hyrcanus probably secured the independence of Judea, but to that point he had not been successful in regaining the port city of Joppa. Only toward the end of his reign did Hyrcanus regain Joppa. Josephus thought this happened in the Decree of Pergamene.[3]

Hyrcanus took territories held by ancient Edom and cities south of Hebron, a territory that thereafter would be known as Idumea. He also destroyed the Samaritan sanctuary on Mt. Gerizim, near Shechem, taking the city of Samaria in the process. The Samaritans appealed to the Seleucids but without results, for one year later Hyrcanus destroyed Samaria (107 B.C.).

Hyrcanus minted bronze coins bearing inscriptions such as "the high priest John and the community of the Judeans." This claim to be a high priest incensed the Pharisees and was the cause of their rejection of the Hasmonean state.

When John Hyrcanus died in 104 B.C., he provided for his consort to succeed him to the throne. But his son Aristobulus would revise that plan. All in all, Hyrcanus left the Hasmonean state with borders that had been extended on all sides. While not all Jews agreed with his policies, his Hasidic background had held his life in check for the most

3. For the Decree of Fannius, see Josephus, *Antiquities* xiii. 9. 2. For the Decree of Pergamene, see Josephus, *Antiquities* xiv. 10. 22. These decrees and their interrelationships are disputed, but they are regaining more attention in recent times.

part. His children, however, were a different story. They had grown up as aristocrats in a palace; their training was more Greek than Hebrew; and they shared a great disdain for the Pharisees.

Aristobulus

John Hyrcanus's oldest son, Aristobulus (his Greek name, though his Hebrew name was Judah, a name he did not prefer), usurped the throne, despite his father's wishes that his consort rule in his stead. He immediately assumed the title of king and began to demonstrate that he indeed was one ambitious and cruel man. He starved his mother to death in prison, where he also had imprisoned three of his brothers, two of whom also starved to death.

Aristobulus continued his father's policy of territorial expansion. In his one-year reign (104–103 B.C.), he pushed the borders as far north as Mt. Lebanon against the Ituraeans.

Josephus gave Aristobulus the surname of *Philohellene*, "friend of the Greeks." [4] However, drink, disease, and a continual fear of insurrection and rebellion brought an early death after a one-year reign. He was not missed by most Jews.

Alexander Jannaeus

When Aristobulus died, only one brother remained alive in prison. His Hebrew name was Jonathan, but he, too, went by his Greek name Alexander Jannaeus (Jannai or Jannaeus being the shortened form of Jonathan). Aristobulus's consort Salome Alexandra released Alexander Jannaeus from prison, made him king, and married him. He ruled from 103–76 B.C.

Jannaeus was likewise a disappointment, for he seems to have evidenced an unstable personality and an ineptitude for the governing processes. However, like his predecessors, he too had a policy of territorial expansion. Jannaeus extended his frontiers along the Philistine coast, toward Egypt, and in the Transjordanian area. The state was now growing to proportions that could begin to rival those of David and Solomon. It stretched from the borders of Egypt to Lake Huleh in the north, from Perea in Transjordan to the coastal plain, including all the Philistine cities except Ashkalon. This latter acquisition was quite important, for the Hasmoneans aspired to be a maritime power. Indeed,

4. Josephus, *Antiquities* xiii. 11. 3. Whether this was an incidental or fixed title is not known.

ships were sculptured on the family tomb near Modein and on the coins minted by later Hasmonean rulers.

The territories that were incorporated into the Hasmonean kingdom were Judaized. Typical of this action were the Nabateans, a people south of the Dead Sea in the Arabah and on the hill country bordering on its east side. Alexander Jannaeus came to friendly terms with King Aretas of the Nabataeans. Later the Idumeans were to exercise an important place in the Jewish national life. However, other cites and peoples, including the Samaritans, resisted assimilation, often retaining their non-Jewish character.

Alexander Jannaeus alienated most of the non-hellenized Jewish population. At one memorable feast where he was acting as king-priest, in contempt for the Pharisees, he poured out a water libation on his own feet instead of on the altar as was prescribed. Outraged by this act of sacrilege, the people in the temple pelted Jannaeus with citrons which they were carrying in honor of the feast. The soldiers were called in to restore order and as a result hundreds lost their lives.

Civil war broke out as a result of this episode. The Pharisees, strange as it may seem, appealed to the Syrians to defend them against the descendants of the Maccabees. The Syrians came, and Jannaeus was forced to retreat to the Judean hills. With time to reflect on what they had done, the Pharisees feared that the Syrians would reclaim Judea. Thus, thousands of Pharisees deserted the Syrian army and went over to Alexander Jannaeus, thinking that by now he had been punished enough for his deed, and thus the Syrians were defeated in this shift of soldier alignment.

Jannaeus seemed to gain very little wisdom from the whole experience, for he hunted down the leaders of the rebellion and used them to teach a lesson to all others who dared to oppose him. He gave a banquet for the leaders of the Sadducees in honor of his victory, but he had eight hundred Pharisees crucified in the presence of his celebrating guests. Jannaeus may be the one known in the Dead Sea Scrolls as the "wicked priest" who persecuted the pious one known as the "teacher of righteousness."

Most feel that the Hasmonean degeneracy reached its all-time low under Alexander Jannaeus. Some suggest that Jannaeus knew his passing would not be mourned and that history would not regard him well; therefore, he instructed his wife to dismiss his Sadducean advisers and to reign with the aid of the Pharisees.

Alexander Jannaeus died in Transjordania at the siege of a fortress just north of the Jabbok in 76 B.C. He was forty-nine years old, an alcoholic, according to Josephus, and one who had foreseen his own death.[5] His successor was his wife Salome Alexandra.

Salome Alexandra

In her nine-year reign (76–67 B.C.), Salome Alexandra followed the alleged advice of her husband by coming to terms with the Pharisees. She had been married successively to Aristobulus and to Alexander Jannaeus, and apparently she had been a major force behind the rule of both men. Once on the throne, she initiated new domestic policies that reversed the prevailing forces and opinions behind the government. She was almost seventy when she began to reign, but she carried out all the secular duties of government, though she could not be high priest because she was a woman. This task she gave to her eldest son, Hyrcanus (II). His brother Aristobulus (II) she made military commander. In the meantime, she kept both brothers at bay so they did not come into open conflict with each other.

Alexandra's brother, Simeon ben Shetah, was a leader of the Pharisees—a fact that greatly aided her efforts to bring peace between herself and the ones her husband had viciously offended. Her new policies favored the Pharisees rather than the Sadducees, as had been the case up to this point. Under the presidency of Simeon ben Shetah, the Sanhedrin (the Jewish council of state) decreed that every young man should be educated, with primary emphasis being placed on training in the Hebrew Scriptures. Thus a comprehensive system of elementary education was installed in most of the larger villages, towns, and cities in Judea.

Compared to the reigns of her predecessors, the reign of Alexandra was rather peaceful. This did not mean that all the hostilities ceased. While the Pharisees were happy over their newly won recognition, the Sadducees resented having lost the power they once held. The Pharisees used their increased power to settle old scores such as the massacre laid on them by Alexander Jannaeus. The spilling of more blood only set the scene for more civil strife.

Alexandra's son Aristobulus led an expedition against Damascus, but this accomplished little. Another threatened invasion from Armenia was stopped, not by armed resistance, but by bribes and diplomacy.

5. Josephus, *Antiquities* xiii. 15. 5

The seventy-three-year-old Alexandra died at an inopportune moment. Her two sons scrambled to seize the reigns of government. The Nabataeans were advancing from the south as the Romans were approaching from the north and west. From Rome's standpoint, the time had arrived to attend to matters in the east, for Rome's long period of internal strife was coming to an end.

Hyrcanus II

Hyrcanus II was made king when his mother Salome Alexandra died. Hyrcanus II had been serving as high priest during the reign of his mother. His brother Aristobulus would not let matters stand.

Aristobulus, with the help of the disenfranchised Sadducees, laid siege to Jerusalem. After a short siege, they persuaded Hyrcanus II to renounce his throne and to surrender it to Aristobulus. Hyrcanus could not appeal to the Pharisees for help, for they had neither the means, ability, or desire to carry out a war. Therefore Hyrcanus II appealed to Antipas, governor of Idumea, who gave him refuge and helped him obtain refuge and help from the Nabataeans. The cost of winning this favor from the Nabataean king Aretas III, with his royal residence at Petra, was the promise of the territory of Moab. Thus, with this Nabataean support, Hyrcanus appeared outside Jerusalem and laid siege to the city where Aristobulus had taken up residence. The populace of Jerusalem was largely on Hyrcanus's side, once again opening more wounds with the Sadducees.

In this tension and contest between the two brothers, another dramatic turn of events would lead to a major shift in power in the Near East. Both Hyrcanus II and Aristobulus appealed to Pompey's representative in Damascus for help in settling who was the legitimate heir to the throne—this with the parties of the Jews divided inside Jerusalem and the Nabataeans perched outside the gates of Jerusalem!

The Roman legate in Damascus, M. Aemilius Scaurus, sided with Aristobulus and ordered the Nabataeans to withdraw from Jerusalem.

Aristobulus II

Aristobulus II continued Hasmonean rule in Judea, but he was no longer the sole ruler. He had become the puppet of Rome by appealing for their help and presence in settling the matter with his brother Hyrcanus II.

Rome had not intended to intervene in Judea's internal disputes at first. Pompey had recently risen to power when the unfortunate L. Licinius Lucullus had tripped up in Armenia and was no longer able to gain Roman support. His replacement was none other than Pompey in 67 B.C. Pompey had been given unusually broad powers by Caesar, against the will of the Senate. In addition, he had been given the provinces of Bithynia and Cilicia, with an order to halt the war against Mithridates. Pompey demanded an unconditional surrender, then defeated Midridates's troops near the Euphrates, causing their king to commit suicide after attempting a counterattack in 63 B.C. Now the province of Pontus was added to his sphere of influence and oversight.

Pompey sent the legate M. Aemilius Scaurus to Syria in 65 B.C., in effect doing away with the Seleucid state. There the legate learned of the dispute between Hyrcanus and Aristobulus in Judea, but he could not make a final decision. Pompey wintered in Syria in 64/63 B.C. and arrived in Damascus in 63 B.C., where both Hyrcanus and Aristobulus appeared in person to win Rome's favor. Antipater sent an envoy to plead the case for Hyrcanus, while another Jerusalem delegation demanded that Rome end the Hasmonean rule altogether and strengthen instead the priesthood.

Pompey hestiated. To him the Nabataeans were the more pressing problem and danger. But when Aristobulus showed that he was in a position to unify all the forces of Judea behind himself and that he had organized resistance in Jerusalem, Pompey decided something had to be done in Judea.

Pompey marched directly to Judea, avoiding Transjordan, and to the Alexandreion, a citadel that Alexander Jannaeus had built on a unique height near the Jordan Rift Valley, near Beth-Shean, where Aristobulus had entrenched himself. Pompey forced Aristobulus to surrender Alexandreion, pursuing him to the vicinity of Jerusalem. There Aristobulus appeared in the Roman camp and promised to hand over the city to Pompey. Pompey kept Aristobulus as his prisoner while Gabinius went ahead of Pompey to Jerusalem, where he was denied entrance. When the populace of Jerusalem realized the danger they were in, they opened the gates of the city, but bitter resistance ensued for the next three months in the fortified temple precinct area. Eventually, that too fell to Pompey, and he entered the temple and the Holy of Holies, to the outrage of the people, but Pompey destroyed nothing, and sacrifices continued the next day with Hyrcanus as high priest.

Accordingly, in 63 B.C., Roman rule came to Jerusalem, and Judea became subject to Roman tribute. Hyrcanus II continued to play a limited role as high priest in Jerusalem. But his brother Aristobulus was taken to Rome as a captive and featured in Pompey's triumphal procession in 61 B.C. Hasmonean rule had come to an end.

EPILOGUE

"With the arrival of the Romans in the old territory of Israel and Judah and the formation of the province of Syria, the history of Israel in Old Testament times comes to its ultimate end," argued Siegfried Herrmann.[1] And so it did!

Rome had first appeared as a city-state on the Tiber River, according to tradition, some thirty years before the fall of Samaria in 722 B.C. Legend assures us that Remus and Romulus founded the city of Rome in 753 B.C. By the fifth century B.C., it was functioning as a thriving republic. But by 250 B.C., Rome had brought under subjection the Etruscans and other tribes on the Italian peninsula.

Later the Carthaginians tried to tackle Rome in three successive wars, known as the Punic Wars, but finally Rome gained control of the western Mediterranean in 146 B.C. These Carthaginians had roots that went back to the Phoenician city of Tyre, but the Roman general Scipio Africanus demolished the Carthaginians and ended their threat to Roman power by repulsing Hannibal's invasion of Italy.[2]

Now that Carthage was no longer a threat, Rome extended her rule to Macedonia, Corinth, and all Achaia. In 133 B.C., King Attalus of Pergamum bequeathed all his lands to the Romans. Now the Romans were in Asia as well.

---

1. Siegfried Herrmann, *A History of Israel*, p. 378.
2. Donald Harden, *The Phoenicians* (London: Thames and Hudson, 1962), chap. V: "Carthage: Her Origin and History," pp. 66–75.

They were poised to begin a new chapter in the history of the successive empires of the world and the ancient Near East.

APPENDIXES

CHRONOLOGY OF THE HISTORY OF ISRAEL

The Ancient World before the Patriarchs

Approximate Date	Event
8500–7500 B.C.	Pre-Pottery Neolithic A
7500–6000 B.C.	Pre-Pottery Neolithic B
6000–5000 B.C.	Pottery Neolithic A
5000–4300 B.C.	Pottery Neolithic B
4300–3300 B.C.	Chalcolithic

The Early Bronze Age to Middle Bronze II

Approximate Date	Event
3300–3050 B.C.	Early Bronze I
3050–2300 B.C.	Early Bronze II–III
2300–2000 B.C.	Early Bronze IV/Middle Bronze I
2000–1800/1750	Middle Bronze IIA

The Patriarchs to the Divided Monarchy

Approximate Date	Event	Biblical Reference
ca. 2092 B.C.	Abraham's journey into Canaan	Genesis 12
ca. 2092–1875 B.C.	Age of biblical patriarchs	Genesis 12–50
ca. 1876 B.C.	Jacob and his sons go to Egypt to join Joseph	Genesis 37–50
1720–1570 B.C.	Hyksos domination of Egypt	
ca. 1447 B.C.	Exodus from Egypt	Exodus 1–15
ca. 1407–1400 B.C.	Conquest of Canaan	Joshua 1–13
ca. 1360–1350 B.C.	Transition period between Joshua and the judges	Judges 1–3:6
1360–1084 B.C.	The period of the judges	Judges 3:7–1 Samuel 7
1051–1011 B.C.	The reign of King Saul	1 Samuel 8–31
ca. 1029 B.C.	David anointed by Samuel	1 Samuel 16
ca. 1011–971 B.C.	The reign of King David	1 Samuel 16–1 Kings 2
971–931 B.C.	The reign of King Solomon	1 Kings 3–11

The Divided Monarchy

Israel		Judah	
Jeroboam I	931–910	931–913	Rehoboam
Nadab	910–909	913–911	Abijah
Baasha	909–886	911–870	Asa
Elah	886–885		
Zimri	885		
Omri	885–874		
Ahab	874–853	873–848	Jehoshaphat
Ahaziah	853–852		
Joram	852–841	848–841	Jehoram

Israel		Judah	
Jehu	841–814	841	Ahaziah
		841–835	Athaliah
Jehoahaz	814–798	835–796	Joash
Jehoash	798–782	796–767	Amaziah
Jeroboam II	793–753	792–740	Uzziah
Zechariah	753		
Shallum	752		
Menahem	752–742	750–731	Jotham
Pekahiah	742–740		
Pekah	752–732	735–715	Ahaz
Hoshea	732–722	729–686	Hezekiah
		696–642	Manasseh
		642–640	Amon
		640–609	Josiah
		609	Jehoahaz
		608–598	Jehoiakim
		598–597	Jehoiachin
		597–586	Zedekiah

Exilic and Postexilic Era (586–331 B.C.)

Approximate Date	Event	Biblical Reference
586 B.C.	The fall of Jerusalem	2 Kings 25; 2 Chronicles 36
606/5–536 B.C.	70-year Babylonian Captivity	Jeremiah 25
539 B.C.	Fall of Babylon	Daniel 5
538 B.C.	Cyrus decree	2 Chronicles 36:22–23; Ezra 1:1–4
536 B.C.	First return under Zerubbabel	Ezra 1–6

Approximate Date	Event	Biblical Reference
520 B.C.	Rebuilding temple starts	Haggai 1–2; Zechariah 1
458 B.C.	Second return under Ezra	Ezra 7–10
445 B.C.	Third return under Nehemiah	Nehemiah 1–10
516 B.C.	Temple completed	
331 B.C.	Battle of Issus; Persia falls to Greece	

The Hellenistic Era (331–64 B.C.)

Approximate Date	Event	Biblical Reference
333–323 B.C.	Alexander the Great conquers most of the known world	1 Maccabees 1
167–134 B.C.	Maccabean revolt	1 Maccabees 1–2
142–63 B.C.	The Hasmonean kingdom	
63 B.C.	Pompey makes Judea part of the Roman Empire	1 Maccabees
ca. 4 B.C.–A.D. 30	Jesus of Nazareth ministers	Gospels
A.D. 70	Temple is destroyed	

GLOSSARY

Ahasuerus (Xerxes). The son of Darius Hystaspes and Atossa, daughter of Cyrus the Great, who married Esther as queen. He is the Xerxes I (486–465 B.C.) who led the second Persian invasion of Greece and was soundly defeated in the battle of Salamis (480 B.C.).

Akhenaton. The Egyptian pharaoh (1379–1362 B.C.), also spelled as Ikhnaton and known as Amenhotep IV, who introduced a monotheistic religion of the solar deity Aton, thereby disaffecting the priests of the Theban state god Amun.

Akkad (Accad). A narrow plain of Babylonia that was just north of Sumer where the founders of the Akkad Dynasty (2360–2180 B.C.) began the first empire in world history. This dynasty was named for its capital city of Akkad.

Akkadian (Accadian). The language written in cuneiform script that shares many common features with Hebrew, Aramaic, and Arabic. This Semitic language was used in Mesopotamia from approximately the twenty-eighth to the first centuries B.C.

Alexander the Great. The son of King Philip of Macedonia. He was born in 356 B.C. and he died in Babylon in 323 B.C. after having conquered most of the world of that day from Greece to India.

Amalekites. A desert people, hostile to Israel through much of her history, living in the Negev south of Canaan who trace their ancestry back to Amalek, the son of Esau (Gen. 36:12).

Amarna Age. The title given to the reign of Pharaoh Akhenaton, Amenhotep IV, whose government centered in his new capital at Amarna, Egypt.

Ammonites. A Semitic people who lived in Transjordania along the lands that drained into the Jabbok River. Though descended from Lot, they were hostile to Israel (Gen. 19:38).

Amorites. A Semitic people called "Westerners" (Babylonian) or "Highlanders" (Hebrew) who may have moved into the ancient Near East around 2000 B.C. and founded the states of Mari and Babylon. Hammurabi was the best known Amorite ruler.

Amphictony. A confederation of tribes (usually six or twelve) organized around a particular shrine or sanctuary. Scholars have applied this term to Israel's organization during the period of the judges around the center in Shiloh or Shechem, but that designation is losing popularity in recent scholarship.

Anatolia. The ancient geographic name for Asia Minor, present-day Turkey.

Anat. The Canaanite goddess and sister-consort of the fertility god Baal.

Antiochus. The name shared by several Syrian rulers who inherited their power from Seleucus I, one of Alexander the Great's generals who divided up his empire at his death.

'Apiru. See Habiru.

Arabah. The arid desert plain that stretches from the Dead Sea to the Gulf of Aqabah.

Aramaic. The West Semitic language of the Syrians (Arameans) spoken earlier by the inhabitants of Mesopotamia, then the official language of the Persian Empire, and used by the Jews during the Babylonian Exile.

Arameans. The descendants of Aram, son of Shem (Gen. 10:22), and the Semitic people who established small kingdoms in Syria.

Artaxerxes. The son of the Persian king Xerxes and ruler of Persia from 465–423 B.C. He commissioned Nehemiah to return to Jerusalem to rebuild the walls of Jerusalem in 445 B.C. (Neh. 2).

Asherah. The Canaanite goddess of war and fertility who was another one of Baal's consorts. A wooden image, pole, or a tree was her symbol.

Ashurbanipal. The Assyrian monarch who was the grandson of Sennacherib, son and successor of Esarhaddon. He ruled from 668–627 B.C.

Assur (Asshur). The chief deity of the Assyrians, the god of war. Assur was also the name of the capital city on the west bank of the Tigris. The Assyrians called their country by this same name—Assur.

Assyria. The territory located in the upper Tigris River that embraced the major cities of Assur, Calah, and Nineveh. It dominated the Near East from the eleventh to the seventh centuries B.C., when it was destroyed by the Babylonians and the Medes in 611 B.C.

Augustus. The first Caesar of Rome (30 B.C.-A.D. 14).

Atonement, Day of. See Fast Day.

Baal. The Canaanite deity, meaning "lord" or "master," who personified the rain, dew, storm, and fertility of nature. He is also known as Hadad in various cultures.

Babel. The "Gate of God," where the languages were confused, according to the story in Genesis 11:1–9. The tower that was under construction in that story was probably a ziggurat.

Babylon. A city on the Euphrates River that served as the capital of the old Babylonian and Neo-Babylonian Empires.

Babylonian Chronicle. A clay tablet that recorded the Battle of Carchemish and the capture of Jerusalem in 597 B.C.

Babylonian Exile. The seventy years between 606/05 and 536 B.C. that Judah spent in captivity in Babylon after Jerusalem was destroyed in 586 B.C.

B.C.E. A substitute designation for B.C., "Before Christ," meaning "Before the Common Era," as a term considered more politically correct in some circles.

Behistun Stone. The trilingual inscription authorized by Darius I of Persia that became the key to deciphering the cuneiform script.

Belshazzar. The final king of Babylon who ruled as a coregent with his father Nabonidus (Dan. 5:1–31).

Booths, Feast of. See Feasts

Caesar. A name for the Roman emperors that commemorated the first emperor Augustus Caesar.

Canaan. The name of the land between the Mediterranean Sea and the Dead Sea, bounded by Egypt to the south and Syria to the north. The name may mean "purple," from the purple dye that came from the murex shellfish found along the coast of this area later known as Palestine.

C.E. "Common Era," a more neutral designation preferred today by some who object to the long-standing *anno Domini*, A.D.

Circumcision. The ancient Semitic rite that removed the male foreskin either on the eighth day (as a sign of the covenant; Gen. 17:10–14) or at puberty at the time of the beginning of manhood or marriage.

Cosmology. The conception of the structure of the universe.

Covenant. The promise God made with certain individuals or groups or an agreement or a compact made between individuals. It may be one-sided (unilateral). with all responsibility for maintaining it left on the promising party (e.g., Yahweh); or it may be two-sided (bilateral), with responsibility for its maintenance resting on both contracting parties.

Cuneiform. The wedge-shaped writing that began in Sumer around 3200 B.C. and spread throughout Mesopotamia.

Dagon. The Canaanite agricultural deity worshiped by the Philistines in the cities of Ashdod and Gaza (1 Sam. 5:1–7), whose temple Samson destroyed (Judg. 16:23–30).

Darius. The name of several Persian rulers. Darius I continued Cyrus's favorable treatment of the Jews. Darius the Mede, mentioned in Daniel 5:31; 9:1, has not yet been certainly attested in sources outside the Bible.

Dead Sea Scrolls. A collection of biblical and nonbiblical manuscripts that have been found since 1947 in caves on the northwest side of the Dead Sea. They probably belonged to the library of the Essene community of Qumran.

Decalogue. The "ten Words" or "Ten Commandments" recorded in Exodus 20 and Deuteronomy 5.

Ebla. A large ancient Canaanite city in modern Syria that contains a large library of clay tablets in cuneiform and dating to the late third millennium B.C.

Edomites. A Semitic people living in the Arabah and Negev, south of the Dead Sea, descendants of Esau (Gen. 36:1).

El. The Semitic root for "God." The name is used for the high god in the Canaanite pantheon, as an indiscriminate designation for all gods in the Hebrew Bible when it is in the plural form of *Elohim*, or as a designation for Israel's God.

Elam. The country east of Sumer now known as the territory of Iran. The Elamites were descendants of Elam, son of Shem (Gen. 10:22). Elam's king, Chedorlaomer (Gen. 14:1–11) headed several states that attacked the five cities of the plain in Genesis 14.

Eponym. The person from whom a family, race, city, nation, or year took its name.

Esarhaddon. The son of the Assyrian king Sennacherib who ruled from 681–669 B.C.

Fast Day. Only one day was officially declared as a day of fasting in the Bible—the Day of Atonement; this was a day most sacred, when atonement for all the sins of all the people who afflicted their souls was effected. Israel later added other fast days in recognition of the tragedies surrounding the fall of Jerusalem.

Feast Days. There are three major festivals in the Israelite calendar: the Feast of Passover, or Unleavened Bread, celebrating the Exodus deliverance; the Feast of Weeks, or Pentecost in later days, coming fifty days after the previous feast at the end of the barley harvest; and the Feast of Ingathering, or Feast of Booths, or Tabernacles, celebrating the harvest festival at the time of New Year. Other minor festivals included the Feast of Purim, celebrating the deliverance recorded in the Book of Esther; and Hanukkah, of the Feast of Dedication, celebrating the rededication of the temple during the days of the Maccabean revolt.

Fertile Crescent. A term first coined by the Egyptologist James H. Breasted for the semi-circular region that extends from the Nile River valley through Palestine, Phoenicia, Syria, and the Tigris-Euphrates river valley to the northern tip of the Persian Gulf.

Gemara. The Aramaic commentary on the Mishna (oral law) that appears in the second part of the Talmud. The Mishna and the Gemara comprise the Talmud.

Habiru. A broad term embracing a group of persons of varied ethnic background who operated outside the urban and legal structures of the third and second millennia. Even though many have made a good case for the term being cognate with the term *Hebrew*, it is now regarded as having a wider application both in time and geography.

Hammurabi. The sixth king (1792–1750 B.C.) of Babylon's First Dynasty and founder of the first Amorite Empire in Mesopotamia. His law code was inscribed on an eight-foot-high stone monument in Akkadian cuneiform.

Hanukkah. See Feasts.

Hasidim. The devout or "pious" Jews who both actively and passively resisted the oppressive measures of the Selucids, beginning with Antiochus IV.

Hasmoneans. The Jewish royal dynasty named for Hasmon, the ancestor of Mattathias Maccabees. This line ended with the Roman conquest of Palestine in 63 B.C.

Hazael. "God sees." An Aramaean murderer of Ben-Hadad II and usurper of the Damascus throne.

Hebrew. The Aramaean branch of Semitic descendants of Eber, descendant of Shem (1 Chron. 1:18). The term is used for the preexilic Israelite. It is also the Semitic tongue of the Israelites, which was obtained from the lip of the Canaanites.

Hellenism. The language, values, and culture of classical Greek thought that inundated the ancient Near East after Alexander the Great's conquest.

Herod. The name of seven Palestinian rulers from 40 B.C. to A.D. 50.

Herodians. An influential political party in the first century B.C. that supported Herod's dynasty and opposed messianic hopes.

Hieroglyphic. The Egyptian system of writing that used pictorial script; it was first deciphered by using the trilingual Rosetta Stone found by Napoleon's troops in Egypt.

Hittites. Possible Aryan people who formed a kingdom in central Anatolia (Asia Minor) in the second millennium B.C. (ca. 1700–1400 B.C.).

Holiness Law. The name for the laws set forth in Leviticus 18–20 emphasizing separateness (holiness) in lifestyle and behavior for Israel.

Hyksos. The Egyptian designation for the racially mixed (but with heavy Semitic) populations that infiltrated and overran Egypt from 1720–1570 B.C. (the Fifteenth and Sixteenth Dynasties of Egypt). They were finally expelled from Egypt by Kamose and his brother Ahmose I. Whether the Israelites entered Egypt during the rule of these rulers friendly to the Semites is still warmly debated by scholars.

Hyrcanus. The name of Simon Maccabees's son, who was the Hasmonean king and high priest of Judah from 134–104 B.C. He was John I. John II (63–40 B.C. was high priest and puppet ruler for Rome.

Idumea. Meaning "pertaining to Edom." The name the Greeks and Romans used for the country of Edom, from whence Herod the Great came (1 Macc. 4:29; 5:65; Mark 3:8).

Ishmaelites. Caravan merchants from the land of Midian that traded with Egypt (Gen 37:25–28, 36; 39:1).

Ishtar. The Assyrian and Babylonian goddess of love and war (Jer. 44).

Isis. The Egyptian goddess who was wife of Osiris and mother of Horus.

Israel. Name given to Jacob in Transjordania (Gen. 32:28) and by Yahweh at Bethel (Gen. 35:10), and thus to the twelve tribes descended from him. It is also used of the northern ten tribes in contradistinction to the southern two tribes of Benjamin and Judah, which are known together as Judah when distinguished from Israel.

Jebel Musa. The mountain in the southern part of the Sinai Peninsula usually thought to be the mountain where Moses received the Ten Commandments.

Jebusites. The early inhabitants of the city of Jebus, later known as Jerusalem.

Jezreel. A town on the edge of Mt. Gilboa that served as the summer palace and residence of the kings of northern Israel. It overlooks the plain of Esdraelon or Jezreel, which extends from Mt. Carmel in the west to Beth-shean in the east.

Jordan Rift Valley. The geological fissure through which the Jordan River runs, extending from the valley between the Lebanon and Anti-Lebanon mountains in the north to the Gulf of Aqabah in the south.

Judah. The fourth son of Jacob and Leah (Gen. 29:35), who became the progenitor of the tribe of Judah. Later, joined by the tribe of Benjamin, Judah was the designation for the Southern Kingdom that lasted until it was destroyed in 586 B.C.

Judaism. The religion of the Jews that emerged while Judah was in the Babylonian Exile.

Judea. The Greco-Roman term for the land of Judah after Judah returned from the Babylonian Exile.

Judges in Israel. The twelve charismatic leaders who led Israel during the period of Israel's occupation of the land after the days of Joshua until Saul was chosen as king. They included Othniel, Ehud, Shamgar, Deborah, Gideon, Tola, Jair, Jephthah, Ibzan, Elon, Abdon, and Samson, with Eli and Samuel also being spoken of as being judges.

Jupiter. The Latin name for the chief Roman deity, known as Zeus in the Greek pantheon.

Kenites. Midianite nomadic metal workers who lived in the Arabah and worshiped Yahweh. The best-known member of this group was Jethro, Moses' father-in-law (Exod. 18:1–12).

Kethu'vim. The Hebrew term for the third main division of the Hebrew Bible. It includes the poets: Psalms, Job, Proverbs; the five "scrolls" (*megilloth*): Song of Songs, Ecclesiastes, Esther, Ruth, Lamentations; and the histories: Daniel, Ezra-Nehemiah, and Chronicles.

Levites. The tribe that served as ministers at the tabernacle and later at the temple; they were descendants of the third son of Jacob and Leah. The Aaronic family in the tribe of Levi was the family that served as the priests of Israel and Judah.

LXX. The popular abbreviation for the Septuagint, the Greek translation of the Hebrew Bible that was made in Alexandria, Egypt, some time during the third to the first centuries B.C.

Maccabees. The name given to the family that successfully won independence for the Jews from the Syrian-Selucid hellenistic oppressors between 165 and 142 B.C. Also known as Hasmoneans, they remained in power until 63 B.C. The name *Maccabeus* means "hammerer," a name first given to Judas.

Mesopotamia. The area "between the rivers" of the Euphrates and Tigris, present-day Iraq, at the head of the Persian Gulf. It was the birthplace of the Sumerian, Akkadian, Assyrian, and Neo-Babylonian civilizations.

Midianites. A nomadic people inhabiting the northwestern Arabian desert, east of the Gulf of Aqabah and east of the Sinai Peninsula. They were descended from Abraham and his second wife Keturah (Gen. 25:1–4), and were also known as Ishmaelites.

Mishnah. The section of the Talmud that contains the collection of the Jewish oral and legal traditions from the previous centuries, but written down by Rabbi Judah ha-Nasi (ca. A.D. 135–220).

Moabites. The descendants from one of Lot's daughters (Gen. 19:30–38) who lived east of Dead Sea and north of Edom. For most of their history they were inveterate enemies of Israel; yet both David and Jesus were descended from Moab through Ruth.

Molech (Moloch). The god of Ammon that called for human sacrifice, an act specifically prohibited for the Hebrews (Lev. 18:21; 20:2).

Mordecai. The cousin and foster father of Esther (Esther 2:21–23). His name is related probably to the Babylonian deity Marduk (Merodach).

Nabopolassar. The founder of the Neo-Babylonian Empire, who destroyed the Assyrian capital of Nineveh in 611 B.C. and was succeeded by his son Nebuchadnezzar (Nah. 3:1–3; Jer. 46).

Nebuchadnezzar. Son of Nabopolassar, who ruled from 605–562 B.C. over the Neo-Babylonian Empire by bringing most of the Near East under his control.

Nebuzardan. The commander of the Babylonian troops under Nebuchadnezzar who was sent to oversee the destruction of Jerusalem in 586 B.C. and the deportation of Judah's populace to Babylon (2 Kings 25:8–20).

Necho. The son of Pharaoh Psammetichus I and second king of the Twenty-sixth Dynasty in Egypt, who defeated and killed King Josiah of Judah in 609 B.C. (2 Kings 23:29–35; 2 Chron. 35:20–24).

Negev. The mostly arid region that is south of Judah and the city of Beersheba.

Nineveh. The final capital of the Assyrian Empire, located on the east bank of the Tigris River, founded by Nimrod (Gen. 10:11). It is most famous for the extensive library discovered there that belonged to Ashurbanipal, including the famous Babylonian Genesis story (*Enuma Elish*) and flood story (*Gilgamesh Epic*).

Ophel. The southeastern portion of the temple site in Jerusalem, where David's city was located (2 Chron. 27:3; 33:14).

Ostracon. A piece of ancient pottery on which writing is found.

Palestine. The land bordered by the Mediterranean Sea on the east, the Jordan rift valley on the west, Syria on the north and the Sinai Peninsula on the south. In the times of the patriarchs, it was known as Canaan (Gen. 12:6–7; 15:18–21). It is named after the Philistines and was first called Palestine by the Greek historian Herodotus around 450 B.C.

Passover. See Feasts.

Patriarch. The male head of a family or tribe in the ancient Near East.

Pentateuch. The Greek word meaning "five scrolls," for the first five books of the Hebrew Bible.

Persia. The territory southeast of Elam inhabited by Indo-European (Ayrian, i.e, "Iran") peoples, who came to world domination under Cyrus the Great as he conquered Babylon in 539 B.C.

Pharaoh. The title of the Egyptian king, meaning "great house."

Pharisees. The religious group that arose in post-Maccabean times in Judea, probably descended from the Hasidim who resisted Antiochus IV's program of Hellenization of the Jews. Their name comes from the Hebrew *parûš*, meaning "separated," because they insisted on a vigorous observance of the Law.

Philistines. A non-Semitic people that migrated from the Aegean islands (Caphtor in Amos 9:7) to the southern coast of Palestine along with the Sea People's migration of 1200 B.C. It also seems that they used this same area earlier for farming during the days of the patriarchs and their permanent settling there.

Phoenicia. The coastal territory along the northeast shore of the Mediterranean Sea, squeezed between the sea on the west and the Lebanon mountain range on the east. Its most famous seaports were Tyre and Sidon.

Ptolemy. A Macedonian general who received the rulership of Egypt after the sudden and unexpected death of Alexander the Great. The Ptolemaic Dynasty controlled Egypt until 31 B.C., when the Romans came to power.

Purim. See Feasts.

Qarqar. The spot where the pivotal battles took place between Shalmaneser III of Assyria and a coalition of kings from Syria-Palestine under Benhadad of Syria in 853 B.C., a crucial date for biblical chronologies.

Qumran. The site of a monastic community of Essenes in the foothills of the Judean desert just west of the northern end of the Dead Sea. This community was responsible for producing the Dead Sea Scrolls.

Ras Shamra. The Syrian site where in A.D. 1929 the Ugaritic Tablets containing the texts of Canaanite religion were found.

Rosetta Stone. The stone discovered by the Napoleonic troops in A.D. 1799 that had the trilingual inscription that unlocked the translation of the Egyptian hieroglyphic texts.

Sadducees. The conservative and aristocratic religious group of Jews that arose in the first century B.C.; they recognized only the Torah as binding on them for faith and practice. They denied the resurrection of the body, a future judgment, and the relevance of the Prophets and the Writings.

Samaria. The village that King Omri made the capital of the northern ten tribes (1 Kings 16:24–25). The Assyrians destroyed it in 721 B.C. (2 Kings 17).

Samaritans. A mixed group of peoples living in the region of Samaria after the fall of Samaria as a result of the Assyrian policy of ethnic and national assimilation of conquered peoples.

Sanhedrin. The final judicial body of the Jews from the third century B.C. until the Romans destroyed Jerusalem in A.D. 70.

Scythians. A warlike nomadic people living on the north and east of the Black Sea who swept south as far as Egypt some time around 626 B.C. in the days when Jeremiah began his ministry. Pharaoh Psammetichus I bribed the Scythians so that they returned by the coastal route without attacking Palestine.

Seleucids. The name of the Macedonian rulers of Syria, who received this area after the unexpected death of Alexander the Great. The dynasty was named after Seleucid I.

Semites. The descendants of Noah's son "Shem" (Gen. 10; 21–31), whose progeny included Elam, Asshur, Arpacshad (Hebrews and Arabs), Lud (Lydians), and Aram (Syria).

Sennacherib. The son of Sargon II and king of Assyria, who besieged Jerusalem in the days of Hezekiah, wherein he lost 185,000 troops in a single night due to the direct intervention of Yahweh (2 Kings 19:9–35).

Shalmaneser. Two of the most famous of the five Assyrian kings that bore this name are Shalmaneser III, who defeated a coalition of Syrian and Palestinian kings that came against him in 853 B.C., and Shalmaneser V, who succeeded Tiglath-Pileser and laid siege to Samaria for three years, but died just before the city fell (2 Kings 17:3–5; 18:9).

Septuagint. See LXX.

Shephelah. The low-lying hills that emerge from the Philistine Plain and rise to meet the Judean hill country further east. The word is Hebrew for "low."

Sinai. See Jebul Musa.

Stele. An upright stone pillar that bears an inscription, carving, or design and memorializes a person, deity, or event.

Succoth (Sukkoth). See Feasts. The Jewish Feast of Tabernacles or Booths.

Synagogue. The gathering place for Jews in instruction or worship that arose during and after the Babylonian Exile.

Syria. The territory from northern Palestine to the Upper Euphrates River, including Phoenicia on the coast and the inland kingdom of Aram, with its capital in Damascus.

Talmud. The collection of Jewish religious and legal traditions that comes in two parts: the Mishnah (the written form of the early oral interpretations of the Torah) and the Gemara (the extensive commentary on the Mishnah). The Palestinian version produced about A.D. 450 is incomplete, but the Babylonian Talmud, which is about four times as long, was finished about A.D. 500.

Targum. The Aramaic paraphrase of the Hebrew Bible completed some time early in the Christian era.

Tell. An artificial mount that served as the site of an ancient Israelite city. With the accumulation of centuries of debris, and the encircling walls that prevented erosion, the mound rose higher over the years.

Torah. The Hebrew term for the "instruction," "teaching," or "law" found in the first five books of the Hebrew Bible. It may also refer in a general sense to all the canonical writings in the Tenak (= the Old Testament).

Transjordan. The plateau area east of the Jordan rift valley and the arid area of the Arabian desert. This area was assigned by Moses to the tribes of Reuben and Gad and the half tribe of Manasseh.

Ugarit. See Ras Shamra.

Ur. Two different sites have been suggested for this place from which Abraham began his journey to the land of Israel: the Ur in Sumerian, which was excavated by Sir Leonard Woolly, and the northern Ur in Upper Mesopotamia, as advocated by Cyrus H. Gordon.

Vulgate. The late fourth-century-A.D. Latin translation of the Bible by Jerome with the Apocrypha, which became the official version of the Roman Catholic Church.

Writings. See Kethu'vim.

Yahweh. The personal name for God in Israel, which was usually not pronounced by the Jews. Most commonly it is thought that the name derives from the Hebrew verb "to be" and means "he will be [there]." The Masoretes took the Hebrew consonantal YHWH and attached the vowels from *Adonai*, meaning "my Lord," to give an artificial pronunciation to the name since the original sound of the name had presumably been lost.

Ziggurat. A Sumerian or Babylonian multi-tiered tower resembling a pyramid with a chapel at the apex dedicated to a chief god, and a broad staircase leading up to this chapel for ceremonial and liturgical processions. The tower of Babel in Genesis 11:1–9 is in this same tradition.

Zion. The "citadel" or rocky ridge in old Jerusalem that later became the poetical way of referring to the city of Jerusalem itself.

BIBLIOGRAPHY

GENERAL WORKS

Albright, William Foxwell. *From Stone Age to Christianity*. 2nd ed. Garden City: Doubleday Anchor, 1957.

———. *Archaeology and the Religion of Israel*. 5th ed. Garden City: Doubleday Anchor, 1969.

———. *Yahweh and the Gods of Canaan*. New York: Doubleday and Co., 1968.

Ahlström, Gösta F. *The History of Ancient Palestine*. Minneapolis: Fortress, 1993.

Avi-Yonah, Michael, ed. *Encyclopedia of Archaeological Excavations in the Holy Land*. 5 vols. Englewood Cliffs, N.J.: Prentice Hall, 1976.

Bright, John. *A History of Israel*. 3rd ed. Philadelphia: Westminster, 1981.

________. *Early Israel in Recent History Writing*. London, SCM, 1956.

Coote, Robert. *Early History: A New Horizon*. Minneapolis: Fortress Press, 1990.

Davies, Philip R. *In Search of Ancient Israel*. Sheffield: JSOT Press, 1992.

Gottwald, Norman. *The Tribes of Yahweh: A Sociology of the Religion of Liberated Israel*. Maryknoll, N.Y.: Orbis, 1979.

Hayes, John H. and J. Maxwell Miller, eds. *Israelite and Judean History* Philadelphia: Westminster Press, 1977.

Herrmann, Siegfried. *A History of Israel in the Old Testament Times*. Translated by John Bowden. Revised and enlarged edition. Philadelphia: Fortress, 1981.

Kaufmann, Y. *The Religion of Israel, from Its Beginnings to the Babylonian Exile*. Chicago: University of Chicago Press, 1960.

Long, V. Phillips. *The Art of Biblical History*. Grand Rapids: Zondervan, 1994.

Mazar, Amihai. *Archaeology of the Land of the Bible: 10,000-586 B.C.E.* New York: Doubleday, 1992.

Millard, Alan R., James K. Hoffmeier, and David W. Baker, eds. *Faith, Tradition and History: Old Testament Historiography in Its Near Eastern Context*. Winona Lake, Ind.: Eisenbrauns, 1994.

Miller, J. H., and John H. Hayes. A *History of Ancient Israel and Judah* Philadelphia: Westminster, 1986.

Miller, J.M. *The Old Testament and the Historian*. Philadelphia: Fortress, 1976.

Merrill, Eugene M. *Kingdom of Priests: A History of Old Testament Israel*. Grand Rapids: Baker, 1987.

Noth, Martin. *The History of Israel*. 2nd English translation. New York: Harper & Brothers, 1960.

Pfeiffer, Charles F. *Old Testament History*. Grand Rapids: Baker, 1973.

Pritchard, James B. *Ancient Near Eastern Texts Relating to the Old Testament*. Princeton: Princeton University Press, 1950.

———. *The Ancient Near East in Pictures*. Princeton: Princeton University Press, 1954.

———. *The Ancient Near East: Supplementary Texts and Pictures Relating to the Old Testament*. Princeton: Princeton University Press, 1969.

Soggin, J. A. A *History of Israel: From the Beginnings to the Bar* Kochba Revolt, tr. John Bowden. London: SCM Press, 1984.

Thomas, D. Winton. *Documents from Old Testament Times*. Nashville: Thomas Nelson & Sons, 1958.

———. *Archaeology and Old Testament Study*. Oxford: Clarendon Press, 1967.

Thompson, Thomas L. *Early History of the Israelite People*. Leiden: Brill, 1992.

Wood, Leon J. A *Survey of Israel's History*. Grand Rapids: Zondervan, 1973.

Vaux, Roland de. *Ancient Israel*, English translation. New York: McGraw-Hill, 1961.

———. *The Early History of Israel*, English translation. Philadelphia: Westminster, 1978.

VanSeters, John. *Abraham, History and Tradition*. New Haven: Yale University Press, 1975.

Younger, Lawson, Jr. *Ancient Conquest Accounts: A Study in Ancient Near Eastern and Biblical History Writing*. JSOT Sup 98: Sheffield: JSOT Press, 1990.

Geography of the Bible Lands

Aharoni, Y. *The Land of the Bible: A Historical Geography*. Translated by Anson F. Rainey, revised edition. Philadelphia: Westminster Press, 1979.

Aharoni, Y., and M. Avi-Yonah. *The Macmillan Bible Atlas New* York: The Macmillan Co., 1968.

Baly, Dennis. *The Geography of the Bible*. New York: Harper & Brothers, 1957.

Beitzel, Barry. *The Moody Atlas of the Bible*. Chicago: Moody Press, 1985.

Grollenberg, L. H. *Atlas of the Bible*. Eng tr. Nashville: Thomas Nelson & Sons, 1956.

May, H. G., ed. *Oxford Bible Atlas*. New York: Oxford University Press, 1962.

Ancient Near Eastern Lands, Peoples, and Civilizations

Dothan, Trude, and Moshe Dothan. *People of the Sea: The Search for the Philistines*. New York: Macmillan, 1992.

Flanders, Henry J. Jr., Robert W. Crapps, and David A. Smith. *People of the Covenant: An Introduction to the Hebrew Bible*. New York: Oxford, 1996.

Frankfort, Henri. *Ancient Egyptian Religion New York*: Columbia University Press, 1948.

Gardiner, Alan. *Egypt of the Pharaohs*. New York: Oxford University Press, 1961.

Ghirshman, R. *Iran*, English translation. Hammondsworth: Penguin Books, 1954.

Gray, John, *The Canaanites*. London: Thames and Hudson, 1964.

Gurney, O. R. *The Hittites*. Hammondsworth: Penguin Books, 1952.

Hoerth, Alfred J., William Mattingly, and Edwin M. Yamauchi, eds. *People of the Old Testament World*. Grand Rapids: Baker, 1994.

Kitchen, Kenneth A. *The Ancient Orient and the Old Testament*. Chicago: InterVarsity Press, 1966.

Kramer, Samuel Noah. *The Sumerians*. Chicago: University of Chicago Press, 1963.

Mallowan, M. E. L. *Early Mesopotamia and Iran*. London: Thames and Hudson, 1965.

Mellaart, J. Earliest *Civilizations of the Near East*. New York: McGraw-Hill Book Company, 1965.

Moscati, S. *The World of the Phoenicians*, English translation. London: George Weidenfeld & Nicolson, 1968.

Olmstead, A. T. *The History of the Persian Empire*. Chicago: University of Chicago Press, 1948.

Oppenheim, A. L. *Ancient Mesopotamia: Portrait of a Dead Civilization*. Chicago: University of Chicago Press, 1964.

Redford, Donald B. *A Study of the Biblical Story of Joseph*. Leiden: Brill, 1970.

Saggs, H. W. F. *The Greatness That Was Babylon: A Sketch of the Ancient Civilization of the Tigris-Euphrates Valley*. New York: Hawthorne Books, 1962.

Unger, Merrill F. *Israel and the Arameans of Damascus*. Grand Rapids: Baker, 1980.

Wilson, John. *The Burden of Egypt*. Chicago: University of Chicago Press, 1951.

Wiseman, Donald J., ed. *Peoples of Old Testament Times*. Oxford: Clarendon Press, 1973.

Yadin, Y. *The Art of Warfare in Biblical Lands*. 2 vols. New York: McGraw-Hill Book Co., 1963.

Wooley, Leonard. *Abraham: Recent Discoveries and Hebrew Origins*. London, 1936.

Specialized Studies

Bimson, John. *Redating the Exodus and Conquest*. Sheffield: JSOT Press, 1978.

Finkelstein, Israel. *The Archaeology of the Israelites Settlement*. Jerusalem: Israel Exploration Society, 1988.

Garstang, John. *Joshua, Judges: Foundations of Bible History*. London: 1931.

Grabbe, Lester L. *Judaism From Cyrus to Hadrian*. Vol. 1 of The Persian and Greek Periods. Minneapolis: Fortress, 1992.

Greenberg, Moshe. *The Hab/piru*. New Haven: American Oriental Society, 1955.

Kaufmann, Y. *The Biblical Account of the Conquest of Palestine*. Jerusalem: Magnes Press, 1953.

Kenyon, Kathleen. *Digging Up Jericho*. London: Ernst Benn, 1957.

Thiele, Edwin R. *The Mysterious Numbers of the Hebrew Kings*. Chicago: University of Chicago Press, 1953.

Author Index

D

E

F

G

H

I

J

K

L

R

S

T

U

V

W

X

Y

Z

SUBJECT INDEX

Scripture Index

Exodus

Leviticus

Numbers

Deuteronomy

Joshua

Judges

Ruth

1 Samuel

2 Samuel

1 Kings

2 Kings

1 Chronicles

2 Chronicles

Ezra

Nehemiah

Esther

Psalms

Proverbs

Ecclesiastes

Isaiah

Jeremiah

Ezekiel

Daniel

Hosea